15

PROGRAMMING IN
VISUAL BASIC .NET

Visual Basic .NET 2003 Update Edition

Julia Case Bradley
Mt. San Antonio College

Anita C. Millspaugh
Mt. San Antonio College

D1299461

 **Technology Education**

Boston   Burr Ridge, IL   Dubuque, IA   Madison, WI   New York   San Francisco   St. Louis
Bangkok   Bogotá   Caracas   Kuala Lumpur   Lisbon   London   Madrid   Mexico City
Milan   Montreal   New Delhi   Santiago   Seoul   Singapore   Sydney   Taipei   Toronto

Technology Education

PROGRAMMING IN VISUAL BASIC .NET:
VISUAL BASIC .NET 2003 UPDATE EDITION

Published by McGraw-Hill Technology Education, a business unit of The McGraw-Hill
Companies, Inc. 1221 Avenue of the Americas, New York, NY, 10020. Copyright © 2005 by
The McGraw-Hill Companies, Inc. All rights reserved. No part of this publication may be
reproduced or distributed in any form or by any means, or stored in a database or retrieval
system, without the prior written consent of The McGraw-Hill Companies, Inc., including, but
not limited to, in any network or other electronic storage or transmission, or broadcast for
distance learning.

Some ancillaries, including electronic and print components, may not be available to customers
outside the United States.

This book is printed on acid-free paper.

1 2 3 4 5 6 7 8 9 0 QPD/QPD 0 9 8 7 6 5 4

ISBN 0-07-297039-1

Editor in chief: *Bob Woodbury*
Sponsoring editor: *Marc Chernoff*
Director, Marketing and Sales: *Paul Murphy*
Producer, Media technology: *Mark Molsky*
Senior project manager: *Lori Koetters*
Senior production supervisor: *Rose Hepburn*
Coordinator freelance design: *Artemio Ortiz Jr.*
Supplement producer: *Joyce J. Chappetto*
Senior digital content specialist: *Brian Nacik*
Cover and interior design: *Artemio Ortiz Jr.*
Typeface: *11/13 Bodoni*
Compositor: *GAC Indianapolis*
Printer: *Quebecor World Dubuque Inc.*

Library of Congress Cataloging-in-Publication Data
Bradley, Julia Case.
    Programming in Visual Basic.Net / Julia Case Bradley, Anita C. Millspaugh.—Update ed.
        p. cm.
    Includes index.
    ISBN 0-07-297039-1 (alk. paper)
    1. Microsoft Visual BASIC. 2. BASIC (Computer program language) 3. Microsoft
.NET. I. Millspaugh, A. C. (Anita C.) II. Title.
    QA76.76.B3B75 2005
    005.2'768—dc22
                                                            2004044890

www.mhhe.com

PREFACE

Visual Basic (VB) has become the most popular programming language for several reasons. VB is easy to learn, which makes it an excellent tool for understanding elementary programming concepts. In addition, it has evolved into such a powerful and popular product that skilled Visual Basic programmers are in demand in the job market.

Visual Basic .NET, the latest version of VB, is practically a new language. Microsoft has completely rewritten the language to be fully object-oriented, compatible with many other languages using the .NET Framework. This book incorporates the object-oriented concepts throughout, as well as the syntax and terminology of the language.

Visual Basic .NET is designed to allow the programmer to develop applications that run under Windows and/or in a Web browser without the complexity generally associated with programming. With very little effort, the programmer can design a screen that holds standard elements such as buttons, check boxes, radio buttons, text boxes, and list boxes. Each of these objects operates as expected, producing a "standard" Windows or Web user interface.

About This Text

This textbook is intended for use in an introductory programming course, which assumes no prior knowledge of computer programming. The later chapters are also appropriate for professional programmers who are learning a new language to upgrade their skills.

This text assumes that the student is familiar with the Windows operating environment and can use an Internet browser application.

Approach

This text incorporates the basic concepts of programming, problem solving, and programming logic, as well as the design techniques of an object-oriented, event-driven language. VB .NET is a fully object-oriented language, which includes inheritance and polymorphism. Object-oriented programming (OOP) is introduced in Chapter 1 and its features appear in every chapter of the book.

Chapter topics are presented in a sequence that allows the programmer to learn how to deal with a visual interface while acquiring important programming skills such as creating projects with objects, decisions, loops, and data management.

A high priority is given to writing applications that are easy for the user to understand and to use. Students are presented with interface design guidelines throughout the text.

Features of This Text

Hands-On Programming Examples

The complete programming exercises guide students through the process of planning, writing, and executing Visual Basic programs.

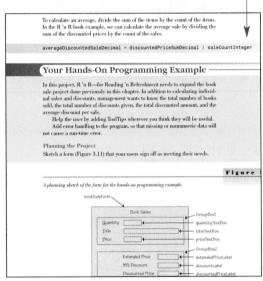

To calculate an average, divide the sum of the items by the count of the items. In the R 'n R book example, we can calculate the average sale by dividing the sum of the discounted prices by the count of the sales.

```
averageDiscountedSaleDecimal = discountedPriceSumDecimal / saleCountInteger
```

Your Hands-On Programming Example

In this project, R 'n R—for Reading 'n Refreshment needs to expand the book sale project done previously in this chapter. In addition to calculating individual sales and discounts, management wants to know the total number of books sold, the total number of discounts given, the total discounted amount, and the average discount per sale.

Help the user by adding ToolTips wherever you think they will be useful.

Add error handling to the program, so that missing or nonnumeric data will not cause a run-time error.

Planning the Project

Sketch a form (Figure 3.11) that your users sign off as meeting their needs.

Figure

A planning sketch of the form for the hands-on programming example.

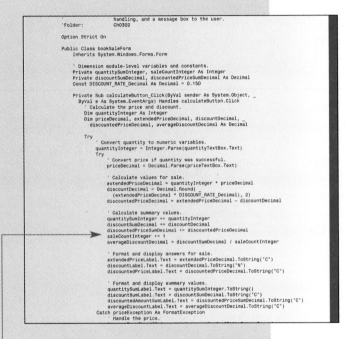

```
                    handling, and a message box to the user.
'Folder:        Ch0302

Option Strict On

Public Class bookSaleForm
    Inherits System.Windows.Forms.Form

    ' Dimension module-level variables and constants.
    Private quantitySumInteger, saleCountInteger As Integer
    Private discountSumDecimal, discountedPriceSumDecimal As Decimal
    Const DISCOUNT_RATE_Decimal As Decimal = 0.15D

    Private Sub calculateButton_Click(ByVal sender As System.Object, _
        ByVal e As System.EventArgs) Handles calculateButton.Click
        ' Calculate the price and discount.
        Dim quantityInteger As Integer
        Dim priceDecimal, extendedPriceDecimal, discountDecimal, _
            discountedPriceDecimal, averageDiscountDecimal As Decimal

        Try
            ' Convert quantity to numeric variables.
            quantityInteger = Integer.Parse(quantityTextBox.Text)
            Try
                ' Convert price if quantity was successful.
                priceDecimal = Decimal.Parse(priceTextBox.Text)

                ' Calculate values for sale.
                extendedPriceDecimal = quantityInteger * priceDecimal
                discountDecimal = Decimal.Round( _
                    (extendedPriceDecimal * DISCOUNT_RATE_Decimal), 2)
                discountedPriceDecimal = extendedPriceDecimal - discountDecimal

                ' Calculate summary values.
                quantitySumInteger += quantityInteger
                discountSumDecimal += discountDecimal
                discountedPriceSumDecimal += discountedPriceDecimal
                saleCountInteger += 1
                averageDiscountDecimal = discountSumDecimal / saleCountInteger

                ' Format and display answers for sale.
                extendedPriceLabel.Text = extendedPriceDecimal.ToString("C")
                discountLabel.Text = discountDecimal.ToString("N")
                discountedPriceLabel.Text = discountedPriceDecimal.ToString("C")

                ' Format and display summary values.
                quantitySumLabel.Text = quantitySumInteger.ToString()
                discountSumLabel.Text = discountSumDecimal.ToString("C")
                discountedAmountSumLabel.Text = discountedPriceSumDecimal.ToString("C")
                averageDiscountLabel.Text = averageDiscountDecimal.ToString("C")
            Catch priceException As FormatException
                ' Handle the price.
```

Naming Conventions Updated

Naming conventions now conform to .NET recommended standards and industry trends.

Switch from VB Functions to .NET Methods

The .NET methods can be used by all languages that operate in the common language run time.

All Code Updated

All programs in the text are modified to conform to the new standards.

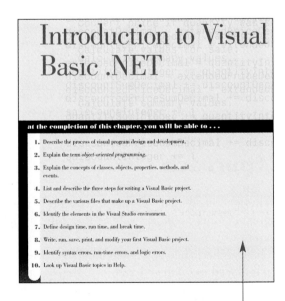

Introduction to Visual Basic .NET

at the completion of this chapter, you will be able to . . .

1. Describe the process of visual program design and development.
2. Explain the term *object-oriented programming.*
3. Explain the concepts of classes, objects, properties, methods, and events.
4. List and describe the three steps for writing a Visual Basic project.
5. Describe the various files that make up a Visual Basic project.
6. Identify the elements in the Visual Studio environment.
7. Define design time, run time, and break time.
8. Write, run, save, print, and modify your first Visual Basic project.
9. Identify syntax errors, run-time errors, and logic errors.
10. Look up Visual Basic topics in Help.

Learning Objectives

These specific objectives tell students what will be covered in the chapter and what they will be able to do after completing the chapter.

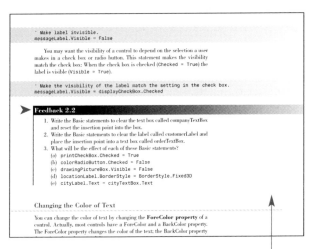

```
' Make label invisible.
messageLabel.Visible = False
```

You may want the visibility of a control to depend on the selection a user makes in a check box or radio button. This statement makes the visibility match the check box: When the check box is checked (Checked = True) the label is visible (Visible = True).

```
' Make the visibility of the label match the setting in the check box.
messageLabel.Visible = displayCheckBox.Checked
```

▶ **Feedback 2.2**

1. Write the Basic statements to clear the text box called companyTextBox and reset the insertion point into the box.
2. Write the Basic statements to clear the label called customerLabel and place the insertion point into a text box called orderTextBox.
3. What will be the effect of each of these Basic statements?
   (a) printCheckBox.Checked = True
   (b) colorRadioButton.Checked = False
   (c) drawingPictureBox.Visible = False
   (d) locationLabel.BorderStyle = BorderStyle.Fixed3D
   (e) cityLabel.Text = cityTextBox.Text

Changing the Color of Text

You can change the color of text by changing the **ForeColor property** of a control. Actually, most controls have a ForeColor and a BackColor property. The ForeColor property changes the color of the text; the BackColor property

Feedback Questions

The Feedback Questions give students time to reflect on the current topic and to evaluate their understanding of the details.

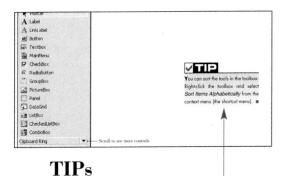

TIPs

Tips in the margins help students avoid potential trouble spots in their programs and encourage them to develop good programming habits from the start.

Case Studies

The Case Studies provide continuing-theme exercises that may be used throughout the course.

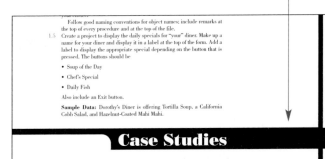

Follow good naming conventions for object names; include remarks at the top of every procedure and at the top of the file.
1.5 Create a project to display the daily specials for "your" diner. Make up a name for your diner and display it in a label at the top of the form. Add a label to display the appropriate special depending on the button that is pressed. The buttons should be

• Soup of the Day

• Chef's Special

• Daily Fish

Also include an Exit button.

Sample Data: Dorothy's Diner is offering Tortilla Soup, a California Cobb Salad, and Hazelnut-Coated Mahi Mahi.

Case Studies

Very Busy (VB) Mail Order

If you don't have the time to look for all those hard-to-find items, tell us what you're looking for. We'll send you a catalog from the appropriate company or order for you.

We can place an order and ship it to you. We also help with shopping for gifts; your order can be gift wrapped and sent anywhere you wish.

The company title will be shortened to VB Mail Order. Include this name on the title bar of the first form of each project that you create for this case study.

Your first job is to create a project that will display the name and telephone number for the contact person for the customer relations, marketing, order processing, and shipping departments.

Include a button for each department. When the user clicks on the button for a department, display the name and telephone number for the contact person in

two labels. Also include identifying labels with Text "Department Contact" and "Telephone Number".

Be sure to include a button for Exit.

Include a label at the bottom of the form that holds your name.

Test Data

Department	Department Contact	Telephone Number
Customer Relations	Tricia Mills	500-1111
Marketing	Michelle Rigner	500-2222
Order Processing	Kenna DeVoss	500-3333
Shipping	Eric Andrews	500-4444

Programming Exercises

The Programming Exercises test students' understanding of the programming skills covered in the chapter.

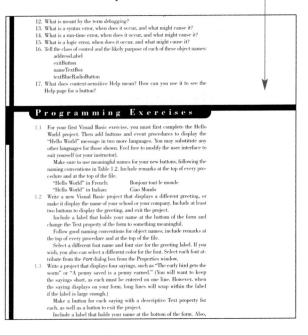

12. What is meant by the term *debugging*?
13. What is a syntax error, when does it occur, and what might cause it?
14. What is a run-time error, when does it occur, and what might cause it?
15. What is a logic error, when does it occur, and what might cause it?
16. Tell the class of control and the likely purpose of each of these object names:
    addressLabel
    exitButton
    nameTextBox
    textBlueRadioButton
17. What does context-sensitive Help mean? How can you use it to see the Help page for a button?

Programming Exercises

1.1 For your first Visual Basic exercise, you must first complete the Hello World project. Then add buttons and event procedures to display the "Hello World" message in two more languages. You may substitute any other languages for those shown. Feel free to modify the user interface to suit yourself (or your instructor).

Make sure to use meaningful names for your new buttons, following the naming conventions in Table 1.2. Include remarks at the top of every procedure and at the top of the file.
"Hello World" in French: Bonjour tout le monde
"Hello World" in Italian: Ciao Mondo

1.2 Write a new Visual Basic project that displays a different greeting, or make it display the name of your school or your company. Include at least two buttons to display the greeting, and exit the project.

Include a label that holds your name at the bottom of the form and change the Text property of the form to something meaningful.

Follow good naming conventions for object names; include remarks at the top of every procedure and at the top of the file.

Select a different font name and font size for the greeting label. If you wish, you also can select a different color for the font. Select each font attribute from the *Font* dialog box from the Properties window.

1.3 Write a project that displays four sayings, such as "The early bird gets the worm" or "A penny saved is a penny earned." (You will want to keep the sayings short, as each must be entered on one line. However, when the saying displays on your form, long lines will wrap within the label if the label is large enough.)

Make a button for each saying with a descriptive Text property for each, as well as a button to exit the project.

Include a label that holds your name at the bottom of the form. Also,

Changes in This Edition

This revision of the text brings the VB programmer more in line with the .NET Framework and the various languages it supports. We have dropped the older-style Hungarian notation and adopted naming conventions that conform to the .NET recommended standards and industry trends. In instances where the .NET Framework provides an OOP solution, we have dropped the older VB language solutions in favor of the object-oriented approach. This change is most evident in our switch from VB conversion functions to .NET methods.

All programs in the text are modified to conform to the new standards. The code for all in-chapter projects is available to instructors.

We have reorganized and expanded some sections of the text. Chapter 6, the OOP concepts chapter, has been rewritten and expanded to clarify the ideas. The `Case` structure now appears in Chapter 4, the selection chapter, rather than in Chapter 8.

Database coverage is significantly changed. The selection programs are simplified and the update has been removed. The consensus of professors teaching the course is that updating belongs in an advanced course rather than in the introductory course.

A new section in Chapter 9 covers navigating Web pages, including adding a second page and using HyperLink controls. Chapter 13 has a new section on field-level validation using ErrorProviders and the Validating event of controls.

The narrative, step-by-step exercises; screen captures; and appendices have all been updated to VB .NET 2003. The screen captures are all based on Windows XP.

Changes to coding conventions include declaring all module-level variables using the `Private` keyword, taking advantage of the feature to declare multiple variables on one statement, and reducing the number of end-line comments. Program comments are now more readable and complete.

A new appendix presents security issues appropriate to an introductory programming text.

Features of This Text

Each chapter begins with identifiable objectives and a brief overview. Numerous coding examples as well as hands-on projects with guidance for the planning and coding appear throughout. Thought-provoking feedback questions give students time to reflect on the current topic and to evaluate their understanding of the details. The end-of-chapter items include a chapter review, questions, programming exercises, and four case studies.

> ***Chapter 1, "Introduction to Visual Basic .NET,"*** introduces Microsoft's Visual Studio integrated development environment (IDE). The single environment is now used for multiple languages. A step-by-step program gets students into programming very quickly (quicker than most books). The chapter introduces the OOP concepts of objects, properties, methods, and events. The elements of debugging and using the Help system are also introduced.

> ***Chapter 2, "User Interface Design,"*** demonstrates techniques for good program design, including making the interface easy for users as well as guidelines for designing maintainable programs. Several controls

are introduced, including text boxes, group boxes, check boxes, radio buttons, and picture boxes.

Chapter 3, "Variables, Constants, and Calculations," presents the concepts of using data and declaring the data type. Students learn to follow standards to indicate the data type and scope of variables and constants and always to use `Option Strict`, which forces adherence to strong data typing.

Error handling is accomplished using structured exception handling. The `Try/Catch/Finally` structure is introduced in this chapter along with calculations. The student learns to display error messages using the new MessageBox class and also learns about the OOP concept of overloaded constructors.

Chapter 4, "Decisions and Conditions," introduces taking alternate actions based on conditions formed with the relational and logical operators. This chapter uses the `If` statement to validate input data. Multiple decisions are handled with both nested `If` statements and the `Select Case` structure.

The debugging features of the IDE are covered, including a step-by-step exercise covering stepping through program statements and checking intermediate values during execution.

Chapter 5, "Menus, Common Dialog Boxes, Sub Procedures, and Function Procedures," covers the concepts of writing and calling general sub procedures and function procedures. Students learn to include both menus and context menus in projects, display the Windows common dialog boxes, and use the input provided by the user.

Chapter 6, "OOP: Creating Object-Oriented Programs," explains more of the theory of object-oriented programming. Although we have been using OOP concepts since Chapter 1, in this chapter students learn the terminology and application of OOP. Inheritance is covered for visual objects (forms) and for extending existing classes. The samples are kept simple enough for an introductory class.

Chapter 7, "Lists, Loops, and Printing," incorporates list boxes and combo boxes into projects, providing the opportunity to discuss looping procedures and printing lists of information. Printing is accomplished in .NET using a graphics object and a callback event. The printing controls also include a Print Preview, which allows students and instructors to view output without actually printing it.

Chapter 8, "Arrays," introduces arrays, which follow logically from the lists covered in Chapter 7. Students learn to use single- and multi-dimension arrays, table lookups, and arrays of structures.

Chapter 9, "Programming with Web Forms," introduces Web applications using VB .NET Web Forms. Students learn to design and develop simple Web applications that consist of Web pages that execute in a browser application.

Chapter 10, "Accessing Database Files," introduces ADO.NET, which is Microsoft's latest technology for accessing data in a database. This chapter shows how to create connections, data adapters, and datasets. Programs include accessing data from both Windows Forms and Web Forms. Students learn to bind data tables to a data grid and bind individual data fields to controls such as labels and text boxes.

Chapter 11, "Saving Data and Objects in Files," presents the .NET object-oriented techniques for data file handling. Students learn to save and read small amounts of data using streams. The StreamWriter and StreamReader objects are used to store and reload the contents of a combo box.

Object serialization is used to persist objects. The hands-on example includes both serialization (saving) and deserialization (restoring) objects.

Chapter 12, "Graphics in Windows and the Web," covers the classes and methods of GDI+. The chapter covers graphics objects, pens, and brushes for drawing shapes and lines. Animation is accomplished using the Timer control and the `SetBounds` method for moving controls.

Chapter 13, "Additional Topics in Visual Basic," introduces some advanced VB topics. This final chapter covers field-level validation of user input using Error Providers and the Validating event of controls. Students learn to create applications using multiple document interfaces (MDI), add toolbars and status bars, and create reports from databases using Crystal Reports.

The appendices offer important additional material. Appendix A holds the answers to all Feedback Questions. Appendix B covers methods and functions for math, string handling, and date manipulation. In the new OOP style, most actions that were formerly done with functions are now accomplished with methods of the Math class and String class. Appendix C, on mastering the Visual Studio environment, is based on the .NET 2003 IDE. The new Appendix D discusses security issues for both Windows and Web programming.

Acknowledgments

Many people have worked very hard to design and produce this text. We would like to thank our editor, Marc Chernoff, and the publisher, Bob Woodbury. Our thanks also to the many people who produced this text, including Lori Koetters, Artemio Ortiz, Rose Hepburn, Joyce Chappetto, Mark Molsky, and the director, marketing and sales, Paul Murphy.

We greatly appreciate Robert Price of Antelope Valley Community College, Deanna Tague of Scott Community College, Avram Malkin of DeVry College, Joann Cook of College of DuPage, and Christy McCloskey of International Academy of Design and Technology for their thorough technical reviews, constructive criticism, and many valuable suggestions. And most importantly, we are grateful to Dennis, Richard, Tricia, Eric, and Kenna for their support and understanding through the long days and busy phone lines.

The Authors

We have had fun teaching and writing about Visual Basic. We hope that this feeling is evident as you read this book and that you will enjoy learning or teaching this outstanding programming language.

Julia Case Bradley
Anita C. Millspaugh

TO THE STUDENT

The best way to learn to program in Visual Basic is to do it. If you enter and run the sample projects, you will be on your way to writing applications. Reading the examples without trying to run them is like trying to learn a foreign language or mathematics by just reading about it. Enter the projects, look up your questions in the extensive MSDN Help files, and make those projects *run*.

Installing Visual Basic

For the programs in this text, you need to install the .NET Framework, IIS (Internet Information Services), Visual Basic, and the MSDN (Microsoft Developers Network) library, which contains all of Help and many instructive articles. You do not need to install C++ or C#.

You need IIS if you want to write any Web applications that run in a browser. All of the programs in Chapter 9 require IIS, as well as some programs in Chapter 10.

The order of installation is important. You must install the .NET Framework and IIS before installing VB.

Format Used for Visual Basic Statements

Visual Basic statements, methods, and functions are shown in `this font`. Any values that you must supply are in `italics`. Optional items are in [square brackets]. Braces and a vertical bar indicate that you must choose one or the other value {one | other}.

Examples:
```
Const Identifier [As Datatype] = Value
Do {While | Until} Condition
```

As you work your way through this textbook, note that you may see a subset of the available options for a Visual Basic statement or method. Generally, the options that are included reflect those covered in the chapter. If you want to see the complete format for any statement or all versions of a method, refer to Help.

J.C.B.
A.C.M.

BRIEF CONTENTS

CONTENTS

Variables, Constants, and Calculations 85

Decisions and Conditions 135

1

Introduction to Visual Basic .NET

1. Describe the process of visual program design and development.

2. Explain the term *object-oriented programming*.

3. Explain the concepts of classes, objects, properties, methods, and events.

4. List and describe the three steps for writing a Visual Basic project.

5. Describe the various files that make up a Visual Basic project.

6. Identify the elements in the Visual Studio environment.

7. Define design time, run time, and break time.

8. Write, run, save, print, and modify your first Visual Basic project.

9. Identify syntax errors, run-time errors, and logic errors.

10. Look up Visual Basic topics in Help.

Writing Windows Applications with Visual Basic

Using this text, you will learn to write computer programs that run in the Microsoft Windows environment. Your projects will look and act like standard Windows programs. You will use the tools in Visual Basic .NET (VB) and Windows Forms to create windows with familiar elements such as labels, text boxes, buttons, radio buttons, check boxes, list boxes, menus, and scroll bars. Figure 1.1 shows some sample Windows user interfaces.

F i g u r e   1 . 1

Graphical user interfaces for application programs designed with Visual Basic .NET and Windows Forms.

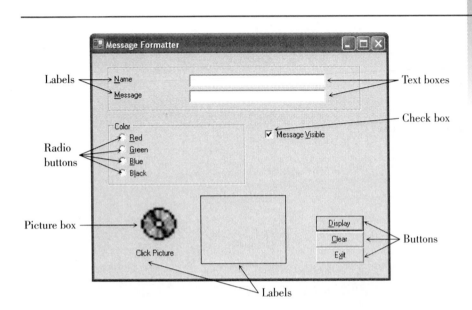

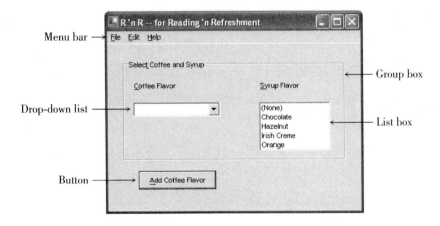

Beginning in Chapter 10 you will create programs using Web Forms. You can run Web applications in a browser such as Internet Explorer, on the Internet, or on a company intranet. Figure 1.2 shows a Web Form application.

The Windows Graphical User Interface

Microsoft Windows uses a **graphical user interface**, or **GUI** (pronounced "gooey"). The Windows GUI defines how the various elements look and function.

Figure 1.2

A Web Form application
created with Visual Basic
.NET, running in a browser.

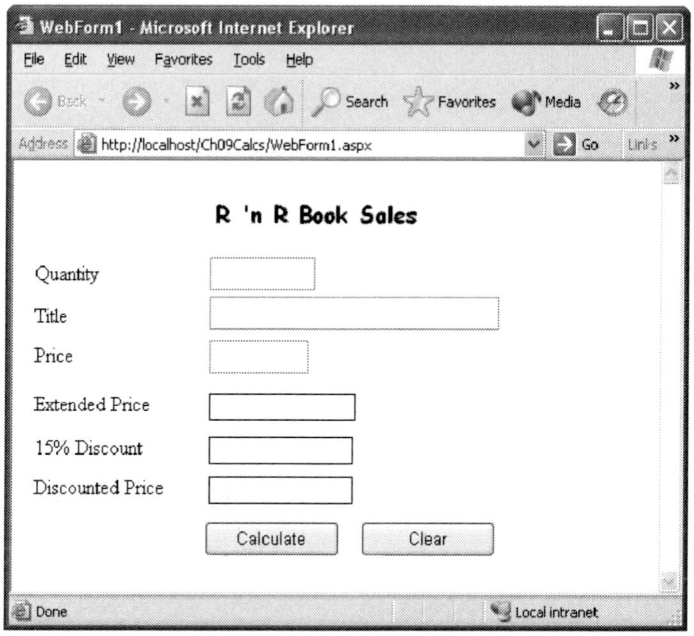

As a Visual Basic programmer, you have available a toolbox of these elements. You will create new windows, called **forms**. Then you will use the toolbox to add the various elements, called **controls**. The projects that you will write follow a programming technique called **object-oriented programming (OOP)**.

Programming Languages—Procedural, Event Driven, and Object Oriented

There are literally hundreds of programming languages. Each was developed to solve a particular type of problem. Most traditional languages, such as BASIC, C, COBOL, FORTRAN, PL/I, and Pascal, are considered *procedural* languages. That is, the program specifies the exact sequence of all operations. Program logic determines the next instruction to execute in response to conditions and user requests.

The newer programming languages, such as Visual Basic .NET, C#, and Java, use a different approach: object-oriented programming (OOP). As a stepping stone between procedural programming and object-oriented programming, the early versions of Visual Basic provided many (but not all) elements of an object-oriented language. For that reason, Microsoft referred to Visual Basic (version 6 and earlier) as an event-driven programming language rather than an object-oriented language. But with the release of Visual Studio .NET, which includes Visual Basic .NET, C#, and J#, Microsoft has produced three programming languages that are truly object-oriented. (Another language, C++, has elements of OOP and of procedural programming, and doesn't conform fully to either paradigm.)

In the OOP model, programs are no longer procedural. They do not follow a sequential logic. You, as the programmer, do not take control and determine the sequence of execution. Instead, the user can press keys and click various buttons and boxes in a window. Each user action can cause an event to occur, which triggers a Basic procedure that you have written. For example, the user clicks on a button labeled Calculate. The clicking causes the button's Click event to occur, and the program automatically jumps to a procedure you have written to do the calculation.

The Object Model

In Visual Basic you will work with **objects**, which have **properties**, **methods**, and **events**. Each object is based on a **class**.

Objects

Think of an object as a thing, or a noun. Examples of objects are forms and controls. *Forms* are the windows and dialog boxes you place on the screen; *controls* are the components you place inside a form, such as text boxes, buttons, and list boxes.

Properties

Properties tell something about or control the behavior of an object such as its name, color, size, or location. You can think of properties as adjectives that describe objects.

When you refer to a property, you first name the object, add a period, and then name the property. For example, refer to the Text property of a form called salesForm as salesForm.Text (pronounced "sales form dot text").

Methods

Actions associated with objects are called *methods*. Methods are the verbs of object-oriented programming. Some typical methods are Close, Show, and Clear. Each of the predefined objects has a set of methods that you can use. You will learn to write additional methods to perform actions in your programs.

You refer to methods as Object.Method ("object dot method"). For example, a Show method can apply to different objects: billingForm.Show shows the form object called billingForm; exitButton.Show shows the button object called exitButton.

Events

You can write procedures that execute when a particular event occurs. An event occurs when the user takes an action, such as clicking a button, pressing a key, scrolling, or closing a window. Events also can be triggered by actions of other objects, such as repainting a form or a timer reaching a preset point.

The term *members* is used to refer to both properties and methods. ■

Classes

A class is a template or blueprint used to create a new object. Classes contain the definition of all available properties, methods, and events.

Each time that you create a new object, it must be based on a class. For example, you may decide to place three buttons on your form. Each button is based on the Button class and is considered one object, called an *instance* of the class. Each button (or instance) has its own set of properties, methods, and events. One button may be labeled "OK", one "Cancel", and one "Exit". When the user clicks the OK button, that button's Click event occurs; if the user clicks on the Exit button, that button's Click event occurs. And of course, you have written different program instructions for each of the button's Click events.

An Analogy

If the concepts of classes, objects, properties, methods, and events are still a little unclear, maybe an analogy will help. Consider an Automobile class. When we say *automobile*, we are not referring to a particular auto, but we know that an automobile has a make and model, a color, an engine, and a number of doors. These elements are the *properties* of the Automobile class.

Each individual car is an object, or an instance of the Automobile class. Each Automobile object has its own settings for the available properties. For example, each object has a Color property, such as myCar.Color = Blue and yourCar.Color = Red.

The methods, or actions, of the Automobile class might be `Start`, `SpeedUp`, `SlowDown`, and `Stop`. To refer to the methods of a specific object of the class, use `myCar.Start` and `yourCar.Stop`.

The events of an Automobile class could be Arrive or Crash. In a VB program you write procedures that specify the actions you want to take when a particular event occurs for an object. For example, you might write a procedure for the yourCar.Crash event.

Note: Chapter 6 presents object-oriented programming in greater depth.

Microsoft's Visual Studio .NET

The latest version of Microsoft's Visual Studio, called Visual Studio .NET 2003, includes Visual Basic, Visual C++, the new languages C# (C sharp) and J# (J sharp), and the .NET Framework. Visual Studio .NET 2003 includes enhancements to each of the languages.

The .NET Framework

The programming languages in Visual Studio .NET run in the .NET Framework. The Framework provides for easier development of Web-based and Windows-based applications, allows objects from different languages to operate together, and standardizes how the languages refer to data and objects. Several third-party vendors have announced or released versions of other programming languages to run in the .NET Framework, including .NET versions of FORTRAN, COBOL, and Java. See http://www.gotdotnet.com/team/lang/ for the latest details.

The .NET languages all compile to (are translated to) a common machine language, called Microsoft Intermediate Language (MSIL). The MSIL code, called *managed code*, runs in the Common Language Runtime (CLR), which is part of the .NET Framework.

Visual Basic .NET

Microsoft Visual Basic .NET comes with Visual Studio .NET. You also can purchase VB .NET by itself (without the other languages but *with* the .NET

Framework). VB .NET is available in a **Standard Edition**, a **Professional Edition**, an **Enterprise Developer Edition**, and an **Enterprise Architect Edition**. Anyone planning to do professional application development that includes the advanced features of database management should use the Professional Edition or one of the Enterprise editions. You can find a matrix showing the features of each edition in Help. The trial version packaged with this book is the Standard Edition. The Professional Edition is available to educational institutions through the Microsoft Academic Alliance program.

This text is based on Visual Basic .NET 2003, the current version. You cannot run the projects in this text in any earlier version of VB.

Writing Visual Basic Projects

When you write a Visual Basic application, you follow a three-step process for planning the project and then repeat the process for creating the project. The three steps involve setting up the user interface, defining the properties, and then creating the code.

The Three-Step Process

Planning

1. *Design the user interface.* When you plan the **user interface**, you draw a sketch of the screens the user will see when running your project. On your sketch, show the forms and all the controls that you plan to use. Indicate the names that you plan to give the form and each of the objects on the form. Refer to Figure 1.1 for examples of user interfaces.

    Before you proceed with any more steps, consult with your user and make sure that you both agree on the look and feel of the project.
2. *Plan the properties.* For each object, write down the properties that you plan to set or change during the design of the form.
3. *Plan the Basic code.* In this step you plan the classes and procedures that will execute when your project runs. You will determine which events require action to be taken and then make a step-by-step plan for those actions.

Later, when you actually write the Visual Basic **code**, you must follow the language syntax rules. But during the planning stage, you will write out the actions using **pseudocode**, which is an English expression or comment that describes the action. For example, you must plan for the event that occurs when the user clicks on the Exit button. The pseudocode for the event could be *Terminate the project*.

Programming

After you have completed the planning steps and have approval from your user, you are ready to begin the actual construction of the project. Use the same three-step process that you used for planning.

1. *Define the user interface.* When you define the user interface, you create the forms and controls that you designed in the planning stage.

Think of this step as defining the objects you will use in your application.

2. *Set the properties*. When you set the properties of the objects, you give each object a name and define such attributes as the contents of a label, the size of the text, and the words that appear on top of a button and in the form's title bar.

   You might think of this step as describing each object.

3. *Write the Basic code*. You will use Basic programming statements (called *Basic code*) to carry out the actions needed by your program. You will be surprised and pleased by how few statements you need to create a powerful Windows program.

   You can think of this third step as defining the actions of your program.

Visual Basic Application Files

A Visual Basic application, called a ***solution***, can consist of one or more projects. Since all of the solutions in this text have only one project, you can think of one solution = one project. Each project can contain one or more form files. In Chapters 1 through 6, all projects have only one form, so you can think of one project = one form. Starting in Chapter 7, your projects may contain multiple forms and additional files. For example, the HelloWorld application that you will create later in this chapter creates these files:

HelloWorld.sln	The **solution file**. A text file that holds information about the solution and the projects it contains. This is the primary file for the solution—the one that you open to work on or run your project.
HelloWorld.suo	Solution user options file. Stores information about the selected options, so that all customizations can be restored each time you open the solution.
helloForm.vb	A .vb file. Holds the definition of a form, its controls, and code procedures. This is a text file that you can open in any editor. *Warning*: You should not modify this file unless you are using the editor in the Visual Studio environment.
helloForm.resx	A resource file for the form. This text file defines all resources used by the form, including strings of text, numbers, and any graphics.
HelloWorld.vbproj	A **project file**. A text file that describes the project and lists the files that are included in the project.
HelloWorld.vbproj.user	The project user option file. This text file holds project option settings, so that the next time you open the project, all selected options will be restored.

After you run your project, you will find several more files created by the system. The only file that you will open directly is the .sln, or solution file.

The Visual Studio Environment

The **Visual Studio environment** is where you create and test your projects. A development environment such as Visual Studio is called an ***integrated development environment* (IDE)**. The IDE consists of various tools, including a form designer, which allows you to visually create a form; an editor, for entering and modifying program code; a compiler, for translating the Visual Basic statements into the intermediate machine code; a debugger, to help locate and correct program errors; an object browser, to view the available classes, objects, properties, methods, and events; and a Help facility.

In earlier versions of Visual Studio, each language had its own IDE. For example, to create a VB project you would use the VB IDE and to create a C++ project you would use the C++ IDE. But in Visual Studio .NET, you use the one IDE to create projects in any of the .NET languages.

The IDE Start Page

When you open the Visual Studio IDE, you see its Start Page (Figure 1.3). Recent projects appear on the list, enabling you to open an existing project, or you can select *New Project* to begin a new project.

Figure 1.3

The Visual Studio IDE Start Page.

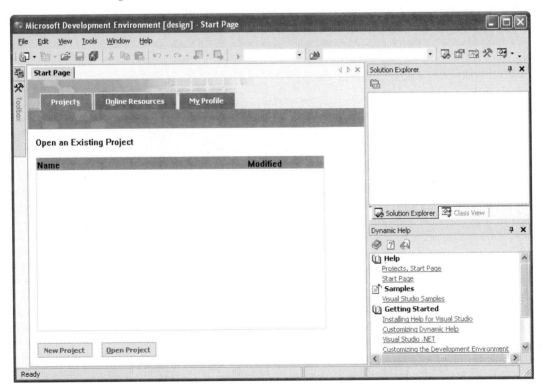

The New Project Dialog

You will create your first Visual Basic projects based on Windows Forms. In the *New Project* dialog (Figure 1.4), select *Visual Basic Projects* in the *Project Types* box and *Windows Application* in the *Templates* box. You also give the project a name and a path on this dialog box.

Figure 1.4

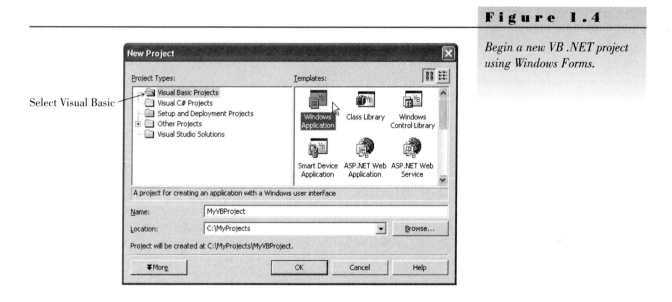

Begin a new VB .NET project using Windows Forms.

The IDE Main Window

Figure 1.5 shows the Visual Studio environment's main window and its various child windows. Note that each window can be moved, resized, opened, closed, and customized. Some windows have tabs that allow you to display different

Figure 1.5

The Visual Studio environment. Each window can be moved, resized, closed, or customized.

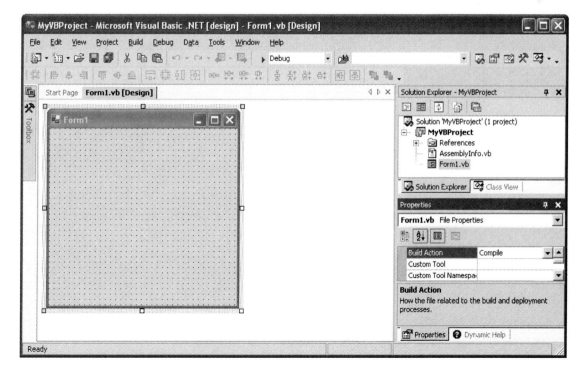

contents. Your screen may not look exactly like Figure 1.5; in all likelihood you will want to customize the placement of the various windows.

The IDE main window holds the Visual Studio menu bar and the toolbars.

The Toolbars

You can use the buttons on the **toolbars** as shortcuts for frequently used operations. Each button represents a command that also can be selected from a menu. Figure 1.6*a* shows the toolbar buttons on the Standard toolbar, which displays in the main window of the IDE; Figure 1.6*b* shows the Layout toolbar, which displays in the Form Designer; and Figure 1.6*c* shows the Text Editor toolbar, which appears when the Editor window is displayed.

Figure 1.6

The Visual Studio toolbars contain buttons that are shortcuts for menu commands. You can display or hide each of the toolbars: a. the Standard toolbar; b. the Layout toolbar; and c. the Text Editor toolbar.

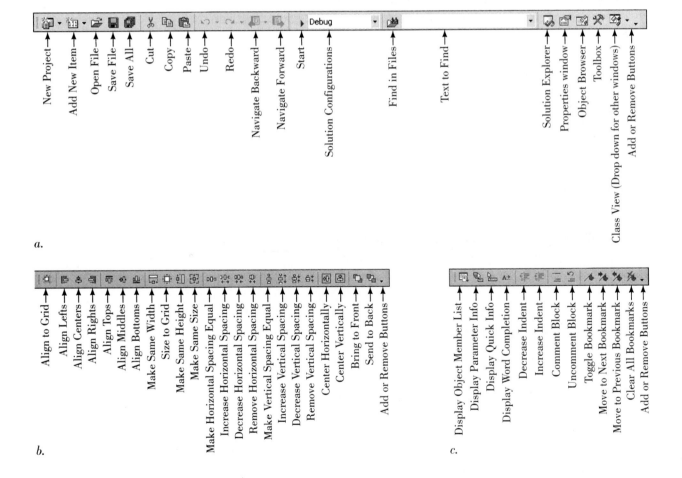

a.

b.   *c.*

The Document Window

The largest window in the center of the screen is the **Document window**. Notice the tabs across the top of the window, which allow you to switch between open documents. The items that display in the Document window include the

Form Designer, the Code Editor, the Object Browser, and the pages of Help that you request.

You can switch from one tab to another, or close any of the documents using its Close button.

The Form Designer

The **Form Designer** is where you design a form that makes up your user interface. In Figure 1.5, the Form Designer for Form1 is currently displaying. You can drag the form's sizing handles to change the size of the form.

When you begin a new Visual Basic Windows project, a new form is added to the project with the default name Form1. In the step-by-step exercise later in the chapter, you will learn to change the form's name.

The Solution Explorer Window

The **Solution Explorer window** holds the filenames for the files included in your project and a list of the classes it references. The window's title bar holds the name of your solution (.sln) file, which is WindowsApplication1 by default unless you give it a new value in the *New Project* dialog box.

The Properties Window

You use the **Properties window** to set the properties for the objects in your project. See "Set Properties" later in this chapter for instructions on changing properties.

The Toolbox

The **toolbox** holds the tools you use to place controls on a form. You may have more or different tools in your toolbox, depending on the edition of Visual Basic you are using (Standard, Professional, or Enterprise). Figure 1.7 shows the toolbox.

Help

Visual Studio has an extensive **Help** feature that is greatly expanded for .NET. Help includes the Microsoft Developer Network library (MSDN), which contains reference materials for Visual Basic, C++, C#, J#, and Visual Studio; several books; technical articles; and the Microsoft Knowledge Base, a database of frequently asked questions and their answers.

Help includes the entire reference manual, as well as many coding examples. See the topic "Visual Studio Help" later in this chapter for help on Help.

When you select *Contents*, *Index*, or *Search* from the *Help* menu, the requested item appears as another tabbed window on top of the Solution Explorer window. It's a good idea to set the *Filtered By* entry to *Visual Basic*. Once you select a topic, the corresponding Help page appears in the main Document window.

In Figure 1.8 notice the tabs across the bottom of the Solution Explorer window and on the top of the Document window. The window for the Solution

Figure 1.7

The toolbox for Visual Studio Windows Forms. Your toolbox may have more or fewer tools, depending on the edition you are using.

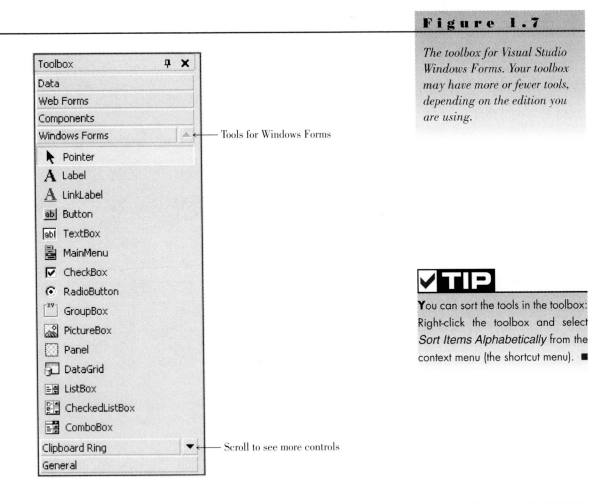

Tools for Windows Forms

Scroll to see more controls

✓TIP

You can sort the tools in the toolbox: Right-click the toolbox and select *Sort Items Alphabetically* from the context menu (the shortcut menu). ■

Figure 1.8

The Help Index displays on a tab in the Solution Explorer window and the Help text appears on a tab in the Document window.

Form Designer   Code Editor   Help Topic

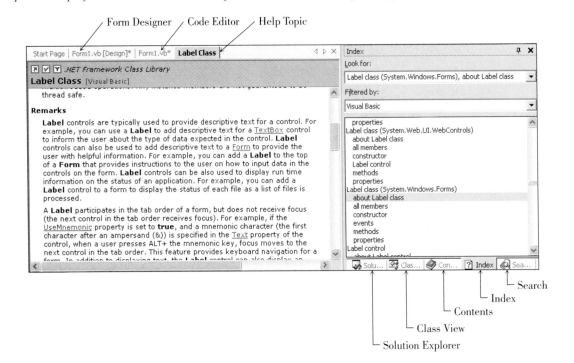

Search

Index

Contents

Class View

Solution Explorer

Explorer now shows the Help Index and the tabs allow you to switch between the Help Index, Help Contents, Help Search, the Class View, and the Solution Explorer. Use the tabs on the Document window to switch back to the Form Designer (*Form1.vb [Design]**), the Code Editor (*Form1.vb**), or the Help topic (*Label Class*).

Design Time, Run Time, and Break Time

Visual Basic has three distinct modes. While you are designing the user interface and writing code, you are in **design time**. When you are testing and running your project, you are in **run time**. If you get a run-time error or pause project execution, you are in **break time**. The window title bar in Figure 1.5 indicates that the project is currently in design time.

Writing Your First Visual Basic Project

For your first VB project, you will create a form with three controls (see Figure 1.9). This simple project will display the message "Hello World" in a label when the user clicks the Push Me button and will terminate when the user clicks the Exit button.

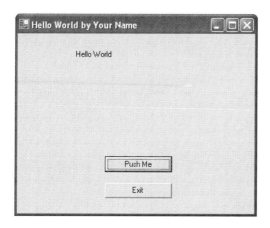

Figure 1.9

The Hello World form. The "Hello World" message will appear in the label when the user clicks on the Push Me button.

Set Up Your Workspace

Before you can begin a project, you must run the Visual Studio IDE. You also may need to customize your workspace.

Run Visual Studio

These instructions assume that Visual Studio .NET is installed in the default location. If you are running in a classroom or lab, the program may be installed in an alternate location, such as directly on the desktop.

STEP 1: Click the Windows *Start* button and move the mouse pointer to *All Programs*.

STEP 2: Locate *Microsoft Visual Studio .NET 2003*.

STEP 3: In the submenu that pops up, select *Microsoft Visual Studio .NET 2003*.

Visual Studio will start and display the Start Page (refer to Figure 1.3).
Note: The VS IDE can be customized to not show the Start Page.

Start a New Project

STEP 1: Click on the New Project button. The *New Project* dialog box opens (refer to Figure 1.4). Make sure that *Visual Basic Projects* is selected for *Project Types* and *Windows Application* is selected for *Templates*.

Note: If the My Profile screen appears, rather than the Start Page, click on the *Projects* tab to find the New Project button.

STEP 2: For *Location*, browse to select the path for your new project and click *Open*. *Note*: You may use a path on the hard drive, a network, or a diskette.

Do not create a new folder for your project; the VS IDE automatically creates a new folder for each new solution. If you create a folder yourself, you will have a folder within a folder.

STEP 3: Enter "HelloWorld" (without the quotes) for the name of the new project (Figure 1.10) and click the OK button. The new project opens (Figure 1.11).

Note: Your screen may look significantly different from the figure, since the environment can be customized.

Figure   1.10

Select the path and enter the name for the new project.

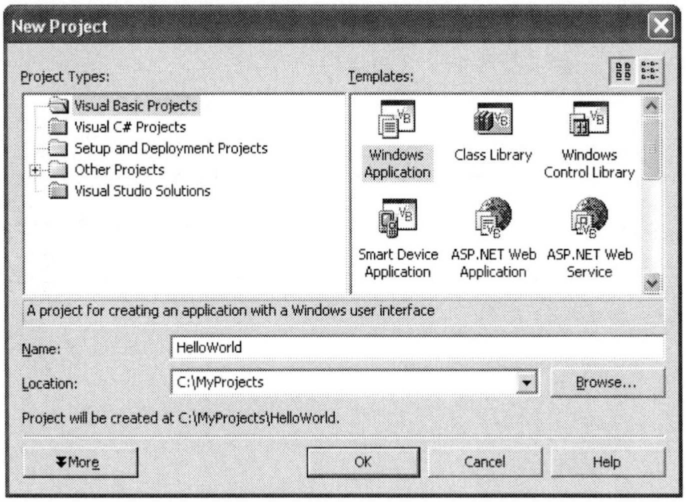

Set Up Your Environment

In this section you will customize the environment. For more information on customizing windows, floating and docking windows, and altering the location and contents of the various windows, see Appendix C.

STEP 1: Reset the IDE's default layout by choosing *Tools / Options / Environment / General / Reset Window Layout*; click OK on both dialogs.

The Server Explorer and toolbox are both set to AutoHide in the same location. You don't need the Server Explorer, but you do need the toolbox.

Figure 1.11

The Visual Studio IDE with a new project.

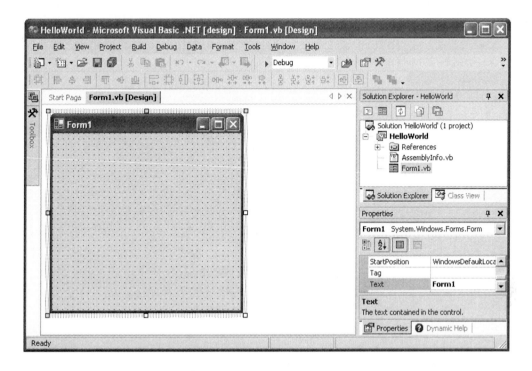

STEP 2: Point to the icon for the Server Explorer at the top of the hidden window's title bar (Figure 1.12). The Server Explorer will open.

Figure 1.12

Server Explorer icon

Toolbox icon

The title bar of the hidden window for the Server Explorer and the toolbox. Point to the correct icon to display the desired window.

STEP 3: Point to the icon for the toolbox at the bottom of the window's title bar. The Toolbox window opens. Notice the pushpin icon at the top of the window (Figure 1.13); clicking this icon makes the window remain on the screen rather than AutoHide.

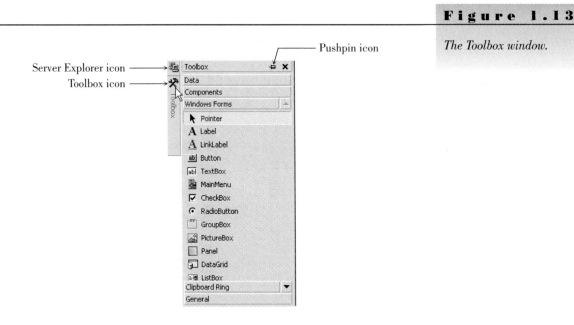

STEP 4: Click the AutoHide pushpin icon for the Toolbox window. The toolbox will remain open and tabs appear at the bottom of the window for the toolbox and the Server Explorer.

STEP 5: Click on the tab for the Server Explorer to make its window appear. Then click on the window's Close button to permanently close the window.

    Note: You can reopen the Server Explorer from the *View* menu if you wish.

STEP 6: In the lower-right corner of the screen, click on the tab for *Dynamic Help* to bring its tabbed window to the top (Figure 1.14). Then click the window's Close button to close the Dynamic Help window. Later you can experiment with Dynamic Help turned on, but the feature slows the environment significantly.

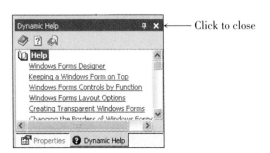

Plan the Project

The first step in planning is to design the user interface. Figure 1.15 shows a sketch of the form that includes a label and two buttons. You will refer to the sketch as you create the project.

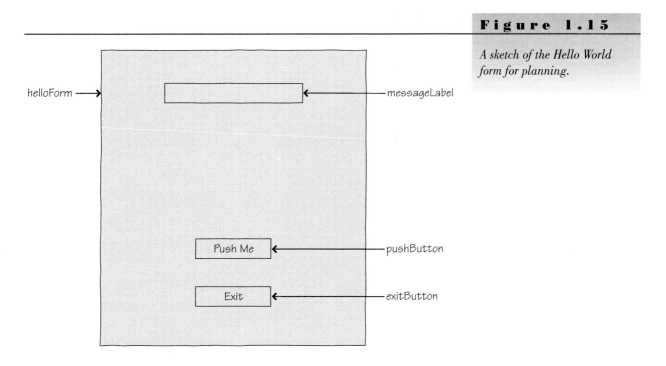

A sketch of the Hello World form for planning.

The next two steps, planning the properties and the code, have already been done for this first sample project. You will be given the values in the steps that follow.

Define the User Interface

Set Up the Form

Notice that the new form in the Document window has all the standard Windows features, such as a title bar, maximize and minimize buttons, and a Close button. The grid of dots on the form is there to help you align the controls; the grid does not appear when you run the program.

STEP 1: Resize the form in the Document window: Drag the handle in the lower-right corner down and to the right (see Figure 1.16).

Figure 1.16

Make the form larger by dragging its lower-right handle diagonally. The handles disappear as you drag the corner of the form.

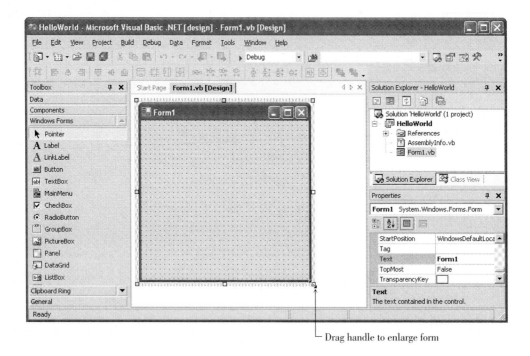

└─ Drag handle to enlarge form

Place Controls on the Form

You are going to place three controls on the form: a **Label** and two **Buttons**.

STEP 1: Point to the Label tool in the toolbox and click. Then move the pointer over the form. Notice that the pointer becomes a crosshair with a big A, and the Label tool looks as if it has been pressed, indicating it is the active tool (Figure 1.17).

Figure 1.17

When you click on the Label tool in the toolbox, the tool's button is activated and the mouse pointer becomes a crosshair.

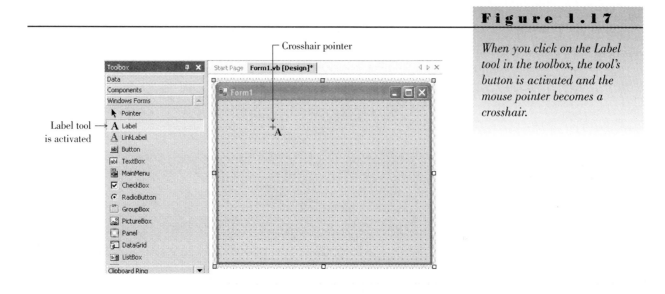

STEP 2: Point to a spot where you want one corner of the label, press the mouse button, and drag the pointer to the opposite corner (Figure 1.18). When you release the mouse button, the label and its default contents (Label1) will appear (Figure 1.19).

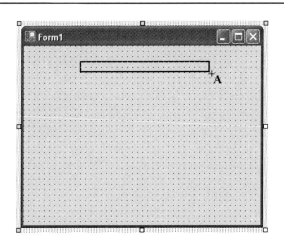

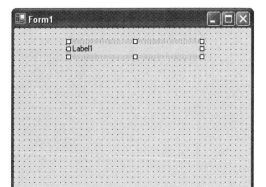

The label has eight small square **handles**, indicating that the control is currently selected. While a control is selected, you can delete it, resize it, or move it. Refer to Table 1.1 for instructions for selecting, deleting, resizing, and moving controls. Click outside of a control to deselect it.

Selecting, Deleting, Resizing, and Moving Controls on a Form   **T a b l e   1 . 1**

Select a control	Click on the control.
Delete a control	Select the control and then press the Delete key on the keyboard.
Move a control	Select the control, point inside the control (not on a handle), press the mouse button, and drag it to a new location.
Resize a control	Make sure the control is selected; then point to one of the handles, press the mouse button, and drag the handle. Drag a side handle to change the width, a bottom or top handle to change the height, or a corner handle to resize in two directions.

STEP 3: Draw a button on the form: Click on the Button tool in the toolbox, position the crosshair pointer for one corner of the button, and drag to the diagonally opposite corner (Figure 1.20). The new button should have selection handles.

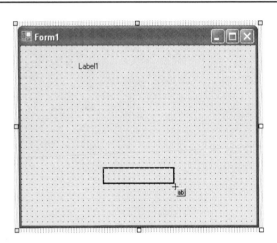

Figure 1.20

Select the Button tool and drag diagonally to create a new Button control.

STEP 4: Create another button using this alternative technique: Point to the Button tool in the toolbox and double-click. A new button of the default size will appear on top of the last-drawn control (Figure 1.21).

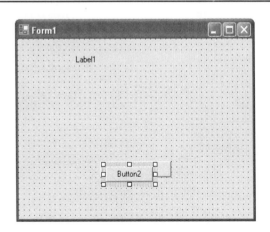

Figure 1.21

Place a new button on the form by double-clicking the Button tool in the toolbox. The new button appears on top of the previously selected control.

STEP 5: Keep the new button selected, point anywhere inside the button (not on a handle), and drag the button below your first button (Figure 1.22). As you drag the control, you see only its outline; when you release the mouse button, the control is actually moved to its new location.

STEP 6: Select each control and move and resize the controls as necessary. Make the two buttons the same size and line them up. Notice that the controls automatically snap to the grid dots.

✔**TIP**

If no control is selected when you double-click a tool, the new control is added to the upper-left corner of the form. ■

Figure 1.22

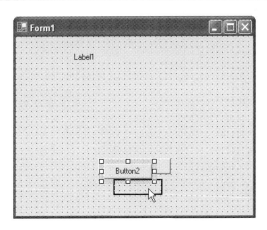

Drag the new button (Button2) below Button1. An outline of the control shows the new location for the control.

STEP 7: Point to one of the controls and click the right mouse button to display a **context menu**. On the context menu, select *Lock Controls* (Figure 1.23). Locking prevents you from accidentally moving the controls. When your controls are locked, a selected control has no handles.

Figure 1.23

After the controls are placed into the desired location, lock them in place by selecting Lock Controls from the context menu.

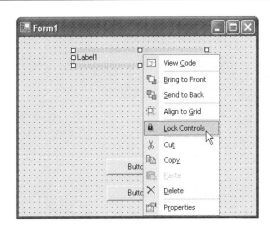

Note: You can unlock the controls at any time if you wish to redesign the form. Just click again on *Lock Controls* on the context menu to deselect it.

At this point you have designed the user interface and are ready to set the properties.

Set Properties

Set the Name and Text Properties for the Label

STEP 1: Click on the label you placed on the form; a shaded outline appears around the control. Next click on the title bar of the Properties window to make it the active window (Figure 1.24).

Figure 1.24

The currently selected control is shown in the Properties window.

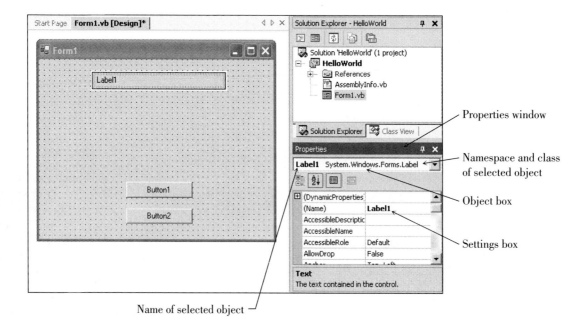

Properties window

Namespace and class of selected object

Object box

Settings box

Name of selected object

Notice that the Object box at the top of the Properties window is showing *Label1* (the name of the object) and *System.Windows. Forms.Label* as the class of the object. The actual class is Label; System.Windows.Forms is called the **namespace**, or the hierarchy used to locate the class.

STEP 2: Select the Name property. You may have to scroll up; Name is located near the top of the list. Click on *(Name)* and notice that the Settings box shows *Label1*, the default name of the label (Figure 1.25).

The **Name property** is used to refer to the control in program code.

☑ TIP

If the Properties window is not visible, you can press the F4 key to show it. ■

Figure 1.25

The Properties window. Click on the Name property to change the value in the Settings box.

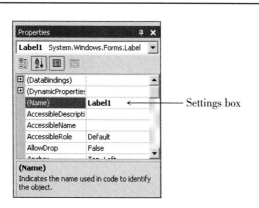

Settings box

STEP 3: Type "messageLabel" (without the quotation marks). See Figure 1.26.
After you change the name of the control and press Enter or Tab, you can see the new name in the Object box's drop-down list.

Figure 1.26

Type "messageLabel" into the Settings box for the Name property.

Sort the Properties list alphabetically

Properties	🔧 ✕
Label1 System.Windows.Forms.Label ▼	

⊞ (DataBindings)
⊞ (DynamicPropertie:
(Name)   **messageLabel** ◄——— The new name appears in the Settings box
AccessibleDescripti
AccessibleName
AccessibleRole   Default
AllowDrop   False

(Name)
Indicates the name used in code to identify the object.

STEP 4: Click on the Text property to select it. (Scroll the list if necessary.) Following the Name property, all properties should be in alphabetic order; if not, click the Alphabetic button at the top of the Properties window.
The **Text property** of a control determines what will be displayed on the form. Because nothing should display when the program begins, you must delete the value of the Text property (as described in the next two steps).

STEP 5: Double-click on *Label1* in the Settings box; the entry should appear selected (highlighted). See Figure 1.27.

STEP 6: Press the Delete key to delete the value of the Text property. Then press Enter and notice that the label on the form now appears empty

☑ **TIP**

Don't confuse the Name property with the Text property. You will use the Name property to refer to the control in your Basic code. The Text property determines what the user will see on the form. Visual Basic sets both of these properties to the same value by default, and it is easy to confuse them. ∎

Figure 1.27

Double-click in the Settings box to select the entry.

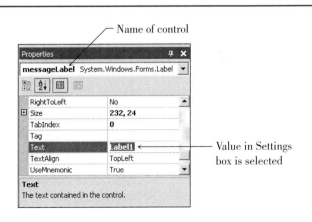

Name of control

Properties	🔧 ✕
messageLabel System.Windows.Forms.Label ▼	

RightToLeft   No
⊞ Size   **232, 24**
TabIndex   **0**
Tag
Text   **Label1** ◄——— Value in Settings box is selected
TextAlign   TopLeft
UseMnemonic   True

Text
The text contained in the control.

(Figure 1.28). Changes do not appear until you press Enter or move to another property or control.

Figure 1.28

Delete the value for the Text property from the Settings box; the label on the form also appears empty.

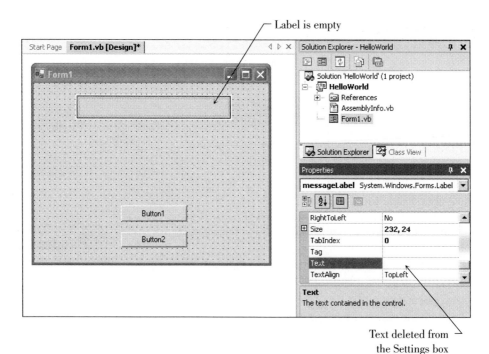

Label is empty

Text deleted from the Settings box

As an alternate technique, you can double-click on the property name, which automatically selects the entry in the Settings box. Then you can press the Delete key or just begin typing to change the entry.

Set the Name and Text Properties for the First Button

STEP 1: Click on the first button (Button1) to select it and then look at the Properties window. The Object box should show the name (*Button1*) and class (*System.Windows.Forms.Button*) of the button. See Figure 1.29.

Figure 1.29

Change the properties of the first button.

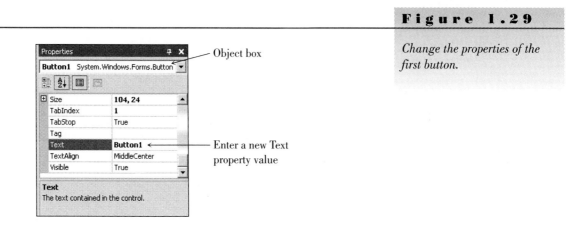

Object box

Enter a new Text property value

Problem? If you should double-click and code appears in the Document window, simply click on the *Form1.vb [Design]* tab at the top of the window.

STEP 2: Change the Name property of the button to "pushButton" (without the quotation marks).

Although the project would work fine without this step, we prefer to give this button a meaningful name, rather than use Button1, its default name. The guidelines for naming controls appear later in this chapter in the section "Naming Rules and Conventions for Objects."

STEP 3: Change the Text property to "Push Me" (without the quotation marks). This step changes the words that appear on top of the button.

Set the Name and Text Properties for the Second Button

STEP 1: Select Button2 and change its Name property to "exitButton".

STEP 2: Change the Text property to "Exit".

Change Properties of the Form

STEP 1: Click anywhere on the form, except on a control. The Properties window Object box should now show the form as the selected object (*Form1* as the object's name and *System.Windows.Forms.Form* as its class).

STEP 2: Change the Text property to "Hello World by Your Name" (again, no quotation marks and use your own name).

The Text property of a form determines the text to appear in the title bar. Your screen should now look like Figure 1.30.

TIP

Always set the Name property of controls before writing code. Although the program will still work if you reverse the order, the method names won't match the control names, which can cause confusion. ■

The form's Text property appears in the title bar

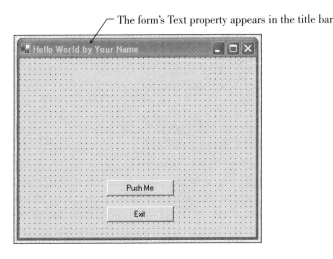

Figure 1.30

Change the form's Text property to set the text that appears in the form's title bar.

STEP 3: Click on the StartPosition property and notice the arrow on the property setting, indicating a drop-down list. Drop down the list and select *CenterScreen*. This will make your form appear in the center of the screen when the program runs.

STEP 4: Change the form's Name property to "helloForm". This step changes the name of the form's class, but not the name of the form's disk file, which is still Form1.

STEP 5: In the Solution Explorer, right-click on Form1.vb and choose *Rename* from the context menu. Change the filename to "helloForm.vb", making sure to retain the .vb extension. Press Enter when finished. The name of the file appears on the tab at the top of the editor window. Now the form's class and its file should both be renamed (Figure 1.31).

Figure 1.31

Change the name of the form class and the name of the form's file.

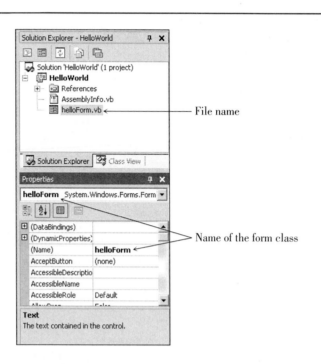

File name

Name of the form class

Set the Project's Startup Object

Whenever you change the name of the form, you must take one more step so that VB knows which form to run when the project begins. Each project has a Startup Object—the object with which to begin execution. By default, the Startup Object is Form1. If you change the name of the form, you must set the project's Startup Object property to the new name of the form.

STEP 1: In the Solution Explorer, click on HelloWorld to select the project. Then you can either select *Project / Properties* or right-click on the project name in the Solution Explorer and select *Properties* from the shortcut menu. In the project's *Property Pages* dialog box, drop down the list for *Startup object* and select helloForm (Figure 1.32).

Figure 1.32

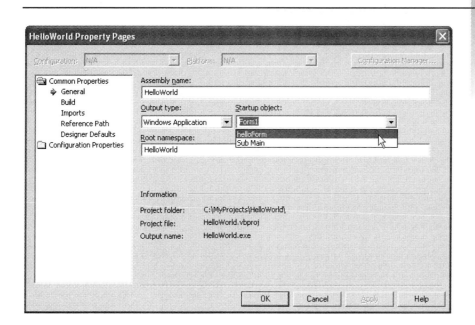

If you ever receive an error message when you attempt to run a project telling you that it can't find Sub Main, you know that you have forgotten this step. Figure 1.33 shows the message that appears in the Task List. You can double-click on the message line and the box in Figure 1.34 appears, where you can select your form name as the new startup object.

Figure 1.33

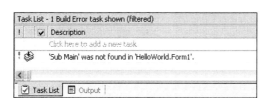

Figure 1.34

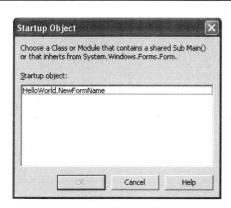

Write Code

Visual Basic Events

While your project is running, the user can do many things, such as move the mouse around; click on either button; move, resize, or close your form's window; or jump to another application. Each action by the user causes an event to occur in your Visual Basic project. Some events (like clicking on a button) you care about, and some events (like moving the mouse and resizing the window) you do not care about. If you write Basic code for a particular event, then Visual Basic will respond to the event and automatically execute your procedure. *VB ignores events for which no procedures are written.*

Visual Basic Event Procedures

You write code in Visual Basic in **procedures**. For now, each of your procedures will be a **sub procedure**, which begins with the words `Private Sub` and ends with `End Sub`. (Later you will also learn about other types of procedures.) Note that many programmers refer to sub procedures as subprograms or subroutines. Subprogram is acceptable; subroutine is not, because Basic actually has a different statement for a subroutine, which is not the same as a sub procedure.

Visual Basic automatically names your **event procedures**. The name consists of the object name, an underscore (_), and the name of the event. For example, the Click event for your button called pushButton will be pushButton_Click. For the sample project you are writing, you will have a pushButton_Click procedure and an exitButton_Click procedure.

Visual Basic Code Statements

This first project requires two Visual Basic statements: the **remark** and the **assignment statement**. You also will execute a method of an object.

The Remark Statement

Remark statements, sometimes called *comments*, are used for project documentation only. They are not considered "executable" and have no effect when the project runs. The purpose of remarks is to make the project more readable and understandable by the people who read it.

Good programming practices dictate that programmers include remarks to clarify their projects. Every procedure should begin with a remark that describes its purpose. Every project should have remarks that explain the purpose of the program and provide identifying information such as the name of the programmer and the date the program was written and/or modified. In addition, it is a good idea to place remarks within the logic of a project, especially if the purpose of any statements might be unclear.

When you try to read someone else's code, or your own after a period of time, you will appreciate the generous use of remarks.

Visual Basic remarks begin with an apostrophe. Most of the time your remarks will be on a separate line that starts with an apostrophe. You can also add an apostrophe and a remark to the right end of a line of code.

The Remark Statement—Examples

```
' This project was written by Jonathon Edwards.
' Exit the project.
messageLabel.Text = "Hello World" ' Assign the message to the Text property.
```

The Assignment Statement

The **assignment statement** assigns a value to a property or variable (you learn about variables in Chapter 3). Assignment statements operate from right to left; that is, the value appearing on the right side of the equal sign is assigned to the property named on the left of the equal sign. It is often helpful to read the equal sign as "is replaced by." For example, the following assignment statement would read "messageLabel.Text is replaced by Hello World."

```
messageLabel.Text = "Hello World"
```

The Assignment Statement—General Form

```
Object.Property = value
```

The value named on the right side of the equal sign is assigned to (or placed into) the property named on the left.

The Assignment Statement—Examples

```
titleLabel.Text = "A Snazzy Program"
addressLabel.Text = "1234 South North Street"
messageLabel.AutoSize = True
numberInteger = 12
```

Notice that when the value to assign is some actual text (called a *literal*), it is enclosed in quotation marks. This convention allows you to type any combination of alpha and numeric characters. If the value is numeric, do not enclose it in quotation marks. And do not place quotation marks around the terms True and False, which Visual Basic recognizes as special key terms.

Ending a Program by Executing a Method

To execute a method of an object, you write:

```
Object.Method()
```

Notice that methods always have parentheses. Although this might seem like a bother, it's helpful to distinguish between properties and methods: Methods always have parentheses; properties don't.

Examples

```
helloButton.Hide()
messageLabel.Show()
```

To execute a method of the current object (the form itself), you use the `Me` keyword for the object. And the method that terminates execution is `Close`.

```
Me.Close()
```

In most cases, you will include `Me.Close()` in the sub procedure for an Exit button or an *Exit* menu choice.

Note: The keyword `Me` refers to the current object. You can omit `Me`, since a method without an object reference defaults to the current object.

TIP

If you don't type the parentheses after a method, the editor adds it for you, for most (but not all) methods. ■

Code the Event Procedures for Hello World

Code the Click Event for the Push Me Button

STEP 1: Double-click the Push Me button. The Visual Studio editor opens with the first and last lines of your sub procedure already in place, with the insertion point indented inside the sub procedure (Figure 1.35).

For now, you can ignore the extra lines of code that appear above your sub procedure.

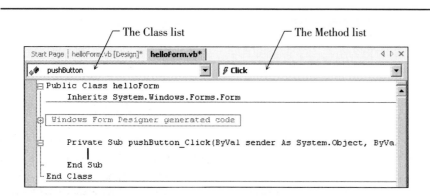

Figure 1.35

The Editor window, showing the first and last lines of the pushButton_Click sub procedure.

STEP 2: Type this remark statement:

```
' Display the Hello World message.
```

Notice that the editor automatically displays remarks in green (unless you or someone else has changed the color with the Environment option).

Follow good coding conventions and indent all lines between `Private Sub` and `End Sub`. The smart editor attempts to help you follow this convention. Also, always leave a blank line after the remarks at the top of a sub procedure.

STEP 3: Press Enter twice and then type this assignment statement:

```
messageLabel.Text = "Hello World"
```

Note: When you type the period after messageLabel, an IntelliSense list pops up showing the properties and methods available for a Label control. Although you can type the entire word *Text*, you can allow

IntelliSense to help you. As soon as you type the *T*, the list automatically scrolls to the first word that begins with *T*. Type the next letter, *e*, and the property *Text* appears highlighted. You can press the spacebar to select the word and continue typing the rest of the statement.

This assignment statement assigns the literal "Hello World" to the Text property of the control called messageLabel. Compare your screen to Figure 1.36.

STEP 4: Return to the form (Figure 1.30) by clicking on the *helloForm.vb [Design]* tab on the Document window (Figure 1.36).

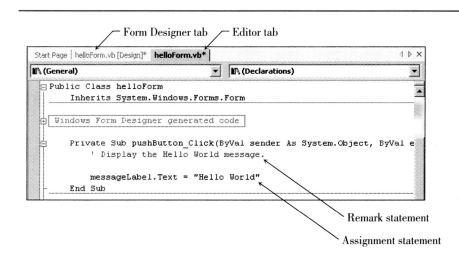

Figure 1.36

Type the remark and assignment statement for the pushButton_Click event procedure.

You may have noticed messages appearing at the bottom of the screen in the Task List as you typed the statements. The smart editor is trying to help you by telling you about any statements that are in error or incomplete. You may want to wait until you complete a statement before you look at any messages.

Code the Click Event for the Exit Button

STEP 1: Double-click the Exit button to open the editor for the exitButton_Click event.

STEP 2: Type this remark:

```
' Exit the project.
```

STEP 3: Press Enter twice and type this Basic statement:

```
Me.Close()
```

☑ TIP

Allow the editor and IntelliSense to help you. If the IntelliSense list does not pop up, likely you misspelled the name of the control. And don't worry about capitalization when you type the name of an object; if the name matches a defined object, the editor fixes the capitalization. ∎

STEP 4: Make sure your code looks like the code shown in Figure 1.37.

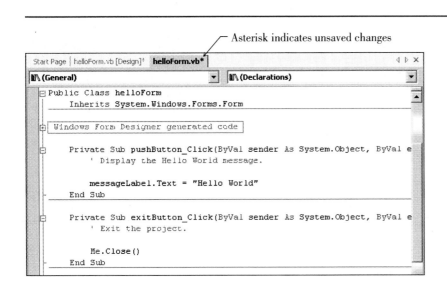

Asterisk indicates unsaved changes

F i g u r e   1 . 3 7

*Type the code for the
exitButton_Click event
procedure. Notice that an
asterisk appears on the tab at
the top of the window,
indicating that there are
unsaved changes in the file.*

Run the Project

After you have finished writing the code, you are ready to run the project. Use one of these three techniques:

1. Open the *Debug* menu and choose *Start*.
2. Press the Start button on the toolbar.
3. Press F5, the shortcut key for the *Start* command.

Start the Project Running

STEP 1: Choose one of the three methods previously listed to start your project running.

Problems? See "Finding and Fixing Errors" later in this chapter. You must correct any errors and restart the program.

If all went well, the Visual Studio title bar now indicates that you are in run time and the grid dots have disappeared from your form (Figure 1.38). (The grid dots help you align the controls; you may turn them off if you prefer.)

TIP

Accept an entry from the Intelli-Sense popup list by typing the punctuation that follows the entry or by pressing the Enter key. You also can scroll the list and select with your mouse. ∎

TIP

If your form disappears during run time, click its button on the task bar. ∎

F i g u r e   1 . 3 8

*When you run the project, the
form's grid dots disappear.*

Click the Push Me Button

STEP 1: Click the Push Me button. Your "Hello World" message appears in the label (Figure 1.39).

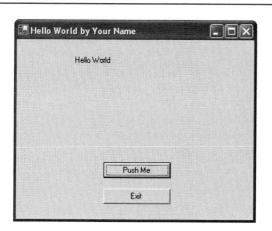

Click the Exit Button

STEP 1: Click the Exit button. Your project terminates, and you return to design time.

Save Your Work

Of course, you must always save your work often. Except for a very small project like this one, you will usually save your work as you go along. Unless you (or someone else) has changed the setting in the IDE's *Options* dialog box, your files are automatically saved each time you build (compile) or execute (run) your project. You also can save the files as you work.

Save the Files

STEP 1: Open the Visual Studio *File* menu and choose *Save All*. This option saves the current form, project, and solution files. You already selected the path for the files when you first created the project. (You cannot change the path after beginning a project. If you want to move or rename the project, it must be closed. See Appendix C for help.)

Close the Project

STEP 1: Open the *File* menu and choose *Close Solution*. If you haven't saved since your last change, you will be prompted to save.

After your project closes, you should again see the Visual Studio Start Page. This time you may see your project on the list.

Note: If the Start Page does not appear, display it with *Help / Show Start Page*.

Open the Project

Now is the time to test your save operation by opening the project from disk. You can choose one of four ways to open a saved project:

- If your project appears on the Start Page, you can open it by clicking on its name.

- Click the Open Project button on the Start Page and browse to find your .sln file.

- Select *Open Solution* from the Visual Studio *File* menu and browse to find your .sln file.

- Choose the solution from the *Files / Recent Projects* menu item.

Open the Project File

STEP 1: Open your project by choosing one of the previously listed methods. Remember that the file to open is the .sln file.

STEP 2: If you do not see your form on the screen, check the Solution Explorer window—it should say *HelloWorld* for both the solution and the project. Select the icon for your form: helloForm.vb. You can double-click the icon or single-click and click on the View Designer button at the top of the Solution Explorer (Figure 1.40); your form will appear in the Form Designer. Notice that you also can click on the View Code button to display your form's code in the Editor window.

Figure 1.40

To display the form layout, select the form name and click on the View Designer button, or double-click on the form name. Click on the View Code button to display the code in the editor.

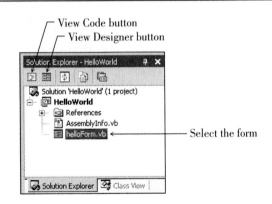

View Code button
View Designer button

Select the form

Modify the Project

Now it's time to make some changes to the project. We'll change the size of the "Hello World" message, display the message in two different languages, and display the programmer name (that's you) on the form.

Change the Size and Alignment of the Message

STEP 1: Right-click one of the form's controls to display the context menu. If your controls are currently locked, select *Lock Controls* to unlock the controls so that you can make changes.

STEP 2: Click on the label on your form, which will make selection handles appear. (If you see a dark border instead of selection handles, you must unlock the controls, as described in Step 1.)

STEP 3: Widen the label on both ends by dragging the handles wider. (Drag the right end farther right and the left end farther left.)

STEP 4: With the label still selected, scroll to the Font property in the Properties window. The Font property is actually a Font object that has a number of properties. To see the Font properties, click on the small plus sign on the left (Figure 1.41); the Font properties will appear showing the current values (Figure 1.42).

Click to expand → the Font list

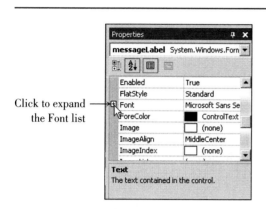

Figure 1.41

Click on the Font's plus sign to view the properties of the Font object.

Figure 1.42

You can change the individual properties of the Font object.

Font properties —

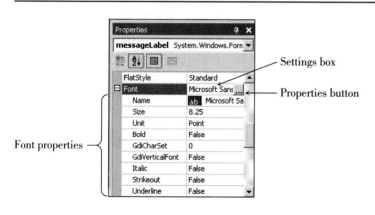

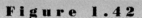

— Settings box

— Properties button

You can change any of the Font properties in the Properties window, such as setting the Font's Size, Bold, or Italic properties. You also can display the *Font* dialog box and make changes there.

To display the *Font* dialog box, click on the button with an ellipsis on top, which appears in the Settings box. The button is called the *Properties button*; the ellipsis indicates that clicking on the button will display a dialog box with choices.

STEP 5: Click the Properties button to display the *Font* dialog box (Figure 1.43). Select 12 point if it is available. (If it isn't available, choose another number larger than the current setting.) Click OK to close the *Font* dialog box.

Figure 1.43

Choose 12 point on the Font dialog box.

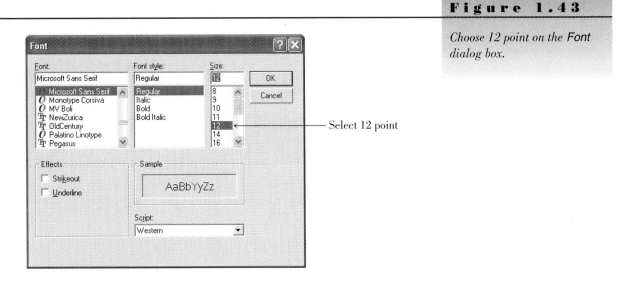

Select 12 point

STEP 6: Select the TextAlign property. The Properties button that appears with the down-pointing arrow indicates a drop-down list of choices. Drop down the list (Figure 1.44) and choose the center box; the alignment property changes to *MiddleCenter*.

✓TIP

You can change the Font property of the form, which sets the default Font for all objects on the form. ■

Figure 1.44

Select the center box for the TextAlign property.

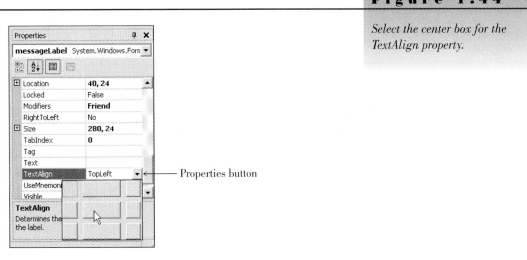

Properties button

Add a New Label for Your Name

STEP 1: Click on the Label tool in the toolbox and create a new label along the bottom edge of your form (Figure 1.45). (You can resize the form if necessary.)

Figure 1.45

Add a new label for your name at the bottom of the form.

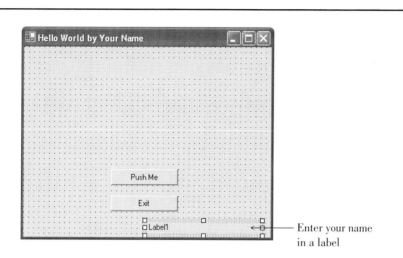

Enter your name in a label

STEP 2: Change the label's Text property to "by Your Name". (Use your name and omit the quotation marks.)

Note: You do not need to name this label because it will never be referred to in the code.

Change the Location and Text of the Push Me Button

Because we plan to display the message in one of two languages, we'll change the text on the Push Me button to "English" and move the button to allow for a second button.

STEP 1: Select the Push Me button and change its Text property to English.
STEP 2: Move the English button to the left to make room for a Spanish button (see Figure 1.46).

Figure 1.46

Move the English button to the left and add a Spanish button.

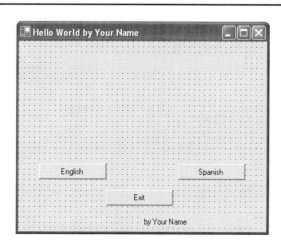

Add a Spanish Button

STEP 1: Add a new button. Move and resize it as necessary, referring to Figure 1.46.

STEP 2: Change the Name property of the new button to spanishButton.

STEP 3: Change the Text property of the new button to Spanish.

Add an Event Procedure for the Spanish Button

STEP 1: Double-click on the Spanish button to open the editor for spanish-Button_Click.

STEP 2: Add a remark:

```
' Display the Hello World message in Spanish.
```

STEP 3: Press Enter twice and type the following Basic code line:

```
messageLabel.Text = "Hola Mundo"
```

STEP 4: Return to design view.

Lock the Controls

STEP 1: When you are satisfied with the placement of the controls on the form, display the context menu and select *Lock Controls* again.

Save and Run the Project

STEP 1: Save your project again. You can use the *File / Save All* menu command or the Save All toolbar button.

STEP 2: Run your project again. Try clicking on the English button and the Spanish button.

Problems? See "Finding and Fixing Errors" later in this chapter.

STEP 3: Click the Exit button to end program execution.

Add Remarks

Good documentation guidelines require some more remarks in the project. Always begin each procedure with remarks that tell the purpose of the procedure. In addition, each project file needs identifying remarks at the top.

The **Declarations section** at the top of the file is a good location for these remarks.

STEP 1: Display the code in the editor and click in front of the first line (Public Class helloForm). Make sure that you have an insertion point; if the entire first line is selected, press the left arrow to set the insertion point.

Press Enter to create a blank line.

Warning: If you accidentally deleted the first line, click Undo (or press Ctrl + Z) and try again.

STEP 2: Move the insertion point up to the blank line and type the following remarks, one per line (Figure 1.47):

```
'Project:       Hello World
'Programmer:    Your Name (Use your own name here.)
'Date:          (Fill in today's date.)
'Description:   This project will display a "Hello World"
'               message in two different languages.
```

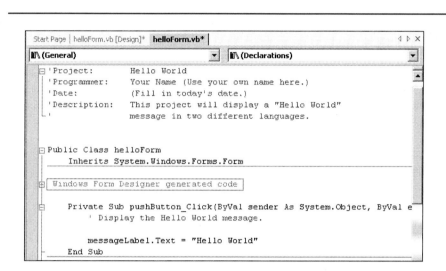

Figure 1.47

Enter remarks at the top of the form file.

Explore the Editor Window

STEP 1: Notice the two drop-down list boxes at the top of the Editor window, called the *Class list* and the *Method list*. You can use these lists to move to any procedure in your code.

STEP 2: Click on the left down-pointing arrow to view the Class list. Notice that every object in your form is listed there (Figure 1.48). At the top of the list, you see the name of your form: *helloForm*.

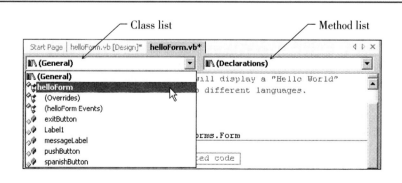

Figure 1.48

View the list of objects in this form by dropping down the Class list. Select an object from the list to display the sub procedures for that object.

STEP 3: Click on *helloForm* to select it. Then notice the Method list on the right, which says *(Declarations)*. Clicking on *(Declarations)* is the quick way to jump to the Declarations section of a file.

STEP 4: Drop down the Class list (the left list) and select spanishButton.

STEP 5: Drop down the Method list (the right list); it shows all possible events for a Button control. Notice that the Click event is bold and the rest are not. Any event for which you have written an event procedure appears in bold.

STEP 6: Select the Click event from the Method list; the insertion point jumps to the event procedure for spanishButton. You are currently viewing the spanishButton_Click event procedure.

To write code for more than one event for an object, use the Method drop-down list. You can jump to another procedure by selecting its name from the list. Selecting a new event from the Method list causes the editor to generate the `Sub` and `End Sub` lines for that procedure.

Finish Up

STEP 1: Save the project again.

Print the Code

Select the Printing Options

STEP 1: Make sure that the Editor window is open, showing your form's code. The *File / Print* command is disabled unless the code is displaying and its window selected.

STEP 2: Open the *File* menu and choose *Print.* Click OK.

A Sample Printout

This output is produced when you print the form's code. Notice the ↙ symbol used to continue long lines on the printout. On the screen, those long lines are not split, but scroll off the right side of the screen.

If you are using a color printer, the colors on the screen also will appear on the printed output.

```
A:\HelloWorld\helloForm.vb                                                    1
'Project:         Hello World
'Programmer:      Your Name
'Date:            Today's Date
'Description:     This project will display a "Hello World"
'                 message in two different languages.

Public Class helloForm
  Inherits System.Windows.Forms.Form

Windows Form Designer generated code

    Private Sub pushButton_Click(ByVal sender As System.Object, ByVal e As
    System.EventArgs) ↙
```

```
Handles pushButton.Click
    ' Display the Hello World Message.

    messageLabel.Text = "Hello World"
End Sub

Private Sub exitButton_Click(ByVal sender As System.Object, ByVal e As
System.EventArgs) ↙
Handles exitButton.Click
    ' Exit the project.

    Me.Close()
End Sub

Private Sub spanishButton_Click(ByVal sender As System.Object, ByVal e As System.↙
EventArgs) Handles spanishButton.Click
    ' Display the Hello World message in Spanish.

    messageLabel.Text = "Hola Mundo"
End Sub
End Class
```

Finding and Fixing Errors

You already may have seen some errors as you entered the first sample project. Programming errors come in three varieties: **syntax errors**, **run-time errors**, and **logic errors**.

Syntax Errors

When you break VB's rules for punctuation, format, or spelling, you generate a syntax error. Fortunately, the smart editor finds most syntax errors and even corrects many of them for you. The syntax errors that the editor cannot identify are found and reported by the compiler as it attempts to convert the code into intermediate machine language. A compiler-reported syntax error may be referred to as a *compile error*.

The editor can correct some syntax errors by making assumptions, and not even report the error to you. For example, if you type the opening quote of

"Hello World" but forget the closing quote, the editor automatically adds the closing quote when you move to the next line. And if you forget the opening and closing parentheses after a method name, such as *Close()*, again the editor will add them for you when you move off the line. Of course, sometimes the editor will make a wrong assumption, but you will be watching, right?

The editor identifies syntax errors as you move off the offending line. A blue squiggly line appears under the part of the line that the editor cannot interpret and a message appears in the Task list at the bottom of the screen (Figure 1.49). Notice also that the Task list shows the line number of the statement that caused the error. You can display line numbers on the source code (Figure 1.50) with *Tools / Options / Text Editor / Basic / Display / Line Numbers*. You also can pause the mouse pointer over the error line to pop up an error message (refer to Figure 1.50).

Figure   1.49

The editor identifies a syntax error with a squiggly blue line and places a message in the Task list.

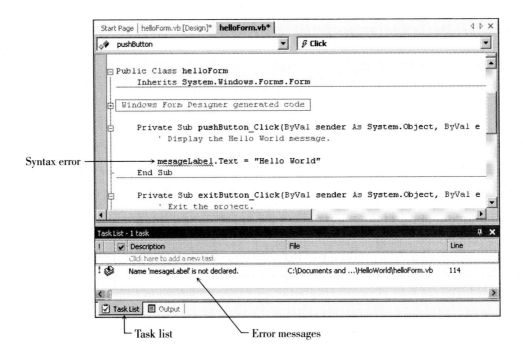

Syntax error

Task list

Error messages

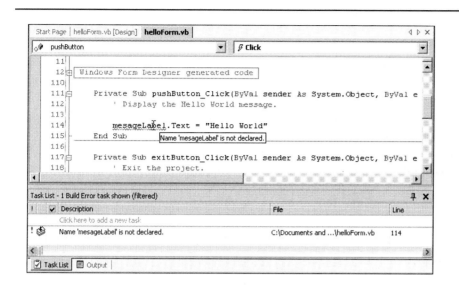

Figure 1.50

You can display line numbers in the source code to help identify the lines, and you can point to an error to pop up the error message.

Note: If the Task list does not appear, show it with *View / Other Windows / Task List.*

The quickest way to jump to an error line is to point to a message in the Task list and double-click. The line in error will display in the Editor window with the error highlighted (Figure 1.51).

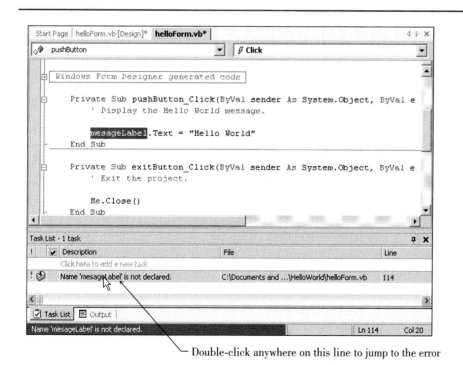

Figure 1.51

Quickly jump to the line in error by double-clicking on the error message in the Task list.

Double-click anywhere on this line to jump to the error

If a syntax error is found by the compiler, you will see the dialog box shown in Figure 1.52. Click No and return to the editor, correct your errors, and run the program again.

Figure 1.52

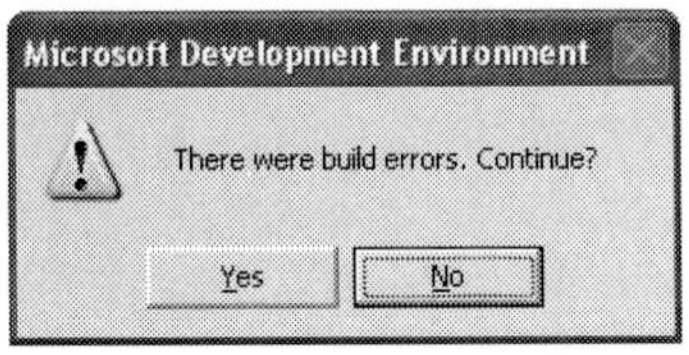

Run-Time Errors

If your project halts during execution, it is called a *run-time error* or an *exception*. Visual Basic displays a dialog box and highlights the statement causing the problem.

Statements that cannot execute correctly cause run-time errors. The statements are correctly formed Basic statements that pass the syntax checking; however, the statements fail to execute due to some serious issue. You can cause run-time errors by attempting to do impossible arithmetic operations, such as calculating with nonnumeric data, dividing by zero, or finding the square root of a negative number.

In Chapter 3 you will learn to catch exceptions, so that the program does not come to a halt when an error occurs.

Logic Errors

When your program contains logic errors, your project runs but produces incorrect results. Perhaps the results of a calculation are incorrect or the wrong text appears or the text is okay but appears in the wrong location.

Beginning programmers often overlook their logic errors. If the project runs, it must be right—right? All too often, that statement is not correct. You may need to use a calculator to check the output. Check all aspects of the project output: computations, text, and spacing.

For example, the Hello World project in this chapter has event procedures for printing "Hello World" in English and in Spanish. If the contents of the two procedures were switched, the program would work, but the results would be incorrect.

The following code does not give the proper instructions to display the message in Spanish:

```
Private Sub spanishButton_Click
    ' Display the Hello World Message in Spanish.

    messageLabel.Text = "Hello World"
End Sub
```

Project Debugging

If you talk to any computer programmer, you will learn that programs don't have errors, but that programs get "bugs" in them. Finding and fixing these bugs is called ***debugging***.

For syntax errors and run-time errors, your job is easier. Visual Basic displays the Editor window with the offending line highlighted. However, you must identify and locate logic errors yourself.

A Clean Compile

After you locate the problem and fix it, you must recompile the program and run it again. Each time you compile the program, you must have a **clean compile**, which means zero errors (Figure 1.53). You are looking for this line in the Output window:

```
Build: 1 succeeded, 0 failed, 0 skipped
```

Figure 1.53

Zero build errors means that you have a clean compile.

You can confuse yourself if you try to run a program without first getting a clean compile. For example, say you *do* get a clean compile and run the program once; then you make some modifications to the program and tell it to run again. If you ignore the error message (refer to Figure 1.52) and attempt to run it anyway, you will actually be running the last cleanly compiled version, without the changes that you just made.

The Visual Studio IDE has some very helpful tools to aid in debugging your projects. The debugging tools are covered in Chapter 4.

TIP

If you get the message "There were build errors. Continue?" always say *No*. If you say *Yes*, the last cleanly compiled version runs, rather than the current version. ■

Naming Rules and Conventions for Objects

Using good consistent names for objects can make a project easier to read and understand, as well as easier to debug. You *must* follow the Visual Basic rules for naming objects, procedures, and variables. In addition, conscientious programmers also follow certain naming conventions.

Most professional programming shops have a set of standards that their programmers must use. Those standards may differ from the ones you find in this book, but the most important point is this: *Good programmers follow standards. You should have a set of standards and always follow them.*

The Naming Rules

When you select a name for an object, Visual Basic requires the name to begin with a letter or an underscore. The name can contain letters, digits, and underscores. An object name cannot include a space or punctuation mark and cannot be a reserved word, such as Exit or If, but can contain one. For example, ExitCalculation and IfGood are legal.

The Naming Conventions

This text follows standard naming conventions, which help make projects more understandable. When naming controls, use **camel casing**, which means that you begin the name with a lowercase character and capitalize each additional word in the name. Make up a meaningful name and append the full name of the control's class. Do not use abbreviations unless it is a commonly used term that everyone will understand. All names must be meaningful and indicate the purpose of the object.

Examples
messageLabel
exitButton
dataEntryForm
discountRateLabel

Do not keep the default names assigned by Visual Basic, such as Button1 and Label3. Also, do not name your objects with numbers. The exception to this rule is for labels that never change during project execution. These labels usually hold items such as titles, instructions, and labels for other controls. Leaving these labels with their default names is perfectly acceptable and is practiced in this text.

Refer to Table 1.2 for sample object names.

Recommended Naming Conventions for Visual Basic Objects   **T a b l e   1 . 2**

Object Class	Example
Form	dataEntryForm
Button	exitButton
TextBox	paymentAmountTextBox
Label	totalLabel
Radio button	boldRadioButton
CheckBox	printSummaryCheckBox
Horizontal scroll bar	rateHorizontalScrollBar
Vertical scroll bar	temperatureVerticalScrollBar
PictureBox	landscapePictureBox
ComboBox	bookListComboBox
ListBox	ingredientsListBox

Visual Studio Help

Visual Studio has an extensive Help facility, which contains much more information than you will ever use. You can look up any Basic statement, class, property, method, or programming concept. Many coding examples are available, and you can copy and paste the examples into your own project, modifying them if you wish.

The VS Help facility is greatly changed and expanded in the .NET version. Help includes all of the Microsoft Developer Network library (MSDN), which contains several books, technical articles, and the Microsoft Knowledge Base, a database of frequently asked questions and their answers. MSDN includes reference materials for the VS IDE, the .NET Framework, Visual Basic, C#, J#, and C++. You will want to filter the information to display only the VB information.

Installing and Running MSDN

You can run MSDN from a hard drive, a network drive, a CD, or the Web. If you run from a CD, you must keep the CD in the drive while you develop programs, and, of course, if you plan to access MSDN from the Web, you must have a live Internet connection as you work.

When you install Visual Studio, by default MSDN is installed on the hard drive. If you don't want to install it there, you must specifically choose this option. You can access MSDN on the Web at http://msdn.microsoft.com.

Or, if you want to go directly to VB Help, add this link to your favorites: http://msdn.microsoft.com/library/default.asp?url=/library/en-us/vblr7/html/vboriVBlangRefTopNode.asp

The expanded Help is a two-edged sword: You have available a wealth of materials, but it may take some time to find the topic you want.

Viewing Help Topics

You view the Help topics in various windows in the VS IDE. When you choose *Contents*, *Index*, or *Search* from the *Help* menu, a new tabbed window opens in the same location as the Solution Explorer (Figure 1.54). Select a topic and the correct page appears in the Document window. Notice the new tab at the top of the Document window in Figure 1.54.

F i g u r e   1 . 5 4

The Help Index, Contents, and Search windows appear as tabs in the Solution Explorer window. Note that this window was widened to show the text in the tabs.

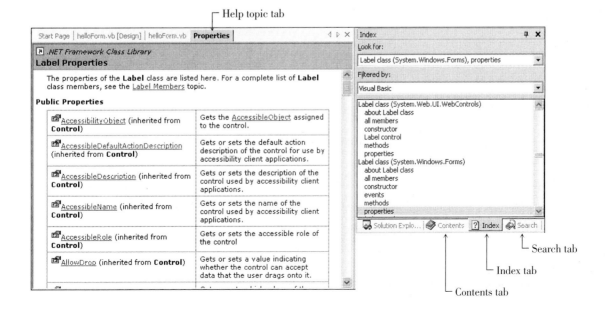

You can choose to filter the Help topics so that you don't have to view topics for all of the languages when you search for a particular topic. Drop down the *Filtered by* list and choose *Visual Basic* (Figure 1.55).

Figure 1.55

Filter the Help topics so that only the Visual Basic topics appear.

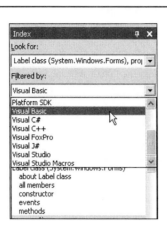

Sometimes you may select a topic that has several pages from which to choose. When that happens, a new tabbed window opens in the Task List window (Figure 1.56). Double-click the topic you wish to view and the selected page appears in the Document window.

Figure 1.56

Multiple matching topics appear in a tabbed window at the bottom of the screen. Select a topic from the list and the corresponding page appears in the Document window.

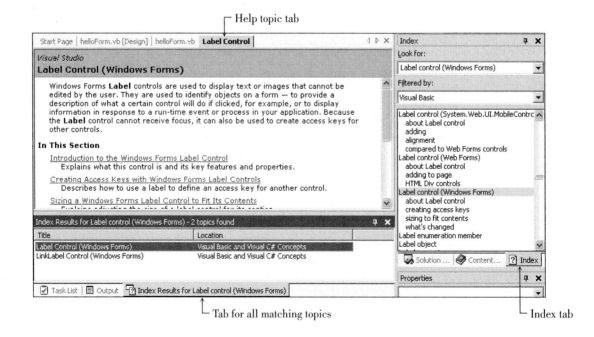

Many Help topics have entries for both Windows Forms and Web Forms. For now, always choose Windows Forms. Chapters 1 through 8 deal with Windows Forms exclusively; Web Forms are introduced in Chapter 9.

A good way to start using Help is to view the topics that demonstrate how to look up topics in Help. Select *Help / Contents* and *(no filter)*. Then choose *Visual Studio .NET / Getting Assistance / Using Help in Visual Studio .NET.*

Context-Sensitive Help

A quick way to view Help on any topic is to use **context-sensitive Help**. Select a VB object, such as a form or control, or place the insertion point in a word in the editor and press F1. The corresponding Help topic will appear in the Document window, if possible, saving you a search. You can display context-sensitive Help about the environment by clicking in an area of the screen and pressing Shift + F1.

Managing Windows

At times you may have more windows and tabs open than you want. You can hide or close any window, or switch to a different window.

- To close a window that is a part of a tabbed window, click the window's Close button. Only the top window will close.

- To hide a window that is a part of a tabbed window, right-click the tab and select *Hide* from the context menu.

- To switch to another window that is part of a tabbed window, click on its tab.

For additional help with the environment, see Appendix C, "Tips and Shortcuts for Mastering the Visual Studio Environment."

▶ Feedback 1.1

Note: Answers for Feedback questions appear in Appendix A.

1. Use the *Help* menu's *Index*, filter by *Visual Basic*, and type "button control". In the Index list, notice that one heading covers Web Forms and another covers Windows Forms. Click on the main topic *Button control (Windows Forms)*. In the Document window the topic "Introduction to the Windows Forms Button Control" topic displays. Click this topic and the corresponding page should appear in the Document window. Notice that additional links appear in the text in the Document window. You can click on a link to view another topic.
2. Display the Editor window of your Hello World project. Click on the `Close` method to place the insertion point. Press the F1 key to view context-sensitive help.
3. Display the *Help* menu and view all of the options. Try the *Contents, Index, Search, Index Results,* and *Search Results* options. Notice the *Next Topic* and *Previous Topic* items and the *Show Start Page* item; you can use this command to show the Start Page if its tab does not appear in the Document window.

Summary

1. Visual Basic is an object-oriented language used to write application programs that run in Windows or on the Internet using a graphical user interface (GUI).
2. In the OOP object model, classes are used to create objects that have properties, methods, and events.
3. The current release of Visual Basic is called .NET 2003. Visual Basic .NET is part of Visual Studio .NET. VB .NET has a Standard Edition, a Professional Edition, an Enterprise Developer Edition, and an Enterprise Architect Edition.
4. The .NET Framework provides an environment for the objects from many languages to interoperate. Each language compiles to Microsoft Intermediate Language (MSIL) and runs in the Common Language Runtime (CLR).
5. To plan a project, first sketch the user interface and then list the objects and properties needed. Then plan the necessary event procedures.
6. The three steps to creating a Visual Basic project are (1) define the user interface, (2) set the properties, and (3) write the Basic code.
7. A Visual Basic application is called a *solution*. Each solution can contain multiple projects, and each project may contain multiple forms and additional files. The solution file has an extension of .sln, a project file has an extension of .vbproj, and form files and additional VB files have an extension of .vb. In addition, the Visual Studio environment and the VB compiler both create several more files.
8. The Visual Studio integrated development environment (IDE) consists of several tools, including a form designer, an editor, a compiler, a debugger, an object browser, and a Help facility.
9. VB has three modes: design time, run time, and break time.
10. You can customize the Visual Studio IDE and reset all customizations back to their default state.
11. You create the user interface for an application by adding controls from the toolbox to a form. You can move, resize, and delete the controls.
12. The Name property of a control is used to refer to the control in code. The Text property holds the words that the user sees on the screen.
13. Visual Basic code is written in procedures. Sub procedures begin with the word `Sub` and end with `End Sub`.
14. Project remarks are used for documentation. Good programming practice requires remarks in every procedure and in the Declarations section of a file.
15. Assignment statements assign a value to a property or a variable. Assignment statements work from right to left, assigning the value on the right side of the equal sign to the property or variable named on the left side of the equal sign.
16. The `Me.Close()` method terminates program execution.
17. Each event to which you want to respond requires an event procedure.
18. You can print out the Visual Basic code for documentation.
19. Three types of errors can occur in a Visual Basic project: syntax errors, which violate the syntax rules of the Basic language; run-time errors, which contain a statement that cannot execute properly; and logic errors, which produce erroneous results.
20. Finding and fixing program errors is called *debugging*.

21. You must have a clean compile each time you modify a program before you can run the program.
22. Following good naming conventions can help make a project easier to debug.
23. Visual Basic Help has very complete descriptions of all project elements and their uses. You can use the *Contents*, *Index*, *Search*, or context-sensitive Help.

Key Terms

assignment statement   *28*

break time   *13*

Button   *18*

camel casing   *46*

class   *4*

clean compile   *45*

code   *6*

context menu   *21*

context-sensitive Help   *49*

control   *3*

debugging   *45*

Declarations section   *38*

design time   *13*

Document window   *10*

Enterprise Architect Edition   *6*

Enterprise Developer Edition   *6*

event   *4*

event procedure   *28*

form   *3*

Form Designer   *11*

graphical user interface (GUI)   *2*

handle   *19*

Help   *11*

integrated development environment
   (IDE)   *8*

Label   *18*

logic error   *41*

method   *4*

Name property   *22*

namespace   *22*

object   *4*

object-oriented programming
   (OOP)   *3*

procedure   *28*

Professional Edition   *6*

project file   *7*

Properties window   *11*

property   *4*

pseudocode   *6*

remark   *28*

run time   *13*

run-time error   *41*

solution   *7*

Solution Explorer window   *11*

solution file   *7*

Standard Edition   *6*

sub procedure   *28*

syntax error   *41*

Text property   *23*

toolbar   *10*

toolbox   *11*

user interface   *6*

Visual Studio environment   *8*

Review Questions

1. What are objects and properties? How are they related to each other?
2. What are the three steps for planning and creating Visual Basic projects? Describe what happens in each step.
3. What is the purpose of these Visual Basic file types: .sln, .suo, and .vb?
4. When is Visual Basic in design time? run time? break time?
5. What is the purpose of the Name property of a control?
6. Which property determines what appears on the form for a Label control?
7. What is the purpose of the Text property of a button? the Text property of a form?
8. What does pushButton_Click mean? To what does pushButton refer? To what does Click refer?

9. What is a Visual Basic event? Give some examples of events.
10. What property must be set to center text in a label? What should be the value of the property?
11. What is the Declarations section of a file? What belongs there?
12. What is meant by the term *debugging*?
13. What is a syntax error, when does it occur, and what might cause it?
14. What is a run-time error, when does it occur, and what might cause it?
15. What is a logic error, when does it occur, and what might cause it?
16. Tell the class of control and the likely purpose of each of these object names:
    addressLabel
    exitButton
    nameTextBox
    textBlueRadioButton
17. What does context-sensitive Help mean? How can you use it to see the Help page for a button?

Programming Exercises

1.1 For your first Visual Basic exercise, you must first complete the Hello World project. Then add buttons and event procedures to display the "Hello World" message in two more languages. You may substitute any other languages for those shown. Feel free to modify the user interface to suit yourself (or your instructor).

Make sure to use meaningful names for your new buttons, following the naming conventions in Table 1.2. Include remarks at the top of every procedure and at the top of the file.

"Hello World" in French: Bonjour tout le monde
"Hello World" in Italian: Ciao Mondo

1.2 Write a new Visual Basic project that displays a different greeting, or make it display the name of your school or your company. Include at least two buttons to display the greeting, and exit the project.

Include a label that holds your name at the bottom of the form and change the Text property of the form to something meaningful.

Follow good naming conventions for object names; include remarks at the top of every procedure and at the top of the file.

Select a different font name and font size for the greeting label. If you wish, you also can select a different color for the font. Select each font attribute from the *Font* dialog box from the Properties window.

1.3 Write a project that displays four sayings, such as "The early bird gets the worm" or "A penny saved is a penny earned." (You will want to keep the sayings short, as each must be entered on one line. However, when the saying displays on your form, long lines will wrap within the label if the label is large enough.)

Make a button for each saying with a descriptive Text property for each, as well as a button to exit the project.

Include a label that holds your name at the bottom of the form. Also, make sure to change the form's title bar to something meaningful.

You may change the Font properties of the large label to the font and size of your choice.

Make sure the label is large enough to display your longest saying and that the buttons are large enough to hold their entire Text properties.

Follow good naming conventions for object names; include remarks at the top of every procedure and at the top of the file.

1.4   Write a project to display company contact information. Include buttons and labels for the contact person, department, and phone. When the user clicks on one of the buttons, display the contact information in the corresponding label. Include a button to exit.

Include a label that holds your name at the bottom of the form and change the title bar of the form to something meaningful.

You may change the Font properties of the labels to the font and size of your choice.

Follow good naming conventions for object names; include remarks at the top of every procedure and at the top of the file.

1.5   Create a project to display the daily specials for "your" diner. Make up a name for your diner and display it in a label at the top of the form. Add a label to display the appropriate special depending on the button that is pressed. The buttons should be

- Soup of the Day

- Chef's Special

- Daily Fish

Also include an Exit button.

Sample Data: Dorothy's Diner is offering Tortilla Soup, a California Cobb Salad, and Hazelnut-Coated Mahi Mahi.

Case Studies

Very Busy (VB) Mail Order

If you don't have the time to look for all those hard-to-find items, tell us what you're looking for. We'll send you a catalog from the appropriate company or order for you.

We can place an order and ship it to you. We also help with shopping for gifts; your order can be gift wrapped and sent anywhere you wish.

The company title will be shortened to VB Mail Order. Include this name on the title bar of the first form of each project that you create for this case study.

Your first job is to create a project that will display the name and telephone number for the contact person for the customer relations, marketing, order processing, and shipping departments.

Include a button for each department. When the user clicks on the button for a department, display the name and telephone number for the contact person in

two labels. Also include identifying labels with Text "Department Contact" and "Telephone Number".

Be sure to include a button for Exit.

Include a label at the bottom of the form that holds your name.

Test Data

Department	Department Contact	Telephone Number
Customer Relations	Tricia Mills	500-1111
Marketing	Michelle Rigner	500-2222
Order Processing	Kenna DeVoss	500-3333
Shipping	Eric Andrews	500-4444

Valley Boulevard (VB) Auto Center

Valley Boulevard Auto Center will meet all of your automobile needs. The center has facilities with everything for your vehicles including sales and leasing for new and used cars and RVs, auto service and repair, detail shop, car wash, and auto parts.

The company title will be shortened to VB Auto Center. This name should appear as the title bar on the first form of every project that you create throughout the text for this case study.

Your first job is to create a project that will display current notices.

Include four buttons labeled "Auto Sales", "Service Center", "Detail Shop", and "Employment Opportunities". One Label will be used to display the information when the buttons are clicked. Be sure to include a button for Exit.

Include your name in a label at the bottom of the form.

Test Data

Button	Label Text
Auto Sales	Family wagon, immaculate condition $12,995
Service Center	Lube, oil, filter $25.99
Detail Shop	Complete detail $79.95 for most cars
Employment Opportunities	Sales position, contact Mr. Mann 551-2134 x475

Video Bonanza

This neighborhood store is an independently owned video rental business. The owners would like to allow their customers to use the computer to look up the aisle number for movies by category.

Create a form with a button for each category. When the user clicks on a button, display the corresponding aisle number in a label. Include a button to exit.

Include a label that holds your name at the bottom of the form and change the title bar of the form to Video Bonanza.

You may change the font properties of the labels to the font and size of your choice. Include additional categories, if you wish.

Follow good programming conventions for object names; include remarks at the top of every procedure and at the top of the file.

Test Data

Button	Location
Comedy	Aisle 1
Drama	Aisle 2
Action	Aisle 3
Sci-Fi	Aisle 4
Horror	Aisle 5
New Releases	Back Wall

Very Very Boards

This chain of stores features a full line of clothing and equipment for snowboard and skateboard enthusiasts. Management wants a computer application to allow their employees to display the address and hours for each of their branches.

Create a form with a button for each store branch. When the user clicks on a button, display the correct address and hours.

Include a label that holds your name at the bottom of the form and change the title bar of the form to Very Very Boards.

You may change the font properties of the labels to the font and size of your choice.

Follow good programming conventions for object names; include remarks at the top of every procedure and at the top of the file.

Store Branches: The three branches are Downtown, Mall, and Suburbs. Make up hours and locations for each.

2

User Interface Design

at the completion of this chapter, you will be able to . . .

1. Use text boxes, group boxes, check boxes, radio buttons, and picture boxes effectively.

2. Set the BorderStyle property to make controls appear flat or three-dimensional.

3. Select multiple controls and move them, align them, and set common properties.

4. Make your projects easy for the user to understand and operate by defining access keys, setting an accept and a cancel button, controlling the tab sequence, resetting the focus during program execution, and causing ToolTips to appear.

5. Clear the contents of text boxes and labels.

6. Change text color during program execution.

7. Code multiple statements for one control using the `With` and `End With` statements.

8. Concatenate (join) strings of text.

9. Make a control visible or invisible at run time by setting its Visible property.

Introducing More Controls

In Chapter 1 you learned to use labels and buttons. In this chapter you will learn to use several more control types: text boxes, group boxes, check boxes, radio buttons, and picture boxes. Figure 2.1 shows the toolbox with the tools for these controls labeled. Figure 2.2 shows some of these controls on a form.

Each class of controls has its own set of properties. To see a complete list of the properties for any class of control, you can (1) place a control on a form and examine the properties list or (2) click on a tool or a control and press F1 for context-sensitive Help. Visual Studio will display the Help page for that control, and you can view a list of the properties and an explanation of their use.

Figure 2.1

The toolbox showing the controls that are covered in this chapter.

Figure 2.2

This form uses text boxes, a check box, radio buttons, group boxes, and a picture box.

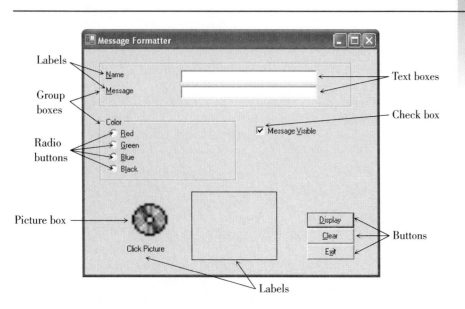

Text Boxes

Use a **text box** control when you want the user to type some input. The form in Figure 2.2 has two text boxes. The user can move from one box to the next, make corrections, cut and paste if desired, and click the Display button when finished. In your program code you can use the **Text property** of each text box.

Example

```
nameLabel.Text = nameTextBox.Text
```

In this example whatever the user enters into the text box is assigned to the Text property of nameLabel. If you want to display some text in a text box during program execution, assign a literal to the Text property:

```
messageTextBox.Text = "Watson, come here."
```

You can set the **TextAlign property** of text boxes to change the alignment of text within the box. In the Properties window, set the property to Left, Right, or Center. In code, you can set the property using these values:

HorizontalAlignment.Left
HorizontalAlignment.Right
HorizontalAlignment.Center

```
messageTextBox.TextAlign = HorizontalAlignment.Left
```

Example Names for Text Boxes

```
titleTextBox
companyTextBox
```

Group Boxes

Group boxes are used as containers for other controls. Usually, groups of radio buttons or check boxes are placed in group boxes. Using group boxes to group controls can make your forms easier to understand by separating the controls into logical groups.

Set a group box's Text property to the words you want to appear on the top edge of the box.

Example Names for Group Boxes

```
colorGroupBox
styleGroupBox
```

Check Boxes

Check boxes allow the user to select (or deselect) an option. In any group of check boxes, any number can be selected. The **Checked property** of a check box is set to False if unchecked or True if checked.

You can write an event procedure for the CheckedChanged event, which executes when the user clicks in the box. In Chapter 4, when you learn about

`If` statements, you can take one action when the box is checked and another action when it is unchecked.

Use the Text property of a check box for the text you want to appear next to the box.

Example Names for Check Boxes

```
boldCheckBox
italicCheckBox
```

Radio Buttons

Use **radio buttons** when only one button of a group may be selected. Any radio buttons that you place directly on the form (not in a group box) function as a group. A group of radio buttons inside a group box function together. The best method is to first create a group box and then create each radio button inside the group box.

The Checked property of a radio button is set to True if selected or to False if unselected. You can write an event procedure to execute when the user selects a radio button using the control's CheckedChanged event. In Chapter 4 you will learn to determine in your code whether or not a button is selected.

Set a radio button's Text property to the text you want to appear next to the button.

Example Names for Radio Buttons

```
redRadioButton
blueRadioButton
```

Picture Boxes

A **PictureBox control** can hold an image. You can set a picture box's **Image property** to a graphic file with an extension of .bmp, .gif, .jpg, .jpeg, .png, .ico, .emf, or .wmf. First place the PictureBox control on a form and then select its Image property in the Properties window. Click on the Properties button (Figure 2.3) to display an *Open* dialog box where you can select a filename (Figure 2.4).

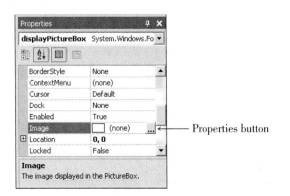

Properties button

Figure 2.3

Click on the Image property for a PictureBox control, and a Properties button appears. Click on the Properties button to view the Open dialog box.

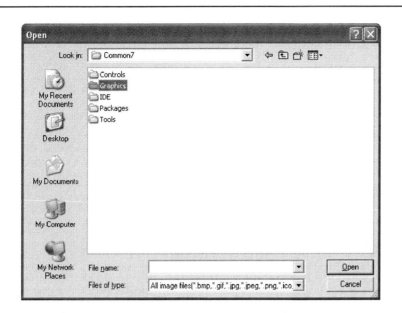

Note: It's a good idea to place the graphic file into the folder with your project before you assign it to your picture box. However, the picture is actually saved in the form's .resx file.

You can use any graphic file (with the proper format) that you have available. You will find many icon files included with Visual Studio. This is the default location (Figure 2.5):

```
Program Files
 Microsoft Visual Studio .NET 2003
  Common7
   Graphics
    Icons
```

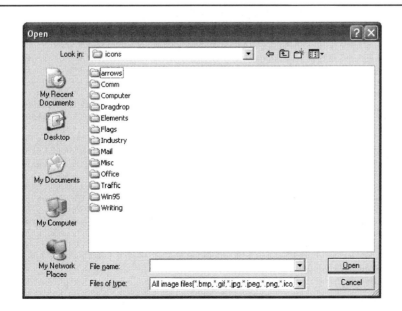

Note: The Standard Edition of Visual Basic .NET does not include the graphic files. You will find many icon files in `StudentData\Graphics` on the text CD.

PictureBox controls have several useful properties that you can set at design time or run time. For example, set the **SizeMode property** to **StretchImage** to make the picture resize to fill the control. You can set the **Visible property** to False to make the picture box disappear.

For example, to make a picture box invisible at run time, use this code statement:

```
logoPictureBox.Visible = False
```

Setting a Border and Style

Most controls can appear to be three-dimensional (refer to Figure 2.2) or flat. Labels, text boxes, and picture boxes all have a **BorderStyle property** with choices of *None*, *FixedSingle*, or *Fixed3D*. Text boxes default to Fixed3D; labels and picture boxes default to None. Of course, you can change the property to the style of your choice.

Feedback 2.1

Create a picture box control that displays an enlarged icon and appears in a 3D box. Make up a name that conforms to this textbook's naming convention.

Property	Setting
Name	
BorderStyle	
SizeMode	
Visible	

Drawing a Line

You can draw a line on a form by using the Label control. You may want to include lines when creating a logo or you may simply want to divide the screen by drawing a line. To create the look of a line, set the Text property of your label to blank, set the BorderStyle to None, and change the Backcolor to the color you want for the line. You can control the size of the line with the Width and Height properties, located beneath the Size property.

You also can draw a line on the form using the graphics methods. Drawing graphics is covered in Chapter 12.

Working with Multiple Controls

You can select more than one control at a time, which means that you can move the controls as a group, set similar properties for the group, and align the controls.

Selecting Multiple Controls

There are several methods of selecting multiple controls. If the controls are near each other, the easiest method is to use the mouse to drag a selection box around the controls. Point to a spot that you want to be one corner of a box surrounding the controls, press the mouse button, and drag to the opposite corner (Figure 2.6). When you release the mouse button, each control will have selection handles (Figure 2.7).

Figure 2.6

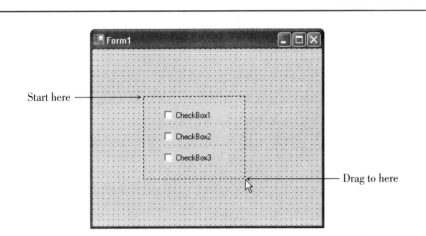

Use the pointer to drag a selection box around the controls you wish to select.

Figure 2.7

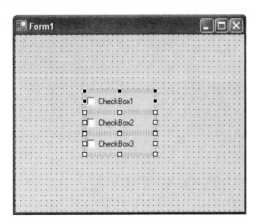

When multiple controls are selected, each has selection handles.

You also can select multiple controls, one at a time. Click on one control to select it, hold down the Ctrl key or the Shift key, and click on the next control. You can keep the Ctrl or Shift key down and continue clicking on controls you wish to select. Ctrl–click (or Shift–click) on a control a second time to deselect it without changing the rest of the group.

When you want to select most of the controls on the form, use a combination of the two methods. Drag a selection box around all of the controls to select them and then Ctrl–click on the ones you want to deselect. You also can select all of the controls using the *Select All* option on the *Edit* menu or its keyboard shortcut: Ctrl + A.

Deselecting a Group of Controls

When you are finished working with a group of controls, it's easy to deselect them. Just click anywhere on the form (not on a control) or select another previously unselected control.

Moving Controls as a Group

After selecting multiple controls, you can move them as a group. To do this, point inside one of the selected controls, press the mouse button, and drag the entire group to a new location (Figure 2.8). As you drag the mouse pointer, an outline of the controls moves. When you release the mouse button, the controls move to their new location.

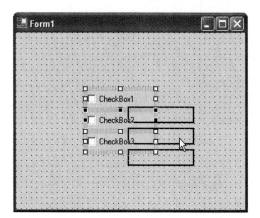

Drag a group of selected controls. An outline of the controls moves as you drag, and then the group moves when you release the mouse button.

Setting Properties for Multiple Controls

You can set some common properties for groups of controls. After selecting the group, check the Properties window. Any properties that appear in the window are shared by all of the controls and can be changed all at once. For example, you may want to set the BorderStyle property for all your controls to three-dimensional or change the font used for a group of labels. Some properties appear empty; those properties do not share a common value. You can enter a new value that will apply to all selected controls.

☑ TIP

Make sure to read Appendix C for tips and shortcuts for working with controls. ■

Aligning Controls

After you select a group of controls, it is easy to resize and align them using the buttons on the Layout toolbar (Figure 2.9) or the corresponding items on the *Format* menu. Select your group of controls and choose any of the resizing buttons. These can make the controls equal in width, height, or both. Then click another button to align the tops, bottoms, or centers of the controls. You also can move the entire group to a new location.

To set the spacing between controls, use the buttons for horizontal and/or vertical spacing. These buttons enable you to create equal spacing between controls or to increase or decrease the space between controls.

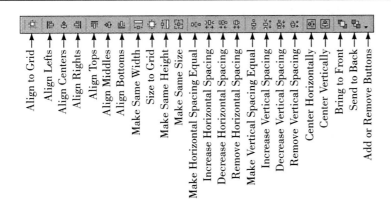

Figure 2.9

Resize and align multiple controls using the Layout toolbar.

Designing Your Applications for User Convenience

One of the goals of good programming is to create programs that are easy to use. Your user interface should be clear and consistent. One school of thought says that if users misuse a program, it's the fault of the programmer, not the users. Because most of your users will already know how to operate Windows programs, you should strive to make your programs look and behave like other Windows programs. Some of the ways to accomplish this are to make the controls operate in the standard way, define keyboard access keys, set a default button, and make the Tab key work correctly. You also can define ToolTips, which are those small labels that pop up when the user pauses the mouse pointer over a control.

Designing the User Interface

The design of the screen should be easy to understand and "comfortable" for the user. The best way that we can accomplish these goals is to follow industry standards for the color, size, and placement of controls. Once users become accustomed to a screen design, they will expect (and feel more familiar with) applications that follow the same design criteria.

You should design your applications to match other Windows applications. Microsoft has done extensive program testing with users of different ages, genders, nationalities, and disabilities. We should take advantage of this research and follow their guidelines. Take some time to examine the screens and dialog boxes in Microsoft Office as well as those in Visual Studio.

One recommendation about interface design concerns color. You have probably noticed that Windows applications are predominantly gray. A reason for this choice is that many people are colorblind. Also, gray is easiest for the majority of users. Although you may personally prefer brighter colors, you will stick with gray, or the system palette the user chooses, if you want your applications to look professional.

Colors can indicate to the user what is expected. Use a white background for text boxes to indicate that the user should input information. Use a gray background for labels, which the user cannot change. Labels that will display a message or the result of a calculation should have a border around them; labels that provide text on the screen should have no border (the default).

Group your controls on the form to aid the user. A good practice is to create group boxes to hold related items, especially those controls that require user input. This visual aid helps the user understand the information that is being presented or requested.

Use a sans serif font on your forms, such as the default MS Sans Serif, and do not make them boldface. Limit large font sizes to a few items, such as the company name.

Defining Keyboard Access Keys

Many people prefer to use the keyboard, rather than a mouse, for most operations. Windows is set up so that most functions can be done with either the keyboard or a mouse. You can make your projects respond to the keyboard by defining **access keys**, also called *hot keys*. For example, in Figure 2.10 you can select the OK button with Alt + o and the Exit button with Alt + x.

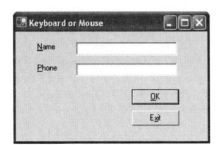

F i g u r e 2 . 1 0

The underlined character defines an access key. The user can select the OK button by pressing Alt + o and the Exit button with Alt + x.

You can set access keys for buttons, radio buttons, and check boxes when you define their Text properties. Type an ampersand (&) in front of the character you want for the access key; Visual Basic underlines the character. You also can set an access key for a label; see "Setting the Tab Sequence" later in this chapter.

For examples of access keys on buttons, type the following for the button's Text property:

&OK   for OK

E&xit   for Exit

When you define access keys, you need to watch for several pitfalls. First, try to use the Windows-standard keys whenever possible. For example, use the x of Exit and the S of Save. Second, make sure you don't give two controls the same access key. It confuses the user and doesn't work correctly. Only the next control (from the currently active control) in the tab sequence is activated when the user presses the access key.

Note: To view the access keys on controls or menus in Windows 2000 or Windows XP, you may have to press the Alt key, depending on your system settings.

Use two ampersands when you want to make an ampersand appear in the Text property: &Health && Welfare for "Health & Welfare".

■

Setting the Accept and Cancel Buttons

Are you a keyboard user? If so, do you mind having to pick up the mouse and click a button after typing text into a text box? Once a person's fingers are on the keyboard, most people prefer to press the Enter key, rather than to click the mouse. If one of the buttons on the form is the accept button, pressing Enter is the same as clicking the button. You can always identify the accept button on a form by its darker outline. In Figure 2.10, the OK button is the accept button.

You can make one of your buttons the accept button by setting the **AcceptButton property** of the form to the button name. When the user presses Enter, that button is automatically selected.

You also can select a *cancel button*. The cancel button is the button that is selected when the user presses the Esc key. You can make a button the cancel button by setting the form's **CancelButton property**. An example of a good time to set the CancelButton property is on a form with OK and Cancel buttons. You may want to set the form's AcceptButton to OKButton and the CancelButton property to cancelButton.

Setting the Tab Order for Controls

In Windows programs one control on the form always has the **focus**. You can see the focus change as you Tab from control to control. For controls such as buttons, the focus appears as a light dotted line. For text boxes, the insertion point (also called the *cursor*) appears inside the box.

Some controls can receive the focus; others cannot. For example, text boxes and buttons can receive the focus, but labels and picture boxes cannot.

The Tab Order

Two properties determine whether the focus stops on a control and the order in which the focus moves. Controls that are capable of receiving focus have a **TabStop property**, which you can set to True or False. If you do not want the focus to stop on a control when the user presses the Tab key, set the TabStop property to False.

The **TabIndex property** determines the order the focus moves as the Tab key is pressed. As you create controls on your form, Visual Studio assigns the TabIndex property in sequence. Most of the time that order is correct, but if you want to Tab in some other sequence or if you add controls later, you will need to modify the TabIndex properties of your controls.

When your program begins running, the focus is on the control with the lowest TabIndex (usually 0). Since you generally want the insertion point to appear in the first control on the form, its TabIndex should be set to 0. The next control should be set to 1; the next to 2; and so forth.

You may be puzzled by the properties of labels, which have a TabIndex property but not a TabStop. A label cannot receive focus, but it has a location in the tab sequence. This fact allows you to create keyboard access keys for text boxes. When the user types an access key, such as Alt + N, the focus jumps to the first TabIndex following the label. See Figure 2.11.

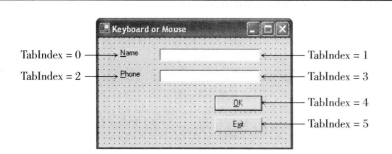

Figure 2.11

To use a keyboard access key for a text box, the TabIndex of the label must precede the TabIndex of the text box.

By default, buttons and text boxes have their TabStop property set to True, but radio buttons have their TabStop property set to False. If you want the tab sequence to include radio buttons, you must set their TabStop property to True. Be aware that the behavior of radio buttons in the tab sequence is different from other controls: The Tab key takes you only to one radio button in a group, even though all buttons in the group have their TabStop and TabIndex properties set. If you are using the keyboard to select radio buttons, you must tab to the group and then use your Up and Down arrow keys to select the correct button.

✔ TIP

Make sure to not have duplicate numbers for the TabIndex properties or duplicate keyboard access keys. You may hear a "ding" at run time if there is duplication. ∎

Setting the Tab Order

To set the tab order for controls, you can set each control's TabIndex property in the Properties window. Or you can use Visual Studio's great feature that helps you set TabIndexes automatically. To use this feature, make sure that the Design window is active and select *View / Tab Order*. (The *Tab Order* item does not appear on the menu unless the Design window is active.) Small numbers appear in the upper-left corner of each control; these are the current TabIndex properties of the controls. Click first in the control that you want to be TabIndex zero, then click on the control for TabIndex one, then click on the next control until you have set the TabIndex for all controls (Figure 2.12).

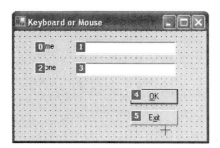

Figure 2.12

Click on each control, in sequence, to set the TabIndex property of the controls automatically.

When you have finished setting the TabIndex for all controls, the white numbered boxes change to blue. Select *View / Tab Order* again to hide the sequence numbers or press the Esc key. If you make a mistake and want to change the tab order, turn the option off and on again, and start over with TabIndex zero again.

Setting the Form's Location on the Screen

When your project runs, the form appears in the upper-left corner of the screen by default. You can set the form's screen position by setting the **StartPosition property** of the form. Figure 2.13 shows your choices for the property setting. To center your form on the user's screen, set the StartPosition property to *CenterScreen*.

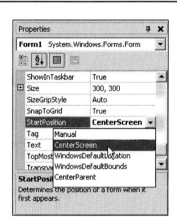

Figure   2 . 1 3

Set the StartPosition property of the form to CenterScreen to make the form appear in the center of the user's screen when the program runs.

Creating ToolTips

If you are a Windows user, you probably appreciate and rely on **ToolTips,** those small labels that pop up when you pause your mouse pointer over a toolbar button or control. You can easily add ToolTips to your projects by adding a **ToolTip component** to a form. After you add the component to your form, each of the form's controls has a new property: **ToolTip on ToolTip1,** assuming that you keep the default name, ToolTip1, for the control.

To define ToolTips, select the ToolTip tool from the toolbox (Figure 2.14) and click anywhere on the form. The new control appears in a new pane that

Figure   2 . 1 4

Add a ToolTip component to your form; each of the form's controls will have a new property to hold the text of the ToolTip.

opens at the bottom of the Form Designer (Figure 2.15). This pane, called the **component tray**, holds controls that do not have a visual representation at run time. You will see more controls that use the component tray later in this text.

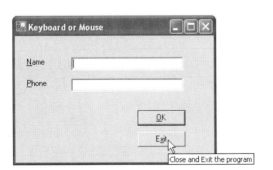

F i g u r e   2 . 1 5

The new ToolTip component goes in the component tray at the bottom of the Form Designer window.

After you add the ToolTip component, examine the properties list for other controls on the form, such as buttons, text boxes, labels, radio buttons, check boxes, and even the form itself. Each has a new ToolTip on ToolTip1 property.

Try this example: Add a button to any form and add a ToolTip component. Change the button's Text property to "Exit" and set its ToolTip on ToolTip1 property to "Close and Exit the program". Now run the project, point to the Exit button and pause; the ToolTip will appear (Figure 2.16).

F i g u r e   2 . 1 6

Use the ToolTip on ToolTip1 property to define a ToolTip.

Coding for the Controls

You already know how to set initial properties for controls at design time. You also may want to set some properties in code as your project executes. You can clear out the contents of text boxes and labels; reset the focus (the active control); and change the color of text.

Clearing Text Boxes and Labels

You can clear out the contents of a text box or label by setting the property to an **empty string**. Use "" (no space between the two quotation marks). This empty string is also called a *null string* or *zero-length string*. You also can clear out a text box using the `Clear` method or set the Text property to `String.Empty`.

Examples

```
' Clear the contents of text boxes and labels.
nameTextBox.Text = ""
messageLabel.Text = ""
dataTextBox.Clear()
messageLabel.Text = String.Empty
```

Resetting the Focus

As your program runs, you want the insertion point to appear in the text box where the user is expected to type. The *focus* should therefore begin in the first text box. But what about later? If you clear the form's text boxes, you should reset the focus to the first text box. The **Focus method** handles this situation. Remember, the convention is Object.Method, so the statement to set the insertion point in the text box called nameTextBox is as follows:

```
' Make the insertion point appear in this text box.
nameTextBox.Focus()
```

Setting the Checked Property of Radio Buttons and Check Boxes

Of course, the purpose of radio buttons and check boxes is to allow the user to make selections. However, often you need to select or deselect a control in code. You can select or deselect radio buttons and check boxes at design time (to set initial status) or at run time (to respond to an event).

To make a radio button or check box appear selected initially, set its Checked property to True in the Properties window. In code, assign True to its Checked property:

```
' Make button selected.
redRadioButton.Checked = True

' Make box checked.
displayCheckBox.Checked = True

' Make box unchecked.
displayCheckBox.Checked = False
```

Setting Visibility at Run Time

You can set the visibility of a control at run time.

```
' Make label invisible.
messageLabel.Visible = False
```

You may want the visibility of a control to depend on the selection a user makes in a check box or radio button. This statement makes the visibility match the check box: When the check box is checked (`Checked = True`) the label is visible (`Visible = True`).

```
' Make the visibility of the label match the setting in the check box.
messageLabel.Visible = displayCheckBox.Checked
```

Feedback 2.2

1. Write the Basic statements to clear the text box called companyTextBox and reset the insertion point into the box.
2. Write the Basic statements to clear the label called customerLabel and place the insertion point into a text box called orderTextBox.
3. What will be the effect of each of these Basic statements?
   (a) `printCheckBox.Checked = True`
   (b) `colorRadioButton.Checked = False`
   (c) `drawingPictureBox.Visible = False`
   (d) `locationLabel.BorderStyle = BorderStyle.Fixed3D`
   (e) `cityLabel.Text = cityTextBox.Text`

Changing the Color of Text

You can change the color of text by changing the **ForeColor property** of a control. Actually, most controls have a ForeColor and a BackColor property. The ForeColor property changes the color of the text; the BackColor property determines the color around the text.

The Color Constants

Visual Basic provides an easy way to specify a large number of colors. These **color constants** are in the Color class. If you type the keyword `Color` and a period in the editor, you can see a full list of colors. Some of the colors are listed below.

```
Color.AliceBlue
Color.AntiqueWhite
Color.Bisque
Color.BlanchedAlmond
Color.Blue
```

Examples

```
nameTextBox.ForeColor = Color.Red
messageLabel.ForeColor = Color.White
```

Changing Multiple Properties of a Control

By now you can see that there are times when you will want to change several properties of a single control. In versions of Visual Basic previous to version 4, you had to write out the entire name (Object.Property) for each statement.

Examples

```
titleTextBox.Visible = True
titleTextBox.ForeColor = Color.White
titleTextBox.Focus()
```

Of course, you can still specify the statements this way, but Visual Basic provides a better way: the **With and End With statements**.

The With and End With Statements—General Form

```
With ObjectName
    ' Statement(s).
End With
```

You specify an object name in the With statement. All subsequent statements until the End With relate to that object.

The With and End With Statements—Example

```
With titleTextBox
  .Visible = True
  .ForeColor = Color.White
  .Focus()
End With
```

The statements beginning with With and ending with End With are called a *With block*. The statements inside the block are indented for readability. Although indentation is not required by VB, it *is* required by good programming practices and aids in readability.

The real advantage of using the With statement, rather than spelling out the object for each statement, is that With is more efficient. Your Visual Basic projects will run a little faster if you use With. On a large, complicated project, the savings can be significant.

Concatenating Text

At times you need to join strings of text. For example, you may want to join a literal and a property. You can "tack" one string of characters to the end of another in the process called **concatenation**. Use an ampersand (&), preceded and followed by a space, between the two strings.

TIP

Although in some situations Basic allows concatenation with the + operator, the practice is not advised. Depending on the contents of the text box, the compiler may interpret the + operator as an addition operator rather than a concatenation operator, giving unpredictable results. ■

Examples

```
messageLabel.Text = "Your name is: " & nameTextBox.Text
nameAndAddressLabel.Text = nameTextBox.Text & addressTextBox.Text
```

Continuing Long Program Lines

Basic interprets the code on one line as one statement. You can type very long lines in the Editor window; the window scrolls sideways to allow you to keep typing. However, this method is inconvenient; it isn't easy to see the ends of the long lines.

When a Basic statement becomes too long for one line, use a **line-continuation character**. You can type a space and an underscore, press Enter, and continue the statement on the next line. It is OK to indent the continued lines. The only restriction is that the line-continuation character must appear between elements; you cannot place a continuation in the middle of a literal or split the name of an object or property.

Example

```
greetingsLabel.Text = "Greetings " & nameTextBox.Text & ": " & _
    "You have been selected to win a free prize. " & _
    "Just send us $100 for postage and handling."
```

Your Hands-On Programming Example

For this example you will write a program that uses many of the new controls and topics introduced in this chapter. The program will input the user's name and a message and display the two items concatenated in a label. The user can change the color of the label's text by selecting the color with radio buttons, and hide or display the output by checking a check box.

In your program you will include buttons to display the message in the label, clear the text boxes and label, and exit. Include keyboard access keys; make the Display button the accept button and make the Clear button the cancel button.

Place a logo on the form. Actually, you will place two picture boxes with different sizes for the logo on the form. Each time the user clicks on the logo, it will toggle the large and small versions of the logo.

Add a ToolTip to the logo that says "Click here".

Planning the Project

Sketch a form (Figure 2.17), which your users sign off as meeting their needs.

Note: Although this step may seem unnecessary, having your users sign off is standard programming practice and documents that your users have been involved and have approved the design.

Figure 2.17

A planning sketch of the form for the hands-on programming example.

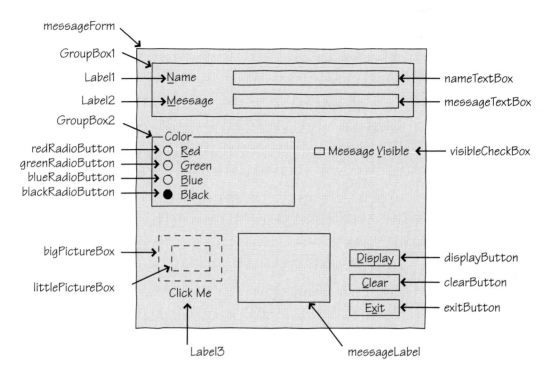

Plan the Objects and Properties Plan the property settings for the form and for each control.

Object	Property	Setting
messageForm	Name	messageForm
	Text	Message Formatter
	AcceptButton	displayButton
	CancelButton	clearButton
	StartPosition	CenterScreen
GroupBox1	Text	(blank)
Label1	Text	&Name Hint: Do not change the name of this label.
nameTextBox	Name	nameTextBox
	Text	(blank)
Label2	Text	&Message
messageTextBox	Name	messageTextBox
	Text	(blank)
GroupBox2	Text	Color

redRadioButton	Name	redRadioButton
	Text	&Red
greenRadioButton	Name	greenRadioButton
	Text	&Green
blueRadioButton	Name	blueRadioButton
	Text	&Blue
blackRadioButton	Name	blackRadioButton
	Text	B&lack
	Checked	True
visibleCheckBox	Name	visibleCheckBox
	Text	Message &Visible
	Checked	True
bigPictureBox	Name	bigPictureBox
	SizeMode	StretchImage
	Image	Microsoft Visual Studio .NET \ Common7 \ Graphics \ Icons \ Computer \ Cdrom01.ico (or StudentData folder on text CD)
	ToolTip on ToolTip1	Click here
	Visible	True
littlePictureBox	Name	littlePictureBox (Note that the two picture boxes are in the same location, one on top of the other.)
	SizeMode	StretchImage
	Image	Microsoft Visual Studio .NET \ Common7 \ Graphics \ Icons \ Computer \ Cdrom02.ico (or StudentData folder on text CD)
	ToolTip on ToolTip1	Click here
	Visible	False
Label3	Text	Click Me
ToolTip1	Name	ToolTip1
messageLabel	Name	messageLabel
	Text	(blank)
	TextAlign	MiddleCenter
	BorderStyle	Fixed Single
displayButton	Name	displayButton
	Text	&Display
clearButton	Name	clearButton
	Text	&Clear

exitButton	Name	exitButton
	Text	E&xit

Plan the Event Procedures You will need event procedures for each button, radio button, check box, and picture box.

Procedure	Actions—Pseudocode
displayButton_Click	Set messageLabel to both the name and message from the text boxes (concatenate them).
clearButton_Click	Clear the two text boxes and label. Reset the focus in the first text box.
exitButton_Click	End the project.
redRadioButton_CheckedChanged	Make the ForeColor of messageLabel red.
greenRadioButton_CheckedChanged	Make the ForeColor of messageLabel green.
blueRadioButton_CheckedChanged	Make the ForeColor of messageLabel blue.
blackRadioButton_CheckedChanged	Make the ForeColor of messageLabel black.
bigPictureBox_Click	Make bigPictureBox invisible (`Visible = False`). Make littlePictureBox visible (`Visible = True`).
littlePictureBox_Click	Make littlePictureBox invisible. Make bigPictureBox visible.
visibleCheckBox_CheckedChanged	Make label's visibility match that of check box.

Write the Project Follow the sketch in Figure 2.17 to create the form. Figure 2.18 shows the completed form.

Figure 2.18

The form for the hands-on programming example.

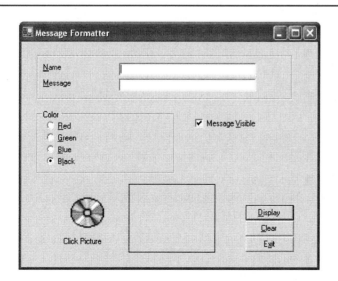

- Set the properties of each object, as you have planned. Make sure to set the tab order of the controls.

- Working from the pseudocode, write each event procedure.

- When you complete the code, thoroughly test the project.

The Project Coding Solution

```
'Project:      Ch0201
'Programmer:   Bradley/Millspaugh
'Date:         January 2004
'Description:  This project uses labels, text boxes, radio buttons,
'              a check box, images in picture boxes, and buttons
'              to change the display.

Public Class messageForm
    Inherits System.Windows.Forms.Form

    Private Sub displayButton_Click(ByVal sender As System.Object, _
     ByVal e As System.EventArgs) Handles displayButton.Click
        ' Display the text in the message area.

        messageLabel.Text = nameTextBox.Text & ": " & messageTextBox.Text
    End Sub

    Private Sub clearButton_Click(ByVal sender As System.Object, _
     ByVal e As System.EventArgs) Handles clearButton.Click
        ' Clear the text controls.

        With nameTextBox
            ' Clear the text box.
            .Clear()
            ' Reset the insertion point.
            .Focus()
        End With
        messageTextBox.Clear()
        messageLabel.Text = ""
    End Sub

    Private Sub exitButton_Click(ByVal sender As System.Object, _
     ByVal e As System.EventArgs) Handles exitButton.Click
        ' Exit the project.

        Me.Close()
    End Sub

    Private Sub blackRadioButton_CheckedChanged(ByVal sender As System.Object, _
     ByVal e As System.EventArgs) Handles blackRadioButton.CheckedChanged
        ' Make the label black.

        messageLabel.ForeColor = Color.Black
    End Sub

    Private Sub blueRadioButton_CheckedChanged(ByVal sender As System.Object, _
     ByVal e As System.EventArgs) Handles blueRadioButton.CheckedChanged
        ' Make the label blue.

        messageLabel.ForeColor = Color.Blue
    End Sub
```

```
Private Sub greenRadioButton_CheckedChanged(ByVal sender As System.Object, _
 ByVal e As System.EventArgs) Handles greenRadioButton.CheckedChanged
    ' Make the label green.

    messageLabel.ForeColor = Color.Green
End Sub

Private Sub redRadioButton_CheckedChanged(ByVal sender As System.Object, _
 ByVal e As System.EventArgs) Handles redRadioButton.CheckedChanged
    ' Make the label red.

    messageLabel.ForeColor = Color.Red
End Sub

Private Sub bigPictureBox_Click(ByVal sender As System.Object, _
 ByVal e As System.EventArgs) Handles bigPictureBox.Click
    ' Switch the icon.

    bigPictureBox.Visible = False
    littlePictureBox.Visible = True
End Sub

Private Sub littlePictureBox_Click(ByVal sender As System.Object, _
 ByVal e As System.EventArgs) Handles littlePictureBox.Click
    ' Switch the icon.

    littlePictureBox.Visible = False
    bigPictureBox.Visible = True
End Sub

Private Sub visibleCheckBox_CheckedChanged(ByVal sender As System.Object, _
 ByVal e As System.EventArgs) Handles visibleCheckBox.CheckedChanged
    ' Set Visibility for messageLabel.

    messageLabel.Visible = visibleCheckBox.Checked
End Sub
End Class
```

Good Programming Habits

1. To make the text in a text box right justified or centered, set the TextAlign property.
2. You can use the Checked property of a check box to set other properties that must be True or False.
3. Always test the tab order on your forms. Fix it if necessary by changing the TabIndex properties.
4. You can create multiple controls of the same type without clicking on the tool in the toolbox every time. To create the first of a series, Ctrl–click on the tool; the tool will remain active and allow you to keep drawing more controls. Click on the pointer tool (the arrow) or press Esc when you are finished.
5. Use text boxes when you want the user to enter or change the text. Use label controls when you do not want the user to change the data.

Summary

1. Text boxes are used primarily for user input. The Text property holds the value input by the user. You also can assign a literal to the text property during design time or run time.

2. Group boxes are used as containers for other controls and to group like items on a form.

3. Check boxes and radio buttons allow the user to make choices. In a group of radio buttons, only one can be selected; but in a group of check boxes, any number of the boxes may be selected.

4. The current state of check boxes and radio buttons is stored in the Checked property; the CheckedChanged event occurs when the user clicks on one of the controls.

5. Picture box controls hold a graphic, which is assigned to the Image property. Set the SizeMode property to StretchImage to make the image resize to fit the control.

6. The BorderStyle property of many controls can be set to None, Fixed Single, or Fixed3D, to determine whether the control appears flat or three-dimensional.

7. Use a Label control to create a line on a form.

8. You can select multiple controls and treat them as a group, including setting common properties at once, moving them, or aligning them.

9. Make your programs easier to use by following Windows standard guidelines for colors, control size and placement, access keys, default and cancel buttons, and tab order.

10. Define keyboard access keys by including an ampersand in the Text property of buttons, radio buttons, check boxes, and labels.

11. Set the AcceptButton property of the form to the desired button so that the user can press Enter to select the button. If you set the form's CancelButton property to a button, that button will be selected when the user presses the Esc key.

12. The focus moves from control to control as the user presses the Tab key. The sequence for tabbing is determined by the TabIndex properties of the controls. The Tab key stops only on controls that have their TabStop property set to True.

13. Add a ToolTip control to a form and then set the ToolTip on ToolTip1 property of a control to make a ToolTip appear when the user pauses the mouse pointer over the control.

14. Clear the Text property of a text box or a label by setting it to an empty string.

15. To make a control have the focus, which makes it the active control, use the `Focus` method. Using the `Focus` method of a text box makes the insertion point appear in the text box.

16. You can set the Checked property of a radio button or check box at run time and also set the Visible property of controls in code.

17. Change the color of text in a control by changing its ForeColor property.

18. You can use the color constants to change colors during run time.

19. The `With` and `End With` statements provide an easy way to refer to an object multiple times without repeating the object's name.

20. Joining two strings of text is called *concatenation* and is accomplished by placing an ampersand between the two elements. (A space must precede and follow the ampersand.)

21. Use a space and an underscore to continue a long statement on another line.

Key Terms

AcceptButton property   *65*
access key   *64*
BorderStyle property   *60*
CancelButton property   *65*
check box   *57*
Checked property   *57*
color constant   *70*
component tray   *68*
concatenation   *71*
empty string   *69*
focus   *65*
Focus method   *69*
ForeColor property   *70*
group box   *57*
Image property   *58*
line-continuation character   *72*

PictureBox control   *58*
radio button   *58*
SizeMode property   *60*
StartPosition property   *67*
StretchImage   *60*
TabIndex property   *65*
TabStop property   *65*
text box   *57*
Text property   *57*
TextAlign property   *57*
ToolTip   *67*
ToolTip component   *67*
ToolTip on ToolTip1 property   *67*
Visible property   *60*
With and End With statements   *71*

Review Questions

1. You can display program output in a text box or a label. When should you use a text box? When is a label appropriate?
2. How does the behavior of radio buttons differ from the behavior of check boxes?
3. If you want two groups of radio buttons on a form, how can you make the groups operate independently?
4. Explain how to make a graphic appear in a picture box control.
5. Describe how to select several labels and set them all to 12-point font size at once.
6. What is the purpose of keyboard access keys? How can you define them in your project? How do they operate at run time?
7. Explain the purpose of the AcceptButton and CancelButton properties of the form. Give an example of a good use for each.
8. What is a ToolTip? How can you make a ToolTip appear?
9. What is the focus? How can you control which object has the focus?
10. Assume you are testing your project and don't like the initial position of the insertion point. Explain how to make the insertion point appear in a different text box when the program begins.
11. During program execution you want to return the insertion point to a text box called addressTextBox. What Basic statement will you use to make that happen?

12. What Basic statements will clear the current contents of a text box and a label?

13. How are the `With` and `End With` statements used? Give an example.

14. What is concatenation and when would it be useful?

15. Explain how to continue a very long Basic statement onto another line.

Programming Exercises

Graphics Files: When you install any edition of Visual Basic .NET other than the Standard Edition, the graphic files are installed by default in `Program Files\Microsoft Visual Studio .NET\Common7\Graphics\Icons`.

You may need to find the exact location of the Graphics folder on your system. If you are using the Standard Edition (the one packaged with this text), the graphic files are not included. You can find the icon files in the `StudentData\Graphics\MicrosoftIcons` folder of the text CD.

2.1   Create a project that will switch a light bulb on and off, using the user interface shown below as a guide.

Form: Include a text box for the user to enter his or her name. Create two picture boxes, one on top of the other. Only one will be visible at a time. Use radio buttons to select the color of the text in the label beneath the light bulb picture box.

Include keyboard access keys for the radio buttons and the buttons. Make the Exit button the cancel button. Create ToolTips for both light bulb picture boxes; make the ToolTips say "Click here to turn the light on or off".

Project Operation: The user will enter a name and click a radio button for the color (not necessarily in that order). When the light bulb is clicked, display the other picture box and change the message below it. Concatenate the user name to the end of the message.

The two icon files are Lightoff.ico and Lighton.ico and are found in the following folder:

```
Microsoft Visual Studio .NET\Common7\Graphics\Icons\Misc
```

(See the note at the top of the exercises for graphic file locations.)

Coding: In the click event procedure for each Color radio button, change the color of the message below the light bulb.

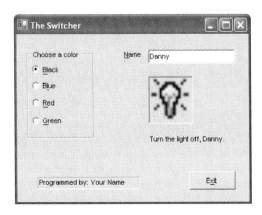
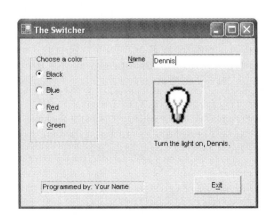

2.2 Write a project to display the flags of four different countries, depending on the setting of the radio buttons. In addition, display the name of the country in the large label under the flag picture box. The user also can choose to display or hide the form's title, the country name, and the name of the programmer. Use check boxes for the display/hide choices.

Include keyboard access keys for all radio buttons, check boxes, and buttons. Make the Exit button the cancel button. Include ToolTips.

You can choose the countries and flags. You will find more than 20 flag icons in `Microsoft Visual Studio .NET\Common7\Graphics\Icons\ Flags`. (See the note at the top of the exercises for graphic file locations.)

Hints: When a project begins running, the focus goes to the control with the lowest TabIndex. Because that control likely is a radio button, one button will appear selected. You must either display the first flag to match the radio button or make the focus begin in a different control. You might consider beginning the focus on the button.

Set the Visible property of a control to the Checked property of the corresponding check box. That way when the check box is selected, the control becomes visible.

Because all three selectable controls will be visible when the project begins, set the Checked property of the three check boxes to True at design time. Set the flag picture boxes to `Visible = False` so they won't appear at startup. (If you plan to display one picture box at startup, its Visible property must be set to True.)

Rather than stacking the picture boxes as was done in the chapter example, consider another method of setting up the four flag picture boxes. Try placing four small invisible flag icons near the bottom of the form. When the user selects a different country's flag, set the Image property of the large flag picture box to the Image property of one of the small, invisible picture boxes. For example:

```
flagPictureBox.Image = mexicoPictureBox.Image
```

Make sure to set the SizeMode property of the large picture box control to StretchImage.

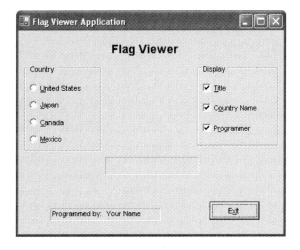

2.3   Write a project to display a weather report. The user can choose one of the radio buttons and display an icon and a message. The message should give the weather report in words and include the person's name (taken from the text box at the top of the form). For example, if the user chooses the Sunny button, you might display "It looks like sunny weather today, John" (assuming that the user entered *John* in the text box).

Include keyboard access keys for the buttons and radio buttons. Make the Exit button the cancel button and include ToolTips.

You might consider the method of hiding and displaying picture boxes described in the hints for Exercise 2.2. The four icons displayed are in the `Microsoft Visual Studio .NET\Common7\Graphics\Icons\Elements` folder and are called `Cloud.ico`, `Rain.ico`, `Snow.ico`, and `Sun.ico`. (See the note at the top of the exercises for graphic file locations.)

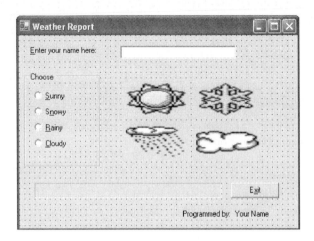

2.4   Write a project that will input the user name and display a message of the day in a label, along with the user's name. Include buttons (with keyboard access keys) for Display, Clear, and Exit. Make the Display button the accept button and the Clear button the cancel button. Include ToolTips where appropriate.

Include a group of radio buttons for users to select the color of the message. Give them a choice of three different colors.

Make your form display a changeable picture box. You can use the happy face icon files or any other images you have available (`Microsoft Visual Studio .NET\Common7\Graphics\Icons\Misc\Face01.ico`, `Face02.ico`, and `Face03.ico`). (See the note at the top of the exercises for graphic file locations.)

You may choose to have only one message of the day, or you can have several that the user can select with radio buttons. You might want to choose messages that go with the different face icons.

2.5   Create a project that allows the user to input information and then display the lines of output for a mailing label.

Remember that fields to be input by the user require text boxes, but information to be displayed belongs in labels. Use text boxes for the first name, last name, street address, city, state, and ZIP code; give meaningful names to the text boxes; and set the initial Text properties to blank. Add appropriate labels to each text box to tell the user which data will be entered into each box and also provide ToolTips.

Use buttons for Display Label Info, Clear, and Exit. Make the Display button the accept button and the Clear button the cancel button.

Use three labels for displaying the information for Line 1, Line 2, and Line 3.

A click event on the Display Label Info button will display the following:

Line 1—The first name and last name concatenated together.
Line 2—The street address.
Line 3—The city, state, and ZIP code concatenated together. (Make sure to concatenate a comma and a space between the city and state, using ", " and two spaces between the state and ZIP code.)

Case Studies

VB Mail Order

Design and code a project that has shipping information.

Use an appropriate image in a picture box in the upper-left corner of the form.

Use text boxes with labels attached for Catalog Code, Page Number, and Part Number.

Use two groups of radio buttons on the form; enclose each group in a group box. The first group box should have a Text of Shipping and contain radio buttons for Express and Ground. Make the second group box have a Text property of Payment Type and include radio buttons for Charge, COD, and Money Order.

Use a check box for New Customer.

Add buttons for Clear and Exit. Make the Clear button the cancel button.

Add ToolTips as appropriate.

VB Auto Center

Modify the project from the Chapter 1 VB Auto Center case study, replacing the buttons with images in picture boxes. (See "Move and Copy Projects" in Appendix C for help in making a copy of the Chapter 1 project to use for this project.) Above each picture box place a label that indicates which department or command the graphic represents. A click on a picture box will produce the appropriate information in the special notices label.

Add an image in a picture box that clears the special notices label. Include a ToolTip for each picture box to help the user understand the purpose of the graphic.

Add radio buttons that will allow the user to view the special notices label in different colors.

Include a check box labeled Hours. When the check box is selected, a new label will display the message "Open 24 Hours--7 days a week".

By default, the images are all stored in `Microsoft Visual Studio .NET\Common7\Graphics\Icons`. (See the note at the top of the exercises for graphic file locations.)

Department/Command	Image for Picture box
Auto Sales	Industry\Cars.ico
Service Center	Industry\Wrench.ico
Detail Shop	Elements\Water.ico
Employment Opportunities	Mail\Mail12.ico
Exit	Computer\Msgbox1.ico

Video Bonanza

Design and code a project that displays the location of videos using radio buttons. Use a radio button for each of the movie categories and a label to display the aisle number. A check box will allow the user to display or hide a message for members. When the check box is selected, a message stating "All Members Receive a 10% Discount" will appear.

Include buttons (with keyboard access keys) for Clear and Exit. The Clear button should be set as the accept button and the Exit as the cancel button.

Place a label on the form in a 24-point font that reads *Video Bonanza*. Use a line to separate the label from the rest of the interface. Include an image in a picture box.

Radio Button	Location
Comedy	Aisle 1
Drama	Aisle 2
Action	Aisle 3
Sci-Fi	Aisle 4
Horror	Aisle 5

Very Very Boards

Create a project that will display an advertising screen for Very Very Boards. Include the company name, a slogan (use "The very best in boards" or make up your own slogan), and a graphic image for a logo. You may use the graphic included with the text materials (Skateboard.gif) or one of your own.

Allow the user to select the color for the slogan text using radio buttons. Additionally, the user may choose to display or hide the company name, the slogan, and the logo. Use check boxes for the display options so that the user may select each option independently.

Include keyboard access keys for the radio buttons and the buttons. Make the Exit button the cancel button. Create ToolTips for the company name ("Our company name"), the slogan ("Our slogan"), and the logo ("Our logo").

When the project begins execution, the slogan text should be red and the Red radio button selected. When the user selects a new color, change the color of the slogan text to match.

Each of the check boxes must appear selected initially, since the company name, slogan, logo, and programmer name display when the form appears. Each time the user selects or deselects a check box, make the corresponding item display or hide.

Make the form appear in the center of the screen.

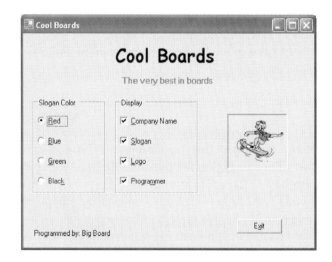

3

Variables, Constants, and Calculations

1. Distinguish between variables, constants, and controls.

2. Differentiate among the various data types.

3. Apply naming conventions that incorporate standards and indicate the data type.

4. Declare variables and constants.

5. Select the appropriate scope for a variable.

6. Convert text input to numeric values.

7. Perform calculations using variables and constants.

8. Convert between numeric data types using implicit and explicit conversions.

9. Round decimal values using the `Decimal.Round` method.

10. Format values for output using the `ToString` method.

11. Use `Try/Catch` blocks for error handling.

12. Display message boxes with error messages.

13. Accumulate sums and generate counts.

In this chapter you will learn to do calculations in Visual Basic. You will start with text values input by the user, convert them to numeric values, and perform calculations on them. You also learn to format the results of your calculations and display them for the user.

Although the calculations themselves are quite simple (addition, subtraction, multiplication, and division), there are some important issues to discuss first. You must learn about variables and constants, the various types of data used by Visual Basic, and how and where to declare variables and constants. Variables are declared differently, depending on where you want to use them and how long you need to retain their values.

The code below is a small preview to show the calculation of the product of two text boxes. The first group of statements (the `Dims`) declares the variables and their data types. The second group of statements converts the text box contents to numeric and places the values into the variables. The last line performs the multiplication and places the result into a variable. The following sections of this chapter describe how to set up your code for calculations.

```
' Dimension the variables.
Dim quantityInteger As Integer
Dim priceDecimal, extendedPriceDecimal As Decimal

' Convert input text to numeric and assign values to variables.
quantityInteger = Integer.Parse(quantityTextBox.Text)
priceDecimal = Decimal.Parse(priceTextBox.Text)

' Calculate the product.
extendedPriceDecimal = quantityInteger * priceDecimal
```

Data—Variables and Constants

So far, all data you have used in your projects have been properties of objects. You have worked with the Text property of Text Boxes and Labels. Now you will work with values that are not properties. Basic allows you to set up locations in memory and give each location a name. You can visualize each memory location as a scratch pad; the contents of the scratch pad can change as the need arises. In this example, the memory location is called *maximumInteger*.

```
maximumInteger = 100
```

maximumInteger
100

After executing this statement, the value of maximumInteger is 100. You can change the value of maximumInteger, use it in calculations, or display it in a control.

In the preceding example, the memory location called maximumInteger is a **variable**. Memory locations that hold data that can be changed during project execution are called *variables*; locations that hold data that cannot change during execution are called **constants**. For example, the customer's name will vary as the information for each individual is processed. However, the name of the company and the sales tax rate will remain the same (at least for that day).

When you declare a variable or a **named constant**, Visual Basic reserves an area of memory and assigns it a name, called an **identifier**. You specify identifier names according to the rules of Basic as well as some recommended naming conventions.

The **declaration** statements establish your project's variables and constants, give them names, and specify the type of data they will hold. The statements are not considered executable; that is, they are not executed in the flow of instructions during program execution. An exception to this rule occurs when you initialize a variable on the same line as the declaration.

Here are some sample declaration statements:

```
' Declare a string variable.
Dim nameString As String

' Declare integer variables.
Dim counterInteger As Integer
Dim MaxInteger As Integer = 100

' Declare a named constant.
Const DISCOUNT_RATE_Decimal As Decimal = .15D
```

The next few sections describe the data types, the rules for naming variables and constants, and the format of the declarations.

Data Types

The **data type** of a variable or constant indicates what type of information will be stored in the allocated memory space: perhaps a name, a dollar amount, a date, or a total. The data types in VB .NET are actually classes and the variables are objects of the class. Table 3.1 shows the VB data types.

The Visual Basic Data Types, the Kind of Data Each Type Holds, and the Amount of Memory Allocated for Each **Table 3.1**

Data Type	Use For	Storage Size in Bytes
Boolean	True or False values	2
Byte	0 to 255, binary data	1
Char	Single Unicode character	2
Date	1/1/0001 through 12/31/9999	8
Decimal	Decimal fractions, such as dollars and cents	16
Single	Single-precision floating-point numbers with six digits of accuracy	4
Double	Double-precision floating-point numbers with 14 digits of accuracy	8
Short	Small integer in the range –32,768 to 32,767	2
Integer	Whole numbers in the range –2,147,483,648 to +2,147,483,647	4
Long	Larger whole numbers	8
String	Alphanumeric data: letters, digits, and other characters	varies
Object	Any type of data	4

The most common types of variables and constants we will use are String, Integer, and Decimal. When deciding which data type to use, follow this guideline: If the data will be used in a calculation, then it must be numeric (usually Integer or Decimal); if it is not used in a calculation, it will be String. Use Decimal as the data type for any decimal fractions in business applications; Single and Double data types are generally used in scientific applications.

Consider the following examples:

Contents	Data Type	Reason
Social Security number	String	Not used in a calculation.
Pay rate	Decimal	Used in a calculation; contains a decimal point.
Hours worked	Decimal	Used in a calculation; may contain a decimal point. (Decimal can be used for any decimal fraction, not just dollars.)
Phone number	String	Not used in a calculation.
Quantity	Integer	Used in calculations; contains a whole number.

Naming Rules

A programmer has to name (identify) the variables and named constants that will be used in a project. Basic requires identifiers for variables and named constants to follow these rules: names may consist of letters, digits, and underscores; they must begin with a letter; they cannot contain any spaces or periods; and they may not be reserved words. (Reserved words, also called *keywords*, are words to which Basic has assigned some meaning, such as *print*, *name*, and *value*.)

Identifiers in VB are not case sensitive. Therefore, the names sumInteger, SumInteger, suminteger, and SUMINTEGER all refer to the same variable.

Note: In earlier versions of VB, the maximum length of an identifier was 255 characters. In VB .NET, you can forget about the length limit, since the maximum is now 16,383.

Naming Conventions

When naming variables and constants, you *must* follow the rules of Basic. In addition, you *should* follow some naming conventions. Conventions are the guidelines that separate good names from bad (or not so good) names. The meaning and use of all identifiers should always be clear.

Just as we established conventions for naming objects in Chapter 1, in this chapter we adopt conventions for naming variables and constants. The following conventions are widely used in the programming industry:

1. *Identifiers must be meaningful.* Choose a name that clearly indicates its purpose. Do not abbreviate unless the meaning is obvious and do not use very short identifiers, such as *X* or *Y*.
2. *Include the class (data type) of the variable.*

3. *Make the first letter lowercase and then capitalize each successive word of the name.* Always use mixed case for variables, uppercase for constants.

Sample identifiers

Field of Data	Possible Identifier
Social Security number	socialSecurityNumberString
Pay rate	payRateDecimal
Hours worked	hoursWorkedDecimal
Phone number	phoneNumberString
Quantity	quantityInteger
Tax rate (constant)	TAX_RATE_Decimal
Quota (constant)	QUOTA_Integer
Population	populationLong

Feedback 3.1

Indicate whether each of the following identifiers conforms to the rules of Basic and to the naming conventions. If the identifier is invalid, give the reason. Remember, the answers to Feedback questions are found in Appendix A.

1. omitted
2. #SoldInteger
3. Number Sold Integer
4. Number.Sold.Integer
5. amount$Decimal
6. Sub
7. subString
8. Text
9. maximum
10. minimumRateDecimal
11. maximumCheckDecimal
12. companyNameString

Constants: Named and Intrinsic

Constants provide a way to use words to describe a value that doesn't change. In Chapter 2 you used the Visual Studio constants Color.Blue, Color.Red, Color.Yellow, and so on. Those constants are built into the environment and called *intrinsic constants*; you don't need to define them anywhere. The constants that you define for yourself are called *named constants*.

Named Constants

You declare named constants using the keyword Const. You give the constant a name, a data type, and a value. Once a value is declared as a constant, its value cannot be changed during the execution of the project. The data type that you declare and the data type of the value must match. For example, if you declare an integer constant, you must give it an integer value.

You will find two important advantages to using named constants rather than the actual values in code. The code is easier to read; for example, seeing the identifier MAXIMUM_PAY_Decimal is more meaningful than seeing a

number, such as 1,000. In addition, if you need to change the value at a later
time, you need to change the constant declaration only once; you do not have to
change every reference to it throughout the code.

Const Statement—General Form

```
Const Identifier [As Datatype] = Value
```

Naming conventions for constants require that you include the data type in the
name as well as the `As` clause that actually declares the data type. Use all uppercase for the name with individual words separated by underscores.

This example sets the company name, address, and the sales tax rate as
constants:

Const Statement—Examples

```
Const COMPANY_NAME_String As String = "R 'n R -- for Reading 'n Refreshment"
Const COMPANY_ADDRESS_String As String = "101 S. Main Street"
Const SALES_TAX_RATE_Decimal As Decimal = .08D
```

Assigning Values to Constants

The values you assign to constants must follow certain rules. You have already
seen that a text (string) value must be enclosed in quotation marks; numeric
values are not enclosed. However, you must be aware of some additional rules.

Numeric constants may contain only the digits (0–9), a decimal point, and
a sign (+ or –) at the left side. You cannot include a comma, dollar sign, any
other special characters, or a sign at the right side. You can declare the data
type of numeric constants by appending a type-declaration character. If you do
not append a type-declaration character to a numeric constant, any whole number is assumed to be Integer and any fractional value is assumed to be Double.
The type-declaration characters are

Decimal	D
Double	R
Integer	I
Long	L
Short	S
Single	F

String literals (also called string constants) may contain letters, digits, and
special characters, such as $#@%&*. You may have a problem when you want
to include quotation marks inside a string literal, since quotation marks enclose
the literal. The solution is to use two quotation marks together inside the literal.
Visual Basic will interpret the pair as one symbol. For example, `"He said,
""I like it."""` produces this string: `He said, "I like it."`

Although you can use numeric digits inside a string literal, remember that
these numbers are text and cannot be used for calculations.

The string values are referred to as ***string literals*** because they contain
exactly (literally) whatever is inside the quotation marks.

The following table lists example constants.

Data Type	Constant Value Example
Integer	5 125 2170 2000 −100 12345678I
Single	101.25F −5.0F
Decimal	850.50D −100D
Double	52875.8 52875.8R −52875.8R
Long	134257987L −8250758L
String literals	"Visual Basic" "ABC Incorporated" "1415 J Street" "102" "She said, ""Hello."""

Intrinsic Constants

Intrinsic constants are system-defined constants. Many sets of intrinsic constants are declared in system class libraries and are available for use in your VB programs. For example, the color constants that you used in Chapter 2 are intrinsic constants.

You must specify the class name or group name as well as the constant name when you use intrinsic constants. For example, Color.Red is the constant "Red" in the class "Color." Later in this chapter you will learn to use constants from the MessageBox class for displaying message boxes to the user.

Declaring Variables

Although there are several ways to declare a variable, inside a procedure you must use the Dim statement. Later in this chapter you will learn to declare variables outside of a procedure, using the Public, Private, or Dim statements.

Declaration Statements—General Form

```
Public | Private | Dim Identifier [As Datatype]
```

If you omit the optional data type, the variable's type defaults to object. It is recommended practice to *always* declare the data type.

Declaration Statement—Examples

```
Dim customerNameString As String
Private totalSoldInteger As Integer
Dim temperatureSingle As Single
Dim priceDecimal As Decimal
Private priceDecimal As Decimal
```

The reserved word `Dim` is really short for dimension, which means "size." When you declare a variable, the amount of memory reserved depends on its data type. Refer to Table 3.1 (page 85) for the size of each data type.

You also can declare several variables in one statement; the data type you declare in the `As` clause applies to all of the variables on the line. Separate the variable names with commas. Here are some sample declarations:

```
Dim nameString, addressString, phoneString As String
Dim priceDecimal, totalDecimal As Decimal
```

Entering Declaration Statements

Visual Basic's IntelliSense feature helps you enter `Private`, `Public`, and `Dim` statements. After you type the space that follows `VariableName As`, a list pops up (Figure 3.1). This list shows the possible entries for data type to complete the statement. The easiest way to complete the statement is to begin typing the correct entry; the list automatically scrolls to the correct section (Figure 3.2). When the correct entry is highlighted, press Enter, Tab, or the Spacebar to select the entry, or double-click if you prefer using the mouse.

Note: Some people find the IntelliSense feature annoying rather than helpful. You can turn off the feature by selecting the *Tools / Options / Text Editor / All Languages* and deselecting *Auto list members*.

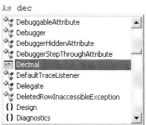

```
Dim priceDecimal As
```

| AcceptRejectRule |
| AccessibleEvents |
| AccessibleNavigation |
| AccessibleObject |
| AccessibleRole |
| AccessibleSelection |
| AccessibleStates |
| Activator |
| AmbientProperties |
| AnchorStyles |

Figure 3.1

As soon as you type the space after **As**, *the IntelliSense menu pops up. You can make a selection from the list with your mouse or the keyboard.*

```
Dim priceDecimal As dec
```

| DebuggableAttribute |
| Debugger |
| DebuggerHiddenAttribute |
| DebuggerStepThroughAttribute |
| Decimal |
| DefaultTraceListener |
| Delegate |
| DeletedRowInaccessibleException |
| {} Design |
| {} Diagnostics |

Figure 3.2

Type the first few characters of the data type and the IntelliSense list quickly scrolls to the correct section. When the correct word is highlighted, press Enter, Tab, or the Spacebar to select the entry.

Feedback 3.2

Write a declaration using the `Dim` statement for the following situations; make up an appropriate variable identifier.

1. You need variables for payroll processing to store the following:
   (a) Number of hours, which can hold a decimal point.
   (b) String employee's name.
   (c) Department number (not used in calculations).
2. You need variables for inventory control to store the following:
   (a) Integer quantity.
   (b) Description of the item.
   (c) Part number.
   (d) Cost.
   (e) Selling price.

Scope and Lifetime of Variables

A variable may exist and be visible for an entire project, for only one form, or for only one procedure. The visibility of a variable is referred to as its **scope**. Visibility really means "this variable can be used or 'seen' in this location". The scope is said to be namespace, module level, local, or block. A **namespace** variable may be used in all procedures of the namespace, which is generally the entire project. **Module-level** variables are accessible from all procedures of a form. A **local** variable may be used only within the procedure in which it is declared and a **block-level** variable is used only within a block of code inside a procedure.

You declare the scope of a variable by choosing where to place the declaration statement.

Note: Previous versions of VB and some other programming languages refer to namespace variables as *global variables*.

Variable Lifetime

When you create a variable, you must be aware of its **lifetime**. The *lifetime* of a variable is the period of time that the variable exists. The lifetime of a local or block variable is normally one execution of a procedure. For example, each time you execute a sub procedure, the local `Dim` statements are executed. Each variable is created as a "fresh" new one, with an initial value of 0 for numeric variables and an empty string for string variables. When the procedure finishes, its variables disappear; that is, their memory locations are released.

The lifetime of a module-level variable is the entire time the form is loaded, generally the lifetime of the entire project. If you want to maintain the value of a variable for multiple executions of a procedure, for example, to calculate a running total, you must use a module-level variable (or a variable declared as `Static`, which is discussed in Chapter 7).

Local Declarations

Any variable that you declare inside a procedure is local in scope, which means that it is known only to that procedure. Use the keyword `Dim` for local declarations. A `Dim` statement may appear anywhere inside the procedure as long as it appears prior to the first use of the variable in a statement. However, good programming practices dictate that all `Dims` appear at the top of the procedure, prior to all other code statements (after the remarks).

```
' Module-level declarations.
Const DISCOUNT_RATE_Decimal As Decimal = 0.15D

Private Sub calculateButton_Click(ByVal sender As System.Object, _
  ByVal e As Systerm.EventArgs) _
  Handles calculateButton.Click)
    ' Calculate the price and discount.

    Dim quantityInteger As Integer
    Dim priceDecimal, extendedPriceDecimal, discountDecimal, discountedPriceDecimal _
      As Decimal

    ' Convert input values to numeric variables.
    quantityInteger = Integer.Parse(quantityTextBox.Text)
    priceDecimal = Decimal.Parse(priceTextBox.Text)

    ' Calculate values.
    extendedPriceDecimal = quantityInteger * priceDecimal
    discountDecimal = Decimal.Round((extendedPriceDecimal * DISCOUNT_RATE_Decimal), 2)
    discountedPriceDecimal = extendedPriceDecimal – discountDecimal
```

Notice the `Const` statement in the preceding example. Although you can declare named constants to be local, block level, module level, or namespace in scope, just as you can variables, good programming practices dictate that constants should be declared at the module level. This technique places all constant declarations at the top of the code and makes them easy to find in case you need to make changes.

Module-Level Declarations

At times you need to be able to use a variable or constant in more than one procedure of a form. When you declare a variable or constant as module level, you can use it anywhere in that form. When you write module-level declarations, you can use the `Dim`, `Public`, or `Private` keywords. The preferred practice is to use either the `Public` or `Private` keyword for module-level variables, rather than `Dim`. In Chapter 6 you will learn how and why to choose `Public` or `Private`. Until then we will declare all module-level variables using the `Private` keyword.

Place the declarations (`Private` or `Const`) for module-level variables and constants in the Declarations section of the form. (Recall that you have been using the Declarations section for remarks since Chapter 1.) **If you wish to accumulate a sum or count items for multiple executions of a procedure, you should declare the variable at the module level.**

Figure 3.3 illustrates the locations for coding local variables and module-level variables.

```
' Declarations section of a form.

' Dimension module-level variables and constants.
Private quantitySumInteger, saleCountInteger As Integer
Private discountSumDecimal As Decimal
Const MAXIMUM_DISCOUNT_Decimal As Decimal = 100.0D
```

Figure 3.3

Coding Module-Level Declarations

To enter module-level declarations, you must be in the Editor window at the top of your code (Figure 3.4). Place the `Private` and `Const` statements after the Form Designer generated code section but before your first procedure.

Figure 3.4

Block-Level and Namespace Declarations

You won't use block-level or namespace-level declarations in this chapter. Block-level variables and constants have a scope of a block of code, such as `If / End If` or `Do / Loop`. These statements are covered later in this text.

Namespace-level variables and constants can sometimes be useful when a project has multiple forms and/or modules, but good programming practices exclude the use of namespace-level variables.

► **Feedback 3.3**

Write the declarations (`Dim`, `Private`, or `Const` statements) for each of the following situations and indicate where each statement will appear.

1. The total of the payroll that will be needed in a Calculate event procedure and in a Summary event procedure.
2. The sales tax rate that cannot be changed during execution of the program but will be used by multiple procedures.
3. The number of participants that are being counted in the Calculate event procedure, but not displayed until the Summary event procedure.

Calculations

In programming you can perform calculations with variables, with constants, and with the properties of certain objects. The properties you will use, such as the Text property of a text box or a label, are usually strings of text characters. These character strings, such as "Howdy" or "12345", cannot be used directly in calculations unless you first convert them to the correct data type.

Converting Strings to a Numeric Data Type

You can use a `Parse` method to convert the Text property of a control to its numeric form before you use the value in a calculation. The class that you use depends on the data type of the variable to which you are assigning the value. For example, to convert text to an integer, use the `Integer.Parse` method; to convert to a decimal value, use `Decimal.Parse`. Pass the text string that you want to convert as an **argument** of the `Parse` method.

```
' Convert input values to numeric variables.
quantityInteger = Integer.Parse(quantityTextBox.Text)
priceDecimal = Decimal.Parse(priceTextBox.Text)

' Calculate the extended price.
extendedPriceDecimal = quantityInteger * priceDecimal
```

Converting from one data type to another is sometimes called *casting*. In the preceding example, quantityTextBox.Text is cast into an Integer data type and priceTextBox.Text is cast into a Decimal data type.

Using the Parse Methods

As you know, objects have methods that perform actions, such as the `Focus` method for a text box. The data types that you use to declare variables are classes, which have properties and methods. Each of the numeric data type classes has a `Parse` method that you will use to convert text strings into the correct numeric value for that type. The Decimal class has a `Parse` method that converts the value inside the parentheses to a decimal value, while the Integer class has a `Parse` method to convert the value to an integer.

The Parse Methods—General Forms

General Forms

```
' Convert to Integer.
Integer.Parse(StringToConvert)

' Convert to Decimal.
Decimal.Parse(StringToConvert)
```

The expression you wish to convert can be the property of a control, a string variable, or a string constant. The **Parse** method returns (produces) a value that can be used as a part of a statement, such as the assignment statements in the following examples.

The Parse Methods—Examples

Examples

```
quantityInteger = Integer.Parse(quantityTextBox.Text)
priceDecimal = Decimal.Parse(priceTextBox.Text)
wholeNumberInteger = Integer.Parse(digitString)
```

The **Parse** methods examine the value stored in the argument and attempt to convert to a number in a process called *parsing*, which means to pick apart, character by character, and convert to another format. The **Parse** methods can be used in any .NET application, including the Microsoft Compact Framework, which is used to program portable devices.

When a **Parse** method encounters a value that it cannot parse to a number, such as a blank or nonnumeric character, an error occurs. You will learn how to avoid those errors later in this chapter in the section titled "Handling Exceptions".

You will use the **Integer.Parse** and **Decimal.Parse** methods for most of your programs. But in case you need to convert to Long, Single, or Double, VB also has a **Parse** method for each data type class.

Converting to String

When you assign a value to a variable, you must take care to assign like types. For example, you assign an integer value to an Integer variable and a decimal value to a Decimal variable. Any value that you assign to a String variable or the Text property of a control must be string. You can convert any of the numeric data types to a string value using the **ToString** method. Later in this chapter you will learn to format numbers for output using parameters of the **ToString** method.

Note: The rule about assigning only like types has some exceptions. See "Implicit Conversions" later in this chapter.

Examples

```
resultLabel.Text = resultDecimal.ToString()
countTextBox.Text = countInteger.ToString()
idString = idInteger.ToString()
```

Arithmetic Operations

The arithmetic operations you can perform in Visual Basic include addition, subtraction, multiplication, division, integer division, modulus, and exponentiation.

Operator	Operation
+	Addition
–	Subtraction
*	Multiplication
/	Division
\	Integer division
Mod	Modulus—Remainder of division
^	Exponentiation

The first four operations are self-explanatory, but you may not be familiar with \, Mod, or ^.

Integer Division (\)

Use integer division (\) to divide one integer by another giving an integer result, truncating (dropping) any remainder. For example, if `totalMinutesInteger` = 150, then

```
hoursInteger = totalMinutesInteger \ 60
```

returns 2 for hoursInteger.

Mod

The Mod operator returns the remainder of a division operation. For example, if `intTotalMinutes` = 150, then

```
minutesInteger = totalMinutesInteger Mod 60
```

returns 30 for minutesInteger.

Exponentiation (^)

The exponentiation operator (^) raises a number to the power specified and returns (produces) a result of the Double data type. The following are examples of exponentiation.

```
squaredDouble = numberDecimal ^ 2      'Square the number--Raise to the 2nd power
cubedDouble = numberDecimal ^ 3        'Cube the number--Raise to the 3rd power
```

Order of Operations

The order in which operations are performed determines the result. Consider the expression 3 + 4 * 2. What is the result? If the addition is done first, the result is 14. However, if the multiplication is done first, the result is 11.

The hierarchy of operations, or **order of precedence**, in arithmetic expressions from highest to lowest is

1. Any operation inside parentheses
2. Exponentiation
3. Multiplication and division
4. Integer division
5. Modulus
6. Addition and subtraction

In the previous example, the multiplication is performed before the addition, yielding a result of 11. To change the order of evaluation, use parentheses. The expression

$$(3 + 4) * 2$$

will yield 14 as the result. One set of parentheses may be used inside another set. In that case, the parentheses are said to be *nested*. The following is an example of nested parentheses:

```
((score1Integer + score2Integer + score3Integer) / 3) * 1.2
```

Extra parentheses can always be used for clarity. The expressions

```
2 * costDecimal * rateDecimal
```

and

```
(2 * costDecimal) * rateDecimal
```

are equivalent, but the second is easier to understand.

Multiple operations at the same level (such as multiplication and division) are performed from left to right. The example 8 / 4 * 2 yields 4 as its result, not 1. The first operation is 8 / 4, and 2 * 2 is the second.

Evaluation of an expression occurs in this order:

1. All operations within parentheses. Multiple operations within the parentheses are performed according to the rules of precedence.
2. All exponentiation. Multiple exponentiation operations are performed from left to right.
3. All multiplication and division. Multiple operations are performed from left to right.
4. All integer division. Multiple operations are performed from left to right.
5. Mod operations. Multiple operations are performed from left to right.
6. All addition and subtraction are performed from left to right.

TIP

Use extra parentheses to make the precedence clearer. The operation will be easier to understand and the parentheses have no negative effect on execution. ∎

Although the precedence of operations in Basic is the same as in algebra, take note of one important difference: There are no implied operations in Basic. The following expressions would be valid in mathematics, but they are not valid in Basic:

Mathematical Notation	Equivalent Basic Function
2A	2 * A
3(X + Y)	3 * (X + Y)
(X + Y)(X − Y)	(X + Y) * (X − Y)

Feedback 3.4

What will be the result of the following calculations using the order of precedence?

Assume that: xInteger = 2, yInteger = 4, zInteger = 3

1. xInteger + yInteger ^ 2
2. 8 / yInteger / xInteger
3. xInteger * (xInteger + 1)
4. xInteger * xInteger + 1
5. yInteger ^ xInteger + zInteger * 2
6. yInteger ^ (xInteger +zInteger) * 2
7. (yInteger ^ xInteger) + zInteger * 2
8. ((yInteger ^ xInteger) + zInteger) * 2

Using Calculations in Code

You perform calculations in assignment statements. Recall that whatever appears on the right side of an = (assignment operator) is assigned to the item on the left. The left side may be the property of a control or a variable. It cannot be a constant.

Examples

```
averageDecimal = sumDecimal / countInteger
amountDueLabel.Text = (priceDecimal − (priceDecimal * discountRateDecimal)).ToString()
commissionTextBox.Text = (salesTotalDecimal * commissionRateDecimal).ToString()
```

In the preceding examples, the results of the calculations were assigned to a variable, the Text property of a label, and the Text property of a text box. In most cases you will assign calculation results to variables or to the Text properties of labels. Text boxes are usually used for input from the user rather than for program output.

Assignment Operators

In addition to the equal sign (=) as an **assignment operator**, VB .NET has several operators that can perform a calculation and assign the result as one operation. The new assignment operators are +=, −=, *=, /=, \=, and &=. Each of these assignment operators is a shortcut for the standard method; you can use the standard (longer) form or the newer shortcut. The shortcuts allow you to type a variable name only once instead of having to type it on both sides of the equal sign.

For example, to add salesDecimal to totalSalesDecimal, the long version is

```
' Accumulate a total.
totalSalesDecimal = totalSalesDecimal + salesDecimal
```

Instead you can use the shortcut assignment operator:

```
' Accumulate a total.
totalSalesDecimal += salesDecimal
```

The two statements have the same effect.
To subtract 1 from a variable, the long version is

```
' Subtract 1 from a variable.
countDownInteger = countDownInteger − 1
```

And the shortcut, using the −= operator:

```
' Subtract 1 from variable.
countDownInteger −= 1
```

The assignment operators that you will use most often are += and −=. The following are examples of other assignment operators:

```
' Multiply resultInteger by 2 and assign the result to resultInteger.
resultInteger *= 2

' Divide sumDecimal by countInteger and assign the result to sumDecimal.
sumDecimal /= countInteger

' Concatenate smallString to the end of bigString.
bigString &= smallString
```

▶ ## Feedback 3.5

1. Write two statements to add 5 to countInteger, using (a) the standard, long version and (b) the assignment operator.
2. Write two statements to subtract withdrawalDecimal from balanceDecimal, using (a) the standard, long version and (b) the assignment operator.
3. Write two statements to multiply priceDecimal by countInteger and place the result into priceDecimal. Use (a) the standard, long version and (b) the assignment operator.

Option Explicit and Option Strict

Visual Basic provides two options that can significantly change the behavior of the editor and compiler. Not using these two options, **Option Explicit** and

Option Strict, can make coding somewhat easier but provide opportunities for hard-to-find errors and very sloppy programming.

Option Explicit

When Option Explicit is turned off, you can use any variable name without first declaring it. The first time you use a variable name, VB allocates a new variable of Object data type. For example, you could write the line

```
Z = myTotal + 1
```

without first declaring either Z or myTotal. This is a throwback to very old versions of Basic that did not require variable declaration. In those days, programmers spent many hours debugging programs that had just a small misspelling or typo in a variable name.

You should always program with Option Explicit turned on. In VB .NET, the option is turned on by default for all new projects. If you need to turn it off (not a recommended practice), place the line

```
Option Explicit Off
```

before the first line of code in a file.

Option Strict

Option Strict is a new option introduced in VB .NET. This option makes VB more like other strongly typed languages, such as C++, Java, and C#. When Option Strict is turned on, the editor and compiler try to help you keep from making hard-to-find mistakes. Specifically, Option Strict does not allow any implicit (automatic) conversions from a wider data type to a narrower one, or between String and numeric data types.

All of the code you have seen so far in this text has been written with Option Strict turned on. With this option you must convert to the desired data type from String or from a wider data type to a narrower type, such as from Decimal to Integer.

With Option Strict turned off, code such as this is legal:

```
quantityInteger = quantityTextBox.Text
```

and

```
amountInteger = amountLong
```

and

```
totalInteger += saleAmountDecimal
```

With each of these legal (but dangerous) statements, the VB compiler makes assumptions about your data. And the majority of the time, the assumptions are correct. But bad input data or very large numbers can cause erroneous results or run-time errors.

The best practice is to always turn on Option Strict. This technique will save you from developing poor programming habits and will also likely save you hours of debugging time. You can turn on Option Strict either in code or in the *Project Properties* dialog box. Place the line

```
Option Strict On
```

before the first line of code, after the general remarks at the top of a file.

Example

```
'Project:        MyProject
'Date:           Today
'Programmer:     Your Name
'Description:    This project calculates correctly.

Option Strict On

Public Class myForm
 Inherits System.Windows.Forms.Form
```

To turn on Option Strict or Option Explicit for all files of a project, open the *Project Properties* dialog box and select *Common Properties / Build*. There you will find settings for both Option Explicit and Option Strict. By default, Option Explicit is turned on and Option Strict is turned off. And beginning with Visual Basic 2003, you can set Option Strict On by default: Select *Tools / Options / Projects* and set the defaults.

Note: Option Strict includes all of the requirements of Option Explicit. If Option Strict is turned on, variables must be declared, regardless of the setting of Option Explicit.

Converting Between Numeric Data Types

In VB you can convert data from one numeric data type to another. Some conversions can be performed implicitly (automatically) and some you must specify explicitly. And some cannot be converted if the value would be lost in the conversion.

Implicit Conversions

If you are converting a value from a narrower data type to a wider type, where there is no danger of losing any precision, the conversion can be performed by an **implicit conversion**. For example, the statement

```
bigNumberDouble = smallNumberInteger
```

does not generate any error message, assuming that both variables are properly declared. The value of smallNumberInteger is successfully converted and stored in bigNumberDouble. However, to convert in the opposite direction could cause problems and cannot be done implicitly.

The following list shows selected data type conversions that can be performed implicitly in VB:

From	To
Byte	Short, Integer, Long, Single, Double, or Decimal
Short	Integer, Long, Single, Double, or Decimal
Integer	Long, Single, Double, or Decimal
Long	Single, Double, or Decimal
Decimal	Single, Double
Single	Double

Notice that Double does not convert to any other type and you cannot convert implicitly from floating point (Single or Double) to Decimal.

Explicit Conversions

If you want to convert between data types that do not have implicit conversions, you must use an **explicit conversion**, also called *casting*. But beware: If you perform a conversion that causes significant digits to be lost, an exception is generated. (Exceptions are covered later in this chapter in the section titled "Handling Exceptions.")

Use methods of the Convert class to convert between data types. The Convert class has methods that begin with "To" for each of the data types: `ToDecimal`, `ToSingle`, and `ToDouble`. However, you must specify the integer data types using their .NET class names, rather than the VB data types.

For the VB data type:	Use the method for the .NET data type:
Short	`ToInt16`
Integer	`ToInt32`
Long	`ToInt64`

The following are examples of explicit conversion. For each, assume that the variables are already declared following the textbook naming standards.

```
numberDecimal = Convert.ToDecimal(numberSingle)
valueInteger = Convert.ToInt32(valueDouble)
amountSingle = Convert.ToSingle(amountDecimal)
```

You should perform a conversion from a wider data type to a narrower one only when you know that the value will fit, without losing significant digits. Fractional values are rounded to fit into integer data types, and a single or double value converted to decimal is rounded to fit in 28 digits.

Performing Calculations with Unlike Data Types

When you perform calculations with unlike data types, VB performs the calculation using the wider data type. For example, `countInteger / numberDecimal` produces a decimal result. If you want to convert the result to a different data type, you must perform a cast: `Convert.ToInt32(countInteger / numberDecimal)` or `Convert.ToSingle(countInteger / numberDecimal)`. Note however that VB does not convert to a different data type until it is necessary. The expression `countInteger / 2 * amountDecimal` is evaluated as integer division for `countInteger / 2`, producing an integer intermediate result; then the multiplication is performed on the integer and decimal value (amountDecimal), producing a decimal result.

Rounding Numbers

At times you may want to round decimal fractions. You can use the `Decimal.Round` method to round decimal values to the desired number of decimal positions.

The Round Method—General Form

```
Decimal.Round(DecimalValue, IntegerNumberOfDecimalPositions)
```

The `Decimal.Round` method returns a decimal result, rounded to the specified number of decimal positions, which can be an integer in the range 0–28.

The Round Method—Examples

```
' Round to two decimal positions.
resultDecimal = Decimal.Round(amountDecimal, 2)

' Round to zero decimal positions.
wholeDollarsDecimal = Decimal.Round(dollarsAndCentsDecimal, 0)

' Round the result of a calculation.
discountDecimal = Decimal.Round(extendedPriceDecimal * DISCOUNT_RATE_Decimal, 2)
```

The `Decimal.Round` method and the `Convert` methods round using a technique called "rounding toward even." If the digit to the right of the final digit is exactly 5, the number is rounded so that the final digit is even.

Examples

Decimal Value to Round	Number of Decimal Positions	Result
1.455	2	1.46
1.445	2	1.44
1.5	0	2
2.5	0	2

In addition to the `Decimal.Round` method, you can use the `Round` method of the Math class to round either decimal or double values. See Appendix B for the methods of the Math class.

Note: Visual Basic provides many functions for mathematical operations, financial calculations, and string manipulation. These functions can simplify many programming tasks. When Microsoft created Visual Basic .NET and moved to object-oriented programming, they made the decision to keep many functions from previous versions of VB, although the functions do not follow the OOP pattern of *object.method.* You can find many of these helpful functions in Appendix B. The authors of this text elected to consistently use OOP methods, rather than mix methods and functions.

Formatting Data for Display

When you want to display numeric data in the Text property of a label or text box, you must first convert the value to string. You also can **format** the data for display, which controls the way the output looks. For example, 12 is just a number, but $12.00 conveys more meaning for dollar amounts. Using the `ToString` method and formatting codes, you can choose to display a dollar sign, a percent sign, and commas. You also can specify the number of digits to appear to the right of the decimal point. VB rounds the value to return the requested number of decimal positions.

If you use the `ToString` method with an empty argument, the method returns an unformatted string. This is perfectly acceptable when displaying integer values. For example, the following statement converts numberInteger to a string and displays it in displayLabel.Text:

```
displayLabel.Text = numberInteger.ToString()
```

Using Format Specifier Codes

You can use the **format specifier** codes to format the display of output. These predefined codes can format a numeric value to have commas and dollar signs, if you wish.

Note: The default format of each of the formatting codes is based on the computer's regional setting. The formats presented here are for the default English (United States) values.

```
' Display as currency.
extendedPriceLabel.Text = (quantityInteger * priceDecimal).ToString("C")
```

The `"C"` code specifies *currency*. By default, the string will be formatted with a dollar sign, commas separating each group of three digits, and two digits to the right of the decimal point.

```
' Display as numeric.
discountLabel.Text = discountDecimal.ToString("N")
```

The `"N"` code stands for *number*. By default, the string will be formatted with commas separating each group of three digits and two digits to the right of the decimal point.

You can specify the number of decimal positions by placing a numeric digit following the code. For example, `"C0"` displays as currency with zero digits to the right of the decimal point. The value is rounded to the specified number of decimal positions.

Format Specifier Codes	Name	Description
C or c	Currency	Formats with a dollar sign, commas, and two decimal places. Negative values are enclosed in parentheses.
F or f	Fixed-point	Formats as a string of numeric digits, no commas, two decimal places, and a minus sign at the left for negative values.
N or n	Number	Formats with commas, two decimal places, and a minus sign at the left for negative values.
D or d	Digits	Use only for *integer* data types. Formats with a left minus sign for negative values. Usually used to force a specified number of digits to display.
P or p	Percent	Multiplies the value by 100, adds a space and a percent sign, and rounds to two decimal places; negative values have a minus sign at the left.

Examples

Variable	Value	Format Specifier Code	Output
totalDecimal	1125.6744	`"C"`	$1,125.67
totalDecimal	1125.6744	`"N"`	1,125.67
totalDecimal	1125.6744	`"N0"`	1,126
balanceDecimal	1125.6744	`"N3"`	1,125.674
balanceDecimal	1125.6744	`"F0"`	1126
pinInteger	123	`"D6"`	000123
rateDecimal	0.075	`"P"`	7.50 %
rateDecimal	0.075	`"P3"`	7.500 %
rateDecimal	0.075	`"P0"`	8 %
valueInteger	-10	`"C"`	($10.00)
valueInteger	-10	`"N"`	-10.00
valueInteger	-10	`"D3"`	-010

Note that the formatted value returned by the `ToString` method is no longer purely numeric and cannot be used in further calculations. For example, consider the following lines of code:

```
amountDecimal += chargesDecimal
amountLabel.Text = amountDecimal.ToString("C")
```

Assume that amountDecimal holds 1050 after the calculation and amount-Label.Text displays $1,050.00. If you want to do any further calculations with this amount, such as adding it to a total, you must use amountDecimal, not amountLabel.Text. The variable amountDecimal holds a numeric value; amountLabel.Text holds a string of (nonnumeric) characters.

You also can format DateTime values using format codes and the `ToString` method. Unlike the numeric format codes, the date codes are case sensitive. The strings returned are based on the computer's regional settings and can be changed. The following are default values for English (United States) in Windows XP.

Date Specifier Code	Name	Description	Example of Default Setting
d	Short date	Mm/dd/yyyy	6/16/2003
D	Long date	Day, Month dd, yyyy	Monday, June 16, 2003
t	Short time	hh:mm AM|PM	4:55 PM
T	Long time	hh:mm:ss AM|PM	4:55:45 PM
f	Full date/time (short time)	Day, Month dd, yyyy hh:mm AM|PM	Monday, June 16, 2003 4:55 PM
F	Full date/time (long time)	Day, Month dd, yyyy hh:mm:ss AM|PM	Monday, June 16, 2003 4:55:45 PM
g	General (short time)	Mm/dd/yyyy hh:mm AM|PM	6/16/2003 11:00 AM
G	General (long time)	Mm/dd/yyyy hh:mm:ss AM|PM	6/16/2003 11:00:15 AM
M or m	Month	Month dd	June 16
R or r	GMT pattern	Day, dd mmm yyyy hh:mm:ss GMT	Mon, 16 Jun 2003 11:00:15 GMT

Note that you can also use methods of the DateTime structure for formatting dates: `ToLongDateString`, `ToShortDateString`, `ToLongTimeString`, `ToShortTimeString`. See Appendix B or MSDN for additional information.

Feedback 3.6

Give the line of code that assigns the formatted output and tell how the output will display for the specified value.

1. A calculated variable called averagePayDecimal has a value of 123.456 and should display in a label called averagePayLabel.
2. The variable quantityInteger, which contains 176123, must be displayed in the label called quantityLabel.
3. The total amount collected in a fund drive is being accumulated in a variable called totalCollectedDecimal. What statement will display the variable in a label called totalLabel with commas and two decimal positions but no dollar signs?

A Calculation Programming Example

R 'n R—for Reading 'n Refreshment needs to calculate prices and discounts for books sold. The company is currently having a big sale, offering a 15 percent discount on all books. In this project you will calculate the amount due for a quantity of books, determine the 15 percent discount, and deduct the discount, giving the new amount due—the discounted amount.

Planning the Project

Sketch a form (Figure 3.5) that meets the needs of your users.

Figure 3.5

A planning sketch of the form for the calculation programming example.

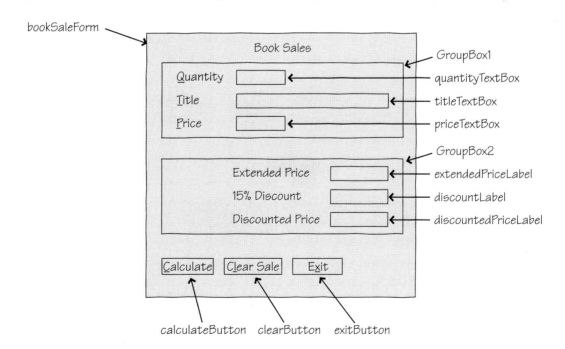

Plan the Objects and Properties

Plan the property settings for the form and each of the controls.

Object	Property	Setting
bookSaleForm	Name Text AcceptButton CancelButton	bookSaleForm R 'n R for Reading 'n Refreshment calculateButton clearButton
Label1	Text Font	Book Sales Bold, 12 point
GroupBox1	Name Text	GroupBox1 (blank)
Label2	Text	&Quantity
quantityTextBox	Name Text	quantityTextBox (blank)
Label3	Text	&Title
titleTextBox	Name Text	titleTextBox (blank)
Label4	Text	&Price
priceTextBox	Name Text	priceTextBox (blank)
GroupBox2	Name Text	GroupBox2 (blank)
Label5	Text	Extended Price
extendedPriceLabel	Name Text TextAlign BorderStyle	extendedPriceLabel (blank) TopRight Fixed3D
Label6	Text	15% Discount
discountLabel	Name Text TextAlign BorderStyle	discountLabel (blank) TopRight Fixed3D
Label7	Text	Discounted Price
discountedPriceLabel	Name Text TextAlign BorderStyle	discountedPriceLabel (blank) TopRight Fixed 3D
calculateButton	Name Text	calculateButton &Calculate
clearButton	Name Text	clearButton C&lear Sale
exitButton	Name Text	exitButton E&xit

Plan the Event Procedures

Since you have three buttons, you need to plan the actions for three event procedures.

Event Procedure	Actions—Pseudocode
calculateButton_Click	Dimension the variables and constants. Convert the input Quantity and Price to numeric. Calculate Extended Price = Quantity * Price. Calculate Discount = Extended Price * Discount Rate. Calculate Discounted Price = Extended Price – Discount. Format and display the output in labels.
clearButton_Click	Clear each text box and output label. Set the focus in the first text box.
exitButton_Click	Exit the project.

Write the Project

Follow the sketch in Figure 3.5 to create the form. Figure 3.6 shows the completed form.

1. Set the properties of each object, as you have planned.
2. Write the code. Working from the pseudocode, write each event procedure.
3. When you complete the code, use a variety of test data to thoroughly test the project.

Figure 3.6

The form for the calculation programming example.

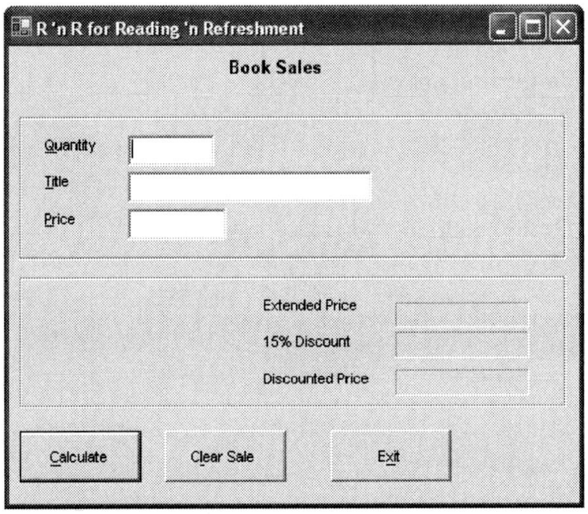

Note: If the user enters nonnumeric data or leaves a numeric field blank, the program will cancel with a run-time error. In the "Handling Exceptions" section that follows this program, you will learn to handle the errors.

The Project Coding Solution

```
'Project:        Chapter Example 3.1
'Date:           January 2004
'Programmer:     Bradley/Millspaugh
'Description:    This project inputs sales information for books.
'                It calculates the extended price and discount for
'                a sale.
'                Uses variables, constants, and calculations.
'                Note that no error trapping is included in this version
'                of the program.
'Folder:         Ch0301

Option Strict On

Public Class bookSaleForm
    Inherits System.Windows.Forms.Form

    ' Declare the constant.
    Const DISCOUNT_RATE_Decimal As Decimal = 0.15D

    Private Sub calculateButton_Click(ByVal sender As System.Object, _
        ByVal e As System.EventArgs) _
        Handles calculateButton.Click
        ' Calculate the price and discount.

        Dim quantityInteger As Integer
        Dim priceDecimal, extendedPriceDecimal, discountDecimal, _
            discountedPriceDecimal As Decimal

        ' Convert input values to numeric variables.
        quantityInteger = Integer.Parse(quantityTextBox.Text)
        priceDecimal = Decimal.Parse(priceTextBox.Text)

        ' Calculate values.
        extendedPriceDecimal = quantityInteger * priceDecimal
        discountDecimal = Decimal.Round( _
            (extendedPriceDecimal * DISCOUNT_RATE_Decimal), 2)
        discountedPriceDecimal = extendedPriceDecimal - discountDecimal

        ' Format and display answers.
        extendedPriceLabel.Text = extendedPriceDecimal.ToString("C")
        discountLabel.Text = discountDecimal.ToString("N")
        discountedPriceLabel.Text = discountedPriceDecimal.ToString("C")
    End Sub

    Private Sub clearButton_Click(ByVal sender As System.Object, _
        ByVal e As System.EventArgs) Handles clearButton.Click
        ' Clear previous amounts from the form.

        titleTextBox.Clear()
        priceTextBox.Clear()
        extendedPriceLabel.Text = ""
        discountLabel.Text = ""
        discountedPriceLabel.Text = ""
        With quantityTextBox
            .Clear()
            .Focus()
        End With
    End Sub
```

```
        Private Sub exitButton_Click(ByVal sender As System.Object, _
           ByVal e As System.EventArgs) Handles exitButton.Click
              ' Exit the project.

              Me.Close()
        End Sub
End Class
```

Handling Exceptions

When you allow users to input numbers and use those numbers in calculations, lots of things can go wrong. The Parse methods, Integer.Parse and Decimal.Parse, fail if the user enters nonnumeric data or leaves the text box blank. Or your user may enter a number that results in an attempt to divide by zero. Each of those situations causes an **exception** to occur, or as programmers like to say, *throws an exception.*

You can easily "catch" program exceptions by using structured exception handling. You catch the exceptions before they can cause a run-time error, and handle the situation, if possible, within the program. Catching exceptions as they happen is generally referred to as *error trapping*, and coding to take care of the problems is called *error handling*. The error handling in Visual Studio .NET is standardized for all of the languages using the Common Language Runtime, which greatly improves on the old error trapping in previous versions of VB.

Try/Catch Blocks

To trap or catch exceptions, enclose any statement(s) that might cause an error in a **Try/Catch block**. If an exception occurs while the statements in the Try block are executing, program control transfers to the Catch block; if a Finally statement is included, the code in that section executes last, whether or not an exception occurred.

The Try Block—General Form

General Form

```
Try
    ' Statements that may cause error.
Catch [VariableName As ExceptionType]
    ' Statements for action when exception occurs.
[Finally
    ' Statements that always execute before exit of Try block]
End Try
```

The Try Block—Example

Example

```
Try
    quantityInteger = Integer.Parse(quantityTextBox.Text)
    quantityLabel.Text = quantityInteger.ToString()
Catch
    messageLabel.Text = "Error in input data."
End Try
```

The `Catch` as it appears in the preceding example will catch any exception. You also can specify the type of exception that you want to catch, and even write several `Catch` statements, each to catch a different type of exception. For example, you might want to display one message for bad input data and a different message for a calculation problem.

To specify a particular type of exception to catch, use one of the predefined exception classes, which are all based on, or derived from, the SystemException class. Table 3.2 shows some of the common exception classes.

To catch bad input data that cannot be converted to numeric, write this `Catch` statement:

```
Catch theException As FormatException
    messageLabel.Text = "Error in input data."
```

The Exception Class

Each exception is an instance of the Exception class. The properties of this class allow you to determine the code location of the error, the type of error, and the cause. The Message property contains a text message about the error and the Source property contains the name of the object causing the error. The Stack-Trace property can identify the location in the code where the error occurred.

Common Exception Classes   **T a b l e   3 . 2**

Exception	Caused By
FormatException	Failure of a numeric conversion, such as `Integer.Parse` or `Decimal.Parse`. Usually blank or nonnumeric data.
InvalidCastException	Failure of a conversion operation. May be caused by loss of significant digits or an illegal conversion.
ArithmeticException	A calculation error, such as division by zero or overflow of a variable.
System.IO.EndOfStreamException	Failure of an input or output operation such as reading from a file.
OutOfMemoryException	Not enough memory to create an object.
Exception	Generic.

You can include the text message associated with the type of exception by specifying the Message property of the Exception object, as declared by the variable you named on the `Catch` statement. Be aware that the messages for exceptions are usually somewhat terse and not oriented to users, but they can sometimes be helpful.

```
Catch theException As FormatException
    messageLabel.Text = "Error in input data: " & theException.Message
```

Handling Multiple Exceptions

If you want to trap for more than one type of exception, you can include multiple Catch blocks (handlers). When an exception occurs, the Catch statements are checked in sequence. The first one with a matching exception type is used.

```
Catch theException As FormatException
    ' Statements for nonnumeric data.
Catch theException As ArithmeticException
    ' Statements for calculation problem.
Catch theException As Exception
    ' Statements for any other exception.
```

The last Catch will handle any exceptions that do not match either of the first two exception types. Note that it is acceptable to use the same variable name for multiple Catch statements; each Catch represents a separate code block, so the variable's scope is only that block.

Later in this chapter in the "Testing Multiple Fields" section, you will see how to nest one Try/Catch block inside another one.

Displaying Messages in Message Boxes

You may want to display a message when the user has entered invalid data or neglected to enter a required data value. You can display a message to the user in a message box, which is a special type of window. You can specify the message, an optional icon, title bar text, and button(s) for the message box (Figure 3.7).

Figure 3.7

Two sample message boxes created with the MessageBox class.

a.

b.

You use the **Show method** of the **MessageBox** object to display a message box. The MessageBox object is a predefined instance of the MessageBox class that you can use any time you need to display a message.

The MessageBox Object—General Form

There is more than one way to call the Show method. Each of the following statements is a valid call; you can choose the format you want to use. It's very important that the arguments you supply exactly match one of the formats. For example, you cannot reverse, transpose, or leave out any of the arguments. When there are multiple ways to call a method, the method is said to be *overloaded*. See the section "Using Overloaded Methods" later in this chapter.

```
MessageBox.Show(TextMessage)
MessageBox.Show(TextMessage, TitleBarText)
MessageBox.Show(TextMessage, TitleBarText, MessageBoxButtons)
MessageBox.Show(TextMessage, TitleBarText, MessageBoxButtons, MessageBoxIcon)
```

The TextMessage is the message you want to appear in the message box. The TitleBarText appears on the title bar of the MessageBox window. The MessageBoxButtons argument specifies the buttons to display. And the MessageBoxIcon determines the icon to display.

The MessageBox Statement—Examples

```
MessageBox.Show("Enter numeric data.")

MessageBox.Show("Try again.", "Data Entry Error")

MessageBox.Show("This is a message.", "This is a title bar", MessageBoxButtons.OK)

Try
    quantityInteger = Integer.Parse(quantityTextBox.Text)
    quantityLabel.Text = quantityInteger.ToString()
Catch err As FormatException
    MessageBox.Show("Nonnumeric Data.", "Error", _
      MessageBoxButtons.OK, MessageBoxIcon.Exclamation)
End Try
```

The TextMessage String

The message string you display may be a string literal enclosed in quotes or it may be a string variable. You also may want to concatenate several items, for example, combining a literal with a value from a variable. If the message you specify is too long for one line, Visual Basic will wrap it to the next line.

The Title Bar Text

The string that you specify for TitleBarText will appear in the title bar of the message box. If you choose the first form of the Show method, without the TitleBarText, the title bar will appear empty.

MessageBox Buttons

When you show a message box, you can specify the button(s) to display. In Chapter 4, after you learn to make selections using the If statement, you will display more than one button and take alternate actions based on which button the user clicks. You specify the buttons using the MessageBoxButtons constants from the MessageBox class. The choices are OK, OKCancel, RetryCancel, YesNo, YesNoCancel, and AbortRetryIgnore. The default for the Show method is OK, so unless you specify otherwise, you will get only the OK button in your message box.

MessageBox Icons

The easy way to select the icon to display is to type MessageBoxIcon and a period into the editor; the IntelliSense list pops up with the complete list. The actual appearance of the icons varies from one operating system to another. You can see a description of the icons in Help under "MessageBoxIcon Enumeration."

Constants for MessageBoxIcon
Asterisk
Error
Exclamation
Hand
Information
None
Question
Stop
Warning

Using Overloaded Methods

As you saw earlier, you can call the Show method with several different argument lists. This OOP feature, called **overloading**, allows the Show method to act differently for different arguments. Each argument list is called a **signature**, so you can say that the Show method has several signatures.

When you call the Show method, the arguments that you supply must exactly match one of the signatures provided by the method. You must supply the correct number of arguments of the correct data type and in the correct sequence.

Fortunately the smart Visual Studio editor helps you enter the arguments; you don't have to memorize or look up the argument lists. Type "MessageBox.Show(" and IntelliSense pops up with the first of the signatures for the Show method (Figure 3.8). Notice in the figure that there are 12 possible forms of the argument list, or 12 signatures for the Show method. (We only showed 4 of the 12 signatures in the previous example, to simplify the concept.)

To select the signature that you want to use, use the up or down arrows at the left end of the IntelliSense popup. For example, to select the signature that

Figure 3.8

IntelliSense pops up the first of 12 signatures for the Show method. Use the up and down arrows to see the other possible argument lists.

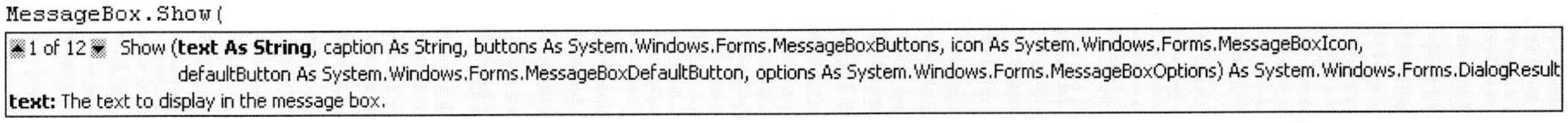

```
MessageBox.Show(
  1 of 12   Show (text As String, caption As String, buttons As System.Windows.Forms.MessageBoxButtons, icon As System.Windows.Forms.MessageBoxIcon,
            defaultButton As System.Windows.Forms.MessageBoxDefaultButton, options As System.Windows.Forms.MessageBoxOptions) As System.Windows.Forms.DialogResult
  text: The text to display in the message box.
```

needs only the text of the message and the title bar caption, select the fifth format (Figure 3.9). The argument that you are expected to enter is shown in bold and a description of that argument appears in the last line of the popup. After you type the text of the message and a comma, the second argument appears in bold and the description changes to tell you about that argument (Figure 3.10).

```
MessageBox.Show(
 ▓5 of 12▓  Show (text As String, caption As String) As System.Windows.Forms.DialogResult
 text: The text to display in the message box.
```

Select the fifth signature to see the argument list. The currently selected argument is shown in bold and the description of the argument appears in the last line of the popup.

```
MessageBox.Show("Error in Input Data",|
 ▓5 of 12▓  Show (text As String, caption As String) As System.Windows.Forms.DialogResult
 caption: The text to display in the title bar of the message box.
```

Type the first argument and a comma, and IntelliSense bolds the second argument and displays a description of the needed data.

Testing Multiple Fields

When you have more than one input field, each field presents an opportunity for an exception. If you would like your exception messages to indicate the field that caused the error, you can nest one Try/Catch block inside another one.

Nested Try/Catch Blocks

One Try/Catch block that is completely contained inside another one is called a **nested Try/Catch block**. You can nest another Try/Catch block within the Try block or the Catch block.

TIP

Use the keyboard Up and Down arrow keys rather than the mouse to view and select the signature. The on-screen arrows jump around from one signature to the next, making mouse selection difficult. ∎

```
Try     ' Outer try block for first field.
        ' Convert first field to numeric.

   Try     ' Inner Try block for second field.
           ' Convert second field to numeric.

        ' Perform the calculations for the fields that passed conversion.

   Catch secondException As FormatException
   ' Handle any exceptions for the second field.

        ' Display a message and reset the focus for the second field.

   End Try ' End of inner Try block for second field.

Catch firstException As FormatException
' Handle exceptions for first field.
```

```
         ' Display a message and reset the focus for the first field.

    Catch anyOtherException as Exception
    ' Handle any generic exceptions.

         ' Display a message.

    End Try
```

You can nest the `Try/Catch` blocks as deeply as you need. Make sure to place the calculations within the most deeply nested `Try`; you do not want to perform the calculations unless all of the input values are converted without an exception.

By testing each `Parse` method individually, you can be specific about which field caused the error and set the focus back to the field in error. Also, by using the `SelectAll` method of the text box, you can make the text appear selected to aid the user. Here are the calculations from the earlier program, rewritten with nested `Try/Catch` blocks.

```
Private Sub calculateButton_Click(ByVal sender As System.Object, _
   ByVal e As System.EventArgs) Handles calculateButton.Click
     ' Calculate the price and discount.
     Dim quantityInteger As Integer
     Dim priceDecimal, extendedPriceDecimal, discountDecimal, _
        discountedPriceDecimal, averageDiscountDecimal As Decimal

     Try
         ' Convert quantity to numeric variables.
         quantityInteger = Integer.Parse(quantityTextBox.Text)
         Try
             ' Convert price if quantity was successful.
             priceDecimal = Decimal.Parse(priceTextBox.Text)

             ' Calculate values for sale.
             extendedPriceDecimal = quantityInteger * priceDecimal
             discountDecimal = Decimal.Round( _
                (extendedPriceDecimal * DISCOUNT_RATE_Decimal), 2)
             discountedPriceDecimal = extendedPriceDecimal - discountDecimal

             ' Format and display answers for sale.
             extendedPriceLabel.Text = extendedPriceDecimal.ToString("C")
             discountLabel.Text = discountDecimal.ToString("N")
             discountedPriceLabel.Text = discountedPriceDecimal.ToString("C")

         Catch priceException As FormatException
             ' Handle price exception.
             MessageBox.Show("Price must be numeric.", "Data Entry Error", _
                MessageBoxButtons.OK, MessageBoxIcon.Exclamation)
             With priceTextBox
                 .Focus()
                 .SelectAll()
             End With
         End Try
     Catch quantityException As FormatException
         ' Handle quantity exception.
         MessageBox.Show("Quantity must be numeric.", "Data Entry Error", _
            MessageBoxButtons.OK, MessageBoxIcon.Exclamation)
```

```
        With quantityTextBox
            .Focus()
            .SelectAll()
        End With
    Catch anyException As Exception
        MessageBox.Show("Error: " & anyException.Message)
    End Try
End Sub
```

Counting and Accumulating Sums

Programs often need to calculate the sum of numbers. For example, in the previous programming exercise, each sale is displayed individually. If you want to accumulate totals of the sales amounts, of the discounts, or of the number of books sold, you need some new variables and new techniques.

As you know, the variables you declare inside a procedure are local to that procedure. They are recreated each time the procedure is called; that is, their lifetime is one time through the procedure. Each time the procedure is entered, you have a new fresh variable with an initial value of 0. If you want a variable to retain its value for multiple calls, in order to accumulate totals, you must declare the variable as module level. (Another approach, using Static variables, is discussed in Chapter 7.)

Summing Numbers

The technique for summing the sales amounts for multiple sales is to declare a module-level variable for the total. Then in the calculateButton_Click event procedure for each sale, add the current amount to the total:

```
discountedPriceSumDecimal += discountedPriceDecimal
```

This assignment statement adds the current value for discountedPrice-Decimal into the sum held in discountedPriceSumDecimal.

Counting

If you want to count something, such as the number of sales in the previous example, you need another module-level variable. Declare a counter variable as integer:

```
Private saleCountInteger as Integer
```

Then in the calculateButton_Click event procedure, add 1 to the counter variable:

```
saleCountInteger += 1
```

This statement adds 1 to the current contents of saleCountInteger. The statement will execute one time for each time the calculateButton_Click event procedure executes. Therefore, saleCountInteger will always hold a running count of the number of sales.

Calculating an Average

To calculate an average, divide the sum of the items by the count of the items. In the R 'n R book example, we can calculate the average sale by dividing the sum of the discounted prices by the count of the sales.

```
averageDiscountedSaleDecimal = discountedPriceSumDecimal / saleCountInteger
```

Your Hands-On Programming Example

In this project, R 'n R—for Reading 'n Refreshment needs to expand the book sale project done previously in this chapter. In addition to calculating individual sales and discounts, management wants to know the total number of books sold, the total number of discounts given, the total discounted amount, and the average discount per sale.

Help the user by adding ToolTips wherever you think they will be useful.

Add error handling to the program, so that missing or nonnumeric data will not cause a run-time error.

Planning the Project

Sketch a form (Figure 3.11) that your users sign off as meeting their needs.

Figure 3.11

A planning sketch of the form for the hands-on programming example.

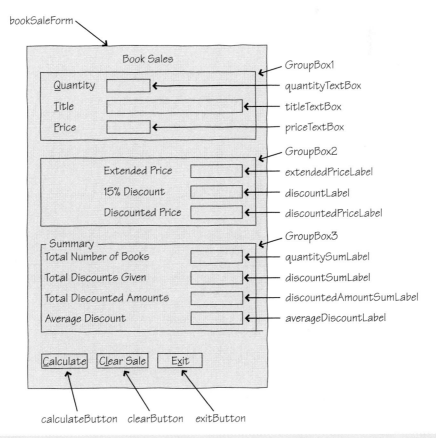

Plan the Objects and Properties Plan the property settings for the form and each control. These objects and properties are the same as the previous example, with the addition of the summary information beginning with GroupBox3.

Note: The ToolTips have not been added to the planning forms. Make up and add your own.

Object	Property	Setting
bookSaleForm	Name	bookSaleForm
	Text	R 'n R for Reading 'n Refreshment
	AcceptButton	calculateButton
	CancelButton	clearButton
Label1	Text	Book Sales
	Font	Bold, 12 point
GroupBox1	Name	GroupBox1
	Text	(blank)
Label2	Text	&Quantity
quantityTextBox	Name	quantityTextBox
	Text	(blank)
Label3	Text	&Title
titleTextBox	Name	titleTextBox
	Text	(blank)
Label4	Text	&Price
priceTextBox	Name	priceTextBox
	Text	(blank)
GroupBox2	Name	GroupBox2
	Text	(blank)
Label5	Text	Extended Price
extendedPriceLabel	Name	extendedPriceLabel
	Text	(blank)
	BorderStyle	Fixed3D
	TextAlign	TopRight
Label6	Text	15% Discount
discountLabel	Name	discountLabel
	Text	(blank)
	BorderStyle	Fixed3D
	TextAlign	TopRight
Label7	Text	Discounted Price
discountedPriceLabel	Name	discountedPriceLabel
	Text	(blank)
	TextAlign	TopRight
	BorderStyle	Fixed 3D
calculateButton	Name	calculateButton
	Text	&Calculate

clearButton	Name	clearButton
	Text	C&lear Sale
exitButton	Name	exitButton
	Text	E&xit
GroupBox3	Name	GroupBox3
	Text	Summary
Label8	Text	Total Number of Books
quantitySumLabel	Name	quantitySumLabel
	Text	(blank)
	BorderStyle	Fixed3D
	TextAlign	TopRight
Label9	Text	Total Discounts Given
discountSumLabel	Name	discountSumLabel
	Text	(blank)
	BorderStyle	Fixed3D
	TextAlign	TopRight
Label10	Text	Total Discounted Amounts
discountAmountSumLabel	Name	discountAmountSumLabel
	Text	(blank)
	BorderStyle	Fixed3D
	TextAlign	TopRight
Label11	Text	Average Discount
averageDiscountLabel	Name	averageDiscountLabel
	Text	(blank)
	BorderStyle	Fixed3D
	TextAlign	TopRight

Plan the Event Procedures The planning that you did for the previous example will save you time now. The only procedure that requires more steps is the calculateButton_Click event.

Event Procedure	Actions—Pseudocode
calculateButton_Click	Declare the variables.
	Try
	Convert the input Quantity to numeric.
	Try
	Convert the input Price to numeric.
	Calculate Extended Price = Quantity * Price.
	Calculate Discount = Extended Price * Discount Rate.
	Calculate Discounted Price = Extended Price − Discount.
	Calculate the summary values:
	Add Quantity to Quantity Sum.
	Add Discount to Discount Sum.
	Add Discounted Price to Discounted Price Sum.
	Add 1 to Sale Count.
	Calculate Average Discount = Discount Sum / Sale Count.
	Format and display sale output in labels.
	Format and display summary values in labels.

Event Procedure	Actions—Pseudocode

calculateButton_Click (continued)	Catch any Quantity exception
	    Display error message and reset the focus to Quantity.
	Catch any Price exception
	    Display error message and reset the focus to Price.
	Catch any generic exception
	    Display error message.

clearButton_Click	Clear each text box and label. Set the focus in the first text box.
exitButton_Click	Exit the project.

Write the Project Following the sketch in Figure 3.11, create the form. Figure 3.12 shows the completed form.

- Set the properties of each of the objects, as you have planned.

- Write the code. Working from the pseudocode, write each event procedure.

- When you complete the code, use a variety of test data to thoroughly test the project. Test with nonnumeric data and blank entries.

Figure 3.12

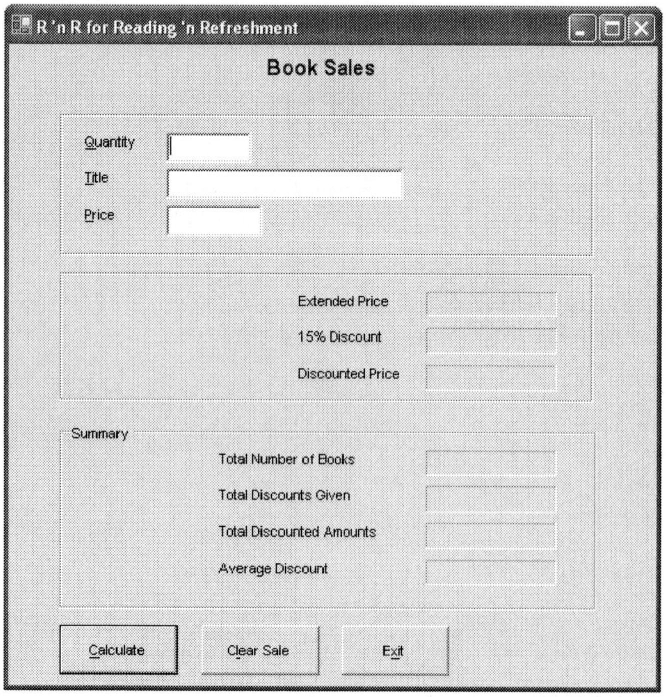

The form for the hands-on programming example.

The Project Coding Solution

```
'Project:        Chapter Example 3.2
'Date:           January 2004
'Programmer:     Bradley/Millspaugh
```

```vbnet
'Description:        This project inputs sales information for books.
'                    It calculates the extended price and discount for
'                    a sale and maintains summary information for all
'                    sales.
'                    Uses variables, constants, calculations, error
'                    handling, and a message box to the user.
'Folder:             Ch0302

Option Strict On

Public Class bookSaleForm
    Inherits System.Windows.Forms.Form

    ' Dimension module-level variables and constants.
    Private quantitySumInteger, saleCountInteger As Integer
    Private discountSumDecimal, discountedPriceSumDecimal As Decimal
    Const DISCOUNT_RATE_Decimal As Decimal = 0.15D

    Private Sub calculateButton_Click(ByVal sender As System.Object, _
      ByVal e As System.EventArgs) Handles calculateButton.Click
        ' Calculate the price and discount.
        Dim quantityInteger As Integer
        Dim priceDecimal, extendedPriceDecimal, discountDecimal, _
          discountedPriceDecimal, averageDiscountDecimal As Decimal

        Try
            ' Convert quantity to numeric variables.
            quantityInteger = Integer.Parse(quantityTextBox.Text)
            Try
                ' Convert price if quantity was successful.
                priceDecimal = Decimal.Parse(priceTextBox.Text)

                ' Calculate values for sale.
                extendedPriceDecimal = quantityInteger * priceDecimal
                discountDecimal = Decimal.Round( _
                  (extendedPriceDecimal * DISCOUNT_RATE_Decimal), 2)
                discountedPriceDecimal = extendedPriceDecimal - discountDecimal

                ' Calculate summary values.
                quantitySumInteger += quantityInteger
                discountSumDecimal += discountDecimal
                discountedPriceSumDecimal += discountedPriceDecimal
                saleCountInteger += 1
                averageDiscountDecimal = discountSumDecimal / saleCountInteger

                ' Format and display answers for sale.
                extendedPriceLabel.Text = extendedPriceDecimal.ToString("C")
                discountLabel.Text = discountDecimal.ToString("N")
                discountedPriceLabel.Text = discountedPriceDecimal.ToString("C")

                ' Format and display summary values.
                quantitySumLabel.Text = quantitySumInteger.ToString()
                discountSumLabel.Text = discountSumDecimal.ToString("C")
                discountedAmountSumLabel.Text = discountedPriceSumDecimal.ToString("C")
                averageDiscountLabel.Text = averageDiscountDecimal.ToString("C")
            Catch priceException As FormatException
                ' Handle the price.
                MessageBox.Show("Price must be numeric.", "Data Entry Error", _
                  MessageBoxButtons.OK, MessageBoxIcon.Exclamation)
```

```
            With priceTextBox
                .Focus()
                .SelectAll()
            End With
        End Try
    Catch quantityException As FormatException
        ' Handle quantity exception.
        MessageBox.Show("Quantity must be numeric.", "Data Entry Error", _
            MessageBoxButtons.OK, MessageBoxIcon.Exclamation)
        With quantityTextBox
            .Focus()
            .SelectAll()
        End With
    Catch anyException As Exception
        MessageBox.Show("Error: " & anyException.Message)
    End Try
End Sub

Private Sub clearButton_Click(ByVal sender As System.Object, _
  ByVal e As System.EventArgs) Handles clearButton.Click
    ' Clear previous amounts from the form.

    titleTextBox.Clear()
    priceTextBox.Clear()
    extendedPriceLabel.Text = ""
    discountLabel.Text = ""
    discountedPriceLabel.Text = ""
    With quantityTextBox
        .Clear()
        .Focus()
    End With
End Sub

Private Sub exitButton_Click(ByVal sender As System.Object, _
    ByVal e As System.EventArgs) Handles exitButton.Click
    ' Exit the project.

    Me.Close()
End Sub
End Class
```

S u m m a r y

1. Variables are temporary memory locations that have a name (called an *identifier*), a data type, and a scope. A constant also has a name, data type, and scope, but also must have a value assigned to it. The value stored in a variable can be changed during the execution of the project; the values stored in constants cannot change.
2. The data type determines what type of values may be assigned to a variable or constant. The most common data types are String, Integer, Decimal, Single, and Boolean.
3. Identifiers for variables and constants must follow the Visual Basic naming rules and should follow good naming standards, called *conventions*. An identifier should be meaningful and have the data type appended at the

end. Variable names should begin with a lowercase character and be mixed upper- and lowercase while constants are all uppercase.

4. Intrinsic constants, such as Color.Red and Color.Blue, are predefined and built into the .NET Framework. Named constants are programmer-defined constants and are declared using the `Const` statement. The location of the `Const` statement determines the scope of the constant.

5. Variables are declared using the `Private` or `Dim` statement; the location of the statement determines the scope of the variable. Use the `Dim` statement to declare local variables inside a procedure; use the `Private` statement to declare module-level variables at the top of the program, outside of any procedure.

6. The scope of a variable may be namespace, module level, local, or block. Block and local variables are available only within the procedure in which they are declared; module-level variables are accessible in all procedures within a form; namespace variables are available in all procedures of all classes in a namespace, which is usually the entire project.

7. The lifetime of local and block-level variables is one execution of the procedure in which they are declared. The lifetime of module-level variables is the length of time that the form is loaded.

8. Identifiers should include the data type of the variable or constant.

9. Use the `Parse` methods to convert text values to numeric before performing any calculations.

10. Calculations may be performed using the values of numeric variables, constants, and the properties of controls. The result of a calculation may be assigned to a numeric variable or to the property of a control.

11. A calculation operation with more than one operator follows the order of precedence in determining the result of the calculation. Parentheses alter the order of operations.

12. To explicitly convert between numeric data types, use the Convert class. Some conversions can be performed implicitly.

13. The `Decimal.Round` method rounds a decimal value to the specified number of decimal positions.

14. The `ToString` method can be used to specify the appearance of values for display. By using formatting codes, you can specify dollar signs, commas, percent signs, and the number of decimal digits to display. The method rounds values to fit the format.

15. `Try / Catch / Finally` statements provide a method for checking for user errors such as blank or nonnumeric data or an entry that might result in a calculation error.

16. An error is called an *exception*; catching and taking care of exceptions is called *error trapping* and *error handling*.

17. You can trap for different types of errors by specifying the exception type on the `Catch` statement, and can have multiple `Catch` statements to catch more than one type of exception. Each exception is an instance of the Exception class; you can refer to the properties of the Exception object for further information.

18. A message box is a window for displaying information to the user.

19. The `Show` method of the MessageBox class is overloaded, which means that the method may be called with different argument lists.

20. You can calculate a sum by adding each transaction to a module-level variable. In a similar fashion, you can calculate a count by adding to a module-level variable.

Key Terms

Review Questions

1. Name and give the purpose of five data types available in Visual Basic.
2. What does *declaring a variable* mean?
3. What effect does the location of a declaration statement have on the variable it declares?
4. Explain the difference between a constant and a variable.
5. What is the purpose of the `Integer.Parse` method? The `Decimal.Parse` method?
6. Explain the order of precedence of operators for calculations.
7. What statement(s) can be used to declare a variable?
8. Explain how to make an interest rate stored in rateDecimal display in rateLabel as a percentage with three decimal digits.
9. What are implicit conversions? Explicit conversions? When would each be used?
10. When should you use `Try/Catch` blocks? Why?
11. What is a message box and when should you use one?
12. Explain why the `MessageBox.Show` method has multiple signatures.
13. Why must you use module-level variables if you want to accumulate a running total of transactions?

Programming Exercises

3.1 Create a project that calculates the total of fat, carbohydrate, and protein calories. Allow the user to enter (in text boxes) the grams of fat, the grams of carbohydrate, and the grams of protein. Each gram of fat is nine calories; a gram of protein or carbohydrate is four calories.

Display the total calories for the current food item in a label. Use two other labels to display an accumulated sum of the calories and a count of the items entered.

Form: The form should have three text boxes for the user to enter the grams for each category. Include labels next to each text box indicating what the user is to enter.

Include buttons to Calculate, to Clear the text boxes, and to Exit.

Make the form's Text property "Calorie Counter".

Code: Write the code for each button. Make sure to catch any bad input data and display a message box to the user.

3.2 Lennie McPherson, proprietor of Lennie's Bail Bonds, needs to calculate the amount due for setting bail. Lennie requires something of value as collateral, and his fee is 10 percent of the bail amount. He wants the screen to provide boxes to enter the bail amount and the item being used for collateral. The program must calculate the fee.

Form: Include text boxes for entering the amount of bail and the description of the collateral. Label each text box.

Include buttons for Calculate, Clear, and Exit.

The text property for the form should be "Lennie's Bail Bonds".

Code: Include event procedures for the click event of each button. Calculate the amount due as 10 percent of the bail amount and display it in a label, formatted as currency. Make sure to catch any bad input data and display a message to the user.

3.3 In retail sales, management needs to know the average inventory figure and the turnover of merchandise. Create a project that allows the user to enter the beginning inventory, the ending inventory, and the cost of goods sold.

Form: Include labeled text boxes for the beginning inventory, the ending inventory, and the cost of goods sold. After calculating the answers, display the average inventory and the turnover formatted in labels.

Include buttons for Calculate, Clear, and Exit. The formulas for the calculations are

$$\text{Average inventory} = \frac{\text{Beginning inventory} + \text{Ending inventory}}{2}$$

$$\text{Turnover} = \frac{\text{Cost of goods sold}}{\text{Average inventory}}$$

Note: The average inventory is expressed in dollars; the turnover is the number of times the inventory turns over.

Code: Include procedures for the click event of each button. Display the results in labels. Format the average inventory as currency and the turnover as a number with one digit to the right of the decimal. Make sure to catch any bad input data and display a message to the user.

Test Data

Beginning	Ending	Cost of Goods Sold
58500	47000	400000
75300	13600	515400
3000	19600	48000

Check Figures

Average Inventory	Turnover
$52,750.00	7.6
44,450.00	11.6
11,300.00	4.2

3.4 A local recording studio rents its facilities for $200 per hour. Management charges only for the number of minutes used. Create a project in which the input is the name of the group and the number of minutes it used the studio. Your program calculates the appropriate charges, accumulates the total charges for all groups, and computes the average charge and the number of groups that used the studio.

Form: Use labeled text boxes for the name of the group and the number of minutes used. The charges for the current group should display formatted in a label. Create a group box for the summary information. Inside the group box, display the total charges for all groups, the number of groups, and the average charge per group. Format all output appropriately. Include buttons for Calculate, Clear, and Exit.

Code: Use a constant for the rental rate per hour; divide that by 60 to get the rental rate per minute. Do not allow bad input data to cancel the program.

Test Data

Group	Minutes
Pooches	95
Hounds	5
Mutts	480

Check Figures

Total Charges for Group	Total Number of Groups	Average Charge	Total Charges for All Groups
$316.67	1	$316.67	$316.67
$16.67	2	$166.67	$333.33
$1,600.00	3	$644.44	$1,933.33

3.5 Create a project that determines the future value of an investment at a given interest rate for a given number of years. The formula for the calculation is

Future value = Investment amount * (1 + Interest rate) ^ Years

Form: Use labeled text boxes for the amount of investment, the interest rate (as a decimal fraction), and the number of years the investment will be held. Display the future value in a label formatted as currency.

Include buttons for Calculate, Clear, and Exit. Format all dollar amounts. Display a message to the user for nonnumeric or missing input data.

Test Data

Amount	Rate	Years
2000.00	.15	5
1234.56	.075	3

Check Figures

Future Value

$4.022.71

$1,533.69

Hint: Remember that the result of an exponentiation operation is a Double data type.

3.6   Write a project that calculates the shipping charge for a package if the shipping rate is $0.12 per ounce.

Form: Use labeled text boxes for the package-identification code (a six-digit code) and the weight of the package—one box for pounds and another one for ounces. Use a label to display the shipping charge.

Include buttons for Calculate, Clear, and Exit.

Code: Include event procedures for each button. Use a constant for the shipping rate, calculate the shipping charge, and display it formatted in a label. Display a message to the user for any bad input data.

Calculation hint: There are 16 ounces in a pound.

ID	Weight	Shipping Charge
L5496P	0 lb. 5 oz.	$0.60
J1955K	2 lb. 0 oz.	$3.84
Z0000Z	1 lb. 1 oz.	$2.04

3.7 Create a project for the local car rental agency that calculates rental charges. The agency charges $15 per day plus $0.12 per mile.

Form: Use text boxes for the customer name, address, city, state, ZIP code, beginning odometer reading, ending odometer reading, and the number of days the car was used. Use labels to display the miles driven and the total charge. Format the output appropriately.

Include buttons for Calculate, Clear, and Exit.

Code: Include an event procedure for each button. For the calculation, subtract the beginning odometer reading from the ending odometer reading to get the number of miles traveled. Use a constant for the $15 per day charge and the $0.12 mileage rate. Display a message to the user for any bad input data.

3.8 Create a project that will input an employee's sales and calculate the gross pay, deductions, and net pay. Each employee will receive a base pay of $900 plus a sales commission of 6 percent of sales.

After calculating the net pay, calculate the budget amount for each category based on the percentages given.

Pay

Base pay	$900; use a named constant
Commission	6% of sales
Gross pay	Sum of base pay and commission
Deductions	18% of gross pay
Net pay	Gross pay minus deductions

Budget

Housing	30% of net pay
Food and clothing	15% of net pay
Entertainment	50% of net pay
Miscellaneous	5% of net pay

Form: Use text boxes to input the employee's name and the dollar amount of the sales. Use labels to display the results of the calculations.

Provide buttons for Calculate, Clear, and Exit. Display a message to the user for any bad input data.

Case Studies

VB Mail Order

The company has instituted a bonus program to give its employees an incentive to sell more. For every dollar the store makes in a four-week period, the employees receive 2 percent of sales. The amount of bonus each employee receives is based upon the percentage of hours he or she worked during the bonus period (a total of 160 hours).

The form will allow the user to enter the employee's name, the total hours worked, and the amount of the store's total sales. The amount of sales needs to be entered only for the first employee. (*Hint:* Don't clear it.)

The Calculate button will determine the bonus earned by this employee, and the Clear button will clear only the name and hours-worked fields. Do not allow missing or bad input data to cancel the program; instead display a message to the user.

VB Auto Center

Salespeople for used cars are compensated using a commission system. The commission is based on the costs incurred for the vehicle.

Commission = Commission rate * (Sales price − Cost value)

The form will allow the user to enter the salesperson's name, the selling price of the vehicle, and the cost value of the vehicle. Use a constant of 20 percent for the commission rate.

The Calculate button will determine the commission earned by the salesperson; the Clear button will clear the text boxes. Do not allow bad input data to cancel the program; instead display a message to the user.

Video Bonanza

Design and code a project to calculate the amount due and provide a summary of rentals. All movies rent for $1.80 and all customers receive a 10 percent discount.

The form should contain input for the member number and the number of movies rented. Inside a group box, display the rental amount, the 10 percent discount, and the amount due. Inside a second group box, display the number of customers served and the total rental income (after discount).

Include buttons for Calculate, Clear, and Exit. The Clear button clears the information for the current rental but does not clear the summary information. Do not allow bad input data to cancel the program; instead display a message to the user.

Very Very Boards

Very Very Boards rents snowboards during the snow season. A person can rent a snowboard without boots or with boots. Create a project that will calculate and print the information for each rental. In addition, calculate the summary information for each day's rentals.

For each rental, input the person's name, the driver's license or ID number, the number of snowboards, and the number of snowboards with boots. Snowboards without boots rent for $20; snowboards with boots rent for $30.

Calculate and display the charges for snowboards and snowboards with boots, and the rental total. In addition, maintain summary totals. Use constants for the snowboard rental rate and the snowboard with boots rental rate.

Create a summary frame with labels to indicate the day's totals for the number of snowboards and snowboards with boots rented, total charges, and average charge per customer.

Include buttons for Calculate Order, Clear, Clear All, and Exit. The Clear All command should clear the summary totals to begin a new day's summary. *Hint*:

You must set each of the summary variables to zero as well as clear the summary labels.

Make your buttons easy to use for keyboard entry. Make the Calculate button the accept button and the Clear button the cancel button.

Do not allow bad input data to cancel the program; instead display a message to the user.

4

Decisions and Conditions

at the completion of this chapter, you will be able to . . .

1. Use If statements to control the flow of logic.

2. Understand and use nested If statements.

3. Read and create flowcharts indicating the logic in a selection process.

4. Evaluate conditions using the relational operators.

5. Combine conditions using And and Or.

6. Test the Checked property of radio buttons and check boxes.

7. Perform validation on numeric fields.

8. Use a Case structure for multiple decisions.

9. Use one event procedure to respond to the events for multiple controls and determine which control caused the event.

10. Call an event procedure from another procedure.

11. Create message boxes with multiple buttons and choose alternate actions based on the user response.

12. Debug projects using breakpoints, stepping program execution, and displaying intermediate results.

In this chapter you will learn to write applications that can take one action or another, based on a condition. For example, you may need to keep track of sales separately for different classes of employees, different sections of the country, or different departments. You also will learn alternate techniques for checking the validity of input data and how to display multiple buttons in a message box and take different actions depending on the user response.

If Statements

A powerful capability of the computer is its ability to make decisions and to take alternate courses of action based on the outcome.

A decision made by the computer is formed as a question: Is a given condition true or false? If it is true, do one thing; if it is false, do something else.

If *the sun is shining* Then	(condition)
go to the beach	(action to take if condition is true)
Else	
go to class	(action to take if condition is false)
End If (See Figure 4.1.)	

or

If *you don't succeed* Then	(condition)
try, try again	(action)
End If (See Figure 4.2.)	

Notice in the second example that no action is specified if the condition is not true.

In an `If` statement, when the condition is true, only the `Then` clause is executed. When the condition is false, only the `Else` clause, if present, is executed.

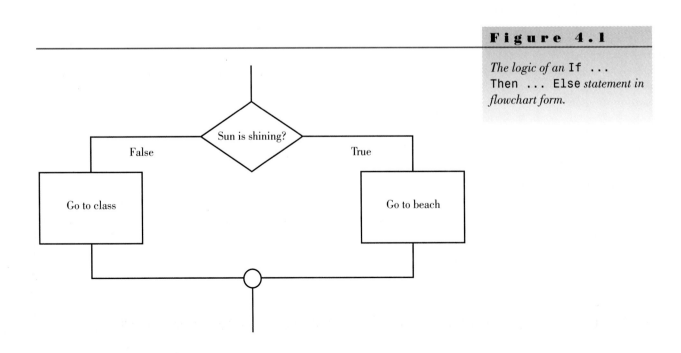

F i g u r e   4 . 1

The logic of an `If` ... `Then` ... `Else` statement in flowchart form.

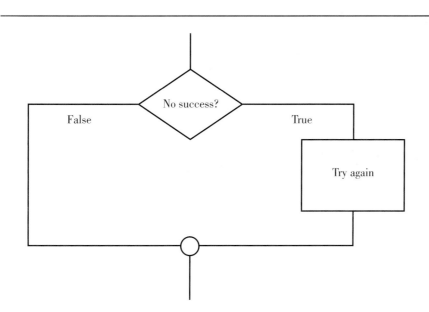

If ... Then ... Else Statement—General Form

```
If (condition) Then
    statement(s)
[ElseIf (condition) Then
    statement(s)]
[Else
    statements(s)]
End If
```

A block **If ... Then ... Else** must always conclude with **End If**. The word Then must appear on the same line as the If with nothing following Then (except a remark). End If and Else (if used) must appear alone on a line. The statements under the Then and Else clauses are indented for readability and clarity.

Note: The keyword ElseIf is all one word, but End If is two words.

If ... Then ... Else Statement—Example

When the number of units in unitsDecimal is less than 32, select the radio button for Freshman; otherwise, make sure the button is unselected (see Figure 4.3). Remember that when a radio button is selected, the Checked property has a Boolean value of True.

```
unitsDecimal = Decimal.Parse(unitsTextBox.Text)
If unitsDecimal < 32D Then
    freshmanRadioButton.Checked = True
Else
    freshmanRadioButton.Checked = False
End If
```

Figure 4.3

The `If` *statement logic in flowchart form. If the number of units is fewer than 32, the Freshman radio button will be selected; otherwise the Freshman radio button will be deselected.*

```
                    Units < 32?
        False                       True
   Turn Freshman              Turn Freshman
   option off                 option on
```

Flowcharting If Statements

A flowchart is a useful tool for showing the logic of an `If` statement. It has been said that one picture is worth a thousand words. Many programmers find that a flowchart helps them organize their thoughts and design projects more quickly.

The symbols used in this text are a subset of the available flowcharting symbols. The diamond-shape symbol (called a *decision symbol*) represents a condition. The two branches from the symbol indicate which path to take when the condition evaluates True or False (see Figure 4.4).

Figure 4.4

The flowcharting symbols used for program decisions and processes.

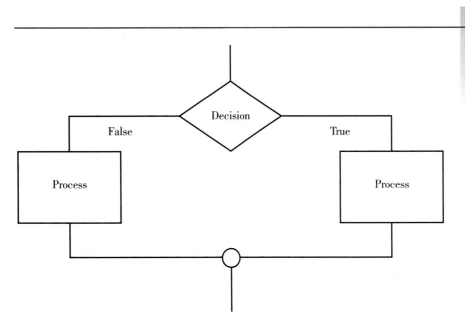
```
                    Decision
        False                       True
      Process                    Process
```

The Helpful Editor

You will find that the VS code editor is very helpful as you enter `If` statements. When you type an `If` statement and press Enter, the editor automatically adds the `End If` statement and places the insertion point on a blank line, indented from the `If`. And if you type `EndIf` without the space, the editor adds the space for you.

The editor also attempts to correct some errors for you. If you type the word `Else` and another statement on the same line, which is illegal syntax, the editor adds a colon. A colon is a statement terminator, which allows you to have multiple statements on one line. However, good programming practices dictate that you should have only one statement per line, so if you find an extra colon in your code, remove it and correct the syntax.

Here is an example of illegal syntax:

```
' Illegal syntax.
If unitsDecimal < 32D Then
    freshmanRadioButton.Checked = True
Else freshmanRadioButton.Checked = False
End If
```

The editor's solution, which you will fix, is

```
If unitsDecimal < 32D Then
    freshmanRadioButton.Checked = True
Else : freshmanRadioButton.Checked = False
End If
```

Fix this poor solution by separating the two statements into two separate lines:

```
' The preferred syntax.
If unitsDecimal < 32D Then
    freshmanRadioButton.Checked = True
Else
    freshmanRadioButton.Checked = False
End If
```

Conditions

The test in an `If` statement is based on a **condition**. To form conditions, six **relational operators** (Table 4.1) are used to compare values. The result of the comparison is either True or False.

The conditions to be tested can be formed with numeric variables and constants, string variables and constants, object properties, and arithmetic expressions. However, it is important to note that comparisons must be made on like types; that is, strings can be compared only to other strings, and numeric values can be compared only to other numeric values, whether a variable, constant, property, or arithmetic expression.

Comparing Numeric Variables and Constants

When numeric values are involved in a test, an algebraic comparison is made; that is, the sign of the number is taken into account. Therefore, negative 20 is less than 10, and negative 2 is less than negative 1.

The Six Relational Operators   T a b l e   4 . 1

Symbol	Relation Tested	Examples
>	Greater than	`Decimal.Parse(amountTextBox.Text) > limitDecimal` `correctInteger > 75`
<	Less than	`Integer.Parse(salesTextBox.Text) < 10000` `nameTextBox.Text < nameString`
=	Equal to	`passwordTextBox.Text = "101"`
<>	Not equal to	`freshmanRadioButton.Checked <> True` `nameTextBox.Text <> ""`
>=	Greater than or equal to	`Integer.Parse(quantityTextBox.Text) >= 500`
<=	Less than or equal to	`nameTextBox1.Text <= nameTextBox2.Text`

Although an equal sign (=) means replacement in an assignment statement, in a relation test, the equal sign is used to test for equality. For example, the condition `If Decimal.Parse(priceTextBox.Text) = maximumDecimal Then` means "Is the current numeric value stored in priceTextBox.Text equal to the value stored in maximumDecimal?"

Sample Comparisons

alphaInteger	bravoInteger	charlieInteger
5	4	−5

Condition	Evaluates
alphaInteger = bravoInteger	False
charlieInteger < 0	True
bravoInteger > alphaInteger	False
charlieInteger <= bravoInteger	True
alphaInteger >= 5	True
alphaInteger <> charlieInteger	True

Comparing Strings

String variables can be compared to other string variables, string properties, or string literals enclosed in quotation marks. The comparison begins with the left-most character and proceeds one character at a time from left to right. As soon as a character in one string is not equal to the corresponding character in the second string, the comparison is terminated, and the string with the lower-ranking character is judged less than the other.

The determination of which character is less than another is based on the code used to store characters internally in the computer. The code, called the **ANSI code**, has an established order (called the *collating sequence*) for all letters, numbers, and special characters. (ANSI stands for American National Standards Institute.) In Table 4.2, A is less than B, L is greater than K, and all numeric digits are less than all letters. Some special symbols are lower than the numbers, some are higher, and the blank space is lower than the rest of the characters shown.

Note: VB actually stores string characters in Unicode, a coding system that uses two bytes to store every character. Using Unicode, all characters and symbols in foreign languages can be represented. For systems that do not use the foreign symbols, only the first byte of each character is used. And the first byte of Unicode is the same as the ANSI code. For comparison, Unicode can store 65,536 unique characters; ANSI code can store 256 unique characters; and ASCII, the earlier coding method, can store 128 unique characters. The first 128 characters of ANSI and Unicode are the same as the ASCII characters.

person1TextBox.Text
JOHN

person2TextBox.Text
JOAN

The condition `person1TextBox.Text < person2TextBox.Text` evaluates False. The *A* in JOAN is lower ranking than the *H* in JOHN.

word1TextBox.Text
HOPE

word2TextBox.Text
HOPELESS

The condition `word1TextBox.Text < word2TextBox.Text` evaluates True. When one string is shorter than the other, it compares as if the shorter string is padded with blanks to the right of the string, and the blank space is compared to a character in the longer string.

car1Label.Text
300ZX

car2Label.Text
Porsche

The condition `car1Label.Text < car2Label.Text` evaluates True. When the number 3 is compared to the letter P, the 3 is lower, since all numbers are lower ranking than all letters.

Feedback 4.1

countOneInteger	countTwoInteger	countThreeInteger	fourTextBox.Text	fiveTextBox.Text
5	5	−5	"Bit"	"Bite"

Determine which conditions will evaluate True and which ones will evaluate False.

1. `countOneInteger >= countTwoInteger`
2. `countThreeInteger < 0`
3. `countThreeInteger < countTwoInteger`
4. `countOneInteger <> countTwoInteger`
5. `countOneInteger + 2 > countTwoInteger + 2`

The ANSI Collating Sequence

Code	Character	Code	Character	Code	Character
32	Space (blank)	64	@	96	'
33	!	65	A	97	a
34	"	66	B	98	b
35	#	67	C	99	c
36	$	68	D	100	d
37	%	69	E	101	e
38	&	70	F	102	f
39	' (apostrophe)	71	G	103	g
40	(	72	H	104	h
41	)	73	I	105	i
42	*	74	J	106	j
43	+	75	K	107	k
44	, (comma)	76	L	108	l
45	–	77	M	109	m
46	.	78	N	110	n
47	/	79	O	111	o
48	0	80	P	112	p
49	1	81	Q	113	q
50	2	82	R	114	r
51	3	83	S	115	s
52	4	84	T	116	t
53	5	85	U	117	u
54	6	86	V	118	v
55	7	87	W	119	w
56	8	88	X	120	x
57	9	89	Y	121	y
58	:	90	Z	122	z
59	;	91	[	123	{
60	<	92	\	124	|
61	=	93	]	125	}
62	>	94	^	126	~
63	?	95	_	127	Del

```
 6. fourTextBox.Text < fiveTextBox.Text
 7. fourTextBox.Text <> fiveTextBox.Text
 8. fourTextBox.Text > "D"
 9. "2" <> "Two"
10. "$" <= "?"
```

Testing for True or False

You can use shortcuts when testing for True or False. Visual Basic evaluates the condition in an `If` statement. If the condition is a Boolean variable name, it holds the values True or False.

For example:

```
If successfulOperationBoolean = True Then ...
```

is equivalent to

```
If successfulOperationBoolean Then ...
```

Comparing Uppercase and Lowercase Characters

When comparing strings, the case of the characters is important. An uppercase *Y* is not equal to a lowercase *y*. Because the user may type a name or word in uppercase, in lowercase, or as a combination of cases, we must check all possibilities. The best way is to use the **ToUpper** and **ToLower methods** of the String class, which return the uppercase or lowercase equivalent of a string, respectively.

The ToUpper and ToLower Methods—General Forms

```
TextString.ToUpper()
TextString.ToLower()
```

The ToUpper and ToLower Methods—Examples

An example of a condition using the `ToUpper` method follows.

nameTextBox.Text Value	nameTextBox.Text.ToUpper()	nameTextBox.Text.ToLower()
Basic	BASIC	basic
PROGRAMMING	PROGRAMMING	programming
Robert Jones	ROBERT JONES	robert jones
hello	HELLO	hello

```
If nameTextBox.Text.ToUpper() = "BASIC" Then
    ' Do something.
End If
```

Note that when you convert nameTextBox.Text to uppercase, you must compare it to an uppercase literal ("BASIC") if you want it to evaluate as True.

Compound Conditions

You can use **compound conditions** to test more than one condition. Create compound conditions by joining conditions with **logical operators**. The logical operators are Or, And, and Not.

Logical Operator	Meaning	Example	Explanation
Or	If one condition or both conditions are True, the entire condition is True.	`Integer.Parse(numberLabel.Text) = 1 Or _` `    Integer.Parse(numberLabel.Text) = 2`	Evaluates True when numberLabel.Text is either "1" or "2".
And	Both conditions must be True for the entire condition to be True.	`Integer.Parse(numberTextBox.Text) > 0 And _` `    Integer.Parse(numberTextBox.Text) < 10`	Evaluates True when numberTextBox.Text is "1", "2", "3", "4", "5", "6", "7", "8", or "9".
Not	Reverses the condition so that a true condition will evaluate false and vice versa.	`Not Integer.Parse(numberLabel.Text) = 0`	Evaluates True when numberLabel.Text is any value other than "0".

Compound Condition Examples

```
If maleRadioButton.Checked And Integer.Parse(ageTextBox.Text) < 21 Then
    minorMaleCountInteger += 1
End If

If juniorRadioButton.Checked Or seniorRadioButton.Checked Then
    upperClassmanInteger += 1
End If
```

The first example requires that both the radio button test and the age test be True for the count to be incremented. In the second example, only one of the conditions must be True.

One caution when using compound conditions: Each side of the logical operator must be a complete condition. For example,

```
countInteger > 10 Or < 0
```

is incorrect. Instead, it must be

```
countInteger > 10 Or countInteger < 0
```

Combining And and Or

You can create compound conditions that combine multiple And and Or conditions. When you have both an And and an Or, the And is evaluated before the Or. However, you can change the order of evaluation by using parentheses; any condition inside parentheses will be evaluated first.

For example, will the following condition evaluate True or False? Try it with various values for saleDecimal, discountRadioButton, and stateTextBox.Text.

```
If saleDecimal > 1000.0 Or discountRadioButton.Checked _
  And stateTextBox.Text.ToUpper <> "CA" Then
    ' Code here to calculate the discount.
End If
```

saleDecimal	discountRadioButton.Checked	stateTextBox.Text.ToUpper	Evaluates
1500.0	False	CA	True
1000.0	True	OH	True
1000.0	True	CA	False
1500.0	True	NY	True
1000.0	False	CA	False

Short-Circuit Operations

When evaluating a compound condition, sometimes the second condition is never evaluated. If a compound condition has an Or and the first condition evaluates True, there is no reason to evaluate the second condition. For example, if you have the condition

```
totalInteger < 0 Or totalInteger > 10
```

and totalInteger = −1 (negative 1), as soon as the first condition is tested, the entire condition is deemed True and the comparison stops, called *short circuiting* the operation. Likewise, if you have a compound condition with an And and the first condition evaluates False, there is no reason to evaluate the second condition.

```
countInteger >= 0 And countInteger <=10
```

If CountInteger = −1, the first condition is evaluated False and the comparison stops.

Nested If Statements

In many programs another If statement is one of the statements to be executed when a condition tests True or False. If statements that contain additional If statements are said to be **nested If** statements. The following example shows a nested If statement in which the second If occurs in the Then portion of the first If (Figure 4.5).

Figure 4.5

Flowcharting a nested If *statement.*

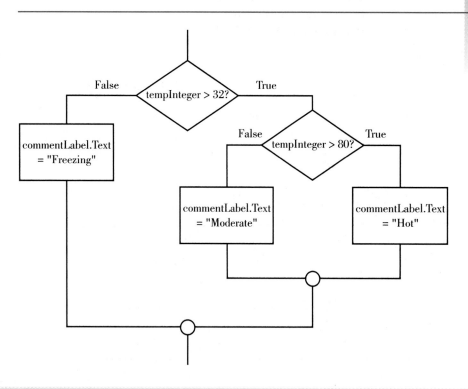

```
If tempInteger > 32 Then
    If tempInteger > 80 Then
        commentLabel.Text = "Hot"
    Else
        commentLabel.Text = "Moderate"
    End If
Else
    commentLabel.Text = "Freezing"
End If
```

To nest If statements in the Else portion, you may use either of the following approaches; however, your code is simpler if you use the second method (using ElseIf ... Then).

```
If tempInteger <= 32 Then
    commentLabel.Text = "Freezing"
Else
    If tempInteger > 80 Then
        commentLabel.Text = "Hot"
    Else
        commentLabel.Text = "Moderate"
    End If
End If
```

```
If tempInteger <= 32 Then
    commentLabel.Text = "Freezing"
ElseIf tempInteger > 80 Then
    commentLabel.Text = "Hot"
Else
    commentLabel.Text = "Moderate"
End If
```

You can nest Ifs in both the Then and Else. In fact, you may continue to nest Ifs within Ifs as long as each If has an End If. However, projects become very difficult to follow (and may not perform as intended) when Ifs become too deeply nested (Figure 4.6).

Figure 4.6

A flowchart of a nested If statement with Ifs nested on both sides of the original If.

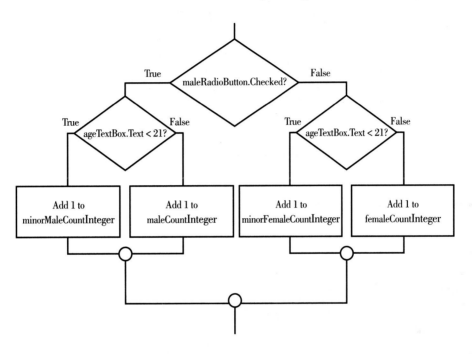

```
If maleRadioButton.Checked Then
    If Integer.Parse(ageTextBox.Text) < 21 Then
        minorMaleCountInteger += 1
    Else
        maleCountInteger += 1
    End If
Else
    If Integer.Parse(ageTextBox.Text) < 21 Then
        minorFemaleCountInteger += 1
    Else
        femaleCountInteger += 1
    End If
End If
```

Indentation can help you catch errors. Visual Basic always matches an Else with the last unmatched If, regardless of the indentation. ■

Feedback 4.2

Assume that frogsInteger = 10, toadsInteger = 5, and polliwogs-Integer = 6. What will be displayed for each of the following statements?

```
1. If frogsInteger > polliwogsInteger Then
       frogsRadioButton.Checked = True
   Else
       frogsRadioButton.Checked = False
   End If
```

2. ```
If frogsInteger > toadsInteger + polliwogsInteger Then
    resultLabel.Text = "It's the frogs"
Else
    resultLabel.Text = "It's the toads and the polliwogs"
End If
```
3. ```
If polliwogsInteger > toadsInteger And frogsInteger <> 0 _
   Or toadsInteger = 0
Then
    resultLabel.Text = "It's true"
Else
    resultLabel.Text = "It's false"
End If
```
4. Write the statements necessary to compare the numeric values stored in applesTextBox.Text and orangesTextBox.Text. Display in mostLabel.Text which has more, the apples or the oranges.
5. Write the Basic statements that will test the current value of balance-Decimal. When balanceDecimal is greater than zero, the check box for Funds Available, called fundsCheckBox, should be selected, the balanceDecimal set back to zero, and countInteger incremented by one. When balanceDecimal is zero or less, fundsCheckBox should not be selected (do not change the value of balanceDecimal or increment the counter).

Using If Statements with Radio Buttons and Check Boxes

In Chapter 2 you used the CheckedChanged event for radio buttons and check boxes to carry out the desired action. Now that you can use If statements, you should not take action in the CheckedChanged event procedures for these controls. Instead, use If statements to determine which options are selected.

To conform to good programming practice and make your programs consistent with standard Windows applications, place your code in the Click event of buttons, such as an OK button or an Apply button. For example, refer to the Visual Studio *Tools / Options* dialog box (Figure 4.7); no action will occur when

Figure 4.7

The Options dialog box. When the user clicks OK, the program checks the state of all radio buttons and check boxes.

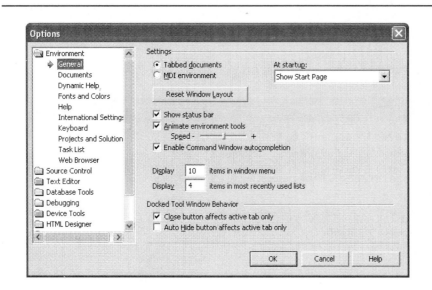

you click on a radio button or check box. Instead, when you click on the OK button, VS checks to see which options are selected.

In an application such as the message formatter project in Chapter 2 (refer to Figure 2.18), you could modify the code for the Display button to include code similar to the following:

```
If redRadioButton.Checked Then
    nameLabel.BackColor = Color.Red
ElseIf greenRadioButton.Checked Then
    nameLabel.BackColor = Color.Green
ElseIf blueRadioButton.Checked Then
    nameLabel.BackColor = Color.Blue
Else
    nameLabel.BackColor = Color.Black
End If
```

Additional Examples

```
If fastShipCheckBox.Checked Then
    totalDecimal += fastShipRateDecimal
End If

If giftWrapCheckBox.Checked Then
    totalDecimal += wrapAmountDecimal
End If
```

A "Simple Sample"

Test your understanding of the use of the If statement by coding some short examples.

Test the Value of a Check Box

Create a small project that contains a check box, a label, and a button. Name the button testButton, the check box testCheckBox, and the label messageLabel. In the Click event procedure for testButton, check the value of the check box. If the check box is currently checked, display "Check box is checked" in messageLabel.

```
Private Sub testButton_Click(ByVal sender As System.Object, ByVal e As System.EventArgs) _
    Handles testButton.Click

    ' Test the value of the check box.

    If testCheckBox.Checked Then
        messageLabel.Text = "Check box is checked"
    End If
```

Test your project. When it works, add an Else to the code that displays "Check box is not checked".

Test the State of Radio Buttons

Remove the check box from the previous project and replace it with two radio buttons, named freshmanRadioButton and sophomoreRadioButton and labeled "< 30 units" and ">= 30 units". Now change the If statement to display "Freshman" or "Sophomore" in the label.

```
If freshmanRadioButton.Checked Then
    messageLabel.Text = "Freshman"
Else
    messageLabel.Text = "Sophomore"
End If
```

Can you modify the sample to work for Freshman, Sophomore, Junior, and Senior? In the sections that follow, you will see code for testing multiple radio buttons and check boxes.

Checking the State of a Radio Button Group

Nested `If` statements work very well for determining which button of a radio button group is selected. Recall that in any group of radio buttons, only one button can be selected. Assume that your form has a group of radio buttons for Freshman, Sophomore, Junior, or Senior. In a calculation procedure, you want to add 1 to one of four counter variables, depending on which radio button is selected:

```
If freshmanRadioButton.Checked Then
    freshmanCountInteger += 1
ElseIf sophomoreRadioButton.Checked Then
    sophomoreCountInteger += 1
ElseIf juniorRadioButton.Checked Then
    juniorCountInteger += 1
ElseIf seniorRadioButton.Checked Then
    seniorCountInteger += 1
End If
```

Note that in most situations the final condition is unnecessary. You should be able to add to seniorRadioButton if the first three conditions are false. You might prefer to code the condition to make the statement more clear, or if no radio button is set initially, or if the program sets all radio buttons to False.

Checking the State of Multiple Check Boxes

Although nested `If` statements work very well for groups of radio buttons, the same is not true for a series of check boxes. Recall that if you have a series of check boxes, any number of the boxes may be selected. In this situation assume that you have check boxes for Discount, Taxable, and Delivery. You will need separate `If` statements for each condition.

```
If discountCheckBox.Checked Then
    ' Calculate the discount.
End If
If taxableCheckBox.Checked Then
    ' Calculate the tax.
End If
If deliveryCheckBox.Checked Then
    ' Deliver it.
End If
```

Enhancing Message Boxes

In Chapter 3 you learned to display a message box to the user. Now it's time to add such features as controlling the format of the message, displaying multiple buttons, checking which button the user clicks, and performing alternate actions depending on the user selection.

Displaying the Message String

The message string you display in a message box may be a string literal enclosed in quotes or it may be a string variable. You also may want to concatenate several items, for example, combining a literal with a value from a variable. It's usually a good idea to create a variable for the message and format the message before calling the Show method; if nothing else, it makes your code easier to read and follow.

Combining Values into a Message String

You can concatenate a literal such as "Total Sales: " with the value from a variable. You may need to include an extra space inside the literal to make sure that the value is separated from the literal.

```
Dim messageString As String

messageString = "Total Sales: " & totalSalesDecimal.ToString("C")
MessageBox.Show(messageString, "Sales Summary", MessageBoxButtons.OK)
```

Specify only the message for a "quick and dirty" message box for debugging purposes. It will display an OK button and an empty title bar: MessageBox.Show("I'm here."). ■

Creating Multiple Lines of Output

If your message is too long for one line, VB wraps it to a second line. But if you would like to control the line length and position of the split, you can insert a **NewLine character** into the string message. Use the Visual Studio constant ControlChars.NewLine to determine line endings. You can concatenate this constant into a message string to set up multiple lines.

In this example, a second line is added to the MessageBox from the previous example.

```
Dim formattedTotalString   As String
Dim messageString          As String
Dim formattedAvgString     As String

formattedTotalString = totalSalesDecimal.ToString("N")
formattedAvgString = averageSaleDecimal.ToString("N")
messageString = "Total Sales: " & formattedTotalString & ControlChars.NewLine & _
  "Average Sale: " & formattedAvgString

MessageBox.Show(messageString, "Sales Summary", MessageBoxButtons.OK)
```

You can combine multiple NewLine constants to achieve double spacing and create multiple message lines (Figure 4.8).

Figure 4.8

A message box with multiple lines of output, created by concatenating two NewLine characters at the end of each line.

```
' Concatenate the message string.
messageString = "Number of Orders: " & customerCount.ToString() _
  & ControlChars.NewLine & ControlChars.NewLine _
  & "Total Sales: " & grandTotalDecimal.ToString("C") _
  & ControlChars.NewLine & ControlChars.NewLine _
  & "Average Sale: " & averageDecimal.ToString("C")
' Display the message box.

MessageBox.Show(messageString, "Coffee Sales Summary", MessageBoxButtons.OK)
```

Using the ControlChars Constants

You can use several other constants from the ControlChars list, in addition to the NewLine constant. Type "ControlChars" and a period into the editor to see the complete list.

ControlChar Constant	Description
CrLf	Carriage return/linefeed character combination
Cr	Carriage return
Lf	Line feed
NewLine	NewLine character; same effect as a carriage return/line feed character combination
NullChar	Character with a value of zero
Tab	Tab character
Back	Backspace character
FormFeed	Formfeed character (not useful in Microsoft Windows)
VerticalTab	VerticalTab character (not useful in Microsoft Windows)
Quote	Quotation mark character

TIP

To prevent the user from clicking a Summary button before the first calculation, disable the button at design time (Enable = False). After the first calculation enable the button (Enable = True). ∎

Displaying Multiple Buttons

You can choose the buttons to display on the message box using the MessageBoxButtons constants (Figure 4.9). Figure 4.10 shows a MessageBox with two buttons using the MessageBoxButtons.YesNo constant. The Show method returns a **DialogResult object** that you can check to see which button the user clicked.

Figure 4.9

Choose the button(s) to display from the MessageBoxButtons constants.

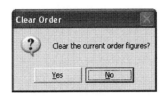

Figure 4.10

Display Yes and No buttons on a message box using `MessageBoxButtons.YesNo`.

Determining the Return Type of a Method

How do you know that the `Show` method returns an object of the DialogResult class? An easy way is to click in the word `Show` and press F1; Help will open to the correct page and show all of the possible argument lists along with the return type (Figure 4.11). Or another easy way is to point to the `Show` keyword and pause; the argument list that you are using pops up (Figure 4.12).

Declaring an Object Variable for the Method Return

To capture the information about the outcome of the `Show` method, you must declare a variable that can hold an instance of the DialogResult type.

Figure 4.11

Click on the keyword `Show` *and press F1 to pop up the* `Show` *method's Help page. All possible argument lists appear along with the method's return type.*

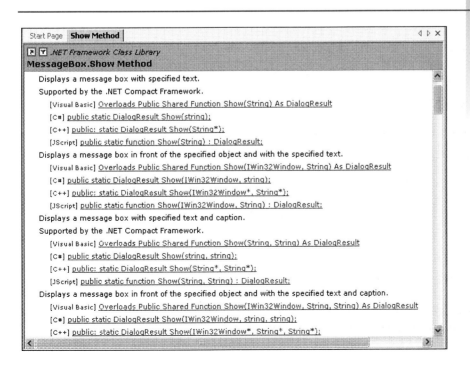

Figure   4.12

```
MessageBox.Show(messageString, "Coffee Sales Summary")
    Public Shared Function Show(text As String, caption As String) As System.Windows.Forms.DialogResult
```

*Pause the mouse pointer over the **Show** keyword and IntelliSense pops up with the argument list you are using. It also shows the method's return type.*

```
Dim whichButtonDialogResult As DialogResult
```

Then you assign the return value of the **Show** method to the new variable.

```
whichButtonDialogResult = MessageBox.Show("Clear the current order figures?", _
    "Clear Order", MessageBoxButtons.YesNo, MessageBoxIcon.Question)
```

The next step is to check the value of the return, comparing to the DialogResult constants, such as **Yes, No, OK, Retry, Abort**, and **Cancel**.

```
If whichButtonDialogResult = DialogResult.Yes Then
    ' Code to clear the order.
End If
```

Specifying a Default Button and Options

Two additional signatures for the MessageBox.Show method are as follows:

```
MessageBox.Show(TextMessage, TitlebarText, MessageBoxButtons, MessageBoxIcons, _
    MessageBoxDefaultButton)
MessageBox.Show(TextMessage, TitlebarText, MessageBoxButtons, MessageBoxIcons, _
    MessageBoxDefaultButton, MessageBoxOptions)
```

When you display multiple buttons, you may want one of the buttons to be the default (the accept button). For example, to make the second button (the No button) the default, use this statement:

```
responseDialogResult = MessageBox.Show("Clear the current order figures?", _
    "Clear Order", MessageBoxButtons.YesNo, MessageBoxIcon.Question, _
    MessageBoxDefaultButton.Button2)
```

You can right-align the message in the message box by setting the MessageBoxOptions argument:

```
responseDialogResult = MessageBox.Show("Clear the current order figures?", _
    "Clear Order", MessageBoxButtons.YesNo, MessageBoxIcon.Question, _
    MessageBoxDefaultButton.Button2, MessageBoxOptions.RightAlign)
```

Input Validation

Careful programmers check the values entered into text boxes before beginning the calculations. Validation is a form of self-protection; it is better to reject bad data than to spend hours (and sometimes days) trying to find an error only to discover that the problem was caused by a "user error." Finding and correcting the error early can often keep the program from producing erroneous results or halting with a run-time error.

Checking to verify that appropriate values have been entered for a text box is called *validation*. The validation may include making sure that the input is numeric, checking for specific values, checking a range of values, or making sure that required items are entered.

In Chapter 3 you learned to use `Try/Catch` blocks to trap for nonnumeric values. This chapter presents some additional validation techniques using `If` statements.

Note: Chapter 13 has some advanced validation techniques using the Validating event and error providers.

Checking for a Range of Values

Data validation may include checking the reasonableness of a value. Assume you are using a text box to input the number of hours worked in a day. Even with overtime, the company does not allow more than 10 work hours in a single day. You could check the input for reasonableness with this code:

```
If Integer.Parse(hoursTextBox.Text) > 10 Then
    MessageBox.Show("Too many hours", "Invalid Data", MessageBoxButtons.OK)
End If
```

Checking for a Required Field

Sometimes you need to be certain that a value has been entered into a text box before proceeding. You can compare a text box value to an empty string literal.

```
If nameTextBox.Text <> "" Then
    ' Do Something.
Else
    MessageBox.Show("Required Entry", "Sales Summary", MessageBoxButtons.OK)
End If
```

By checking separately for blank or nonnumeric data, you can display a better message to the user. Make sure to check for blanks first, since a blank field will throw an exception with a parsing method. For example, if you reverse the order of the `If` and `Try` blocks in the following example, blanks in quantityTextBox will always trigger the nonnumeric message in the `Catch` block.

```
If quantityTextBox.Text <> "" Then                ' Not blank.
    Try
        quantityDecimal = Decimal.Parse(quantityTextBox.Text)
    Catch ' Nonnumeric data.
        messageString = "Nonnumeric data entered for quantity."
        MessageBox.Show(messageString, "Data Entry Error")
    End Try
Else                    ' Missing data.
    messageString = "Enter the quantity."
    MessageBox.Show(messageString, "Data entry error")
End If
```

Performing Multiple Validations

When you need to validate several input fields, how many message boxes do
you want to display for the user? Assume that the user has neglected to fill five
text boxes and clicked on Calculate. You can avoid displaying five message
boxes in a row by using a nested `If` statement. This way you check the second
value only if the first one passes, and you can exit the processing if a problem
is found with a single field.

```
If nameTextBox.Text <> "" Then
    Try
        unitsDecimal = Decimal.Parse(unitsTextBox.Text)
        If freshmanRadioButton.Checked Or sophomoreRadioButton.Checked _
           Or juniorRadioButton.Checked Or seniorRadioButton.Checked Then

            ' Data valid — Do calculations or processing here.

        Else
            MessageBox.Show("Please select a Grade Level.", "Data Entry Error", _
                MessageBoxButtons.OK)
        End If

    Catch
        MessageBox.Show("Enter number of units.", "Data Entry Error", _
            MessageBoxButtons.OK)
        unitsTextBox.Focus()
    End Try
Else
    MessageBox.Show("Please enter a name", "Data Entry Error", MessageBoxButtons.OK)
    nameTextBox.Focus()
End If
```

The Case Structure

Earlier you used the `If` statement for testing conditions and making decisions.
Whenever you want to test a single variable for multiple values, the **Case
structure** provides a flexible and powerful solution. Any decisions that you
can code with a `Case` structure also can be coded with nested `If` statements,
but usually the `Case` structure is simpler and clearer.

The Select Case Statement—General Form

```
Select Case expression
    Case ConstantList
        [Statement(s)]
    [Case ConstantList
        [Statement(s)]]
    .
    .
    .
    [Case Else]
        [Statement(s)]
End Select
```

The expression in a `Case` structure is usually a variable or property that you wish to test.

The constant list is the value that you want to match; it may be a numeric or string constant or variable, a range of values, a relational condition, or a combination of these.

There is no limit to the number of statements that can follow a `Case` statement.

The Select Case Statement—Examples

```
Select Case scoreInteger
    Case Is >= 100
        messageLabel1.Text = "Excellent Score"
        messageLabel2.Text = "Give yourself a pat on the back."
    Case 80 To 99
        messageLabel1.Text = "Very Good"
        messageLabel2.Text = "You should be proud."
    Case 60 To 79
        messageLabel1.Text = "Satisfactory Score"
        messageLabel2.Text = "You should have a nice warm feeling."
    Case Else
        messageLabel1.Text = "Your score shows room for improvement."
        messageLabel2.Text = ""
End Select

Select Case listIndexInteger
    Case 0
        ' Handle Item Zero
    Case 1, 2, 3
        ' Handle Items
    Case Else
        ' Handle No Selection
End Select
```

The examples show a combination of relational operators, constant ranges, and multiple constants. Notice these points from the examples:

- When using a relational operator (e.g., `Is >= 100`), the word `Is` must be used.

- To indicate a range of constants, use the word `To` (e.g., `80 To 99`).

- Multiple constants should be separated by commas.

The elements used for the constant list may have any of these forms:

```
constant [, constant...]         Case 2, 5, 9
constant To constant             Case 25 To 50
Is relational-operator constant  Case Is < 10
```

When you want to test for a string value, you must include quotation marks around the literals.

Example

```
Select Case teamNameTextBox.Text
    Case "Tigers"
        ' Code for Tigers.
    Case "Leopards"
        ' Code for Leopards.
    Case "Cougars", "Panthers"
        ' Code for Cougars and Panthers.
    Case Else
        ' Code for any nonmatch.
End Select
```

Note that in the previous example, the capitalization also must match exactly. A better solution would be

```
Select Case teamNameTextBox.Text.ToUpper()
    Case "TIGERS"
        ' Code for Tigers.
    Case "LEOPARDS"
        ' Code for Leopards.
    Case "COUGARS", "PANTHERS"
        ' Code for Cougars and Panthers.
    Case Else
        ' Code for any nonmatch.
End Select
```

Although the `Case Else` clause is optional, generally you will want to include it in **Select Case** statements. The statements you code beneath `Case Else` execute only if none of the other `Case` conditions is matched. This clause provides checking for any invalid or unforeseen values of the expression being tested. If the `Case Else` clause is omitted and none of the `Case` conditions is True, the program continues execution at the statement following the `End Select`.

If more than one `Case` value is matched by the expression, only the statements in the *first* `Case` clause execute.

Feedback 4.3

Convert the following `If` statements to `Select Case` statements

```
1. If tempInteger <=32 Then
        commentLabel.Text = "Freezing"
    ElseIf tempInteger > 80 Then
        commentLabel.Text = "Hot"
    Else
        commentLabel.Text = "Moderate"
    End If
```

```
2. If countInteger = 0 Then
       MessageBox.Show("No items were entered.")
   ElseIf countInteger < 11 Then
       MessageBox.Show("1 - 10 items were entered.")
   ElseIf countInteger < 21 Then
       MessageBox.Show("11 - 20 items were entered.")
   Else
       MessageBox.Show("More than 20 items were entered.")
   End If
```

Sharing an Event Procedure

A very handy feature of VB .NET is the ability to share an event procedure for several controls. For example, assume that you have a group of five radio buttons to allow the user to choose a color (Figure 4.13). Each of the radio buttons must have its own name and will ordinarily have its own event procedure. But you can add events to the Handles clause at the top of an event procedure to make the procedure respond to events of other controls.

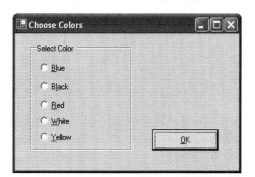

Figure 4.13

The five radio buttons allow the user to choose the color.

```
Private Sub blueRadioButton_CheckedChanged(ByVal sender As System.Object, _
    ByVal e As System.EventArgs) _
    Handles blueRadioButton.CheckedChanged, blackRadioButton.CheckedChanged, _
    redRadioButton.CheckedChanged, whiteRadioButton.CheckedChanged, _
    yellowRadioButton.CheckedChanged
```

After you have added the additional events to the Handles clause, this event procedure will execute when the user selects *any* of the radio buttons.

A good, professional technique is to set up a module-level variable to hold the selection that the user makes. Then, in the OK button's event procedure, you can take action based on which of the buttons was selected.

The key to using the shared event procedure is the sender argument that is passed to the CheckedChanged event procedure. The sender is defined as an object, which has a Name property. However, if you refer to sender.Name with Option Strict turned on, you generate a compiler error telling you that late binding is not allowed. **Late binding** means that the type cannot be determined at compile time, but must be determined at run time. Late binding is allowed with Option Strict turned off, but should be avoided if possible for performance reasons.

You can use the properties of the `sender` argument if you first cast (convert) `sender` to a specific object type, instead of the generic object. You can use VB's **CType function** to convert from one object type to another:

```
CType(ValueToConvert, NewType)
```

The `CType` function returns an object of the new type. If the `ValueToConvert` is not in the range of legal values for `NewType`, an exception is generated at run time.

For the radio button example, declare a variable as RadioButton data type, cast the `sender` argument to a RadioButton object type, and assign it to the new variable:

```
Dim selectedRadioButton As RadioButton
selectedRadioButton = CType(sender, RadioButton)
```

After these statements, you can refer to `selectedRadioButton.Name` to determine which radio button was selected:

```
Select Case selectedRadioButton.Name
    Case "blueRadioButton"
        ' Code for blue button.
```

You can declare a module-level variable as a Color data type, assign the chosen color in the shared event procedure, and then apply the color in the OK button's click event.

```
' Declare a module-level variable.
Dim selectedColor As Color

Private Sub blueRadioButton_CheckedChanged(ByVal sender As System.Object, _
    ByVal e As System.EventArgs) Handles yellowRadioButton.CheckedChanged, _
    whiteRadioButton.CheckedChanged, redRadioButton.CheckedChanged, _
    blackRadioButton.CheckedChanged, blueRadioButton.CheckedChanged
    'Save the name of the selected button

    Dim selectedRadioButton As RadioButton

    selectedRadioButton = CType(sender, RadioButton)
    Select Case selectedRadioButton.Name
        Case "blueRadioButton"
            selectedColor = Color.Blue
        Case "blackRadioButton"
            selectedColor = Color.Black
        Case "redRadioButton"
            selectedColor = Color.Red
        Case "whiteRadioButton"
            selectedColor = Color.White
        Case "yellowRadioButton"
            selectedColor = Color.Yellow
    End Select
End Sub
```

Calling Event Procedures

If you wish to perform a set of instructions in more than one location, you don't have to duplicate the code. Write the instructions once, in an event procedure, and "call" the procedure from another procedure. When you **call** an event procedure, the entire procedure is executed and then execution returns to the statement following the call.

The Call Statement—General Form

```
[Call] ProcedureName()
```

Notice that the keyword **Call** is optional and rarely used. You must include the parentheses; if the procedure that you are calling requires arguments, then place the arguments within the parentheses; otherwise leave them empty.

The Call Statement—Examples

```
Call clearButton_Click(sender, e)
clearButton_Click(sender, e)    ' Equivalent to the previous statement.
```

Notice the arguments for both of the example **Call** statements. You are passing the same two arguments that were passed to the calling procedure. If you examine any of the editor-generated event procedure headers, you can see that every event procedure requires these two arguments, which can be used to track the object that generated the event.

```
Private Sub summaryButton_Click( _
  ByVal sender As System.Object, ByVal e As System.EventArgs) Handles summaryButton.Click
        ...
        newOrderButton_Click(sender, e)        ' Call the event procedure.
```

In the programming example that follows, you will accumulate individual items for one customer. When that customer's order is complete, you need to clear the entire order and begin an order for the next customer. Refer to the interface in Figure 4.14; notice the two buttons: *Clear for Next Item* and *New Order*. The button for next item clears the text boxes on the screen. The button for a new order must clear the screen text boxes and clear the subtotal fields. Rather than repeat the instructions to clear the individual screen text boxes, we can call the event procedure for clearButton_Click from the newOrderButton_Click procedure.

```
Private Sub newOrderButton_Click(ByVal sender As System.Object, _
  ByVal e As System.EventArgs) Handles newOrderButton.Click
    ' Clear the current order and add to totals.

    clearButton_Click(sender, e)    ' Call the clearButton_Click event procedure.
    ' Continue with statements to clear subtotals.
```

Figure 4.14

A form with buttons that perform overlapping functions. The New Order *button must do the same tasks as* Clear for Next Item.

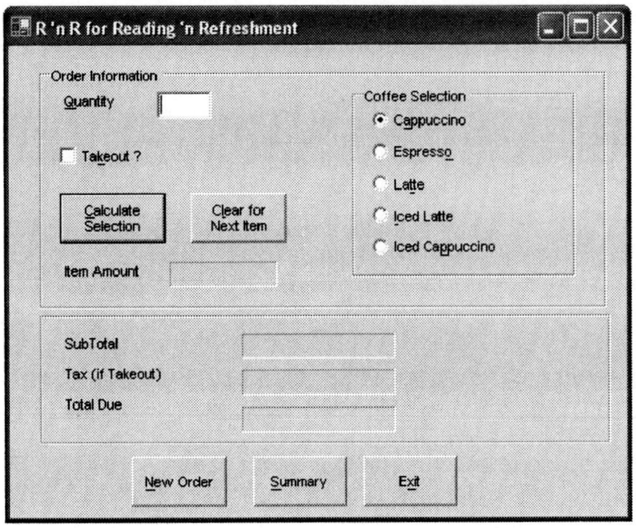

In the newOrderButton_Click procedure, all the instructions in clearButton_Click are executed. Then execution returns to the next statement following the call.

Your Hands-On Programming Example

Create a project for R 'n R—for Reading 'n Refreshment that calculates the amount due for individual orders and maintains accumulated totals for a summary. Have a check box for takeout items, which are taxable at 8 percent; all other orders are nontaxable. Include radio buttons for the five coffee selections: Cappuccino, Espresso, Latte, Iced Cappuccino, and Iced Latte. The prices for each will be assigned using these constants:

Cappuccino	2.00
Espresso	2.25
Latte	1.75
Iced (either)	2.50

Use a button for *Calculate Selection*, which will calculate and display the amount due for each item. Display appropriate error messages for missing or nonnumeric data.

A button for *Clear for Next Item* will clear the selections and the amount for the current item and set the focus back to the quantity. The Clear button should be disabled when the program begins and be enabled after the user begins an order.

Additional labels in a separate group box will display the summary information for the current order, including subtotal, tax, and total.

Buttons at the bottom of the form will be used for *New Order*, *Summary*, and *Exit*. The *New Order* button will confirm that the user wants to clear the current order. If the user agrees, clear the current order and add to the summary totals. The *Summary* button should display a message box with the number of orders, the total dollar amount, and the average sale amount per order.

Planning the Project

Sketch a form (Figure 4.15), which your users sign as meeting their needs.

Figure 4.15

The planning sketch of the form for the hands-on programming exercise example.

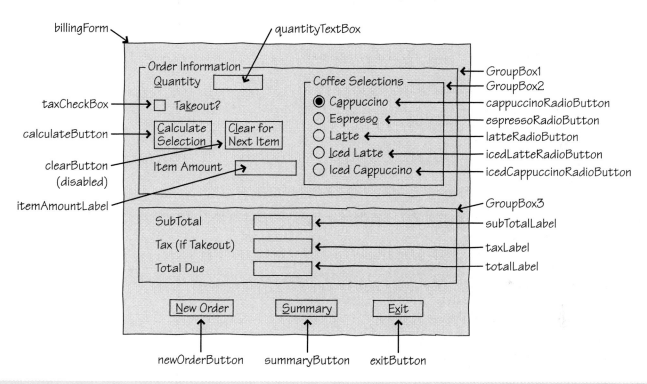

Plan the Objects and Properties Plan the property settings for the form and each of the controls.

Object	Property	Setting
billingForm	Name	billingForm
	Text	R 'n R—for Reading 'n Refreshment
	AcceptButton	calculateButton
	CancelButton	clearButton
GroupBox1	Text	Order Information
GroupBox2	Text	Coffee Selections
GroupBox3	Text	(blank)
cappuccinoRadioButton	Name	cappuccinoRadioButton
	Text	C&appuccino
	Checked	True

Object	Property	Setting
espressoRadioButton	Name	espressoRadioButton
	Text	Espress&o
latteRadioButton	Name	latteRadioButton
	Text	La&tte
icedLatteRadioButton	Name	icedLatteRadioButton
	Text	&Iced Latte
icedCappuccinoRadioButton	Name	icedCappuccinoRadioButton
	Text	Iced Ca&ppuccino
Label1	Text	&Quantity
quantityTextBox	Name	quantityTextBox
	Text	(blank)
taxCheckBox	Name	taxCheckBox
	Text	Ta&keout?
Label2	Text	Item Amount
Label3	Text	SubTotal
Label4	Text	Tax (if Takeout)
Label5	Text	Total Due
itemAmountLabel	Name	itemAmountLabel
	Text	(blank)
	BorderStyle	Fixed3D
subTotalLabel	Name	subTotalLabel
	Text	(blank)
	BorderStyle	Fixed3D
taxLabel	Name	taxLabel
	Text	(blank)
	BorderStyle	Fixed3D
totalLabel	Name	totalLabel
	Text	(blank)
	BorderStyle	Fixed3D
calculateButton	Name	calculateButton
	Text	&Calculate Selection
clearButton	Name	clearButton
	Text	C&lear for Next Item
	Enabled	False
newOrderButton	Name	newOrderButton
	Text	&New Order
summaryButton	Name	summaryButton
	Text	&Summary
exitButton	Name	exitButton
	Text	E&xit

Plan the Event Procedures You need to plan the actions for five event procedures for the buttons.

Object	Procedure	Action
calculateButton	Click	Validate for blank or nonnumeric quantity. Find price of drink selection. Multiply price by quantity. Add amount to subtotal. Calculate tax if needed. Calculate total = subtotal + tax. Format and display the values. Enable the Clear button.
clearButton	Click	Clear the coffee selections. Clear the quantity and the item price. Set the focus to the quantity.
summaryButton	Click	If current order not added to totals call newOrderButton_Click Calculate the average. Display the summary totals in a message box.
newOrderButton	Click	Confirm clearing current order. Clear the current order. Accumulate total sales and count. Set subtotal and total due to 0. Enable takeout check box.
exitButton	Click	Terminate the project.

Write the Project Follow the sketch in Figure 4.15 to create the form. Figure 4.16 shows the completed form.

• Set the properties of each object as you have planned.

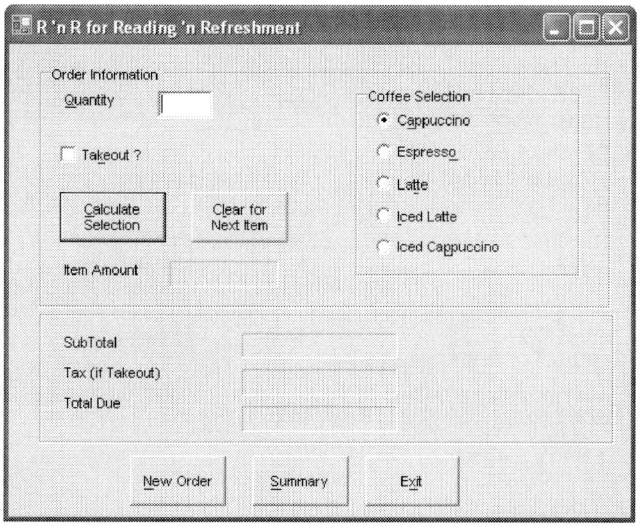

Figure 4.16

The form for the hands-on programming exercise.

- Write the code. Working from the pseudocode, write each event procedure.

- When you complete the code, use a variety of data to thoroughly test the project. Make sure the tab order is set correctly so that the insertion point begins in quantityTextBox.

The Project Coding Solution

```
'Program Name:    Billing
'Programmer:      Bradley/Millspaugh
'Date:            January 2004
'Description:     This project calculates the amount due
'                 based on the customer selection
'                 and accumulates summary data for the day.
'Folder:          Ch0401

Option Strict On

Public Class billingForm
 Inherits System.Windows.Forms.Form

    ' Declare constants.
    Const TAX_RATE_Decimal As Decimal = 0.08D
    Const CAPPUCCINO_PRICE_Decimal As Decimal = 2D
    Const ESPRESSO_PRICE_Decimal As Decimal = 2.25D
    Const LATTE_PRICE_Decimal As Decimal = 1.75D
    Const ICED_PRICE_Decimal As Decimal = 2.5D

    ' Declare variables for summary information.
    Dim subtotalDecimal, totalDecimal, grandTotalDecimal As Decimal
    Dim customerCountInteger As Integer

    Private Sub calculateButton_Click(ByVal sender As System.Object, _
      ByVal e As System.EventArgs) Handles calculateButton.Click
        ' Calculate and display the current amounts and add to totals.

        Dim priceDecimal, taxDecimal, itemAmountDecimal As Decimal
        Dim quantityInteger As Integer

        ' Find the price.
        If cappuccinoRadioButton.Checked Then
            priceDecimal = CAPPUCCINO_PRICE_Decimal
        ElseIf espressoRadioButton.Checked Then
            priceDecimal = ESPRESSO_PRICE_Decimal
        ElseIf LatteRadioButton.Checked Then
            priceDecimal = LATTE_PRICE_Decimal
        ElseIf icedCappuccinoRadioButton.Checked Or icedLatteRadioButton.Checked Then
            priceDecimal = ICED_PRICE_Decimal
        End If

        ' Calculate extended price and add to order total.
        Try
            quantityInteger = Integer.Parse(quantityTextBox.Text)
            itemAmountDecimal = priceDecimal * quantityInteger
            subtotalDecimal += itemAmountDecimal
```

```vbnet
            If taxCheckBox.Checked Then
                taxDecimal = subtotalDecimal * TAX_RATE_Decimal
            Else
                taxDecimal = 0
            End If
            totalDecimal = subtotalDecimal + taxDecimal
            itemAmountLabel.Text = itemAmountDecimal.ToString("C")
            subtotalLabel.Text = subtotalDecimal.ToString("N")
            taxLabel.Text = taxDecimal.ToString("N")
            totalLabel.Text = totalDecimal.ToString("C")
            ' Allow a change only for new order.
            taxCheckBox.Enabled = False
            ' Allow Clear after an order is begun.
            clearButton.Enabled = True

        Catch quantityException As FormatException
            MessageBox.Show("Quantity must be numeric.", "Data Entry Error", _
                MessageBoxButtons.OK, MessageBoxIcon.Information)
            With quantityTextBox
                .Focus()
                .SelectAll()
            End With
        End Try
    End Sub

    Private Sub clearButton_Click(ByVal sender As System.Object, _
        ByVal e As System.EventArgs) Handles clearButton.Click
        ' Clear the appropriate controls.

        cappuccinoRadioButton.Checked = True    'All others are False
        itemAmountLabel.Text = ""
        With quantityTextBox
            .Clear()
            .Focus()
        End With
    End Sub

    Private Sub exitButton_Click(ByVal sender As System.Object, _
      ByVal e As System.EventArgs) Handles exitButton.Click
        ' Terminate the project.

        Me.Close()
    End Sub

    Private Sub newOrderButton_Click(ByVal sender As System.Object, _
      ByVal e As System.EventArgs) Handles newOrderButton.Click
        ' Clear the current order and add to the totals.

        Dim returnDialogResult As DialogResult
        Dim messageString As String

        ' Confirm clear of current order.
        messageString = "Clear the current order figures?"
        returnDialogResult = MessageBox.Show(messageString, "Clear Order", _
            MessageBoxButtons.YesNo, MessageBoxIcon.Question, _
            MessageBoxDefaultButton.Button2)
```

```vbnet
        If returnDialogResult = DialogResult.Yes Then    'User said Yes.
            clearButton_Click(sender, e)              'Clear the screen fields.
            subtotalLabel.Text = ""
            taxLabel.Text = ""
            totalLabel.Text = ""

            Try
                ' Add to Totals.
                ' Adds only if not a new order/customer.
                If subtotalDecimal <> 0 Then
                    grandTotalDecimal += totalDecimal
                    customerCountInteger += 1
                    ' Reset totals for next customer.
                    subtotalDecimal = 0
                    totalDecimal = 0
                End If
            Catch
                messageString = "Error in calculations."
                MessageBox.Show(messageString, "Error", _
                    MessageBoxButtons.OK, MessageBoxIcon.Error)
            End Try

            ' Clear appropriate display items and enable check box.
            With taxCheckBox
                .Enabled = True
                .Checked = False
            End With
            clearButton.Enabled = False
        End If
    End Sub

    Private Sub summaryButton_Click(ByVal sender As System.Object, _
      ByVal e As System.EventArgs) Handles summaryButton.Click
        ' Calculate the average and display the totals.

        Dim averageDecimal As Decimal
        Dim messageString As String

        If totalDecimal <> 0 Then
            ' Make sure last order is counted.
            newOrderButton_Click(sender, e)
        End If

        If customerCountInteger > 0 Then
            Try
                ' Calculate the average.
                averageDecimal = grandTotalDecimal / customerCountInteger

                ' Concatenate the message string.
                messageString = "Number of Orders: " _
                    & customerCountInteger.ToString() _
                    & ControlChars.NewLine & ControlChars.NewLine _
                    & "Total Sales: " & grandTotalDecimal.ToString("C") _
                    & ControlChars.NewLine & ControlChars.NewLine _
                    & "Average Sale: " & averageDecimal.ToString("C")
                MessageBox.Show(messageString, "Coffee Sales Summary", _
                    MessageBoxButtons.OK, MessageBoxIcon.Information)
```

```
        Catch
            messageString = "Error in calculations."
            MessageBox.Show(messageString, "Error", _
                MessageBoxButtons.OK, MessageBoxIcon.Error)
        End Try
    Else
        messageString = "No sales data to summarize."
        MessageBox.Show(messageString, "Coffee Sales Summary", _
            MessageBoxButtons.OK, MessageBoxIcon.Information)
    End If
End Sub
End Class
```

Debugging Visual Basic Projects

One of the advantages of programming in the Visual Studio environment is the availability of debugging tools. You can use these tools to help find and eliminate logic and run-time errors. The debugging tools also can help you follow the logic of existing projects to better understand how they work.

Sometimes it's helpful to know the result of a condition, the value of a variable or property, or the sequence of execution of your program. You can follow program logic in Break mode by single-stepping through code; you also can get information about execution without breaking the program run, using the WriteLine method of the Debug class.

In the following sections, you will learn to use many of the debugging tools on the Debug toolbar (Figure 4.17) and the *Debug* menu (Figure 4.18). Note that the Debug toolbar appears automatically when you choose the Start command; you also can make the toolbar display full-time by right-clicking on any toolbar and choosing *Debug* from the popup menu.

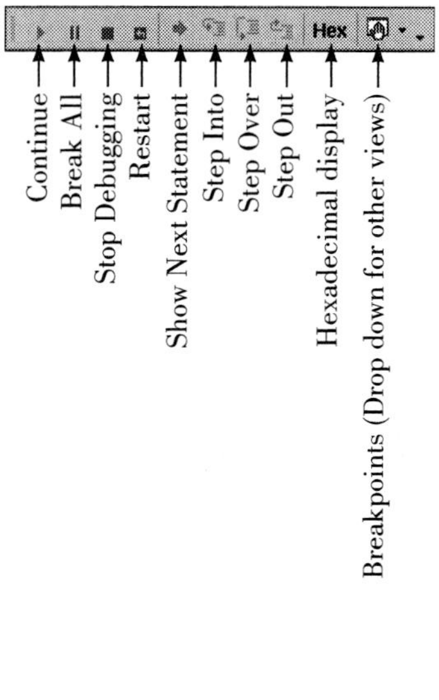

Figure 4.17

The Debug toolbar with its tools for debugging programs.

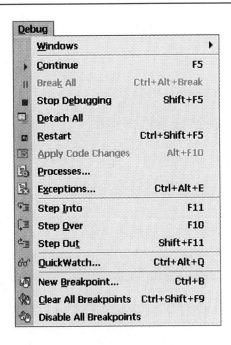

Writing to the Output Window

You can place a **Debug.WriteLine method** in your code. In the argument you can specify a message to write or an object that you want tracked.

The Debug.WriteLine Method—General Form

```
Debug.WriteLine(TextString)
Debug.WriteLine(Object)
```

The Debug.WriteLine method is overloaded, so you can pass it a string argument or the name of an object.

The Debug.WriteLine Method—Examples

```
Debug.WriteLine("calculateButton procedure entered.")
Debug.WriteLine(quantityTextBox)
```

When the Debug.WriteLine method executes, its output appears in the Output window. Figure 4.19 shows the output of the two example statements above. Notice the second line of output, for quantityTextBox—the class of the object displays along with its current contents.

Figure 4.19

The Output window shows the output of the Debug.WriteLine method.

Output

Debug

```
calculateButton procedure entered.
System.Windows.Forms.TextBox, Text: 100
```

Call Stack | Breakpoints | Command Window | Output

You may find it useful to place `WriteLine` methods in `If` statements, so that you can see which branch the logic followed.

```
If countInteger > 10 Then
    Debug.WriteLine("Count is greater than 10.")
    ' Other processing.
Else
    Debug.WriteLine("Count is not greater than 10.")
    ' Other processing.
End If
```

An advantage of using `WriteLine`, rather than the other debugging techniques that follow, is that you do not have to break program execution.

Clearing the Output Window

New to the VS IDE, you can clear the Output window. Right-click in the window and choose *Clear All*.

Pausing Execution with the Break Button

You can click on the Break button to pause execution. This step places the project into break time at the current line. However, you will generally prefer to break in the middle of a procedure. To choose the location of the break, you can force a break with a breakpoint.

Forcing a Break

During the debugging process, often you want to stop at a particular location in code and watch what happens (e.g., which branch of an `If ... Then ... Else`; which procedures were executed; the value of a variable just before or just after a calculation). You can force the project to break by inserting a **breakpoint** in code.

```
Try
    amountDueLabel.Text = (priceDecimal * Decimal.Parse(quantityTextBox.Text)).ToString()
Catch
    MessageBox.Show( "Please Enter a Numeric Value.", "Error", MessageBoxButtons.OK)
End Try
```

To set a breakpoint, place the mouse pointer in the gray margin indicator area at the left edge of the Editor window and click; the line will be highlighted in red and a large red dot will display in the margin indicator (Figure 4.20).

After setting a breakpoint, start execution. When the project reaches the breakpoint, it will halt, display the line, and go into break time.

You can remove a breakpoint by clicking again in the gray margin area, or clear all breakpoints from the *Debug* menu.

TIP

Place the insertion point in the line you want as a breakpoint and press F9. Press F9 again to toggle the breakpoint off. ∎

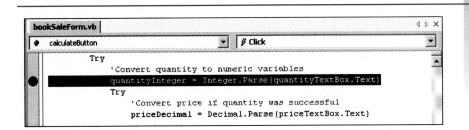

Figure 4.20

A program statement with a breakpoint set appears highlighted, and a dot appears in the gray margin indicator area.

Checking the Current Values of Expressions

You can quickly check the current value of an expression such as a variable, a control, a condition, or an arithmetic expression. During break time, display the Editor window and point to the name of the expression that you want to view; a small label will pop up, similar to a ToolTip, that displays the current contents of the expression. If you want to view the contents of an expression of more than one word, such as a condition or arithmetic expression, highlight the entire expression and then point to the highlighted area; the current value will display.

The steps for viewing the contents of a variable during run time are as follows:

1. Break the execution using a breakpoint.
2. If the code does not appear in the editor, click on the editor's tab in the Document window.
3. Point to the variable or expression you wish to view.

The current contents of the expression will pop up in a label (Figure 4.21).

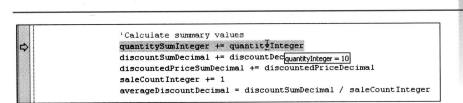

Figure 4.21

Point to a variable name in code, and its current value displays.

Stepping through Code

The best way to debug a project is to thoroughly understand what the project is doing every step of the way. Previously, this task was performed by following each line of code manually to understand its effect. You can now use the Visual Studio stepping tools to trace program execution line by line and see the progression of the program as it executes through your code.

You step through code at break time. You can use one of the techniques already mentioned to break execution or choose one of the stepping commands at design time; the program will begin running and immediately transfer to break time.

The three stepping commands on the *Debug* menu are *Step Into*, *Step Over*, and *Step Out*. You also can use the toolbar buttons for stepping or the keyboard shortcuts shown on the menu (refer to Figure 4.18).

These commands force the project to execute a single line at a time and to display the Editor window with the current statement highlighted. As you execute the program, by pressing a button, for example, the Click event occurs. Execution transfers to the Click event procedure, the Editor window for that procedure appears on the screen, and you can follow line-by-line execution.

Step Into

Most likely you will use the **Step Into** command more than the other two stepping commands. When you choose *Step Into* (from the menu, the toolbar button, or F11), the next line of code executes and the program pauses again in break time. If the line of code is a call to another procedure, the first line of code of the other procedure displays.

To continue stepping through your program execution, continue choosing the *Step Into* command. When a procedure is completed, your form will display again, awaiting an event. You can click on one of the form's buttons to continue stepping through code in an event procedure. If you want to continue execution without stepping, choose the *Continue* command (from the menu, the toolbar button, or F5).

Step Over

The **Step Over** command also executes one line of code at a time. The difference between *Step Over* and *Step Into* occurs when your code has calls to other procedures. *Step Over* displays only the lines of code in the current procedure being analyzed; it does not display lines of code in the called procedures.

You can choose *Step Over* from the menu, from the toolbar button, or by pressing F10. Each time you choose the command, one more program statement executes.

Step Out

You use the third stepping command when you are stepping through a called procedure. The **Step Out** command continues rapid execution until the called procedure completes, and then returns to break mode at the statement following the call, that is, the next line of the calling procedure.

Continuing Program Execution

When you have seen what you want to see, continue rapid execution by pressing F5 or choosing *Continue* from the Debug toolbar or the *Debug* menu. If you want to restart execution from the beginning, choose the *Restart* command.

Stopping Execution

Once you have located a problem in the program's code, usually you want to stop execution, correct the error, and run again. Stop execution by selecting *Stop Debugging* from the *Debug* menu or the toolbar button, or press the keyboard shortcut: Shift + F5.

The Locals Window

Sometimes you may find that the **Locals window** displays just the information that you want (Figure 4.22). The Locals window displays all objects and variables that are within scope at break time. That means that if you break execution in the calculateButton_Click event procedure, all variables local to that

Figure 4.22

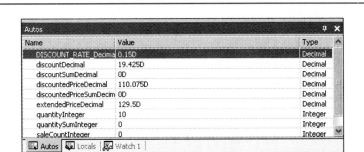

procedure display. You also can expand the Me entry to see the state of the form's controls and the values of module-level variables.

The Autos Window

Another helpful debugging window is the **Autos window**. The Autos window "automatically" displays all variables and control contents that are referenced in the current statement and a few statements on either side of the current one (Figure 4.23). Note that the highlighted line is about to execute next; the "current" statement is the one just before the highlighted one.

    You can view the Autos window when your program stops at a breakpoint. Click on the Autos window tab or open it from the *View* menu.

To use any of the debugging windows, you must be in break mode. ■

Figure 4.23

Debugging Step-by-Step Tutorial

In this exercise you will learn to set a breakpoint; pause program execution; single step through program instructions; display the current values in properties, variables, and conditions; and debug a Visual Basic project.

Test the Project

STEP 1: Open the debugging project on your student CD. The project is found in the Ch04Debug folder.

STEP 2: Run the program.

STEP 3: Enter color Blue, quantity 100, and press Enter or click on the Calculate button.

STEP 4: Enter another color Blue, quantity 50, and press Enter. Are the totals correct?

STEP 5: Enter color Red, quantity 30, and press Enter.

STEP 6: Enter color Red, quantity 10, and press Enter. Are the totals correct?

STEP 7: Enter color White, quantity 50, and press Enter.

STEP 8: Enter color White, quantity 100, and press Enter. Are the totals correct?

STEP 9: Exit the project. You are going to locate and correct the errors in the red and white totals.

Break and Step Program Execution

STEP 1: Display the program code. Scroll to locate this line, which is the first calculation line in the calculateButton_Click event procedure:

```
quantityDecimal = Decimal.Parse(quantityTextBox.Text)
```

STEP 2: Click in the gray margin indicator area to set a breakpoint on the selected line. Your screen should look like Figure 4.24.

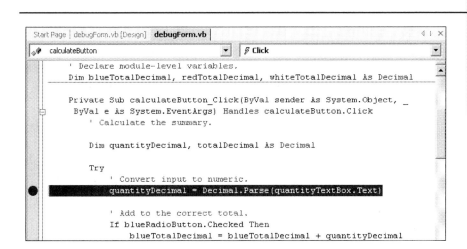

Figure 4.24

A program statement with a breakpoint set appears highlighted, and a dot appears in the gray margin indicator area.

STEP 3: Run the project, enter Red, quantity 30, and press Enter.

The project will transfer control to the calculateButton_Click procedure, stop when the breakpoint is reached, highlight the current line, and enter break time (Figure 4.25).

Note: The highlighted line has not yet executed.

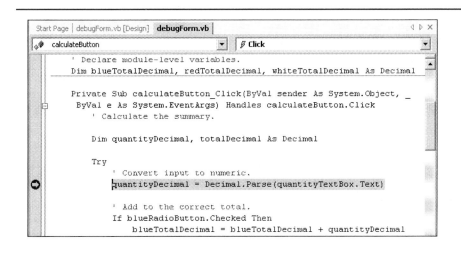

Figure 4.25

When a breakpoint is reached during program execution, Visual Basic enters break time, displays the Editor window, and highlights the breakpoint line.

Press the F11 key, which causes VB to execute the current program statement (the assignment statement). (F11 is the keyboard shortcut for *Debug / Step Into.*) The statement is executed, and the highlight moves to the next statement (the `If` statement).

STEP 4: Press F11 again; the condition (`blueRadioButton.Checked`) is tested and found to be False.

STEP 5: Continue pressing F11 a few more times and watch the order in which program statements execute.

View the Contents of Properties, Variables, and Conditions

STEP 1: Scroll up if necessary and point to the `.Text` portion of `quantity-TextBox.Text` in the breakpoint line; the contents of the Text property pop up (Figure 4.26). Note that if you instead point to the object name (quantityTextBox), the class of the selected object pops up (quantity-TextBox = {System.Windows.Forms.TextBox}).

F i g u r e　4 . 2 6

Point to a property reference in code and the current content pops up.

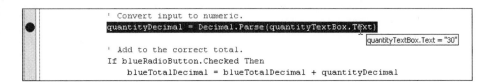

```
' Convert input to numeric.
quantityDecimal = Decimal.Parse(quantityTextBox.Text)
                                                      quantityTextBox.Text = "30"
' Add to the correct total.
If blueRadioButton.Checked Then
    blueTotalDecimal = blueTotalDecimal + quantityDecimal
```

STEP 2: Point to quantityDecimal and view the contents of that variable. Notice that the Text property is enclosed in quotes and the numeric variable is not. The 30D means 30 Decimal.

STEP 3: Point to `blueRadioButton.Checked` in the `If` statement, taking care to point to the property name, not the object name. Then point to `redRadioButton.Checked`. You can see the Boolean value for each of the radio buttons.

STEP 4: Point to redTotalDecimal to see the current value of that total variable. This value looks correct, since you just entered 30, which was added to the total.

Continue Program Execution

STEP 1: Press F5, the keyboard shortcut for the *Continue* command. The *Continue* command continues rapid execution.

If the current line is any line other than `End Sub`, execution continues and your form reappears. If the current line is `End Sub`, you may have to click on your project's Taskbar button to make the form reappear.

STEP 2: Enter color Red and quantity 10. When you press Enter, program execution will again break at the breakpoint.

The 10 you just entered should be added to the 30 previously entered for Red, producing 40 in the Red total.

Use the Step Into button on the Debug toolbar to step through execution. Keep pressing Step Into until the 10 is added to redTotal-Decimal. Display the current contents of the total. Can you see what the problem is?

✓TIP

You can change the current line of execution in debugging mode by dragging the current line indicator arrow on the left side. ■

Hint: redTotalDecimal has only the current amount, not the sum of the two amounts. The answer will appear a little later; try to find it yourself first.

You will fix this error soon, after testing the White total.

Test the White Total

STEP 1: Press F5 to continue execution. If the form does not reappear, click the project's Taskbar button.

STEP 2: Enter color White, quantity 100, and press Enter.

STEP 3: When execution halts at the breakpoint, press F5 to continue. This returns to rapid execution until the next breakpoint is reached.

STEP 4: Enter color White, quantity 50, and press Enter.

STEP 5: Press F11 several times when execution halts at the breakpoint until you execute the line that adds the quantity to the White total. Remember that the highlighted line has not yet executed; press Step Into (F11) one more time, if necessary, to execute the addition statement.

STEP 6: Point to each variable name to see the current values (Figure 4.27). Can you see the problem?

Figure 4.27

Point to the variable name in code and its current value displays as 50 Decimal.

```
          ' Add to the correct total.
        If blueRadioButton.Checked Then
            blueTotalDecimal = blueTotalDecimal + quantityDecimal
        ElseIf redRadioButton.Checked Then
            redTotalDecimal = quantityDecimal
        ElseIf whiteRadioButton.Checked Then
            whiteTotalDecimal = whiteTotalDecimals + quantityDecimal
        End If          whiteTotalDecimal = 50D
```

STEP 7: Display the Autos window by clicking on its tab. Here you can see the current value of all properties and variables referred to by the previous two statements and the following three statements (Figure 4.28).

Figure 4.28

The Autos window displays the current contents of variables and properties in the statements before and after the current statement.

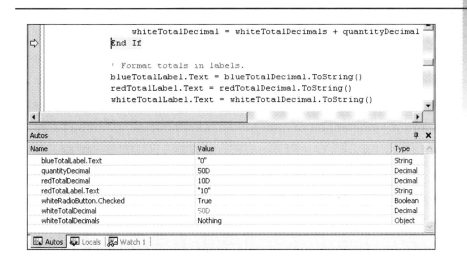

```
            whiteTotalDecimal = whiteTotalDecimals + quantityDecimal
        End If

        ' Format totals in labels.
        blueTotalLabel.Text = blueTotalDecimal.ToString()
        redTotalLabel.Text = redTotalDecimal.ToString()
        whiteTotalLabel.Text = whiteTotalDecimal.ToString()
```

Autos			🔲 ✕
Name	Value		Type
blueTotalLabel.Text	"0"		String
quantityDecimal	50D		Decimal
redTotalDecimal	10D		Decimal
redTotalLabel.Text	"10"		String
whiteRadioButton.Checked	True		Boolean
whiteTotalDecimal	50D		Decimal
whiteTotalDecimals	Nothing		Object

🔲 Autos 🔲 Locals 🔲 Watch 1

STEP 8: Identify all the errors. When you are ready to make the corrections, continue to the next step.

Correct the Red Total Error

STEP 1: Stop program execution by clicking on the Stop Debugging toolbar button (Figure 4.29).

Figure 4.29

Click on the Stop Debugging button on the Debug toolbar to halt program execution.

☑TIP

Display keyboard shortcuts on ToolTips, as in Figure 4.29, by selecting *Tools / Customize / Options / Other / Show shortcut keys in ScreenTips.* ∎

STEP 2: Locate this line:

```
redTotalDecimal = quantityDecimal
```

This statement replaces the value of redTotalDecimal with quantity-Decimal rather than adding to the total.

STEP 3: Change the line to read:

```
redTotalDecimal += quantityDecimal
```

(*or* `redTotalDecimal = redTotalDecimal + quantityDecimal` if you prefer.)

Correct the White Total Error

STEP 1: Locate this line:

```
whiteTotalDecimal = whiteTotalDecimals + quantityDecimal
```

Have you found the problem with this line? Look carefully at the spelling of the variable names. The compiler would find this error if Option Explicit were turned on. Unfortunately, someone turned it off, which means that VB will allow you to use variables without first declaring them.

STEP 2: Scroll up to the top of the code and find this statement (just below the comments in the Declarations section).

```
Option Explicit Off
```

STEP 3: Change the statement to read:

```
Option Explicit On
```

Note: Option Explicit defaults to the setting in Project Properties. If the option is turned on in Project Properties, you can just remove this line, if you prefer.

STEP 4: Run the project again. This time the compiler identifies the error in the variable name. Click No to the Continue question.

The error appears in the Task List (Figure 4.30).

F i g u r e   4 . 3 0

Display the Task List to view the error. Double-click on the error line to jump to that error in code.

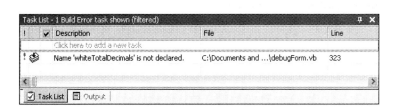

STEP 5: Double-click on the error line in the Task List; the error line in code is highlighted.

STEP 6: Remove the *s* from whiteTotalDecimals. The line should read:

```
whiteTotalDecimal += quantityDecimal
```

Or you can change it to read

```
whiteTotalDecimal = whiteTotalDecimal + quantityDecimal
```

STEP 7: Press F5 to start program execution. Enter color White and 100 and press Enter.

STEP 8: Press F5 to continue when the project halts at the breakpoint.

STEP 9: Enter White, 50, and Enter.

STEP 10: At the breakpoint, clear the breakpoint by clicking on the red margin dot for the line.

STEP 11: Press F5 to continue and check the total on the form. It should be correct now.

STEP 12: Test the totals for all three colors carefully and then click Exit.

Test the Exception Handling

STEP 1: Set a breakpoint again on the first calculation line in the calculate-Button_Click event procedure.

STEP 2: Run the program, this time entering nonnumeric characters for the amount. Click on Calculate; when the program stops at the breakpoint, press F11 repeatedly and watch program execution. The message box should appear.

Force a Run-Time Error

For this step, you will use a technique called *commenting out* code. Programmers often add apostrophes to the beginning of code lines, to test the code without those lines. Sometimes it works well to copy a section of code, comment out the original to keep it unchanged, and modify only the copy. You'll find it easy to uncomment the code later, after you finish testing.

STEP 1: Select *Clear All Breakpoints* from the *Debug* menu if the menu item is available. The item is available only when there are breakpoints set in the program.

STEP 2: At the left end of the line with the Try statement, add an apostrophe, turning the line into a comment.

STEP 3: Scroll down and locate the exception-handling code. Highlight the lines beginning with Catch and ending with End Try.

```
Catch
    MessageBox.Show("Enter numeric data.", "Data Error", MessageBoxButtons.OK, _
        MessageBoxIcon.Information)
    With quantityTextBox
        .Focus()
        .SelectAll()
    End With
End Try
```

STEP 4: Click on the *Comment out the selected lines* button on the Editing toolbar (Figure 4.31). The editor adds an apostrophe to the start of each of the selected lines.

Figure 4.31

Click the Comment out the selected lines *toolbar button to temporarily make program lines into comments.*

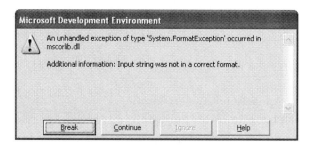

STEP 5: Run the project. This time click the Calculate button without entering a quantity.

A run-time error will occur (Figure 4.32).

Figure 4.32

The missing data cause an exception and run-time error. Click on the Break button to correct the problem.

Microsoft Development Environment

An unhandled exception of type 'System.FormatException' occurred in mscorlib.dll

Additional information: Input string was not in a correct format.

[Break] [Continue] [Ignore] [Help]

STEP 6: Click *Break* on the error dialog box, and the Editor window will display with the offending line highlighted in green (Figure 4.33). You can click on the tab for the Output window to see more description of the error.

You can click *Stop Debugging* or *Continue*, if you wish. Either will cancel execution.

Figure 4.33

For a run-time error, the offending line is highlighted in green and the Output window shows a description of the error.

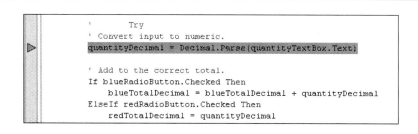

```
'        Try
' Convert input to numeric.
quantityDecimal = Decimal.Parse(quantityTextBox.Text)

' Add to the correct total.
If blueRadioButton.Checked Then
    blueTotalDecimal = blueTotalDecimal + quantityDecimal
ElseIf redRadioButton.Checked Then
    redTotalDecimal = quantityDecimal
```

STEP 7: After you are finished testing the program, select the commented lines and click on the *Uncomment the selected lines* button (Figure 4.34).

Note: You can just click an insertion point in a line or select the entire line when you comment and uncomment lines.

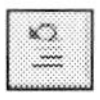

Figure 4.34

Click the Uncomment the selected lines toolbar button after testing the program.

Summary

1. Visual Basic uses the `If ... Then ... Else` statement to make decisions. An `Else` clause is optional and specifies the action to be taken if the condition evaluates as false. An `If ... Then ... Else` statement must conclude with an `End If`.
2. Flowcharts can help visualize the logic of an `If ... Then ... Else` statement.
3. The conditions for an `If` statement are evaluated for True or False.
4. Conditions can be composed of the relational operators, which compare items for equality, greater than, or less than. The comparison of numeric values is based on the quantity of the number, while string comparisons are based on the ANSI code table.
5. The `ToUpper` and `ToLower` methods of the String class can convert a text value to upper- or lowercase.
6. The `And` and `Or` logical operators may be used to combine multiple conditions. With the `And` operator, both conditions must be true for the entire condition to evaluate True. For the `Or` operator, if either or both conditions are true, the entire condition evaluates as True. When both `And` and `Or` are used in a condition, the `And` condition is evaluated before the `Or` condition.
7. A nested `If` statement contains an `If` statement within either the true or false actions of a previous `If` statement. Nesting an `If` statement inside of another requires the use of the `End If` clause. An `Else` clause always applies to the last unmatched `If` regardless of indentation.
8. The state of radio buttons and check boxes is better tested with `If` statements in the event procedure for a button, rather than coding event procedures for the radio button or check box.
9. The `MessageBox.Show` method can display a multiple-line message if you concatenate a NewLine character to specify a line break.
10. You can choose to display multiple buttons on a message box. The `MessageBox.Show` method returns an object of the DialogResult class, which you can check using the DialogResult constants.
11. Data validation checks the reasonableness or appropriateness of the value in a variable or property.
12. The same event procedure can be assigned to multiple controls, so that the controls share the procedure.
13. You can use the `sender` argument in an event procedure to determine which control caused the procedure to execute.

14. One procedure can call another procedure. To call an event procedure, you must supply the sender and e arguments.
15. A variety of debugging tools are available in Visual Studio. These include writing to the Output window, breaking program execution, displaying the current contents of variables, and stepping through code.

Key Terms

ANSI code   *141*
Autos window   *174*
breakpoint   *171*
call   *161*
Case structure   *156*
compound condition   *144*
condition   *139*
CType function   *160*
Debug.WriteLine method   *170*
DialogResult object   *152*
End If   *137*
If ... Then ... Else   *137*
late binding   *160*

Locals window   *173*
logical operator   *144*
nested If   *145*
NewLine character   *151*
relational operator   *139*
Select Case   *158*
short circuit   *145*
Step Into   *173*
Step Out   *173*
Step Over   *173*
ToLower method   *143*
ToUpper method   *143*
validation   *155*

Review Questions

1. What is the general format of the statement used to code decisions in an application?
2. What is a condition?
3. Explain the purpose of relational operators and logical operators.
4. Differentiate between a comparison performed on numeric data and a comparison performed on string data.
5. How does Visual Basic compare the Text property of a text box?
6. Why would it be useful to include the ToUpper method in a comparison?
7. Name the types of items that can be used in a comparison.
8. Explain a Boolean variable test for True and False. Give an example.
9. Give an example of a situation where nested Ifs would be appropriate.
10. Define the term *validation*. When is it appropriate to do validation?
11. Define the term *checking a range*.
12. When would it be appropriate to use a Case structure? Give an example.
13. Explain the difference between *Step Into* and *Step Over*.
14. What steps are necessary to view the current contents of a variable during program execution?

Programming Exercises

4.1   Lynette Rifle owns an image consulting shop. Her clients can select from the following services at the specified regular prices: Makeover $125, Hair Styling $60, Manicure $35, and Permanent Makeup $200. She has distributed discount coupons that advertise discounts of 10 percent and 20 percent off the regular price. Create a project that will allow the receptionist to select a discount rate of 10 percent, 20 percent, or none, and then select a service. Display the price for the individual service in a label and have another label to display the total due after each visit is completed. A visit may include several services. Include buttons for *Calculate*, *Clear*, and *Exit*.

4.2   Modify Programming Exercise 4.1 to allow for sales to additional patrons. Include buttons for *Next Patron* and *Summary*. When the receptionist clicks the *Summary* button, display in a summary message box the number of clients and the total dollar value for all services rendered. For *Next Patron*, confirm that the user wants to clear the totals for the current customer.

4.3   Create a project to compute your checking account balance.

Form: Include radio buttons to indicate the type of transaction: deposit, check, or service charge. A text box will allow the user to enter the amount of the transaction. Display the new balance in a label. Calculate the balance by adding deposits and subtracting service charges and checks. Include buttons for *Calculate*, *Clear*, and *Exit*.

4.4   Add validation to Programming Exercise 4.3. Display a message box if the new balance would be a negative number. If there is not enough money to cover a check, do not deduct the check amount. Instead, display a message box with the message "Insufficient Funds" and deduct a service charge of $10.

4.5   Modify Programming Exercise 4.3 or 4.4 by adding a *Summary* button that will display the total number of deposits, the total dollar amount of deposits, the number of checks, and the dollar amount of the checks. Do not include checks that were returned for insufficient funds, but do include the service charges. Use a message box to display the Summary information.

4.6   (Select Case) Piecework workers are paid by the piece. Workers who produce a greater quantity of output are often paid at a higher rate.

Form: Use text boxes to obtain the person's name and the number of pieces completed. Include a *Calculate* button to display the dollar amount earned. You will need a *Summary* button to display the total number of pieces, the total pay, and the average pay per person. A *Clear* button should clear the name and the number of pieces for the current employee and a *Clear All* button should clear the summary totals after confirming the operation with the user.

Include validation to check for missing data. If the user clicks on the *Calculate* button without first entering a name and the number of pieces, display a message box. Also, you need to make sure to not display a summary before any data are entered; you cannot calculate an average when no items have been calculated. You can check the number of employees in the Summary event procedure or disable the *Summary* button until the first order has been calculated.

Pieces Completed	Price Paid per Piece for All Pieces
1–199	.50
200–399	.55
400–599	.60
600 or more	.65

4.7   Modify Programming Exercise 2.3 (the weather report) to treat radio buttons the proper way. Do not have an event procedure for each radio button; instead use an *OK* button to display the correct image and message.

   Note: For help in basing a new project on an existing project, see "Copy and Move a Windows Project" in Appendix C.

4.8   Modify Programming Exercise 2.2 (the flag viewer) to treat radio buttons and check boxes in the proper way. Include a *Display* button and check the settings of the radio buttons and check boxes in the button's event procedure, rather than code event procedures for each radio button and check box.

   Note: For help in basing a new project on an existing project, see "Copy and Move a Windows Project" in Appendix C.

4.9   Create an application to calculate sales for Catherine's Catering. The program must determine the amount due for a party based on the number of guests, the menu selected, and the bar options. Additionally, the program maintains summary figures for multiple parties.

   Form: Use a text box to input the number of guests and radio buttons to allow a selection of Prime Rib, Chicken, or Pasta. Check boxes allow the user to select an Open Bar and/or Wine with Dinner. Include buttons for *Calculate*, *Clear*, *Summary*, and *Exit*. Display the amount due for the event in a label.

Rates per Person

Prime Rib	25.95
Chicken	18.95
Pasta	12.95
Open Bar	25.00
Wine with Dinner	8.00

   Summary: Display the number of parties and the total dollar amount in a message box. Prompt the user to determine if he or she would like to clear the summary information. If the response is Yes, set the number of parties and the total dollar amount to zero. Do not display the summary message box if there is no summary information. (Either disable the *Summary* button until a calculation has been made or test the total for a value.)

Case Studies

VB Mail Order

Calculate the amount due for an order. For an order, the user should enter the following information into text boxes: customer name, address, city, state (two-letter abbreviation), and ZIP code. An order may consist of multiple items. For each item, the user will enter the product description, quantity, weight, and price into text boxes.

You will need buttons for *Add This Item*, *Update Summary*, *Clear*, and *Exit*.

For the *Add This Item* button, validate the quantity, weight, and price. Each must be present and numeric. For any bad data, display a message box. Calculate the charge for the current item and add the charge and weight into the appropriate totals. Do not calculate shipping and handling on individual items; rather, calculate shipping and handling on the entire order.

When the *Update Summary* button is clicked, calculate the sales tax, shipping and handling, and the total amount due for the order. Sales tax is 8 percent of the total charge and is charged only for shipments to a California address. Do not charge sales tax on the shipping and handling charges.

The shipping and handling charges depend on the weight of the products. Calculate the shipping charge as $0.25 per pound and add that amount to the handling charge (taken from the following table).

Weight	Handling
Less than 10 pounds	$1.00
10 to 100 pounds	3.00
Over 100 pounds	5.00

Display the entire amount of the bill in labels titled Subtotal, Sales tax, Shipping and handling, and Total amount due.

Test Data

Description	Quantity	Weight	Price
Planter	2	3	19.95
Mailbox	1	2	24.95
Planter	2	3	19.95

Test Data Output for Taxable

Dollar Amount Due	$104.75
Sales Tax	8.38
Shipping and Handling	6.50
Total Amount Due	119.63

Test Data Output for Nontaxable

Dollar Amount Due	$104.75
Sales Tax	0.00
Shipping and Handling	6.50
Total Amount Due	111.25

VB Auto Center

Create a project that determines the total amount due for the purchase of a vehicle. Include text boxes for the base price and the trade-in allowance. Check boxes will indicate if the buyer wants additional accessories: stereo system, leather interior, and/or computer navigation. A group box for the exterior finish will contain radio buttons for Standard, Pearlized, or Customized detailing.

Have the trade-in allowance default to zero; that is, if the user does not enter a trade-in value, use zero in your calculation. Validate the values from the text boxes, displaying a message box if necessary.

To calculate, add the price of selected accessories and finish to the base price and display the result in a label called Subtotal. Calculate the sales tax on the subtotal and display the result in a Total label. Then subtract any trade-in value from the total and display the result in an Amount Due label.

Include buttons for *Calculate*, *Clear*, and *Exit*. The *Calculate* button must display the total amount due after trade-in.

Hint: Recall that you can make an ampersand appear in the Text property of a control by including two ampersands. See the tip on page 62 (Chapter 2).

Item	Price
Stereo System	425.76
Leather Interior	987.41
Computer Navigation	1,741.23
Standard	No additional charge
Pearlize	345.72
Customized Detailing	599.99
Tax Rate	8%

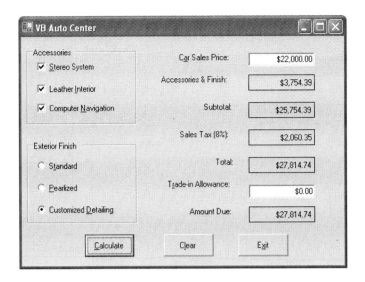

Video Bonanza

Design and code a project to calculate the amount due for rentals. Movies may be in VHS (videotape) format or DVD format. Videotapes rent for $1.80 each and DVDs rent for $2.50. New releases are $3 for DVD and $2 for videotape.

On the form include a text box to input the movie title and radio buttons to indicate whether the movie is in DVD or videotape format. Use one check box to indicate whether the person is a member; members receive a 10 percent discount. Another check box indicates a new release.

Use buttons for *Calculate*, *Clear for Next Item*, *Order Complete*, *Summary*, and *Exit*. The *Calculate* button should display the item amount and add to the sub-total. The *Clear for Next Item* clears the check box for new releases, the movie title, and the radio buttons; the member check box cannot be changed until the current order is complete. Include validation to check for missing data. If the user clicks on the *Calculate* button without first entering the movie title and selecting the movie format, display a message box.

For the *Order Complete* button, first confirm the operation with the user and clear the controls on the form for a new customer.

The *Summary* button displays the number of customers and the sum of the rental amounts in a message box. Make sure to add to the customer count and rental sum for each customer order.

Very Very Boards

Very Very Boards does a big business in shirts, especially for groups and teams. They need a project that will calculate the price for individual orders, as well as a summary for all orders.

The store employee will enter the orders in an order form that has text boxes for customer name and order number. To specify the shirts, use a text box for the quantity, radio buttons to select the size (small, medium, large, extra large, and XXL), and check boxes to specify a monogram and/or a pocket. Display the shirt price for the current order and the order total in labels.

Include buttons to add a shirt to an order, clear the current item, complete the order, and display the summary of all orders. Do not allow the summary to display if the current order is not complete. Also, disable the text boxes for customer name and order number after an order is started; enable them again when the user clicks on the button to begin a new order. Confirm the operation before clearing the current order.

When the user adds shirts to an order, validate the quantity, which must be greater than zero. If the entry does not pass the validation, do not perform any calculations but display a message box and allow the user to correct the value. Determine the price of the shirts from the radio buttons and check boxes for the monogram and pockets. Multiply the quantity by the price to determine the extended price, and add to the order total and summary total.

Use constants for the shirt prices.

Display the order summary in a message box. Include the number of shirts, the number of orders, and the dollar total of the orders.

Prices for the Shirts

Small, medium, and large	$10
Extra large	11
XXL	12
Monogram	Add $2
Pocket	Add $1

5

Menus, Common Dialog Boxes, Sub Procedures, and Function Procedures

1. Create menus and submenus for program control.

2. Display and use the Windows common dialog boxes.

3. Write reusable code in sub procedures and function procedures and call the procedures from other locations.

Menus

You have undoubtedly used menus quite extensively while working with the computer. **Menus** consist of a menu bar that contains menus, each of which drops down to display a list of menu items. You can use menu items in place of or in addition to buttons to execute a procedure.

Menu items are actually controls; they have properties and events. Each menu item has a Name property, a Text property, and a Click event, similar to a button. When the user selects a menu item, either with the mouse or the keyboard, the menu item's Click event procedure executes.

It is easy to create menus for a Windows form using the Visual Studio environment's **Menu Designer**. Your menus will look and behave like standard Windows menus.

Defining Menus

The Visual Studio Menu Designer allows you to add menus and menu items to your forms. You must add a MainMenu control from the toolbox (Figure 5.1), which appears in the component tray below the form. Once you have added the MainMenu control, it is extremely easy to create the menu items for your menu bar. The words "Type Here" appear at the top of the form, so that you can enter the text for your first menu (Figure 5.2). After you type the text for the first menu name, the words "Type Here" appear both below the menu name and to

---

Figure 5.1

Add a MainMenu control to the form using the MainMenu tool from the toolbox.

Figure 5.2

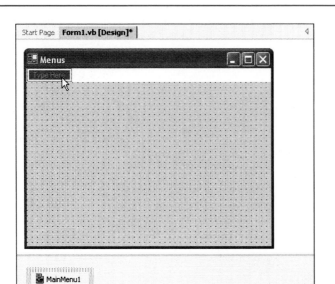

The MainMenu control appears in the component tray below the form and the Menu Designer allows you to begin typing the text for the menu items.

the right of the menu name. You can choose next to enter menu items for the first menu or to type the words for the second menu (Figure 5.3).

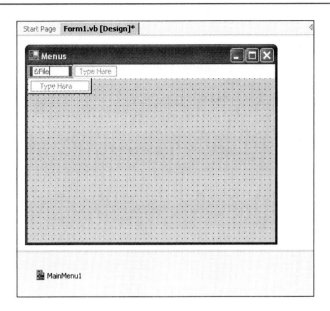

After typing the text for the first menu, you can add a second menu or add menu items below the menu name.

Note: If you click elsewhere on the form, you deactivate the Menu Designer. You can click on the menu at the top of the form to activate the Menu Designer again.

The Text Property

When you type the words for a menu or menu item, you are entering the Text property for a MenuItem object. The Text property holds the words that you want to appear on the screen (just like the Text property of a label or button). To conform to Windows standards, your first menu's Text property should be Ḟile, with a keyboard access key. Use the ampersand (&) in the text to specify the key to use for keyboard access, as you learned to do in Chapter 2. For example, for Ḟile, the Text property should be &File.

Do not use the same access key on a main menu name as you use on a form control. However, access keys on menu items and submenus do not conflict with menu or control access keys. ■

You can enter and change the Text property for each of your menu items using the Menu Designer. You can also change the Text property using the Properties window (Figure 5.4).

Modify the Text property of a menu item in the Properties window or the Menu Designer.

The Name

After you create menu items using the Menu Designer, you will find each
MenuItem object listed in the Properties window, where you can view or change
the properties. The Name property gives the MenuItem a name, similar to naming other controls.

Follow good consistent naming conventions for your menu items. Append
the suffix "Menu" for top-level menu names and "MenuItem" for the items on
the menu. Therefore, the name for the *File* menu should be fileMenu. For the
items on a menu, use the name of the menu plus the name of the item. (You can
abbreviate long names, if you do so consistently and clearly.) The name for the
Print item on the *File* menu should be filePrintMenuItem. The *Exit* item should
be called fileExitMenuItem, which will trigger the fileExitMenuItem_Click
event when the user selects it.

You also can use the Menu Designer to name your controls. Right-click on
the Designer and select the option *Edit Names*. The menu items will display the
name property and can be changed in place. Right-clicking again shows a
check mark next to *Edit Names*; by selecting the option a second time, you
switch back to displaying the Text property.

Submenus

The drop-down list of items below a menu name is called a *menu*. When an item
on the menu has another list of items that pops up, the new list is called a **submenu**. A filled triangle to the right of the item indicates that a menu item has a
submenu (Figure 5.5). You create a submenu by moving to the right of a menu
item and typing the next item's text (Figure 5.6).

Figure 5.5

*A filled triangle on a menu
item indicates that a submenu
will appear.*

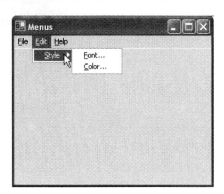

Figure 5.6

*Create a submenu by typing
to the right of the parent
menu item.*

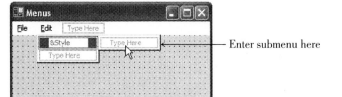

Enter submenu here

Separator Bars

When you have many items in a menu, you should group the items according to their purpose. You can create a **separator bar** in a menu, which draws a bar across the entire menu.

You can choose one of two ways to create a separator bar: (1) type a single hyphen (-) for the text or (2) right-click on the Menu Designer where you want the separator bar to appear and choose *Insert Separator* from the context menu. The Menu Designer will create a new MenuItem for the separator bar, which you can see in the Properties window. It isn't necessary to change the Name property of a separator bar control.

Creating a Menu—Step-by-Step

You are going to create a project with one form and a menu bar that contains these menu items:

File	*Help*
Exit	*About*

Create the Menu Items

STEP 1: Begin a new Windows Forms project (or open an existing one to which you want to add a menu).

STEP 2: Add a MainMenu control to the form. You can double-click or drag the tool to the form; the control will appear in the component tray at the bottom of the form (Figure 5.7).

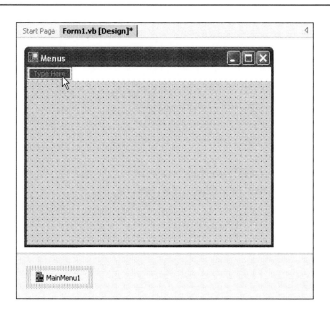

Figure 5.7

Add a MainMenu control to the form. It will appear in the component tray at the bottom of the form.

STEP 3: With the words "Type Here" selected, type "&File" over the words.

STEP 4 Move down to the "Type Here" words below the *File* menu and type "E&xit".

STEP 5: Move up and to the right and add the *Help* menu ("&Help").

STEP 6: Below the *Help* menu, add the *About* menu item ("&About").

The menu bar is complete. Now we'll change the Name property of each of the controls.

Change the Properties of the Menu Items

STEP 1: Drop down the Object list in the Properties window (Figure 5.8). You can see a MainMenu object and a series of MenuItem objects.

The MenuItem controls are listed in the Object list of the Properties window.

STEP 2: In the Properties window, select the MenuItem1 object. This should be the *File* menu—check the highlighted entry in the Menu Designer to make sure. Then change the Name property to fileMenu.

STEP 3: Next you will change the name of the *Exit* menu item. You can select the menu item on the form to make it appear in the Properties window, or select MenuItem2 in the Object list. Change the Name property to fileExitMenuItem.

STEP 4: Change the name of the *Help* menu item (MenuItem3) to helpMenu.

STEP 5: Change the name of the *About* menu item (MenuItem4) to helpAboutMenuItem.

✓TIP

Drag and drop a menu item to change the location and sequence of the items. Right-click the Menu Designer to insert an item. ■

You also can use the Menu Designer to name your controls. Right-click on the Menu Designer and select the option *Edit Names*. The menu items display the Name properties, which you can change in place. Right-click again to see a check mark next to *Edit Names*; select the option a second time to switch back to displaying only the Text properties.

Just as you always name buttons before writing the code, you should always name menu items before writing code, so that the event procedures are correctly named.

Coding for Menu Items

After you create your form's menu bar, it appears on the form in design time. Double-click any menu item and the Editor window opens in the control's Click event procedure, where you can write the code. For example, in design time, open your form's *File* menu and double-click on *Exit*. The Editor window will open with the fileExitMenuItem_Click procedure displayed (assuming you have followed the suggested naming conventions and named the *Exit* item fileExitMenuItem).

Write the Code

STEP 1: Code the procedure for the *Exit* by pulling down the menu and double-clicking on the word *Exit*. Type in the remark and the `Me.Close` statement.

STEP 2: Open the helpAboutMenuItem_Click event procedure. Use a `MessageBox.Show` statement to display the *About* box. The message string should say "Programmer: " followed by your name (Figure 5.9).

Figure 5.9

Display a message box for an About box.

STEP 3: Test your menu items.

Modifying Menu Items

You can use the Menu Designer to modify menu items. To add a new menu and menu items, right-click on the menu bar. Options include *Delete*, *Insert New*, *Insert Separator*, and *Edit Names*. The *Edit Names* option displays the names of the menu items instead of the Text properties. You can modify the names of the menu items here, rather than in the Properties window, if you prefer. To redisplay the menu text, select *Edit Names* from the context menu a second time. You also can rearrange menu items: Drag and drop an item in its new location.

The Enabled Property

By default, all new menu items have their **Enabled property** set to True. An enabled menu item appears in black text and is available for selection, whereas the grayed out or **disabled** (Enabled = False) items are not available (Figure 5.10). You can set the Enabled property at design time or run time, in code.

```
displayInstructionsMenuItem.Enabled = False
```

Figure 5.10

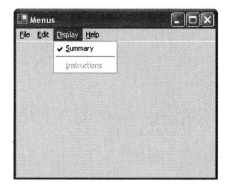

Menu items can be disabled (grayed) or checked. A check mark usually indicates that the item is currently selected.

The Checked Property

A menu item may contain a check mark beside it (indicating that the item is **checked**). Usually a check mark next to a menu item indicates that the option is currently selected (refer to Figure 5.10). By default the **Checked property** is set to False; you can change it at design time or in code.

```
displaySummaryMenuItem.Checked = True
```

Toggling Check Marks On and Off

If you create a menu item that can be turned on and off, you should include a check mark to indicate the current state. You set the initial state of the check mark in the Properties window. In code you can change its state by setting the menu item's Checked property. For example, for a menu item that displays or hides a summary, called displaySummaryMenuItem, a check mark indicates that the summary is currently selected. Choosing the menu item a second time should remove the check mark and hide the summary.

```
Private Sub displaySummaryMenuItem_Click(ByVal sender As System.Object, _
    ByVal e As System.EventArgs) Handles displaySummaryMenuItem.Click
    ' Hide or display the summary.

    If displaySummaryMenuItem.Checked Then
        ' Hide the summary information.
        displaySummaryMenuItem.Checked = False
    Else
        ' Show the summary information.
        displaySummaryMenuItem.Checked = True
    End If
End Sub
```

TIP

You can toggle a Boolean value on and off using the Not operator: displaySummaryMenuItem. Checked = Not display-SummaryMenuItem.Checked.

■

Setting Keyboard Shortcuts

Many computer users prefer to use keyboard shortcuts for selecting menu items. For example, most applications from Microsoft use Ctrl + P for the *Print* menu item and Ctrl + S for *Save*. You can create keyboard shortcuts for your menu items and choose whether or not to display the shortcuts on the menu. (For example, you can exit most Windows applications using Alt + F4, but the keyboard shortcut rarely appears on the menu.)

To set a keyboard shortcut for a menu item, first select the menu item in the designer. Then in the Properties window, select the Shortcut property. Drop down the list to see the available choices and make your selection. You can use many combinations of function keys, the Alt key, and the Ctrl key. By default the ShowShortcut property is set to True; you can change it to False if you don't want the shortcut to show up on the menu.

Standards for Windows Menus

When you write applications that run under Windows, your programs should follow the Windows standards. You should always include keyboard access keys; if you include keyboard shortcuts, such as Ctrl + key, stick with the standard keys, such as Ctrl + P for printing. Also follow the Windows standards for placing the *File* menu on the left end of the menu bar and ending the menu with an *Exit* command. If you have a *Help* menu, it belongs at the right end of the menu bar.

Any menu item that will display a dialog box asking for more information from the user should have "..." appended to its Text property. Following Windows standards, the "..." indicates that a dialog box will appear if the user selects the menu item. You do not use the "..." for menu items that display dialog boxes that are informational only, such as an *About* box or a Summary form.

Plan your menus so that they look like other Windows programs. Your users will thank you.

Common Dialog Boxes

You can use a set of predefined standard dialog boxes in your projects for such tasks as specifying colors and fonts, printing, opening, and saving. Use the **common dialog** components to display the dialog boxes that are provided as part of the Windows environment. The common dialog components provided with Visual Studio are OpenFileDialog, SaveFileDialog, FontDialog, Color-Dialog, PrintDialog, and PrintPreviewDialog (Figure 5.11).

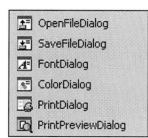

Figure 5.11

The common dialog tools in the toolbox.

To use a common dialog component, add the component to the form, placing it in the component tray. You can keep the default names for the components, such as ColorDialog1 and FontDialog1, since you will have only one component of each type.

Displaying a Windows Common Dialog Box

After you place a common dialog component on your form, you can display the dialog box at run time using the **ShowDialog method**.

ShowDialog Method—General Form

```
DialogObject.ShowDialog()
```

The DialogObject is the name of the common dialog component that you placed on the form. The name will be the default name, such as ColorDialog1 or FontDialog1.

ShowDialog Method—Examples

```
ColorDialog1.ShowDialog()
FontDialog1.ShowDialog()
```

Place the code to show the dialog in the event procedure for a menu item or button.

Modal versus Modeless Windows

You probably have noticed that when you display a Windows dialog box, it remains on top until you respond. But in many applications, you can display additional windows and switch back and forth between the windows. A dialog box is said to be **modal**, which means that it stays on top of the application and must be responded to. You use the `ShowDialog` method to display a dialog box, which is just a window displayed modally. In Chapter 6 you will learn to display additional windows that are **modeless**, which do not demand that you respond. You will use the `Show` method to display a modeless window.

Using the Information from the Dialog Box

Displaying the *Color* dialog box (Figure 5.12) doesn't make the color of anything change. You must take care of that in your program code. When the user clicks on OK, the selected color is stored in a property that you can access. You can assign the value to the properties of controls in your project.

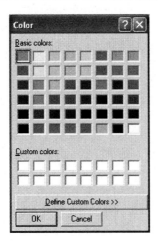

Figure 5.12

The Color common dialog box.

Using the Color Dialog Box

The color selected by the user is stored in the Color property. You can assign this property to another object, such as a control.

```
titleLabel.BackColor = ColorDialog1.Color
```

Because Basic executes the statements in sequence, you would first display the dialog box with the ShowDialog method. (Execution then halts until the user responds to the dialog box.) Then you can use the Color property:

```
Public Sub editColorMenuItem_Click(ByVal sender As System.Object, _
    ByVal e As System.EventArgs) Handles editColorMenuItem.Click
    ' Change the color of the total labels.

    With ColorDialog1
        .ShowDialog()
        subTotalLabel.ForeColor = .Color
        taxLabel.ForeColor = .Color
        totalLabel.ForeColor = .Color
    End With
End Sub
```

Using the Font Dialog Box

When you display the *Font* common dialog box (Figure 5.13), the available fonts for the system display. After the user makes a selection, you can use the Font property of the dialog box object. You may want to assign the Font property to the Font property of other objects on your form.

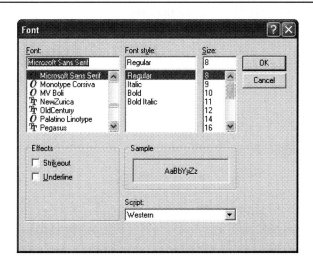

Figure 5.13

The Font common dialog box. The fonts that display are those installed on the user's system.

```
Public Sub editFontMenuItem_Click(ByVal sender As System.Object, _
    ByVal e As System.EventArgs) Handles editFontMenuItem.Click
    ' Change the font name for the subtotal labels.

    With FontDialog1
        .ShowDialog()
        subTotalLabel.Font = .Font
        taxLabel.Font = .Font
        totalLabel.Font = .Font
    End With
End Sub
```

When the user clicks on the *Font* menu item, the *Font* dialog box appears on the screen. Execution halts until the user responds to the dialog box, either by clicking *OK* or *Cancel.*

Setting Initial Values

When a common dialog box for colors or fonts appears, what color or font do you want to display? It's best to assign initial values before showing the dialog box. Before executing the `ShowDialog` method, you should assign the existing values of the object's properties that will be altered. This step makes the current values selected when the dialog box appears. It also means that if the user selects the Cancel button, the property settings for the objects will remain unchanged.

```
FontDialog1.Font = subTotalLabel.Font
```

or

```
ColorDialog1.Color = Me.BackColor
```

Creating Context Menus

You also can add **context menus** to your applications. Context menus are the **shortcut menus** that pop up when you right-click. Generally, the items in a context menu are specific to the component to which you are pointing, reflecting the options available for that component or that situation.

Creating a context menu is similar to creating a menu bar. You add a ContextMenu component, which appears in the component tray below the form. At the top of the form, in the Menu Designer, the words say "Context Menu" (Figure 5.14). A context menu does not have a top-level menu, only the menu items. Click on the words "Context Menu" and the words "Type Here" appear underneath, where you can type the text of your first menu item (Figure 5.15).

Your application can have more than one context menu. You assign the context menu to the form or control using its ContextMenu property. For example, a

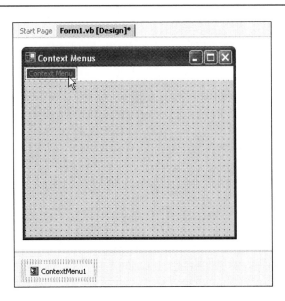

Figure 5.14

Add a ContextMenu component to the component tray and create the context menu using the Menu Designer.

Figure 5.15

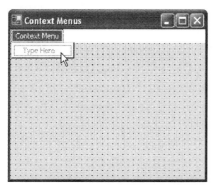

form has a ContextMenu property, a button has a ContextMenu property, and all visible controls have ContextMenu properties. You can assign the same context menu to each of the components, or a different context menu to each. If you have only one context menu and attach it to the form, it will pop up if the user right-clicks anywhere on the form, including on a control.

Creating a Context Menu—Step-by-Step

You are going to create a context menu that contains these menu items:

Color...
Font...
Exit

Add the Context Menu to a Form

STEP 1: Begin a new Windows Forms project (or open an existing one to which you want to add a context menu). Change the form name and set the project's startup object to the new form name.

STEP 2: Add a ContextMenu component to the form; the component will appear in the component tray at the bottom of the form (refer to Figure 5.14).

STEP 3: Click on the words "Context Menu" in the Menu Designer to make a "Type Here" menu item appear.

STEP 4: Click on the words "Type Here" and type the text for the first menu item: "&Color...".

STEP 5: Type the text for the second and third menu items: "&Font..." and "E&xit".

STEP 6: Set the Name properties for the context menu items as follows:

- Color   colorContextMenuItem

- Font   fontContextMenuItem

- Exit   exitContextMenuItem

STEP 7: Add a label named messageLabel to your form and set the Text property to "Right click for the Context Menu". Enlarge the label so that if the font is changed to something larger, the entire message can display.

STEP 8: Set the form's ContextMenu property to ContextMenu1. Notice that the property box has a drop-down list. If you have more than one context menu defined, you can choose from the list.

STEP 9: Add a ColorDialog component from the toolbox.

STEP 10: Add a FontDialog component from the toolbox.

In this example, right-clicking anywhere on the form allows you to change the foreground color or the font of the form. As you know, if you haven't set those properties for individual controls, the form's properties apply to all controls on the form.

STEP 11: Code the form as follows:

TIP

It's a good idea to set a Context-Menu property for all controls and for the form to allow users the option of using context menus. ∎

```vb
'Program:        Ch05ContextMenus
'Programmer:     Your Name
'Date:           Today's Date
'Description:    Create and apply a context menu.

Option Strict On

Public Class contextMenuForm
  Inherits System.Windows.Forms.Form

    Private Sub exitContextMenuItem_Click(ByVal sender As System.Object, _
      ByVal e As System.EventArgs) Handles exitContextMenuItem.Click
        ' Terminate the project.

        Me.Close()
    End Sub

    Private Sub colorContextMenuItem_Click(ByVal sender As System.Object, _
      ByVal e As System.EventArgs) Handles colorContextMenuItem.Click
        ' Change the form's ForeColor.
        ' Applies to all controls on the form that haven't had their
        ' ForeColorchanged.

        With ColorDialog1
            ' Initialize the dialog box.
            .Color = Me.ForeColor
            .ShowDialog()
            ' Assign the new color.
            Me.ForeColor = .Color
        End With
    End Sub

    Private Sub fontContextMenuItem_Click(ByVal sender As System.Object, _
      ByVal e As System.EventArgs) Handles fontContextMenuItem.Click
        ' Change the label's font.

        With FontDialog1
            ' Initialize the dialog box.
            .Font = messageLabel.Font
            .ShowDialog()
            ' Assign the new font.
            messageLabel.Font = .Font
        End With
    End Sub

End Class
```

Test the Program

STEP 1: Experiment with right-clicking on the form and on the label. Test each of the options.

After you have the program working, experiment with adding more controls and setting the ContextMenu property of controls. You can determine which object the user right-clicked by referring to the context menu's SourceControl property.

```
'Set the color of the selected control
contextMenu.SourceControl.ForeColor = ColorDialog1.Color
```

Sharing Procedures

Most frequently a context menu is added as an additional way to access a feature that is also available from another menu or a button. Recall from Chapter 4 that you can use the same procedure for several events by adding to the Handles clause.

```
Private Sub fontContextMenuItem_Click(ByVal sender As System.Object, _
   ByVal e As System.EventArgs) _
   Handles fontContextMenuItem.Click, fontButton.Click, editFontMenuItem.Click
   ' Change the label's font.

   With FontDialog1
      ' Initialize the dialog box.
      .Font = messageLabel.Font
      .ShowDialog()
      ' Assign the new font.
      messageLabel.Font = .Font
   End With
End Sub
```

Writing General Procedures

Often you will encounter programming situations in which multiple procedures perform the same operation. This condition can occur when the user can select either a button or a menu item to do the same thing. Rather than retyping the code, you can write reusable code in a **general procedure** and call it from both event procedures.

General procedures are also useful in breaking down large sections of code into smaller units that perform a specific task. By breaking down your calculations into smaller tasks, you simplify any maintenance that needs to be done in a program in the future. For example, bowling statistics for a league may require calculations for handicap and series total. If the formula for calculating handicaps changes, wouldn't it be nice to have a procedure that calculates handicaps only instead of one that performs all the calculations?

You can choose from two types of general procedures: **sub procedures** and **function procedures**:

- A sub procedure performs actions.

- A function procedure performs actions and returns a value (the **return value**).

You will likely use a sub procedure if you need to set property values for a series of objects. However, if you need to calculate a result, then a function procedure is the appropriate choice. Both sub procedures and function procedures are considered the **methods** of object-oriented programming.

Creating a New Sub Procedure

You can create a sub procedure in your code window by enclosing the desired lines of code within a set of `Sub` and `End Sub` statements.

Sub ... End Sub Statements—General Form

```
Private Sub ProcedureName()
    ' ... Statements in the procedure.
End Sub
```

When you type the line

```
Private Sub ProcedureName
```

and press Enter, the editor automatically adds the parentheses to the `Sub` statement, adds the `End Sub` statement, and places the insertion point on the line between the two new lines.

Sub ... End Sub Statements—Example

```
Private Sub SelectColor()
    ' Display the color dialog box.

    ColorDialog1.ShowDialog()
End Sub
```

Note that VB .NET has choices other than `Private` for the access, such as `Public`, `Friend`, and `Protected`. In a later chapter you will learn about the other types of procedures; for now use `Private` for all general procedures.

The coding for the new procedure is similar to the other procedures we have been coding, but is not attached to any event. Therefore, this code cannot be executed unless we specifically **call** the procedure from another procedure. To call a sub procedure, just give the procedure name, which in this case is `SelectColor`.

```
Private Sub changeMessageButton_Click(ByVal sender As System.Object, _
    ByVal e As System.EventArgs) Handles changeMessageButton.Click
    ' Change the color of the message.

    SelectColor()
    messageLabel.ForeColor = ColorDialog1.Color
End Sub
```

```
Private Sub changeTitleButton_Click(ByVal sender As System.Object, _
    ByVal e As System.EventArgs) Handles changeTitleButton.Click
      ' Change the color of the title.

      SelectColor()
      titleLabel.ForeColor = ColorDialog1.Color
End Sub
```

Passing Arguments to Procedures

At times you may need to use the value of a variable in one procedure and then again in a second procedure that is called from the first. In this situation, you could declare the variable as module level, but that approach makes the variable visible to all other procedures. To keep the scope of a variable as narrow as possible, consider declaring the variable as local and passing it to any called procedures.

As an example, we will expand the capabilities of the previous Select-Color sub procedure to display the original color when the dialog box appears. Because the SelectColor procedure can be called from various locations, the original color must be passed to the procedure.

```
Private Sub SelectColor(incomingColor As Color)
      ' Allow the user to select a color.

      With ColorDialog1
          ' Set the initial color.
          .Color = incomingColor
          .ShowDialog()
      End With
End Sub

Private Sub changeMessageButton_Click(ByVal sender As System.Object, _
    ByVal e As System.EventArgs) Handles changeMessageButton.Click
      ' Change the color of the message.
      Dim originalColor As Color

      originalColor = messageLabel.ForeColor
      SelectColor(originalColor)
      messageLabel.ForeColor = ColorDialog1.Color
End Sub

Private Sub changeTitleButton_Click(ByVal sender As System.Object, _
    ByVal e As System.EventArgs) Handles changeTitleButton.Click
      ' Change the color of the title.
      Dim originalColor As Color

      originalColor = titleLabel.ForeColor
      SelectColor(originalColor)
      titleLabel.ForeColor = ColorDialog1.Color
End Sub
```

Notice that in this example the SelectColor procedure now has an argument inside the parentheses. This syntax specifies that when called, an argument must be supplied.

When a sub procedure definition names an argument, any call to that procedure must supply the argument. In addition, the argument value must be the same data type in both locations. Notice that in the two calling procedures (changeMessageButton_Click and changeTitleButton_Click), the variable originalColor is declared as a Color data type.

Another important point is that the name of the argument does not have to be the same in both locations. The ShowColor sub procedure will take whatever Color value it is passed and refer to it as incomingColor inside the procedure.

You may specify multiple arguments in both the sub procedure header and the call to the procedure. The number of arguments, their sequence, and their data types must match in both locations. You will see some examples of multiple arguments in the sections that follow.

Passing Arguments ByVal or ByRef

When you pass a value to a procedure you may pass it **ByVal** or **ByRef** (for *by value* or *by reference*). ByVal sends a copy of the argument's value to the procedure so that the procedure cannot alter the original value. ByRef sends a reference indicating where the value is stored in memory, allowing the called procedure to actually change the argument's original value. You can specify how you want to pass the argument by using the ByVal or ByRef keyword before the argument. If you don't specify ByVal or ByRef, arguments are passed by value.

```
' Argument passed by reference.
Private Sub SelectColor(ByRef incomingColor As Color)

' Argument passed by value.
Private Sub SelectColor(ByVal incomingColor As Color)

' Argument passed by value (the default).
Private Sub SelectColor(incomingColor As Color)
```

Writing Function Procedures

As a programmer, you may need to calculate a value that will be needed in several different procedures or programs. You can write your own function that will calculate a value and call the function from the locations where it is needed. As an example, we will create a function procedure called Commission that calculates and returns a salesperson's commission.

Typing in a block of code using the Function ... End Function statements creates a function procedure. Since the procedure returns a value, you must specify a data type for the value.

Function ... End Function Statements—General Form

General Form
```
Private Function ProcedureName() As Datatype

End Function
```

Functions also can be declared as Public, Protected, or Friend, which you will learn about later. Private is appropriate for all functions for now.

Function ... End Function Statements—Example

Example

```
Private Function Commission() As Decimal
    ' Statements in function.
End Function
```

Notice that this procedure looks just like a sub procedure except that the word `Function` replaces the word `Sub` on both the first line and the last line. The procedure header also includes a data type, which is the type of the value returned by the function.

Remember that functions also have arguments. You supply arguments to a function when you call the function by placing a value or values inside the parentheses. You can choose to pass the arguments `ByVal` or `ByRef`.

When you write a function, you declare the argument(s) that the function needs. You give each argument an identifier and a data type. The name that you give an argument in the function procedure header is the identifier that you will use inside the function to refer to the value of the argument (Figure 5.16).

Figure 5.16

A procedure header for a function procedure.

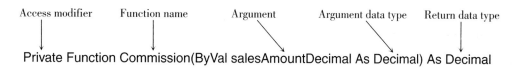

Access modifier   Function name   Argument   Argument data type   Return data type

Private Function Commission(ByVal salesAmountDecimal As Decimal) As Decimal

Examples

```
Private Function Commission(ByVal salesAmountDecimal As Decimal) As Decimal
Private Function Payment(rateDecimal As Decimal, timeDecimal As Decimal, _
    amountDecimal As Decimal) As Decimal
```

In the function procedure, the argument list you enter establishes the number of arguments, their type, and their sequence. When using multiple arguments, the sequence of the arguments is critical, just as when you use the predefined Visual Basic functions.

Returning the Result of a Function

The main difference between coding a function procedure and coding a sub procedure is that in a function procedure you must set up the return value. This return value is placed in a variable that Visual Basic names with the same name as the function name. In the first of the preceding examples, the variable name is Commission.

You can choose from two techniques for returning the result of the function:

- Somewhere inside the `Commission` function, set the function name to a value. Example: `Commission = 0.15D * salesAmountDecimal`

- Use the `Return` statement. If you use the `Return` statement, you do not use the function's name as a variable name.
  Example: `Return 0.15D * salesAmountDecimal`

Writing a Commission Function

Here is the `Commission` function procedure coded using the first technique for returning a value.

```
Private Function Commission(ByVal salesAmountDecimal As Decimal) As Decimal
    ' Calculate the sales commission.

    If salesAmountDecimal < 100D Then
        Commission = 0D
    ElseIf salesAmountDecimal <= 200D Then
        Commission = 0.15D * salesAmountDecimal
    Else
        Commission = 0.2D * salesAmountDecimal
    End If
End Function
```

And here is the same `Commission` function procedure using the `Return` statement.

```
Private Function Commission(ByVal salesAmountDecimal As Decimal) As Decimal
    ' Calculate the sales commission.

    If salesAmountDecimal < 100D Then
        Return 0D
    ElseIf salesAmountDecimal <= 200D Then
        Return 0.15D * salesAmountDecimal
    Else
        Return 0.2D * salesAmountDecimal
    End If
End Function
```

Calling the Commission Function

In another procedure in the project, you can call your function by using it in an expression.

```
Private Sub calculateButton_Click(ByVal sender As System.Object, _
  ByVal e As System.EventArgs) Handles calculateButton.Click
    ' Calculate the commission.
    Dim salesDecimal As Decimal

    salesDecimal = Decimal.Parse(salesTextBox.Text)
    commissionLabel.Text = Commission(salesDecimal).ToString("C")
End Sub
```

Notice in the preceding example that the argument named in the function call does not have the same name as the argument named in the function definition. When the function is called, a copy of salesDecimal is passed to the function and is assigned to the named argument, in this case salesAmount-Decimal. As the calculations are done (inside the function), for every reference to salesAmountDecimal, the value that was passed in for salesDecimal is actually used.

You can nest the functions, if you wish:

```
commissionLabel.Text = Commission(Decimal.Parse(salesTextBox.Text)).ToString("C")
```

To read this statement, begin with the inner parentheses: `sales-TextBox.Text` is passed to `Decimal.Parse` for conversion to Decimal; the result of that conversion is passed as an argument to the `Commission` function; the value returned by the `Commission` function is formatted as it is converted to a string and then assigned to `commissionLabel.Text`.

Functions with Multiple Arguments

A function can have multiple arguments. The sequence and data type of the arguments in the `Call` must exactly match the arguments in the function procedure header.

Writing a Function with Multiple Arguments

When you create a function with multiple arguments such as a `Payment` function, you enclose the list of arguments within the parentheses. The following example indicates that three arguments are needed in the call: The first argument is the interest rate, the second is the time, and the third is the loan amount. All three argument values will have a data type of decimal, and the return value will be decimal. Look carefully at the following formula and notice how the identifiers in the parentheses are used.

```
Private Function Payment(ByVal rateDecimal As Decimal, ByVal timeDecimal As Decimal, _
   ByVal amountDecimal As Decimal) As Decimal
   ' Calculate the monthly payment on an amortized loan.

   Dim ratePerMonthDecimal As Decimal
   ratePerMonthDecimal = rateDecimal / 12D

   ' Calculate and set the return value of the function.
   Payment = Convert.ToDecimal((amountDecimal * ratePerMonthDecimal) _
      / ((1 - (1 / (1 + ratePerMonthDecimal) ^ (timeDecimal * 12D)))))
End Function
```

Calling a Function with Multiple Arguments

To call this function from another procedure, use these statements:

```
principalDecimal = Decimal.Parse(principalTextBox.Text)
rateDecimal = Decimal.Parse(rateTextBox.Text)
yearsDecimal = Decimal.Parse(yearsTextBox.Text)
paymentDecimal = Payment(rateDecimal, yearsDecimal, principalDecimal)
```

You can format the result, as well as pass the value of the text boxes, by nesting functions:

```
paymentLabel.Text = Payment(Decimal.Parse(rateTextBox.Text), _
   Decimal.Parse(yearsTextBox.Text), Decimal.Parse(principalTextBox.Text)).ToString()
```

When you call the function, the VS smart editor shows you the arguments of your function (Figure 5.17), just as it does for built-in functions (assuming that you have already entered the function procedure).

```
principalDecimal = Decimal.Parse(principalTextBox.Text)
rateDecimal = Decimal.Parse(rateTextBox.Text)
yearsDecimal = Decimal.Parse(yearsTextBox.Text)
paymentDecimal = Payment(
        Payment (rateDecimal As Decimal, timeDecimal As Decimal, amountDecimal As Decimal) As Decimal
```

*The Visual Studio IntelliSense
feature pops up with the list of
arguments for your own newly
written procedure.*

Breaking Calculations into Smaller Units

A project with many calculations can be easier to understand and to write if you break the calculations into small units. Each unit should perform one program function or block of logic. In the following example that calculates bowling statistics, separate function procedures calculate the average, handicap, and series total, and find the high game.

```
'Project:        Chapter 5 Bowling Example
'Programmer:     Bradley/Millspaugh
'Date:           January 2004
'Folder:         Ch05Bowling
'Description:    This project calculates bowling statistics using
'                multiple function procedures.

Option Strict On

Public Class bowlingForm
   Inherits System.Windows.Forms.Form

    Private Sub editClearMenuItem_Click(ByVal sender As System.Object, _
      ByVal e As System.EventArgs) Handles editClearMenuItem.Click
        ' Clear the input area and individual bowler info.

        With nameTextBox
            .Clear()
            .Focus()
        End With
        maleRadioButton.Checked = False
        femaleRadioButton.Checked = False
        scoreTextBox1.Clear()
        scoreTextBox2.Clear()
        scoreTextBox3.Clear()
        seriesLabel.Text = ""
        averageLabel.Text = ""
        highGameLabel.Text = ""
        handicapLabel.Text = ""
    End Sub

    Private Sub fileCalculateMenuItem_Click(ByVal sender As System.Object, _
      ByVal e As System.EventArgs) Handles fileCalculateMenuItem.Click
        ' Calculate individual and summary info.
        Dim averageDecimal, handicapDecimal As Decimal
        Dim seriesInteger, game1Integer, game2Integer, game3Integer As Integer
        Dim highGameString As String

        Try
            game1Integer = Integer.Parse(scoreTextBox1.Text)
            game2Integer = Integer.Parse(scoreTextBox2.Text)
            game3Integer = Integer.Parse(scoreTextBox3.Text)
```

```
            ' Perform all calculations.
            averageDecimal = FindAverage(game1Integer, game2Integer, game3Integer)
            seriesInteger = FindSeries(game1Integer, game2Integer, game3Integer)
            highGameString = FindHighGame(game1Integer, game2Integer, game3Integer)
            handicapDecimal = FindHandicap(averageDecimal)

            ' Format the output.
            averageLabel.Text = averageDecimal.ToString("N1")
            highGameLabel.Text = highGameString
            seriesLabel.Text = seriesInteger.ToString()
            handicapLabel.Text = handicapDecimal.ToString("N1")
        Catch
            MessageBox.Show("Please Enter three numeric scores", _
                "Missing Data", MessageBoxButtons.OK)
        End Try
    End Sub

    Private Sub fileExitMenuItem_Click(ByVal sender As System.Object, _
      ByVal e As System.EventArgs) Handles fileExitMenuItem.Click
        ' Terminate the project.

        Me.Close()
    End Sub

    Private Function FindAverage(ByVal score1Integer As Integer, _
      ByVal score2Integer As Integer, ByVal score3Integer As Integer) As Decimal
        ' Return the average of three games.

        Return (score1Integer + score2Integer + score3Integer) / 3D
    End Function

    Private Function FindHandicap(ByVal averageDecimal As Decimal) As Decimal
        ' Calculate the handicap.

        Return (200D - averageDecimal) * 0.8D
    End Function

    Private Function FindSeries(ByVal game1Integer As Integer, _
      ByVal game2Integer As Integer, ByVal game3Integer As Integer) As Integer
        ' Calculate the series total.

        Return game1Integer + game2Integer + game3Integer
    End Function

    Private Function FindHighGame(ByVal game1Integer As Integer, _
      ByVal game2Integer As Integer, ByVal game3Integer As Integer) As String
        ' Find the highest game in the series.

        If game1Integer > game2Integer And game1Integer > game3Integer Then
            Return "1"
        ElseIf game2Integer > game1Integer And game2Integer > game3Integer Then
            Return "2"
        ElseIf game3Integer > game1Integer And game3Integer > game2Integer Then
            Return "3"
        Else
            Return "Tie"
        End If
    End Function
End Class
```

Feedback 5.1

You need to write a procedure to calculate and return the average of three integer values.

1. Should you write a sub procedure or a function procedure?
2. Write the header line of the procedure.
3. Write the calculation.
4. How is the calculated average passed back to the calling procedure?

Your Hands-On Programming Example

Modify the hands-on programming example from Chapter 4 by replacing some of the buttons with menus. Write a function procedure to calculate the sales tax, and allow the user to select the font and color of the summary labels.

The project for R 'n R—for Reading 'n Refreshment calculates the amount due for individual orders and maintains accumulated totals for a summary. Use a check box for takeout items, which are taxable (8 percent); all other orders are nontaxable. Include radio buttons for the five coffee selections: Cappuccino, Espresso, Latte, Iced Latte, and Iced Cappuccino. The prices for each will be assigned using these constants:

Cappuccino	2.00
Espresso	2.25
Latte	1.75
Iced (either)	2.50

Use a button for *Calculate Selection*, which will calculate and display the amount due for each item. A button for *Clear for Next Item* will clear the selections and amount for the single item. Additional labels in a separate group box will maintain the summary information for the current order to include subtotal, tax, and total.

The *New Order* menu item will clear the bill for the current customer and add to the totals for the summary. The menu item for *Summary* should display the total of all orders, the average sale amount per customer, and the number of customers in a message box.

The *Edit* menu contains options that duplicate the Calculate and Clear buttons. The *Font* and *Color* options change the properties of the subtotal, tax, and total labels.

The *About* selection on the *Help* menu will display a message box with information about the programmer.

File	Edit	Help
New Order	Calculate Selection	About
Summary	Clear Item	
Exit	———	
	Font...	
	Color...	

Planning the Project

Sketch a form (Figure 5.18) that your users sign as meeting their needs.

Figure   5.18

A sketch of the form for the hands-on programming example.

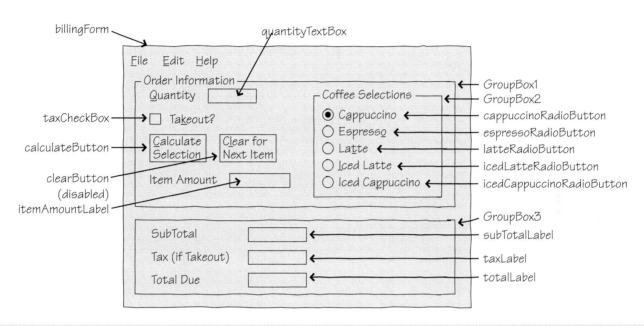

Plan the Objects and Properties Plan the property settings for the form and each of the controls.

Object	Property	Setting
billingForm	Name	billingForm
	Text	R 'n R—for Reading 'n Refreshment
	AcceptButton	calculateButton
	CancelButton	clearButton
GroupBox1	Text	Order Information
GroupBox2	Text	Coffee Selections
GroupBox3	Text	(blank)
cappuccinoRadioButton	Name	cappuccinoRadioButton
	Text	C&appuccino
	Checked	True
espressoRadioButton	Name	espressoRadioButton
	Text	Espress&o
latteRadioButton	Name	latteRadioButton
	Text	La&tte
icedLatteRadioButton	Name	icedLatteRadioButton
	Text	&Iced Latte

Object	Property	Setting
icedCappuccinoRadioButton	Name	icedCappuccinoRadioButton
	Text	Iced Ca&ppuccino
Label1	Text	&Quantity
quantityTextBox	Name	quantityTextBox
	Text	(blank)
taxCheckBox	Name	taxCheckBox
	Text	Ta&keout?
Label2	Text	Item Amount
Label3	Text	SubTotal
Label4	Text	Tax (if Takeout)
Label5	Text	Total Due
itemAmountLabel	Name	itemAmountLabel
	Text	(blank)
	BorderStyle	Fixed3D
subTotalLabel	Name	subTotalLabel
	Text	(blank)
	BorderStyle	Fixed3D
taxLabel	Name	taxLabel
	Text	(blank)
	BorderStyle	Fixed3D
totalLabel	Name	totalLabel
	Text	(blank)
	BorderStyle	Fixed3D
calculateButton	Name	calculateButton
	Text	&Calculate Selection
clearButton	Name	clearButton
	Text	C&lear for Next Item
fileMenu	Name	fileMenu
	Text	&File
fileNewOrderMenuItem	Name	fileNewOrderMenuItem
	Text	&New Order
fileSummaryMenuItem	Name	fileSummaryMenuItem
	Text	&Summary
fileExitMenuItem	Name	fileExitMenuItem
	Text	E&xit
editMenu	Name	editMenu
	Text	&Edit
editCalcMenuItem	Name	editCalcMenuItem
	Text	Calculate &Selection
editClearMenuItem	Name	editClearMenuItem
	Text	C&lear Item

Object	Property	Setting
editFontMenuItem	Name Text	editFontMenuItem &Font
editColorMenuItem	Name Text	editColorMenuItem &Color
helpMenu	Name Text	helpMenu &Help
helpAboutMenuItem	Name Text	helpAboutMenuItem &About
ColorDialog1	Name	ColorDialog1
FontDialog1	Name	FontDialog1

Plan the Event Procedures You need to plan the actions for the buttons and the actions of the menu items, as well as the function for the sales tax.

Object	Procedure	Action
calculateButton	Click	Validate for blank or nonnumeric amount. Find price of drink selection. Multiply price by quantity. Add amount to subtotal. Call tax function if needed. Calculate total = subtotal + tax. Format and display the values. Enable the Clear button. Disable the Takeout check box.
clearButton	Click	Check that there are data to clear. Clear the coffee selections. Clear the quantity and the item price. Set the focus to the quantity. Disable the Clear button.
fileNewOrderMenuItem	Click	Confirm clearing the current order. Clear the current order. Accumulate total sales and count. Set subtotal and total due to 0. Enable Takeout check box. Disable the Clear button.
fileSummaryMenuItem	Click	If current order not added to totals Call newOrderButton_Click. Calculate the average. Display the summary totals in a message box.
fileExitMenuItem	Click	Terminate the project.
editCalcMenuItem	Click	Call the calculate event procedure.
editClearMenuItem	Click	Call the clear event procedure.
helpAboutMenuItem	Click	Display the About message box.
(Function procedure)	FindTax	Calculate the sales tax.

Write the Project Follow the sketch in Figure 5.18 to create the form. Figure 5.19 shows the completed form.

- Set the properties of each object according to your plan. If you are modifying the project from Chapter 4, add the menus and the common dialog components and remove the extra buttons.

- Write the code. Working from the pseudocode, write each event procedure.

- When you complete the code, use a variety of data to thoroughly test the project.

Figure 5.19

The form for the hands-on programming example.

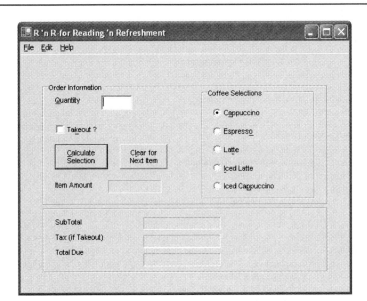

The Project Coding Solution

```
'Program Name:     Billing
'Programmer:       Bradley/Millspaugh
'Date:             January 2004
'Description:      This project calculates the amount due
'                  based on the customer selection
'                  and accumulates summary data for the day.
'                  Incorporates menus and common dialog boxes,
'                  which allow the user to change the font and
'                  color of labels.
'Folder:           Ch0501

Option Strict On

Public Class billingForm
  Inherits System.Windows.Forms.Form

    ' Declare module-level variables and constants.
    Private subtotalDecimal, totalDecimal, grandTotalDecimal As Decimal
    Private customerCountInteger As Integer
    Const TAX_RATE_Decimal As Decimal = 0.08D
    Const CAPPUCCINO_PRICE_Decimal As Decimal = 2D
    Const ESPRESSO_PRICE_Decimal As Decimal = 2.25D
```

```vb
Const LATTE_PRICE_Decimal As Decimal = 1.75D
Const ICED_PRICE_Decimal As Decimal = 2.5D

Private Sub calculateButton_Click(ByVal sender As System.Object, _
  ByVal e As System.EventArgs) Handles calculateButton.Click
    ' Calculate and display the current amounts and add to totals.
    Dim priceDecimal, taxDecimal, itemAmountDecimal As Decimal
    Dim quantityInteger As Integer

    ' Find the price.
    If cappuccinoRadioButton.Checked Then
        priceDecimal = CAPPUCCINO_PRICE_Decimal
    ElseIf espressoRadioButton.Checked Then
        priceDecimal = ESPRESSO_PRICE_Decimal
    ElseIf LatteRadioButton.Checked Then
        priceDecimal = LATTE_PRICE_Decimal
    ElseIf icedCappuccinoRadioButton.Checked _
      Or icedLatteRadioButton.Checked Then
        priceDecimal = ICED_PRICE_Decimal
    Else
        MessageBox.Show("Please make a drink selection", _
          "Selection Required", MessageBoxButtons.OK, MessageBoxIcon.Information)
    End If

    ' Calculate the extended price and add to order total.
    Try
        quantityInteger = Integer.Parse(quantityTextBox.Text)
        itemAmountDecimal = priceDecimal * quantityInteger
        subtotalDecimal += itemAmountDecimal
        If taxCheckBox.Checked Then
            ' Call a function procedure.
            taxDecimal = FindTax(subtotalDecimal)
        Else
            taxDecimal = 0
        End If
        totalDecimal = subtotalDecimal + taxDecimal
        itemAmountLabel.Text = itemAmountDecimal.ToString("C")
        subTotalLabel.Text = subtotalDecimal.ToString("N")
        taxLabel.Text = taxDecimal.ToString("N")
        totalLabel.Text = totalDecimal.ToString("C")
        ' Allow change for new order only.
        taxCheckBox.Enabled = False
        ' Allow Clear after an order is begun.
        clearButton.Enabled = True
    Catch
        MessageBox.Show("Enter the quantity.", "Data entry error", _
          MessageBoxButtons.OK, MessageBoxIcon.Information)
        With quantityTextBox
            .Focus()
            .SelectAll()
        End With
    End Try
End Sub

Private Sub clearButton_Click(ByVal sender As System.Object, _
  ByVal e As System.EventArgs) Handles clearButton.Click
    ' Clear the appropriate controls.

    cappuccinoRadioButton.Checked = True
    itemAmountLabel.Text = ""
```

```vb
    With quantityTextBox
        .Clear()
        .Focus()
    End With
End Sub

Private Sub fileNewMenuItem_Click(ByVal sender As System.Object, _
  ByVal e As System.EventArgs) Handles fileNewMenuItem.Click
    ' Clear the current order and add to the totals.
    Dim responseDialogResult As DialogResult

    ' Confirm clear of the current order.
    responseDialogResult = MessageBox.Show("Clear the current order figures?", _
      "Clear Order", MessageBoxButtons.YesNo, MessageBoxIcon.Question, _
      MessageBoxDefaultButton.Button2)

    If responseDialogResult = DialogResult.Yes Then
        ' User said Yes; clear the screen fields.
        clearButton_Click(sender, e)
        subTotalLabel.Text = ""
        taxLabel.Text = ""
        totalLabel.Text = ""

        Try
            ' Add to the totals only if not a new order/customer.
            If subtotalDecimal <> 0 Then
                grandTotalDecimal += totalDecimal
                customerCountInteger += 1
                ' Reset totals for the next customer.
                subtotalDecimal = 0
                totalDecimal = 0
            End If
        Catch
            MessageBox.Show("Error in calculations.", "Error", _
              MessageBoxButtons.OK, MessageBoxIcon.Error)
        End Try

        ' Clear the appropriate display items and enable the check box.
        With taxCheckBox
            .Enabled = True
            .Checked = False
        End With
        clearButton.Enabled = False
    End If
End Sub

Private Sub fileSummaryMenuItem_Click(ByVal sender As System.Object, _
  ByVal e As System.EventArgs) Handles fileSummaryMenuItem.Click
    ' Calculate the average and display the totals.

    Dim averageDecimal As Decimal
    Dim messageString As String

    If totalDecimal <> 0 Then
        ' Make sure the last order is counted.
        fileNewMenuItem_Click(sender, e)
        ' Pass incoming arguments to the called procedure.
    End If
```

```
        If customerCountInteger > 0 Then
            Try
                ' Calculate the average.
                averageDecimal = grandTotalDecimal / customerCountInteger

                ' Concatenate the message string.
                messageString = "Number of Orders: " _
                    & customerCountInteger.ToString() _
                    & ControlChars.NewLine & ControlChars.NewLine _
                    & "Total Sales: " & grandTotalDecimal.ToString("C") _
                    & ControlChars.NewLine & ControlChars.NewLine _
                    & "Average Sale: " & averageDecimal.ToString("C")
                MessageBox.Show(messageString, "Coffee Sales Summary", _
                    MessageBoxButtons.OK, MessageBoxIcon.Information)
            Catch
                messageString = "Error in calculations."
                MessageBox.Show(messageString, "Error", MessageBoxButtons.OK, _
                    MessageBoxIcon.Error)
            End Try
        Else
            messageString = "No sales data to summarize."
            MessageBox.Show(messageString, "Coffee Sales Summary", _
                MessageBoxButtons.OK, MessageBoxIcon.Information)
        End If

    End Sub

    Private Sub fileExitMenuItem_Click(ByVal sender As System.Object, _
      ByVal e As System.EventArgs) Handles fileExitMenuItem.Click
        ' Terminate the project.

        Me.Close()
    End Sub

    Private Sub editCalcMenuItem_Click(ByVal sender As System.Object, _
      ByVal e As System.EventArgs) Handles editCalcMenuItem.Click
        ' Call the Calculate event procedure.

        ' Pass the incoming arguments to the called procedure.
        calculateButton_Click(sender, e)
    End Sub

    Private Sub editClearMenuItem_Click(ByVal sender As System.Object, _
      ByVal e As System.EventArgs) Handles editClearMenuItem.Click
        ' Call the Clear event procedure.

        ' Pass the incoming arguments to the called procedure.
        clearButton_Click(sender, e)
    End Sub

    Private Sub editFontMenuItem_Click(ByVal sender As System.Object, _
      ByVal e As System.EventArgs) Handles editFontMenuItem.Click
        ' Allow the user to select a new font for the summary totals.

        With FontDialog1
            .Font = subTotalLabel.Font
            .ShowDialog()
            subTotalLabel.Font = .Font
            taxLabel.Font = .Font
            totalLabel.Font = .Font
        End With
```

```
    End Sub

    Private Sub editColorMenuItem_Click(ByVal sender As System.Object, _
        ByVal e As System.EventArgs) Handles editColorMenuItem.Click
        ' Allow the user to select a new color for the summary totals.

        With ColorDialog1
            .Color = subTotalLabel.ForeColor
            .ShowDialog()
            subTotalLabel.ForeColor = .Color
            taxLabel.ForeColor = .Color
            totalLabel.ForeColor = .Color
        End With
    End Sub

    Private Sub helpAboutMenuItem_Click(ByVal sender As System.Object, _
        ByVal e As System.EventArgs) Handles helpAboutMenuItem.Click
        ' Display the About message box.
        Dim messageString As String

        messageString = "R 'n R Billing" & ControlChars.NewLine _
            & ControlChars.NewLine & "Programmed by Bradley and Millspaugh"

        MessageBox.Show(messageString, "About R 'n R Billing", _
            MessageBoxButtons.OK, MessageBoxIcon.Information)
    End Sub

    Private Function FindTax(ByVal amountDecimal As Decimal) As Decimal
        ' Calculate the sales tax.

        Return amountDecimal * TAX_RATE_Decimal
    End Function
End Class
```

Summary

1. The Visual Studio Menu Designer enables you to create menus, menu items, and submenus, each with keyboard access keys.
2. In the Menu Designer you can set and modify the order and level of menu items.
3. Each menu item has a Click event. The code to handle selection of a menu item belongs in the item's Click event procedure.
4. Common dialog boxes allow Visual Basic programs to display the predefined Windows dialog boxes for *Print*, *PrintPreview*, *File Open*, *File Save*, *Font*, and *Color*. These dialog boxes are part of the operating environment; therefore, it is an unnecessary duplication of effort to have each programmer create them again.
5. Context menus, or shortcut menus, are created using a ContextMenu control and the Menu Designer. Context menus pop up when the user right-clicks.

6. The programmer can write reusable code in general procedures. These procedures may be sub procedures or function procedures and may be called from any other procedure in the form module.

7. Both sub procedures and function procedures can perform an action. However, function procedures return a value and sub procedures do not. The value returned by a function procedure has a data type.

8. Arguments can be passed `ByRef` or `ByVal` (the default). `ByRef` passes a reference to the actual data item; `ByVal` passes a copy of the data.

9. A function procedure must return a value, which can be accomplished using the `Return` statement or by setting the name of the function to the result.

Key Terms

`ByRef` *206*	menu *190*
`ByVal` *206*	Menu Designer *190*
`Call` (procedure call) *204*	method *204*
checked *196*	modal *198*
Checked property *196*	modeless *198*
common dialog *197*	return value *204*
context menu *200*	separator bar *193*
disabled *195*	shortcut menu *200*
Enabled property *195*	`ShowDialog` method *197*
function procedure *203*	sub procedure *203*
general procedure *203*	submenu *192*

Review Questions

1. Explain the difference between a menu and a submenu.
2. How can the user know if a menu item contains a submenu?
3. What is a separator bar and how is it created?
4. Name at least three types of common dialog boxes.
5. What is a context menu? How would you attach a context menu to a control?
6. Why would you need procedures that are not attached to an event?
7. Code the necessary statements to produce a *Color* dialog box and use it to change the background color of a label.
8. Explain the difference between a sub procedure and a function procedure.
9. What is a return value? How can it be used?
10. Explain the differences between `ByRef` and `ByVal`. When would each be used?

Programming Exercises

5.1 Modify Programming Exercise 4.6 (Piecework Pay) to replace buttons with menus and add a function procedure.

   This project will input the number of pieces and calculate the pay for multiple employees. It also must display a summary of the total number of pieces, the total pay, and the average pay for all employees.

Menu: The menu bar must have these items:

<u>F</u>ile	<u>E</u>dit	<u>H</u>elp
<u>C</u>alculate Pay	C<u>l</u>ear	<u>A</u>bout
<u>S</u>ummary	————	
E<u>x</u>it	<u>F</u>ont...	
	<u>C</u>olor...	

Piecework workers are paid by the piece. Workers who produce a greater quantity of output may be paid at a higher rate.

Use text boxes to obtain the name and the number of pieces completed. The *Calculate Pay* menu item calculates and displays the dollar amount earned. The *Summary* menu item displays the total number of pieces, the total pay, and the average pay per person in a message box. The *Clear* menu choice clears the name, the number of pieces, and the dollar amount earned for the current employee, and resets the focus.

The *Color* and *Font* items should change the color and font of the information displayed in the Amount Earned label.

Use a message box to display the program name and your name for the *About* option on the *Help* menu.

Write a function procedure to find the pay rate and return a value to the proper event procedure.

Pieces Completed	Price Paid per Piece for All Pieces
1 to 199	.50
200 to 399	.55
400 to 599	.60
600 or more	.65

Note: For help in basing a new project on an existing project, see "Copy and Move a Windows Project" in Appendix C.

5.2 Redo the checking account programming exercises from Chapter 4 (4.3, 4.4, and 4.5) using menus and sub procedures.

Menu:

<u>F</u>ile	<u>E</u>dit	<u>H</u>elp
<u>T</u>ransaction	C<u>l</u>ear	<u>A</u>bout
<u>S</u>ummary	————	
E<u>x</u>it	<u>F</u>ont...	
	<u>C</u>olor...	

Form: Use radio buttons to indicate the type of transaction—deposit, check, or service charge. Use a text box to allow the user to enter the amount of the transaction. Display the balance in a label.

Include validation that displays a message box if the amount of the transaction is a negative number. If there is not enough money to cover a check, display a message box with the message "Insufficient Funds." Do not pay the check, but deduct a service charge of $10.

Write function procedures for processing deposits, checks, and service charges. The deposit function adds the deposit to the balance; the check function subtracts the transaction amount from the balance; the service charge function subtracts $10 from the balance. Each of the functions must return the updated balance.

The *Summary* menu item displays the total number of deposits and the dollar amount of deposits, the number of checks, and the dollar amount of the checks in a message box.

The *Clear* menu item clears the radio buttons and the amount and re-sets the focus.

The *Color* and *Font* menu items change the color and font of the information displayed in the balance label.

Use a message box to display the program name and your name as the programmer for the *About* option on the *Help* menu.

Note: For help in basing a new project on an existing project, see "Copy and Move a Windows Project" in Appendix C.

5.3 A salesperson earns a weekly base salary plus a commission when sales are at or above quota. Create a project that allows the user to input the weekly sales and the salesperson name, calculates the commission, and displays summary information.

Form: The form should have text boxes for the salesperson name and his or her weekly sales.

Menu:

File	Edit	Help
Pay	Clear	About
Summary	———	
Exit	Font...	
	Color...	

Use constants to establish the base pay, the quota, and the commission rate.

The *Pay* menu item calculates and displays in labels the commission and the total pay for that person. However, if there is no commission, do not display the commission amount (do not display a zero-commission amount).

Write a function procedure to calculate the commission. The function must compare sales to the quota. When the sales are equal to or greater than the quota, calculate the commission by multiplying sales by the commission rate.

Each salesperson receives the base pay plus the commission (if one has been earned). Format the dollar amounts to two decimal places; do not display a dollar sign.

The *Summary* menu item displays a message box that holds total sales, total commissions, and total pay for all salespersons. Display the numbers with two decimal places and dollar signs.

The *Clear* menu item clears the name, sales, and pay for the current employee and then resets the focus.

The *Color* and *Font* menu items should change the color and font of the information displayed in the amount earned label.

Use a message box to display the program name and your name as programmer for the *About* option on the *Help* menu.

Test Data: Quota = 1000; Commission rate = .15; and Base pay = $250.

Name	Sales
Sandy Smug	1,000.00
Sam Sadness	999.99
Joe Whiz	2,000.00

Totals should be:

Sales	$3,999.99
Commissions	450.00
Pay	1,200.00

5.4   The local library has a summer reading program to encourage reading. The staff keeps a chart with readers' names and bonus points earned. Create a project using a menu and a function procedure that determines and returns the bonus points.

Menu:

File	Edit	Help
Points	Clear	About
Summary		
Exit	Font...	
	Color...	

Form: Use text boxes to obtain the reader's name and the number of books read. Use a label to display the number of bonus points.

The *Points* menu item should call a function procedure to calculate the points using this schedule: the first three books are worth 10 points each. The next three books are worth 15 points each. All books over six are worth 20 points each.

The *Summary* menu item displays the average number of books read for all readers that session.

The *Clear* menu item clears the name, the number of books read, and the bonus points and then resets the focus.

The *Color* and *Font* menu items change the color and font of the information displayed in the bonus points label.

Use a message box to display the program name and your name as programmer for the *About* option on the *Help* menu.

5.5 Modify Programming Exercise 2.2 (the flag viewer) to use a menu instead of radio buttons, check boxes, and buttons. Include check marks next to the name of the currently selected country and next to the selected display options.

Menu:

File	Country	Display	Help
Exit	United States	Title	About
	Canada	Country Name	
	Japan	Programmer	
	Mexico		

Note: For help in basing a new project on an existing project, see "Copy and Move a Windows Project" in Appendix C.

Case Studies

VB Mail Order

Modify the case study project from Chapter 4 to use menus and a function procedure. Refer to Chapter 4 for project specifications.

Write a function procedure to calculate and return the shipping and handling based on the weight for an entire order. (Do not calculate shipping and handling on individual items—wait until the order is complete.)

Note: For help in basing a new project on an existing project, see "Copy and Move a Windows Project" in Appendix C.

Menu:

File	Edit	Help
Update Summary	Add This Item	About
Exit	Clear	
	———	
	Font...	
	Color...	

VB Auto Center

Modify the case study project from Chapter 4 to use menus and a function procedure. Refer to Chapter 4 for project specifications.

Write a function procedure to calculate and return the sales tax.

Consider adding keyboard shortcuts to the menu commands.

Note: For help in basing a new project on an existing project, see "Copy and Move a Windows Project" in Appendix C.

Menu:

File	Edit	Help
Exit	Calculate Item	About
	Clear	
	———	
	Font...	
	Color...	

Video Bonanza

Modify the case study project from Chapter 4 to use menus and a function procedure. Refer to Chapter 4 for project specifications.

Use a function procedure to calculate the rental fee based on the type of video.

The *Help* menu *About* option should display a message box with information about the program and the programmer. The *Color* option should change the background color of the form.

Optional extra: Set keyboard shortcuts for the menu commands.

Menu:

File	Edit	Help
Summary	Calculate	About
Exit	Clear for Next Item	
	Order Complete	
	———	
	Font...	
	Color...	

Very Very Boards

Modify your case study project from Chapter 4 to add a menu and a function procedure. Refer to Chapter 4 for the project specifications.

Write a function procedure to calculate and return the price of shirts; display the *About* box in a message box.

Allow the user to change the font size and font color of the labels that display the company slogan.

Include keyboard shortcuts for the menu commands.

Menu:

File	Sale	Display	Help
Summary	Clear This Item	Font...	About
———	Display Order Total	Color...	
Exit	Order Complete	———	
		Slogan	
		Logo	

The slogan and logo: Make up a slogan for the company, such as "We're Number One" or "The Best in Boards." The logo should be a graphic; you can use an icon, any graphic you have available, or a graphic you create yourself with a draw or paint program.

The *Slogan* and *Logo* menu choices must toggle and display a check mark when selected. For example, when the slogan is displayed, the *Slogan* menu command is checked. If the user selects the *Slogan* command again, hide the slogan and uncheck the menu command. The *Slogan* and *Logo* commands operate independently; that is, the user may select either, both, or neither item.

When the project begins, the slogan and logo must both be displayed and their menu commands appear checked.

Note: For help in basing a new project on an existing project, see "Copy and Move a Windows Project" in Appendix C.

6

OOP: Creating Object-Oriented Programs

at the completion of this chapter, you will be able to . . .

1. Use object-oriented terminology correctly.

2. Create a two-tier application that separates the user interface from the business logic.

3. Differentiate between a class and an object.

4. Create a class that has properties and methods.

5. Use property procedures to set and retrieve properties of a class.

6. Declare object variables and assign values to the properties with a constructor or property procedures.

7. Instantiate an object in a project using your class.

8. Differentiate between shared members and instance members.

9. Understand the purpose of the constructor and destructor methods.

10. Inherit a new class from your own class.

11. Apply visual inheritance by deriving a form from another form.

Object-Oriented Programming

You have been using objects since Chapter 1. As you know quite well by now, **objects** have properties and methods and generate events that you can respond to (or ignore) if you choose. Up until now, the classes for all objects in your projects have been predefined; that is, you could choose to create a new object of the form class, a button class, a text box class, or any other class of control in the toolbox. In this chapter you will learn to define your own new class and create objects based on that class.

Object-oriented programming (OOP) is currently the most accepted style of programming. Some computer languages, such as Java, C#, and SmallTalk, were designed to be object-oriented (OO) from their inception. Other languages, such as Visual Basic and C++, have been modified over the last few years to accommodate OOP. Visual Basic .NET is the first version of Visual Basic to be truly object-oriented.

Writing object-oriented programs is a mindset—a different way of looking at a problem. You must think in terms of using objects. As your projects become more complex, using objects becomes increasingly important.

Objects

Beyond the many built-in choices you have for objects to include in your projects, Visual Basic allows you to create your own new object type by creating a **class**. Just like other object types, your class may have both properties and methods. *Remember:* Properties are characteristics, and methods are actions that can be performed by a class of object.

An object is a *thing* such as a button. You create a button object from the button tool in the toolbox. In other words, *button* is a class but *exitButton* is an actual occurrence or **instance** of the class; the instance is the object. Just as you may have multiple buttons in a project, you may have many objects of a new class type.

Defining your own class is like creating a new tool for the toolbox; the process does not create the object, only a definition of what that type of object looks like and how it behaves. You may then create as many instances of the class as you need. Your class may be a student, an employee, a product, or any other type of object that would be useful in a project.

Many people use a cookie analogy to describe the relationship of a class and an object. The cookie cutter is the class. You can't eat a cookie cutter, but you can use it to make cookies; the cookie is the object. When you make a cookie using a cookie cutter, you **instantiate** an object of the cookie class. You can use the same cookie cutter to make various kinds of cookies. Although all the cookies made will have the same shape, some may be chocolate, while others are lemon or vanilla; some may be frosted or have colored sprinkles on top. The characteristics of the cookie, such as flavor and topping, are the properties of the object. You could refer to the properties of your cookie object as

```
Cookie1.Flavor = "Lemon"
Cookie1.Topping = "Cream Frosting"
```

What about methods? Recall that a method is an action or behavior—something the object can do or have done to it, such as Move, Clear, or Print.

Possible methods for our cookie object might be Eat, Bake, or Crumble. Using object terminology, you can refer to `Object.Method`:

```
Cookie1.Crumble
```

Sometimes the distinction between a method and an event is somewhat fuzzy. Generally, anything you tell the object to do is a method; if the object does an action and needs to inform you, that's an event. So if you tell the cookie to crumble, that is a method; if the cookie crumbles on its own and needs to inform you of the fact, that's an event.

Object-Oriented Terminology

Key features of an object-oriented language are encapsulation, inheritance, and polymorphism.

Encapsulation

Encapsulation refers to the combination of characteristics of an object along with its behaviors. You have one "package" that holds the definition of all properties, methods, and events. For example, when you create a button, you can set or retrieve its properties, such as Text, Name, or BackColor. You can execute its methods, such as `Focus`, `Hide`, or `Show`, and you can write code for its events, such as Click or Double-click. But you cannot make up new properties or tell it to do anything that it doesn't already know how to do. It is a complete package; you can think of all of the parts of the package as being in a capsule.

You can witness encapsulation by looking at any program. The form is actually a class. All of the methods and events that you code are enclosed within the `Class` and `End Class` statements. The variables that you place in your code are actually properties of the specific form class that you are generating.

Encapsulation is sometimes referred to as data hiding. Each object keeps its data (properties) and procedures (methods) hidden. Through use of the `Public` and `Private` keywords, an object can "expose" only those data elements and procedures that it wishes to allow the outside world to see.

Inheritance

Inheritance is the ability to create a new class from an existing class. You can add enhancements to an existing class without modifying the original. By creating a new class that inherits from an existing class, you can add or modify class variables and methods. For example, each of the forms that you create is inherited from, or derived from, the existing Form class. The original class is known as the **base class, superclass,** or **parent class**. The inherited class is called a **subclass, derived class,** or **child class**. Of course, a new class can inherit from a subclass—that subclass becomes a superclass as well as a subclass.

Look closely at the first line of code for a form:

```
Public Class Form1
    Inherits System.Windows.Forms.Form
```

The base class is System.Windows.Forms.Form and Form1 is the derived class. Inherited classes have an "is a" relationship with the base class. In the form example, the new Form1 "is a" Form.

The real purpose of inheritance is **reusability**. You may need to reuse or obtain the functionality from one class or object when you have another similar situation. The new Form1 class that you create has all of the characteristics and actions of the base class, System.Windows.Forms.Form. From there you can add the functionality for your own new form.

You can create your own hierarchy of classes. You place the code you want to be common in a base class. You then create other classes from it, which inherit the base class methods. This concept is very helpful if you have features that are similar in two classes. Rather than writing two classes that are almost identical, you can create a base class that contains the similar procedures.

An example of reusing classes could be a Person class, where you might have properties for name, address, and phone number. The Person class can be a base class, from which you derive an Employee class, a Customer class, or a Student class (Figure 6.1). The derived classes could call shared procedures from the base class and contain any procedures that are unique to the derived class. In inheritance, typically the classes go from general to the more specific.

The derived classes inherit from the base class.

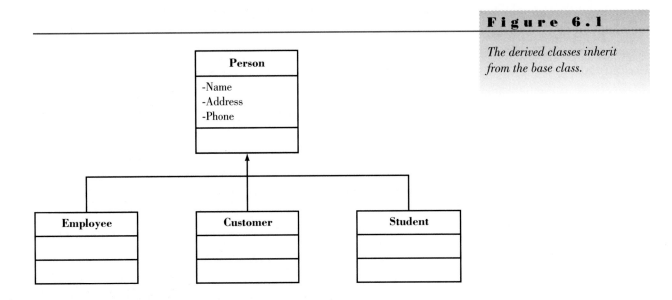

Polymorphism

The term *polymorphism* actually means the ability to take on many shapes or forms. As applied to OOP, polymorphism refers to methods having identical names but different implementations, depending on the situation. For example, radio buttons, check boxes, and list boxes all have a `Select` method. In each case, the `Select` method operates appropriately for its class.

Polymorphism also allows a single class to have more than one method with the same name. When the method is called, the argument type determines which version of the method to use. Each of the identically named methods should perform the same task in a slightly different manner, depending on the arguments.

Later in this chapter you will use both **overloading** a method and **overriding** a method to implement polymorphism. You have already seen examples of *overloading*, such as the `MessageBox.Show` method that gives you several argument lists for calling the method. *Overriding* refers to a method that has the same name as a method in its base class. The method in the subclass, or derived class, takes precedence, or overrides the identically named method in the base class.

Reusable Classes

A big advantage of object-oriented programming over traditional programming is the ability to reuse classes. When you create a new class, you can then use that class in multiple projects. Each object that you create from the class has its own set of properties. This process works just like the built-in VB controls you have been using all along. For example, you can create two PictureBox objects: PictureBox1 and PictureBox2. Each has its own Visible property and Image property, which will probably be set differently from each other.

As you begin creating classes in your projects, you will find many situations in which classes are useful. You might want to create your own class to provide database access. You could include methods for adding and deleting data members. If you work frequently with sales, you might create a Product class. The Product class would likely have properties such as description, quantity, and cost. The methods would probably include finding the current value of the product.

Multitier Applications

A common practice for writing professional applications is to write independent components that work in multiple "tiers" or layers. Each of the functions of a **multitier application** can be coded in a separate component and the components may be stored and run on different machines.

One of the most popular approaches is a three-tier application. The tiers in this model are the Presentation tier, Business tier, and Data tier (Figure 6.2). You also hear the term "n-tier" application, which is an expansion of the three-tier model. The middle tier, which contains all of the business logic, may be written in multiple classes that can be stored and run from multiple locations.

Figure 6.2

The three-tier model for application design.

Presentation Tier	Business Tier	Data Tier
User Interface Forms, controls, menus	**Business Objects** Validation Calculations Business logic Business rules	**Data Retrieval** Data storage

In a multitier application, the goal is to create components that can be combined and replaced. If one part of an application needs to change, such as a redesign of the user interface or a new database format, the other components do not need to be replaced. A developer can simply "plug in" a new user interface and continue using the rest of the components of the application

The Presentation tier refers to the user interface, which in VB is the form. Consider that in the future the user interface could be redesigned or even converted to a Web page.

The Business tier is a class or classes that handle the data. This layer can include validation to enforce business rules as well as the calculations.

The Data tier includes retrieving and storing the data in a database. Occasionally an organization will decide to change database vendors or will need to retrieve data from several different sources. The Data tier retrieves the data and passes the results to the Business tier, or takes data from the Business tier and writes them in the appropriate location. Database handling is covered in Chapters 10 and 11.

Classes

The classes that you have worked with up until now have generated visual objects such as text boxes and labels. These were easily created from the toolbox at design time. You also can create objects at run time. One example of a class that you would instantiate at run time is the Font class.

Instantiating an Object

To create an object based on a class, you must create an instance of the class using the **New keyword**. This step is referred to as *instantiating* an object.

The New Keyword—General Form

```
New className()
```

You can give the new object a variable name, if you will need to refer to it in the future, or you can instantiate and use the new object without naming it.

The New Keyword—Examples

```
Dim arialFont As Font = New Font("Arial", 12)
messageLabel.Font = arialFont

messageLabel.Font = New Font("Arial", 12)
```

Notice that when the object is created, two arguments are passed: the name of the font and the point size.

The New keyword creates a new instance of an object class. The object can be instantiated either from a class that you create or a standard Visual Basic class such as a form or a control.

Specifying a Namespace

You may have noticed that when VB creates a new form class, the Inherits clause says

```
Inherits System.Windows.Forms.Form
```

The name of the class is Form; the **namespace** is System.Windows.Forms. Actually this is a bit of overkill; the entire namespace isn't needed for any classes in the namespaces that are automatically included in a Windows Forms project, which include System, System.Windows.Forms, and System.Drawing. A fully qualified name consists of the complete namespace and class name, such as System.Windows.Forms.TextBox.

When you refer to a class in a different namespace, you have two choices. You can write out the entire namespace and class, such as

```
messageLabel.Font = New System.Drawing.Font("Arial", 12)
```

or you can add an `Imports` statement at the top of the code file to specify the namespace, and then refer only to the class name. For example:

```
Imports System.Drawing.Font

messageLabel.Font = New Font("Arial", 12)
```

For specifying fonts, both of these techniques are overkill, since the System.Drawing namespace is automatically imported into all Windows Forms projects. However, you will need to use these techniques for other classes and namespaces, and if you examine the code generated by the Windows Form Designer, you will see examples with the namespaces spelled out.

Before you can refer to most properties and methods of a class, you must instantiate an object of the class. The exception is shared members, which you will see later in this chapter. ∎

Designing Your Own Class

To design your own class, you need to analyze the characteristics and behaviors that your object needs. The characteristics or properties are defined as variables, and the behaviors (methods) are sub procedures or function procedures. For a simple example, assume that you have a user interface (form) that gathers the price and the quantity of a product. You can design a class to perform the calculations. For the class to calculate the extended price, it must know the price and the quantity. The form needs to retrieve the extended price. The price, quantity, and extended price are stored in private variables in the class; those variables are accessed through property procedures.

Creating Properties in a Class

Inside your class you define private member variables, which store the values for the properties of the class. Theoretically, you could declare all variables as `Public` so that all other project code could set and retrieve their values. However, this approach violates the rules of encapsulation that require each object to be in charge of its own data. Remember that encapsulation is also called data hiding. To accomplish encapsulation, you will declare all variables in a class as `Private`. As a private variable, the value is available only to procedures within the class, the same way that module-level variables are available only to procedures within a form's class code.

When your program creates objects from your class, you will need to assign values to the properties. Because the properties are private variables, you will use special property procedures to pass the values to the class module and to return values from the class module.

Property Procedures

The way that your class allows its properties to be accessed is with **accessor methods** in a **property procedure**. The procedure may contain a `Get` accessor method to retrieve a property value and/or a `Set` accessor method to assign a value to the property. The name that you use for the `Property` procedure becomes the name of the property to the outside world. Create "friendly" property names that describe the property, such as LastName or EmployeeNumber.

The Property Procedure—General Form

```
Private ClassVariable As DataType

[Public] Property PropertyName() As DataType
    Get
        Return ClassVariable [|PropertyName = ClassVariable]
    End Get

    Set(ByVal Value As DataType)

        [Statements, such as validation]
        ClassVariable = Value
    End Set
End Property
```

The `Set` statement uses the **Value keyword** to refer to the incoming value for the property. Property procedures are public by default, so you can omit the optional `Public` keyword. `Get` blocks are similar to function procedures in at least one respect: Somewhere inside the procedure, before the `End Get`, you must assign a return value to the procedure name or use a `Return` statement to return a value. The data type of the incoming value for a `Set` must match the type of the return value of the corresponding `Get`.

The Property Procedure—Example

```
Private lastNameString As String

Property LastName() As String
    Get
        Return lastNameString
    End Get

    Set(ByVal Value As String)
        lastNameString = Value
    End Set
End Property
```

Remember, the private module-level variable holds the value of the property. The `Property Get` and `Set` retrieve the current value and assign a new value to the property.

Read-Only Properties

In some instances you may wish to have a property that can be retrieved by an object but not changed. You can write a property procedure to create a read-only property: Use the **ReadOnly** modifier and write only the Get portion of the property procedure.

```
' Define the property at the module level.
Private totalPayDecimal As Decimal

' The property procedure for a read-only property.
ReadOnly Property TotalPay() As Decimal
    Get
        TotalPay = totalPayDecimal
    End Get
End Property
```

Write-Only Properties

At times you may need to have a property that can be assigned by an object but not retrieved. You can create a property block that contains only a Set to create a write-only property.

```
' Private class-level variable to hold the property value.
Private priceDecimal As Decimal

Public WriteOnly Property Price() As Decimal
    Set(ByVal Value As Decimal)
        If Value >= 0 Then
            priceDecimal = Value
        End If
    End Set
End Property
```

Class Methods

You create methods of the new class by coding public methods within the class. Any methods that you declare with the Private keyword are available only within the class. Any methods that you declare with the Public keyword are available to external objects created from this class or other classes.

```
' Private method used for internal calculations.

Private Sub CalculateExtendedPrice()
' Calculate the extended price.

    ExtendedPrice = quantityInteger * priceDecimal
End Sub
```

Constructors and Destructors

A **constructor** is a method that executes automatically when an object is instantiated. A **destructor** is a method that executes automatically when an object is destroyed. A constructor method is named New.

Constructors

The constructor executes automatically when you instantiate an object of the class. Because the constructor method executes before any other code in the class, the constructor is an ideal location for any initialization tasks that you need to do, such as setting the initial values of variables and properties.

The constructor must be public, because the objects that you create must execute this method.

Note: If a class does not contain a constructor, the compiler creates an implicit method called the *default constructor*. The default constructor has an empty argument list.

Overloading the Constructor

Recall from Chapter 3 that *overloading* means that two methods have the same name but a different list of arguments (the signature). You can create overloaded procedures in your class by giving the same name to multiple procedures, each with a different argument list. The following example shows an empty constructor (one without arguments) and a constructor that passes arguments to the class.

```
Sub New()

    ' Empty constructor.

End Sub


Sub New(ByVal Title As String, ByVal Quantity As Integer, _
  ByVal Price As Decimal)

    ' Code statements to assign property values.

End Sub
```

Parameterized Constructor

The term ***parameterized constructor*** refers to a constructor that requires arguments. This popular technique allows you to pass arguments as you create the new object.

```
' Instantiate the object and set the properties.
aBookSale = New BookSale(titleTextBox.Text, _
  Integer.Parse(quantityTextBox.Text), Decimal.Parse(priceTextBox.Text))
```

Within the class code, use the `Me` object to refer to the current class. So `Me.Quantity` refers to the Quantity property of the current class. This technique is preferable to just assigning the passed argument to the class-level property variables, since validation is often performed in the `Set` methods.

```
Sub New(ByVal Title As String, ByVal Quantity As Integer, _
  ByVal Price As Decimal)
    ' Assign property values.

    Me.Title = Title
    Me.Quantity = Quantity
    Me.Price = Price
    CalculateExtendedPrice()
End Sub
```

When your class has both an empty constructor and a parameterized constructor, the program that creates the object can choose which method to use.

Creating a New Class—Step-by-Step

In this step-by-step tutorial, you will create a new class to hold book sale information for R 'n R.

Begin the Project
A class file is part of a Visual Basic project, so the first step is to create a new project.

STEP 1: Create a new project called Ch06SBS.

Begin a New Class
STEP 1: Select *Add Class* from the *Project* menu. The *Add New Item* dialog box will appear (Figure 6.3).

Figure 6.3

Add a new class to a project in the Add New Item dialog box.

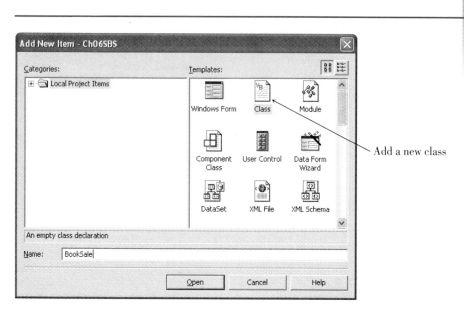

STEP 2: In the *Add New Item* dialog, choose *Class*, type "BookSale" for the class name, and click on *Open*. You will see a new tab in the Editor window for the new class.

Define the Class Properties
STEP 1: In the Editor window, right after the Class statement, declare the Private variables. These module-level variables will hold the values for the properties of your new class.

```
Private titleString As String
Private quantityInteger As Integer
Private priceDecimal, extendedPriceDecimal As Decimal
```

This class has private module-level variables: titleString, quantityInteger, priceDecimal, and extendedPriceDecimal (Figure 6.4). Because the variables

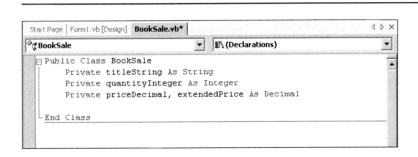

Declare module-level variables for the class properties.

Follow variable naming conventions for the module-level variable to hold the property value; use a friendly name for the property name in the Property procedure. ∎

are declared as `Private`, they can be accessed only by procedures within the class module. To allow access from outside the class module, you must add property procedures.

Add the Title Property Procedure

STEP 1: In the Editor window, after the property declarations, type "Property Title As String". Press Enter.

The `Get` and `Set` blocks will appear, as well as the parentheses on the property name.

Note: The smart editor takes care of the capitalization of keywords. However, the new property name that you declare will be capitalized exactly as you enter it. You can save a little time by typing the line: "property Title as string".

STEP 2: Write the code for the `Property` procedures, indenting as shown.

```
Property Title() As String
    Get
        Return titleString
    End Get

    Set(ByVal Value As String)
        titleString = Value
    End Set
End Property
```

Add the Quantity Property Procedure

STEP 1: After the `End Property` for Title, type "Property Quantity As Integer" and press Enter.

STEP 2: The `Get` and `Set` blocks will appear.

STEP 3: Write the code for the `Property` procedure.

```
Property Quantity() As Integer
    Get
        Return quantityInteger
    End Get

    Set(ByVal Value As Integer)
        If Value >= 0 Then
            quantityInteger = Value
        End If
    End Set
End Property
```

Notice the code to validate the incoming `Value` in the `Set`.

Add the Price Property Procedure

STEP 1: After the `End Property` for Quantity, add the `Property` procedure for Price.

STEP 2: Write the code.

```
Property Price() As Decimal
    Get
        Return priceDecimal
    End Get

    Set(ByVal Value As Decimal)
        If Value >= 0 Then
            priceDecimal = Value
        End If
    End Set
End Property
```

Add the ExtendedPrice Property Procedure

STEP 1: After the `End Property` for Price, add the `Property` procedure for ExtendedPrice.

STEP 2: Write the code.

```
Property ExtendedPrice() As Decimal
    Get
        Return extendedPriceDecimal
    End Get

    Set(ByVal Value As Decimal)
        If Value >= 0 Then
            extendedPriceDecimal = Value
        End If
    End Set
End Property
```

Write the Constructor

STEP 1: Above the property procedures, type in "Public Sub New(Title As String, Quantity As Integer, Price As Decimal)" and press Enter.

Notice that the editor adds the `ByVal` before each argument.

The constructor can actually appear anywhere in the code, as long as it's inside the class and not inside another procedure. A good convention is to place the constructors near the top of the class, right after the module-level declarations.

STEP 2: Type the code for the procedure.

```
Public Sub New(ByVal Title As String, ByVal Quantity As Integer, _
    ByVal Price As Decimal)
    ' Assign the property values.

    Me.Title = Title
    Me.Quantity = Quantity
    Me.Price = Price
    CalculateExtendedPrice()
End Sub
```

The call to `CalculateExtendedPrice` is flagged as an error. You will code that procedure next.

Code a Method

You can create methods by adding sub procedures and functions for the behaviors needed by the class. For this class, you will add a sub procedure to calculate the extended price, which is the price per book multiplied by the quantity.

STEP 1: After the property procedures, type in "Private Sub Calculate-ExtendedPrice " and press Enter. (Do not type the hyphen.)
      Notice that the editor adds the parentheses after the procedure name.
STEP 2: Type the code for the procedure.

```
Private Sub CalculateExtendedPrice()
    ' Calculate the extended price.

    extendedPriceDecimal = quantityInteger * priceDecimal
End Sub
```

Add General Remarks

STEP 1: Type the remarks at the top of the file, before the Class declaration line.

```
'Class Name:     BookSale
'Programmer:     Your Name
'Date:           Today's Date
'Description:    Handle book sale information.
'Folder:         Ch06SBS
```

STEP 2: Save your project.

The Complete Class Code

```
'Class Name:     BookSale
'Programmer:     Your Name
'Date:           Today's Date
'Description:    Handle book sale information.
'Folder:         Ch06SBS

Option Strict On

Public Class BookSale
    Private titleString As String
    Private quantityInteger As Integer
    Private priceDecimal, extendedPriceDecimal As Decimal

    Sub New(ByVal Title As String, ByVal Quantity As Integer, _
      ByVal Price As Decimal)
        ' Assign the property values.

        Me.Title = Title
        Me.Quantity = Quantity
        Me.Price = Price
        CalculateExtendedPrice()
    End Sub
```

```
    Property Title() As String
        Get
            Title = titleString
        End Get

        Set(ByVal Value As String)
            titleString = Value
        End Set
    End Property

    Property Quantity() As Integer
        Get
            Quantity = quantityInteger
        End Get

        Set(ByVal Value As Integer)
            If Value >= 0 Then
                quantityInteger = Value
            End If
        End Set
    End Property

    Property Price() As Decimal
        Get
            Price = priceDecimal
        End Get

        Set(ByVal Value As Decimal)
            If Value >= 0 Then
                priceDecimal = Value
            End If
        End Set
    End Property

    Property ExtendedPrice() As Decimal
        Get
            Return extendedPriceDecimal
        End Get
        Set(ByVal Value As Decimal)
            extendedPriceDecimal = Value
        End Set
    End Property

    Private Sub CalculateExtendedPrice()
    ' Calculate the extended price.

        extendedPriceDecimal = quantityInteger * priceDecimal
    End Sub

End Class
```

Feedback 6.1

1. What is the difference between an object and a class?
2. Given the statement

```
Private aProduct As Product
```

Is aProduct an object or class? What about Product?

3. What actions are performed by the following statement?

```
aProduct.Quantity = Integer.Parse(quantityTextBox.Text)
```

4. Write the property declarations for a class module for a Student class that will contain the properties LastName, FirstName, StudentID-Number, and GPA. Where will these statements appear?
5. Code the `Property` procedure to set and retrieve the value of the LastName property.
6. Code the `Property` procedure to retrieve the value of the read-only GPA property.

Creating a New Object Using a Class

Creating a new class defines a new type; it does not create any objects. This is similar to creating a new tool for the toolbox but not yet creating an instance of the class.

Generally you will create new objects of your class in a two-step operation: first declare a variable for the new object and then instantiate the object using the `New` keyword. Use `Dim`, `Public`, or `Private` to declare the identifier that refers to the object of the class.

```
Private aBookSale As BookSale
```

This line merely states that the name aBookSale is associated with the BookSale class, but it does not create an instance of the object. You must use the `New` keyword to actually create the object.

```
aBookSale = New BookSale()
```

In Visual Basic it is legal to declare and instantiate an object at the same time:

```
Dim aBookSale As New BookSale()
```

If you will need to use the object variable in multiple procedures, you should declare the object at the class level. But when you instantiate an object, you may need to include the `New` statement in a `Try/Catch` block to allow error checking, and a `Try/Catch` block *must* be inside a procedure. Make sure to enclose the instantiation in a `Try/Catch` block if you are converting and passing values that a user enters in a text box, so that you catch any bad input data.

The preferred technique is to include the `New` statement inside of a procedure at the time the object is needed. And if the object is never needed, it won't be created needlessly.

If you *do* choose to declare the variable and instantiate it at the same time, these two statements are equivalent:

```
Private aBookSale As BookSale = New BookSale()
Private aBookSale as New BookSale()
```

The second statement is a coding shortcut for the first (more complete) statement.

If you are using a parameterized constructor, you must pass the values for the arguments when you instantiate the object.

```
Private aBookSale As BookSale

' Instantiate the BookSale object and set the properties.
aBookSale = New BookSale(titleTextBox.Text, Integer.Parse(quantityTextBox.Text), _
    Decimal.Parse(priceTextBox.Text))
```

Defining and Using a New Object—Step-by-Step

To continue the step-by-step tutorial for the BookSale class, the next step is to design the form for the user interface. The form has text boxes for the user to enter the title, quantity, and price; a menu choice to calculate the sale (the extended price); and another menu item to exit.

In the Calculate Sale event procedure, you will create an instance of the BookSale class and assign the input values for title, quantity, and price to the properties of the BookSale object. The ExtendedPrice property in the BookSale class retrieves the amount of the sale, which appears in a label on the form. Figure 6.5 shows the completed form.

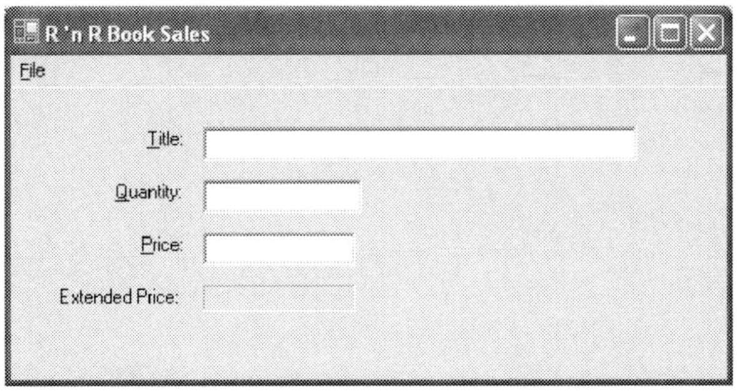

Figure 6.5

The user interface that uses the new BookSale class; the completed form for the step-by-step exercise.

Placing all calculations in a separate class is a good thing. You are seeing your first example of dividing a program into a Presentation tier and a Business tier.

Create the Form

This is a continuation of the step-by-step tutorial for this chapter. If the project is not still open, open it now.

STEP 1: Open the form designer for Form1. Referring to Figure 6.5, create the user interface with text boxes for the title, quantity, and price, and a label for the extended price. Set appropriate properties for the form and the controls.

STEP 2: Change the form name to "salesForm". Open the *Project Properties* dialog box and set the startup object to "salesForm".

STEP 3: Create menu items on the *File* menu for *Calculate Sale*, *Clear*, and *Exit*. Make sure to follow naming guidelines for the items, such as fileCalculateSaleMenuItem and fileExitMenuItem. You may want to create keyboard shortcuts for the menu items to simplify testing.

Add General Remarks

STEP 1: Type the remarks at the top of the code.

```
'Program:      Chapter 6 BookSale Step-by-Step
'Programmer:   Your Name
'Date:         Today's Date
'Description:  Calculate sales price using the BookSale class.
'              Instantiate aBookSale as a new object of the BookSale class.
'Folder:       Ch06SBS
```

Declare the New Object

STEP 1: Declare the object variable in the Declarations section, right under the Windows Form Designer–generated code.

```
' Declare the new object.
Private aBookSale As BookSale
```

Write the Code

STEP 1: In the fileCalculateSaleMenuItem event procedure, write the code to instantiate the BookSale object, assign the values to the properties, calculate the extended price, and assign the result to extended-PriceLabel. Notice that IntelliSense pops up with the properties and method of your new BookSale class.

```
Private Sub fileCalculateSaleMenuItem_Click(ByVal sender As System.Object, _
  ByVal e As System.EventArgs) Handles fileCalculateSaleMenuItem.Click
    ' Calculate the extended price for the sale.

    Try
        ' Instantiate the object and set the properties
        aBookSale = New BookSale(titleTextBox.Text, _
          Integer.Parse(quantityTextBox.Text), Decimal.Parse(priceTextBox.Text))

        ' Calculate and format the result.
        extendedPriceLabel.Text = aBookSale.ExtendedPrice.ToString("N")
    Catch ex As Exception
        MessageBox.Show("Enter numeric data.", "R 'n R Book Sales", _
          MessageBoxButtons.OK, MessageBoxIcon.Exclamation)
    End Try
End Sub
```

STEP 2: Code the fileClearMenuItem_Click procedure.

```
Private Sub fileClearMenuItem_Click(ByVal sender As System.Object, _
  ByVal e As System.EventArgs) Handles fileClearMenuItem.Click
    ' Clear the screen controls.

    priceTextBox.Clear()
    quantityTextBox.Clear()
    extendedPriceLabel.Text = ""
    With titleTextBox
        .Clear()
        .Focus()
    End With
End Sub
```

STEP 3: Code the fileExitMenuItem_Click procedure.

```
Private Sub fileExitMenuItem_Click(ByVal sender As System.Object, _
    ByVal e As System.EventArgs) Handles fileExitMenuItem.Click
    ' Exit the program.

    Me.Close()
End Sub
```

Save Your Work

STEP 1: Click the *Save All* toolbar button to save the project, class, and form.

Run the Project

The next step is to watch the project run—hopefully without errors.

STEP 1: Run the program; your form should appear.
STEP 2: Fill in test values for the title, quantity, and price. Select the *Calculate Sale* menu item. What did you get for the extended price? Is it correct?

Single-Step the Execution

If you get an error message or an incorrect answer in the output, you will need to debug the project. The quickest and easiest way to debug is to single-step program execution. Single-stepping is an interesting exercise, even if you *did* get the right answer.

To single-step, you need to be in break time. Place a breakpoint on the first line in the fileCalculateSaleMenuItem_Click procedure (the `Try` statement). Run the program, enter test values for quantity and price, and select *File / Calculate Sale*. When the program stops at the breakpoint, press the F11 key repeatedly and watch each step; you will see execution transfer to the code for the BookSale class for each property and for the `CalculateExtendedPrice` method. If an error message halts program execution, point to the variable names and property names on the screen to see their current values.

When the Click event procedure finishes, click on your project's task bar button, if necessary, to make the form reappear.

Instance Variables versus Shared Variables

The class properties that you have created up to this point belong to each instance of the class. Therefore, if you create two BookSale objects, each object has its own set of properties. This is exactly what you want for properties such as quantity and price, but what if you need to find a total or count for all of the BookSale objects? You don't want each new object to have its own count property; there would be nothing to increment.

The variables and properties that we have declared thus far are called *instance variables*, or *instance properties*. A separate memory location exists for each instance of the object. Now we will create **shared variables**, also called *shared properties*. A shared property is a single variable that exists, or is available, for all objects of a class.

Terminology varies from one OOP language to another. In some languages, shared members are called *class variables* or *static variables*. Microsoft documentation refers to *instance members* and *shared members*, which include both properties and methods. In general, a shared member has one copy for all objects of the class, and an instance member has one copy for *each* instance or object of the class. Methods also can be declared as shared and are considered shared members.

Another important point is that you can access shared members without instantiating an object of the class. When you display class documentation in MSDN Help, shared members display with a yellow *S* next to the name (Figure 6.6). You must reference these shared members with `ClassName.Property` or `ClassName.Method()`, whether or not you have instantiated an object from the class.

F i g u r e   6 . 6

Shared members display in MSDN Help with a yellow S.

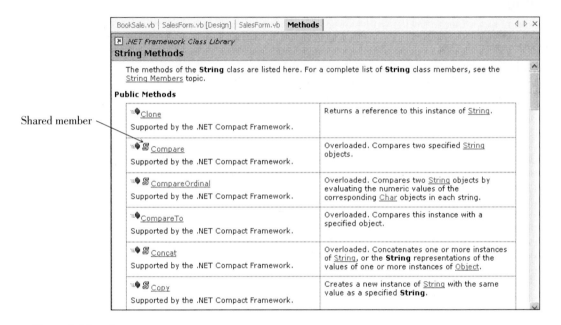

Creating Shared Members

Use the `Shared` keyword to create a shared member.

```
[Public|Private] Shared VariableName As Datatype
[Public|Private] Shared FunctionName(ArgumentList) As Datatype
```

If we want to accumulate a total of all sales and a count of the number of sales for our BookSale class, we need shared properties:

```
Private Shared salesTotalDecimal As Decimal
Private Shared salesCountInteger As Integer
```

You will want to make these shared properties read-only, so that their values can be retrieved but not set directly. The values of the properties are accumulated inside the class; each time a new sale is calculated, the extended price is added to the total sales and the sales count is incremented by one.

```
Shared ReadOnly Property SalesTotal() As Decimal
    Get
        Return salesTotalDecimal
    End Get
End Property
```

```
Shared ReadOnly Property SalesCount() As Integer
    Get
        Return salesCountInteger
    End Get
End Property
```

Note that the `Shared` keyword on the private module-level variable makes it a shared member; the `Shared` keyword on the property procedure is optional. You need to use it if you plan to retrieve the property without first creating an instance of the class.

Adding Shared Properties to the Step-by-Step Tutorial

You will now make the BookSale class calculate the total of all sales and a count of the number of sales. You will need shared properties for the sales total and sales count in the class. Then, on the form, you will add a menu option for *Summary* that displays the totals in a message box.

Add Shared Properties to the Class

If the chapter step-by-step exercise is not still open, open it now.

STEP 1: In the BookSale class, add the private module-level declarations for salesTotalDecimal and salesCountInteger.

```
Private Shared salesTotalDecimal As Decimal
Private Shared salesCountInteger As Integer
```

STEP 2: Add the property procedures for these two shared read-only properties.

```
Shared ReadOnly Property SalesTotal() As Decimal
    Get
        Return salesTotalDecimal
    End Get
End Property

Shared ReadOnly Property SalesCount() As Integer
    Get
        Return salesCountInteger
    End Get
End Property
```


Modify the Code to Calculate the Totals

STEP 1: Add a private procedure for calculating the totals. This method will be called inside the class but cannot be called from an object outside the class.

```
Private Sub AddToTotals()
    ' Add to summary information.

    salesTotalDecimal += extendedPriceDecimal
    salesCountInteger += 1
End Sub
```

STEP 2: Modify the constructor procedure to call the `AddToTotals` procedure.

```
Sub New(ByVal Title As String, ByVal Quantity As Integer, _
    ByVal Price As Decimal)
        ' Assign property values.

        Me.Title = Title
        Me.Quantity = Quantity
        Me.Price = Price
        CalculateExtendedPrice()
        AddToTotals()
End Sub
```

Modify the Form

STEP 1: Add a menu item for *File / Summary* to the form.

STEP 2: Write the event procedure for fileSummaryMenuItem to display the sales total and sales count from the properties of the class. Use a message box and format the sales total to display dollars and cents. Note that you retrieve the shared members of the BookSale class without using an instance of the class: BookSale.SalesTotal.

```
Private Sub fileSummaryMenuItem_Click(ByVal sender As System.Object, _
    ByVal e As System.EventArgs) Handles fileSummaryMenuItem.Click
        ' Display the sales summary information.
    Dim messageString As String

    messageString = "Sales Total: " & BookSale.SalesTotal.ToString("C") & _
        ControlChars.NewLine & "Sales Count: " & BookSale.SalesCount.ToString()
    MessageBox.Show(messageString, "R 'n R Book Sales Summary", _
        MessageBoxButtons.OK, MessageBoxIcon.Information)
End Sub
```

STEP 3: Test the program. Try entering several sales and checking the totals. Also try selecting *Summary* without first calculating a sale. If the program throws an exception, it means that you probably left the `Shared` modifier off the property procedures for the two shared properties.

Save This Version of the Program

STEP 1: This program will be used in Chapter 11. After you save and close the project, make a copy of the project folder. Name the folder copy "Ch11SBS".

Destructors

If there is special processing that you need to do when an object goes out of scope, you can write a Finalize procedure, which is also called a *destructor*. However, Microsoft recommends against writing Finalize procedures unless you need to do something special that the system doesn't know how to handle, such as closing some types of database connections.

Garbage Collection

The **garbage collection** feature of the .NET Common Language Runtime cleans up unused components. Periodically the garbage collector checks for unreferenced objects and releases all memory and system resources used by the objects. If you have written a Finalize procedure, it executes during garbage collection. Microsoft recommends that you rely on garbage collection to release resources and not try to finalize objects yourself. Using this technique, you don't know exactly when your objects will be finalized, since the CLR performs garbage collection on its own schedule, when it needs to recover the resources or has spare time.

Inheritance

When you create a class, the new class can be based on another class. You can make the new class inherit from one of the .NET existing classes or from one of your own classes. Recall that a form uses inheritance using the statement

```
Public Class Form1
    Inherits System.Windows.Forms.Form
```

The `Inherits` statement must follow the class header prior to any comments.

```
Public Class NewClass
    Inherits BaseClass
```

Inheriting Properties and Methods

All public and protected data members and methods of the base class are inherited in the derived class. If you want the derived class to have a different implementation for a base-class method, you must write the method in the derived class that overrides the base-class method.

Constructors in Inheritance

Although a derived class can inherit all public and private methods, there is one exception: A subclass cannot inherit constructors from the base class. Each class must have its own constructors, unless the only constructor needed is an empty constructor. (Visual Basic automatically creates an empty constructor for all classes, so you don't need to write one if that's the only constructor that you need.)

Calling the Base Class Constructor

Often an inherited class needs to make sure that the constructor for the base class executes as well as the constructor for the inherited class. You can call the base-class constructor with the statement

```
MyBase.New()
```

You generally place this code in the constructor for the inherited class, before any additional statements.

```
Sub New(ByVal Title As String, ByVal Quantity As Integer, ByVal Price As Decimal)
    ' Assign property values.

    ' Call the base-class constructor.
    MyBase.New(Title, Quantity, Price)
End Sub
```

Overriding Methods

You can create a method with the same name and the same argument list as a method in the base class. The new method is said to override the base-class method. The derived class will use the new method rather than the method in the base class.

To override a method in Visual Basic .NET, you must declare the original method with the `Overridable` keyword and declare the new method with the `Overrides` keyword. The access modifier for the base-class procedure can be **Private** or **Protected** (not Public).

Base Class

```
Protected Overridable Sub CalculateExtendedPrice()
```

Inherited Class

```
Protected Overrides Sub CalculateExtendedPrice()
```

In a base class, you can actually use the `Overridable`, `Overrides`, or **MustOverride** keyword on a method that can be overridden. Use `Overridable` when you are writing a new method that has code. Use `Must Override` for an **abstract** method, which is an empty method. Abstract methods are designed to be overridden by subclasses and have no implementation of their own. The only time that you declare a base-class method with the `Overrides` keyword is when the method is overriding a method in *its* base class.

When you use the word `Overridable` for a base-class method, in the derived class you have the option of using the base-class implementation for the method or overriding the method by supplying new code. However, if you use the `MustOverride` keyword on a base-class method, the method does not have any code; the derived class *must* provide its own code for the method. A class that has any method declared as `MustOverride` is considered an abstract class, which can be used only for inheritance. You cannot instantiate objects from a class that contains abstract methods.

Accessing Properties

Your derived class can set and retrieve the properties of the base class by using the property accessor methods. Usually your derived class needs to make use of properties and methods of the base class. You can call the base-class constructor from the derived-class constructor, which allows you to use the property values from the base class. In the following example, the derived StudentBookSale class inherits from BookSale. Notice the constructor, which uses the `MyBase.New()` statement to call the constructor of the base class. If the constructor requires arguments, you can pass the argument values when you call the constructor:

```
Sub New(ByVal Title As String, ByVal Quantity As Integer, _
   ByVal Price As Decimal)
    ' Assign property values.

    ' Call base-class constructor and pass the property values.
   MyBase.New(Title, Quantity, Price)
End Sub
```

After you have assigned values to the properties of the base class, you can refer to the properties in methods in the derived class. In the following example, the `CalculateExtendedPrice` method in the derived class uses properties of the base class by property name.

```
' Procedure in the derived class that overrides the procedure in the base class:
Protected Overrides Sub CalculateExtendedPrice()
    ' Calculate the extended price and add to the totals.

    discountDecimal = Quantity * Price * DISCOUNT_RATE_Decimal
    ExtendedPrice = Quantity * Price — discountDecimal
    discountTotalDecimal += discountDecimal
End Sub
```

Note that to use base-class properties in the derived class as in this example, the properties must have both a `Get` and a `Set` accessor method. Read-only or write-only properties cannot be accessed by name from a derived class.

Creating a Derived Class Based on BookSale

The BookSale class could be considered a generic class, which is appropriate for most sales. But now we want another similar class, but with some differences. The new class should have all of the same properties and methods of the BookSale class but will calculate sales with a student discount of 15 percent. We also want a new shared property in the new class to hold the total of the student discounts.

Our new derived class will be called StudentBookSale; the base class is BookSale. Figure 6.7 shows the diagram to indicate the inherited class. The inherited class automatically has all public and protected properties and methods

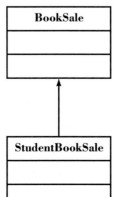

of the base class; in this case, StudentBookSale automatically has six properties and one method.

Adding Inheritance to the Step-by-Step Tutorial

This continuation of the chapter step-by-step tutorial includes a new subclass class, overriding a method, and adding a new property.

Note: If you haven't already done so, save a copy of the project folder for use in Chapter 11. The Chapter 11 step-by-step uses this project without the new class that you will add in the next sections.

Add the New Class

STEP 1: Open your project, if necessary, and select *Add Class* from the *Project* menu.

STEP 2: In the *Add New Item* dialog, choose *Class*, type "StudentBookSale" for the class name, and click on *Open*. You will see a new tab in the Editor window for the new class.

STEP 3: Add a new line after the class declaration and type the Inherits statement.

```
Public Class StudentBookSale
    Inherits BookSale
```

All of the public and protected properties and methods of the base class will be inherited by the subclass.

Add the Constructor

STEP 1: The subclass must have its own constructors, since constructors are not inherited.

```
Sub New(ByVal Title As String, ByVal Quantity As Integer, _
    ByVal Price As Decimal)
    ' Assign property values.

    ' Call the base-class constructor.
    MyBase.New(Title, Quantity, Price)
End Sub
```

Add the New Property

STEP 1: Add a module-level variable to hold the value of a new shared property for the total of discounts.

```
Shared discountTotalDecimal As Decimal
```

STEP 2: Add the Property procedure for DiscountTotal .

```
Shared ReadOnly Property DiscountTotal() As Decimal
    Get
        DiscountTotal = discountTotalDecimal
    End Get
End Property
```

Add a Constant

STEP 1: Add a constant at the module level to hold the discount rate of 15 percent.

```
Const DISCOUNT_RATE_Decimal As Decimal = 0.15D
```

Override a Method

When you override a method from the base class in an inherited class, the method name and the argument list must exactly match.

STEP 1: Open the BookSale base class in the editor and modify the procedure header for CalculateExtendedPrice.

```
Protected Overridable Sub CalculateExtendedPrice()
```

STEP 2: In the StudentBookSale inherited class, write the new Calculate-ExtendedPrice procedure, using the Overrides keyword. You can copy and paste the method from the base class and make the modifications, or type the entire method.

```
Protected Overrides Sub CalculateExtendedPrice()
    ' Calculate the discount, extended price, and add to the total.
    Dim discountDecimal As Decimal

    discountDecimal = Quantity * Price * DISCOUNT_RATE_Decimal
    ExtendedPrice = Quantity * Price - discountDecimal
    discountTotalDecimal += discountDecimal
End Sub
```

Allow a Method to Be Inherited

The AddToTotals method in the base class was declared with the Private keyword, which does not allow it to be inherited. If you want to be able to inherit a method, it must be declared as Protected or Public.

STEP 1: Open the BookSale base class and modify the AddToTotals procedure header.

```
Protected Sub AddToTotals()
```

Modify the Form to Use the Inherited Class

STEP 1: Add a check box to the form, named studentCheckBox, with the Text set to "Student". You can set the RightToLeft property to True if you want the text to appear to the left of the box (Figure 6.8). Rearrange the controls to keep the input fields together.

STEP 2: In the code editor window, add a module-level variable for an object of the new StudentBookSale class.

```
Private aStudentBookSale As StudentBookSale
```

STEP 3: Modify the fileCalculateSaleMenuItem event procedure to create the correct object, depending on the state of studentCheckBox.

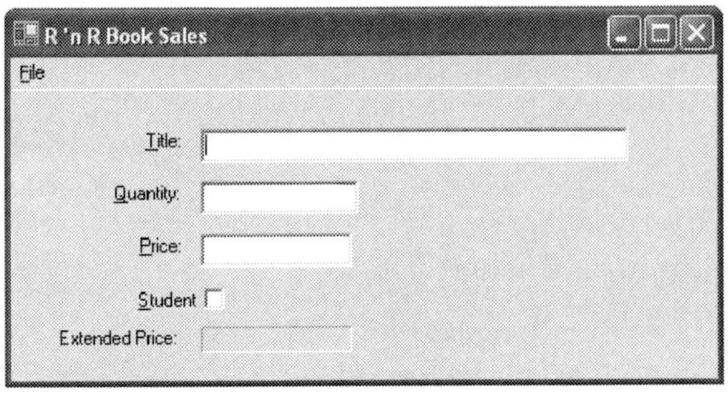

Figure 6.8

Add a Student check box to the form.

R 'n R Book Sales

File

Title:

Quantity:

Price:

Student ☐

Extended Price:

```
Try
    If studentCheckBox.Checked Then

        ' Instantiate the StudentBookSale object and set the properties.
        aStudentBookSale = New StudentBookSale(titleTextBox.Text, _
            Integer.Parse(quantityTextBox.Text), Decimal.Parse(priceTextBox.Text))
        ' Calculate and format the result.
        extendedPriceLabel.Text = aStudentBookSale.ExtendedPrice.ToString("C")
    Else
        ' Instantiate the BookSale object and set the properties.
        aBookSale = New BookSale(titleTextBox.Text, _
            Integer.Parse(quantityTextBox.Text), Decimal.Parse(priceTextBox.Text))
        ' Calculate and format the result.
        extendedPriceLabel.Text = aBookSale.ExtendedPrice.ToString("C")
    End If
Catch ' Rest of code for procedure goes here
```

Notice that the code uses the `ExtendedPrice` method in either case. But when studentCheckBox is checked, the `ExtendedPrice` method of the subclass is retrieved; when the check box is not checked, the `ExtendedPrice` method of the base class is used. Both classes add to the shared SalesTotal and SalesCount properties of the base class, which will hold the totals for both classes.

STEP 4: Modify the fileSummaryMenuItem event procedure to include the discount total.

```
messageString = "Sales Total: " & aBookSale.SalesTotal.ToString("N") & _
    ControlChars.NewLine & "Sales Count: " & aBookSale.SalesCount.ToString() & _
    ControlChars.NewLine & "Total of Student Discounts: " & _
    aStudentBookSale.DiscountTotal.ToString("C")
```

Creating a Base Class Strictly for Inheritance

Sometimes you may want to create a class solely for the purpose of inheritance by two or more similar classes. For example, you might create a Person class that you don't intend to instantiate. Instead you will create subclasses of the Person class, such as Employee, Customer, and Student.

For a base class that you intend to inherit, include the **MustInherit** modifier on the class declaration, which creates an abstract class. In each of the methods in the base class that must be overridden, include the `MustOverride` modifier. The method that must be overridden does not contain any code in the base class.

Base Class

```
MustInherit Class BaseClass
    Public MustOverride Sub SomeProcedure()
        ' No code allowed here.
    End Sub
End Class
```

Inherited Class

```
Class DerivedClass
    Inherits BaseClass
    Public Overrides Sub SomeProcedure()
        ' Code goes here.
    End Sub
End Class
```

Inheriting Form Classes

Some projects require that you have several forms. You may want to use a similar design from one form to the next. You can use **visual inheritance** by designing one form and then inheriting any other forms from the first (Figure 6.9).

Once you have designed the form that you want to use for a pattern, you can add more forms that inherit from your design master, called your *base class*. Your base class inherits from System.Windows.Forms.Form, and your new forms inherit from your base class.

When you design the base class, you can include design elements and other controls, such as labels, text boxes, and buttons. You also can write procedures and declare variables in the base class. Just as you saw earlier, all public and protected procedures and variables are inherited from the base class to the sub class. You can write procedures in the base class and specify Overridable or MustOverride, and then in the subclass write the identically named procedure with the Overrides keyword.

You can create an inherited form class in two ways:

1. Select *Project / Add Windows Form* and type in a name for the new Windows form. Then modify the Inherits statement to inherit from your base form using your project name as the namespace.

```
Public Class MyDerivedForm
    Inherits ProjectName.BaseFormName
```

2. Select *Project / Add Inherited Form* and type the name of the new form. After naming your form, you are shown a dialog displaying the forms in the project from which to select.

Form Inheritance Example

This example has three forms that inherit from a base class. The base class has an OK button, a picture box, and labels. All forms that inherit from the base

Figure 6.9

Create a base form and inherit the visual interface to new forms. a. The base form; b. and c., inherited forms.

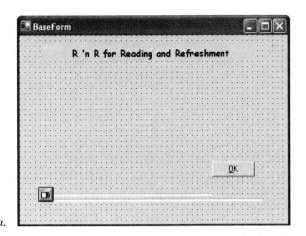

a.

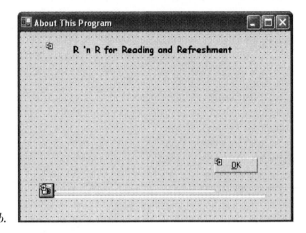

b.

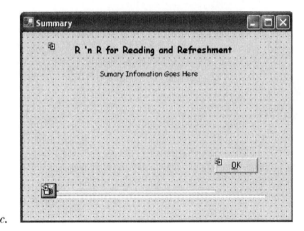

c.

class will have all of these controls, but the Text property of the base class is
not inherited. You cannot delete any of the controls on the inherited forms, but
you can make a control invisible. For example, in mainForm, the OK button's
Visible property is set to False.

The base class has an okButton_Click event procedure, which can be overridden in the sub classes.

All forms are in the same project, called Ch06Multiforms.

baseForm

```
Public Class baseForm
    Inherits System.Windows.Forms.Form

    Public Overridable Sub okButton_Click(ByVal sender As System.Object, _
        ByVal e As System.EventArgs) Handles okButton.Click
        ' Allow inherited classes to override this method.

    End Sub
End Class
```

aboutForm

```
Public Class aboutForm
    Inherits ChO6Multiforms.baseForm

    Public Overrides Sub okButton_Click(ByVal sender As System.Object, _
      ByVal e As System.EventArgs) Handles okButton.Click
        ' Override the base class method.

        Me.Close()
    End Sub
End Class
```

mainForm

```
Public Class mainForm
    Inherits ChO6Multiforms.baseForm

    Private Sub mainForm_Load(ByVal sender As System.Object, _
      ByVal e As System.EventArgs) Handles MyBase.Load
        ' Hide the OK button for this form.

        okButton.Visible = False
    End Sub

    Private Sub fileExitMenuItem_Click(ByVal sender As Object, _
      ByVal e As System.EventArgs) Handles fileExitMenuItem.Click
        ' Exit the application.

        Me.Close()
    End Sub

    Private Sub fileAboutMenuItem_Click(ByVal sender As Object, _
      ByVal e As System.EventArgs) Handles fileAboutMenuItem.Click
        ' Show the About form.

        Dim anAboutForm As New aboutForm()
        anAboutForm.ShowDialog()
    End Sub

    Private Sub fileSummaryMenuItem_Click(ByVal sender As Object, _
      ByVal e As System.EventArgs) Handles fileSummaryMenuItem.Click
        ' Show the Summary form.

        Dim aSummaryForm As New summaryForm()
        aSummaryForm.ShowDialog()
    End Sub
End Class
```

summaryForm

```
Public Class summaryForm
    Inherits ChO6Multiforms.baseForm

    Public Overrides Sub okButton_Click(ByVal sender As System.Object, _
      ByVal e As System.EventArgs) Handles okButton.Click
        ' Override the base class method.
```

```
        Me.Close()
    End Sub
End Class
```

Coding for Events of an Inherited Class

When you derive a new form class from an existing form, you often want to write code for events of inherited controls. Unfortunately, you can't double-click on an inherited control and have the event procedure open, like you can for most controls. In the previous example of form inheritance, for the ok-Button_Click event procedure header, we copied the procedure from the base class into the derived class and made the modifications.

Note: An alternate solution would be to use the inherited okButton_Click event handler in the derived class.

Managing Multiclass Projects

This chapter has examples of projects with multiple forms and multiple classes. In each case, every class is stored in a separate file. Although you must keep form classes in separate files, other classes do not have that requirement. You can code multiple classes in one file.

Namespaces

A VB project is automatically assigned to a namespace, which defaults to the name of the project. You can view and modify the project's namespace, called the root namespace, in the *Project Properties* dialog box (Figure 6.10). If you

Change the project's root namespace in the Project Properties dialog box.

make a copy of a VB project, you need to modify the root namespace of the copy. Even though the folder locations are different, Visual Studio groups classes by their namespace and will confuse the two projects with the same root namespace.

Adding an Existing Class File to a Project

If you have an existing form or other class file that you want to include in a project, you can choose to reference the file in its original location or move or copy it into your project folder. Unless you need to share a class among several projects, it's best to place the class file into the project folder. After you move or copy the desired file into the project folder, add the file to the project by selecting *Project / Add Existing Item* (or right-click the project name in the Solution Explorer and select from the context menu).

Displaying Values on a Different Form

When you have multiple forms in a project, you may want to reference controls on one form from another form. For example, maybe the code in the main form calculates information that you want to display on a summary form. Earlier you displayed summary information in a message box; in this chapter you will display the summary information on another form.

You can easily refer to the controls on another form by using the identifier for the form instance. Write the reference as `FormInstance.ControlName.Property`.

```
Dim aSummaryForm As New summaryForm()
aSummaryForm.salesLabelTotal.Text = aBookSale.SalesTotal.ToString("C")
```

If the form to which you refer is in a different namespace, you also must include a reference to the namespace or include the namespace in a `Using` statement.

Using the Object Browser

The Object Browser is an important tool for working with objects. The Object Browser can show you the names of objects, properties, methods, events, and constants for VB objects, your own objects, and objects available from other applications.

If you don't see a tab for the Object Browser in the Editor window, you can open it easily. Select the Object Browser toolbar button (Figure 6.11). In the Object Browser window (Figure 6.12), you can choose the libraries/namespaces

F i g u r e   6 . 1 1

Open the Object Browser from the toolbar button.

Figure 6.12

The Object Browser window; notice the icons to indicate the member type.

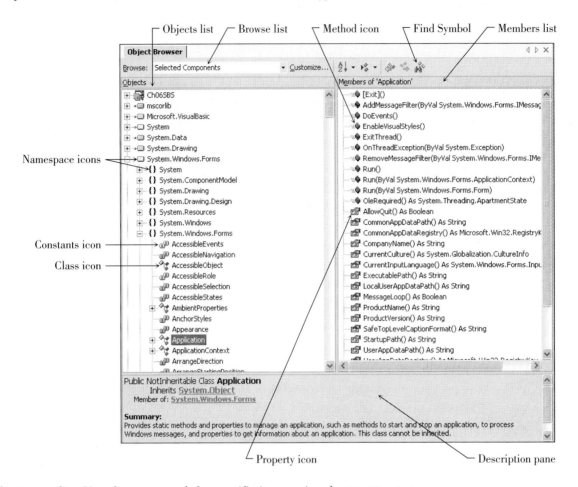

in the *Browse* list. You also can search for specific items using the *Find Symbol* button.

The Object Browser uses several icons to represent items. Notice in Figure 6.12 the icons that represent properties, methods, constants, classes, and namespaces. At the bottom of the window you can see a description of any item you select.

Examining VB Classes

You can look up the available properties, methods, events, or constants of a Visual Basic class. You can see which elements are defined in the class, what is the base class, and which properties, methods, and events are inherited. In Figure 6.13 notice the entries for System.Windows.Forms.MessageBox; the overloaded constructors appear in the *Members* list. And in Figure 6.14, you can see the constants for MessageBoxButtons.

Examining Your Own Classes

You can see your own classes listed in the Object Browser. With the chapter step-by-step project open, select your project name in the Object Browser. Try

Figure 6.13

Display the members of the System.Windows.Forms.MessageBox class.

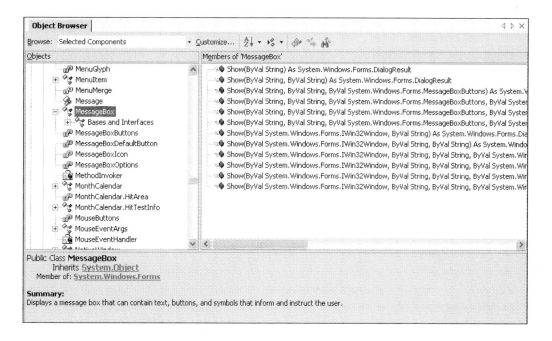

Figure 6.14

Display the MessageBoxButtons constants.

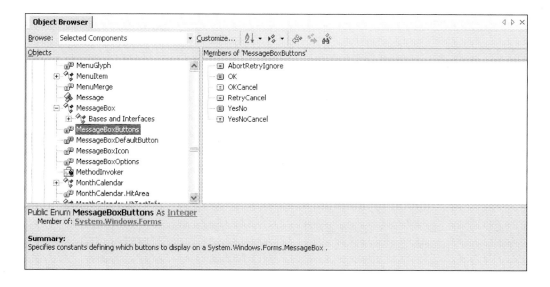

clicking on each class name and viewing the list of properties and methods (Figure 6.15).

You can use the Object Browser to jump to the definition of any property or method by double-clicking on its name in the *Members* list. This technique is also a great way to jump to any of the procedures in your forms. Select your

Figure 6.15

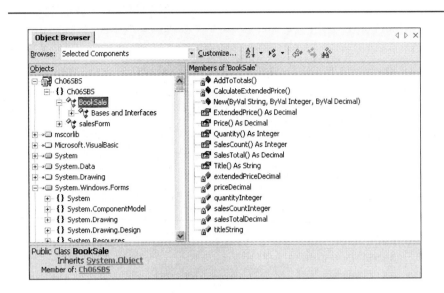

form name in the *Objects* list and double-click on the name of the procedure you want to view.

Your Hands-On Programming Example

This program must calculate book sales for R 'n R, with a discount of 15 percent for students. The project will use the BookSale and StudentBookSale classes developed in the chapter step-by-step.

Create a project with multiple forms that have a shared design element. Include a main form, an About form, and a Summary form that displays the sales summary information.

Design a base form to use for inheritance and make the other three forms inherit from the base form. The About form and Summary form must have an OK button, which closes the form. The main form will have menus and no OK button.

Main Form Menu

File	Help
Calculate Sale	About
Clear	
Summary	
————	
Exit	

Planning the Project

Sketch a base form for inheritance, a main form, an About form, and a Summary form (Figure 6.16) for your users. The users approve and sign off the forms as meeting their needs.

Figure 6.16

The planning sketches of the forms for the hands-on programming example. a. *The base form;* b. *the main form;* c. *the About form; and* d. *the Summary form.*

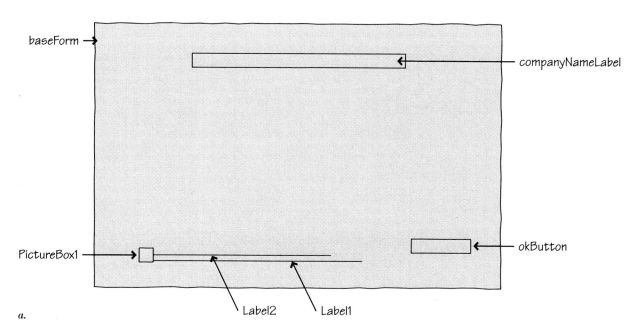

a.

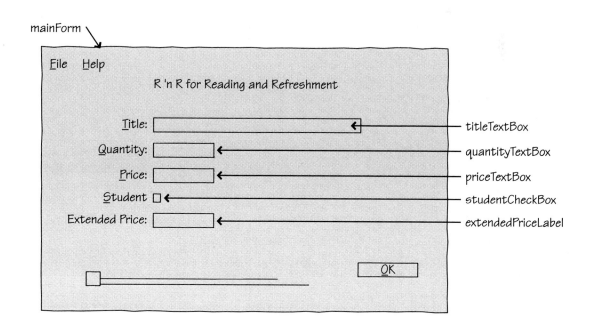

b.

Figure 6.16

(continued)

aboutForm

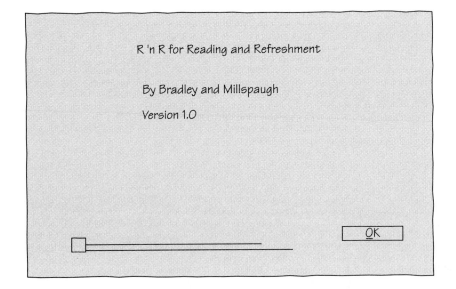

R 'n R for Reading and Refreshment

By Bradley and Millspaugh

Version 1.0

OK

c.

summaryForm

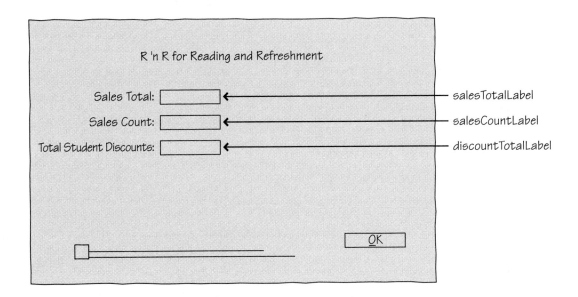

R 'n R for Reading and Refreshment

Sales Total: ⟵ salesTotalLabel

Sales Count: ⟵ salesCountLabel

Total Student Discounts: ⟵ discountTotalLabel

OK

d.

Plan the Objects and Properties for the Main Form

Object	Property	Setting
mainForm	Name	mainForm
	Text	R 'n R Book Sales
	AcceptButton	okButton
Label1	Name	Label1
	Text	&Title:
titleTextBox	Name	titleTextBox
	Text	(blank)
Label2	Name	Label2
	Text	&Quantity:
quantityTextBox	Name	quantityTextBox
	Text	(blank)
Label3	Name	Label3
	Text	&Price:
priceTextBox	Name	priceTextBox
	Text	(blank)
studentCheckBox	Name	studentCheckBox
	Text	&Student
	RightToLeft	Yes
Label4	Name	Label4
	Text	Extended Price:
extendedPriceLabel	Name	extendedPriceLabel
	Text	(blank)
	BorderStyle	Fixed3D
fileMenu	Name	fileMenu
	Text	&File
fileCalculateSaleMenuItem	Name	fileCalculateSaleMenuItem
	Text	&Calculate Sale
fileClearMenuItem	Name	fileClearMenuItem
	Text	C&lear
fileSummaryMenuItem	Name	fileSummaryMenuItem
	Text	&Summary
fileExitMenuItem	Name	fileExitMenuItem
	Text	E&xit
helpMenu	Name	helpMenu
	Text	&Help
helpAboutMenuItem	Name	helpAboutMenuItem
	Text	&About

Plan the Procedures for the Main Form

Procedure	Actions
Form_Load	Hide the inherited OK button.

fileCalculateSaleMenuItem_Click	If student sale then
	    Create a StudentBookSale object.
	    Calculate and format the extended price.
	Else
	    Create a BookSale object.
	    Calculate and format the extended price.
	End If

fileClearMenuItem_Click	Clear text boxes and labels. Uncheck the check box. Set the focus on first text box.
fileSummaryMenuItem_Click	Declare an instance of the Summary form. Format and display the summary information on the Summary form. Show the Summary form.
fileExitMenuItem_Click	End the project
helpAboutMenuItem_Click	Declare an instance of the About form. Show the About form.

Plan the Objects and Properties for the About Form

Object	Property	Setting
aboutForm	Name Text	aboutForm About this Program
okButton	Name Text	(Inherited) okButton &OK

Plan the Procedures for the About Form

Procedure	Actions
okButton_Click	Close this form.

Plan the Objects and Properties for the Summary Form

Object	Property	Setting
summaryForm	Name Text	summaryForm Summary
Label1	Name Text	Label1 Sales Total:

Object	Property	Setting
salesTotalLabel	Name	salesTotalLabel
	Text	(blank)
	BorderStyle	Fixed3D
Label2	Name	Label2
	Text	Sales Count:
salesCountLabel	Name	salesCountLabel
	Text	(blank)
	BorderStyle	Fixed3D
Label3	Name	Label3
	Text	Total Student Discounts:
discountTotalLabel	Name	discountTotalLabel
	Text	(blank)
	BorderStyle	Fixed3D
okButton	Name	(Inherited) okButton
	Text	&OK

Plan the Procedures for the Summary Form

Procedure	Actions
okButton_Click	Close this form.

Plan the BookSale Object Class

Properties

Declare private module-level variables and write property procedures
for all public properties:

>Instance:
>>Title
>>Quantity
>>Price

>Shared:
>>SalesTotal
>>SalesCount

Methods

Procedure	Actions
ExtendedPrice	Calculate extended price = Quantity * Price.
	Add extended price to SalesTotal.
	Add 1 to SalesCount.
	Return extended price.

Plan the StudentBookSale Object Class

Inherit from BookSale.

Additional Properties

   Shared:
      DiscountTotal

Methods

Procedure	Actions
ExtendedPrice	Calculate discount = price * quantity * discount rate.
	Calculate extended price = quantity * price – discount.
	Add extended price to SalesTotal.
	Add 1 to SalesCount.
	Add discount to DiscountTotal.
	Return extended price.

Write the Project Follow the sketches in Figure 6.16 to create the forms. Create the base form first and inherit the other three forms from the base form. Figure 6.17 shows the completed forms.

- Set the properties of each of the objects according to your plan.

- Create the BookSale and StudentBookSale classes, or copy them into your project folder and add them to the project.

- Write the code. Working from the pseudocode, write each procedure.

- When you complete the code, use a variety of data to thoroughly test the project.

The Project Coding Solution

baseForm

```
'Program:        Chapter 6 BookSale Hands-On Program
'Programmer:     Bradley/Millspaugh
'Date:           January 2004
'Description:    Base form for hands-on project.
'Folder:         Ch06HandsOn

Option Strict On

Public Class baseForm
    Inherits System.Windows.Forms.Form

    Public Overridable Sub okButton_Click(ByVal sender As System.Object, _
        ByVal e As System.EventArgs) Handles okButton.Click
            ' Allow inherited classes to override this method.

    End Sub
End Class
```

Figure 6.17

The completed forms for the hands-on programming example. a. *The base form;* b. *the main form;* c. *the About form; and* d. *the Summary form.*

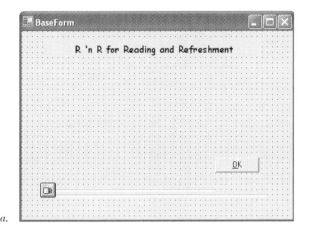

a.

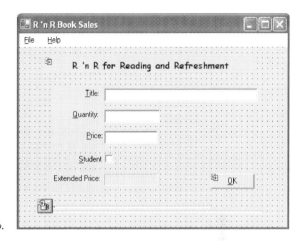

b.

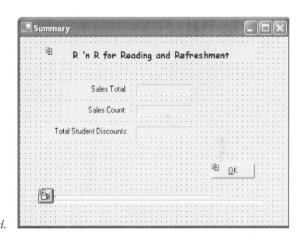

c.

d.

mainForm

```
'Program:        Chapter 6 BookSale Hands-On Program
'Programmer:     Bradley/Millspaugh
'Date:           January 2004
'Description:    Calculate sales price using the BookSale and StudentBookSale classes.
'                Main form for hands-on project.
'Folder:         Ch06HandsOn

Option Strict On

Public Class mainForm
    Inherits Ch06HandsOn.baseForm

    ' Declare the new objects.
    Private aBookSale As BookSale
    Private aStudentBookSale As StudentBookSale
```

```vb
Private Sub mainForm_Load(ByVal sender As Object, _
  ByVal e As System.EventArgs) Handles MyBase.Load
    ' Make the OK button invisible on this form.

    okButton.Visible = False
End Sub

Private Sub fileCalculateSaleMenuItem_Click(ByVal sender As System.Object, _
  ByVal e As System.EventArgs) Handles fileCalculateSaleMenuItem.Click
    ' Calculate the extended price for the sale.

    Try
        If studentCheckBox.Checked Then

            ' Instantiate the StudentBookSale object and set the properties.
            aStudentBookSale = New StudentBookSale(titleTextBox.Text, _
                Integer.Parse(quantityTextBox.Text), Decimal.Parse(priceTextBox.Text))
            ' Calculate and format the result.
            extendedPriceLabel.Text = aStudentBookSale.ExtendedPrice.ToString("N")
        Else
            ' Instantiate the BookSale object and set the properties.
            aBookSale = New BookSale(titleTextBox.Text, _
                Integer.Parse(quantityTextBox.Text), _
                Decimal.Parse(priceTextBox.Text))
            ' Calculate and format the result.
            extendedPriceLabel.Text = aBookSale.ExtendedPrice.ToString("N")
        End If
    Catch
        MessageBox.Show("Error in quantity or price field.", "R 'n R Book Sales", _
            MessageBoxButtons.OK, MessageBoxIcon.Exclamation)
    End Try
End Sub

Private Sub fileClearMenuItem_Click(ByVal sender As System.Object, _
  ByVal e As System.EventArgs) Handles fileClearMenuItem.Click
    ' Clear screen controls.

    quantityTextBox.Clear()
    priceTextBox.Clear()
    extendedPriceLabel.Text = ""
    studentCheckBox.Checked = False
    With titleTextBox
        .Clear()
        .Focus()
    End With
End Sub

Private Sub fileSummaryMenuItem_Click(ByVal sender As System.Object, _
  ByVal e As System.EventArgs) Handles fileSummaryMenuItem.Click
    ' Display the sales summary information.
    Dim aSummaryForm As New summaryForm()

    With aSummaryForm
        .salesLabelTotal.Text = aBookSale.SalesTotal.ToString("C")
        .salesLabelCount.Text = aBookSale.SalesCount.ToString()
        .discountTotalLabel.Text = aStudentBookSale.DiscountTotal.ToString("C")
        .ShowDialog()
    End With
End Sub
```

```
    Private Sub fileExitMenuItem_Click(ByVal sender As Object, _
        ByVal e As System.EventArgs) Handles fileExitMenuItem.Click
            ' Exit the application.

            Me.Close()
    End Sub

    Private Sub fileAboutMenuItem_Click(ByVal sender As System.Object, _
        ByVal e As System.EventArgs) Handles fileAboutMenuItem.Click
            ' Display the About form.
            Dim anAboutForm As New aboutForm()

            anAboutForm.Show()
    End Sub
End Class
```

aboutForm

```
'Program:           Chapter 6 BookSale Hands-On Program
'Programmer:        Bradley/Millspaugh
'Date:              January 2004
'Description:       Calculate sales price using the BookSale class.
'                   About form for hands-on project.
'Folder:            Ch06HandsOn

Option Strict On

Public Class aboutForm
    Inherits Ch06HandsOn.baseForm

    Public Overrides Sub okButton_Click(ByVal sender As System.Object, _
        ByVal e As System.EventArgs) Handles okButton.Click
            ' Override the base class method.

            Me.Close()
    End Sub
End Class
```

summaryForm

```
'Program:           Chapter 6 BookSale Hands-On Program
'Programmer:        Bradley/Millspaugh
'Date:              January 2004
'Description:       Calculate sales price using the BookSale class.
'                   Summary form for hands-on project.
'Folder:            Ch06HandsOn

Option Strict On

Public Class summaryForm
    Inherits Ch06HandsOn.baseForm

    Public Overrides Sub okButton_Click(ByVal sender As System.Object, _
        ByVal e As System.EventArgs) Handles okButton.Click
            ' Override the base class method.

            Me.Close()
    End Sub
End Class
```

BookSale Class

```
'Class Name:        BookSale
'Programmer:        Bradley/Millspaugh
'Date:              January 2004
'Description:       Handle book sale information.
'Folder:            Ch06HandsOn

Public Class BookSale
    Private titleString As String
    Private quantityInteger As Integer
    Private priceDecimal, extendedPriceDecimal As Decimal
    Private Shared salesTotalDecimal As Decimal
    Private Shared salesCountInteger As Integer

    ' Parameterized Constructor.
    Sub New(ByVal Title As String, ByVal Quantity As Integer, _
      ByVal Price As Decimal)
        ' Assign property values.

        Me.Title = Title
        Me.Quantity = Quantity
        Me.Price = Price
        CalculateExtendedPrice()
        AddToTotals()
    End Sub

    Property Title() As String
        Get
            Return titleString
        End Get

        Set(ByVal Value As String)
            titleString = Value
        End Set
    End Property

    Property Quantity() As Integer
        Get
            Return quantityInteger
        End Get

        Set(ByVal Value As Integer)
            If Value >= 0 Then
                quantityInteger = Value
            End If
        End Set
    End Property

    Property Price() As Decimal
        Get
            Return priceDecimal
        End Get

        Set(ByVal Value As Decimal)
            If Value >= 0 Then
                priceDecimal = Value
            End If
        End Set
    End Property
```

```
        Public Property ExtendedPrice() As Decimal
            Get
                Return extendedPriceDecimal
            End Get

            Set(ByVal Value As Decimal)
                extendedPriceDecimal = Value
            End Set
        End Property

        Shared Property SalesTotal() As Decimal
            Get
                Return salesTotalDecimal
            End Get

            Set(ByVal Value As Decimal)
                salesTotalDecimal = Value
            End Set
        End Property

        Shared Property SalesCount() As Integer
            Get
                Return salesCountInteger
            End Get

            Set(ByVal Value As Integer)
                salesCountInteger = Value
            End Set
        End Property

        Protected Overridable Sub CalculateExtendedPrice()
            ' Calculate the extended price.

            extendedPriceDecimal = quantityInteger * priceDecimal
        End Sub

        Protected Overridable Sub AddToTotals()
            ' Add to the summary information.

            salesTotalDecimal += extendedPriceDecimal
            salesCountInteger += 1
        End Sub
End Class
```

StudentBookSale Class

```
'Class Name:        StudentBookSale
'Programmer:        Bradley/Millspaugh
'Date:              January 2004
'Description:       Handle book sale information for student sales,
'                   which receive a discount.
'Folder:            Ch06HandsOn

Option Strict On

Public Class StudentBookSale
    Inherits BookSale

    Shared discountTotalDecimal As Decimal
    Const DISCOUNT_RATE_Decimal As Decimal = 0.15D
    Private discountDecimal, extendedPriceDecimal As Decimal
```

```
Sub New(ByVal Title As String, ByVal Quantity As Integer, _
    ByVal Price As Decimal)
        ' Assign property values.

        ' Call the base-class constructor and pass the property values.
        MyBase.New(Title, Quantity, Price)
    End Sub

    Shared ReadOnly Property DiscountTotal() As Decimal
        Get
            Return discountTotalDecimal
        End Get
    End Property

    Protected Overrides Sub CalculateExtendedPrice()
        ' Calculate the extended price and add to the totals.

        discountDecimal = Quantity * Price * DISCOUNT_RATE_Decimal
        ExtendedPrice = Quantity * Price — discountDecimal
        discountTotalDecimal += discountDecimal
    End Sub

End Class
```

Summary

1. Objects have properties and methods and can trigger events.
2. You can create a new class that can then be used to create new objects.
3. Creating a new object is called *instantiating* the object; the object is called an *instance* of the class.
4. In object-oriented terminology, encapsulation refers to the combination of the characteristics and behaviors of an item into a single class definition.
5. Polymorphism allows different classes of objects in an inheritance hierarchy to have similarly named methods that behave differently for that particular object.
6. Inheritance provides a means to derive a new class based on an existing class. The existing class is called a *base class*, *superclass*, or *parent class*. The inherited class is called a *subclass*, *derived class*, or *child class*.
7. One of the biggest advantages of object-oriented programming is that classes that you create for one application may be reused in another application.
8. Multitier applications separate program functions into a Presentation tier (the user interface), Business tier (the logic of calculations and validation), and Data tier (accessing stored data).
9. The variables inside a class used to store the properties should be private, so that data values are accessible only by procedures within the class.
10. The way to make the properties of a class available to code outside the class is to use `Property` procedures. The `Get` portion returns the value of the property and the `Set` portion assigns a value to the property. Validation is often performed in the `Set` portion.

11. Read-only properties are declared with the `ReadOnly` keyword and have only a `Get` accessor method. Write-only properties are written with the `WriteOnly` keyword and have only a `Set` accessor method.

12. The public functions and sub procedures of a class module are its methods.

13. To instantiate an object of a class, you must use the `New` keyword either on the declaration statement or an assignment statement. The location of the `New` keyword determines when the object is created.

14. A constructor is a method that automatically executes when an object is created; a destructor method is triggered when an object is destroyed.

15. A constructor method must be named `New` and may be overloaded.

16. A parameterized constructor requires arguments to create a new object.

17. Shared members (properties and methods) have one copy that can be used by all objects of the class, generally used for totals and counts. Instance members have one copy for each instance of the object. Declare shared members with the `Shared` keyword.

18. The garbage collection feature periodically checks for unreferenced objects, destroys the object references, and releases resources.

19. A subclass inherits all public and protected properties and methods of its base class, except for the constructor.

20. To override a method from a base class, the original method must be declared as `Overridable` or `MustOverride`, and the new method must use the `Overrides` keyword.

21. A base class used strictly for inheritance is called an abstract class and cannot be instantiated. The class should be declared as `MustInherit` and the methods that must be overridden should be declared as `MustOverride`.

22. You can use visual inheritance to derive new forms from existing forms.

23. Each project has a default namespace, called the root namespace. Change the root namespace for a VB project in the *Project Properties* dialog box.

24. Refer to controls on a different form with the form instance name, control name, and property.

25. You can use the Object Browser to view classes, properties, methods, events, and constants in system classes as well as your own classes.

Key Terms

Review Questions

1. What is an object? a property? a method?
2. What is the purpose of a class?
3. Why should property variables of a class be declared as private?
4. What are property procedures and what is their purpose?
5. Explain how to create a new object.
6. What steps are needed to assign property values to an object?
7. What actions trigger the constructor and destructor methods of an object?
8. How can you write methods for a new class?
9. What is a shared member? How is it created?
10. Explain the steps necessary to inherit a class from another class.
11. Differentiate between overriding and overloading.
12. What is a parameterized constructor?
13. When might you use the `Protected` keyword on a constructor?
14. What is visual inheritance?

Programming Exercises

Note: For help in basing a new project on an existing project, see "Copy and Move a Windows Project" in Appendix C.

6.1   Modify the program for Programming Exercise 5.1 (the piecework pay) to separate the business logic into a separate class. The class should have properties for Name and Pieces, as well as shared read-only properties to maintain the summary information.

6.2   Modify Programming Exercise 6.1 to include multiple forms. Create a base form that you can use for visual inheritance. Display the summary information and the *About* box on separate forms, rather than in message boxes.

6.3   *Extra Challenge:* Modify Programming Exercise 6.2 to have an inherited class. Create a derived class for senior workers, who receive 10 percent higher pay for 600 or more pieces. Add a check box to the main form to indicate a senior worker.

6.4   Modify Programming Exercise 5.3 (the salesperson commissions) to separate the business logic into a separate class. The class should have properties for Name and Sales, as well as shared read-only properties to maintain the summary information.

6.5   Modify Programming Exercise 6.4 to include multiple forms. Create a base form that you can use for visual inheritance. Display the summary information and the *About* box on separate forms, rather than message boxes.

6.6   *Extra Challenge:* Modify Exercise 6.5 to have an inherited class. Create a derived class for supervisors, who have a different pay scale. The supervisor quota is $2,000; the commission rate is 20 percent; and the base pay is $500. Include a check box on the main form to indicate a supervisor and calculate separate totals for supervisors.

6.7 Modify Programming Exercise 5.5 (the check transactions) to separate the business logic from the user interface. Create a Transaction class and derived classes for Deposit, Check, and Service Charges. Display the summary information on a separate form rather than a message box.
Optional extra: Use visual inheritance for the forms.

6.8 Modify Programming Exercise 5.4 (the library reading program) to separate the business logic from the user interface. Create a class with properties for Name and Number of Books. Display the summary information and *About* box in separate forms rather than message boxes.
Optional extra: Use visual inheritance for the forms.

6.9 *Extra Challenge:* Modify Programming Exercise 6.8 to have inherited classes. Have separate classes and separate totals for elementary, intermediate, and high school. Include radio buttons on the form to select the level; display totals for all three groups on the summary.

6.10 Create a project that contains a class for sandwich objects. Each sandwich object should have properties for Name, Bread, Meat, Cheese, and Condiments. Use a form for user input. Assign the input values to the properties of the object and display the properties on a separate form.

6.11 Create a project that contains a Pet class. Each object will contain pet name, animal type, breed, and color. The form should contain text boxes to enter the information for the pets. A button or menu item should display the pet information on a separate form.

6.12 Modify the project that you created in Chapter 3 to separate the user interface from the business logic (calculations) and return the results through a property.

Case Studies

VB Mail Order

Modify your VB Mail Order project from Chapter 5 to separate the user interface from the business logic. Create two new classes: one for customer information and one for order items. The order item class should perform the calculations and maintain the summary information.

Add a menu option to display the customer information. Display the properties of the Customer object on a separate form.

Display the *About* box and the summary information on forms, rather than message boxes.

Optional extra: Use visual inheritance for the forms.
Need a bigger challenge? Create an inherited class for preferred customers. Preferred customers receive an automatic 5 percent discount on all purchases. Use a check box to determine if the customer is a preferred customer and instantiate the appropriate class. Maintain and display separate totals for preferred customers.

Note: For help in basing a new project on an existing project, see "Copy and Move a Windows Project" in Appendix C.

VB Auto Center

Modify your VB Auto Center project from Chapter 5 to separate the business logic from the user interface. Create a class for purchases, with properties for each of the options. The methods of the class will calculate the subtotal, total, and amount due.

Make the *About* box display on a separate form, rather than a message box.

Need a bigger challenge? Add summary totals for the number of sales, the total sales, and the total trade-ins. Maintain the totals as shared read-only properties of the class and display the summary information on a separate form.

Note: For help in basing a new project on an existing project, see "Copy and Move a Windows Project" in Appendix C.

Video Bonanza

Modify the Video Bonanza project from Chapter 5 to separate the user interface from the business logic. Create a class for each rental. Include a property for Title, Boolean properties for Video Tape format and Members, and shared read-only properties for the summary information.

Display the summary information and the *About* box on forms, rather than message boxes.

Note: For help in basing a new project on an existing project, see "Copy and Move a Windows Project" in Appendix C.

Very Very Boards

Modify the Very Very Boards project from Chapter 5 to separate the user interface from the business logic. Create a class for each shirt sale with properties for Order Number, Quantity, and Size. Use Boolean properties for Monogram and Pocket, and a method to calculate the price. Maintain shared read-only properties for the summary information.

Display the summary information and the *About* box on forms, rather than message boxes.

Optional extra: Use visual inheritance for the forms.

Note: For help in basing a new project on an existing project, see "Copy and Move a Windows Project" in Appendix C.

CHAPTER 7

Lists, Loops, and Printing

at the completion of this chapter, you will be able to . . .

1. Create and use list boxes and combo boxes.

2. Differentiate among the available types of combo boxes.

3. Enter items into list boxes using the Items collection in the Properties window.

4. Add and remove items in a list at run time.

5. Determine which item in a list is selected.

6. Use the Items.Count property to determine the number of items in a list.

7. Display a selected item from a list.

8. Use Do/Loops and For/Next statements to iterate through a loop.

9. Send information to the printer or the Print Preview window using the PrintDocument class.

Often you will want to offer the user a list of items from which to choose. You can use the Windows ListBox and ComboBox controls to display lists on a form. You may choose to add items to a list during design time, during run time, or perhaps a combination of both. Several styles of list boxes are available; the style you use is determined by design and space considerations as well as by whether you will allow users to add items to the list.

List Boxes and Combo Boxes

Both list boxes and combo boxes allow you to have a list of items from which the user can make a selection. Figure 7.1 shows the toolbox tools for creating the controls; Figure 7.2 shows several types of list boxes and combo boxes, including **simple list boxes**, **simple combo boxes**, **drop-down combo boxes**, and **drop-down lists**. The list boxes on the left of the form in Figure 7.2 are all created with the ListBox tool; the boxes on the right of the form are created with the ComboBox tool. Notice the three distinct styles of combo boxes.

    ListBox controls and **ComboBox controls** have most of the same properties and operate in a similar fashion. One exception is that a ComboBox control has a DropDownStyle property, which determines whether or not the list box also has a text box for user entry and whether or not the list will drop down (refer to Figure 7.2).

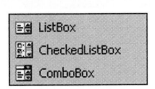

Figure 7.1

Use the ListBox tool and ComboBox tool to create list boxes and combo boxes on your forms.

Figure 7.2

Various styles of list boxes and combo boxes.

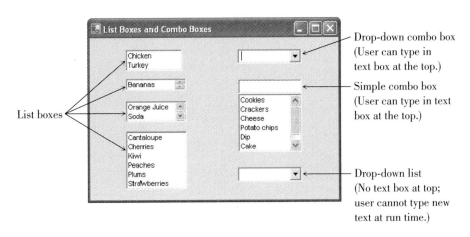

Both list boxes and combo boxes have a great feature. If the box is too small to display all the items in the list at one time, VB automatically adds a scroll bar. You do not have to be concerned with the location of the scroll box in the scroll bar; the scrolling is handled automatically.

When you add a list control to a form, choose the style according to the space you have available and how you want the box to operate. Do you want the user to select from an existing list? If so, use a simple list box or a drop-down list (ComboBox DropDownStyle = DropDownList). Do you want the user to be able to type a new entry if necessary? In this case, use one of the two styles with an added text box: the drop-down combo box (DropDownStyle = DropDown) or the simple combo box (DropDownStyle = Simple).

At design time, the behavior of list boxes and combo boxes differs. For list boxes, Visual Basic displays the Name property in the control; for combo boxes, the Text property displays. Don't spend any time trying to make a list box appear empty during design time; the box will appear empty at run time. Combo boxes have a Text property, which you can set or remove at design time. List boxes also have a Text property, but you can only access it at run time.

The Items Collection

The list of items that displays in a list box or combo box is a **collection**. VB collections are objects that have properties and methods to allow you to add items, remove items, refer to individual elements, count the items, and clear the collection. In the sections that follow, you will learn to maintain and refer to the Items collection.

You can refer to the items in a collection by an index, which is zero based. For example, if a collection holds 10 items, the indexes to refer to the items range from 0 to 9. To refer to the first item in the Items collection, use Items(0).

Filling a List

You can use several methods to fill the Items collection of a list box and combo box. If you know the list contents at design time and the list never changes, you can define the Items collection in the Properties window. If you must add items to the list during program execution, you will use the `Items.Add` or `Items.Insert` method in an event procedure. In Chapter 11 you will learn to fill a list from a data file on disk. This technique allows the list contents to vary from one run to the next.

Using the Properties Window
The **Items property**, which is a collection, holds the list of items for a list box or combo box. To define the Items collection at design time, select the control and scroll the Properties window to the Items property (Figure 7.3). Click on the ellipses button to open the String Collection Editor (Figure 7.4) and type your list items, ending each line with the Enter key. Click OK when finished. You can open the editor again to modify the list, if you wish.

Using the Items.Add Method
To add an item to a list at run time, use the **`Items.Add` method**. You can choose to add a variable, a constant, the contents of the text box at the top of a combo box, or the Text property of another control.

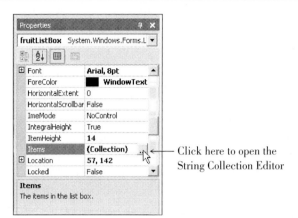

Click here to open the
String Collection Editor

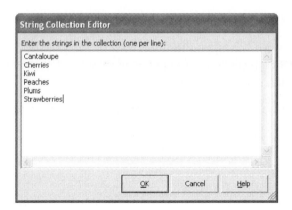

The Items.Add Method—General Form

```
Object.Items.Add(ItemValue)
```

ItemValue is the string value to add to the list. If the value is a string literal, enclose it in quotation marks.

The new item generally goes at the end of the list. However, you can alter the placement by setting the control's **Sorted property** to True. Then the new item will be placed alphabetically in the list.

The Items.Add Method—Examples

```
schoolsListBox.Items.Add("Harvard")
schoolsListBox.Items.Add("Stanford")
schoolsListBox.Items.Add(schoolsTextBox.Text)
majorsComboBox.Items.Add(majorsComboBox.Text)
majorsComboBox.Items.Add(majorString)
```

When the user types a new value in the text box portion of a combo box, that item is not automatically added to the list. If you want to add the newly entered text to the list, use the `Items.Add` method:

```
coffeeComboBox.Items.Add(coffeeComboBox.Text)
```

or the preferable form:

```
With coffeeComboBox
    .Items.Add(.Text)
End With
```

You also can add the contents of a text box to a list box.

```
schoolsListBox.Items.Add(schoolTextBox.Text)
```

Using the Items.Insert Method

You can choose the location for a new item added to the list. In the **Items. Insert method**, you specify the index position for the new item.

The Items.Insert Method—General Form

```
Object.Items.Insert(IndexPosition, ItemValue)
```

The index position is zero based. To insert a new item in the first position, use index position = 0.

The Items.Insert Method—Examples

```
schoolsListBox.Items.Insert(0, "Harvard")
majorsComboBox.Items.Insert(1, majorsComboBox.Text)
```

If you choose the index position of an item using the `Insert` method, do not set the list control's Sorted property to True. A sorted list is always sorted into alphabetic order, regardless of any other order that you request.

The SelectedIndex Property

When a project is running and the user selects (highlights) an item from the list, the index number of that item is stored in the **SelectedIndex property** of the list box. Recall that the index of the first item in the list is 0. If no list item is selected, the SelectedIndex property is set to negative 1 (–1).

You can use the SelectedIndex property to select an item in the list or deselect all items in code.

Examples

```
' Select the fourth item in list.
coffeeTypesListBox.SelectedIndex = 3
```

```
' Deselect all items in list.
coffeeTypesListBox.SelectedIndex = -1
```

The Items.Count Property

You can use the Count property of the Items collection to determine the number of items in the list. We will use the **Items.Count property** later in this chapter to process each element in the list. Items.Count is also handy when you need to display the count at some point in your project.

Remember: Items.Count is always one more than the highest possible SelectedIndex, since the indexes begin with 0. For example, if there are five items in a list, Items.Count is 5 and the highest index is 4 (Figure 7.5).

Examples

```
totalItemsInteger = itemsListBox.Items.Count
MessageBox.Show("The number of items in the list is " & itemsListBox.Items.Count.ToString())
```

Figure 7.5

For a list of five items, the indexes range from 0 to 4.

Items.SelectedIndex	Items.Count = 5
(0)	Harvard
(1)	Stanford
(2)	University of California
(3)	Miami University
(4)	University of New York

Referencing the Items Collection

If you need to display one item from a list, you can refer to one element of the Items collection. The Items collection of a list box or combo box holds the text of all list elements. You specify which element you want by including an index. This technique can be useful if you need to display a list item in a label or on another form. Later in this chapter we will use the Items property to send the contents of the list box to the printer.

Using the Items Collection—General Form

```
Object.Items(IndexPosition) [ = Value]
```

The index of the first list element is 0, so the highest index is Items.Count – 1. You can retrieve the value of a list element or set an element to a new value.

Using the Items Collection—Examples

```
schoolsListBox.Items(2) = "University of California"
majorLabel.Text = majorsComboBox.Items(indexInteger)
selectedMajorLabel.Text = majorsComboBox.Items(majorsComboBox.SelectedIndex)
selectedMajorLabel.Text = majorsComboBox.Text
```

To refer to the currently selected element of a list, you must combine the Items property and the SelectedIndex property:

```
selectedFlavorString = flavorListBox.Items(flavorListBox.SelectedIndex).ToString()
```

You also can retrieve the selected list item by referring to the Text property of the control:

```
selectedMajorLabel.Text = majorsComboBox.Text
```

Note that if you assign a value to a particular item, you replace the previous contents of that position. For example,

```
schoolsListBox.Items(0) = "My School"
```

places "My School" into the first position, replacing whatever was there already. It does not insert the item into the list or increase the value in Items.Count.

Removing an Item from a List

You can remove individual items from a list, by specifying either the index of the item or the text of the item. Use the **Items.RemoveAt method** to remove an item by index and the **Items.Remove method** to remove by specifying the text.

The Items.RemoveAt Method—General Form

```
Object.Items.RemoveAt(IndexPosition)
```

The index is required; it specifies which element to remove. The index of the first list element is 0, and the index of the last element is Items.Count – 1. If you specify an invalid index, the system throws an IndexOutOfRange exception.

The Items.RemoveAt Method—Examples

```
' Remove the first name from the list.
namesListBox.Items.RemoveAt(0)
' Remove the item in position indexInteger.
schoolsComboBox.Items.RemoveAt(indexInteger)
' Remove the currently selected item.
coffeeComboBox.Items.RemoveAt(coffeeComboBox.SelectedIndex)
```

The Items.Remove Method—General Form

```
Object.Items.Remove(TextString)
```

The `Items.Remove` method looks for the named string in the Items collection. If the string is found, it is removed; however, if it is not found, no exception is generated.

The Items.Remove Method—Examples

```
' Remove the specified item.
namesListBox.Items.Remove("My School")
' Remove the matching item.
schoolsComboBox.Items.Remove(schoolTextBox.Text)
' Remove the currently selected item.
coffeeComboBox.Items.Remove(coffeeComboBox.Text)
```

If you remove the currently selected item using either the `RemoveAt` or `Remove` method, make your code more efficient and easier to read by using the `With` statement.

```
With coffeeComboBox
    If .SelectedIndex <> -1 Then
        .Items.RemoveAt(.SelectedIndex)   'Remove by Index
        '.Items.Remove(.Text)             'Alternate -- remove by Text
    Else
        MessageBox.Show("First select the coffee to remove", "No selection made", _
            MessageBoxButtons.OK, MessageBoxIcon.Exclamation)
    End If
End With
```

Clearing a List

In addition to removing individual items at run time, you also can clear all items from a list. Use the **Items.Clear method** to empty a combo box or list box.

The Items.Clear Method—General Form

```
Object.Items.Clear()
```

The Clear Method—Examples

```
schoolsListBox.Items.Clear()
majorsComboBox.Items.Clear()
```

```
' Confirm clearing the majors list.
Dim responseDialogResult As DialogResult

responseDialogResult = MessageBox.Show("Clear the majors list?", "Clear Majors List", _
    MessageBoxButtons.YesNo, MessageBoxIcon.Question)

If responseDialogResult = DialogResult.Yes Then
    majorsComboBox.Items.Clear()
End If
```

List Box and Combo Box Events

Later in the chapter we will perform actions in event procedures for events of list boxes and combo boxes. Some useful events are the SelectedIndexChanged, TextChanged, Enter, and Leave.

Note: Although we haven't used these events up until this point, many other controls have similar events. For example, you can code event procedures for the Enter, Leave, and TextChanged events of text boxes.

The TextChanged Event

As the user types text into the text box portion of a combo box, the TextChanged event occurs. Each keystroke generates another TextChanged event. A list box does not have a TextChanged event, because list boxes do not have associated text boxes.

The Enter Event

When a control receives the focus, an Enter event occurs. As the user tabs from control to control, an Enter event fires for each control. Later you will learn to make any existing text appear selected when the user tabs to a text box or the text portion of a combo box.

The Leave Event

You also can write code for the Leave event of a control. When the user tabs from one control to another, the Leave event is triggered as the control loses focus, before the Enter event of the next control. Programmers often use Leave event procedures to validate input data.

> **✔ TIP**
>
> To write a procedure for an event that isn't the default event, you cannot just double-click the control. Instead, in the Editor window, select the control name in the Class Name list (at the top-left of the window), drop down the Method Name list, and select the event for which you want to write code. The Editor will create the procedure header for you. ■

Feedback 7.1

Describe the purpose of each of the following methods or properties for a ListBox or ComboBox control.

1. Sorted
2. SelectedIndex
3. Items
4. DropDownStyle
5. Items.Count
6. Items.Add
7. Items.Insert
8. Items.Clear
9. Items.RemoveAt
10. Items.Remove

Do/Loops

Until now, there has been no way to repeat the same steps in a procedure without calling them a second time. The computer is capable of repeating a group of instructions many times without calling the procedure for each new set of data. The process of repeating a series of instructions is called *looping*. The group of repeated instructions is called a **loop**. An **iteration** is a single execution of the statement(s) in the loop. In this section, you will learn about the

`Do/Loop`. Later in this chapter, you will learn about another type of loop: a `For/Next` loop.

A **Do/Loop** terminates based on a condition that you specify. Execution of a `Do/Loop` continues *while* a condition is True or *until* a condition is True. You can choose to place the condition at the top or the bottom of the loop. Use a `Do/Loop` when the exact number of iterations is unknown.

Align the **Do and Loop statements** with each other and indent the lines of code to be repeated in between.

The Do and Loop Statements—General Forms

```
Do {While | Until} Condition
    ' Statements in loop.

Loop

or

Do
    ' Statements in loop.

Loop {While | Until} Condition
```

The first form of the `Do/Loop` tests for completion at the top of the loop. With this type of loop, also called a **pretest**, the statements inside the loop may never be executed if the terminating condition is True the first time it is tested.

Example

```
totalInteger = 0
Do Until totalInteger = 0
    ' Statements in loop.
Loop
```

Because totalInteger is 0 the first time the condition is tested, the condition is True and the statements inside the loop will not execute. Control will pass to the statement following the `Loop` statement.

The second form of the `Do/Loop` tests for completion at the bottom of the loop, which means that the statements inside the loop will *always* be executed at least once. This form of loop is sometimes called a **posttest**. Changing the example to a posttest, you can see the difference.

```
totalInteger = 0
Do
    ' Statements in loop.

Loop Until totalInteger = 0
```

In this case the statements inside the loop will be executed at least once. Assuming the value for totalInteger does not change inside the loop, the condition (totalInteger = 0) will be True the first time it is tested and control will pass to the first statement following the `Loop` statement. Figure 7.6 shows flowcharts of pretest and posttest loops, using both `While` and `Until`.

Flowcharts of pretest and posttest loops.

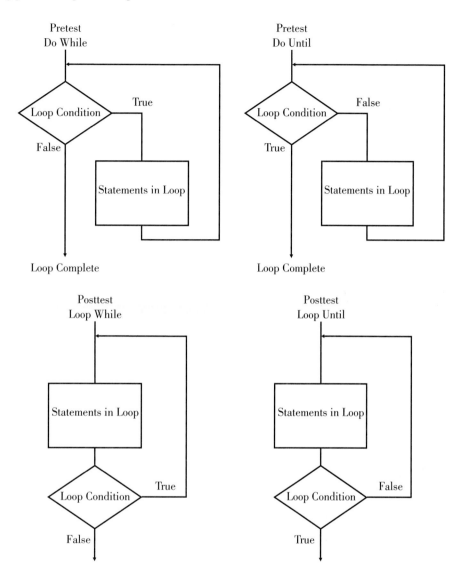

The Do and Loop Statements—Examples

```
Do Until itemIndexInteger = itemsListBox.Items.Count — 1
    ' Statements in loop.

Loop

Do While amountDecimal >= 10D And amountDecimal <= 20D
    ' Statements in loop.

Loop

Do
    ' Statements in loop.

Loop Until totalInteger < 0
```

The Boolean Data Type Revisited

In Chapter 2 you learned about the Boolean data type, which holds only the values True or False. You will find Boolean variables very useful when setting and testing conditions for a loop. You can set a Boolean variable to True when a specific circumstance occurs and then write a loop condition to continue until the variable is True.

An example of using a Boolean variable is when you want to search through a list for a specific value. The item may be found or not found, and you want to quit looking when a match is found.

Using a Boolean variable is usually a three-step process. First, you must dimension a variable and set its initial value (or use the default VB setting of False). Then, when a particular situation occurs, you set the variable to True. A loop condition can then check for True.

```
Dim itemFoundBoolean as Boolean = False

Do Until itemFoundBoolean ' Checks for True.
    ...
```

A Boolean variable is always in one of two states: True or False. Many programmers refer to Boolean variables as *switches* or *flags*. Switches have two states: on or off; flags are considered either up or down.

Using a Do/Loop with a List Box

This small example combines a Boolean variable with a `Do/Loop`. Inside the loop, each element of the list is compared to newItemTextBox.Text for a match. The loop will terminate when a match is found or when all elements have been tested. Follow through the logic to see what happens when there is a match, when there isn't a match, when the match occurs on the first list element, and when the match occurs on the last list element.

```
Private Sub findButton_Click(ByVal sender As System.Object, _
  ByVal e As System.EventArgs) Handles findButton.Click

    ' Look for a match between text box and list items.
    Dim itemFoundBoolean As Boolean = False
    Dim itemIndexInteger As Integer = 0

    Do Until itemFoundBoolean Or itemIndexInteger = itemsListBox.Items.Count
        If newItemTextBox.Text = itemsListBox.Items(itemIndexInteger).ToString() Then
            itemFoundBoolean = True    ' A match was found.
        End If
        itemIndexInteger += 1
    Loop

    If itemFoundBoolean Then
        MessageBox.Show("Item is in the list", "Item match", _
            MessageBoxButtons.OK, MessageBoxIcon.Information)
    Else
        MessageBox.Show("Item is not is the list", "No item match", _
            MessageBoxButtons.OK, MessageBoxIcon.Information)
    End If
End Sub
```

Feedback 7.2

Explain the purpose of each line of the following code:

```
itemFoundBoolean = False
itemIndexInteger = 0
Do Until itemFoundBoolean Or itemIndexInteger = itemsListBox.Items.Count
    If newItemTextBox.Text = itemsListBox.Items(itemIndexInteger).ToString() Then
        itemFoundBoolean = True
    End If
    itemIndexInteger += 1
Loop
```

For/Next Loops

When you want to repeat the statements in a loop a specific number of times, the **For/Next loop** is ideal. The For/Next loop uses the **For and Next statements** and a counter variable, called the *loop index*. The loop index is tested to determine the number of times the statements inside the loop will execute.

```
Dim loopIndexInteger as Integer
Dim maximumInteger as Integer
maximumInteger = schoolsListBox.Items.Count − 1

For loopIndexInteger = 0 To maximumInteger
    'The statements inside of the loop are indented
    ' and referred to as the body of the loop
Next loopIndexInteger
```

When the For statement is reached during program execution, several things occur. The loop index, loopIndexInteger, is established as the loop counter and is initialized to 0 (the initial value). The final value for the loop index is set to the value of maximumInteger, which was assigned the value of schoolsListBox.Items.Count −1 in the previous statement.

Execution is now "controlled by" the For statement. After the value of loopIndexInteger is set, it is tested to see whether loopIndexInteger is greater than maximumInteger. If not, the statements in the body of the loop are executed. The Next statement causes the loopIndexInteger to be incremented by 1. Then control passes back to the For statement. Is the value of loopIndex-Integer greater than maximumInteger? If not, the loop is again executed. When the test is made and the loop index *is* greater than the final value, control passes to the statement immediately following the Next.

A counter-controlled loop generally has three elements (see Figure 7.7 for a flowchart of loop logic):

1. Initialize the counter.
2. Increment the counter.
3. Test the counter to determine when it is time to terminate the loop.

Figure   7.7

A flowchart of the logic of a For/Next *loop.*

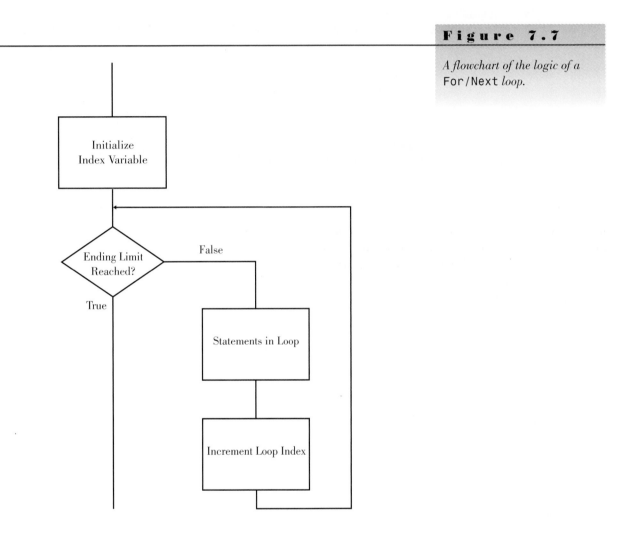

The For and Next Statements—General Form

```
For LoopIndex = InitialValue To TestValue [Step Increment]
    '
    ' Statements in loop.
    '
Next [LoopIndex]
```

LoopIndex must be a numeric variable; InitialValue and TestValue may be constants, variables, numeric property values, or numeric expressions. The optional word Step may be included, along with the value to be added to the loop index for each iteration of the loop. When the Step is omitted, the increment is assumed to be 1.

The For and Next Statements—Examples

Examples

```
For indexInteger = 2 To 100 Step 2
For countInteger = startInteger To endInteger Step incrementInteger
For countInteger = 0 To coffeeComboBoxType.Items.Count − 1
For numberInteger = (numberCorrectInteger − 5) To totalPossibleInteger
For rateDecimal = 0.05 To 0.25 Step 0.05D
For countDownInteger = 10 To 0 Step −1
```

Each `For` statement has a corresponding `Next` statement, which must follow the `For`. All statements between the `For` and `Next` statements are considered to be the body of the loop and will be executed the specified number of times.

The first `For` statement example will count from 2 to 100 by 2. The statements in the body of the loop will be executed 50 times—first with indexInteger = 2, next with indexInteger = 4, next with indexInteger = 6, and so forth.

When the comparison is done, the program checks for *greater than* the test value—not equal to. When indexInteger = 100 in the preceding example, the body of the loop will be executed one more time. Then, at the `Next` statement, indexInteger will be incremented to 102, the test will be made, and control will pass to the statement following the `Next`. If you were to display the value of indexInteger after completion of the loop, its value would be 102.

Note: New to VB .NET 2003, you can declare the loop index variable in the `For` statement. The scope of the variable is block level, so it is available only inside the `For`/`Next` loop. Example:

> ✅**TIP**
>
> **U**se a `For`/`Next` loop when you know the number of iterations needed for the loop. Use a `Do`/`Loop` when the loop should end based on a condition. ∎

```
For indexInteger As Integer = 1 to 10
    ' Statements in loop.
Next indexInteger
```

Negative Increment or Counting Backward

You can use a negative number for the `Step` increment to decrease the loop index rather than increase it. When the `Step` is negative, VB tests for *less than* the test value instead of greater than.

```
' Count Backwards.
For countInteger = 10 To 1 Step −1
    ' Statements in body of loop.
Next countInteger
```

Conditions Satisfied before Entry

At times the final value will be reached before entry into the loop. In that case, the statements in the body of the loop will not be executed at all.

```
' An unexecutable loop.
finalInteger = 5
For indexInteger = 6 to finalInteger
    ' The execution will never reach here.
Next indexInteger
```

Altering the Values of the Loop Control Variables

Once a For loop has been entered, the values for InitialValue, TestValue, and Increment have already been set. Changing the value of these control variables within the loop will have no effect on the number of iterations of the loop. Many texts admonish against changing the values within the loop. However, Visual Basic just ignores you if you try.

```
' Bad Example--Changing the Control Variable.
finalInteger = 10
increaseInteger = 2
For indexInteger = 1 to finalInteger Step increaseInteger
    finalInteger = 25
    increaseInteger = 5
Next indexInteger
```

If you tried this example and displayed the values of indexInteger, you would find that the final value will remain 10 and the increment value will be 2.

The value that you *can* change within the loop is the loop index. However, this practice is considered poor programming.

```
' Poor Programming.
For indexInteger = 1 To 10 Step 1
    indexInteger += 5
Next indexInteger
```

Endless Loops

Changing the value of a loop index variable is not only considered a poor practice but also may lead to an endless loop. Your code could get into a loop that is impossible to exit. Consider the following example; when will the loop end?

```
' More Poor Programming.
For indexInteger = 1 To 10 Step 1
    indexInteger = 1
Next indexInteger
```

Exiting For/Next Loops

In the previous example of an endless loop, you will have to break the program execution manually. You can click on your form's close box or use the Visual Basic menu bar or toolbar to stop the program. If you can't see the menu bar or toolbar, you can usually move or resize your application's form to bring it into view. If you prefer, press Ctrl + Break to enter break time; you may want to step program execution to see what is causing the problem.

Usually For/Next loops should proceed to normal completion. However, on occasion you may need to terminate a loop before the loop index reaches its final value. Visual Basic provides an Exit For statement for this situation. Generally, the Exit For statement is part of an If statement.

The Exit For Statement—General Form

```
Exit For
```

The Exit For Statement—Example

```
For loopIndexInteger = 1 to 10
    If inputTextBox.Text = "" Then ' Nothing was entered into the input textbox.
        MessageBox.Show("You must enter something.")
        Exit For
    End If
    ... ' Statements in loop.
Next loopIndexInteger
```

Feedback 7.3

1. Identify the statements that are correctly formed and those that have errors. For those with errors, state what is wrong and how to correct it.
   (a) ```
       For indexDecimal = 3.5 To 6.0, Step 0.5D
           Next indexDecimal
       ```
   (b) ```
       For indexInteger = beginInteger To endInteger Step incrementInteger
           Next endInteger
       ```
   (c) ```
       For 4 = 1 To 10 Step 2
           Next For
       ```
   (d) ```
       For indexInteger = 100 To 0 Step −25
           Next indexInteger
       ```
   (e) ```
       For indexInteger = 0 To −10 Step −1
           Next indexInteger
       ```
   (f) ```
       For indexInteger = 10 To 1
           Next indexInteger
       ```

2. How many times will the body of the loop be executed for each of these examples? What will be the value of the loop index after normal completion of the loop?
   (a) `For countInteger = 1 To 3`
   (b) `For countInteger = 2 To 11 Step 3`
   (c) `For countInteger = 10 To 1 Step −1`
   (d) `For counterDecimal = 3.0 To 6.0 Step 0.5D`
   (e) `For countInteger = 5 To 1`

Making Entries Appear Selected

You can use several techniques to make the text in a text box or list appear selected.

Selecting the Entry in a Text Box

When the user tabs into a text box that already has an entry, how do you want
the text to appear? Should the insertion point appear at either the left or right
end of the text? Or should the entire entry appear selected? You also can apply
this question to a text box that failed validation; shouldn't the entire entry be
selected? The most user-friendly approach is to select the text, which you can
do with the `SelectAll` method of the text box. A good location to do this is in
the text box's Enter event procedure, which occurs when the control receives
the focus.

```
Private Sub nameTextBox_Enter(ByVal sender As Object, _
    ByVal e As System.EventArgs) Handles nameTextBox.Enter
        ' Select any existing text.

        nameTextBox.SelectAll()
End Sub
```

Selecting an Entry in a List Box

You can make a single item in a list box appear selected by setting the
SelectedIndex property.

```
coffeeListBox.SelectedIndex = indexInteger
```

When a list box has a very large number of entries, you can help users by
selecting the matching entry as they type in a text box. This method is similar
to the way the Help Topics list in Visual Basic works. For example, when you
type *p*, the list quickly scrolls and displays words beginning with *p*. Then if you
next type *r*, the list scrolls down to the words that begin with *pr* and the first
such word is selected. If you type *i* next, the first word beginning with *pri* is selected. The following example implements this feature. See if you can tell what
each statement does.

Notice that this is coded in the TextChanged event procedure for the control
into which the user is typing; the event occurs once for every keystroke entered.

```
Private Sub coffeeTextBox_TextChanged(ByVal sender As System.Object, _
    ByVal e As System.EventArgs) Handles coffeeTextBox.TextChanged

    ' Locate first matching occurrence in the list.

    Dim indexInteger As Integer = 0
    Dim foundBoolean As Boolean = False
    Dim listCompareString As String
    Dim textCompareString As String

    Do While Not foundBoolean And indexInteger < coffeeListBox.Items.Count
        listCompareString = coffeeListBox.Items(indexInteger).ToString()
        listCompareString = listCompareString.ToUpper()
        textCompareString = coffeeTextBox.Text.ToUpper()
```

```
        If listCompareString.StartsWith(textCompareString) Then
            coffeeListBox.SelectedIndex = indexInteger
            foundBoolean = True
        End If
        indexInteger += 1
    Loop
End Sub
```

Sending Information to the Printer

So far, all program output has been on the screen. You can use the .NET PrintDocument and PrintPreviewDialog classes to produce output for the printer and also to preview the output on the screen.

Visual Basic was designed to run under Windows, which is a highly interactive environment. It is extremely easy to create forms for interactive programs, but it is not easy at all to print on the printer. Most professional programmers using Visual Basic use a separate utility program to format printer reports. Several companies sell utilities that do a nice job of designing and printing reports. The VB Professional Edition and Enterprise Edition include Crystal Reports for creating reports from database files.

The PrintDocument Component

You set up output for the printer using the methods and events of the **PrintDocument component**. Add a PrintDocument component to a form; the component appears in the component tray below the form (Figure 7.8).

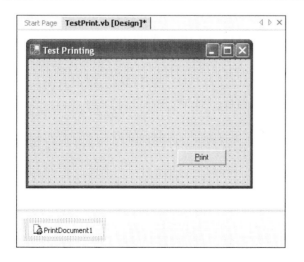

Figure 7.8

Add a PrintDocument component to your application. The component appears in the form's component tray.

Beginning the Print Operation

To start printing output, you execute the **Print method** of the PrintDocument component. This code belongs in the Click event procedure for the Print button or menu item that the user selects to begin printing.

```
Private Sub printButton_Click(ByVal sender As System.Object, _
    ByVal e As System.EventArgs) Handles printButton.Click
    ' Print output on the printer.

    PrintDocument1.Print()          ' Start the print process.
End Sub
```

Setting Up the Print Output

The logic for the actual printing belongs in the PrintDocument's **PrintPage event procedure**. The PrintPage event is fired once for each page to be printed. This technique is referred to as a *callback*, and is different from anything we have done so far. In a callback, the object notifies the program that it needs to do something or that a situation exists that the program needs to handle. The object notifies the program of the situation by firing an event.

The PrintDocument object is activated when you issue its `Print` method. It then fires a PrintPage event for each page to print. It also fires events for BeginPrint and EndPrint, for which you can write code if you wish.

```
Private Sub PrintDocument1_PrintPage(ByVal sender As Object, _
    ByVal e As System.Drawing.Printing.PrintPageEventArgs) _
    Handles PrintDocument1.PrintPage
    ' Set up actual output to print.

End Sub
```

Notice the argument: `e As System.Drawing.Printing.PrintPage-EventArgs`. We will use some of the properties and methods of the `Print-PageEventArgs` argument for such things as determining the page margins and sending a string of text to the page.

The Graphics Page

You set up a graphics page in memory and then the page is sent to the printer. The graphics page can contain strings of text as well as graphic elements.

You must specify the exact location on the graphics page for each element that you want to print. You can specify the upper-left corner of any element by giving its X and Y coordinates, or by using a Point structure or a Rectangle structure. We will stick with the X and Y coordinates in these examples (Figure 7.9).

You can use multiple PrintDocument objects if you have more than one type of output or report. Each PrintDocument has its own PrintPage event. Code the graphics commands to precisely print the page in each document's PrintPage event procedure.

Using the DrawString Method

You use the **DrawString method** to send a line of text to the graphics page. The DrawString method belongs to the Graphics object of the `PrintPage-EventArgs` argument. Refer back to the procedure header for the PrintPage event in "Setting Up the Print Output."

The DrawString Method—General Form

The `DrawString` method is overloaded, which means that there are several forms for calling the method. The form presented here is the least complicated and requires that page coordinates be given in X and Y format.

Figure 7.9

The X coordinate is the horizontal distance across a line from the left edge of the page; the Y coordinate is the vertical distance from the top of the page. The measurements are in pixels.

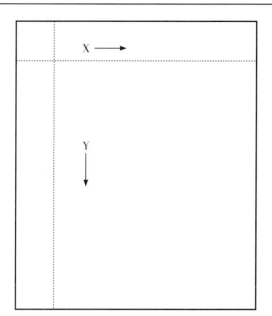

General Form

```
DrawString(StringToPrint, Font, Brush, xSingle, ySingle)
```

You supply the arguments of the `DrawString` method: what to print, what font and color to print it in, and where to print it.

The DrawString Method—Examples

Examples

```
e.Graphics.DrawString(printLineString, printFont, Brushes.Black, _
    horizontalPrintLocationSingle, verticalPrintLocationSingle)
e.Graphics.DrawString("My text string", myFont, Brushes.Black, 100.0, 100.0)
e.Graphics.DrawString(nameTextBox.Text, New Font("Arial", 10), Brushes.Red, _
    leftMarginSingle, currentLineSingle)
```

Before you execute the `DrawString` method, you should set up the font that you want to use and the X and Y coordinates.

Setting the X and Y Coordinates

For each line that you want to print, you must specify the X and Y coordinates. It is helpful to set up some variables for setting these values, which should be declared as Single data type.

```
Dim horizontalPrintLocationSingle As Single
Dim verticalPrintLocationSingle As Single
```

The PrintPageEventArgs argument has several useful properties (Figure 7.10), such as MarginBounds, PageBounds, and PageSettings. You can use these properties to determine present settings. For example, you may want to set the X coordinate to the current left margin and the Y coordinate to the top margin.

Figure 7.10

Use the properties of the
PrintPageEventArgs argument
to determine the current
margin settings.

```
horizontalPrintLocationSingle = e.MarginBounds.Left
verticalPrintLocationSingle = e.MarginBounds.Top
```

To send multiple lines to the print page, you must increment the Y coordinate. You can add the height of a line to the previous Y coordinate to calculate the next line's Y coordinate.

```
' Declarations at the top of the procedure.
Dim printFont As New Font("Arial", 12)
Dim lineHeightSingle As Single = printFont.GetHeight
' ... More declarations here.

' Print a line.
e.Graphics.DrawString(printLineString, printFont, Brushes.Black, _
   horizontalPrintLocationSingle, verticalPrintLocationSingle)
' Increment the Y position for the next line.
verticalPrintLocationSingle += lineHeightSingle
```

Printing the Contents of a List Box

You can combine the techniques for printing, a loop, and the list box properties to send the contents of a list box to the printer. You know how many iterations to make, using the Items.Count property. The Items collection allows you to print out the actual values from the list.

```
' Print out all items in the coffeeComboBox list.
For listIndexInteger = 0 To coffeeComboBox.Items.Count - 1
   ' Set up a line.
   printLineString = coffeeComboBox.Items(listIndexInteger).ToString()
   ' Send the line to the graphics page object.
   e.Graphics.DrawString(printLineString, printFont, Brushes.Black, _
      horizontalPrintLocationSingle, verticalPrintLocationSingle)

   ' Increment the Y position for the next line.
   verticalPrintLocationSingle += lineHeightSingle
Next listIndexInteger
```

Printing the Selected Item from a List

When an item is selected in a list box or a combo box, the Text property holds the selected item. You can use the Text property to print the selected item.

```
' Set up the line for the list selections.
printLineString = "Coffee: " & coffeeComboBox.Text & "  Syrup: " & syrupListBox.Text
' Send the line to the graphics page object.
e.Graphics.DrawString(printLineString, printFont, Brushes.Black, _
    horizontalPrintLocationSingle, verticalPrintLocationSingle)
```

Aligning Decimal Columns

When the output to the printer includes numeric data, the alignment of the decimal points is important. Alignment can be tricky with proportional fonts, where the width of each character varies. The best approach is to format each number as you want it to print and then measure the length of the formatted string. This technique requires a couple more elements: You need an object declared as a SizeF structure, which has a Width property, and you need to use the MeasureString method of the Graphics class. Both the SizeF structure and the MeasureString method work with pixels, which is what you want. It's the same unit of measure as used for the X and Y coordinates of the DrawString method.

The following example prints a left-aligned literal at position 200 on the line and right-aligns a formatted number at position 500. (Assume that all variables are properly declared.)

```
' SizeF structure for font size info.
Dim fontSizeF As New SizeF()

' Set X for left-aligned column.
horizontalPrintLocationSingle = 200
' Set ending position for right-aligned column.
columnEndSingle = 500

' Format the number.
formattedOutputString = amountDecimal.ToString("C")

' Calculate the X position of the amount.

' Measure string in this font.
fontSizeF = e.Graphics.MeasureString(formattedOutputString, printFont)
' Subtract width of string from the column position.
columnXSingle = columnEndSingle - fontSizeF.Width

' Set up the line--each element separately.
e.Graphics.DrawString("The Amount = ", printFont, Brushes.Black, _
    horizontalPrintLocationSingle, verticalPrintLocationSingle)
e.Graphics.DrawString(formattedOutputString, printFont, Brushes.Black, _
    columnXSingle, verticalPrintLocationSingle)
' Increment line for next line.
verticalPrintLocationSingle += lineHeightSingle
```

Displaying a Print Preview

A really great feature of the new VB .NET printing model is **print preview**. You can view the printer's output on the screen and then choose to print or cancel. This is especially helpful for testing and debugging a program, so that you don't have to keep sending pages to the printer and wasting paper.

The **PrintPreviewDialog component** is the key to print preview. You add the component to your form's component tray; the default name is Print-PreviewDialog1 (Figure 7.11). Since you can use the same dialog for all print previews, you do not need to name the component.

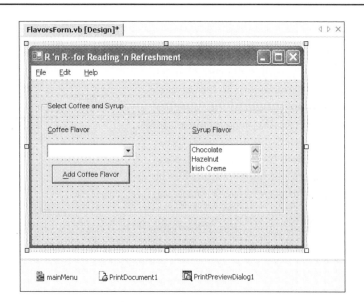

Add a PrintPreviewDialog component to your form's component tray.

You write two lines of code in the event procedure for the button or menu item where the user selects the print preview option. The PrintPreviewDialog class uses the same PrintDocument component that you declared for printer output. You assign the PrintDocument to the Document property of the Print-PreviewDialog and execute the `ShowDialog` method. The same PrintPage event procedure executes as for the PrintDocument.

```
Private Sub filePrintPreviewMenu_Click(ByVal sender As Object, ByVal e As _
    System.EventArgs) Handles filePrintPreviewMenu.Click
    ' Begin the process for print preview.

    PrintPreviewDialog1.Document = PrintDocument1
    PrintPreviewDialog1.ShowDialog()
End Sub
```

Using Static Variables

Static local variables retain their value for as long as the form is loaded, which is generally the life of the project, rather than being reinitialized for each call to the procedure. If you need to retain the value in a variable for multiple calls to a procedure, such as a running total, declare it as `Static`. (In the past we used module-level variables for this task. Using a static local variable is usually better than using a module-level variable because it is best to keep the scope of a variable as narrow as possible.)

When printing multiple pages, you want to know what page you are currently on. This page-number variable can be declared at the local level, but it must retain the value from one execution of the procedure to the next. This is the perfect time to use a static local variable.

```
' Count pages for multiple-page output.
Static pageCountInteger As Integer = 1
```

The format of the Static statement is the same as the format of the Dim statement. However, Static statements can appear only in procedures; Static statements never appear in the Declarations section of a module.

Printing Multiple Pages

You can easily print multiple pages, both to the printer and to the *Print Preview* dialog box. Recall that the PrintDocument's PrintPage event fires once for each page. You indicate that you have more pages to print by setting the HasMore-Pages property of the PrintPageEventArgs argument to True.

The following example prints four pages full of the same line, just to illustrate multiple-page output. Normally you will have a certain amount of data to print and stop when you run out.

```
Private Sub PrintDocument1_PrintPage(ByVal sender As Object, _
  ByVal e As System.Drawing.Printing.PrintPageEventArgs) _
  Handles reportPrintDocument.PrintPage

    ' Print multiple-page output.
    Dim printFont As New Font("Arial", 12)
    Dim lineHeightSingle As Single = printFont.GetHeight + 2
    Dim horizontalPrintLocationSingle As Single = e.MarginBounds.Left
    Dim verticalPrintLocationSingle As Single = e.MarginBounds.Top
    Dim printLineString As String
    ' Count pages for multiple-page output.
    Static pageCountInteger As Integer = 1

    verticalPrintLocationSingle = e.MarginBounds.Top
    printLineString = "This is a line of output"

    ' Print the page number.
    e.Graphics.DrawString("Page " & pageCountInteger.ToString(), printFont, _
      Brushes.Black, 600, verticalPrintLocationSingle)
    verticalPrintLocationSingle += lineHeightSingle * 2

    ' Print a page full of the same line.
    Do
        ' Print a line.
        e.Graphics.DrawString(printLineString, printFont, Brushes.Black, _
          horizontalPrintLocationSingle, verticalPrintLocationSingle)
        verticalPrintLocationSingle += lineHeightSingle
        ' Stop at the bottom margin.
    Loop Until verticalPrintLocationSingle >= e.MarginBounds.Bottom

    ' Increment the page number.
    pageCountInteger += 1

    ' Indicate whether there are more pages to print.
    If pageCountInteger <=4 Then
        e.HasMorePages = True
    Else
        e.HasMorePages = False
        pageCountInteger = 1
    End If
End Sub
```

Feedback 7.4

What is the purpose of each of these elements? Where and how is each used?

1. The PrintDocument component.
2. The `Print` method.
3. The PrintPage event.
4. The `DrawString` method.
5. `System.Drawing.Printing.PrintPageEventArgs`.
6. `MarginBounds.Left`.
7. The PrintPreviewDialog component.

Your Hands-On Programming Example

Create a project for R 'n R—for Reading 'n Refreshment that contains a drop-down combo box of the coffee flavors and a list box of the syrup flavors. Adjust the size of the boxes as needed when you test the project. The controls should have labels above them with the words "Coffee" and "Syrup". Enter the initial values for the syrup flavors and coffee flavors in the Properties window. Set the Sorted property of both lists to True. The user will be able to add more coffee flavors to the list at run time.

Coffee Flavors	Syrup Flavors
Espresso Roast	(None)
Jamaica Blue Mountain	Chocolate
Kona Blend	Hazelnut
Chocolate Almond	Irish Cream
Vanilla Nut	Orange

Include one menu item to print all the flavors and another to print only a selected item from each list. Then include submenus for each of the print options to allow the user to send the output to the printer or the Print Preview window. These print commands belong on the *File* menu, along with the *Exit* command. Use a separator bar between the *Print* and the *Exit*.

Include an *Edit* menu with commands to *Add coffee flavor*, *Remove coffee flavor*, *Clear coffee list*, and *Display coffee count*.

Add an About form to your project and add a *Help* menu with an *About* command.

After you have completed the project, try using different styles for the combo box and rerun the project. As an added challenge, modify the add-coffee-flavor routine so that no duplicates are allowed.

Planning the Project

Sketch a form (Figure 7.12), which your users sign off as meeting their needs.

Figure 7.12

A sketch of the form for the hands-on project.

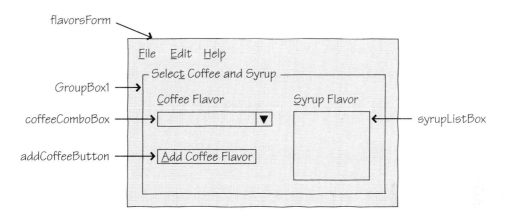

Plan the Objects and Properties

Object	Property	Setting
flavorsForm	Name	flavorsForm
	Text	R 'n R—for Reading 'n Refreshment
GroupBox1	Text	Selec&t Coffee and Syrup
Label1	Text	&Coffee Flavor
Label2	Text	&Syrup Flavor
coffeeComboBox	Name	coffeeComboBox
	DropDownStyle	DropDown
	Items	Chocolate Almond
		Espresso Roast
		Jamaica Blue Mountain
		Kona Blend
		Vanilla Nut
	Sorted	True
	Text	(blank)
syrupListBox	Name	syrupListBox
	Items	(None)
		Chocolate
		Hazelnut
		Irish Creme
		Orange
	Sorted	True
addCoffeeButton	Name	addCoffeeButton
	Text	&Add Coffee Flavor
fileMenu	Name	fileMenu
	Text	&File

Object	Property	Setting
filePrintSelectedMenuItem	Name	filePrintSelectedMenuItem
	Text	Print &Selected Flavors
filePrintSelectedPreviewMenuItem	Name	filePrintSelectedPreviewMenuItem
	Text	Print Pre&view
filePrintSelectedPrintMenuItem	Name	filePrintSelectedPrintMenuItem
	Text	&Print
filePrintAllMenuItem	Name	filePrintAllMenuItem
	Text	Print &All Flavors
filePrintAllPreviewMenuItem	Name	filePrintAllPreviewMenuItem
	Text	Print Pre&view
filePrintAllPrintMenuItem	Name	filePrintAllPrintMenuItem
	Text	&Print
fileExitMenuItem	Name	fileExitMenuItem
	Text	E&xit
editMenu	Name	editMenu
	Text	&Edit
editAddMenuItem	Name	editAddMenuItem
	Text	&Add Coffee Flavor
editRemoveMenuItem	Name	editRemoveMenuItem
	Text	&Remove Coffee Flavor
editClearMenuItem	Name	editClearMenuItem
	Text	&Clear Coffee List
editCountMenuItem	Name	editCountMenuItem
	Text	Count Coffee &List
helpMenu	Name	helpMenu
	Text	&Help
helpAboutMenuItem	Name	helpAboutMenuItem
	Text	&About
printAllPrintDocument	Name	printAllPrintDocument
printSelectedPrintDocument	Name	printSelectedPrintDocument
PrintPreviewDialog1	Name	PrintPreviewDialog1

Plan the Event Procedures

Main Form

Procedure	Actions

addCoffeeButton_Click	If text box in coffeeComboBox not empty then
	    If item is already on the list then
	        Display error message.
	    Else
	        Add contents of coffeeComboBox text box to items.
	        Clear the text box in coffeeComboBox.
	Else
	    Display error message.
	Set the focus to coffeeComboBox.

filePrintSelectedPreviewMenuItem_Click	If both coffee and syrup selected
	    Set Boolean variable for selected item.
	    Set the print preview document.
	    Show the print preview dialog.
	Else
	    Display error message.

filePrintSelectedPrintMenuItem_Click	If both coffee and syrup selected
	    Set Boolean variable for selected item.
	    Start the print operation.
	Else
	    Display error message.

filePrintAllPreviewMenuItem_Click	Set the Boolean variable for entire list. Set the print preview document. Show the print preview dialog.
filePrintAllPrintMenuItem_Click	Set the Boolean variable for entire list. Start the print operation.
printAllPrintDocument_PrintPage	Use a loop to send all flavor names to the printer.

printSelectedPrintDocument_PrintPage	If item is selected
	    Send selected item to the printer.
	Else
	    Display error message.

fileExitMenuItem_Click	Terminate the project.
editAddMenuItem_Click	Add to Handles clause of addCoffeeButton_Click.

editRemoveMenuItem_Click	If coffee flavor selected then
	    Remove selected item.
	Else
	    Display error message.

editClearMenuItem_Click	Display a message box to confirm the clear. If user clicks Yes Clear the coffee list.
editCountMenuItem_Click	Display list count in message box.
helpAboutMenuItem_Click	Display the About box.

About Form	
Procedure	**Actions**
okButton_Click	Close the About box.

Write the Project Follow the sketch in Figure 7.12 to create the form. Figure 7.13 shows the completed form.

- Set the properties of each object as you have planned.

- Write the code. Working from the pseudocode, write each event procedure.

- When you complete the code, use a variety of data to thoroughly test the project.

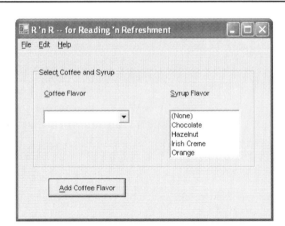

Figure 7.13

The main form for the hands-on project.

The Project Coding Solution

Main Form

```
'Class:        FlavorsForm
'Programmer:   Bradley/Millspaugh
'Date:         January 2004
'Description:  Maintain a list of coffee flavors; print the selected flavor
'              of coffee and syrup or print a list of all of the
'              coffee flavors.
'Folder:       Ch0701

Option Strict On

Public Class FlavorsForm
 Inherits System.Windows.Forms.Form

    Private Sub addCoffeeButton_Click(ByVal sender As System.Object, _
        ByVal e As System.EventArgs) _
        Handles addCoffeeButton.Click, editAddMenuItem.Click
        ' Add a new coffee flavor to the coffee list.
```

```vb
        With coffeeComboBox
            ' Test for blank input.
            If .Text <> "" Then
                ' Make sure item is not already on the list.
                Dim itemFoundBoolean As Boolean
                Dim itemIndexInteger As Integer
                Do Until itemFoundBoolean Or itemIndexInteger = coffeeComboBox.Items.Count
                    If .Text = .Items(itemIndexInteger).ToString() Then
                        itemFoundBoolean = True
                    End If
                    itemIndexInteger += 1
                Loop
                If itemFoundBoolean Then
                    MessageBox.Show("Duplicate item", "Add Failed")
                Else
                    ' If it's not in the list, add it.
                    .Items.Add(.Text)
                    .Text = ""
                End If
            Else
                MessageBox.Show("Enter a coffee flavor to add", _
                    "Missing data", MessageBoxButtons.OK, _
                    MessageBoxIcon.Exclamation)
            End If
            coffeeComboBox.Focus()
        End With
    End Sub

    Private Sub filePrintAllPrintMenuItem_Click(ByVal sender As System.Object, _
      ByVal e As System.EventArgs) Handles filePrintAllPrintMenuItem.Click
        ' Begin the print process to print all items.

        printAllPrintDocument.Print()
    End Sub

    Private Sub filePrintAllPreviewMenuItem_Click(ByVal sender As System.Object, _
      ByVal e As System.EventArgs) Handles filePrintAllPreviewMenuItem.Click
        ' Begin the process for print preview of all items.

        PrintPreviewDialog1.Document = printAllPrintDocument
        PrintPreviewDialog1.ShowDialog()
    End Sub

    Private Sub filePrintSelectedPrintMenuItem_Click(ByVal sender As Object, _
      ByVal e As System.EventArgs) Handles filePrintSelectedPrintMenuItem.Click
        ' Begin the print process to print the selected item.

        If syrupListBox.SelectedIndex = -1 Then
            ' Select (None) if nothing selected.
            syrupListBox.SelectedIndex = 0
        End If
        If coffeeComboBox.SelectedIndex <> -1 Then
            ' Items selected.
            printSelectedPrintDocument.Print()
        Else
            ' No item selected.
            MessageBox.Show("Select a flavor from the coffee list", _
                "Print Selection", MessageBoxButtons.OK, MessageBoxIcon.Exclamation)
        End If
    End Sub
```

```vbnet
Private Sub filePrintSelectPreviewMenuItem_Click(ByVal sender As Object, _
  ByVal e As System.EventArgs) Handles filePrintSelectedPreviewMenuItem.Click
    ' Begin the process for print preview of the selected item.

    If syrupListBox.SelectedIndex = -1 Then
        ' Select (None) if nothing selected.
        syrupListBox.SelectedIndex = 0
    End If
    If coffeeComboBox.SelectedIndex <> -1 Then
        ' Item selected.
        PrintPreviewDialog1.Document = printSelectedPrintDocument
        PrintPreviewDialog1.ShowDialog()
    Else
        ' No item selected.
        MessageBox.Show("Select a flavor from the coffee list", "Print Selection", _
          MessageBoxButtons.OK, MessageBoxIcon.Exclamation)
    End If
End Sub

Private Sub printAllPrintDocument_PrintPage(ByVal sender As Object, _
  ByVal e As System.Drawing.Printing.PrintPageEventArgs) _
  Handles printAllPrintDocument.PrintPage
    ' Handle printing and print previews when printing all.

    Dim printFont As New Font("Arial", 12)
    Dim headingFont As New Font("Arial", 14, FontStyle.Bold)
    Dim lineHeightSingle As Single = printFont.GetHeight + 2
    Dim horizontalPrintLocationSingle As Single = e.MarginBounds.Left
    Dim verticalPrintLocationSingle As Single = e.MarginBounds.Top
    Dim printLineString As String
    Dim listIndexInteger As Integer

    ' Loop through the entire list.
    For listIndexInteger = 0 To coffeeComboBox.Items.Count - 1

        ' Set up a line.
        printLineString = coffeeComboBox.Items(listIndexInteger).ToString()
        ' Send the line to the graphics page object.
        e.Graphics.DrawString(printLineString, printFont, _
          Brushes.Black, horizontalPrintLocationSingle, verticalPrintLocationSingle)
        ' Increment the Y position for the next line.
        verticalPrintLocationSingle += lineHeightSingle
    Next listIndexInteger
End Sub

Private Sub printSelectedPrintDocument_PrintPage(ByVal sender As Object, _
  ByVal e As System.Drawing.Printing.PrintPageEventArgs) _
  Handles printSelectedPrintDocument.PrintPage
    ' Handle printing and print previews when printing selected items.

    Dim printFont As New Font("Arial", 12)
    Dim headingFont As New Font("Arial", 14, FontStyle.Bold)
    Dim lineHeightSingle As Single = printFont.GetHeight + 2
    Dim horizontalPrintLocationSingle As Single = e.MarginBounds.Left
    Dim verticalPrintLocationSingle As Single = e.MarginBounds.Top
    Dim printLineString As String
    Dim listIndexInteger As Integer
```

```
        ' Set up and display heading lines.
        printLineString = "Print Selected Item"
        e.Graphics.DrawString(printLineString, headingFont, _
            Brushes.Black, horizontalPrintLocationSingle, verticalPrintLocationSingle)
        printLineString = "by Programmer Name"
        verticalPrintLocationSingle += lineHeightSingle
        e.Graphics.DrawString(printLineString, headingFont, _
            Brushes.Black, horizontalPrintLocationSingle, verticalPrintLocationSingle)

        ' Leave a blank line between the heading and detail line.
        verticalPrintLocationSingle += lineHeightSingle * 2
        ' Set up the selected line.
        printLineString = "Coffee: " & coffeeComboBox.Text & _
            "  Syrup: " & syrupListBox.Text
        ' Send the line to the graphics page object.
        e.Graphics.DrawString(printLineString, printFont, _
            Brushes.Black, horizontalPrintLocationSingle, verticalPrintLocationSingle)
End Sub

Public Sub fileExitMenuItem_Click(ByVal sender As System.Object, _
    ByVal e As System.EventArgs) Handles fileExitMenuItem.Click
        ' Terminate the project.

    Me.Close()
End Sub

Public Sub editClearMenuItem_Click(ByVal sender As System.Object, _
    ByVal e As System.EventArgs) Handles editClearMenuItem.Click
        ' Clear the coffee list.
        Dim responseDialogResult As DialogResult

        responseDialogResult = MessageBox.Show("Clear the coffee flavor list?", _
            "Clear coffee list", MessageBoxButtons.YesNo, MessageBoxIcon.Question)
        If responseDialogResult = DialogResult.Yes Then
            coffeeComboBox.Items.Clear()
        End If
End Sub

Public Sub editRemoveMenuItem_Click(ByVal sender As System.Object, _
    ByVal e As System.EventArgs) Handles editRemoveMenuItem.Click
        ' Remove the selected coffee from list.

    With coffeeComboBox
        If .SelectedIndex <> -1 Then
            .Items.RemoveAt(.SelectedIndex)
        Else
            MessageBox.Show("First select the coffee to remove", _
                "No selection made", MessageBoxButtons.OK, _
                MessageBoxIcon.Exclamation)
        End If
    End With
End Sub

Public Sub editCountMenuItem_Click(ByVal sender As System.Object, _
    ByVal e As System.EventArgs) Handles editCountMenuItem.Click
        ' Display a count of the coffee list.

    MessageBox.Show("The number of coffee types is " & _
        coffeeComboBox.Items.Count)
End Sub
```

```
    Public Sub helpAboutMenuItem_Click(ByVal sender As System.Object, _
      ByVal e As System.EventArgs) Handles helpAboutMenuItem.Click
        ' Display AboutForm.
        Dim anAboutForm As New AboutForm

        anAboutForm.Show()
    End Sub
End Class
```

About Form

```
'Class:        AboutForm
'Programmer:   Bradley/Millspaugh
'Date:         January 2004
'Description:  Display information about the program
'              and the programmer.
'Folder:       Ch0701

Public Class AboutForm
    Inherits System.Windows.Forms.Form

    Private Sub okButton_Click(ByVal sender As System.Object, ByVal e _
      As System.EventArgs) Handles okButton.Click
        ' Return to the main form.

        Me.Close()
    End Sub
End Class
```

Summary

1. List boxes and combo boxes hold lists of values. The three styles of combo boxes are simple combo boxes, drop-down combo boxes, and drop-down lists.
2. The size of a list box or combo box is determined at design time. If all of the items will not fit into the box, VB automatically adds scroll bars.
3. The values for the items in a list are stored in the Items property, which is a collection. The items can be entered in the Items property in the Properties window. At run time, items are added to lists using the `Items.Add` or `Items.Insert` method.
4. The SelectedIndex property can be used to select an item in the list or to determine which item is selected.
5. The Items.Count property holds the number of elements in the list.
6. The Items collection holds all elements of the list. The individual elements can be referenced by using an index.
7. The `Items.Remove` and `Items.RemoveAt` methods remove one element from a list.
8. The `Items.Clear` method may be used to clear all of the contents of a list box's Items collection at once.

9. Code can be written for several events of list boxes and combo boxes. Combo boxes have a TextChanged event; both combo boxes and list boxes have Enter and Leave events.

10. A loop allows a statement or series of statements to be repeated. Do/Loops continue to execute the statements in the loop until a condition is met. Each pass through a loop is called an iteration.

11. Do/Loops can have the condition test at the top or the bottom of the loop and can use a While or Until to test the condition.

12. A Do/Loop can be used to locate a selected item in a combo box.

13. A loop index controls For/Next loops; the index is initialized to an initial value. After each iteration, the loop index is incremented by the Step value (the increment), which defaults to 1. The loop is terminated when the loop index is greater than the ending value.

14. The PrintDocument component and the PrintPreviewDialog component can be used to send program output to the printer or the screen.

15. The Print method of the PrintDialog control begins a print operation. The control's PrintPage event fires once for each page to print. All printing logic belongs in the PrintPage event procedure. The PrintPage event continues to fire as long as the HasMorePages property of the PrintDocument component has a value of True.

16. The page to print or display is a graphics object. Use the DrawString method to send a string of text to the page, specifying X and Y coordinates for the string.

17. Aligning columns of numbers is difficult using proportional fonts. Numbers can be right-aligned by formatting the number, measuring the length of the formatted string in pixels, and subtracting the length from the right end of the column for the X coordinate.

Key Terms

Review Questions

1. What is a list box? a combo box?
2. Name and describe the three styles of combo boxes.
3. How can you make scroll bars appear on a list box or combo box?
4. Explain the purpose of the SelectedIndex property and the Items.Count property.
5. When and how is information placed inside a list box or a combo box?
6. In what situation would a loop be used in a procedure?
7. Explain the difference between a pretest and a posttest in a Do/Loop.
8. Explain the differences between a Do/Loop and a For/Next loop.
9. What are the steps in processing a For/Next loop?
10. Discuss how and when the values of the loop index change throughout the processing of the loop.
11. What is the purpose of the PrintDocument component? the PrintPreview-Dialog component?
12. In what procedure do you write the logic for sending output to the printer?
13. What is the purpose of the X and Y coordinates on a print page?

Programming Exercises

7.1   Create a project for obtaining student information.
Startup form controls are as follows:

- Text boxes for entering the name and units completed.

- Radio buttons for Freshman, Sophomore, Junior, and Senior.

- Check box for Dean's List.

- A list box for the following majors: Accounting, Business, Computer Information Systems, and Marketing.

- A simple combo box for name of high school—initially loaded with Franklin, Highland, West Highland, and Midtown. If the user types in a new school name, it should be added to the list. *Hint:* Add the school in the combo box's Validate event procedure.

- Print button that prints the data from the form. Use the *Print Preview* dialog box.

- An OK button that clears the entries from the form and resets the focus. The button should be the Accept button for the form.

The Menus: The *File* menu should have an option for *Print Schools* and *Exit*. The *Help* menu should have an option for the *About* box.
  Note: Print your name at the top of the printer output for the schools. Display the printer output in the *Print Preview* dialog box.

7.2   R 'n R—for Reading 'n Refreshment needs a project that contains a form for entering book information.

The Form Controls:

- Text boxes for author and title.

- Radio buttons for type: fiction or nonfiction.

- Drop-down list for Subject that will include Best-Seller, Fantasy, Religion, Romance, Humor, Science Fiction, Business, Philosophy, Education, Self-Help, and Mystery.

- List box for Shelf Number containing RC-1111, RC-1112, RC-1113, and RC-1114.

- Print button that prints the data from the form. Use the *Print Preview* dialog box.

- An OK button that clears the entries from the form and resets the focus. Make this the Accept button.

The Menus: The *File* menu will have an option for *Print Subjects* and *Exit*. The *Help* menu will have an option for the *About* box.

    Note: Print your name at the top of the printer output for the subjects. Display the printer output in the *Print Preview* dialog box.

7.3   Create a project to input chartering information about yachts and print a summary report showing the total revenue and average hours per charter. *The Menus:* The *File* menu will contain commands for *Print Summary, Print Yacht Types,* and *Exit.* Place a separator bar before *Exit.* The *Edit* menu should have commands for *Clear for Next Charter, Add Yacht Type, Remove Yacht Type,* and *Display Count of Yacht Types.* Include a separator bar after the *Clear* command. The *Help* menu will contain an *About* command that displays an About form.

The Form:

- The form should contain text boxes for responsible party and hours chartered. Include a label to show the calculated price of the charter.

- A drop-down combo box will contain the type of yacht: Ranger, Wavelength, Catalina, Coronado, Hobie, C & C, Hans Christian, and Excalibur. Any items that are added to the text box during processing must be added to the list.

- A drop-down list will contain the size: 22, 24, 30, 32, 36, 38, 45. (No new sizes can be entered at run time.)

- An OK button will calculate and display the price and add to the totals. The calculations will require price per hour. Use the following chart:

Size	Hourly Rate
22	95.00
24	137.00
30	160.00
32	192.00
36	250.00
38	400.00
45	550.00

- A Clear button will clear the contents of the screen controls. The functions of the Clear button are the same as for the *Clear for Next Charter* menu item.

- Make the OK button the Accept button and the Clear button the form's Cancel button.

Summary Report: The summary report will print the summary information and send the report to the printer and/or the *Print Preview* dialog box. The summary information will include Number of Charters, Total Revenue, and Average Hours Chartered. Include your name on the output and identifying labels for the summary information.

Yacht Types Report: Display the yacht types in the combo box in the *Print Preview* dialog box. Include your name and a title at the top of the report.

7.4 Create a project that contains a list box with the names of all U.S. states and territories. When the user types the first letters of the state into a text box, set the SelectedIndex property of the list box to display the appropriate name. Include an *Exit* menu item.

Alabama	Kentucky	Oklahoma
Alaska	Louisiana	Oregon
American Samoa	Maine	Pennsylvania
Arizona	Maryland	Puerto Rico
Arkansas	Massachusetts	Rhode Island
California	Michigan	South Carolina
Colorado	Minnesota	South Dakota
Connecticut	Mississippi	Tennessee
Delaware	Missouri	Texas
District of Columbia	Montana	Trust Territories
Florida	Nebraska	Utah
Georgia	Nevada	Vermont
Guam	New Hampshire	Virgin Islands
Hawaii	New Jersey	Virginia
Idaho	New Mexico	Washington
Illinois	New York	West Virginia
Indiana	North Carolina	Wisconsin
Iowa	North Dakota	Wyoming
Kansas	Ohio	

7.5 Maintain a list of bagel types for Bradley's Bagels. Use a drop-down combo box to hold the bagel types and use buttons or menu choices to *Add Bagel Type, Remove Bagel Type, Clear Bagel List, Print Bagel List, Display Bagel Type Count,* and *Exit.* Keep the list sorted in alphabetic order.

Do not allow a blank type to be added to the list. Display an error message if the user selects *Remove* without first selecting a bagel type.

Before clearing the list, display a message box to confirm the operation. Here are some suggested bagel types. You can make up your own list.

Plain	Poppy seed
Egg	Sesame seed
Rye	Banana nut
Salt	Blueberry

7.6 Modify Programming Exercise 7.5 to not allow duplicate bagel types to be added to the list.

Case Studies

VB Mail Order

Create a project for VB Mail Order to maintain a list of catalogs. Use a drop-down combo box for the catalog names and allow the user to enter new catalog names, delete catalog names, display a count of the number of catalogs, clear the catalog list, or print the catalog list.

Do not allow a blank catalog name to be added to the list. Display an error message if the user selects *Remove* without first selecting a catalog name. Before clearing the list, display a message box to confirm the operation.

To begin, the catalog list should hold these catalog names: Odds and Ends, Solutions, Camping Needs, ToolTime, Spiegel, The Outlet, and The Large Size.

Display the printed output in the *Print Preview* dialog box. Include your name and a heading at the top of the report.

VB Auto Center

Create an application for the car wash located at VB Auto Center.

The form will contain three ListBox or ComboBox controls that do not permit the user to type in items at run time. The first list will contain the names of the packages available for detailing a vehicle: Standard, Deluxe, Executive, or Luxury.

The contents of the other two lists will vary depending upon the package selected. Display one list for the interior work and one list for the exterior work. Store the descriptions of the items in string constants. You must clear the lists for the interior and exterior for each order and add new items to the lists each time the user makes a selection from the package list.

Use a drop-down list to allow the user to select the fragrance. The choices are Hawaiian Mist, Baby Powder, Pine, Country Floral, Pina Colada, and Vanilla.

Include menu commands for *Print Order, Clear,* and *Exit.* The print option should send its output to the Print Preview window. Display the printed output in the *Print Preview* dialog box. Include your name and a heading at the top of the report.

The Order printout will contain the package name (Standard, Deluxe, Executive, or Luxury), the interior and exterior items included, and the fragrance selected. Use a `For`/`Next` loop when printing the interior and exterior lists.

	Item Description	S	D	E	L
Exterior	Hand Wash	✓	✓	✓	✓
	Hand Wax		✓	✓	✓
	Check Engine Fluids			✓	✓
	Detail Engine Compartment				✓
	Detail Under Carriage				✓
Interior	Fragrance	✓	✓	✓	✓
	Shampoo Carpets		✓	✓	✓
	Shampoo Upholstery				✓
	Interior Protection Coat (dashboard and console)			✓	
	Scotchgard™				✓

Note: S—Standard; D—Deluxe; E—Executive; L—Luxury

Video Bonanza

Maintain a list of movie categories. Use a drop-down combo box to hold the movie types and use buttons or menu choices to *Add a Category, Remove a Category, Clear All Categories, Print the Category List, Display the Movie Category Count,* and *Exit.* Keep the list sorted in alphabetic order.

Do not allow a blank type to be added to the list. Display an error message if the user selects *Remove* without first selecting a movie category. Before clearing the list, display a message box to confirm the operation.

The starting categories are

- Comedy
- Drama
- Action
- Sci-Fi
- Horror

Display the printed output in the *Print Preview* dialog box. Include your name and a heading at the top of the report.

Very Very Boards

Write a project to maintain a list of shirt styles. Keep the styles in a drop-down combo box, with styles such as crew, turtleneck, or crop top.

Add a *Style* menu with options to *Add Style, Remove Style, Clear Style List, Count Styles,* and *Print Style List.* Include keyboard shortcuts for the menu commands.

Display the printed output in the *Print Preview* dialog box. Include your name and a heading at the top of the report.

8

Arrays

at the completion of this chapter, you will be able to . . .

1. Establish an array and refer to individual elements in the array with subscripts.

2. Use the For Each/Next to traverse the elements of an array.

3. Create a structure for multiple fields of related data.

4. Accumulate totals using arrays.

5. Distinguish between direct access and indirect access of a table.

6. Write a table lookup for matching an array element.

7. Combine the advantages of ListBox controls with arrays.

8. Store and look up data in multidimensional arrays.

Single-Dimension Arrays

An **array** is a list or series of values, similar to a list box or a combo box. You can think of an array as a list box without the box—without the visual representation. Any time you need to keep a series of variables for later processing, such as reordering, calculating, or printing, you need to set up an array.

Consider an example that has a form for entering product information one product at a time. After the user has entered many products, you will need to calculate some statistics, perhaps use the information in different ways, or print it. Of course, each time the user enters the data for the next product, the previous contents of the text boxes are replaced. You could assign the previous values to variables, but they also would be replaced for each new product. Another approach might be to create multiple variables, such as product1String, product2String, product3String, and so on. This approach might be reasonable for a few entries, but what happens when you need to store 50 or 500 products?

When you need to store multiple values, use an array. An array is a series of individual variables, all referenced by the same name. Sometimes arrays are referred to as **tables** or **subscripted variables**. For an array for storing names, you may have nameString(0), nameString(1), nameString(2), and so on.

Each individual variable is called an **element** of the array. The individual elements are treated the same as any other variable and may be used in any statement, such as an assignment statement. The **subscript** (which also may be called an **index**) inside the parentheses is the position of the element within the array. Figure 8.1 illustrates an array of 10 elements with subscripts from 0 to 9.

Figure 8.1

nameString array

(0)	Janet Baker
(1)	George Lee
(2)	Sue Li
(3)	Samuel Hoosier
(4)	Sandra Weeks
(5)	William Macy
(6)	Andy Harrison
(7)	Ken Ford
(8)	Denny Franks
(9)	Shawn James

An array of string variables with 10 elements. Subscripts are 0 through 9.

Subscripts

The real advantage of using an array is not realized until you use variables for subscripts in place of the constants.

```
nameString(indexInteger) = ""

Debug.WriteLine(nameString(indexInteger))
```

Subscripts may be constants, variables, or numeric expressions. Although the subscripts must be integers, Visual Basic rounds any noninteger subscript.

A question has probably occurred to you by now: how many elements are there in the nameString array? The answer is that you must specify the number of elements in a `Dim` statement.

The Dim Statement for Arrays—General Forms

```
Dim ArrayName(UpperSubscript) As Datatype
Dim ArrayName() As Datatype = {InitialValueList}
Dim ArrayName As Datatype() = {InitialValueList}
```

The first form of the `Dim` statement allocates storage for the specified number of elements and initializes each numeric variable to 0. In the case of string arrays, each element is set to an empty string (zero characters).

In the second and third forms of the `Dim` statement, you specify initial values for the array elements, which determines the number of elements. You cannot declare the upper subscript *and* initial values.

The Dim Statement for Arrays—Examples

```
Dim nameString(25) As String
Dim balanceDecimal(10) As Decimal
Dim productString(99) As String
Dim indexInteger() As Integer = {1, 5, 12, 18, 20}
Dim indexInteger As Integer() = {1, 5, 12, 18, 20}
Dim departmentsString() As String = {"Accounting", "Marketing", "Human Relations"}
Private categoryString(10) As String
Public idNumbersString(5) As String
```

Array subscripts are zero based, so the first element is always element zero. The upper subscript is the highest subscript—one less than the number of elements. For example, the statement

```
Dim categoryString(10) As String
```

creates an array of 11 elements with subscripts 0 through 10.

Notice that you declare a data type for the array. All of the array elements must be the same data type. If you omit the data type, just as with single variables, the type defaults to Object.

Valid Subscripts

A subscript must reference a valid element of the array. If a list contains 10 names, it wouldn't make sense to ask: What is the 15th name on the list? *or* What is the 2½th name on the list? Visual Basic rounds fractional subscripts and throws an exception for a subscript that is out of range.

Note: Arrays are derived from System.Array, which is a collection.

► **Feedback 8.1**

```
Dim nameString(20) As String
Const INDEX_Integer As Integer = 10
```

After execution of the preceding statements, which of the following are valid
subscripts?

1. nameString(20)
2. nameString(INDEX_Integer)
3. nameString(INDEX_Integer * 2)
4. nameString(INDEX_Integer * 3)
5. nameString(0)
6. nameString(INDEX_Integer – 20)
7. nameString(INDEX_Integer / 3)
8. nameString(INDEX_Integer / 5 – 2)

For Each/Next Statements

When you use an array, you need a way to reference each element in the array.
For/Next loops, which you learned to use in Chapter 7, work well to traverse
the elements in an array. Another handy loop construct is the **For Each and
Next.** The significant advantage of using the For Each and Next is that you
don't have to manipulate the subscripts of the array.

The For Each and Next Statements—General Form

General Form

```
For Each ElementName In ArrayName
     ' Statement(s) in loop.
Next [ElementName]
```

Visual Basic automatically references each element of the array, assigns its
value to ElementName, and makes one pass through the loop. If the array has
12 elements, for example, the loop will execute 12 times. The variable used for
ElementName must be the same data type as the array elements or an Object
data type.

    In the following example, assume that the array nameString has already
been dimensioned and holds data.

The For Each and Next Statements—Example

Example

```
Dim eachNameString As String
For Each eachNameString In nameString
     ' Write one element of the array.
     Debug.WriteLine(eachNameString)
Next eachNameString
```

The For Each loop will execute if the array has at least one element. All the statements within the loop are executed for the first element. If the array has more elements, the loop continues to execute until all the elements are processed. When the loop finishes, execution of code continues with the line following the Next statement.

   Note: You may use an Exit For statement within a loop to exit early.

Structures

You have been using VB data types such as Integer, String, and Decimal since Chapter 3. Now you will learn to combine multiple fields of related data to create a new **structure**. In many ways, a structure is similar to defining a new data type. For example, an Employee structure may contain last name, first name, Social Security number, street, city, state, ZIP code, date of hire, and pay code. A Product structure might contain a description, product number, quantity, and price. You can combine the fields into a structure using the Structure and End Structure statements.

The Structure and End Structure Statements—General Form

```
[Public | Private] Structure NameOfStructure
    Dim FirstField As DataType
    Dim SecondField As DataType
    . . .
End Structure
```

The Structure declaration cannot go inside a procedure. You generally place the Structure statement at the top of a file with the module-level declarations. You also can place a Structure in a separate file.

The Structure and End Structure Statements—Examples

```
Structure Employee
    Dim lastNameString As String
    Dim firstNameString As String
    Dim socialSecurityNumberString As String
    Dim streetString As String
    Dim stateString As String
    Dim zipCodeString As String
    Dim hireDate As Date
    Dim payCodeInteger As Integer
End Structure

Public Structure Product
    Dim descriptionString As String
    Dim idString As String
    Dim quantityInteger As Integer
    Dim priceDecimal As Decimal
End Structure

Structure SalesDetail
    Dim saleDecimal() As Decimal
End Structure
```

By default, a structure is public. You can declare the structure to be public or private, if you wish.

If you include an array inside a structure, you cannot specify the number of elements. You must use a `ReDim` statement in your code to declare the number of elements.

Declaring Variables Based on a Structure

Once you have created a structure, you can declare variables of the structure, just as if it were another data type.

```
Dim officeEmployee As Employee
Dim warehouseEmployee As Employee
Dim widgetProduct As Product
Dim inventoryProduct(100) As Product
Dim houseWaresSalesDetail As SalesDetail
Dim homeFurnishingsSalesDetail As SalesDetail
```

Accessing the Elements in a Structure Variable

Each field of data in a variable declared as a structure is referred to as an *element* of the structure. To access elements, use the dot notation similar to that used for objects: Specify *Variable.Element*.

```
officeEmployee.lastNameString
officeEmployee.hireDate
warehouseEmployee.lastNameString
widgetProduct.descriptionString
widgetProduct.quantityInteger
widgetProduct.priceDecimal
inventoryProduct(indexInteger).descriptionString
inventoryProduct(indexInteger).quantityInteger
inventoryProduct(indexInteger).priceDecimal
```

Notice the use of indexes in the preceding examples. Each example was taken from the preceding `Structure` and `Dim` statements. A variable that is not an array, such as widgetProduct, does not need an index. However, for inventoryProduct, which was dimensioned as an array of 101 elements, you must specify not only the inventoryProduct item but also the element within the structure.

Including an Array in a Structure

The SalesDetail structure is a little more complicated than the other structures described above. In this structure we want to include an array of seven variables, one for each day of the week. However, VB does not allow you to declare the number of elements in the `Structure` declaration. You must use the `ReDim` statement inside a procedure to give the array a size.

```
' Module-level declarations.
Structure SalesDetail
    Dim saleDecimal() As Decimal
End Structure
```

```
Dim houseWaresSalesDetail As SalesDetail

' Inside a procedure:
' Establish the number of elements in the array.
ReDim houseWaresSalesDetail.saleDecimal(6)

' In processing.
houseWaresSalesDetail.saleDecimal(dayIndexInteger) = currentDaySalesDecimal
```

Because the saleDecimal element of the SalesDetail structure is declared as an array, you must use a subscript to refer to each individual element within the structure.

Feedback 8.2

1. Write a `Structure` statement to hold student data containing last name, first name, student number, number of units completed, and GPA. The new structure should be called "Student".
2. Declare an array of 100 students that will use the structure for student information.
3. Write the `Structure` statement for a structure called "Project" containing a project name, form name, and folder name.
4. Declare a variable called "myProject" based on the Project structure.
5. Declare an array of 100 elements called "ourProjects", based on the Project structure.

Using Array Elements for Accumulators

Array elements are regular variables and perform in the same ways as all variables used so far. You may use the subscripted variables in any way you choose, such as for counters or total accumulators.

To demonstrate the use of array elements as total accumulators, eight totals will be accumulated. For this example, eight scout troops are selling raffle tickets. A separate total must be accumulated for each of the eight groups. Each time a sale is made, the number of tickets must be added to the correct total. The statement

```
Dim totalInteger(7) As Integer
```

declares the eight accumulators with subscripts 0 to 7.

Adding to the Correct Total

Assume that your user inputs a group number into groupTextBox.Text and the number of tickets sold into saleTextBox.Text. The sales may be input in any order with multiple sales for each group. Your problem is to add each ticket sale to the correct total, numbered 0 to 7, for groups numbered 1 to 8.

You can subtract one from the group number to use as the subscript to add to the correct total. For example, if the first sale of 10 tickets is for group 4, the 10 must be added to totalInteger(3). (Figure 8.2 shows the form and the variables used for this example.)

Figure 8.2

The group number entered in groupTextBox is used as a subscript to determine the correct totalInteger array element to which to add.

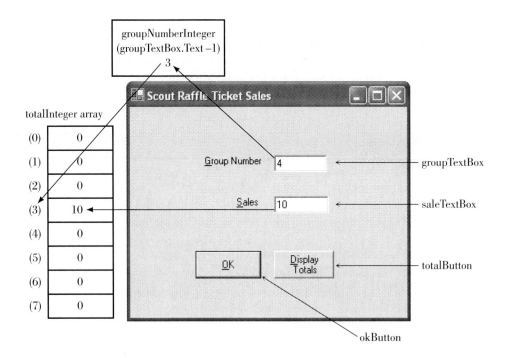

```
' Convert input group number to subscript.
groupNumberInteger = Integer.Parse(groupTextBox.Text) — 1

' Add sale to the correct total.
saleInteger = Integer.Parse(saleTextBox.Text)
totalInteger(groupNumberInteger) += saleInteger
```

Of course, the user might enter an incorrect group number. Because you don't want the program to cancel with an exception, you must validate the group number.

```
Try
    ' Convert input group number to a subscript.
    groupNumberInteger = Integer.Parse(groupTextBox.Text) — 1
    If groupNumberInteger >= 0 And groupNumberInteger <= 7 Then
        'Add sale to correct total
        saleInteger = Integer.Parse(saleTextBox.Text)
        totalInteger(groupNumberInteger) += saleInteger
    Else
        MessageBox.Show("Enter a valid group number (1-8)", "Data Entry Error", _
            MessageBoxButtons.OK, MessageBoxIcon.Exclamation)
    End If
Catch
    MessageBox.Show("Numeric entries required for both group number and sales", _
        "Data Entry Error", MessageBoxButtons.OK, MessageBoxIcon.Exclamation)
End Try
```

Using the group number as an index to the array is a technique called **direct reference**. The groups are assigned numbers from 1 to 8. You can subtract 1 from the group number to create the subscripts, which are 0 to 7.

Debugging Array Programs

You can view the contents of array elements when your program is in break time. Set a breakpoint and view the Autos window (Figure 8.3). You will need to click on the plus sign to the left of the array name to view the individual array elements.

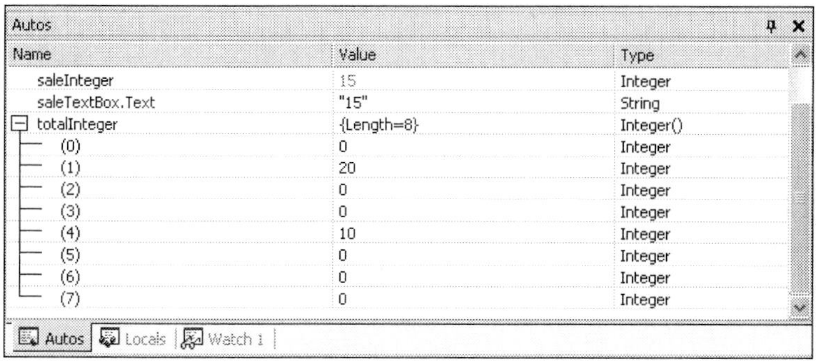

Figure 8.3

View the contents of an array in the Autos window at break time.

Autos			⏸ ✕
Name	Value	Type	
saleInteger	15	Integer	
saleTextBox.Text	"15"	String	
⊟ totalInteger	{Length=8}	Integer()	
(0)	0	Integer	
(1)	20	Integer	
(2)	0	Integer	
(3)	0	Integer	
(4)	10	Integer	
(5)	0	Integer	
(6)	0	Integer	
(7)	0	Integer	

Autos | Locals | Watch 1

Table Lookup

Things don't always work out so neatly as having sequential group numbers that can be used to access the table directly. Sometimes you will have to do a little work to find (look up) the correct value. Reconsider the eight scout troops and their ticket sales. Now the groups are not numbered 1 to 8, but 101, 103, 110, 115, 121, 123, 130, and 145. The group number and the number of tickets sold are still input, and the number of tickets must be added to the correct total. But now you must do one more step: determine to which array element to add the ticket sales, using a **table lookup**.

The first step in the project is to establish a structure with the group numbers and totals and then dimension an array of the structure. Before any processing is done, you must load the group numbers into the table; the best place to do this is in the Form_Load event procedure, which is executed once as the form is loaded into memory.

Place the following statements at the top of a form class:

```
' Declare structure and module-level variables.
Structure Group
    Dim groupNumberString As String
    Dim totalInteger As Integer
End Structure

' Hold group number and total for 8 groups.
Private arrayGroup(7) As Group
```

Then initialize the values of the array elements by placing these statements into the Form_Load procedure:

```
Private Sub salesForm_Load(ByVal sender As System.Object, _
  ByVal e As System.EventArgs) Handles MyBase.Load
  ' Initialize group numbers.

  arrayGroup(0).groupNumberString = "101"
  arrayGroup(1).groupNumberString = "103"
  arrayGroup(2).groupNumberString = "110"
  arrayGroup(3).groupNumberString = "115"
  arrayGroup(4).groupNumberString = "121"
  arrayGroup(5).groupNumberString = "123"
  arrayGroup(6).groupNumberString = "130"
  arrayGroup(7).groupNumberString = "145"
End Sub
```

During program execution, the user still enters the group number and the number of tickets sold into text boxes.

The technique used to find the subscript is called a *table lookup*. In this example, the object is to find the element number (0 to 7) of the group number and add to the corresponding group total. If the user enters the third group number ("110"), the subscript is 2 and the sale is added to the total for subscript 2. If the seventh group number ("130") is entered, the sale is added to the total with the subscript 6, and so on. Hence, you need a way, given the group number in groupTextBox.Text, to find the corresponding subscript of the arrayGroup array.

When Visual Basic executes the statement

```
arrayGroup(groupNumberInteger).totalInteger += saleInteger
```

the value of groupNumberInteger must be a number in the range 0 to 7. The task for the lookup operation is to find the number to place in groupNumberInteger, based on the value of groupTextBox.Text. Figure 8.4 shows the variables used for the lookup. Figure 8.5 shows the flowchart of the lookup logic.

Coding a Table Lookup

For a table lookup, you will find that a Do/Loop works better than For Each. As you compare to each element in the array and eventually find a match, you need to know the subscript of the matching element.

Figure 8.4

A lookup operation: The group number is looked up in the arrayGroup array; the correct subscript is found and used to add the sale to the correct totalInteger.

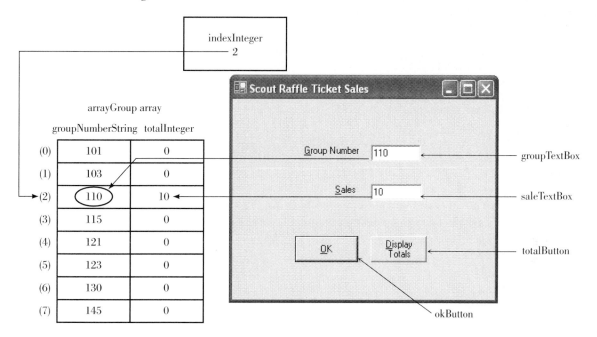

Figure 8.5

A flowchart of the logic of a lookup operation.

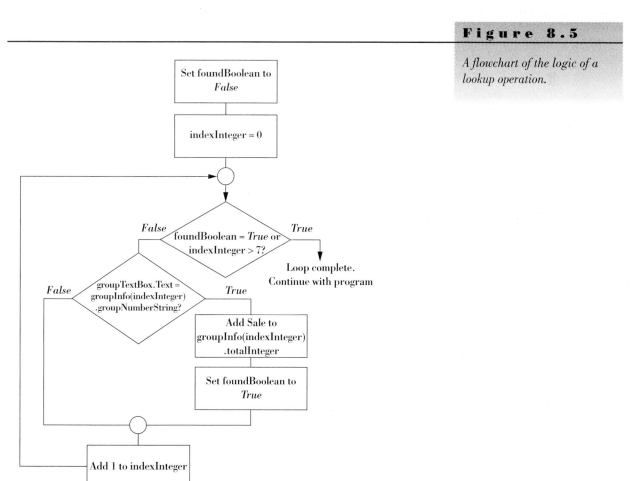

```
' Accumulate the sales by group number.
Dim saleInteger As Integer
Dim indexInteger As Integer = 0
Dim foundBoolean As Boolean = False

' Look up input group number to find subscript.
Do Until foundBoolean Or indexInteger > 7
    If groupTextBox.Text = arrayGroup(indexInteger).groupNumberString Then
        'Add sale to correct total
        saleInteger = Integer.Parse(saleTextBox.Text)
        arrayGroup(indexInteger).totalInteger += saleInteger
        foundBoolean = True
    End If
    indexInteger += 1
Loop
```

Once again, you should do some form of validation. If the user enters an invalid group number, you should display a message box. You can check the value of the Boolean variable foundBoolean after completion of the loop to determine whether the loop terminated because of a match or without a match.

```
If Not foundBoolean Then
    MessageBox.Show("Enter a valid group number", "Data Entry Error", _
        MessageBoxButtons.OK, MessageBoxIcon.Exclamation)
    With groupTextBox
        .Focus()
        .SelectAll()
    End With
End If
```

The table-lookup technique will work for any table, numeric or string. It isn't necessary to arrange the fields being searched in any particular sequence. The comparison is made to one item in the list, then the next, and the next—until a match is found. In fact, you can save processing time in a large table by arranging the elements with the most-often-used entries at the top so that fewer comparisons must be made.

Using List Boxes with Arrays

In the previous example of a lookup, the user had to type some information into a text box, which was used to look up the information in an array. A more efficient and friendly solution might be to substitute a list box for the text box. You can store the eight group numbers in a list box and allow the user to select from the list (Figure 8.6).

The initial Items collection can contain the values 101, 103, 110, 115, 121, 123, 130, and 145.

You have probably already realized that you can use the SelectedIndex property to determine the array subscript. Remember that the SelectedIndex property holds the position or index of the selected item from the list.

In place of the lookup operation, we can use this code:

```
' Declare module-level variables.
' Hold totals for 8 groups.
Dim totalInteger(7) As Integer

Private Sub okButton_Click(ByVal sender As System.Object, _
  ByVal e As System.EventArgs) Handles okButton.Click
    ' Accumulate the sales by group number.
    Dim saleInteger As Integer
    Dim groupNumberInteger As Integer

    If groupListBox.SelectedIndex <> -1 Then
        ' Selection made; Add to the correct total.
        saleInteger = Integer.Parse(saleTextBox.Text)
        groupNumberInteger = groupListBox.SelectedIndex
        totalInteger(groupNumberInteger) += saleInteger

        ' Clear the screen fields.
        groupListBox.SelectedIndex = -1
        saleTextBox.Text = ""
    Else
        MessageBox.Show("Select a group number from the list.", "Data Entry Error", _
            MessageBoxButtons.OK, MessageBoxIcon.Exclamation)
    End If
End Sub
```

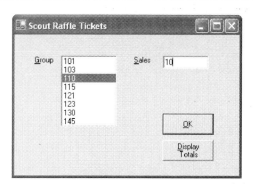

Figure 8.6

Allow the user to select from a list and you can use the list's SelectedIndex property as the subscript of the total array.

Multidimensional Arrays

You may need to use two subscripts to identify tabular data, where data are arranged in **rows** and **columns**.

Many applications of two-dimensional tables quickly come to mind: insurance rate tables, tax tables, addition and multiplication tables, postage rates, foods and their nutritive value, population by region, rainfall by state.

To define a two-dimensional array or table, the `Dim` statement specifies the number of rows and columns in the array. The row is horizontal and the column is vertical. The following table has three rows and four columns:

The Dim Statement for Two-Dimensional Arrays—General Forms

```
Dim ArrayName(HighestSubscript, HighestSubscript) As Datatype
Dim ArrayName( , ) As Datatype = {ListOfValues}
```

The Dim Statement for Two-Dimensional Arrays—Examples

```
Dim nameString(2, 3) As String
Dim nameString( , ) As String = { {"James", "Mary", "Sammie", "Sean"}, _
    {"Tom", "Lee", "Leon", "Larry"}, {"Maria", "Margaret", "Jill", "John"} }
```

Both of these two statements establish an array of 12 elements, with three rows and four columns. Just as with single-dimension arrays, you cannot specify the number of elements within parentheses *and* specify initial values.

Notice the comma inside the parentheses in the second example: You must use a comma to specify that there are two dimensions to the array. Specify the initial values with the first dimension (the row) first and the second dimension (the column) second. The compiler determines the number of elements from the initial values that you supply. The second example above fills the table in this sequence:

(0, 0) James	(0, 1) Mary	(0, 2) Sammie	(0, 3) Sean
(1, 0) Tom	(1, 1) Lee	(1, 2) Leon	(1, 3) Larry
(2, 0) Maria	(2, 1) Margaret	(2, 2) Jill	(2, 3) John

You must always use two subscripts when referring to individual elements of the table. Specify the row with the first subscript and the column with the second subscript.

The elements of the array may be used in the same ways as any other variable—in accumulators, counts, and reference fields for lookup; in statements like assignment and printing; and as conditions. Some valid references to the table include

```
nameString(1, 2) = "New Name"
nameString(rowInteger, columnInteger) = "New Name"
displayLabel.Text = nameString(1, 2)
DrawString(nameString(rowInteger, columnInteger), printFont, Brushes.Black, 100.0, 100.0)
```

Invalid references for the nameString table would include any value greater than 2 for the first subscript or greater than 3 for the second subscript.

Initializing Two-Dimensional Arrays

Numeric array elements are initially set to 0 and string elements are set to empty strings. And, of course, you can assign initial values when you declare the array. But many situations require that you reinitialize arrays to 0 or some other value. You can use nested For/Next loops to set each array element to an initial value.

Nested For/Next Example

The assignment statement in the inner loop will be executed 12 times, once for each element of nameString.

```
Dim rowInteger As Integer
Dim columnInteger As Integer

For rowInteger = 0 To 2
    For columnInteger = 0 To 3
        ' Initialize each element.
        nameString(rowInteger, columnInteger) = ""
    Next columnInteger
Next rowInteger
```

Printing a Two-Dimensional Table

When you want to print the contents of a two-dimensional table, you can use a For Each/Next loop. This code prints one array element per line.

```
' Print one name per line.
For Each elementString In nameString
    ' Set up a line.
    e.Graphics.DrawString(elementString, printFont, _
      Brushes.Black, horizontalPrintLocationSingle, verticalPrintLocationSingle)

    ' Increment the Y position for the next line.
    verticalPrintLocationSingle += lineHeightSingle
Next elementString
```

If you wish to print an entire row in one line, use a For/Next loop and set up the X and Y coordinates to print multiple elements per line.

```
' Print one row per line.
For rowInteger = 0 To 2
    For columnInteger = 0 To 3
        e.Graphics.DrawString(nameString(rowInteger, columnInteger), printFont, _
          Brushes.Black, horizontalPrintLocationSingle, verticalPrintLocationSingle)
        ' Move across the line.
        horizontalPrintLocationSingle += 200
    Next columnInteger
```

```
' Start next line; Reset to left margin.
  horizontalPrintLocationSingle = e.MarginBounds.Left
  ' Move down to next line.
  verticalPrintLocationSingle += lineHeightSingle
Next rowInteger
```

Summing a Two-Dimensional Table

You can find the sum of a table in various ways. You may sum either the columns or the rows of the table; or, as in a cross-foot, you can sum the figures in both directions and double-check the totals.

To sum the array in both directions, each column needs one total field and each row needs one total field. Two one-dimensional arrays will work well for the totals. Figure 8.7 illustrates the variables used in this example.

```
' Crossfoot total a 2D table.

' Give the 6 x 4 array values for testing.
' (Normally you would total values that are accumulated in a program.)
Dim amountDecimal( , ) As Decimal = {{2.5D, 3D, 1.2D, 2.2D, 4.5D, 3.5D}, _
   {2D, 2D, 2D, 2D, 2D, 2D}, _
   {3D, 3.1D, 3.2D, 3.3D, 3.4D, 3.5D}, _
   {4.4D, 4.5D, 4.6D, 4.7D, 4.8D, 4.9D}}
Dim rowTotalDecimal(3) As Decimal
Dim columnTotalDecimal(5) As Decimal
Dim rowInteger As Integer
Dim columnInteger As Integer

For rowInteger = 0 To 3
   For columnInteger = 0 To 5
      rowTotalDecimal(rowInteger) += amountDecimal(rowInteger, columnInteger)
      columnTotalDecimal(columnInteger) += amountDecimal(rowInteger, columnInteger)
   Next columnInteger
Next rowInteger
```

Figure 8.7

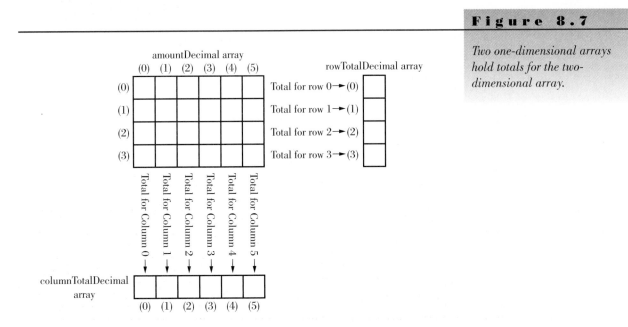

Two one-dimensional arrays hold totals for the two-dimensional array.

> **Feedback 8.3**

Write VB statements to do the following:

1. Dimension a table called temperatureDecimal with five columns and three rows.
2. Set each element in the first row to 0.
3. Set each element in the second row to 75.
4. For each column of the table, add together the elements in the first and second rows, placing the sum in the third row.
5. Print the entire table. (Write only the logic for printing inside the Print-Document_PrintPage event procedure.)

Lookup Operation for Two-Dimensional Tables

When you look up items in a two-dimensional table, you can use the same techniques discussed with single-dimensional arrays: direct reference and table lookup. The limitations are the same.

1. To use a direct reference, row and column subscripts must be readily available. For example, you can tally the hours used for each of five machines (identified by machine numbers 1 to 5) and each of four departments (identified by department numbers 1 to 4).

```
rowInteger = Integer.Parse(machineTextBox.Text) – 1
columnInteger = Integer.Parse(departmentTextBox.Text) – 1
hoursDecimal = Decimal.Parse(hoursTextBox.Text)
machineTotalDecimal(rowInteger, columnInteger) += hoursDecimal
```

2. A table lookup is the most common lookup technique.

Many two-dimensional tables used for lookup require additional one-dimensional arrays or lists to aid in the lookup process. For an example, use a shipping rate table (Figure 8.8) to look up the rate to ship a package. The

F i g u r e   8 . 8

This shipping rate table in a two-dimensional array can be used to look up the correct shipping charge.

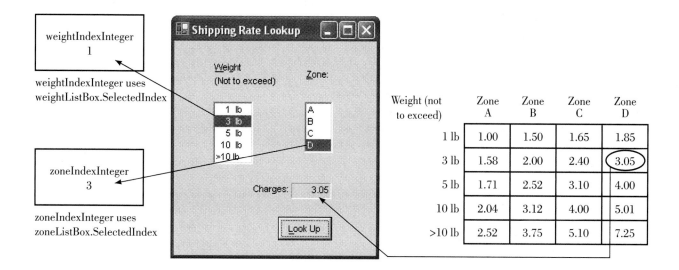

Weight (not to exceed)	Zone A	Zone B	Zone C	Zone D
1 lb	1.00	1.50	1.65	1.85
3 lb	1.58	2.00	2.40	3.05
5 lb	1.71	2.52	3.10	4.00
10 lb	2.04	3.12	4.00	5.01
>10 lb	2.52	3.75	5.10	7.25

shipping rate depends on the weight of the package and the zone to which it is being shipped. You could design the project with the weight and zones in list boxes, or you could use a text box and let the user input the data.

Using List Boxes

In this example, a list box holds the weight limits, and another list holds the zones. The values for the two lists are set with the Items properties at design time. The five-by-four rate table is two-dimensional, and the values are set when the table is declared.

```
' Look up values from list boxes.

' Declare module-level variables.
Dim rateDecimal( , ) As Decimal = {{1D, 1.5D, 1.65D, 1.85D}, {1.58D, 2D, 2.4D, 3.05D}, _
    {1.71D, 2.52D, 3.1D, 4D}, {2.04D, 3.12D, 4D, 5.01D}, {2.52D, 3.75D, 5.1D, 7.25D}}

Private Sub lookupButton_Click(ByVal sender As System.Object, _
    ByVal e As System.EventArgs) Handles lookupButton.Click
        ' Look up the shipping rate.

    Dim weightIndexInteger As Integer
    Dim zoneIndexInteger As Integer

    weightIndexInteger = weightListBox.SelectedIndex
    zoneIndexInteger = zoneListBox.SelectedIndex
    If weightIndexInteger <> -1 And zoneIndexInteger <> -1 Then
        chargesLabel.Text = rateDecimal(weightIndexInteger, zoneIndexInteger).ToString("N")
    Else
        MessageBox.Show("Select the weight and zone.", "Information Missing", _
            MessageBoxButtons.OK, MessageBoxIcon.Exclamation)
    End If
End Sub
```

Using Text Boxes

If you are using text boxes rather than list boxes for data entry, the input requires more validation. You must look up both the weight and zone entries before you can determine the correct rate. The valid zones and weight ranges will be stored in two separate one-dimensional arrays. The first step in the project is to establish and fill the arrays. The five-by-four rate table is two-dimensional, and the values should be preloaded, as in the previous example.

Note that the Try/Catch blocks were omitted to clarify the logic. You should always use error trapping when converting input to numeric values.

```
' Look up values from text boxes.

' Declare module-level variables.
Dim rateDecimal( , ) As Decimal = {{1D, 1.5D, 1.65D, 1.85D}, {1.58D, 2D, 2.4D, 3.05D}, _
    {1.71D, 2.52D, 3.1D, 4D}, {2.04D, 3.12D, 4D, 5.01D}, {2.52D, 3.75D, 5.1D, 7.25D}}
Dim weightInteger() As Integer = {1, 3, 5, 10}
Dim zoneString() As String = {"A", "B", "C", "D"}

Private Sub lookupButton_Click(ByVal sender As System.Object, _
    ByVal e As System.EventArgs) Handles lookupButton.Click
        ' Look up the shipping rate.
```

```
        Dim weightIndexInteger As Integer
        Dim zoneIndexInteger As Integer
        Dim indexInteger As Integer = 0
        Dim weightInputInteger As Integer
        Dim weightFoundBoolean As Boolean = False
        Dim zoneFoundBoolean As Boolean = False

        ' Look up the weight to find the weightIndexInteger.
        weightInputInteger = Integer.Parse(txtWeight.Text)

        Do Until weightFoundBoolean Or indexInteger > 3
            If weightInputInteger <= weightInteger(indexInteger) Then
                weightIndexInteger = indexInteger
                weightFoundBoolean = True
            End If
            indexInteger += 1
        Loop
        If Not weightFoundBoolean Then
            weightIndexInteger = 4
            weightFoundBoolean = True
        End If

        ' Look up the zone to find the zoneIndexInteger.
        indexInteger = 0
        Do Until zoneFoundBoolean Or indexInteger > 3
            If zoneTextBox.Text.ToUpper() = zoneString(indexInteger) Then
                zoneIndexInteger = indexInteger
                zoneFoundBoolean = True
            End If
            indexInteger += 1
        Loop

        ' Display the appropriate rate.
        If weightFoundBoolean And zoneFoundBoolean Then
            chargesLabel.Text = rateDecimal(weightIndexInteger, _
                zoneIndexInteger).ToString("N")
        Else
            MessageBox.Show("Select the weight and zone.", "Information Missing", _
                MessageBoxButtons.OK, MessageBoxIcon.Exclamation)
        End If
End Sub
```

Your Hands-On Programming Example

Create a project for R 'n R—for Reading 'n Refreshment that determines the price per pound for bulk coffee sales. The coffees are divided into categories: regular, decaf, and special blend. The prices are set by the quarter pound, half pound, and full pound. Use a *Find Price* button to search for the appropriate price based on the selections.

	Regular	Decaf	Blend
1/4 pound	2.60	2.90	3.25
1/2 pound	4.90	5.60	6.10
Full pound	8.75	9.75	11.25

Create a structure that contains the coffee type, amount, and price. Set up a module-level variable that is an array of 20 elements of your structure; this array will hold the transactions. Each time the *Find Price* button is pressed, look up and display the price of the coffee selection and add the data to the array.

Include a *Clear* button to clear the selections from the screen and a *Print* button that prints all of the transactions. Using *Print Preview*, print appropriate headings and the data from the transaction array.

When the *Exit* button is pressed, give the user another opportunity to print all the transactions.

Planning the Project

Sketch a form (Figure 8.9), which your users sign off as meeting their needs.

A planning sketch of the form for the hands-on programming example.

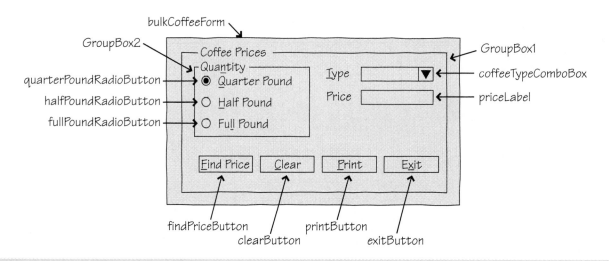

Plan the Objects and Properties

Object	Property	Setting
bulkCoffeeForm	Name	bulkCoffeeForm
	Text	R 'n R — for Reading and Refreshment
	AcceptButton	findPriceButton
GroupBox1	Text	Coffee Prices
GroupBox2	Text	Qua&ntity
coffeeTypeComboBox	Name	coffeeTypeComboBox
	Items	Regular
		Decaffeinated
		Special Blend
	DropDownStyle	DropDownList
Label1	Text	&Type
Label2	Text	Price

Object	Property	Setting
priceLabel	Name	priceLabel
	Text	(blank)
	BorderStyle	Fixed3D
	BackColor	Control
quarterPoundRadioButton	Name	quarterPoundRadioButton
	Text	&Quarter Pound
	Checked	True
halfPoundRadioButton	Name	halfPoundRadioButton
	Text	&Half Pound
fullPoundRadioButton	Name	fullPoundRadioButton
	Text	Fu&ll Pound
findPriceButton	Name	findPriceButton
	Text	&Find Price
clearButton	Name	clearButton
	Text	&Clear
printButton	Name	printButton
	Text	&Print
exitButton	Name	exitButton
	Text	E&it
PrintDocument1	Name	PrintDocument1
PrintPreviewDialog1	Name	PrintPreviewDialog1

Plan the Event Procedures You need to plan the actions for the event procedures.

Procedure	Actions
findPriceButton_Click	Find the column from the list selection.
	Find the row from the radio button selection.
	Look up the price in the table.
	Display the price in the label.
	Store the type, quantity, and price in the transaction array.
clearButton_Click	Select the first radio button.
	Deselect the list entry.
	Clear the price label.
printButton_Click	Set up print preview.
	Print the report.
exitButton_Click	Display message box giving the user opportunity to print.
	If print selected
	Execute printButton_Click procedure.
	End If
	Terminate the project.
All radio buttons_Click	Save the name of the selected button.
PrintDocument1_PrintPage	Print title.
	Loop to print all of the stored transactions.

Write the Project Follow the sketch in Figure 8.9 to create the form. Figure 8.10 shows the completed form and Figure 8.11 shows sample report output.

- Set the properties of each object, according to your plan.

- Write the code. Working from the pseudocode, write each event procedure.

- When you complete the code, use a variety of data to thoroughly test the project.

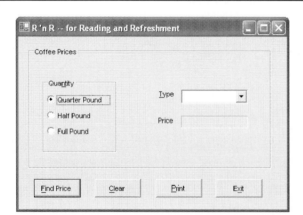

Figure 8.10

The form for the hands-on programming example.

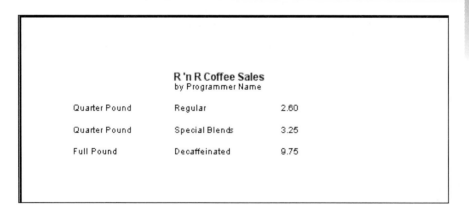

Figure 8.11

A sample report created by the program.

The Project Coding Solution

```
' Program:        Ch0801
' Programmer:     Bradley/Millspaugh
' Date:           January 2004
' Description:    Look up the price for bulk coffee
'                 based upon quantity and type.
'                 Uses a structure and arrays, and prints a report
'                 of the transactions from the array.
' Folder:         Ch0801

Public Class bulkCoffeeForm
    Inherits System.Windows.Forms.Form
```

```vb
' Declare structure and module-level variables.
Structure CoffeeSale
    Dim typeString As String
    Dim quantityString As String
    Dim priceDecimal As Decimal
End Structure

Private transactionCoffeeSale(20) As CoffeeSale
Private numberTransactionsInteger As Integer
Private priceDecimal( , ) As Decimal = _
  {{2.6D, 2.9D, 3.25D}, {4.9D, 5.6D, 6.1D}, {8.75D, 9.75D, 11.25D}}

Private selectedButtonString As String

Private Sub clearButton_Click(ByVal sender As System.Object, _
  ByVal e As System.EventArgs) Handles clearButton.Click
    ' Remove the selection from the list and
    ' Clear the price.

    ' Select first radio button.
    quarterPoundRadioButton.Select()
    ' Clear selection
    typeComboBox.SelectedIndex = -1
    priceLabel.Text = ""
End Sub

Private Sub exitButton_Click(ByVal sender As System.Object, _
  ByVal e As System.EventArgs) Handles exitButton.Click
    ' Terminate the project.
    Dim responseDialogResult As DialogResult

    responseDialogResult = MessageBox.Show("Print the report?", _
      "Terminate the Application", MessageBoxButtons.YesNoCancel, _
      MessageBoxIcon.Question)
    If responseDialogResult = DialogResult.Yes Then
        printButton_Click(sender, e)
        Me.Close()
    ElseIf responseDialogResult = DialogResult.No Then
        Me.Close()
    End If
    ' For a response of Cancel, no action is taken.
End Sub

Private Sub findPriceButton_Click(ByVal sender As System.Object, _
  ByVal e As System.EventArgs) Handles findPriceButton.Click
    ' Look up the price using the quantity and type.
    Dim rowInteger, columnInteger As Integer
    Dim salePriceDecimal As Decimal

    ' Allow only 20 transactions.
    If numberTransactionsInteger < 20 Then
        If typeComboBox.SelectedIndex <> -1 Then
            ' Coffee selection made.
            columnInteger = typeComboBox.SelectedIndex
            ' Determine quantity selected.
```

```
        Select Case selectedButtonString
            Case "quarterPoundRadioButton"
                rowInteger = 0
                transactionCoffeeSale(numberTransactionsInteger).quantityString _
                    = "Quarter Pound"
            Case "halfPoundRadioButton"
                rowInteger = 1
                transactionCoffeeSale(numberTransactionsInteger).quantityString _
                    = "Half Pound"
            Case "fullPoundRadioButton"
                rowInteger = 2
                transactionCoffeeSale(numberTransactionsInteger).quantityString _
                    = "Full Pound"
            Case Else                    'No selection made; use quarter pound
                rowInteger = 0
                transactionCoffeeSale(numberTransactionsInteger).quantityString _
                    = "Quarter Pound"
        End Select

        ' Retrieve price of selection.
        salePriceDecimal = priceDecimal(rowInteger, columnInteger)
        priceLabel.Text = salePriceDecimal.ToString("C")
        ' Save this transaction.
        transactionCoffeeSale(numberTransactionsInteger).typeString _
            = typeComboBox.Text
        transactionCoffeeSale(numberTransactionsInteger).priceDecimal _
            = salePriceDecimal
        numberTransactionsInteger += 1
    Else
        MessageBox.Show("Select the coffee type.", "Selection Incomplete", _
            MessageBoxButtons.OK, MessageBoxIcon.Exclamation)
    End If
    Else
        MessageBox.Show("Only 20 transactions allowed")
    End If
End Sub

Private Sub printButton_Click(ByVal sender As Object, _
  ByVal e As System.EventArgs) Handles printButton.Click
    ' Print the report using Print Preview.

    PrintPreviewDialog1.Document = PrintDocument1
    PrintPreviewDialog1.ShowDialog()
End Sub

Private Sub PrintDocument1_PrintPage(ByVal sender As Object, _
  ByVal e As System.Drawing.Printing.PrintPageEventArgs) _
  Handles PrintDocument1.PrintPage
    ' Handle print and print previews.

    Dim printFont As New Font("Arial", 12)
    Dim headingFont As New Font("Arial", 14, FontStyle.Bold)
    Dim lineHeightSingle As Single = printFont.GetHeight + 2
    Dim column1HorizontalLocationSingle As Single = e.MarginBounds.Left
    Dim verticalPrintLocationString As Single = e.MarginBounds.Top
    Dim column2HorizontalLocationSingle As Single = 300
    Dim column3HorizontalLocationSingle As Single
    Dim printLineString As String
    Dim listIndexInteger As Integer
```

```
        Dim individualCoffeeSale As CoffeeSale
        Dim fontSizeF As New SizeF()
        Dim formattedPriceString As String

        ' Set up and display heading lines.
        printLineString = "R 'n R Coffee Sales"
        e.Graphics.DrawString(printLineString, headingFont, _
          Brushes.Black, column2HorizontalLocationSingle, verticalPrintLocationString)
        printLineString = "by Programmer Name"
        verticalPrintLocationString += lineHeightSingle
        e.Graphics.DrawString(printLineString, printFont, _
          Brushes.Black, column2HorizontalLocationSingle, verticalPrintLocationString)
        verticalPrintLocationString += lineHeightSingle * 2

        ' Loop through the transactions.
        For Each individualCoffeeSale In transactionCoffeeSale
            ' Don't print if blank.
            If individualCoffeeSale.quantityString <> "" Then
                ' Set up a line.

                ' Quantity.
                e.Graphics.DrawString(individualCoffeeSale.quantityString, printFont, _
                  Brushes.Black, column1HorizontalLocationSingle, _
                  verticalPrintLocationString)

                ' Type.
                e.Graphics.DrawString(individualCoffeeSale.typeString, printFont, _
                  Brushes.Black, column2HorizontalLocationSingle, _
                  verticalPrintLocationString)

                ' Right-align the price.
                formattedPriceString = FormatNumber(individualCoffeeSale.priceDecimal)
                ' Measure string in this font.
                fontSizeF = e.Graphics.MeasureString(formattedPriceString, printFont)
                ' Subtract width of string from column position.
                column3HorizontalLocationSingle = 550 - fontSizeF.Width
                e.Graphics.DrawString(formattedPriceString, printFont, _
                  Brushes.Black, column3HorizontalLocationSingle, _
                  verticalPrintLocationString)

                ' Increment the Y position for the next line; Double space.
                verticalPrintLocationString += lineHeightSingle * 2
            End If
        Next
    End Sub

    Private Sub quarterPoundRadioButton_CheckedChanged(ByVal sender As System.Object, _
      ByVal e As System.EventArgs) _
      Handles quarterPoundRadioButton.CheckedChanged, _
      halfPoundRadioButton.CheckedChanged, fullPoundRadioButton.CheckedChanged
        ' Save the name of the selected radio button.
        ' This procedure is executed each time any radio button is selected.

        selectedButtonString = CType(sender, RadioButton).Name
    End Sub
End Class
```

Summary

1. A series of variables with the same name is called an array. The individual values are referred to as elements, and each element is accessed by its subscript, which is a position number.
2. Array subscripts or indexes are zero based; they must be integers in the range of the array elements. VB rounds noninteger values.
3. You can assign initial values in the array declaration *or* specify the highest subscript allowed.
4. A special form of the `For` loop called `For Each` is available for working with arrays. The `For Each` eliminates the need for the programmer to manipulate the subscripts of the array.
5. You can declare a structure to combine related fields and then declare variables and arrays of the structure. `Structure` statements must appear in the declarations section at the top of a file.
6. Arrays can be used like any other variables; they can be used to accumulate a series of totals or to store values for a lookup procedure.
7. The information in arrays may be accessed directly by subscript, or a table lookup may be used to determine the correct table position.
8. You can use the SelectedIndex property of a list box as a subscript of an array.
9. Arrays may be multidimensional. A two-dimensional table contains rows and columns and is processed similarly to a one-dimensional array. Accessing a multidimensional array frequently requires the use of nested loops.

Key Terms

array *320*

column *331*

direct reference *327*

element *320*

`For Each` and `Next` *322*

index *320*

row *331*

structure *323*

subscript *320*

subscripted variable *320*

table *320*

table lookup *327*

Review Questions

1. Define the following terms:
   (a) Array
   (b) Element
   (c) Subscript
   (d) Index
   (e) Subscripted variable
2. What is a structure? When might a structure be useful?
3. Describe the logic of a table lookup.
4. Name some situations in which it is important to perform validation when working with subscripted variables.
5. Compare a two-dimensional table to an array of a structure.
6. How can you initialize values in a two-dimensional table?

Programming   Exercises

8.1 *Array of a structure.* Create a project to analyze an income survey. The statistics for each home include an identification code, the number of members in the household, and the yearly income. A menu will contain *File*, *Reports*, and *Help*. The *File* menu will contain *Enter Data* and *Exit*. As the data are entered, they should be assigned from the text boxes to the elements of a structure.

The reports for the project will be sent to the printer and include the following:

(a) A three-column report displaying the input data.
(b) A listing of the identification number and income for each household that exceeds the average income.
(c) The percentage of households having incomes below the poverty level.

Test Data: Poverty level: 8000 for a family of one or two, plus 2000 for each additional member.

ID Number	Annual Income	Number of Persons
2497	12500	2
3323	13000	5
4521	18210	4
6789	8000	2
5476	6000	1
4423	16400	3
6587	25000	4
3221	10500	4
5555	15000	2
0085	19700	3
3097	20000	8
4480	23400	5
0265	19700	2
8901	13000	3

Check Figures: Households exceeding average income: You should have seven entries on the list.

Households below poverty level: 21.43%

8.2 *Two-Dimensional Table.* Modify Programming Exercise 8.1 to assign the data to a multidimensional array rather than use an array of a structure.

8.3 Create a project to keep track of concert ticket sales by your club. Ticket prices are based on the seating location. Your program should calculate the price for each sale, accumulate the total number of tickets sold in each section, display the ticket price schedule, and print a summary of all sales.

   The form should contain a list box of the sections for seating.

   Do not allow the user to receive an exception for subscript out-of-range.

Section	Price
Orchestra	40.00
Mezzanine	27.50
General	15.00
Balcony	10.00

8.4 *Array of a Structure.* Create a project that will allow a user to look up state names and their two-letter abbreviations. The user will have the options to *Look up the Abbreviation* or *Look up the State Name*. In the event that a match cannot be found for the input, print an appropriate error message.

   Use radio buttons with a shared event procedure and a `Select Case` to determine which text box (state name or abbreviation) should have the focus and which should be disabled.

Data

AL	Alabama		HI	Hawaii
AK	Alaska		ID	Idaho
AS	American Samoa		IL	Illinois
AZ	Arizona		IN	Indiana
AR	Arkansas		IA	Iowa
CA	California		KS	Kansas
CO	Colorado		KY	Kentucky
CT	Connecticut		LA	Louisiana
DE	Delaware		ME	Maine
DC	District of Columbia		MD	Maryland
FL	Florida		MA	Massachusetts
GA	Georgia		MI	Michigan
GU	Guam		MN	Minnesota

MS	Mississippi					PR	Puerto Rico			
MO	Missouri					RI	Rhode Island			
MT	Montana					SC	South Carolina			
NE	Nebraska					SD	South Dakota			
NV	Nevada					TN	Tennessee			
NH	New Hampshire					TX	Texas			
NJ	New Jersey					TT	Trust Territories			
NM	New Mexico					UT	Utah			
NY	New York					VT	Vermont			
NC	North Carolina					VA	Virginia			
ND	North Dakota					VI	Virgin Islands			
OH	Ohio					WA	Washington			
OK	Oklahoma					WV	West Virginia			
OR	Oregon					WI	Wisconsin			
PA	Pennsylvania					WY	Wyoming			

8.5 *Two-Dimensional Table.* Create a project that looks up the driving distance between two cities. Use two drop-down lists that contain the names of the cities. Label one list "Departure" and the other "Destination". Use a *Look Up* button to calculate distance.

Store the distances in a two-dimensional table.

	Boston	Chicago	Dallas	Las Vegas	Los Angeles	Miami	New Orleans	Toronto	Vancouver	Washington, DC
Boston	0	1004	1753	2752	3017	1520	1507	609	3155	448
Chicago	1004	0	921	1780	2048	1397	919	515	2176	709
Dallas	1753	921	0	1230	1399	1343	517	1435	2234	1307
Las Vegas	2752	1780	1230	0	272	2570	1732	2251	1322	2420
Los Angeles	3017	2048	1399	272	0	2716	1858	2523	1278	2646
Miami	1520	1397	1343	2570	2716	0	860	1494	3447	1057
New Orleans	1507	919	517	1732	1858	860	0	1307	2734	1099
Toronto	609	515	1435	2251	2523	1494	1307	0	2820	571
Vancouver	3155	2176	2234	1322	1278	3447	2734	2820	0	2887
Washington, DC	448	709	1307	2420	2646	1057	1099	571	2887	0

8.6   *Two-Dimensional Table.* Create a project in which the user will complete a 10-question survey. Create a form containing labels with each of the questions and a group of radio buttons for each question with the following responses: Always, Usually, Sometimes, Seldom, and Never.

Use a two-dimensional array to accumulate the number of each response for each question.

Have a menu or button option that will print an item analysis on the printer that shows the question number and the count for each response.

Sample of partial output:

Question	Always	Usually	Sometimes	Seldom	Never
1	5	2	10	4	6
2	2	2	10	2	1
3	17	0	10	0	0

Case Studies

VB Mail Order

Create a project that will calculate shipping charges from a two-dimensional table of rates. The rate depends on the weight of the package and the zone to which it will be shipped. The Wt. column specifies the maximum weight for that rate. All weights over 10 pounds use the last row.

	Zone			
Wt.	A	B	C	D
1	1.00	1.50	1.65	1.85
3	1.58	2.00	2.40	3.05
5	1.71	2.52	3.10	4.00
10	2.04	3.12	4.00	5.01
>10	2.52	3.75	5.10	7.25

VB Auto Center

VB Auto sells its own brand of spark plugs. To cross-reference to major brands, it keeps a table of equivalent part numbers. VB Auto wants to computerize the process of looking up part numbers in order to improve its customer service.

The user should be able to enter the part number and brand and look up the corresponding VB Auto part number. You may allow the user to select the brand (Brand A, Brand C, or Brand X) from a list or from radio buttons.

You can choose from two approaches for the lookup table. Store the part numbers either in a two-dimensional table or in an array of a structure. In either case, use the part number and brand entered by the user; look up and display the VB Auto part number.

VB Auto	Brand A	Brand C	Brand X
PR214	MR43T	RBL8	14K22
PR223	R43	RJ6	14K24
PR224	R43N	RN4	14K30
PR246	R46N	RN8	14K32
PR247	R46TS	RBL17Y	14K33
PR248	R46TX	RBL12-6	14K35
PR324	S46	J11	14K38
PR326	SR46E	XEJ8	14K40
PR444	47L	H12	14K44

Video Bonanza

Create a project that displays the aisle number of a movie category in a label. The movie categories will be in a list box. Store the aisle numbers and categories in an array.

A *Search* button should locate the correct location from the array and display it in a label. Make sure that the user has selected a category from the list and use the list box SelectedIndex property to find the appropriate aisle number.

Test Data

Aisle 1	Comedy
Aisle 2	Drama
Aisle 3	Action
Aisle 4	Sci-Fi
Aisle 5	Horror
Back Wall	New Releases

Very Very Boards

Modify your project from Chapter 6 to keep track of each order in an array. You can then print out the entire order with detail lines for each type of shirt. Convert the event handling for the radio buttons to share an event procedure. Use a Case structure for selection.

Create an array of a structure, which holds the quantity, size, monogram (Boolean), pocket (Boolean), price, and extended price for each type of shirt ordered. As each shirt type is added to an order, store the information in the array. Add a menu option to print out the order, which will have the customer name and order number at the top, and one line for each shirt type ordered. Use the following layout as a rough guide for your list. Make sure to align the numeric columns correctly. For the two Boolean fields (Monogram and Pocket), print Yes or No. Do not allow the user to print an invoice until the order is complete.

Very Very Boards Shirt Orders

By Your Name

Customer name: xxxxxxxxxxxxxxxxxxxxx

Order Number: xxxxx

Quantity	Size	Monogram	Pocket	Price Each	Extended Price
=========	======	=========	========	========	==========
xxx	xxx	xxx	xxx	xx	x,xxx

Order Total: xx,xxx

9

Programming with Web Forms

at the completion of this chapter, you will be able to . . .

1. Explain the functions of the server and the client in Web programming.

2. Create a Web Form and run it in a browser.

3. Describe the differences among the various types of Web controls and the relationship of Web controls to controls used on Windows forms.

4. Understand the event structure required for Web programs.

5. Design a Web Form using either a grid layout or a flow layout.

6. Validate Web input using the validator controls.

7. Use elementary techniques to maintain state in Web pages.

8. Include HyperLink controls to provide navigation between Web pages.

9. Define ASP, XML, WSDL, and SOAP.

Visual Basic and Web Programming

So far, all of your projects are based on Windows Forms and run stand-alone in the Windows environment. In this chapter, you learn to program for the Internet. In Visual Basic .NET, you use **Web Forms** to create the user interface for Web projects. A Web Form displays as a document in a **browser**, such as Netscape or Internet Explorer (IE). You also can use Mobile Web Forms to display documents on mobile devices such as cell phones and personal digital assistants (PDAs).

Client/Server Web Applications

Most Windows applications are stand-alone applications; Web applications require a server and a client. The server sends Web pages to the client, where the pages display inside a browser application (Figure 9.1).

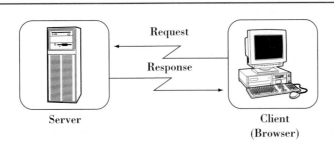

Server   Client
                (Browser)

Figure 9.1

A server delivers Web pages to a client, where the pages display in a browser window. The server can be on a remote machine or on the same machine as the client.

Web Servers

To develop Web applications you must either use a remote Web server or make your local machine a Web server. The most common practice is to make the development machine a server by installing Internet Information Services (IIS). IIS handles the Web server functions and the browser acts as the client.

Note: You should install the IIS *before* installing VB. If you must install IIS after VB .NET, you must register IIS by running aspnet_regiis.exe, which is found in the Windows/Microsoft .NET folder.

Web Clients

Browsers display pages written in hypertext markup language (HTML). The pages also may contain programming logic in the form of script, such as JavaScript, VBScript, or Jscript, or as Java applets. The browser renders the page and displays it on the local system.

You have likely seen Web pages that look different when displayed in different browsers, or even in different versions of the same browser. Although many browser applications are available, the two most common are Internet Explorer and Netscape.

You may know which browser your users are using, such as when you are programming for a network within a company, called an **intranet**. Or you may develop applications that run on the Internet and might display in any browser. If your projects will run on different browsers, you should test and check the output on multiple browsers.

Web Pages

One characteristic of HTML **Web pages** is that they are **stateless**. That is, a page does not store any information about its contents from one invocation to the next. Several techniques have been developed to get around this limitation, including storing cookies on the local machine and sending state information to the server as part of the page's address, called the uniform resource locator (URL). The server can then send the state information back with the next version of the page, if necessary.

When a user requests a Web page, the browser (client) sends a request to the server. The server may send a preformatted HTML file, or a program on the server may dynamically generate the necessary HTML to render the page. One Microsoft technology for dynamically generating HTML pages is active server pages (ASP).

ASP.NET

The latest Web programming technology from Microsoft is ASP.NET, which is their greatly improved and easier-to-use Web development tool that replaces ASP. ASP.NET provides libraries, controls, and programming support that allow you to write programs that interact with the user, maintain state, render controls, display data, and generate appropriate HTML. When you use Web Forms in Visual Basic .NET, you are using ASP.NET.

Using VB and ASP.NET you can create object-oriented, event-driven programs. These programs can have multiple classes and use inheritance.

Visual Basic and ASP.NET

Each Web Form that you design has two distinct pieces: (1) the HTML and instructions needed to render the page and (2) the Visual Basic code. This separation is new to ASP.NET and is a big improvement over the older methods that mix the HTML and programming logic (script or applets). A Web Form generates a file with an .aspx extension for the HTML and another file with an .aspx.vb extension for the Visual Basic code.

Don't panic if you don't know HTML; the HTML is generated automatically by the Visual Studio IDE. This is similar to the automatically generated code in Windows Forms. You visually create the document using the IDE's designer; then you can view and modify the HTML tags in the Visual Studio editor.

The VB code contains the program logic to respond to events. This code file is called the "code-behind" file. The code looks just like the code you have been writing for Windows applications, but many of the events are different.

Creating Web Forms

You begin a Web Forms project in much the same way as a Windows Forms project. In the *New Project* dialog box, select *ASP.NET Web Application* (Figure 9.2). Notice that the project location is set to *http://localhost*, which is the default location on your machine set up by IIS. Also notice that the *Name* box is disabled; you name the project by modifying the location in the *Location* text box. Change the location to *http://localhost/ProjectName*; the ProjectName will become a new folder located in the Inetpub\wwwroot folder, which is by default the physical folder mapped to localhost by IIS.

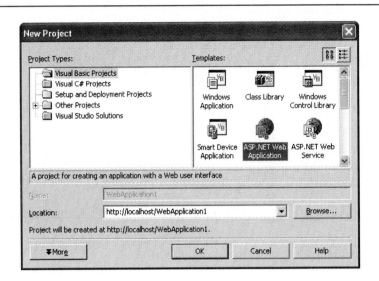

Figure 9.2

Begin a new Web Forms project by selecting ASP.NET Web Application from the New Project dialog box.

Note: You must have correct Web Permissions settings to create Web projects. If the security on your campus network does not allow the proper permissions, you cannot create Web applications.

Web Forms in the Visual Studio IDE

As soon as you open a Visual Basic Web application, you notice many differences from working on a Windows application. As the project opens, a connection to the Web server is established (Figure 9.3). Instead of a Windows form, you see a Web document (Figure 9.4), also called a *Web page* or a *Web Form*. A message appears on the form indicating the layout type, by default a grid layout. The message also tells how to change the layout. As soon as you add a control to the form, the message disappears.

Figure 9.3

The Create New Web dialog box appears briefly to show the Web connection for the new project.

If you look closely at Figure 9.4, you will notice several other differences from Windows Forms. The toolbar is different, as is the list of files in the Solution Explorer. The toolbox has different controls, and even those that look the same, such as TextBoxes, Buttons, and Labels, are actually different from their Windows counterparts and have some different properties and events. For example, Web controls have an ID property rather than a Name property.

Figure 9.4

The Visual Studio IDE with a new Web Form defined.

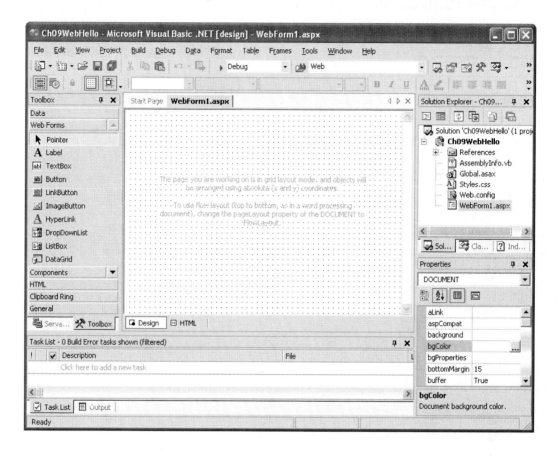

When you look at the code for a Web Form, you see that the form inherits from `System.Web.UI.Page` and a Button control inherits from `System.Web.UI.WebControls.Button`.

Creating Your First Web Form—Step-by-Step

This simple step-by-step exercise creates a Web application that displays "Hello World" on a document in a browser window.

Begin the Project

STEP 1: From the *File* menu select *New* and then *Project*.

STEP 2: Select *Visual Basic Projects* as the project type and *ASP.NET Web Application* as the template.

STEP 3: Notice that the location defaults to *http://localhost/ProjectName*. Change only the project name to "Ch09WebHello". The location should read *http://localhost/Ch09WebHello* (Figure 9.5).

STEP 4: Click *OK*. A *Create New Web* dialog box appears briefly and then WebForm1.aspx appears.

Figure 9.5

The New Project dialog box. Name the new Web application by changing the project name in the Location text box.

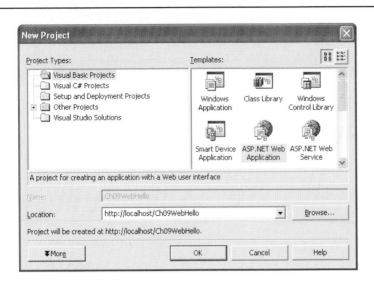

Create the User Interface

STEP 1: Add a Label from the Web Forms section of the toolbox. Notice that the layout message disappears.

STEP 2: Change the Label's ID property to "messageLabel" and the Text property to "Hello World".

Run the Web Application

STEP 1: Run the project. The Internet Explorer browser should launch and open the page with your label showing.

STEP 2: Close the browser window to end execution. Or you can switch back to the VS IDE and click the *Stop Debugging* toolbar button (or select *Debug / Stop Debugging* or press Shift + F5).

Viewing the HTML Code

When you are viewing your Web Form in the designer, you can see two tabs at the bottom of the form: *Design* and *HTML* (refer to Figure 9.4). You can click on the *HTML* tab to see the static HTML code. Don't worry about reading the code; it is automatically generated, like the Windows-generated code in a Windows Form.

Browser View

Sometimes you may want a preview of your Web page in a browser without actually running the project. Right-click on the form and select *View in Browser*. A new tab is added to the Editor window that displays the Web page as it will appear in a browser.

Toolbars

When the Web Form is open, the Design toolbar displays with some new buttons (Figure 9.6). These buttons include *Display Borders*, *Show Details*, *Lock Element*, *Show Grid*, and *Snap to Grid*.

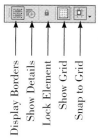

Figure 9.6

The Design toolbar displays while you are creating the user interface for a Web Form.

Controls

Several types of controls are available for Web Forms. You can mix the control types on a single form.

- *HTML controls.* These are the standard HTML elements that operate only on the client. You cannot write any server-side programming logic for HTML controls. As you submit forms to the server, any HTML controls pass to the server and back as static text. You might want to use HTML controls if you have existing HTML pages that are working and you want to convert to ASP.NET for additional capabilities. In this chapter we won't use any HTML controls.

- *HTML server controls.* These controls match HTML controls on a one-for-one basis. They have all of the attributes of HTML (client) controls plus the added capability of object-oriented, event-driven, server-side programming. However, HTML server controls do not provide many of the features of Web server controls, such as type checking for data and customized rendering of the control based on the browser.

    To change an HTML control to an HTML server control, right-click on the control and select *Run As Server Control*.

- *Web server controls*, also called *ASP.NET server controls*. These are the richest, most powerful controls provided by ASP.NET and the .NET framework. Web server controls do not directly correspond to HTML controls, but are rendered differently for different browsers in order to achieve the desired look and feel. Some of the special-purpose Web server controls are validation controls, Calendar, DataGrid, CheckBoxList, and Radio-ButtonList.

    In this chapter we will stick with Web server controls.

You can see the available controls in the toolbox when a Web Form is in Design view. Try clicking in the toolbox on *HTML*, *Web Forms*, and *Components*. The Web server controls on the *Components* list are nonvisual components that appear in the component tray of the Web Form. For your projects, keep your toolbox showing *Web Forms* controls.

In Design view, you can tell the difference between client-side HTML controls and server-side controls. The VS designer adds a small green arrow in the upper-left corner for all server controls (Figure 9.7), whether it is an HTML server control or an ASP.NET server control.

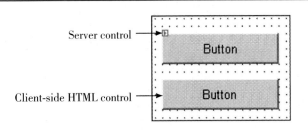

Server control

Client-side HTML control

Event Handling

You write VB code for events of Web controls in the same way that you write for Windows controls. The events may actually occur on either the client or the server. The process of capturing an event, sending it to the server, and executing the required methods is all done for you automatically.

The events of Web Forms and controls are somewhat different from those of Windows Forms. For example, a Web Form has a Page_Load event rather than a Form_Load event. You can see the events of controls using the editor; drop down the Event list for a control such as a button. You will see that you still have a Click event, but the list of events is much shorter than it is for Windows Forms.

Files

The files that you find in a Web application differ greatly from those in a Windows application (Figure 9.8). Two files make up the form: the aspx file and the aspx.vb file. The aspx file holds the specifications for the user interface that are used by the server to render the page. The aspx.vb file holds the Visual Basic code that you write to respond to events. The aspx.vb file is the "code-behind" file for the aspx file. When you are designing the user interface, you select the *FormName.aspx* tab; when you are working on the code procedures, you select the *FormName.aspx.vb* tab.

Figure 9.8

The Solution Explorer window for a Web application. Click on **Show All Files** *and expand the collapsed nodes to see all files.*

Files in a Web Project
Table 9.1

File	File Type	Purpose
FormName.aspx	ASP.NET	Dynamically generates a Web user interface allowing for server-side code.
FormName.aspx.vb	Visual Basic code	Supplies the code procedures for the form. The "code-behind" the aspx file.
FormName.aspx.resx	Resource file	Holds resources for rendering the form, including graphics and text strings.
AssemblyInfo.vb	Project information	Holds information about the project such as assembly names and versions.
ProjectName.vsdisco	XML discovery file	Holds links (URLs) to help locate the necessary Web services.
Global.asax	Text file	Identifies the Global code file and base class.
Global.asax.vb	ASP.NET application file	Supplies any code needed to respond to Application- and Session-level events.
Global.asax.resx	Resource file	Holds resources such as text strings and graphics for the Global.asax file.
Styles.css	Cascading Style Sheet	Formats and positions Web page elements.
Web.config	Configuration	Contains configuration information about each URL resource used in the project.

Several other files are generated for you, as listed in Table 9.1. One of these is the Styles.css or Cascading Style Sheet for positioning and formatting text and elements on a Web page. Another is the Web.config file, which may appear in multiple directories on the server.

When you compile a Web project, the compiler generates .dll (dynamic link library) files in the project's bin folder that hold the compiled code. When a request for the Web page is made by accessing the address (URL) of the Web page, the .dll file produces the HTML output for the page.

Coding Event Procedures—Step-by-Step

In this continuation of the earlier step-by-step tutorial, you will add a text box and a button, and code an event procedure for the button. When the user clicks the button, the page is submitted to the server. The event procedure executes on the server and the page is sent back to the client.

Add Controls and Code

STEP 1: If you closed your project, reopen it. You can choose from several methods to reopen the project:

- Switch to or display the Start page *(Help / Show Start Page)* and select your project.

- Open the *File* menu and select either *Recent Files* or *Recent Projects* and select your project.

- Select *File / Open / Project from Web* to locate your file under *localhost*.

STEP 2: Add a text box to the Web Form and change its ID property to "nameTextBox".

STEP 3: Add a button called submitButton and change its Text property to "Submit" (Figure 9.9).

Figure 9.9

Add a label and a button to the Web Form for the chapter step-by-step exercise.

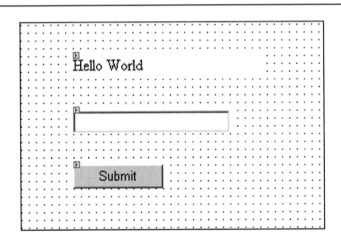

STEP 4: Double-click on the button to open the Editor window for the aspx.vb file. Write the code for the button:

```
' Display the name in the label.
messageLabel.Text = "Hello " & nameTextBox.Text
```

Run the program. Type your name into the text box and click the *Submit* button.

Watch the status bar of the browser after you click on *Submit*. First you should see a message *Web Site Found... Waiting for reply*. You can watch it send the information and then respond.

STEP 5: Close the browser window to stop execution.

Add Remarks

STEP 1: Finish up by adding remarks to the form's code.

```
' Project:        Ch09WebHello
' Programmer:     Your Name
' Date:           Today's Date
```

```
' Description:        Display the user name concatenated to a label.
'                     This is the step-by-step program for creating Web Forms.
```

Debugging

The Visual Studio IDE is designed to debug programs. You can set breakpoints, single-step execution, and display the contents of variables and properties. Try setting a breakpoint in the submitButton event procedure and rerun the program. The project compiles and displays in the browser. After you click on the button, the breakpoint halts execution and you can view the code and the values of properties, just as you can in Windows Forms. Single-step execution using the F11 key and view your objects and properties in the Autos or Locals window.

Testing in Other Browsers

You can test your project in another browser, such as Netscape. First, launch the browser and then type the URL of your page into the Address bar. (As a shortcut, you can copy and paste the URL from the Address bar of Internet Explorer.) For the step-by-step tutorial, assuming that you called the project Ch09WebHello, the URL would be `http://localhost/Ch09WebHello/Web-Form1.aspx`. You also can test the project from within the VS IDE. With the form showing in the Designer window, select *File / Browse With*. You can select from browsers that are installed on your computer.

Feedback 9.1

1. How can you convert an HTML control to an HTML server control?
2. Why might a person *want* to convert an HTML control to an HTML server control?
3. What two files make up a Web Form? What is the purpose of each file?
4. How can you display a preview of how your Web Form will display in a browser without actually running the program?

Laying Out Web Forms

Using Web Forms, you have considerable control over the layout of a page. However, you must always be aware that users may have different browsers, different screen sizes, and different screen resolutions. ASP.NET generates appropriate HTML to render the page in various browsers but cannot be aware of the screen size, resolution, or window size on the target machine.

The Page Layout

The **pageLayout property** of a page determines how and where the controls on a Web page appear. The two choices for layout are **grid layout** (the default) or **flow layout**.

A flow layout works very much like adding text in a word processor. You have an insertion point and each control that you add appears immediately following the insertion point. You can add spaces and press the Enter key to set the location for each control. When the page is displayed in the browser, the user can resize the window and the controls will move to fit in the window, very much like changing the margins in a text file. The advantage of a flow layout is that your Web page can display on any size screen with any resolution; the disadvantage is that you have very little control over the exact placement of the controls.

The default grid layout allows you to determine the exact placement of controls, using an X and Y grid. ASP.NET generates the correct HTML to display the controls in the correct location. However, if your page is large and the user's browser window is small, some controls may not be visible. You can expect a scroll bar to appear on the browser window, giving the user the opportunity to scroll sideways or down to see the rest of the page, but the effect may not be what you had in mind.

Using Tables for Layout

If you want to set up an area on your form with rows and columns, you can add a **table**. You can add controls and text to the table cells to align the columns as you want them. Although you can use tables in either a grid layout or a flow layout, you will find tables most useful in a flow layout. This is because a grid layout already gives you control of the placement of controls.

The table is an HTML control, which doesn't need any server-side programming. Although there is a Web server Table control, that is generally used when you want to write code to add rows, columns, or controls at run time. You can add a table from the HTML controls or from the *Table* menu, which appears when you are designing a Web Form. The *Table / Insert / Table* menu item displays a dialog box (Figure 9.10) that allows you to select the number of rows and columns and set other properties, such as borders, alignment, and background

Figure 9.10

In the Insert Table *dialog box, you can set the number of rows and columns and the properties for the table.*

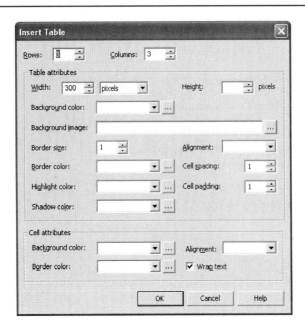

color. Note that you also can set these properties in the Properties window when the table is selected.

You can move a table to a new location. In a grid layout, select the table and move it as you would any other element. For a flow layout, you must insert spaces to move the table.

To add or delete a table row, first select a row. Then right-click and use the context menu. You can use the same technique to add or delete a column.

Entering Data in a Table

You can add controls to any table cell or type text in a cell during design time. If you want to be able to refer to the text in a cell at run time, add a label and give it an ID; otherwise you can type text directly into the cell. Figure 9.11 shows a table in Design view. Although the table's border is set to zero, the borders appear at design time but not at run time (Figure 9.12).

Including Images on Web Pages

You can add graphics to a Web page using the Image control. The concept is similar to the PictureBox control on Windows Forms but the graphic file is

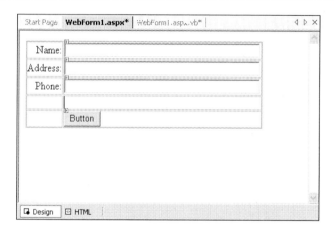

Figure 9.11

Add text and controls to the table cells. Although the Border property is set to zero, the borders still show at design time.

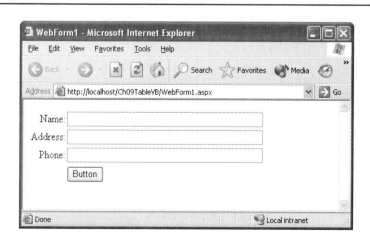

Figure 9.12

The table at run time. With the Border property set to zero, the borders do not appear.

connected differently due to the nature of Web applications. Each Image control has an ImageUrl property that specifies the location of the graphic file.

Many companies keep all Web graphics in a separate folder for organization purposes. For your projects, the best technique is to store your image in the project folder. When you set the ImageUrl property, leave the URL type as "Document Relative". For the URL value on the dialog box, type the name of the image file including the extension (Figure 9.13).

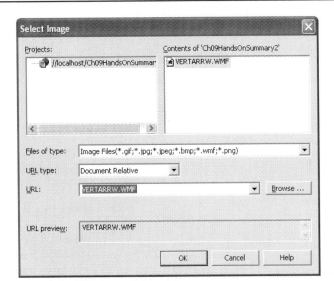

Figure 9.13

Set the URL to "Document Relative" and type the name of the graphic file. The server will look for the graphic in the same folder in which the page is located.

Feedback 9.2

1. List the differences between using a grid layout and a flow layout.
2. Name two ways to place a button at the bottom of a form using a flow layout.
3. What is the difference between an HTML Table control and a Web Table control?
4. Where should you store images for a Web application?

Using the Validator Controls

ASP.NET provides several controls that can automatically validate input data. You add a **validator control**, attach it to an input control such as a text box, and set the error message. At run time, when the user inputs data, the error message displays if the validation rule is violated. These validation controls run on the client-side, so the page does not have to be submitted to the server to view and clear the message. Table 9.2 lists the ASP.NET validator controls.

Note: A blank entry passes the validation for each of the controls except the RequiredFieldValidator. If you want to ensure that the field is not blank *and* that it passes a range check, for example, attach both a RangeValidator and a RequiredFieldValidator control to a field.

Validator Controls

Control	Purpose	Properties to Set
RequiredFieldValidator	Requires that the user enter something into the field.	ControlToValidate ErrorMessage
CompareValidator	Compares the value in the field to the value in another control or to a constant value. You also can set the Type property to a numeric type and the CompareValidator will verify that the input value can be converted to the correct type.	ControlToValidate ControlToCompare *or* ValueToCompare Type (to force type checking) ErrorMessage
RangeValidator	Makes sure that the input value falls in the specified range.	ControlToValidate MinimumValue MaximumValue Type (to force type checking) ErrorMessage
RegularExpressionValidator	Validates against a regular expression, such as a required number of digits, or a formatted value, such as a telephone number or Social Security number. Use the Regular Expression Editor to select or edit expressions; open by selecting the ellipses button on the ValidationExpression property.	ControlToValidate ValidationExpression ErrorMessage
ValidationSummary	Displays a summary of all of the messages from the other validation controls.	DisplayMode (can be set to a list, bulleted list, or message box)

Feedback 9.3

Describe how to validate a text box called numberTextBox using validator controls. A numeric entry is required, in the range 0 to 1000. The field must not be blank.

Maintaining State

As you learned earlier, a Web page holds static data. Each time a page is displayed, or redisplayed, it is a new "fresh" copy of the page. In fact, each time the page is posted back to the server, a new fresh copy of the *program* is loaded.

The server responds to the postback, handles any events that have occurred, sends the page back to the client (the browser), and releases the memory used by the program. Unless steps are taken to maintain the values of variables and the controls on the page, called the *state* of the page, all values will be lost in every postback.

Retaining the Contents of Controls

Although regular HTML does not retain the contents of controls during a postback, ASP.NET *can* retain and redisplay control contents. Web controls have an EnableViewState property, which indicates that you want the server to send the control's contents back with the page. EnableViewState is set to True by default, so control contents reappear for each postback.

Retaining the Values of Variables

Local variables in a Web application work just like local variables in a Windows application: The variables are recreated each time the procedure begins. But module-level variables in Web applications do not work like the ones you are used to in Windows. Because the program is reloaded for each postback, the values of module-level variables are lost unless you take steps to save them. You can store the value of a module-level variable in a control on the Web page; the control's EnableViewState property takes care of holding the value during postback.

Note: More advanced techniques for maintaining state, such as cookies and session variables, are beyond the scope of this text. These techniques are covered in the authors' *Advanced VB .NET* text.

You generally set up a label with its Visible property set to False. Then assign the module-level variable to the invisible control. In the following example, invisibleLabel is a control on the page and discountTotalDecimal is a module-level variable.

```
' Declare a module-level variable
Private discountTotalDecimal As Decimal

Private Sub submitButton_Click(ByVal sender As System.Object, _
  ByVal e As System.EventArgs) Handles submitButton.Click
    ' Perform calculations.
    Dim discountDecimal As Decimal

    ' Omitted code to convert input to numeric and calculate a discount.

    ' Add to the discount total.
    discountTotalDecimal += discountDecimal
    ' Save the discount total in a label.
    invisibleLabel.Text = discountTotalDecimal.ToString()
End Sub
```

Checking for Postback

When an ASP.NET Web application loads, the Page_Load event occurs. But unlike Windows applications, the page is reloaded for each "round-trip" to the server (each postback). Therefore, the Page_Load event occurs many times in a Web application. The page's IsPostBack property is set to False for the initial page load and to True for all page loads following the first. If you want to perform an initialization task once, you can test for IsPostBack = False (or Not IsPostBack) in the Page_Load event procedure. And if you want to make sure that you perform an action only on postback (not the initial page load), you can check for IsPostBack = True.

```
Private Sub Page_Load(ByVal sender As System.Object, _
  ByVal e As System.EventArgs) Handles MyBase.Load

    ' If a value exists for the discount total...
    If IsPostBack And invisibleLabel.Text <> "" Then
        discountTotalDecimal = Decimal.Parse(invisibleLabel.Text)
    End If
```

Notice that the module-level variable discountTotalDecimal is assigned a value only on postback *and* invisibleLabel already has been assigned a value.

Feedback 9.4

Why is it necessary to check for a postback when writing Web applications?

Navigating Web Pages

ASP.NET provides several techniques for navigating from one Web page to another. The easiest form of navigation is to use a HyperLink control.

Using HyperLinks

You may need to allow your user to navigate to another site or to another page in your application. You can add a HyperLink to a Web page. The HyperLink control allows you to enter a Text property for the text to display for the user and a NavigateUrl property that specifies the URL to which to navigate.

When you select the NavigateUrl property for a HyperLink control, the *Builder* button displays the *Select URL* dialog box (Figure 9.14). You can enter an absolute URL, a root-relative URL, or a document-relative URL. Use an "Absolute" URL to enter the complete address of another Web site, such as http://www.microsoft.com. For your Web applications that have all Web pages in a single folder, specify "Document Relative" and select the name of the file at the top of the dialog box (Figure 9.15). If your application is organized into multiple folders, you may want to use "Root Relative".

Adding a Second Web Page

You may want to include multiple Web pages in your application. For example, you can have a separate page to display contact information for your company. You can create a Web Form that contains labels about the company and a HyperLink control to return to the company's home page. To add a page, select *Add Web Form* from the *Project* menu and give the new form an appropriate name. You can add HyperLinks to each page to navigate back and forth.

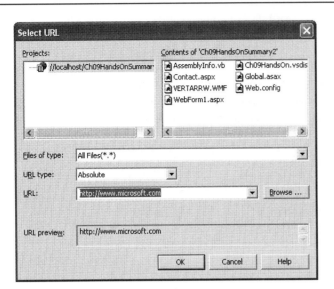

Figure 9.14

Enter the URL to which to navigate in the Select URL dialog box. Select "Absolute" when you want to enter a complete URL.

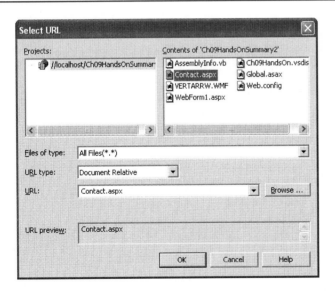

Figure 9.15

To navigate to a page in your application's folder, specify a "Document Relative" URL and select only the file name.

Feedback 9.5

1. What property of a HyperLink control indicates to which Web page the control is linked?
2. Describe how to set up the HyperLinks to navigate from a main page to a second page and back again to the main page.

Managing Web Projects

Managing the files for Web projects can be a challenge, especially if you need to move the project from one computer to another. Unless you are careful, your solution files (.sln and .suo) will be saved in a separate folder in a different location from the rest of your project.

Location of Files

The Visual Studio IDE saves solution files in the default folder that you select in *Tools / Options / Environment*. In the *Projects and Solutions* section, the entry for *Visual Studio projects location* determines the location of the .sln and .suo files. This location is the same for Windows projects and for Web projects.

When you create a new Web project, all files *except the solution files* are stored in a new folder beneath Inetpub\wwwroot. For example, if you create a new Web project called "MyWebProject", two folders called "MyWebProject" are created: one in your default project folder and one in wwwroot.

If you keep your project on a single development machine, the VS IDE can open either the project or solution file and keep track of the files. But if you need to move your project, the file arrangement can cause difficulties.

Recommendation: As soon as you open a new Web project, select the solution file in the Solution Explorer. Then select *File / Save SolutionName As*. Browse to find your folder name in Inetpub\wwwroot and save your solution file there. This will keep all of your files in the same folder.

Moving a Project

When you move a project folder from one computer to another, the project will not run until you take an extra step. To run a Web project from your local Web server (usually IIS), you must have a "virtual folder" defined. Fortunately, the VS IDE makes this happen when you create a new Web application. However, when you move the project to another computer, you must either create a virtual folder on that computer or declare the project folder to be Web-Shared.

To move a project, copy the project folder from Inetpub\wwwroot on the source computer to the same location on the target machine. Then either create a virtual directory or Web-Share the folder.

Note: Remember that the project runs from the bin folder, so you should maintain the same directory structure on the target computer.

Creating a Virtual Directory

After you move a project to a new computer, you must open the Internet Services Manager to create a virtual directory, also called a *virtual folder*. To access the Internet Services Manager, you can right-click on *My Computer*, select *Manage*, then double-click on *Services and Applications*. *Internet Information Services* should be the last item. Click on *Web Sites*, then *Default Web Site*. Select the folder for your project, right-click, and display the *Properties* dialog box. On the *Directory* tab under *Application Settings*, click on the *Create* button and then click on *OK*. Notice that the icon for the folder has changed.

Note: You also can open Internet Services Manager by typing "inetmgr" from the *Run* dialog box.

Open the project in the VS IDE, select the startup page in the Solution Explorer, right-click, and choose *Set as Start Page* from the context menu. Your project should run after creating the IIS virtual directory and setting the start page.

Web Sharing the Project Folder

An alternative to creating an IIS virtual directory on the new computer is to declare the folder as Web-Shared. This procedure is a little easier than creating a virtual directory but can cause security problems on a network. On the target computer, select the folder name using *Explorer* or *My Computer*, right-click, and choose *Properties*. On the *Web Sharing* tab, select the radio button for *Share this folder*. An *Edit Alias* dialog box appears; click *OK* and *OK* again on the *Properties* dialog box. This makes the folder Web-Shared on the new machine.

Running the Relocated Project

After you create a virtual folder or Web-Share your project folder and set the start page, you should be able to open and run your project in the VS IDE using the path Inetpub\wwwroot, or enter the URL of your page in a browser to run it. The URL should be something like this:

```
http://localhost/YourFolderName/YourFormName.aspx
```

Renaming a Web Project

If you rename a Web project, the project won't run until you take one more step. The project file for a Web application (.sln extension) stores the complete path to the folder and project file. You must open the file in an editor such as Notepad and carefully edit the folder and project name to the new name.

Deleting a Web Project

You can delete a Web project; the procedure depends on how the project was created and whether its folder is an IIS virtual directory or a Web-Shared folder. If the project is still in the location created by the VS IDE, it is in an IIS virtual folder. If you have moved or renamed the project, you may have created an IIS virtual folder or a Web-Shared folder (see the previous section). You can easily delete an IIS virtual folder in *Explorer* or *My Computer*. When you try to delete a Web-Shared folder, you receive a message telling you that the folder is in use.

To delete a Web-Shared project folder, first unshare it: Right-click the folder name in *My Computer* or *Explorer* and select *Properties*. On the *Web Sharing* tab, select the button for *Do not share this folder* and answer Yes to the confirmation; then close the *Properties* dialog box. Although it seems like you should be able to delete the folder after this step, the folder is still marked as "In Use". You must either reboot or stop and restart IIS; then you can delete the folder.

Some Web Acronyms

You have seen many acronyms in this chapter, such as HTML, ASP, IIS, and URL. But we have only scratched the surface. As you read the Help files for VB .NET and begin developing Web applications, you will want to know the meaning of many more. These include the following:

XML	*Extensible Markup Language.* This popular tag-based notation is used to define data and their format and transmit the data over the Web. XML is entirely text based, does not follow any one manufacturer's specifications, and can pass through firewalls.
	See the page "XML, Beginner's Guide" in Help for further information.
SOAP	*Simple Object Access Protocol.* An XML-based protocol for exchanging component information among distributed systems of many different types. Since it is based on XML, its messages can pass through network firewalls.
	See `http://www.w3.org/TR/SOAP/`.
HTTP	*HyperText Transfer Protocol.* The protocol used to send and receive Web pages over the Internet using standardized request and response messages.
Web Service	Code in classes used to provide middle-tier services over the Internet.
WSDL	*Web Services Description Language.* An XML document using specific syntax that defines how a Web service behaves and how clients interact with the service.

Your Hands-On Programming Example

R 'n R has decided to start selling books online. Create a Web project to calculate the amount due including discounts. Allow the user to display the total of discounts.

The user enters the quantity, title, and price of a book, and the program calculates the extended price, a 15 percent discount, and the discounted price.

The input must be validated. The quantity and price are required fields, and the quantity must be an integer between 1 and 100.

Additionally, the program will maintain a total of all discounts given and display that total on the page in response to a button click.

Include a second page for contact information.

Note: This project is a Web version of the Book Sales program for R 'n R from Chapter 3.

Planning the Project
Sketch the Web Forms (Figure 9.16), which your users sign off as meeting their needs.

Plan the Objects and Properties

Main Page

Object	Property	Setting
Label1	ID	Label1
	Text	R 'n R Book Sales
	Font	Bold, Arial, Medium
Label2	ID	Label2
	Text	Quantity

Figure 9.16

Sketch the forms for the hands-on programming example. a. The main page and b. the contact page.

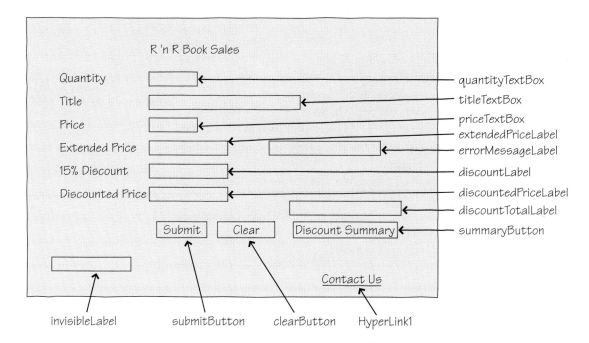

a.

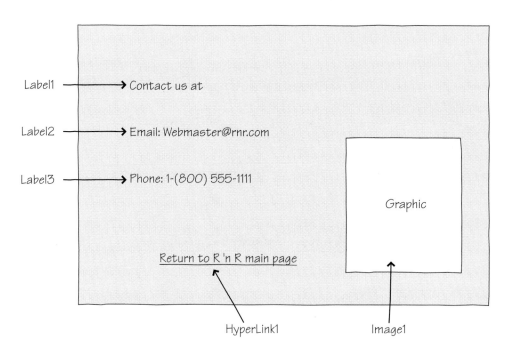

b.

Object	Property	Setting
Label3	ID	Label3
	Text	Title
Label4	ID	Label4
	Text	Price
Label5	ID	Label5
	Text	Extended Price
Label6	ID	Label6
	Text	15% Discount
Label7	ID	Label7
	Text	Discounted Price
quantityTextBox	ID	quantityTextBox
titleTextBox	ID	titleTextBox
priceTextBox	ID	priceTextBox
extendedPriceLabel	ID	extendedPriceLabel
	Text	(blank)
	BorderStyle	Solid
	BorderWidth	1
discountLabel	ID	discountLabel
	Text	(blank)
	BorderStyle	Solid
	BorderWidth	1
discountedPriceLabel	ID	discountedPriceLabel
	Text	(blank)
	BorderStyle	Solid
	BorderWidth	1
discountTotalLabel	ID	discountTotalLabel
	Text	(blank)
invisibleLabel	ID	invisibleLabel
	Text	(blank)
	Visible	False
submitButton	ID	submitButton
	Text	Submit
clearButton	ID	clearButton
	Text	Clear
summaryButton	ID	summaryButton
	Text	Discount Summary
RequiredFieldValidator1	ID	RequiredFieldValidator1
	ControlToValidate	quantityTextBox
	ErrorMessage	Required Field

Object	Property	Setting
RangeValidator1	ID	RangeValidator1
	ControlToValidate	quantityTextBox
	Type	Integer
	MaximumValue	100
	MinimumValue	1
	ErrorMessage	Quantity must be 1-100.
RequiredFieldValidator2	ID	RequiredFieldValidator2
	ControlToValidate	priceTextBox
	ErrorMessage	Required Field
errorMessageLabel	ID	errorMessageLabel
	Text	(blank)
	ForeColor	Red
Hyperlink1	Text	Contact Us
	NavigateUrl	Contact.aspx

Contacts Page

Object	Property	Setting
Label1	Text	Contact us at
Label2	Text	Email: Webmaster@rnr.com
Label3	Text	Phone: 1-(800) 555-1111
Hyperlink1	Text	Return to R 'n R main page
	NavigateUrl	MainPage.aspx
Image1	ImageUrl	VERTARRW.WMF (Stored in project folder)
		(Image found in Graphics\metafile\Arrows and your text CD.)

Plan the Procedures

Procedure	Actions
Page_Load	If PostBack and invisible label has a value
	Load discount total from invisible label.
submitButton_Click	Clear any text in errorMessageLabel.
	Convert input text values to numeric.
	Calculate the extended price = price * quantity.
	Calculate the discount = extended price * discount rate.
	Calculate the discounted price = extended price – discount.
	Add the discount to the discount total.
	Assign the discount total to the invisible label.
	Format and display the results.
	Handle any conversion exceptions.
clearButton_Click	Clear all text boxes and labels.
summaryButton_Click	Display the discount total in a label.

Write the Project Follow the sketch in Figure 9.16 to create the Web pages. Figure 9.17 shows the completed pages and Figure 9.18 shows the pages in Design view.

- Set the properties of each of the objects according to your plan.

- Write the code. Working from the pseudocode, write each procedure.

- When you complete the code, use a variety of data to thoroughly test the project. Make sure to test with empty fields, data out of range, and nonnumeric data in the numeric fields.

Figure 9.17

The finished Web application. a. The main page and b. the contact page.

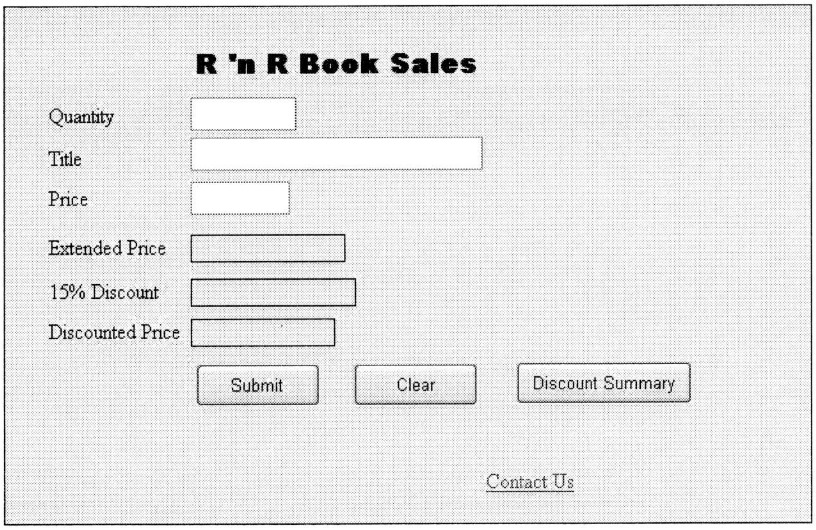

a.

b.

The Project Coding Solution

```
' Program:      Chapter 9 Hands-on
' Programmer:   Bradley/Millspaugh
' Date:         January 2004
```

Figure 9.18

Lay out the controls in Design view. a. The main page and b. the contact page.

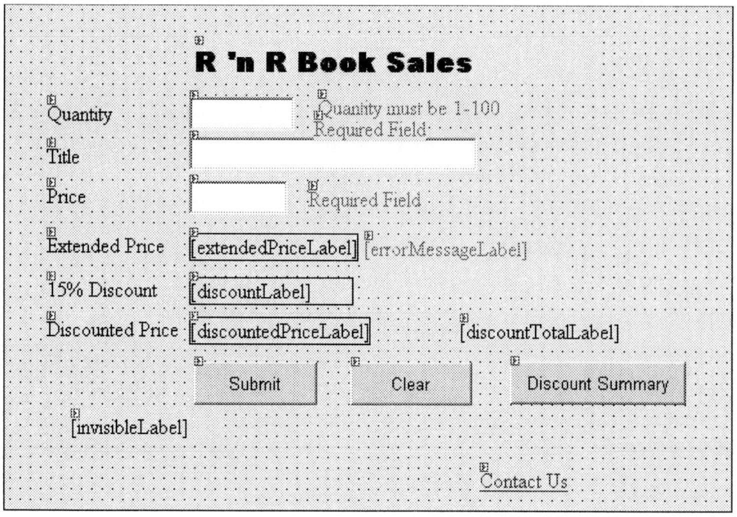

a.

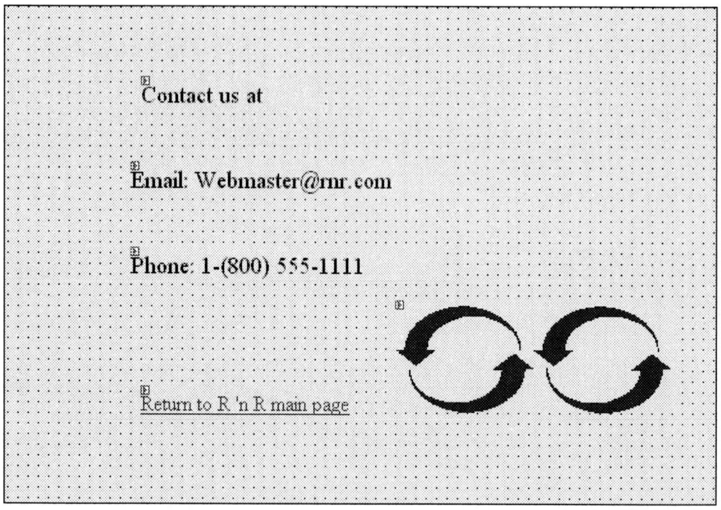

b.

```
' Description:    A Web application to calculate the extended price for books sold,
'                 a discount, and the discounted amount. Calculates and displays
'                 the total discounts.
'                 Uses validator controls for input validation.
' Folder:         Ch09VBHandsOn
'                 Note: This folder must be placed in Inetpub/wwwroot and a virtual
'                 directory created in order to run.

Option Strict On

Public Class MainForm
    Inherits System.Web.UI.Page

'... Automatically generated code appears here.

    Private discountTotalDecimal As Decimal
    Const DISCOUNT_RATE_Decimal As Decimal = 0.15D
```

```vb
Private Sub Page_Load(ByVal sender As System.Object, _
  ByVal e As System.EventArgs) Handles MyBase.Load
    ' Put user code to initialize the page here.

    ' If a value exists for the discount total...
    If IsPostBack And invisibleLabel.Text <> "" Then
       discountTotalDecimal = Decimal.Parse(invisibleLabel.Text)
    End If
End Sub

Private Sub submitButton_Click(ByVal sender As System.Object, _
  ByVal e As System.EventArgs) Handles submitButton.Click
    ' Calculate the price and discount.
    Dim quantityInteger As Integer
    Dim priceDecimal, extendedPriceDecimal As Decimal
    Dim discountDecimal, discountedPriceDecimal As Decimal

    errorMessageLabel.Text = ""
    Try
        ' Convert input values to numeric variables.
        quantityInteger = Integer.Parse(quantityTextBox.Text)
        priceDecimal = Decimal.Parse(priceTextBox.Text)

        ' Calculate values for sale.
        extendedPriceDecimal = quantityInteger * priceDecimal
        discountDecimal = extendedPriceDecimal * DISCOUNT_RATE_Decimal
        discountedPriceDecimal = extendedPriceDecimal - discountDecimal

        ' Add to the discount total.
        discountTotalDecimal += discountDecimal
        ' Save the discount total in a label.
        invisibleLabel.Text = discountTotalDecimal.ToString()

        ' Format and display answers for sale.
        extendedPriceLabel.Text = extendedPriceDecimal.ToString("C")
        discountLabel.Text = discountDecimal.ToString("N")
        discountedPriceLabel.Text = discountedPriceDecimal.ToString("C")

        ' Handle exceptions.
    Catch ErrException As Exception
        errorMessageLabel.Text = "Unable to calculate. Check for numeric values."
    End Try
End Sub

Private Sub clearButton_Click(ByVal sender As System.Object, _
  ByVal e As System.EventArgs) Handles clearButton.Click
    ' Clear previous amounts from the form.

    quantityTextBox.Text = ""
    titleTextBox.Text = ""
    priceTextBox.Text = ""
    extendedPriceLabel.Text = ""
    discountLabel.Text = ""
    discountedPriceLabel.Text = ""
    errorMessageLabel.Text = ""
    discountTotalLabel.Text = ""
End Sub
```

```
Private Sub summaryButton_Click(ByVal sender As System.Object, _
    ByVal e As System.EventArgs) Handles summaryButton.Click
    ' Display the discount summary information.

    discountTotalLabel.Text = "Total discounts: " &  discountTotalDecimal.ToString("C")
End Sub
End Class
```

Summary

1. Web applications run in a browser whereas most Windows applications run stand-alone.
2. A Web application has a client, which is the system running the Web page in a browser, and a server, which is the location of the Web page files.
3. Different browsers may display Web pages differently. Web developers must test their applications on multiple browsers unless they know that all users will use the same browser, such as in a company intranet.
4. Web pages are static and stateless. They require processing to change the appearance of the page and cannot store variables on their own.
5. ASP.NET is the Web technology included in Visual Studio .NET. Web Forms in Visual Basic use ASP.NET.
6. A Web Form consists of two files: the .aspx file that holds the code to render the user interface and the .aspx.vb file that holds the VB code.
7. Web projects running on the local machine are stored in a folder under Inetpub\wwwroot. The URL of the page is `http://localhost/ProjectName`.
8. The controls for Web pages are different from those used on Windows Forms.
9. In Design view, the HTML tab displays the HTML that is automatically generated.
10. You can display a page preview as it will appear in a browser.
11. Controls on Web pages may be HTML (client-side) controls, HTML server controls, or Web server controls, which are the controls provided by ASP.NET. Web server controls are rendered specifically for the browser being used.
12. Although the events of Web controls are somewhat different from those on Windows controls, coding for the events is the same.
13. A different set of files is generated for Web projects than for Windows projects.
14. A page may have a grid layout or a flow layout. In a flow layout, controls are placed one after another, from top to bottom, similar to a word processing document. In a grid layout, controls are placed in absolute X and Y locations.
15. You can use an HTML table to lay out controls and text in rows and columns.
16. Add graphics to a page using an Image control. The control's ImageUrl property holds the location of the file.
17. Validator controls allow testing for a required field, proper type of data, or a range of values.
18. The EnableViewState property of a Web control determines whether the control maintains its value during postback. To maintain the value of a program module-level variable, assign the variable's value to an invisible control.

19. A HyperLink control is used for navigation. Set the NavigateURL property to the page to which to navigate, which can be an absolute, root-relative, or document-relative URL.
20. You can add multiple pages to a Web application and set up navigation between the pages.
21. To move a Web project from one computer to another takes several steps. You must move the folder, create a virtual folder on the target machine, and set the project's start page. If you rename the project folder or place it anywhere other than the localhost location, you must edit the solution file with a text editor to modify the path of the project folder.
22. A compiled Web application is stored in the project's bin folder in a .dll file. If you move the project to another location, you must maintain the directory structure.
23. XML is used to store and transfer data on the Internet. XML is tag-based and text-only and can be transmitted through network firewalls. SOAP and WSDL are based on XML.

Key Terms

browser *352*

flow layout *361*

grid layout *361*

intranet *352*

pageLayout property *361*

stateless *353*

table *362*

validator control *364*

Web Form *352*

Web page *353*

Review Questions

1. Explain the differences between the execution of a Windows application and a Web application.
2. Differentiate between the client and the server for a Web application.
3. What is meant by the statement that Web pages are stateless?
4. What is the localhost?
5. What are the differences between HTML controls and HTML server controls? Between HTML server controls and ASP.NET server controls?
6. How does event handling for Web applications differ from that for Windows applications?
7. What functions are done by validator controls? How can you set up a validator control?
8. What is the purpose of XML? Of SOAP?

Programming Exercises

9.1 Rewrite your project from Chapter 3 to be a Web project; include validation.

9.2 Rough Riders Rodeo wants to sell tickets online. Allow the user to enter the number of tickets needed. The data entry screen also should include the shipping address for the tickets, a credit card number, expiration date, and a drop-down box allowing the user to select the type of credit card. Also include a check box for attending the Awards Event. Include a hyperlink for confirming the order. Make the link invisible to begin but display it after the Submit button has been clicked.

The confirmation page should say "Thank you for your order".

The tickets are $15 for just the rodeo, $25 if they want to attend the Awards Event. Note that all members of the party must select the same type of tickets.

When the user selects the Submit button, display the amount due and display a link to confirm the order (make the existing link visible).

9.3   Create a Web page for entering new customer information. The fields include name, e-mail, username, and password. Include a second text box to confirm the password. Set the TextMode property of the two password fields to "Password". Use a table to lay out your controls in a flow layout.

Validate that all fields contain information. Display appropriate messages for any empty fields. Include a Submit button.

When all information is entered and the Submit button is pressed, compare the two password fields to see if they are equal. If not, clear both text boxes and display a message to reenter the password information. When the passwords match, display a message that says "Welcome" and the name of the customer.

Case Studies

VB Mail Order

Write the VB Mail Order project from Chapter 4 as a Web project. Use validator controls for the validation.

Include a second page with contact information for the company.

VB Auto Center

Write the VB Auto Center project from Chapter 4 as a Web project. Use validator controls for the validation.

Include a second page with contact information for the company.

Video Bonanza

Write the Video Bonanza project from Chapter 3 as a Web project. Use validator controls for the validation.

Include a second page with contact information for the company.

Very Very Boards

Write the Very Very Boards project from Chapter 3 as a Web project. Use validator controls for the valida-

tion. Include a second page with contact information for the company.

Accessing Database Files

1. Use database terminology correctly.

2. Create Windows and Web projects to display database data.

3. Display data in a DataGrid control.

4. Bind data to text boxes and labels.

5. Allow the user to select from a combo box or list box and display the corresponding record in data-bound controls.

Database Files

Most data handling today is done with relational database files. Many manufacturers produce database management systems (DBMS), each with its own proprietary format. One challenge for software developers has been accessing data from multiple sources that are stored in different formats. Most of the new tools available to developers, including Microsoft's Visual Studio .NET, attempt to handle data from multiple locations (servers) and data stored in different formats.

Visual Basic and Database Files

You can use Visual Basic to write projects that display and update the data from database files. Visual Basic .NET uses ADO.NET, which is the next generation of database technology, based on Microsoft's previous version called *ActiveX Data Objects (ADO)*. One big advantage of ADO.NET is that information is stored and transferred in Extensible Markup Language (XML). You will find more information about XML in the section "XML Data" later in this chapter.

ADO.NET allows you to access database data in many formats. The basic types of providers are OleDb, SQLClient for SQL Server (Microsoft's proprietary DBMS), Odbc, and Oracle. Using OleDb you can obtain data from sources such as Access, Oracle, Sybase, and DB2. The examples in this text use an Access database.

Database Terminology

To use database files, you must understand the standard terminology of relational databases. Although there are various definitions of standard database terms, we will stick with those used by Access.

An Access file (with an .mdb extension) can hold multiple tables. Each **table** can be viewed like a spreadsheet, with rows and columns. Each **row** in a table represents the data for one item, person, or transaction and is called a **record**. Each **column** in a table is used to store a different element of data, such as an account number, a name, an address, or a numeric amount. The elements represented in columns are called **fields**. You can think of the table in Figure 10.1 as consisting of rows and columns or of records and fields.

Most tables use a **key field** (or combination of fields) to identify each record. The key field is often a number, such as employee number, account number, identification number, or Social Security number; or it may be a text field, such as last name, or a combination, such as last name and first name.

A relational database generally contains multiple tables and relationships between the tables. For example, an Employee table may have an Employee ID field and the Payroll table also will have an Employee ID field. The two tables are related by Employee ID. You can find the employee information for one payroll record by retrieving the record for the corresponding Employee ID in the Employee table.

Any time a database table is open, one record is considered the current record. As you move from one record to the next, the current record changes.

Figure 10.1

A database table consists of rows (records) and columns (fields).

ISBN	Title	Author	Publisher
0-111-11111-1	89 Years in a Sand Trap	Beck, Fred	Hill and Wang
0-15-500139-6	Business Programming in C	Millspaugh, A. C.	The Dryden Press
0-394-75843-9	Cultural Literacy	Hirsch, E. D. Jr.	Vintage
0-440-22284-2	Five Days in Paris	Steel, Danielle	Dell Publishing
0-446-51251-6	Megatrends	Naisbitt, John	Warner Books
0-446-51652-X	Bridges of Madison County	Waller, Robert James	Warner Books
0-446-60274-4	The Rules	Fein/Schneider	Warner Books
0-451-16095-9	The Stand	King, Stephen	Signet
0-452-26011-6	Song of Solomon	Morrison, Toni	Plume/Penguin
0-517-59905-8	How to Talk to Anyone, Anytime, Anywhere	King, Larry	Crown
0-534-26076-4	A Quick Guide to the Internet	Bradley, Julia Case	Integrated Media Group

— Record or row

Field or column

XML Data

XML is an industry-standard format for storing and transferring data. You can find the specifications for XML at `http://www.w3.org/XML`, which is the site for the World Wide Web Consortium (W3C).

You don't need to know any XML to write database applications in VB. The necessary XML is generated for you automatically, like the automatically generated VB code and HTML. However, a few facts about XML can help you understand what is happening in your programs.

Most proprietary database formats store data in binary, which cannot be accessed by other systems or pass through Internet firewalls. Data stored in XML are all text, identified by tags, similar to HTML tags. An XML file can be edited by any text editor program, such as Notepad.

If you have seen or written any HTML, you know that opening and closing tags define elements and attributes. For example, any text between `<b>` and `</b>` is rendered in bold by the browser.

```
<b>This text is bold.</b> <i>This is italic.</i>
```

The tags in XML are not predefined as they are in HTML. The tags can identify fields by name. For example, following are three records of the Rnr-Books database file exported from Access to XML. (Later in this chapter you will be using the RnrBooks Access database for VB projects.)

```
<?xml version="1.0" encoding="UTF-8"?>
<dataroot xmlns:od="urn:schemas-microsoft-com:officedata">
   <Books>
      <ISBN>0-15-500139-6</ISBN>
      <Title>Business Programming in C</Title>
      <Author>Millspaugh, A. C.</Author>
      <Publisher>The Dryden Press</Publisher>
   </Books>
   <Books>
      <ISBN>0-446-51652-X</ISBN>
      <Title>Bridges of Madison County</Title>
      <Author>Waller, Robert James</Author>
      <Publisher>Warner Books</Publisher>
   </Books>
   <Books>
      <ISBN>0-451-16095-9</ISBN>
      <Title>The Stand</Title>
      <Author>King, Stephen</Author>
      <Publisher>Signet</Publisher>
   </Books>
</dataroot>
```

In addition to an XML data file, you usually also have an XML schema file. The schema describes the fields, data types, and any constraints, such as required fields. ADO.NET validates the data against the schema and checks for constraint violations. The schema also is defined with XML tags and can be viewed or edited in a text editor. You will be able to see the schema for your data files in a VB project by viewing the .xsd file shown in the Solution Explorer.

The format of XML data offers several advantages for programming. Because an XML schema provides for strong data typing, the various data types can be handled properly. And ADO.NET can treat the XML data as objects, allowing the IntelliSense feature of the VS .NET environment to provide information for the programmer. In addition, data handling in XML and ADO.NET executes faster than earlier forms of ADO.

▶ Feedback 10.1

1. Assume you have a database containing the names and phone numbers of your friends. Describe how the terms *file*, *table*, *row*, *column*, *record*, *field*, and *key field* apply to your database.
2. What is an advantage of transferring data as XML, rather than a proprietary format such as Access or SQLServer?

Using ADO.NET and Visual Basic

In Visual Basic, you can display data from a database on a Windows Form or a Web Form. You add controls to the form and bind data to the controls. The controls may be labels or text boxes or one of the special controls designed just for data, such as the DataGrid or DataList. However, just as you found in Chapter 9, the controls for a Windows application are different from the controls for a Web application and have different properties and events. In this chapter you will write database applications using both Windows Forms and Web Forms. Figure 10.2 shows a data table displaying in a DataGrid on a Windows Form.

Figure 10.2

The DataGrid control is bound to a table in a dataset. The data fields display automatically in the cells of the grid.

You must use several classes and objects to set up data access in Visual Basic. This list is an overview—each of the classes is further described in the sections that follow.

- *Connection.* A **connection** establishes a link to a data source, which is a specific file and/or server.

- *Data adapter.* A **data adapter** handles retrieving and updating the data. A data adapter automatically generates SQL statements that you can use to access or update data. SQL, or Structured Query Language, is an industry-standard language that is used to select and update data in a relational database.

- *Dataset.* A **dataset** contains the actual data. The data in a single dataset may come from multiple connections and/ or multiple data adapters.

Figure 10.3 shows a visual representation of the required steps.

Figure 10.3

To display database data in bound controls on a form, you need to define a connection, a data adapter, and a dataset.

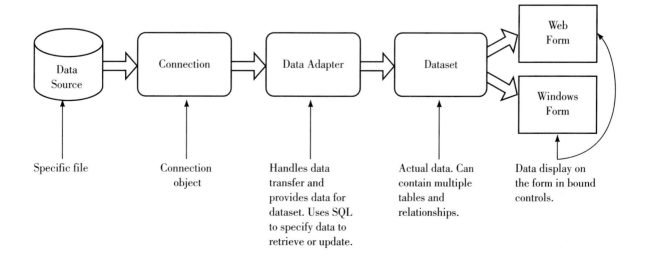

Connections

A Connection object establishes a link from a specific file or database to your program. ADO.NET provides four types of Connection objects: an OleDbConnection, an SqlConnection, an OdbcConnection, and an OracleConnection (Figure 10.4).

The Server Explorer is a great help for working with connections (Figure 10.5). If the Server Explorer is closed, choose *View / Server Explorer*.

Note: The Server Explorer for the VB Standard Edition has fewer options than the VB Professional Edition.

You can choose from several techniques for creating a new connection, the two easiest are

The Data controls in the toolbox. The connection tools provide connections to a data source.

Use the Server Explorer to manage database connections.

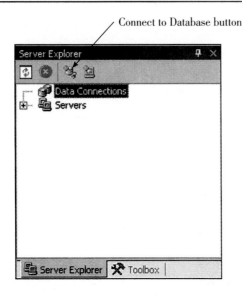

Connect to Database button

1. Click on the *Connect to Database* button in the Server Explorer.
2. Right-click on *Data Connections* in the Server Explorer and select *Add Connection* from the context menu.

No matter which method you use to begin a connection, the *Data Link Properties* dialog box appears (Figure 10.6). The *Provider* tab lists the possible drivers. For an Access 2000 or higher database, select *Microsoft Jet 4.0 OLE DB Provider*. On the *Connection* tab (Figure 10.7), you can enter or browse to the

Figure 10.6

Select the data provider on the *Provider* tab of the *Data Link Properties* dialog box.

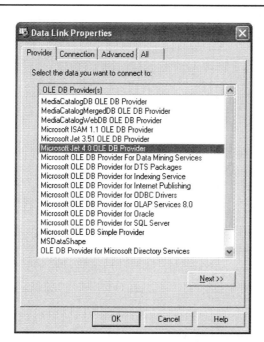

Figure 10.7

Browse to find the database filename on the *Connection* tab of the *Data Link Properties* dialog box.

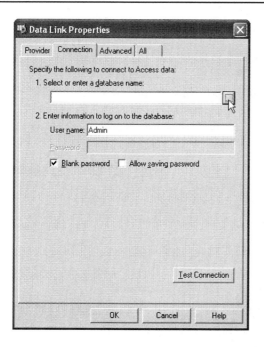

actual database file. The *Test Connection* button can test whether the connection succeeds.

Once you create a connection to a database file on a computer, the connection appears in the Server Explorer for all projects. You can use the same connection for multiple projects. And you can expand the nodes for the connection to view the tables and fields in the database file (Figure 10.8).

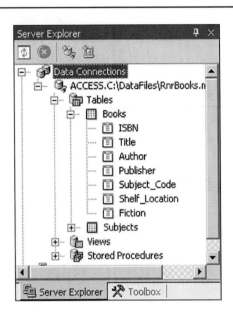

Figure 10.8

Expand the nodes for the connection to see the tables and fields in the database.

Data Adapters

A data adapter does all of the work of passing data back and forth between a data source and a program. The data source for a data adapter does not have to be a database; it also can be a text file, an object, or even an array.

You can add a new data adapter in several ways:

1. Drag a table name from the Server Explorer to the form. This technique adds both a new connection object and a new data adapter to the project.
2. Ctrl + click on the field names that you want to include; then drag the selected fields as a group to the form. This technique, like the previous one, creates both a new connection and a new data adapter in the form's component tray. Figure 10.9 shows a new connection and data adapter added to the component tray of a Windows project.

Datasets

A dataset is a temporary set of data stored in the memory of the computer. In ADO.NET, datasets are disconnected, which means that the copy of data in memory does not keep an active connection to the data source. This technique is a big improvement from the recordsets in previous versions of ADO, which maintain open connections to the data source. A dataset may contain multiple tables; however, the examples in this chapter use only one table per dataset.

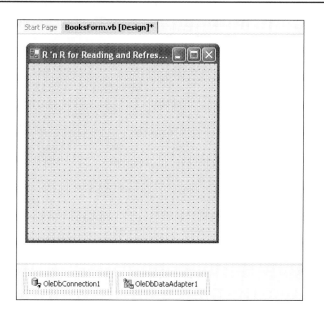

Figure 10.9

Drag the table or selected fields to the form. A new connection and data adapter are added to the form's component tray.

To define a dataset, select the data adapter component in the component tray. Then select *Generate Dataset* from the *Data* menu or right-click and select from the context menu. Name the dataset in the *Generate Dataset* dialog box (Figure 10.10).

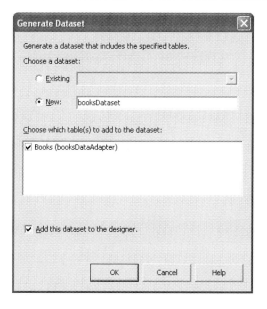

Figure 10.10

In the Generate Dataset dialog box, name the dataset.

When your program runs, you must write code to fill the dataset. This operation actually opens the connection to the data source and retrieves the data into the dataset. Any controls that you have bound to the dataset will automatically fill with data. Figure 10.11 shows how data pass from the data source to the dataset to the user interface.

Figure 10.11

The objects in a three-tier data application.

The Fill Method

To fill the dataset at run time, you must execute the **Fill method** of the data adapter. You generally add this method to the Form_Load event procedure or Page_Load for Web projects. There are several formats for the Fill method; we are using the one that specifies only the dataset name.

The Fill Method—General Form

```
DataAdapterName.Fill(DataSetName)
```

The Fill Method—Example

```
booksDataAdapter.Fill(BooksDataset1)
```

Binding Data to Controls

To bind a dataset to controls, you just set a few properties of the controls. If you are binding to a grid, as in our first step-by-step exercise, you set the grid's DataSource property to the name of the dataset and the DataMember property to the name of the table. Later in the chapter you'll bind individual fields to controls, such as labels and text boxes. In this case, you will set the DataBindings property of each control to the correct dataset field.

Feedback 10.2

Explain the purpose of and the differences between *connections*, *data adapters*, and *datasets*.

Creating a Database Application

In the following step-by-step exercise, you will create a Windows application that displays data from the Books table of the RnrBooks.mdb Access database file. Refer to Figure 10.2 for the finished application.

You will select only a few of the fields from the table and display them in a DataGrid control on a Windows Form. With only a couple of exceptions, the same procedures work for a Web application; in those cases, the differences are noted.

Creating a Bound DataGrid Control—Step by Step

Make sure that you have the RnrBooks.mdb file available before you begin the step-by-step tutorial. If you copy the file from CD to disk, make sure to remove the ReadOnly attribute from the file.

Begin the Project

STEP 1: Begin a new Visual Basic project using the Windows Application template. Name your application "Ch10WindowsGrid".

STEP 2: Move or paste a copy of the RnrBooks.mdb file into the bin folder of your project. In the Solution Explorer, click on the *Show All Files* toolbar button to display the bin folder.

　　　　Note: For a production application, you would never place the database file in the project's bin folder. For these exercises, the practice makes your project portable for testing purposes.

STEP 3: Name the form "BooksForm" and change the startup form in the *Project Properties* dialog box.

STEP 4: Set the Text property of the form to "R 'n R for Reading and Refreshment".

STEP 5: In the Solution Explorer, change the name of the Form1.vb file to BooksForm.vb.

Set Up the Connection

STEP 1: Display the Server Explorer, if necessary, by selecting *View / Server Explorer*.

STEP 2: Click on the *Connect to Database* button in the Server Explorer.

STEP 3: In the *Data Link Properties* dialog, click on the *Provider* tab and select *Microsoft Jet 4.0 OLE DB Provider* (Figure 10.12). Then click *Next*.

Figure 10.12

Select the data provider for an Access database file.

Connect to Database button

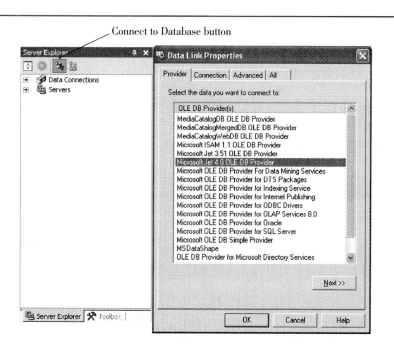

STEP 4: On the *Connection* tab, click the build button (...) and navigate to the bin folder with your RnrBooks.mdb file. Select the file and click on the *Open* button.

STEP 5: Click on *Test Connection;* you should see a message box indicating "Test connection succeeded". Click *OK* on the message box and also on the *Data Link Properties* dialog box.

STEP 6: In the Server Explorer, expand the nodes for the Data Connections, for your new connection, the Tables node, and the Books table. You should see the fields in the Books table.

Add the Connection and Data Adapter to the Form

STEP 1: In the Server Explorer, hold down the Ctrl key and click to select the ISBN, Title, and Author fields (Figure 10.13).

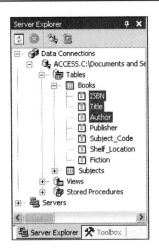

STEP 2: Drag the three selected fields from the Server Explorer to the form. If a dialog box appears asking if you want to include the password, click on *Don't include password*.

New connection and data adapter objects will appear in the component tray (Figure 10.14).

Name the Components

STEP 1: In the component tray you should have OleDbConnection1 and OleDb-DataAdapter1, which are both selected. In the next steps you will rename the connection and the data adapter. Click somewhere away from the two new controls in the component tray to deselect them.

STEP 2: Select the OleDbConnection1 component; in the Properties window change the Name property to "RnRConnection".

STEP 3: Select the OleDbDataAdapter1 component and change the name to "booksDataAdapter".

STEP 4: Press Enter or Tab and make sure the changes appear on the components in the component tray.

Generate a Dataset

STEP 1: Select the booksDataAdapter component and choose *Generate Dataset* from the *Data* menu or right-click and choose the item from the context

Figure 10.14

The new connection and data
adapter appear in the form's
component tray.

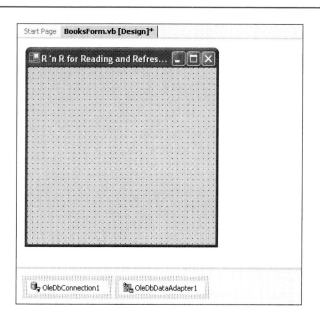

Figure 10.15

Name the new dataset in the
Generate Dataset dialog box.

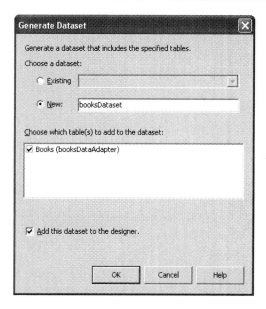

menu. In the *Generate Dataset* dialog box (Figure 10.15), name the new dataset "booksDataset" and click *OK*.

A new DataSet component is added to the component tray. Note in the Properties window that the dataset component name is BooksDataset1 and its class is booksDataset (Ch10WindowsGrid.booksDataset).

STEP 2: Notice in the Solution Explorer that booksDataset.xsd now appears. This is the schema for the new dataset. You can consider the schema a new class and the new component in the component tray an instance of the class. In code you will refer to BooksDataset1, the dataset object, which is an instance of the booksDataset class.

STEP 3: Double-click on booksDataset.xsd to see the schema of the data.

STEP 4: The bottom of the Document window shows two tabs, one for *DataSet* and one for *XML*. Go ahead and take a peek at the *XML* tab and be grateful that it's all generated automatically. You can close the books-Dataset.xsd window or click back on the tab for your form.

Add a Data Grid to the Form

STEP 1: Make sure the form is showing and display the toolbox. Widen the form and add a large DataGrid control to your form. (Refer to Figure 10.2.)

STEP 2: Set the grid's Name property to "booksDataGrid".

STEP 3: Set the grid's DataSource property to "BooksDataset1".

STEP 4: Set the DataMember to "Books", which is the name of the table within the dataset.

Notice that the grid now has column headings for the fields in the table.

Write the Code

STEP 1: Double-click on the form (not on the grid) to display the Editor window.

STEP 2: Type the following code in the Form_Load event procedure:

```
' Fill the dataset.
booksDataAdapter.Fill(BooksDataset1)
```

The Windows DataGrid control is automatically bound when you set the design-time properties, but in a Web application, you must explicitly bind the controls. For a Web application, you need one more statement:

```
booksDataGrid.DataBind() ' (Do not add this statement to your Windows application.)
```

Run the Project

STEP 1: Run the project. The grid should fill with data from the database file. Notice that you can resize the columns by pointing to the divider between columns and dragging the two-headed arrow. You also can click on a field name in the grid's header row and sort the data by that column. Your form should resemble Figure 10.2.

STEP 2: Close the form's window to stop the application.

Modify the Grid Format

STEP 1: Switch back to your form in design view.

STEP 2: Right-click the grid and choose *Auto Format* from the context menu. Select one of the formats and click *OK*.

STEP 3: Run the project again and admire your work. Not too bad for a single line of code, right? (The corresponding Web application requires two lines of code.)

STEP 4: Stop the application.

Displaying a Data Preview

Sometimes it is helpful to see what your data look like while you are designing the user interface. The .NET environment provides a *Data Adapter Preview* dialog to display a preview of a dataset. Select the data adapter component in the Designer window and select *Data / Preview Data* (or right-click and select from the context menu). In the dialog box make sure that your data adapter name displays in the Data Adapters list and click *Fill Dataset*. The data selected by the data adapter's SQL SELECT statement appears in the window (Figure 10.16). Note that you can resize the columns and scroll the window to see all of the data.

Figure 10.16

Display a preview of the dataset in the Data Adapter Preview dialog box.

Click to display → the data

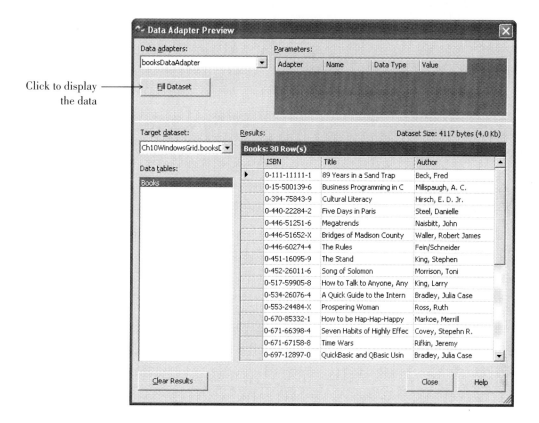

Binding Data

When you connect a control or property to one or more data elements, that is called **data binding**. ADO.NET has two forms of data binding: complex binding and simple binding. You set the binding in the Properties window at design time.

Complex Data Binding

If you need to bind more than one data element to a control, use **complex binding**. This is the technique that you used for binding the data grid in the preceding exercise, and is also used for list boxes and combo boxes. Using complex binding, you set the control's DataSource and DataMember properties; depending on the control type, you may need to set additional properties.

Simple Data Binding

Simple binding connects one control to one data element. Use simple binding to display a field value in a control such as a text box or a label. You also can bind data elements to buttons, check boxes, radio buttons, picture boxes, and any other control that shows *(Data Bindings)* in the Properties window. In the next step-by-step exercise, you will bind data elements to labels.

You can modify the data adapter's SQL SELECT statement by displaying the Query Builder. In the Properties window for the data adapter, expand the node for the SelectCommand and click on the build button for the CommandText. ■

Selecting Records from a Combo Box

Many applications allow the user to select an item to display from a list. You can fill a list box or combo box with values from a database. Consider the previous grid with book titles. A better approach might be to display the list of titles in a drop-down list and allow the user to make a selection. Then, after the title is selected, the corresponding data elements fill the Author and ISBN fields (Figure 10.17).

Figure   10.17

The user can select a book from the drop-down list. Then the labels fill with the field values that correspond to that title.

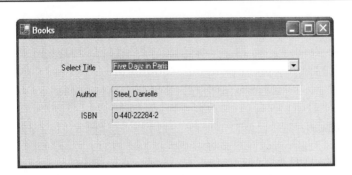

You can use any of the toolbox list controls to automatically fill with values. For Windows Forms, use the ListBox or ComboBox control; for Web Forms, use the ListBox or DropDownList. These controls have the necessary properties to bind to a data source. However, the programming for Windows controls differs from that of Web controls. First we will cover the Windows version, and then show the techniques required for the Web version.

Filling a List—Windows Forms

To automatically fill a list box or combo box with data from a dataset (Figure 10.18), you must set two properties: the DataSource and DisplayMember properties. The DataSource connects to the dataset. The DisplayMember connects to the specific field name for the data element that you want to display in the list.

After you add a list box to a form that has a dataset defined, drop down the Properties list for the DataSource and select the dataset name. Then drop down

Figure   10.18

Automatically fill a drop-down list with the field values from a dataset.

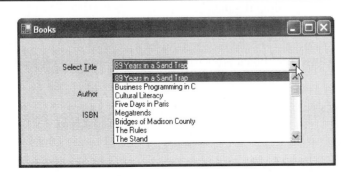

the list for the DisplayMember property; it will show the field names in the
dataset from which to select. For example, for the combo box shown in Figure
10.18, the DataSource is set to "booksDataSet1.Books" (the dataset and table
name) and the DisplayMember property is set to "Title" (the field name). That's
all there is to it. When you run your program, the list automatically fills with
the values from the selected field.

You must still use the Fill method for the dataset, just as you do for filling
grids.

```
' Fill the dataset for the list box.
booksDataAdapter.Fill(BooksDataset1)
```

Binding a Single Data Field

When you are working with a label, text box, radio button, or check box, you
only want to bind a single data field to the control. You can accomplish this
with the DataBindings property at the top of the Properties window. After
you expand the DataBindings property, you can see three additional entries for
(Advanced), *Tag*, and *Text*. You are going to bind a data field to the Text property
of the bound control; expand the Text entry and you will see a list of the fields
in the dataset (Figure 10.19).

Displaying Single Records—Step by Step

This exercise creates the form shown in Figure 10.20. The user can select a title from a combo box; then the values for a single record display in the bound
labels.

Begin a New Project

STEP 1: Begin a new project using the Windows Application template. Name
the project "Ch10WindowsSelection".

STEP 2: Change the form's Name to "booksForm" and its Text property to
"Books". Set the startup object in the *Project Properties* dialog box.

F i g u r e   1 0 . 2 0

This Windows Form displays fields for one record. The user selects the title from the combo box and the labels fill with the field values for that record.

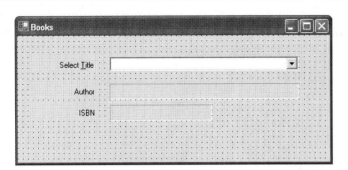

Set Up the Data Adapter and Dataset

STEP 1: If you are using the same computer as for the previous exercise, the Server Explorer should still show the connection for RnrBooks.mdb. If no connection appears in the Server Explorer, click on the *Connect to Database* button and set up the connection, following the instructions in the DataGrid step-by-step.

Note: Both the grid and selection programs can use the same database and the same connection. However, if you will want to move a project from one computer to another, you should place a copy of the database in the project's bin folder and create a new connection for that database.

STEP 2: In the Server Explorer, expand the nodes to see the fields in the Books table. Select ISBN, Title, and Author.

STEP 3: Drag the selected fields to the form to create the connection and data adapter components. If you are presented with a choice, select *Don't include password*.

STEP 4: Name the connection component "RnRConnection".

STEP 5: Name the data adapter component "booksDataAdapter".

STEP 6: Select the data adapter component and generate the dataset, calling it "booksDataset". You will see booksDataset.xsd, which is the dataset's schema, appear in the Solution Explorer, and BooksDataset1, which is the dataset object, appear in the component tray.

Add the Label and Button Controls

STEP 1: Referring to Figure 10.20, add three labels to the form. Set the Text property values to Select &Title, Author, and ISBN.

STEP 2: Add a combo box and two labels next to the labels, naming them title-ComboBox, authorLabel, and ISBNLabel. Change the BorderStyle property of the labels to Fixed3D. You can remove the Text properties or not; the labels will automatically fill with data at run time.

Bind the Data Fields

STEP 1: Set the DataSource property of titleCombobox to "BooksDataset1" and the DisplayMember property to "Books.Title".

STEP 2: Select authorLabel and expand the DataBindings property at the top of the Properties window. Select Text, drop down the list, and then expand BooksDataset1 until you see a list of fields (Figure 10.21). Double-click on Author. (Or you can select Author and press Enter.)

Figure 10.21

Set the DataBindings to bind the Author field to the Text property of authorLabel.

STEP 3: Set the DataBindings Text property for ISBNLabel to ISBN.

Write the Code

STEP 1: Code the Form_Load event procedure.

```
' Fill the dataset.
booksDataAdapter.Fill(BooksDataset1)
```

Run the Project

Run the project. Try selecting a title from the list. Do the labels change?

STEP 1: Because all fields on a form display data from the same record, changing one field (the title) changes all bound controls on the form to the same record.

Problem? If the data values in the labels do not change to match the selection in the combo box, check the combo box data binding. The DataSource must be BooksDataset1 (not BooksDataset1.Books) and the DisplayMember must be Books.Title (not Title).

STEP 2: Stop execution by closing the form.
STEP 3: Adjust the label sizes if necessary.

Question: How many lines of code did it take to write an application to select records from a database?

Sorting the List Data

You cannot sort bound data in a combo box or list box using the Sorted property of the control. However, you can sort the record in the data adapter's SQL SELECT statement, which is part of the data adapter configuration. Select the data adapter and choose *Data / Configure Data Adapter* or the context menu to open the wizard (Figure 10.22). Click *Next* to display the second page of the wizard (Figure 10.23). Generally, the connection is already selected, but you can drop down a list of all connections or even create a new connection on this page. Make sure the correct connection is selected and click *Next* to move to the next page of the wizard.

Figure 10.22

Select Data / Configure Data Adapter to display the Data Adapter Configuration Wizard. Click Next to configure the data adapter.

Figure 10.23

Select the connection or click New Connection to create a new one.

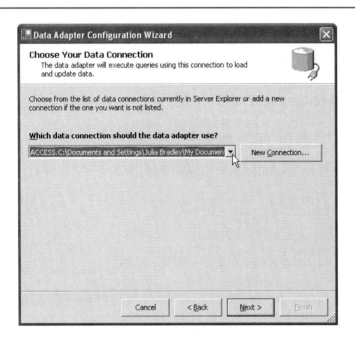

On the next page of the wizard you have only one choice (Figure 10.24) unless you are using a SQLServer database. A data adapter can select the data from a database using an SQL statement or stored procedures. Stored procedures are prewritten SQL statements stored in the database and are not available in an Access database.

The next page of the wizard displays the SQL SELECT statement as it was created originally (Figure 10.25). You can type or edit the SELECT statement yourself or use the Query Builder to help you (the recommended practice).

Figure 10.24

The third page of the wizard provides only one choice when you are configuring a data adapter for an Access database.

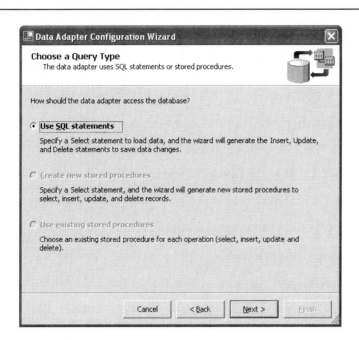

Click on *Query Builder*. If necessary, add the Books table and click to select the desired fields (Author, ISBN, and Title, in this case). Then click in the Sort Type cell for Title, drop down the list, and choose "Ascending". Notice the modification made to the SELECT statement (Figure 10.26).

When you are finished with the Query Builder, click *OK* and *Next* to finish the Data Adapter Configuration Wizard. (If you are presented with the password question, select *Don't save password*.) Any time you change the SQL SE-LECT statement, you need to regenerate the dataset schema. Right-click on the

Figure 10.25

The Query Builder can generate an SQL SELECT statement for you. Select the table(s) and field(s) that you want to include.

Figure 10.26

Specify the Sort Type for the Title field and the Query Builder adds an ORDER BY clause to the SQL SELECT statement.

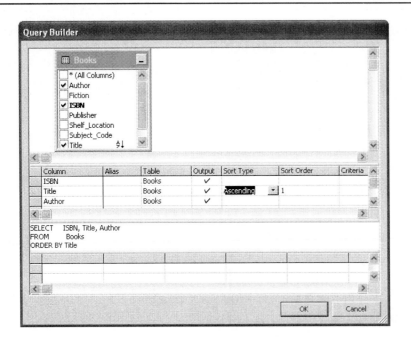

✓**TIP**

You can right-click in the SQL SE-LECT statement pane of the Query Builder and select *Run* from the context menu to see the result of the statement. ■

data adapter, select *Generate Dataset*, and select the existing dataset name. The new schema will replace the existing schema.

By adding the ORDER BY clause to the SQL SELECT statement, the list items will appear in sorted order.

▶ **Feedback 10.3**

1. What properties of a ComboBox control must be set to bind the control to a data field?
2. What properties of a Label control must be set to bind the control to a data field?
3. How can you make the list items in a data-bound combo box appear in sorted order?

Selecting Records Using Web Forms

When you write database programs for the Web, you have a few more considerations. You set up the connection, data adapter, and dataset components in the same manner as in Windows applications. But there are additional security issues and you must modify the program logic due to the nature of Web pages in a client/server environment. Remember that a Web page is stateless. Each time a page displays, it is a "new fresh page." The page's Load event occurs for every round-trip to the server, which happens more often than you might think.

Filling a List—Web Forms

In the Web version of the list selection program (see Figure 10.27), each time the user makes a selection from the list, a **postback** occurs. A postback is a

Figure 10.27

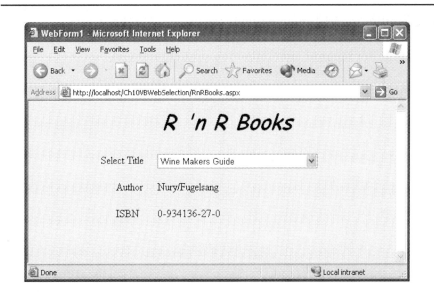

Allow the user to select a book title from the drop-down list; then display the corresponding Author and ISBN for the selected title.

round-trip to the server. After a postback, the Web page redisplays and the Page_Load event occurs. You must modify the logic in the Page_Load event procedure; otherwise the dataset for the list elements will be recreated when the user makes a selection from the list, and the user's selection will be lost.

```
Private Sub Page_Load(ByVal sender As System.Object, _
    ByVal e As System.EventArgs) Handles MyBase.Load
    ' Create the dataset and fill the drop-down list.

    ' Fill the list only the first time the page displays.
    If Not IsPostBack Then
        titlesDataAdapter.Fill(BooksDataset1)
        ' Bind all controls on the page.
        Me.DataBind()
    End If
End Sub
```

Notice the statement `Me.DataBind()` in the preceding procedure. Rather than bind each control by name, you can bind all controls on the page at once.

Setting the List Properties

You must set some different properties of the Web version of the DropDownList control. Set the DataSource property to the Dataset, just as in the Windows version. Then set the DataMember to the name of the table, which appears in a drop-down selection list. You also must set the DataTextField to the name of the field that you want to display in the list.

Another list property that needs setting is the AutoPostBack property. In a Web application, not all events cause a PostBack to the server. By default, when the user makes a selection from a DropDownList, the event is saved for the next postback, which generally occurs when the user clicks a button. If you want to respond to a change in the list selection, you must set the AutoPost-Back property to True. Then when the user selects from the list, a postback occurs and the SelectedIndexChanged event procedure executes immediately.

Retrieving the Selected Record

In a Windows application, when you fill a dataset, the dataset remains in memory; you can display any record and even move from one record to another. But in a Web application, the dataset is created on the server and only one pageful of data is sent to the client. If you request a different record from the dataset on the next postback, the server must recreate the entire dataset in order to send one record with the page. When the user makes a selection from the list, it makes more sense to retrieve only the selected record, rather than a dataset that contains the entire table, especially if the table is very large. Therefore, we will use a technique called a **parameterized query** to create a dataset with only the selected record.

When you want your dataset to contain only selected record(s), you can modify the SQL SELECT statement used by the data adapter. In fact, the Web selection application will have two data adapters: one that selects the titles to fill the drop-down list and one to select a single record. An SQL SELECT statement that selects a particular record requires a WHERE clause.

Examples

```
SELECT Title, Author, ISBN FROM Books
    WHERE Title = "War and Peace"

SELECT Name, AmountDue FROM OverdueAccounts
    WHERE AmountDue > 100
```

Usually you don't know until run time the value that you want to include in the WHERE clause. In that case, you can use a question mark in place of the actual value and supply the value as a parameter in code. This type of query is called a *parameterized query*.

```
SELECT Title, Author, ISBN FROM Books
    WHERE Title = ?
```

You can modify the SQL SELECT statement using the Query Builder in the Data Adapter Configuration Wizard. (Refer to Figures 10.22–26 for instructions on using the Query Builder.) On the Query Builder page, for the Title, type "=?" in the **Criteria** column (Figure 10.28). The Query Builder creates the correct SQL for you. Note that the Query Builder adds the optional parentheses around "(Title = ?)", even when you leave them out.

Displaying the Data for a Selected Item

You supply the value for a parameterized query at run time. The user may enter a value in a text box or, better yet, select an item from a list, as in the previous list box example. For a list box selection, write your code in the control's SelectedIndexChanged event procedure.

Specify the parameter value using the Parameters collection of the data adapter's SelectCommand property. You assign the value from the drop-down list or combo box to a specific parameter:

```
booksDataAdapter.SelectCommand.Parameters("Title").Value = titleDropDownList.Text
```

Figure 10.28

Using the Query Builder, enter "=?" in the Criteria column for Title to create a parameterized query.

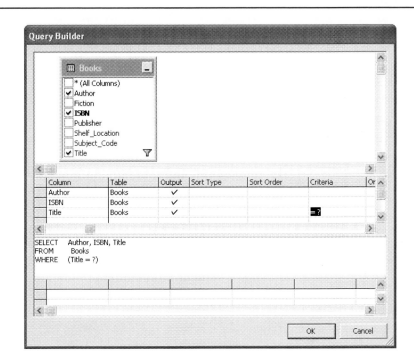

Figure 10.28

Using the Query Builder, enter "=?" in the Criteria column for Title to create a parameterized query.

You must assign the parameter value before executing the `Fill` method. Notice also in the following code example that you clear out any previous contents of the dataset when you create the new dataset.

```
Private Sub titleDropDownList_SelectedIndexChanged(ByVal _
   sender As System.Object, ByVal e As System.EventArgs) _
   Handles titleDropDownList.SelectedIndexChanged
      ' Retrieve the record matching the selection.

   If titleDropDownList.SelectedIndex <> -1 Then
      BooksDataset1.Clear()
      booksDataAdapter.SelectCommand.Parameters("Title").Value _
         = titleDropDownList.SelectedItem.Text
      booksDataAdapter.Fill(BooksDataset1)
      ISBNLabel.DataBind()
      authorLabel.DataBind()
   End If
End Sub
```

If you have the user enter a value into a text box instead of selecting from a list, you must watch out for entries that don't exist in the dataset. Include a button for the event such as *Find*. Then, in the *Find* button's event procedure, check for an empty dataset after the `Fill` method.

```
Private Sub findButton_Click(ByVal sender As System.Object, _
   ByVal e As System.EventArgs) Handles findButton.Click
      'Get record to match the selected title

   BooksDataset1.Clear()
   messageLabel.Text = ""
```

```
booksDataAdapter.SelectCommand.Parameters("Title").Value _
    = titleTextBox.Text
booksDataAdapter.Fill(BooksDataset1)
If booksDataSet1.Tables("Books").Rows.Count = 0 Then
    messageLabel.Text = "Book not found"
Else
    ISBNLabel.DataBind()
    authorLabel.DataBind()
End If
End Sub
```

You don't need to check for an unmatched value when the user selects from a list because all elements are known to be in the database.

The Web Selection Program

The Web version of the selection program uses two data adapters: one for the titles list and one for the selected record. Figure 10.29 shows the Web Form in design time. Refer to Figure 10.27 for the completed program output. In the program listing that follows, notice the connection string specification in the Page_Load event procedure. This statement allows the application to be moved from one computer to another and is discussed in the "Making a Database Project Portable" section later in this chapter.

The Web version of the selection application.

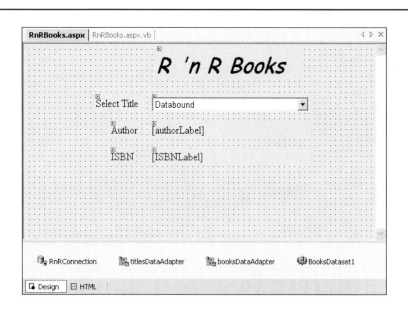

```
'Program:        Ch10VBWebSelection
'Programmer:     Bradley / Millspaugh
'Date:           January 2004
'Description:    A Web application that allows the user to select a book
'                title from a drop-down list and then displays
'                additional fields for the selected record.

Public Class RnRBooks
    Inherits System.Web.UI.Page
```

```
      Private Sub Page_Load(ByVal sender As System.Object, _
        ByVal e As System.EventArgs) Handles MyBase.Load
          ' Fill the titles list.

          RnRConnection.ConnectionString _
            = "Provider=Microsoft.Jet.OLEDB.4.0; " _
            & "Data Source=C:\inetpub\wwwroot\Ch10VBWebSelection\RnrBooks.mdb"
          If Not IsPostBack Then
              titlesDataAdapter.Fill(BooksDataset1)
              Me.DataBind()
          End If
      End Sub

      Private Sub titleDropDownList_SelectedIndexChanged(ByVal _
        sender As System.Object, ByVal e As System.EventArgs) _
        Handles titleDropDownList.SelectedIndexChanged
          ' Retrieve the record matching the selection.

          If titleDropDownList.SelectedIndex <> -1 Then
              BooksDataset1.Clear()
              booksDataAdapter.SelectCommand.Parameters("Title").Value _
                = titleDropDownList.SelectedItem.Text
              booksDataAdapter.Fill(BooksDataset1)
              ISBNLabel.DataBind()
              authorLabel.DataBind()
          End If
      End Sub
End Class
```

Complications with Web Database Applications

Running Web database applications is considerably more complicated than Windows applications, primarily due to security issues. The operating system must take precautions to prevent Web applications from accessing and/or modifying data. The security can make it difficult for you as a developer to test your programs. And Microsoft is constantly updating the Windows security measures, as more issues become known, so techniques that work today may not work tomorrow.

Two common error messages that appear when you try to run a Web database application are

```
"Could not lock file."
```

or

```
"The Microsoft Jet database engine cannot open the file ...... It is already opened
exclusively by another user, or you need permission to view its data."
```

Here are two possible solutions to the error messages:

1. The file's folder may not have proper permissions. To open an .mdb file, even in read-only mode, the user must have Write permission for the folder in which the database resides, since an .ldb file must be created to open the file. In Windows Explorer, display the folder's properties, click on the *Security* tab, and give everyone Write permission. If you

don't have a *Security* tab in the *Properties* dialog box, you can modify a setting in Windows Explorer: Select *Tools / Folder Options*. On the *View* tab, scroll to the bottom of the list and deselect *Use simple file sharing*.

2. The file's connection may be open. Using Windows Explorer you can see an .ldb file in the .mdb file's folder, which means that the file is open. You can right-click on the connection in the VS Server Explorer and select *Close*, or close and reopen the VS IDE.

TIP

If a Web program refuses to run, try *Debug / Start without Debugging*, which often gives better messages about the cause of the problem. ∎

Making a Database Project Portable

If you need to move database projects from one computer to another, you must modify the connection information. Of course, you must have the database file available on the new computer, and you must have a connection to the file.

For a Windows Project

When you know that you must move a Windows database project, store the database file in the project's bin folder. In the Form_Load event procedure, just before filling the dataset, change the data adapter's ConnectionString property to not include the path. Although the automatically generated connection string includes the complete path and many optional parameters, a minimal connection string works just fine for an Access database. In the absence of a path, ADO.NET looks in the folder from which the application is running, which is the project's bin folder.

```
Private Sub lookupForm_Load(ByVal sender As System.Object, _
   ByVal e As System.EventArgs) Handles MyBase.Load
    ' Set up the connection and fill the dataset.

    RnRConnection.ConnectionString = _
      "Provider=Microsoft.Jet.OLEDB.4.0;Data Source=RnrBooks.mbd"
    booksDataAdapter.Fill(BooksDataSet1)
End Sub
```

Setting the connection string in code works great unless you want to make modifications to the database elements at design time. In that case, you must set up a connection on the target computer after moving the project. Here is the easiest way to set up the connection for a moved project:

*   Move the project folder, including the solution file and the database file, to the new computer.

*   Open the project and display the form.

*   Select the Connection component in the component tray and click on the ConnectionString property in the Properties window.

*   Click on the down arrow to display the list of connections on that computer. If your database file shows up in the list, you can select it. Otherwise, scroll to the bottom of the list and select *<New Connection>*. The *Data Link Properties* dialog box appears, and you can set the provider and database information following the steps shown on pages 391–392.

For a Web Project

A Web database project does not run from the bin folder, so it works best to place the database file in the project's folder and include the full path in the connection string. In the Page_Load event procedure, include the code to set the connection string.

```
Private Sub Page_Load(ByVal sender As System.Object, _
  ByVal e As System.EventArgs) Handles MyBase.Load
    ' Set up the connection and fill the dataset.

    RnRConnection.ConnectionString _
      = "Provider=Microsoft.Jet.OLEDB.4.0; " _
      & "Data Source=C:\inetpub\wwwroot\Ch10VBWebGrid\RnrBooks.mdb"
    booksDataAdapter.Fill(BooksDataset1)
    Me.DataBind()
End Sub
```

Follow the steps from Chapter 9 (page 369) for moving a Web project. That is, place the project folder in Inetpub\wwwroot and either create a virtual directory or Web-Share the folder.

After these steps, your moved Web database application should run. If you also want to make modifications to the database elements, you must set up a connection on the new computer. Follow the steps above for a Windows project.

Your Hands-On Programming Example

Create a Windows application that contains a drop-down list of titles from the RnrBooks.mdb database file. When the user selects a title, display the corresponding ISBN, author, and publisher in labels. Include additional labels to identify the contents of the list box and the data fields.

Make the ISBN, Author, and Publisher labels appear empty until the user selects a title from the drop-down list, and make the title list appear in alphabetic order.

Include the database in the project's bin folder and write a connection string in code so that the project can be moved to another computer.

Planning the Project

Sketch the form (Figure 10.30), which your users sign off as meeting their needs. Figure 10.31 shows the form in Design mode.

Plan the Objects and Properties

Object	Property	Setting
RnRConnection	Name	RnRConnection
BooksDataset1	Name	BooksDataset1
booksDataAdapter	Name	booksDataAdapter
Label1	Text	Select &Title

Figure 10.30

A planning sketch of the form for the hands-on programming example.

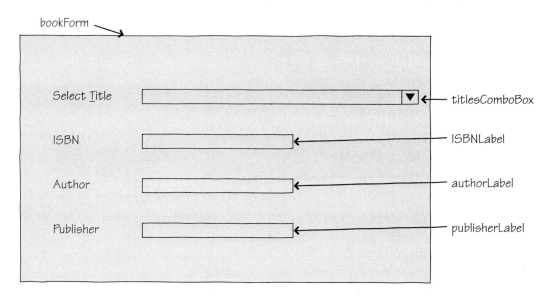

Figure 10.31

The form for the hands-on programming example in Design mode, showing the component tray.

Object	Property	Setting
Label2	Text	ISBN
Label3	Text	Author
Label4	Text	Publisher
titlesComboBox	Name	titlesComboBox
	DataSource	BooksDataset1
	DisplayMember	Books.Title

Object	Property	Setting
ISBNLabel	Name	ISBNLabel
	Text	(blank)
	DataBindings.Text	Books.ISBN
authorLabel	Name	authorLabel
	Text	(blank)
	DataBindings.Text	Books.Author
publisherLabel	Name	publisherLabel
	Text	(blank)
	DataBindings.Text	Books.Publisher

Plan the Procedures

Procedure	Actions
Form_Load	Set up the connection string.
	Fill the dataset.
	Deselect the list entry.
	Clear the labels.

Write the Project

- Create a new Windows project and move a copy of the data file to the project's bin folder. Make sure that the data file is not ReadOnly.

- Create a connection to the data file and create the data adapter for the dataset.

- Follow the sketch in Figure 10.30 and Figure 10.31 to create the form. Figure 10.32 shows the completed form.

- Set the properties of each of the objects according to your plan.

- Write the code. Working from the pseudocode, write the procedure.

- When you complete the code, thoroughly test the project.

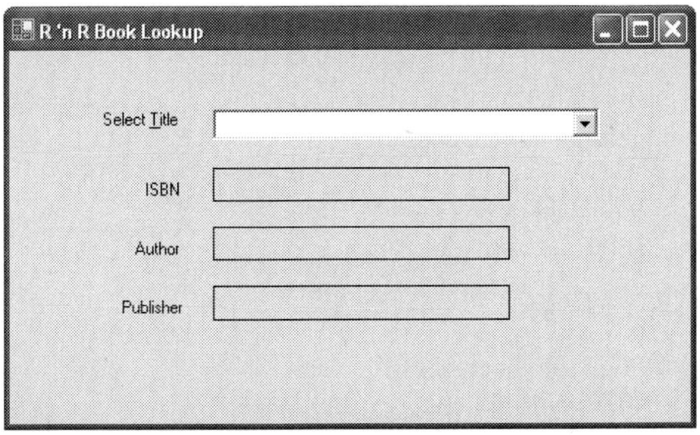

Figure 10.32

The form for the hands-on programming example. Notice that the controls appear empty until the user makes a selection.

The Project Coding Solution

```
'Program:        Ch10HandsOnWindows
'Programmer:     Bradley/Millspaugh
'Date:           Jan 2004
'Description:    Display book information for the title selected from a list.
'Folder:         Ch10HandsOnWindowsForms

'Note:           This version of the program uses a copy of RnrBooks.mdb that is stored
'                in the project's bin folder. The ConnectionString is set in the form's
'                Load event procedure.

Option Strict On

Public Class bookForm
    Inherits System.Windows.Forms.Form

    Private Sub BookForm_Load(ByVal sender As System.Object, _
      ByVal e As System.EventArgs) Handles MyBase.Load
        ' Set up the connection and fill the dataset.

        RnRConnection.ConnectionString = _
          "Provider=Microsoft.Jet.OLEDB.4.0;Data Source=RnrBooks.mdb"
        booksDataAdapter.Fill(BooksDataSet1)

        ' Set the combo box and labels to display without a selection.
        titlesComboBox.SelectedIndex = -1
        authorLabel.Text = ""
        ISBNLabel.Text = ""
        publisherLabel.Text = ""
    End Sub
End Class
```

Summary

1. Visual Studio .NET uses Microsoft's ADO.NET technology to access databases in many different formats.
2. ADO.NET provides several types of connections for databases: OleDb, SQL Server, Odbc, and Oracle.
3. Access databases are composed of tables of related information. Each table is organized into rows representing records and columns containing fields of data.
4. The primary key field uniquely identifies a row or record.
5. ADO.NET stores and transfers data using a format called XML (Extensible Markup Language), which can be used by many different platforms.
6. Many controls can be bound to a database including labels, text boxes, list boxes, and a DataGrid.
7. A connection establishes a link to a data source, which is a specific data file or server.
8. A data adapter handles the transfer of data between a data source and a dataset.
9. A dataset stores information from the database in the memory of the computer. A dataset can contain multiple tables and their relationships.

10. You can create connections and data adapters by dragging table names or field names from the Server Explorer to the form.

11. A data adapter uses an SQL `SELECT` statement to specify the data to retrieve. You can write your own SQL `SELECT` statement or use the Query Builder in the Data Adapter Configuration Wizard.

12. The `Fill` method of the data adapter retrieves the data from the data source and fills the dataset.

13. Simple data binding connects one control to one data element while complex binding is needed for data lists and data grids.

14. To bind a grid to a data source, set the grid's DataSource property to the dataset and the DataMember property to the name of the table. You must fill the dataset in code—usually in the form's Load event procedure.

15. For a Web Forms application, you must execute the data adapter's `Fill` method and the grid's `DataBind` method. A Windows application does not use the `DataBind` method.

16. To bind a single control to a database field, set the control's DataBindings.Text field to the name of the field.

17. You can automatically fill a list box or combo box with the field values from a dataset. Set the DataSource property to the dataset and the DisplayMember property to the name of the field that should display in the list.

18. A common approach is to allow the user to select a value from a list and then display the data values for the selected item in bound labels.

19. A parameterized query is an SQL statement that requires a value to be supplied at run time.

20. When the user selects a value from a list box, display the data in the SelectedIndexChanged event procedure.

21. If the user enters a selection in a text box rather than selecting from a list for a parameterized query, code should be included to test for no records matching the criteria.

22. In Web applications, a list will be refilled automatically for every postback unless code is included in the Page_Load event procedure. Also, the Auto-PostBack property of the list control must be set to True so that the SelectedIndexChanged event will fire when the user makes a selection.

23. When you move a database project to another computer, you must reset the connection used by the data adapter.

Key Terms

Review Questions

1. Explain the purpose of a connection.
2. Explain the purpose of the data adapter component. How does a data adapter differ from a connection?
3. What is a dataset?
4. How is a data grid used?
5. Explain the steps to bind a single control, such as a label, to a field in a dataset.
6. Which properties must be set to bind a combo box to a field in a database and display a drop-down list of the choices for that field?
7. How do a Windows and a Web version of a list selection program vary? Why?
8. What is a parameterized query? When would it be used?
9. What is a postback? When does it occur?
10. How can you keep a Web application from recreating the list data when a postback occurs?

Programming Exercises

Note: Each of these exercises can be written as a Windows application or as a Web application.

10.1 The Rnrbooks.mdb database file holds two tables: the Books table used in this chapter and the Subjects table. The Subjects table has only two fields: the Subject Code (the key field) and the Subject Name. Write a project that displays the Subjects table in a grid.

10.2 Write a project to display a list of the subject names in the Subjects table described in Programming Exercise 10.1. Use a drop-down combo box. Display in a label the Subject Code for the name selected from the list.

10.3 Write a project to display the Publishers table from the Biblio.mdb database from your StudentData folder on the text CD. The Publishers table has the following fields: PubID (the key field), Name, Company Name, Address, City, State, ZIP, Telephone, Fax, and Comments.

Allow the user to select the publisher name from a drop-down list; display the rest of the fields in labels.

Case Studies

VB Mail Order

1. Create a Windows application to display the VB Mail Order Customer table from the VbMail.mdb database on your student CD in a grid.
2. Create a Web application to display the Customer table in a grid on a Web Form.

The Customers table holds these fields:

Fields

CustomerID

LastName

FirstName

Address

City

State

ZipCode

VB Auto Center

Create a Windows application or a Web application to display the VB Auto Center Vehicle table from the VBAuto.mdb database on your student CD. Create a drop-down combo box of manufacturers. Be sure to include each manufacturer only once. (*Hint:* Add DISTINCT to the SQL SELECT statement.)

Display the remaining fields in labels for the selected element.

Fields

InventoryID

Manufacturer

ModelName

Year

VehicleID

CostValue

Video Bonanza

1. Create a Windows application or a Web application to display the information from the Studio table in the VBVideo.mdb database. Allow the user to select the studio name from a drop-down list and display the rest of the fields in labels.
2. Create a Windows or Web application to display the Studio table in a grid.

The Studio table contains these fields:

Studio ID

Studio Name

Contact Person

Phone

Very Very Boards

1. Create a Windows or a Web application to display the Product table from the VeryBoards.mdb database file on your student CD. Allow the user to select the product ID from a drop-down list and display the rest of the fields in labels.

2. Create a Windows or a Web application to display the Product table in a grid.

    The Product table contains these fields:

ProductID

Description

MfgID

Unit

Cost

LastOrderDate

LastOrderQuantity

11

Saving Data and Objects in Files

at the completion of this chapter, you will be able to . . .

1. Store and retrieve data in files using streams.

2. Save the values from a list box and reload for the next program run.

3. Check for the end of file.

4. Test whether a file exists.

5. Display the standard *Open File* or *Save As* dialog box to allow the user to choose the file.

6. Use serialization to store and retrieve objects.

Data Files

Many computer applications require that data be saved from one run to the next. Although the most common technique is to use a database, many times a database is overkill. Perhaps you just need to store a small amount of data, such as the date of the last program run, the highest ID number assigned, a user preference, or the property values of an object to transfer to another application. This chapter deals with techniques to store and retrieve **data files** on disk.

Note that default security policy for the Internet and for intranets does not allow access to disk files. This chapter presents only basic file input and output (I/O) for Windows applications.

Data Files and Project Files

In computer terminology, any data/information that you store on disk is given its own unique name and is called a *file*. In other words, a file is a collection of related data stored together and assigned a name so that it can be accessed later. Each of your Visual Basic projects requires multiple files—for the forms, other classes, code modules, assembly information, and project information. However, the files you will create now are different; they contain actual data, such as names and addresses, inventory amounts, and account balances.

Data File Terminology

The entire collection of data is called a *file*. The file is made up of **records**—one record for each entity in the file. Each record can be broken down further into **fields** (also called data elements). For example, in an employee file, the information for one employee is one record. In a name and address file, the information for one person is a record.

In the name and address file, each person has a last name field, a first name field, address fields, and a phone number field. Each field in a record pertains to the same person. Figure 11.1 illustrates a name and address file.

Figure   11.1

The rows in this data file represent records; the columns represent fields.

Last Name	First Name	Street	City	State	Zip	Phone	Email
Maxwell	Harry	795 W. J Street	Ontario	CA	91764	909-555-1234	
Helm	Jennifer	201 Cortez Way	Pomona	CA	91766	818-555-2222	JHelm@ms.org
Colton	Craig	1632 Granada Place	Pomona	CA	91766	909-555-3333	

A record

A field

File Handling Using Streams

Visual Studio handles data files using streams. A **stream** is designed to transfer a series of bytes from one location to another. Streams are objects that have methods and properties, just like any other object. The stream objects are found in the **System.IO namespace**. Your file-handling project must contain an `Imports` statement before the statement declaring the form's class.

```
Imports System.IO

Public Class fileIOForm
    Inherits System.Windows.Forms.Form
```

File I/O

You can read and write data in a disk file. You may have the user enter data into text boxes that you want to store in a file; that is called *writing* or *output*. At a later time, when you want to retrieve the data from the file, that is *reading* or *input* (Figure 11.2).

Figure 11.2

Write output from a program to a file; read input from the file into a program.

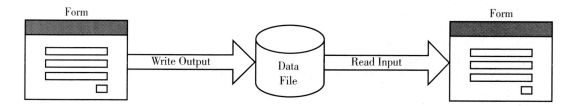

In VB, the simplest way to read and write small amounts of data is to use the **StreamReader** and **StreamWriter** objects. Generally, you write the StreamWriter code first, to create the data file. Then you can write the StreamReader code to read the file that you just created.

Writing Data in a File

To write data to a file, you first have the user input the data into text boxes and then write the data to the disk. The steps for writing data are

- Declare a new StreamWriter object, which also declares the name of the data file.

- Use the StreamWriter's `WriteLine` method to copy the data to a buffer in memory. (A buffer is just a temporary storage location.)

- Call the StreamWriter's `Close` method, which transfers the data from the buffer to the file and releases the system resources used by the stream.

Instantiating a StreamWriter Object—General Form

```
Dim ObjectName As New StreamWriter("FileName")
Dim ObjectName As New StreamWriter("FileName", BooleanAppend)
```

You declare a new StreamWriter object for writing data to a file. The first argument in the constructor specifies the name of the file. The default location for the file is where the program executable is placed, which is the bin folder beneath the folder for the current project. You also can specify the complete path of the file.

In the second version of the StreamWriter constructor, you can specify that you want to append data to an existing file. Specify True to append. By default, the option is set to False, and new data overwrite any existing data.

Declaring a new StreamWriter object opens the file. The file must be open before you can write in the file. If the file does not already exist, a new one is created. Because no exception occurs whether or not the file exists, you can declare the StreamWriter object in the declarations section of your program or in a procedure.

TIP

Use .txt as your file extension to allow for easy viewing of the file in Notepad. ∎

Declaring a StreamWriter Object—Examples

```
Dim phoneStreamWriter As New StreamWriter("Phone.txt")
Dim namesStreamWriter As New StreamWriter("C:\MyFiles\Names.txt")
Dim logFileStreamWriter As New StreamWriter("C:\MyFiles\LogFile.txt", True)
```

The StreamWriter object has both a **Write** and a **WriteLine method**. The difference between the two is a carriage-return character. The Write method places items consecutively in the file with no delimiter (separator). The WriteLine method places an Enter (carriage return) between items. We will use the Write-Line in this chapter because we want to easily retrieve the data elements later.

The WriteLine Method—General Form

```
ObjectName.WriteLine(DataToWrite)
```

The DataToWrite argument may be string or numeric. The WriteLine method converts any numeric data to string and actually writes string data in the file.

The WriteLine Method—Examples

```
phoneStreamWriter.WriteLine(nameTextBox.Text)
phoneStreamWriter.WriteLine(phoneTextBox.Text)

namesStreamWriter.WriteLine("Sammy")

bankBalanceStreamWriter.WriteLine(balanceDecimal.ToString())
```

If you are inputting data from the user and writing in a file, you generally place the WriteLine in a button click event procedure. That way you can write one record at a time. Figure 11.3 shows the form for this phone list example.

```
Private Sub saveButton_Click(ByVal sender As System.Object, _
  ByVal e As System.EventArgs) Handles saveButton.Click
    ' Save the record to the already-open file.

    phoneStreamWriter.WriteLine(nameTextBox.Text)
    phoneStreamWriter.WriteLine(phoneTextBox.Text)
    With nameTextBox
        .Clear()
        .Focus()
    End With
    phoneTextBox.Clear()
End Sub
```

Figure 11.3

The user enters data into the text boxes and clicks the **Save** button, which writes this record in the stream's buffer.

The *Save* button writes the data from the screen to the StreamWriter object and then clears the screen.

Closing a File

After you finish writing data in a file, you must close the file. Closing a file is good housekeeping; it finishes writing all data from the stream's buffer to the disk and releases the system resources. Use the StreamWriter's **Close method**, which is similar to closing a form. A common location for the `Close` method is in your program's Exit command or the form's closing event procedure (see page 432).

```
Private Sub exitButton_Click(ByVal sender As System.Object, _
    ByVal e As System.EventArgs) Handles exitButton.Click
    ' Close the file and the form.

    phoneStreamWriter.Close()
    Me.Close()
End Sub
```

If you fail to close a file when you are finished with it, the file may remain open for an indefinite time and sometimes may become unusable.

Viewing the Contents of a File

After you run your project, you can view the new file using a text editor such as Notepad. You also can view the file in the Visual Studio IDE. In the Solution Explorer, select the project name. If you don't see the *bin* and *obj* folders listed, click on the *Show All Files* button at the top of the window. Then you can expand the *bin* folder, find the data file name, and open it. The contents of the file should appear in the Editor window (Figure 11.4).

It's best to open a file only when it is needed and close it as soon as you are done with it so that you don't tie up system resources unnecessarily. ∎

Reading Data from a File

You use the StreamReader class to read the data from a file that you created with a StreamWriter.

Figure 11.4

View the contents of your new file in the VS IDE.

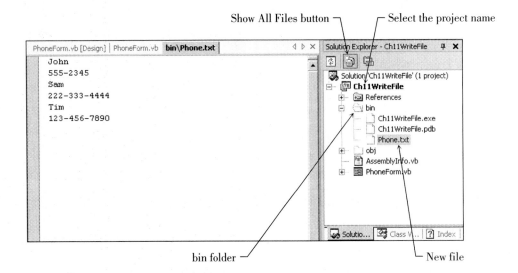

The steps for reading the data from a file are the following:

- Declare an object of the StreamReader class. The constructor declares the file name and optional path. This statement opens the file so that you can read from it.

- Use the `ReadLine` method to read the data. You may need to use a loop to retrieve multiple records.

- When finished, close the stream using the StreamReader's `Close` method.

Instantiating a StreamReader Object—General Form

```
Dim ObjectName As New StreamReader("FileName")
```

The StreamReader class works in much the same way as the StreamWriter. However, the file must exist in the location where the application expects it. If no such file exists, an exception occurs. For this reason, you must declare the StreamReader object in a procedure, so that you can enclose it in a `Try`/`Catch` block.

Instantiating a StreamReader Object—Examples

```
Try
     Dim namesStreamReader As New StreamReader("C:\MyFiles\Names.txt")
Catch
     MessageBox.Show("File does not exist")
End Try


' In declarations section, to create a module-level variable name.
Private phoneStreamReader As StreamReader
. . .
' In a procedure, to catch an exception for a missing file.
Try
     phoneStreamReader = New StreamReader("Phone.txt")
Catch
     MessageBox.Show("File does not exist")
End Try
```

Using the ReadLine Method

Use the StreamReader's **ReadLine method** to read the previously saved data. Each time you execute the method, it reads the next line from the file. Assign the value from the read to the desired location, such as a label, a text box, or a string variable. The ReadLine method has no arguments.

```
nameLabel.Text = phoneStreamReader.ReadLine()
```

Checking for the End of the File

How can you tell when there is no more data in the file? One way is to use the StreamReader's **Peek method**. The Peek method looks at the next element without really reading it. The value returned when you peek beyond the last element is negative 1 (–1).

```
If phoneStreamReader.Peek <> -1 Then
    nameLabel.Text = phoneStreamReader.ReadLine()
    phoneLabel.Text = phoneStreamReader.ReadLine()
End If
```

Note that the ReadLine method does not throw an exception when you attempt to read past the end of the file.

You must always make sure to read the data elements in the same order in which they were written. Otherwise your output will display the wrong values. For example, if you reversed the two lines in the program segment above, the phone number would display for the name and vice-versa. The ReadLine method just reads the next line and assigns it to the variable or property that you specify.

The File Read Program

Here is the completed program that reads the name and phone numbers from a file and displays them on the form (Figure 11.5). Each time the user clicks *Next,* the program reads and displays the next record. Note that for this example program, we copied the Phone.txt file from the *bin* folder of the Ch11WriteFile project to the *bin* folder of this project. You also could specify the exact path of the file.

```
'Program:        Ch11ReadFile
'Programmer:     Bradley/Millspaugh
'Date:           Jan 2004
'Description:    Retrieve the information stored in a data file
'                and display it on the screen.
'                Uses a StreamReader.

Option Strict On
Imports System.IO

Public Class phoneForm
    Inherits System.Windows.Forms.Form

    Private phoneStreamReader As StreamReader

    Private Sub phoneForm_Load(ByVal sender As System.Object, _
      ByVal e As System.EventArgs) Handles MyBase.Load
        ' Open the file and display the first record.

        Try
            phoneStreamReader = New StreamReader("Phone.txt")
            DisplayRecord()
        Catch
            'File is not found
            MessageBox.Show("File does not exist")
        End Try
    End Sub

    Private Sub nextButton_Click(ByVal sender As System.Object, _
      ByVal e As System.EventArgs) Handles nextButton.Click
        ' Read the next record.

        DisplayRecord()
    End Sub

    Private Sub exitButton_Click(ByVal sender As System.Object, _
      ByVal e As System.EventArgs) Handles exitButton.Click
        ' End the project.

        phoneStreamReader.Close()
        Me.Close()
    End Sub
```

```
      Private Sub DisplayRecord()
          ' Read and display the next record.

          If phoneStreamReader.Peek <> -1 Then
              nameLabel.Text = phoneStreamReader.ReadLine()
              phoneLabel.Text = phoneStreamReader.ReadLine()
          End If
      End Sub
End Class
```

Feedback 11.1

1. Write the statement to create an inventory StreamWriter object that will write data to a file called "Inventory.txt".
2. Code the statement to write the contents of descriptionTextBox into the inventory stream.
3. Why should the declaration statement for a StreamReader object be in a `Try/Catch` block? Does the declaration statement for a StreamWriter object need to be in a `Try/Catch` block? Why or why not?
4. Write the statement(s) to read a description and a product number from inventory StreamReader assuming it has been opened as a StreamReader object. Make sure to test for the end of the file.

Using the File Common Dialog Box

In the preceding file read and write programs, the file names are hard-coded into the programs. You may prefer to allow the user to browse and enter the file name at run time. You can display the standard Windows *Open File* dialog box, in which the user can browse for a folder and file name and/or enter a new file-name. Use the **OpenFileDialog** common dialog component to display the dialog box, and then use the object's FileName property to open the selected file.

OpenFileDialog Component Properties

You will find the following properties of the OpenFileDialog component very useful:

Property	Description
Name	Name of the component. You can use the default OpenFileDialog1.
CheckFileExists	Display an error message if the file does not exist. Set to False for saving a file, since you want to create a new file if the file does not exist. Leave at the default True to read an existing file.
CheckPathExists	Display an error message if the path does not exist. Set to False for saving a file, since you want it to create the new folder if necessary.
FileName	The name of the file selected or entered by the user, which includes the file path. Use this property after displaying the dialog box to determine which file to open. You also can give this property an initial value, which places a default file name in the dialog box when it appears.
Filter	Filter file extensions to display. Example: `Text Files (*.txt)|*.txt|All files (*.*)|*.*`
InitialDirectory	Directory to display when the dialog box opens. Set this in code to Application.StartupPath to begin in the same folder as your application.
Title	Title bar of the dialog box

Displaying the Open File Dialog Box

To display an *Open File* dialog box (Figure 11.6), you must first add an Open-FileDialog component to your form. The component appears in the component tray. At design time set initial properties for Name, CheckFileExists, Check-PathExists, Filter, and Title (see the preceding table for the values). In code, set the InitialDirectory property to **Application.StartupPath**, display the dialog box using the `ShowDialog` method, and retrieve the FileName property.

F i g u r e   1 1 . 6

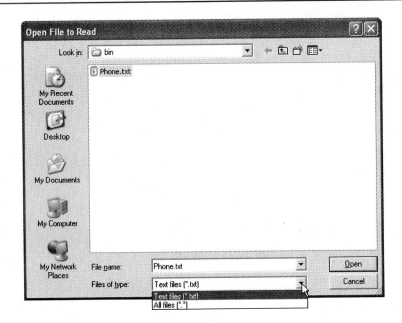

Display the Windows **Open File to Read** *dialog box using the OpenFileDialog component. The Filter property determines the entries for* **Files of type.**

```
Private Sub fileOpenMenuItem_Click(ByVal sender As System.Object, _
   ByVal e As System.EventArgs) Handles fileOpenMenuItem.Click
        ' Open the file.
        Dim responseDialogResult As DialogResult

        ' Begin in the project folder.
        OpenDialog1.InitialDirectory = Application.StartupPath
        ' Display the File Open dialog box.
        responseDialogResult = OpenDialog1.ShowDialog()
        ' Make sure that the user didn't click the Cancel button.
        If responseDialogResult <> DialogResult.Cancel Then
            ' Open the output file.
            phoneStreamWriter = New StreamWriter(OpenDialog1.FileName)
        End If
End Sub
```

Notice that the user may click on the *Cancel* button of the *Open File* dialog box. Check the DialogResult for *Cancel*. And if the user *does* click *Cancel*, that presents one more task for the program: You cannot close a StreamWriter object that isn't open.

Checking for Successful File Open

In the preceding file-open procedure, the statement

```
phoneStreamWriter = New StreamWriter(OpenDialog1.FileName)
```

may not execute. In that case, the StreamWriter is not instantiated. You can verify the object's instantiation using the VB keyword **Nothing**. An object variable that has not been instantiated has a value of Nothing. Notice the syntax: you must use the keyword **Is** rather than the equal sign (=).

```
' Is the file already open?
If Not phoneStreamWriter Is Nothing Then
    phoneStreamWriter.Close()
End If
```

Place this code in the form's Closing event procedure.

Checking for Already Open File

It's possible that the user may select the *File / Open* menu item twice, which can cause a problem. A second open instantiates another file stream, and the Close method never executes for the first file. It's best to check for an active instance of the file stream before instantiating a new one.

```
Private Sub fileOpenMenuItem_Click(ByVal sender As System.Object, _
   ByVal e As System.EventArgs) Handles fileOpenMenuItem.Click
    ' Open the file.
    Dim responseDialogResult As DialogResult

    ' Is the file already open?
    If Not phoneStreamWriter Is Nothing Then
        phoneStreamWriter.Close()
    End If
```

```
    ' Begin in the project folder.
    OpenDialog1.InitialDirectory = Application.StartupPath
    ' Display the File Open dialog box.
    responseDialogResult = OpenDialog1.ShowDialog()
    ' Make sure that the user didn't click the Cancel button.
    If responseDialogResult <> DialogResult.Cancel Then
        ' Open the output file.
        phoneStreamWriter = New StreamWriter(OpenDialog1.FileName)
    End If
End Sub
```

Using the Save File Dialog Component

In addition to the OpenFileDialog, you also can choose to display a SaveFile-
Dialog component, which displays the standard system *Save File* dialog box.
The SaveFileDialog allows the user to browse and enter a filename to save; it
has most of the same properties as the OpenFileDialog component. By default,
the SaveFileDialog component checks for an already-existing file and displays
a dialog box asking the user whether to replace the existing file.

The Write File Program

Here is the complete listing of the Write File program, which allows the user to
select the filename. The user can select the *Open* command from the *File* menu.
But if the *Save* button is clicked and the file is not yet open, the *Open File* dialog box displays automatically.

```
'Program:        Ch11 Open and Write File
'Programmer:     Bradley/Millspaugh
'Date:           Jan 2004
'Description:    Create a file using a StreamWriter.
'                Displays the File Open dialog box for the user to
'                enter the file and path.
'Folder:         Ch11OpenAndWriteFile

Option Strict On
Imports System.IO

Public Class phoneForm
    Inherits System.Windows.Forms.Form

    Dim phoneStreamWriter As StreamWriter

    Private Sub saveButton_Click(ByVal sender As System.Object, _
        ByVal e As System.EventArgs) Handles saveButton.Click
        ' Save the record to the file.

        If Not phoneStreamWriter Is Nothing Then 'Is the file open?
            phoneStreamWriter.WriteLine(nameTextBox.Text)
            phoneStreamWriter.WriteLine(phoneTextBox.Text)
            With nameTextBox
                .Clear()
                .Focus()
            End With
            phoneTextBox.Clear()
```

```
        Else          ' File is not open.
            MessageBox.Show("You must open the file before you can save a record", _
              "File Not Open", MessageBoxButtons.OK, MessageBoxIcon.Information)
            ' Display the File Open dialog box.
            fileOpenMenuItem_Click(sender, e)
        End If
    End Sub

    Private Sub fileExitMenuItem_Click(ByVal sender As System.Object, _
      ByVal e As System.EventArgs) Handles fileExitMenuItem.Click
        ' Close the file and the form.

        If Not phoneStreamWriter Is Nothing Then ' Is the file open?
            phoneStreamWriter.Close()
        End If
        Me.Close()
    End Sub

    Private Sub fileOpenMenuItem_Click(ByVal sender As System.Object, _
      ByVal e As System.EventArgs) Handles fileOpenMenuItem.Click
        ' Open the file.
        Dim responseDialogResult As DialogResult

        ' Is the file already open?
        If Not phoneStreamWriter Is Nothing Then
            phoneStreamWriter.Close()
        End If

        ' Begin in the project folder.
        OpenDialog1.InitialDirectory = Application.StartupPath
        ' Display the File Open dialog box.
        responseDialogResult = OpenDialog1.ShowDialog()
        ' Make sure that the user didn't click the Cancel button.
        If responseDialogResult <> DialogResult.Cancel Then
            ' Open the output file.
            phoneStreamWriter = New StreamWriter(OpenDialog1.FileName)
        End If
    End Sub
End Class
```

> ### Feedback 11.2

1. What is the Filter property setting to display only .txt files?
2. Write the statement to set OpenDialog1 to begin in the same folder as the application.
3. Write the statement to close the StreamWriter phoneStreamWriter; make sure to allow for the possibility that the file is not open.

Saving the Contents of a List Box

In Chapter 7 you wrote a program to maintain a list. The user was allowed to add items and remove items, but the next time the program ran, the list changes were gone. The changes were not saved from one execution to the next.

Now that you know how to save data in a file, you can save the contents of a list when the program exits and reload the list when the program reopens. Use the following techniques for this project:

- Do not give any values to the list's Items collection at design time. Instead, when the program begins, open the data file and read the items into the Items collection.

- If the user makes any changes to the list, ask whether to save the list when the program ends.

- Include a menu option to save the list.

- If the file holding the list elements does not exist when the program begins, give the user the option of creating a new list by adding items.

The examples in this section use the hands-on example from Chapter 7, which allows the user to make changes to the Coffee Flavor list (Figure 11.7). We will load the list from a file in the Form_Load procedure and query the user to save the list if any changes are made.

F i g u r e   1 1 . 7

The form for the list save program, taken from Chapter 7.

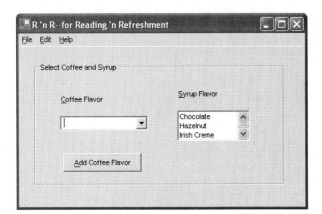

Loading the List Box

Assuming that the list items are stored in a data file, you can read the file into the list in the Form_Load procedure. Loop through the file until all elements are read, placing each item in the list with the `Items.Add` method.

```
Dim coffeeFlavorString As String

' Read all elements into the list.
Do Until flavorsStreamReader.Peek = -1
    coffeeFlavorString = flavorsStreamReader.ReadLine()
    coffeeComboBox.Items.Add(coffeeFlavorString)
Loop
```

Checking for Existence of the File

When you create a StreamReader object, the constructor checks to make sure the file exists. If the file does not exist, what do you want to do? Maybe the user wants to exit the program, locate the file, and try again. Or maybe the user prefers to begin with an empty list, add the list items, and create a new file. This technique is a good way to create the file in the first place.

You can catch the exception for a missing file and display a message box asking if the user wants to create a new file.

```
responseDialogResult = MessageBox.Show("Create a new file?", "File not Found", _
    MessageBoxButtons.YesNo, MessageBoxIcon.Question)
```

If the user says Yes, allow the program to begin running with an empty list; the file will be created when the program exits or the user saves the list. If the user says No, exit the program immediately.

```
Private Sub flavorsForm_Load(ByVal sender As System.Object, _
    ByVal e As System.EventArgs) Handles MyBase.Load
    ' Load the items in the coffeeComboBox list.
    Dim responseDialogResult As DialogResult
    Dim coffeeFlavorString As String

    Try
        ' Open the file.
        Dim flavorsStreamReader As New StreamReader("Coffees.txt")
        ' Read all elements into the list.
        Do Until flavorsStreamReader.Peek = -1
            coffeeFlavorString = flavorsStreamReader.ReadLine()
            coffeeComboBox.Items.Add(coffeeFlavorString)
        Loop
        ' Close the file.
        flavorsStreamReader.Close()
    Catch
        ' File missing.
        responseDialogResult = MessageBox.Show("Create a new file?", "File not Found", _
            MessageBoxButtons.YesNo, MessageBoxIcon.Question)
        If responseDialogResult = DialogResult.No Then
            ' Exit the program.
            fileExitMenuItem_Click(sender, e)
        End If
    End Try
End Sub
```

Saving the File

In this program the user can choose a menu option to save the file. Open a StreamWriter object and loop through the Items collection of the list box, saving each element with a WriteLine method.

```
Private Sub fileSaveMenuItem_Click(ByVal sender As System.Object, _
    ByVal e As System.EventArgs) Handles fileSaveMenuItem.Click
    ' Save the list box contents in a file.
    Dim indexInteger As Integer
    Dim numberItemsInteger As Integer
```

```
    ' Open the file.
    Dim flavorsStreamWriter As New StreamWriter("Coffees.txt")
    ' Save the items in the file.
    numberItemsInteger = coffeeComboBox.Items.Count - 1
    For indexInteger = 0 To numberItemsInteger
        flavorsStreamWriter.WriteLine(coffeeComboBox.Items(indexInteger))
    Next indexInteger
    ' Close the file.
    flavorsStreamWriter.Close()
    isDirtyBoolean = False
End Sub
```

The last line in this procedure needs some explanation. The next section
explains the reason for isDirtyBoolean = False.

Querying the User to Save

If your program allows users to make changes to data during program execution, it's a good idea to ask them if they want to save the changes before the program ends. This is similar to working in a word processing program or the VB
editor. If you close the file after making changes, you receive a message asking
if you want to save the file. But if you haven't made any changes since the last
save, no message appears.

To keep track of data changes during execution, you need a module-level
Boolean variable. Because the standard practice in programming is to refer to
the data as "dirty" if changes have been made, we will call the variable isDirty-
Boolean. In each procedure that allows changes (Add, Remove, Clear), you must
set isDirtyBoolean to True. After saving the file, set the variable to False.

Just before the project ends, you must check the value of isDirtyBoolean; if
True, ask the user if he or she wants to save; if False, you can just exit without
a message.

The Form_Closing Procedure

If you want to do something before the project ends, such as ask the user to
save the file, the best location is the form's **Closing event** procedure. This is a
much better place for such a question than your exit procedure, because the
user can quit the program in more than one way. The Form_Closing event procedure executes before the form closes when the user clicks on your *Exit* button
or menu command, clicks on the window's Close button, or even exits Windows.

```
Private Sub flavorsForm_Closing(ByVal sender As Object, _
   ByVal e As System.ComponentModel.CancelEventArgs) Handles MyBase.Closing
    ' Ask user to save the file.
    Dim responseDialogResult As DialogResult

    If isDirtyBoolean Then
        responseDialogResult = MessageBox.Show("Coffee list has changed. Save the list?", _
          "Coffee List Changed", MessageBoxButtons.YesNo, MessageBoxIcon.Question)
        If responseDialogResult = DialogResult.Yes Then
            fileSaveMenuItem_Click(sender, e)
        End If
    End If
End Sub
```

The List Save Program

This programming example puts together the routines in the previous section. The form, based on the hands-on example in Chapter 7, is shown in Figure 11.7. The user can add new flavors to the list, remove items from the list, or clear the list. Any changes can be saved in a file; the next program run retrieves the elements from the file, so the changes carry through from one run to the next.

```vb
'Program:        Ch11 List Save and Reload
'Programmer:     Bradley/Millspaugh
'Date:           January 2004
'Description:    Maintain a list of coffee flavors. The flavors are stored to disk
'                and reloaded for the next program run.
'Folder:         Ch11ListSave

Option Strict On
Imports System.IO

Public Class flavorsForm
    Inherits System.Windows.Forms.Form

    ' Declare module-level variable.
    Private isDirtyBoolean As Boolean

    Private Sub flavorsForm_Load(ByVal sender As System.Object, _
      ByVal e As System.EventArgs) Handles MyBase.Load
        ' Load the items in the coffeeComboBox list.
        Dim responseDialogResult As DialogResult
        Dim coffeeFlavorString As String

        Try
            ' Open the file.
            Dim flavorsStreamReader As New StreamReader("Coffees.txt")
            ' Read all elements into the list.
            Do Until flavorsStreamReader.Peek = -1
                coffeeFlavorString = flavorsStreamReader.ReadLine()
                coffeeComboBox.Items.Add(coffeeFlavorString)
            Loop
            ' Close the file.
            flavorsStreamReader.Close()
        Catch
            ' File missing.
            responseDialogResult = MessageBox.Show("Create a new file?","File not Found", _
                MessageBoxButtons.YesNo, MessageBoxIcon.Question)
            If responseDialogResult = DialogResult.No Then
                ' Exit the program.
                fileExitMenuItem_Click(sender, e)
            End If
        End Try
    End Sub

    Private Sub flavorsForm_Closing(ByVal sender As Object, _
      ByVal e As System.ComponentModel.CancelEventArgs) Handles MyBase.Closing
        ' Ask user to save the file.
        Dim responseDialogResult As DialogResult
```

```vb
      If isDirtyBoolean Then
          responseDialogResult = MessageBox.Show( _
            "Coffee list has changed. Save the list?","Coffee List Changed.", _
            MessageBoxButtons.YesNo, MessageBoxIcon.Question)
          If responseDialogResult = DialogResult.Yes Then
              fileSaveMenuItem_Click(sender, e)
          End If
      End If
End Sub

Private Sub fileSaveMenuItem_Click(ByVal sender As System.Object, _
  ByVal e As System.EventArgs) Handles fileSaveMenuItem.Click
    ' Save the list box contents in a file.
    Dim indexInteger As Integer
    Dim numberItemsInteger As Integer

    ' Open the file.
    Dim flavorsStreamWriter As New StreamWriter("Coffees.txt")
    ' Save the items in the file.
    numberItemsInteger = coffeeComboBox.Items.Count - 1
    For indexInteger = 0 To numberItemsInteger
        flavorsStreamWriter.WriteLine(coffeeComboBox.Items(indexInteger))
    Next indexInteger
    ' Close the file.
    flavorsStreamWriter.Close()
    isDirtyBoolean = False
End Sub

Public Sub fileExitMenuItem_Click(ByVal sender As System.Object, _
  ByVal e As System.EventArgs) Handles fileExitMenuItem.Click
    ' Terminate the project.

    Me.Close()
End Sub

Private Sub addCoffeeButton_Click(ByVal sender As System.Object, _
  ByVal e As System.EventArgs) Handles addCoffeeButton.Click, editAddMenuItem.Click
    ' Add a new coffee flavor to the coffee list.

    With coffeeComboBox
        If .Text <> "" Then
            .Items.Add(.Text)
            .Text = ""
            isDirtyBoolean = True
        Else
            MessageBox.Show("Enter a coffee flavor to add", "Missing data", _
                MessageBoxButtons.OK, MessageBoxIcon.Exclamation)
        End If
        .Focus()
    End With
End Sub

Public Sub editClearMenuItem_Click(ByVal sender As System.Object, _
  ByVal e As System.EventArgs) Handles editClearMenuItem.Click
    ' Clear the coffee list.
    Dim responseDialogResult As DialogResult
```

```
        responseDialogResult = MessageBox.Show("Clear the coffee flavor list?", _
            "Clear coffee list", MessageBoxButtons.YesNo, MessageBoxIcon.Question)
        If responseDialogResult = DialogResult.Yes Then
            coffeeComboBox.Items.Clear()
            isDirtyBoolean = True
        End If
    End Sub

    Public Sub editCountMenuItem_Click(ByVal sender As System.Object, _
        ByVal e As System.EventArgs) Handles editCountMenuItem.Click
        ' Display a count of the coffee list.

        MessageBox.Show("The number of coffee types is " & _
            coffeeComboBox.Items.Count)
    End Sub

    Public Sub editRemoveMenuItem_Click(ByVal sender As System.Object, _
        ByVal e As System.EventArgs) Handles editRemoveMenuItem.Click
        ' Remove the selected coffee from list.

        With coffeeComboBox
            If .SelectedIndex <> -1 Then
                .Items.RemoveAt(.SelectedIndex)
                isDirtyBoolean = True
            Else
                MessageBox.Show("First select the coffee to remove.", _
                    "No selection made", MessageBoxButtons.OK, MessageBoxIcon.Exclamation)
            End If
        End With
    End Sub
End Class
```

> ## Feedback 11.3

1. Write the loop to save all of the elements from namesListBox using namesStreamWriter, which is a StreamWriter already opened and connected to Names.txt.
2. In what procedure should the code from Question 1 be placed?
3. Write the statements in the Form_Load event procedure to load the list of names into namesListBox.

Serialization

Sometimes you may need to store an object. You can save an object and the current value of all of its properties using **serialization**. The term *serialization* is used in many programming languages and refers to a series or stream of bits. An object's state is converted to a series of bits that can be saved and later used to recreate the object. Reading the saved data back and recreating the object is called *deserialization*.

The .NET framework uses serialization when performing functions such as marshalling (transferring) an object to another application.

If you want to be able to save an object, its class must be declared as `Serializable` and you must have a formatter. Two types of formatters are available: Binary and SOAP. The **Binary formatter** stores data in a binary form. Simple Object Access Protocol (SOAP) is a specification for storing data for transfer across platforms. The data from a **SOAP formatter** are actually stored in an XML format.

You can make any of your projects that contain a class module serializable, allowing the public properties of an object to be saved. To accomplish this you must

- Declare the class as `Serializable`.

In the form's code:

- Declare a Formatter object.

- Declare a FileStream object that includes the name of the file.

- Use the Formatter object's `Serialize` method to save the object's properties.

- Close the FileStream.

Making a Class Serializable

Before you can **serialize** an object, you must modify the class header to include the `Serializable` attribute.

```
<Serializable()> Public Class BookSale
    ' Body of the class.
End Class
```

All that you need to do is to add `<Serializable()>` in front of the class header.

Adding a Formatter Object

You write the code to actually store (serialize) the object in your form's code, not in the serializable class. You declare a new formatter object using either the BinaryFormatter or SoapFormatter class.

```
Dim FormatObject As SoapFormatter = New SoapFormatter
Dim FormatObject As BinaryFormatter = New BinaryFormatter
```

To use a formatter object, you need to include an `Imports` statement for the formatter class. This brings the number of `Imports` statements for saving an object to three: one for the System.IO for saving files, one for serialization, and one for the formatter.

```
Imports System.IO
Imports System.Runtime.Serialization
Imports System.Runtime.Serialization.Formatters.Binary
```

Using a FileStream

Serialization uses the **FileStream** class, rather than the StreamReader and StreamWriter classes that we used earlier. Declaring a FileStream is similar to declaring the other stream classes, but requires a file mode in addition to the path for the file.

Declaring a FileStream Object—Constructor

```
Dim ObjectName As FileStream = New FileStream("file name", FileMode.Open | Create)
```

We will use only the Open and Create modes. Use FileMode.Create when you open the file for output and FileMode.Open when you want to retrieve the file. Note that there is also an OpenOrCreate mode that can be used if the stream is instantiated at the module level and you want to be able to both read and write.

Declaring a FileStream Object—Example

```
Dim booksFileStream As FileStream = New FileStream("Books.txt", FileMode.Create)
```

Saving an Object

After you open the file by declaring an object of the FileStream class and declare the Formatter object, you save your object using the `Serialize` method of the Formatter.

The Serialize Method—General Form

```
FormatterObject.Serialize(StreamObject, ObjectToSave)
```

The Serialize Method—Example

```
bookBinaryFormatter.Serialize(booksFileStream, aBookSale)
```

The `Serialize` method actually writes the data to the buffer. You must code a `Close` method to complete the save operation to disk.

```
Private Sub fileSaveMenuItem_Click(ByVal sender As System.Object, _
   ByVal e As System.EventArgs) Handles fileSaveMenuItem.Click
    ' Save the contents of the object.
    Dim booksFileStream As FileStream = New FileStream("Books.txt", FileMode.Create)
    Dim bookBinaryFormatter As BinaryFormatter = New BinaryFormatter()

    bookBinaryFormatter.Serialize(booksFileStream, aBookSale)
    booksFileStream.Close()
End Sub
```

Recreating an Object

You read an object back in with the `Deserialize` method of the formatter. Following are the necessary steps:

- Create a FileStream object in the Open mode.

- Declare a Formatter object.

- Use the Formatter's `Deserialize` method, converting the input to the desired object type.

- Transfer the fields from the object to the screen.

- Close the stream.

When you are deserializing an object, you must be sure to convert the input data to the correct type.

```
aBookSale = CType(bookBinaryFormatter.Deserialize(booksFileStream), BookSale)
```

Following is the complete method to retrieve an object.

```vb
Private Sub fileRetrieveMenuItem_Click(ByVal sender As System.Object, _
  ByVal e As System.EventArgs) Handles fileRetrieveMenuItem.Click
    ' Retrieve the record from disk.
    Dim bookBinaryFormatter As BinaryFormatter = New BinaryFormatter

    Try
        ' Read the data and convert to the BookSale class.
        Dim booksFileStream As FileStream = New FileStream("Books.txt", FileMode.Open)
        aBookSale = CType(bookBinaryFormatter.Deserialize(booksFileStream), BookSale)
        booksFileStream.Close()

        ' Transfer data to the screen.
        With aBookSale
            titleTextBox.Text = .Title
            quantityTextBox.Text = .Quantity.ToString("N")
            priceTextBox.Text = .Price.ToString("N")
            extendedPriceLabel.Text = .ExtendedPrice.ToString("N")
        End With
    Catch
        MessageBox.Show("No saved object found.", "File Error", _
            MessageBoxButtons.OK, MessageBoxIcon.Exclamation)
    End Try
End Sub
```

Your Hands-On Programming Example

Modify the step-by-step example program from Chapter 6 to store and retrieve a book object using serialization. Note that this program is based on the step-by-step example as it appears on page 248, before adding the inherited class. You renamed this folder as "Ch11SBS" in Chapter 6.

The user enters book sale information, which is assigned to the properties of a BookSale object. The `ExtendedPrice` method of the BookSale object calculates the extended price that displays on the screen.

Include menu options to save the record (the BookSale object), clear the screen, and retrieve the record. The `Clear` method clears the screen so that you can see the data disappear and then redisplay.

Planning the Project

Begin with the Chapter 6 SBS project (in folder Ch11SBS), which contains a form (Figure 11.8) and a BookSale class. Add these new menu items to the *File* menu:

    *S*ave Record
    *C*lear
    *R*etrieve Record

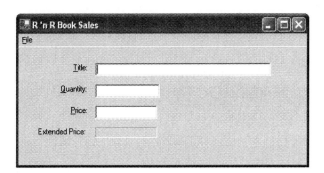

Figure 11.8

The completed form for the hands-on programming example. Note that this form is based on the step-by-step example in Chapter 6.

Plan the Objects and Properties:

Object	Property	Setting
fileSaveMenuItem	Name	fileSaveMenuItem
	Text	S&ave Record
fileClearMenuItem	Name	fileClearMenuItem
	Text	C&lear
fileRetrieveMenuItem	Name	fileRetrieveMenuItem
	Text	&Retrieve Record

Plan the Procedures

Procedure	Actions
fileSaveMenuItem	Declare an instance of a file stream and a formatter.
	Call the **Serialize** method of the formatter.
	Close the file stream.
fileClearMenuItem	Clear the text boxes and labels.
	Set the focus in the first text box.
fileRetrieveMenuItem	Declare an instance of a file stream and a formatter.
	Call the **Deserialize** method of the formatter.
	Close the file stream.
	Transfer data to the text boxes and label.

Write the Project Begin with the step-by-step in Chapter 6, through page 248. (You renamed this folder "Ch11SBS" in Chapter 6.)

- Add the menu items and set the properties according to your plan.

- Make sure to add the three new **Imports** statements:
  ```
  Imports System.IO
  Imports System.Runtime.Serialization
  Imports System.Runtime.Serialization.Formatters.Binary
  ```

- Open the BookSale class and add the **Serializable** attribute:
  ```
  <Serializable()> Public Class BookSale
  ```

- Write the code for the new menu items. Working from the pseudocode, write each procedure.

- When you complete the code, thoroughly test the project. Create an object, save it, clear the form, and retrieve the object. Then close the application, rerun it, and retrieve the saved object.

The Project Coding Solution

The Form

```
'Program:        Chapter 11 Serialization Hands-On
'Programmer:     Bradley/Millspaugh
'Date:           Jan 2004
'Description:    Calculate sales price using the BookSale class.
'                Instantiate aBookSale as a new object of the BookSale class.
'                Store the object to disk using serialization and
'                retrieve and recreate the object using deserialization.
'Folder:         Ch11SerializationHandsOn

Option Strict On
Imports System.IO
Imports System.Runtime.Serialization
Imports System.Runtime.Serialization.Formatters.Binary

Public Class salesForm
    Inherits System.Windows.Forms.Form
```

```vb
' Declare the new object.
Private aBookSale As BookSale

Private Sub fileCalculateSaleMenuItem_Click(ByVal sender As System.Object, _
  ByVal e As System.EventArgs) Handles fileCalculateSaleMenuItem.Click
    ' Calculate the extended price for the sale.

    Try
        ' Instantiate the object and set the properties.
        aBookSale = New BookSale(titleTextBox.Text, _
          Integer.Parse(quantityTextBox.Text), Decimal.Parse(priceTextBox.Text))

        ' Calculate and format the result.
        extendedPriceLabel.Text = aBookSale.ExtendedPrice.ToString("N")

    Catch
        MessageBox.Show("Error in quantity or price field.", "R 'n R Book Sales", _
          MessageBoxButtons.OK, MessageBoxIcon.Exclamation)
    End Try
End Sub

Private Sub fileExitMenuItem_Click(ByVal sender As Object, _
  ByVal e As System.EventArgs) Handles fileExitMenuItem.Click
    ' Exit the application.

    Me.Close()
End Sub

Private Sub fileSummaryMenuItem_Click(ByVal sender As System.Object, _
  ByVal e As System.EventArgs) Handles fileSummaryMenuItem.Click
    ' Display the sales summary information.
    Dim messageString As String

    messageString = "Sales Total: " & aBookSale.SalesTotal.ToString("C") & _
      ControlChars.NewLine & "Sales Count: " & aBookSale.SalesCount.ToString()
    MessageBox.Show(messageString, "R 'n R Book Sales Summary", _
      MessageBoxButtons.OK, MessageBoxIcon.Information)
End Sub

Private Sub fileSaveMenuItem_Click(ByVal sender As System.Object, _
  ByVal e As System.EventArgs) Handles fileSaveMenuItem.Click
    ' Save the contents of the object.
    Dim booksFileStream As FileStream = New FileStream("Books.txt", FileMode.Create)
    Dim bookBinaryFormatter As BinaryFormatter = New BinaryFormatter

    bookBinaryFormatter.Serialize(booksFileStream, aBookSale)
    booksFileStream.Close()
End Sub

Private Sub fileClearMenuItem_Click(ByVal sender As System.Object, _
  ByVal e As System.EventArgs) Handles fileClearMenuItem.Click
    ' Clear the text boxes.

    quantityTextBox.Clear()
    priceTextBox.Clear()
    extendedPriceLabel.Text = ""
    With titleTextBox
        .Clear()
        .Focus()
    End With
End Sub
```

```
    Private Sub fileRetrieveMenuItem_Click(ByVal sender As System.Object, _
      ByVal e As System.EventArgs) Handles fileRetrieveMenuItem.Click
        ' Retrieve the record from disk.
        Dim bookBinaryFormatter As BinaryFormatter = New BinaryFormatter

        Try
            ' Read the data and convert to the BookSale class.
            Dim booksFileStream As FileStream = New FileStream("Books.txt", FileMode.Open)
            aBookSale = CType(bookBinaryFormatter.Deserialize(booksFileStream), BookSale)
            booksFileStream.Close()

            ' Transfer data to the screen.
            With aBookSale
                titleTextBox.Text = .Title
                quantityTextBox.Text = .Quantity.ToString("N")
                priceTextBox.Text = .Price.ToString("N")
                extendedPriceLabel.Text = .ExtendedPrice.ToString("N")
            End With
        Catch
            MessageBox.Show("No saved object found.", "File Error", _
                MessageBoxButtons.OK, MessageBoxIcon.Exclamation)
        End Try
    End Sub
End Class
```

The BookSale Class

```
'Class Name:     BookSale
'Programmer:     Bradley/Millspaugh
'Date:           Jan 2004
'Description:    Handle book sale information.
'Folder:         Ch11SerializationHandsOn

<Serializable()> Public Class BookSale
    Sub New(ByVal Title As String, ByVal Quantity As Integer, _
      ByVal Price As Decimal)
        'Assign property values

        Me.Title = Title
        Me.Quantity = Quantity
        Me.Price = Price
        CalculateExtendedPrice()
        AddToTotals()
    End Sub

    Private titleString As String
    Private quantityInteger As Integer
    Private priceDecimal, extendedPriceDecimal As Decimal
    Private Shared salesTotalDecimal As Decimal
    Private Shared salesCountInteger As Integer

    Property Title() As String
        Get
            Title = titleString
        End Get

        Set(ByVal Value As String)
            titleString = Value
        End Set
    End Property
```

```
Property Quantity() As Integer
    Get
        Quantity = quantityInteger
    End Get

    Set(ByVal Value As Integer)
        If Value >= 0 Then
            quantityInteger = Value
        End If
    End Set
End Property

Property Price() As Decimal
    Get
        Price = priceDecimal
    End Get

    Set(ByVal Value As Decimal)
        If Value >= 0 Then
            priceDecimal = Value
        End If
    End Set
End Property

Property ExtendedPrice() As Decimal
    Get
        ExtendedPrice = extendedPriceDecimal
    End Get

    Set(ByVal Value As Decimal)
        If Value >= 0 Then
            extendedPriceDecimal = Value
        End If
    End Set
End Property

Shared ReadOnly Property SalesTotal() As Decimal
    Get
        SalesTotal = salesTotalDecimal
    End Get
End Property

Shared ReadOnly Property SalesCount() As Integer
    Get
        SalesCount = salesCountInteger
    End Get
End Property

Private Sub CalculateExtendedPrice()
    ' Calculate the extended price.

    extendedPriceDecimal = quantityInteger * priceDecimal
End sub

Private Sub AddToTotals()
    'Add to summary information

    salesTotalDecimal += extendedPriceDecimal
    salesCountInteger += 1
End Sub
```

Summary

1. A data file is made up of records, which can be further broken down into fields or data elements. The field used for organizing the file is the key field.
2. A stream object is used to transfer data to and from a data file. The StreamWriter outputs (writes) the data and the StreamReader inputs (reads) data.
3. The constructors for a StreamWriter and StreamReader take the name of the file, with an optional path, as a parameter.
4. The `WriteLine` method writes a data line to disk.
5. A `Close` method should be used as soon as you are done with the stream. Make sure the stream is closed prior to the termination of a program that uses streams.
6. The `Peek` method looks at the next element, which allows testing for the end of the file. The `Peek` method returns −1 at the end of file.
7. List box data may be saved to a stream. The Items collection should be filled in the Form_Load if the file exists. Any changes are saved back to the file when the program terminates.
8. A Boolean variable is used to track whether changes were made to the data.
9. The form's Closing event procedure is a good location for the code to prompt the users if they wish to save any changes.
10. The OpenFileDialog and SaveFileDialog components can be used to display the *Open File* and *Save File* dialog boxes and allow the user to select the filename.
11. Saving the state of an object is called *serialization;* retrieving and recreating the object is called *deserialization*.
12. You can use different modes for saving files using the FileStream class.
13. An object can be saved to a file stream if the class is declared as `Serializable`.
14. Serialization has two formatters for determining the way the information is stored: binary or SOAP.

Key Terms

Review Questions

1. What is the difference between a Visual Basic project file and a data file?
2. Explain what occurs when a stream object is instantiated.
3. Name two types of stream classes. What is the difference between the two?
4. What is the difference between a `Write` method and a `WriteLine` method?
5. What steps are necessary for storing the list items from a list box into a disk file?
6. What is the format for the statements to read and write streams?
7. What method can be used to determine the end of file?
8. When is exception handling necessary for stream handling?
9. Explain when a form's Closing event occurs and what code might be included in the Closing event procedure.
10. What is serialization and when would it be used?
11. What statement must be included in a class if you want to serialize objects of the class?
12. What is a SOAP formatter?

Programming Exercises

11.1 Rewrite Programming Exercise 8.4 using a file to store the state names and abbreviations. You need two projects: The first will allow the typist to enter the state name and the abbreviation in text boxes and store them in a file. The second project will perform the functions specified in Programming Exercise 8.4.

   Optional extra: Allow the user to select the file to open using the *Open File* dialog box.

11.2 Create a file for employee information and call it Employee.txt. Each record will contain fields for first name, last name, employee number, and hourly pay rate.

   Write a second project to process payroll. The application will load the employee data into an array of structures from the file with an extra field for the pay. The form will contain labels for the information from the array (display one record at a time) and a text box for the hours worked.

   A button called *FindPay* will use a `For/Next` loop to process the array. You will calculate the pay and add the pay to the totals. Then display the labels for the next employee. (Place the pay into the extra field in the array.)

   The *Exit* button will print a report on the printer and terminate the project. (Print the array.)

   Processing: Hours over 40 receive time-and-a-half pay. Accumulate the total number of hours worked, the total number of hours of overtime, and the total amount of pay.

(continued on next page)

Sample Report:

Ace Industries

Employee Name	Hours Worked	Hours Overtime	Pay Rate	Amount Earned
Janice Jones	40	0	5.25	210.00
Chris O'Connel	35	0	5.35	187.25
Karen Fisk	45	5	6.00	285.00
Tom Winn	42	2	5.75	247.25
Totals	162	7		929.50

> *Optional extra:* Allow the user to select the file to open using the *Open File* dialog box.

11.3 Modify Programming Exercise 7.5 to store the list box for Bradley's Bagels in a data file. Load the list during the Form Load event procedure and then close the file. Be sure to use error checking in case the file does not exist.

> In the Closing procedure prompt the user to save the bagel list back to the disk.

> *Note:* For help in basing a new project on an existing project, see "Copy and Move a Windows Project" in Appendix C.

> *Optional extra:* Allow the user to select the file to open using the *Open File* dialog box.

11.4 Create a simple text editor that has one large text box (with its Multiline property set to True) or a RichTextBox control. Set the text control to fill the form and set its Anchor property to all four edges, so that the control fills the form even when it is resized.

> Allow the user to save the contents of the text box in a data file and load a data file into the text box using the *Open File* dialog box.

11.5 Create a project that stores personal information for a little electronic "black book." The fields in the file should include name, phone number, pager number, cell phone number, voice mail number, and email address. Create an object that contains the appropriate fields and text boxes to enter the data.

> Create a second project to load the names into a list box. Perform a "look up" and display the appropriate information for the selected name.

> *Optional extra:* Allow the user to select the file to open using the *Open File* dialog box.

Case Studies

VB Mail Order

Modify your project from Chapter 7 to save the changes to the catalog name combo box from one run to the next. When the program begins, load the list from the data file. If the file does not exist, display a message asking if the user wants to create it.

Allow the user to save changes from a *Save* menu item. When the program terminates, check to see if there are any unsaved changes. If so, prompt the user to save the changes.

Optional extra: Allow the user to select the file to open using the *Open File* dialog box.

VB Auto Center

Write a project to store vehicle information including model, manufacturer, year, and VIN number.

Create a second project that loads the data from the file into memory and loads a drop-down combo box with the VIN numbers. When a number is selected from the combo box, display the appropriate information regarding the vehicle in labels.

Optional extra: Allow the user to select the file to open using the *Open File* dialog box.

Video Bonanza

Modify your project from Chapter 7 to save the changes to the movie combo box from one run to the next. When the program begins, load the list from the data file. If the file does not exist, display a message asking if the user wants to create it.

Allow the user to save changes from a *Save* menu item. When the program terminates, check to see if there are any unsaved changes. If so, prompt the user to save the changes.

Optional extra: Allow the user to select the file to open using the *Open File* dialog box.

Very Very Boards

Modify your project from Chapter 7 to save the changes to the shirt style combo box from one run to the next. When the program begins, load the list from the data file. If the file does not exist, display a message asking if the user wants to create it.

Allow the user to save changes from a *Save* menu item. When the program terminates, check to see if there are any unsaved changes. If so, prompt the user to save the changes.

Optional extra: Allow the user to select the file to open using the *Open File* dialog box.

12

Graphics in Windows and the Web

at the completion of this chapter, you will be able to . . .

1. Use graphics methods to draw shapes, lines, and filled shapes.

2. Create a drawing surface with a Graphics object.

3. Instantiate Pen and Brush objects as needed for drawing.

4. Create animation by changing pictures at run time.

5. Create simple animation by moving images.

6. Use the Timer component to automate animation.

7. Use scroll bars to move an image.

8. Draw a pie chart using the methods of the Graphics object.

You had your first introduction to graphics when you learned to print documents in Chapter 7. In this chapter you will learn to draw shapes, such as lines, rectangles, and ellipses, using the methods of the Graphics object. You can use the graphics methods to draw pictures and charts in a business application.

You will do simple animation by replacing and moving graphics. You also will use a Timer component to cause events to fire, so that you can create your own animation.

Graphics in Windows and the Web

The term *graphics* refers to any text, drawing, image, or icon that you display on the screen. You have placed a graphic image in a PictureBox control to display pictures on your forms. A picture box also can display animated .gif files, so you can easily produce animation on the screen.

You can display a graphics file on either a Web Form or a Windows Form. Recall that the Web control is an Image control and the Windows control is a PictureBox. Both display graphics files, but the Windows control accepts a few more file formats.

Using Windows Forms, you can draw graphics shapes such as circles, lines, and rectangles on a form or control. The graphics methods work only on Windows Forms, not Web Forms. Therefore, the programs in the next section use Windows Forms only.

The Graphics Environment

The .NET Framework uses a technology called *GDI+* for drawing graphics. GDI+ is an advancement and improvement over the previous Graphics Device Interface (GDI) used in previous versions of VB. GDI+ is designed to be device-independent, so the programmer doesn't have to be concerned about the physical characteristics of the output device. For example, the code to draw a circle is the same whether the output goes to a large-screen monitor, a low-resolution monitor, or the printer.

Steps for Drawing Graphics

When you draw a picture, you follow these general steps. The sections that follow describe the steps in more detail.

- Create a Graphics object to use as a drawing surface.

- Instantiate a Pen or Brush object to draw with.

- Call the drawing methods from the Graphics object.

Looking over the steps, you realize that this is what you did for creating printer output in Chapter 7. In that chapter you used the `DrawString` method to place text on the Graphics object; in this chapter you will use methods that draw shapes.

The Paint Event Procedure

You draw lines and shapes on a form or control by drawing on a Graphics object. And where do you place the code for the drawing methods? In the Paint event procedure for the form or the control on which you are drawing.

Each time a window is displayed, resized, moved, maximized, restored, or uncovered, the form's Paint event executes. In the Paint event procedure, the form and its controls are redrawn. If you draw some graphics on the form, in, say, the Form_Load event procedure or the click event of a button, the graphics are not automatically redrawn when the form is repainted. The only way to make sure that the graphics appear is to create them in the Paint event procedure. Then they are redrawn every time the form is rendered.

So far we have ignored the Paint event and allowed the repainting to proceed automatically. Now we will place code in that event procedure. You can write code in the form's Paint event procedure to draw on the form, or code in a control's Paint event procedure to draw graphics on the control.

In the Paint event procedure, you must declare a Graphics object. You assign the Graphics property of the procedure's PaintEventArgs argument to the new Graphics object.

TIP

To write code for the form's Paint event, select *(Base class Events)* from the Object list and then drop down the Method list in the Editor window. ∎

```
Private Sub Form1_Paint(ByVal sender As Object, _
    ByVal e As System.Windows.Forms.PaintEventArgs) Handles MyBase.Paint
    'Create a graphics object
    Dim gr As Graphics = e.Graphics
```

You also can create a graphic object by calling the `CreateGraphics` method of a form or control. You would use this method when you want to display a graphic from a procedure other than the Paint event.

```
' Draw on the form.
Me.CreateGraphics.MethodName

' Draw on a control.
myGroupBox.CreateGraphics.MethodName
```

Pen and Brush Objects

Using a **Pen object** you can draw lines or outlined shapes such as rectangles or circles. A **Brush object** creates filled shapes. You can set the width of a Pen and the color for both a Pen and a Brush. Figure 12.1 shows some lines and shapes created with Pen and Brush objects.

When you create a new Pen object, you set the color using the Color constants, such as Color.Red, Color.Blue, and Color.Aquamarine. You also can set the pen's width, which is measured in pixels. The term *pixel* is an abbreviation of *picture element*—a dot that makes up a picture. You are probably most familiar with pixels in the determination of the resolution of a monitor. A display of 1,280 by 1,024 is a reference to the number of pixels horizontally and vertically.

The Pen Class—Constructors

```
Pen(Color)
Pen(Color, Width)
```

Figure 12.1

Graphic shapes created by drawing with Pen and Brush objects and the methods of the Graphics class.

If you don't set the width of the pen, it defaults to one pixel.

The Pen Class—Examples

```
Dim redPen As New Pen(Color.Red)
Dim widePen As New Pen(Color.Black, 10)
```

You may find that you want several different pens. For each different color or line width, you can create another Pen object or redefine a Pen variable that you are finished with.

If you want to create filled figures, declare Brush objects—one for each different color that you want to use.

The SolidBrush Class—Constructor

```
SolidBrush(Color)
```

Use the Color constants to assign a color to your Brush objects.

The SolidBrush Class—Example

```
Dim blueBrush As New SolidBrush(Color.Blue)
```

You may have deduced from the name of the SolidBrush class that other types of brushes exist. See Help if you are interested in using a TextureBrush, HatchBrush, LinearGradientBrush, or PathGradientBrush.

The Coordinate System

Graphics are measured from a starting point of 0,0 for the X and Y coordinates beginning in the upper-left corner. The *X* is the horizontal position and the *Y* is the vertical measurement. The starting point depends on where the graphic is being placed. If the graphic is going directly on a form, the 0,0 coordinates are the upper-left corner of the form, below the title bar and menu bar. You also can draw graphics in a container, such as a PictureBox, GroupBox, or Button. In this case, the container has its own 0,0 coordinates to be used as the starting point for measuring the location of items inside the container (Figure 12.2).

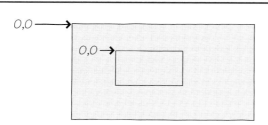

Figure 12.2

The coordinates for graphics begin with 0,0 in the upper-left corner of a form or container.

Each of the drawing methods allows you to specify the starting position using X and Y coordinates. Most of the methods also allow you to specify the position using a Point structure. In some methods it is useful to use a Rectangle structure, and in others a Size structure comes in handy.

The Point Structure

A **Point structure** is designed to hold the X and Y coordinates as a single unit. You can create a Point object, giving it values for the X and Y. Then you can use the object anywhere that accepts a Point as an argument.

```
Dim myStartingPoint As New Point(20, 10)
```

You can see an example of a Point in the design of any of your forms. Examine the Location property of any control; the Location is assigned a Point object, with X and Y properties.

The Size Structure

A **Size structure** has two components: the width and height. Both integers specify the size in pixels. Some graphics methods accept a Size structure as an argument.

```
Dim myPictureSize As New Size(100, 20)     ' Width is 100, height is 20.
```

You also can see an example of a Size structure by examining the design of any of your forms. Each of the controls has a Size property, which has width and height properties.

For an interesting exercise, examine the Windows-generated code for a Button control. The Location is set to a new Point object and the size is set to a new Size object.

The Rectangle Structure

A **Rectangle structure** defines a rectangular region, specified by its upper-left corner and its size.

```
Dim myRectangle As New Rectangle(myStartingPoint, myPictureSize)
```

The overloaded constructor also allows you to declare a new Rectangle by specifying its location in X and Y coordinates and its width and height.

```
Dim myOtherRectangle As New Rectangle(xInteger, yInteger, widthInteger, heightInteger)
```

Note that you also can create Point, Size, and Rectangle structures for single-precision floating-point values. Specify the PointF, SizeF, and RectangleF structures.

Graphics Methods

The drawing methods fall into two basic categories: draw and fill. The draw methods create an outline shape and the fill methods are solid shapes. The first argument in a draw method is a Pen object, whereas the fill methods use Brush objects. Each of the methods also requires the location for the upper-left corner, which you can specify as X and Y coordinates or as a Point object. Some of the methods require the size, which you may supply as width and height or as a Rectangle object.

Graphics Methods—General Forms

```
DrawLine(Pen, x1Integer, y1Integer, x2Integer, y2Integer)
DrawLine(Pen, Point1, Point2)

DrawRectangle(Pen, xInteger, yInteger, widthInteger, heightInteger)
DrawRectangle(Pen, Rectangle)

FillRectangle(Brush, xInteger, yInteger, widthInteger, heightInteger)
FillRectangle(Brush, Rectangle)

FillEllipse(Brush, xInteger, yInteger, widthInteger, heightInteger)
FillEllipse(Brush, Rectangle)
```

The following code draws the outline of a rectangle in red using the **DrawRectangle method** and draws a line with the **DrawLine method**. The **FillEllipse method** is used to draw a filled circle.

```
Private Sub graphicsForm_Paint(ByVal sender As Object, _
  ByVal e As System.Windows.Forms.PaintEventArgs) Handles MyBase.Paint
    ' Create a graphics object.
    Dim gr As Graphics = e.Graphics
    Dim redPen As New Pen(Color.Red)

    ' Draw a red rectangle.
    gr.DrawRectangle(redPen, 10, 10, 30, 30)

    ' Draw a red line.
    gr.DrawLine(redPen, 50, 0, 50, 300)

    ' Draw a blue filled circle.
    Dim blueBrush As New SolidBrush(Color.Blue)
    gr.FillEllipse(blueBrush, 100, 100, 50, 50)

    ' Draw a fat blue line.
    Dim widePen As New Pen(Color.Blue, 15)
    gr.DrawLine(widePen, 300, 0, 300, 300)
End Sub
```

Table 12.1 shows some of the methods in the Graphics class. For excellent help
in using the methods, see the MSDN Help page:

```
Contents
    Visual Studio .NET
        .NET Framework
            Programming with the .NET Framework
                Drawing and Editing Images
                    About GDI+ Managed Code
                        Lines, Curves, and Shapes
```

Note: Microsoft tends to change the organization of MSDN periodically. You
may need to search for the graphics pages.

Selected Methods from the Graphics Class   **T a b l e   1 2 . 1**

Method	Purpose
Clear()	Clear the drawing surface by setting it to the container's background color.
Dispose()	Releases the memory used by a Graphics object.
DrawArc(*Pen, x1Integer, y1Integer, x2Integer, y2Integer, widthInteger, heightInteger*) DrawArc(*Pen, Rectangle, startAngleSingle, angleLengthSingle*)	Draw an arc (segment of an ellipse).
DrawLine(*Pen, x1Integer, y1Integer, x2Integer, y2Integer*) DrawLine(*Pen, Point1, Point2*)	Draw a line from one point to another.
DrawEllipse(*Pen, xInteger, yInteger, widthInteger, heightInteger*) DrawEllipse(*Pen, Rectangle*)	Draw an oval shape. A circle has equal width and height.
DrawRectangle(*Pen, xInteger, yInteger, widthInteger, heightInteger*) DrawRectangle(*Pen, Rectangle*)	Draw a rectangle.
DrawPie(*Pen, xInteger, yInteger, widthInteger, heightInteger, angleStartInteger, angleLengthInteger*) DrawPie(*Pen, Rectangle, angleStartSingle, angleLengthSingle*)	Draw a partial circle (segment of a pie).
DrawString(*textString, Font, Brush, xSingle, ySingle*) DrawString(*textString, Font, Brush, PointF*)	Draw a string of text. Note that coordinates are single-precision.
FillEllipse(*SolidBrush, xInteger, yInteger, widthInteger, heightInteger*) FillEllipse(*SolidBrush, Rectangle*)	Draw a filled oval; a circle for equal width and height.
FillPie(*Brush, xInteger, yInteger, widthInteger, heightInteger, angleStartInteger, angleLengthInteger*) FillPie(*Brush, Rectangle, angleStartSingle, angleLengthSingle*)	Draw a partial-filled oval (segment of a pie).
FillRectangle(*SolidBrush, xInteger, yInteger, widthInteger, heightInteger*) FillRectangle(*SolidBrush, Rectangle*)	Draw a filled rectangle.

Random Numbers

Often it is useful to be able to generate random numbers. The **Random class** contains various methods for returning random numbers of different data types. A Random object is popular for use in games, as well as problems in probability and queuing theory.

```
Dim generateRandom As New Random()
```

Unfortunately, the computer can't really generate random numbers. Each time you run an application, the Random object produces the identical sequence of "random" numbers. To generate a different series for each run, use an integer value when you instantiate an object from the Random class. This is called *seeding* the random number generator. You can use the system date to get a different seed for each execution of the code.

```
' Seed the random number generator.
Dim currentDateTime As DateTime = DateTime.Now
generateRandom = New Random(currentDateTime.Millisecond)
```

You seed the Random object once when you instantiate it and generate the random numbers using the Random object's **Next method**, which returns a positive integer number. You can use one of three overloaded argument lists to choose the range for the random numbers.

The Random.Next Method—General Forms

```
' Any positive integer number.
Object.Next()

' A positive integer up to the value specified.
Object.Next(MaximumValueInteger)

' A positive integer in the range specified.
Object.Next(minimumValueInteger, maximumValueInteger)
```

The Random.Next Method—Examples

```
' Return an integer in the range 0 - 10
randomInteger = generateRandom.Next(10)

' Return an integer in the range 1 to the width of the form.
randomNumberInteger = generateRandom.Next(1, Me.Width)
```

A Random Number Example

This example program draws graphics using the graphics methods and generates snowflakes using the Random.Next method. Figure 12.3 shows the screen generated by this code.

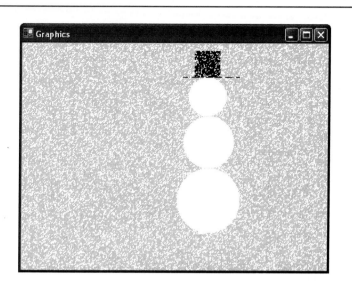

Figure 12.3

This output is produced by the Ch12RandomNumbers example program. The program draws the figure and generates random snowflakes in the form's Paint event handler.

```
'Program         Chapter 12 Random Numbers
'Programmer:     Bradley/Millspaugh
'Date:           Jan 2004
'Description:    Draw a snowman using filled ellipses and then snow using
'                random locations.
'Folder:         Ch12RandomNumbers

Option Strict On

Public Class graphicsForm
    Inherits System.Windows.Forms.Form

    ' Declare module-level variable.
    Private generateRandom As Random

    Private Sub graphicsForm_Load(ByVal sender As Object, _
      ByVal e As System.EventArgs) Handles MyBase.Load
        ' Seed the random number generator.

        Dim currentDateTime As DateTime
        generateRandom = New Random(currentDateTime.Millisecond)
    End Sub

    Private Sub graphicsForm_Paint(ByVal sender As Object, _
      ByVal e As System.Windows.Forms.PaintEventArgs) _
      Handles MyBase.Paint
        ' Generate dots (snowflakes) in random locations.
        ' Draw a snowman at the bottom center of the screen.
        Dim xInteger As Integer = Convert.ToInt32(Me.Width / 2)
        Dim yInteger As Integer = Convert.ToInt32(Me.Height / 2)
        Dim indexInteger As Integer
        Dim gr As Graphics = e.Graphics
        Dim whitePen As New Pen(Color.White, 2)
        Dim whiteBrush As New SolidBrush(Color.White)
        Dim blackPen As New Pen(Color.Black)
        Dim blackBrush As New SolidBrush(Color.Black)

        ' Draw the snowman.
        gr.FillEllipse(whiteBrush, xInteger, yInteger, 100, 100)
```

```
        ' Top of last circle.
        yInteger = yInteger - 80
        ' Offset for smaller circle.
        xInteger = xInteger + 10
        gr.FillEllipse(whiteBrush, xInteger, yInteger, 80, 80)
        yInteger = yInteger - 60
        xInteger = xInteger + 8
        gr.FillEllipse(whiteBrush, xInteger, yInteger, 60, 60)

        ' Add a top hat.
        gr.DrawLine(blackPen, xInteger - 10, yInteger, _
            xInteger + 80, yInteger)
        gr.FillRectangle(blackBrush, xInteger + 10, yInteger - 40, _
            40, 40)

        ' Make it snow in random locations.
        For indexInteger = 1 To 40000
            xInteger = generateRandom.Next(1, Me.Width)
            yInteger = generateRandom.Next(1, Me.Height)
            gr.DrawLine(whitePen, xInteger, yInteger, _
                xInteger + 1, yInteger + 1)
        Next
    End Sub
End Class
```

☑ **TIP**

Use the time as a seed for the Random class to generate different random numbers for each execution of the program. ∎

> ## Feedback 12.1

1. Write the statements necessary to draw a green vertical line down the center of a form.
2. Write the statements to draw one circle inside another one.
3. Write the statements to define three points and draw lines between the points.

Simple Animation

There are several ways to create animation on a form. The simplest way is to display an animated .gif file in a PictureBox control. The animation is already built into the graphic. Other simple ways to create animation are to replace one graphic with another, move a picture, or rotate through a series of pictures. You also can create graphics with the various graphics methods.

If you want to create animation on a Web page, displaying an animated .gif file is the best way. Another way is to write script using a scripting language such as VBScript or JavaScript or to embed a Java applet, which creates the animation on the client side. It doesn't make any sense to create animation using server-side controls, since each movement would require a round-trip to the server.

Displaying an Animated Graphic

You can achieve animation on either a Windows Form or a Web Form by displaying an animated .gif file (Figure 12.4). Use a PictureBox control on a Windows Form and an Image control on a Web Form.

Note: You can find the graphics for the programs in this chapter in the Graphics folder of your text CD.

Figure 12.4

Create animation by displaying an animated .gif file on either a Windows Form or a Web Form.

Controlling Pictures at Run Time

You can add or change a picture at run time. To speed execution, it is usually best to have the pictures loaded into controls that you can make invisible until you are ready to display them. But you can also use the **FromFile method** to load a picture at run time.

If you store a picture in an invisible control, you can change the Visible property to True at run time; or you may decide to copy the picture to another control.

```
logoPictureBox.Visible = True
logoPictureBox.Image = holdPicture.Image
```

You can use the FromFile method to retrieve a file during run time. One problem with this method is that the path must be known. When you are running an application on multiple systems, the path names may vary.

```
logoPictureBox.Image = Image.FromFile("C:\VB\LOGO.BMP")
```

If you store your image file in your project's bin folder, you can omit the path. The bin folder is the default folder for the application's executable file.

To remove a picture from the display, either hide it or use the Nothing constant.

```
logoPictureBox.Visible = False
logoPictureBox.Image = Nothing
```

Switching Images

An easy way to show some animation is to replace one picture with another. Many of the icons in the Visual Studio icon library have similar sizes but opposite states, such as a closed file cabinet and an open file cabinet; a mail box with the flag up and with the flag down; a closed envelope and an open envelope; or a traffic light in red, yellow, or green. (Recall that in Chapter 2 you used the two light bulbs: LightOn and LightOff.)

This sample program demonstrates switching between two phone icons: a phone and a phone being held. The program has three PictureBox controls: one to display the selected image and two, with their Visible property set to false, to hold the two images. The two icons are *Phone12.ico* and *Phone13.ico* in the Graphics\Icons\Comm folder (or the Graphics folder on your text CD). When the user clicks the *Change* button, the icon is switched to the opposite one. (See Figure 12.5.)

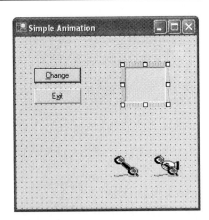

F i g u r e   1 2 . 5

Create animation by switching from one icon to another. Each of these graphics is placed into the upper picture box when the user clicks the Change button.

```
'Program:          Chapter 12 Simple Animation
'Programmer:       Bradley/Millspaugh
'Date:             Jan 2004
'Description:       Change a picture of a phone to show someone holding it.
'Folder:           Ch12SimpleAnimation

Option Strict On

Public Class animationForm
    Inherits System.Windows.Forms.Form

    Private Sub exitButton_Click(ByVal sender As System.Object, _
      ByVal e As System.EventArgs) Handles exitButton.Click
        ' End the program.

        Me.Close()
    End Sub

    Private Sub changeButton_Click(ByVal sender As System.Object, _
      ByVal e As System.EventArgs) Handles changeButton.Click
        ' Toggle the image from one to the other.
        Static switchBoolean As Boolean = True

        If switchBoolean Then
            displayPictureBox.Image = withHandPictureBox.Image
            switchBoolean = False
        Else
            displayPictureBox.Image = phonePictureBox.Image
            switchBoolean = True
        End If
    End Sub
End Sub
```

```
    Private Sub animationForm_Load(ByVal sender As Object, _
        ByVal e As System.EventArgs) Handles MyBase.Load
        ' Set the initial image.

        displayPictureBox.Image = phonePictureBox.Image
    End Sub
End Class
```

Moving a Picture

The best way to move a control is to use the control's **SetBounds method**. The SetBounds method produces a smoother appearing move than the move that is produced by changing the Left and Top properties of controls.

The SetBounds Method—General Form

```
SetBounds(xInteger, yInteger, widthInteger, heightInteger)
```

You can use a control's SetBounds method to move it to a new location and/or to change its size.

The SetBounds Method—Examples

```
planePictureBox.SetBounds(xInteger, yInteger, planeWidth, planeHeight)
enginePictureBox.SetBounds(xInteger, yInteger, widthInteger, heightInteger)
```

The program example in the next section uses a timer and the SetBounds method to move a graphic across the screen.

The Timer Component

Generally events occur when the user takes an action. But what if you want to make events occur at some interval, without user action? You can cause events to occur at a set interval using the **Timer component** and its **Tick event**. Timers are very useful for animation; you can move or change an image each time the Tick event occurs.

When you have a Timer component on a form, it "fires" each time an interval elapses. You can place any desired code in the Tick event procedure; the code executes each time the event occurs. You choose the interval for the timer by setting its **Interval property**, which can have a value of 0 to 65,535. This value specifies the number of milliseconds between the calls to the Tick event. One second is equivalent to 1,000 milliseconds. Therefore, for a three-second delay, set the Timer's Interval property to 3,000. You can set the value at run time or at design time.

You can keep the Tick event from occurring by setting the Timer's Enabled property to False. The default value is False, so you must set it to True when you want to enable the Timer. You can set the Enabled property at design time or run time.

When you add a timer to your form, it goes into the component tray. The tool for the timer is represented by the little stopwatch in the toolbox (Figure 12.6).

Timer

This Timer example program achieves animation in two ways: it moves an animated .gif file for a steam engine across the screen. When the steam engine moves off the left edge of the form, it reappears at the right edge, so it comes around again. Figure 12.7 shows the form. You'll have to use your imagination for the animation.

Timer Animation

```
'Program        Ch12 Timer Animation
'Programmer:    Bradley/Millspaugh
'Date:          Jan 2004
'Description:   Move a steam engine across the screen.
'               It reappears on the other side after leaving the screen.
'Folder:        Ch12TimerAnimation

Option Strict On

Public Class timerForm
    Inherits System.Windows.Forms.Form
```

```
Private Sub trainTimer_Tick(ByVal sender As System.Object, _
  ByVal e As System.EventArgs) Handles trainTimer.Tick
    ' Move the graphic across the form.
    Static xInteger As Integer = enginePictureBox.Left
    Static yInteger As Integer = enginePictureBox.Top
    Static widthInteger As Integer = enginePictureBox.Width
    Static heightInteger As Integer = enginePictureBox.Height

    ' Set new X coordinate.
    xInteger -= 10
    If xInteger <= -enginePictureBox.Width Then  ' Graphic entirely off edge of form.
        xInteger = Me.Width
    End If
    ' Move image.
    enginePictureBox.SetBounds(xInteger, yInteger, widthInteger, heightInteger)
  End Sub
End Class
```

Feedback 12.2

1. Write the statement(s) to move commandButton 10 pixels to the left using the SetBounds method
2. How long is an interval of 450?
3. What fires a Timer's Tick event?

The Scroll Bar Controls

You can add **horizontal scroll bars** and **vertical scroll bars** to your form (Figure 12.8). These scroll bar controls are similar to the scroll bars in Windows that can be used to scroll through a document or window. Often scroll bars are used to control sound level, color, size, and other values that can be changed in small amounts or large increments. The HScrollBar control and VScrollBar control operate independently of other controls and have their own methods, events, and properties.

Figure 12.8

Horizontal scroll bars and vertical scroll bars can be used to select a value over a given range.

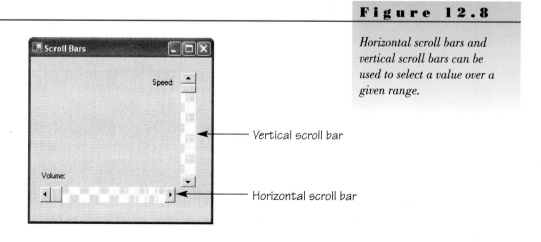

Vertical scroll bar

Horizontal scroll bar

Scroll Bar Properties

Properties for scroll bars are somewhat different from the controls we have worked with previously. Because the scroll bars represent a range of values, they have the following properties: **Minimum** for the minimum value, **Maximum** for the maximum value, **SmallChange** for the distance to move when the user clicks on the scroll arrows, and **LargeChange** for the distance to move when the user clicks on the gray area of the scroll bar or presses the Page-Up or Page-Down keys (Figure 12.9). Each of these properties has a default value (Table 12.2).

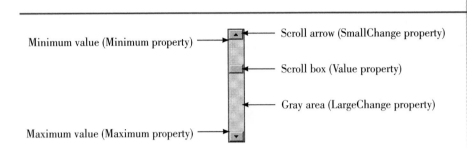

Minimum value (Minimum property) —→

Maximum value (Maximum property) —→

Scroll arrow (SmallChange property)

Scroll box (Value property)

Gray area (LargeChange property)

Figure   12.9

Clicking on the scroll arrow changes the Value property by SmallChange amount; clicking the gray area of the scroll bar changes the Value property by LargeChange amount.

Default Values for Scroll Bar Properties.   **Table   12.2**

Property	Default Value
Minimum	0
Maximum	100
Small Change	1
Large Change	10
Value	0

The **Value property** indicates the current position of the scroll box (also called the *thumb*) and its corresponding value within the scroll bar. When the user clicks the up arrow of a vertical scroll bar, the Value property decreases by the amount of SmallChange (if the Minimum value has not been reached) and moves the scroll box up. Clicking the down arrow causes the Value property to increase by the amount of SmallChange and moves the thumb down until it reaches the bottom or Maximum value.

Figure 12.10 shows the horizontal scroll bar tool and vertical scroll bar tool from the toolbox.

Figure   12.10

The toolbox tools for horizontal scroll bars and vertical scroll bars.

Scroll Bar Events

The events that occur for scroll bars differ from the ones used for other controls. Although a user might click on the scroll bar, there is no Click event; rather, there are two events: a **ValueChanged** event and a **Scroll event**. The Value-Changed event occurs any time that the Value property changes, whether it's changed by the user or by the code.

If the user drags the scroll box, a Scroll event occurs. In fact, multiple scroll events occur, as long as the user continues to drag the scroll box. As soon as the user releases the mouse button, the Scroll events cease and a ValueChanged event occurs. When you write code for a scroll bar, usually you will want to code both a ValueChanged event procedure and a Scroll event procedure.

A Programming Example

This little program uses scroll bars to move an image of a car around inside a container (Figure 12.11). The image is in a PictureBox and a GroupBox is the container. By placing the image inside a container, you use the container's co-ordinates rather than those of the form.

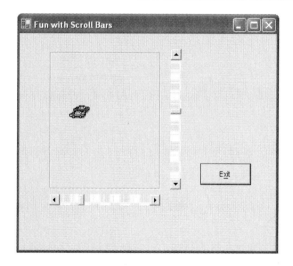

Figure 12.11

The form for the scroll bar programming example. Move the car around inside the container using the scroll bars.

A horizontal scroll bar will make the image move sideways in the container, and the vertical scroll bar will make it move up and down. Although you want the Maximum properties of the scroll bars to reflect the height and width of the container, due to the shape of the image, you may need to set the properties using trial and error. For example, the width of the GroupBox is 176 pixels, but the Maximum property of the horizontal scroll bar is set to 150; that's the point at which the car's bumper touches the edge of the container.

```
'Program:       Scroll
'Programmer:    Bradley/A. Millspaugh
'Date:          Jan 2004
'Description:   Use scroll bars to move an image
'                horizontally and vertically within the
'                limits of a group box.
'Folder:        Ch12ScrollBars
```

```
Option Strict On

Public Class scrollForm
    Inherits System.Windows.Forms.Form

    Private Sub exitButton_Click(ByVal eventSender As System.Object, _
      ByVal eventArgs As System.EventArgs) Handles exitButton.Click
        ' Terminate the project.

        Me.Close()
    End Sub

    Private Sub moveCarHorizontalScrollBar_Scroll(ByVal eventSender As System.Object, _
      ByVal eventArgs As System.Windows.Forms.ScrollEventArgs) _
      Handles moveCarHorizontalScrollBar.Scroll
        ' Control the side-to-side movement.
        ' Used when scroll box is moved.

        carPictureBox.Left = moveCarHorizontalScrollBar.Value
    End Sub

    Private Sub moveCarVerticalScrollBar_Scroll(ByVal eventSender As System.Object, _
      ByVal eventArgs As System.Windows.Forms.ScrollEventArgs) _
      Handles moveCarVerticalScrollBar.Scroll
        ' Position the up and down movement.
        ' Used when scroll box is moved.

        carPictureBox.Top = moveCarVerticalScrollBar.Value
    End Sub

    Private Sub moveCarVerticalScrollBar_ValueChanged(ByVal sender As Object, _
      ByVal e As System.EventArgs) Handles moveCarVerticalScrollBar.ValueChanged
        ' Position the up and down movement.
        ' Used for arrow clicks.

        carPictureBox.Top = moveCarVerticalScrollBar.Value
    End Sub

    Private Sub moveCarHorizontalScrollBar_ValueChanged(ByVal sender As Object, _
      ByVal e As System.EventArgs) Handles moveCarHorizontalScrollBar.ValueChanged
        ' Control the side-to-side movement.
        ' Used for arrow clicks.

        carPictureBox.Left = moveCarHorizontalScrollBar.Value
    End Sub
End Class
```

Your Hands-On Programming Example

Create a project that will draw a pie chart showing the relative amount of sales for Books, Periodicals, and Food for R 'n R—For Reading and Refreshment.

Include text boxes for the user to enter the sales amount for Books, Periodicals, and Food. Include buttons for *Display Chart, Clear,* and *Exit.*

Draw the pie chart in the *Display Chart* button's Click event procedure and use the CreateGraphics.FillPie method to draw each of the pie segments.

```
Me.CreateGraphics.FillPie(Brush, xInteger, yInteger, widthInteger, heightInteger, _
    beginAngleInteger, lengthInteger)
```

Planning the Project

Sketch a form (Figure 12.12) that your users sign off as meeting their needs.

Figure 12.12

A planning sketch of the hands-on programming example.

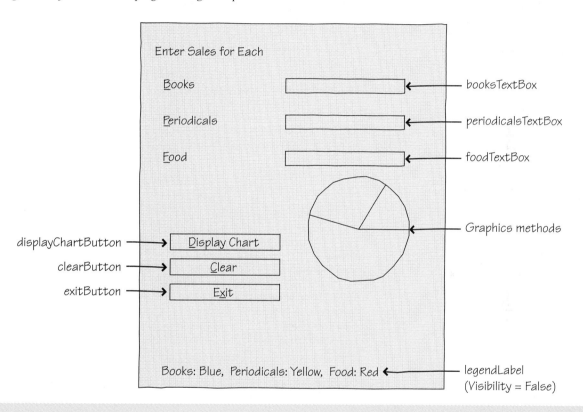

Plan the Objects and Properties

Plan the property settings for the form and each control.

Object	Property	Setting
Form	Name	pieChartForm
	Text	R 'n R Sales Pie Chart
	AcceptButton	displayChartButton
	CancelButton	clearButton
Label1	Name	Label1
	Text	Enter Sales for Each
Label2	Name	Label2
	Text	&Books
booksTextBox	Name	booksTextBox
	Text	(blank)

Object	Property	Setting
Label3	Name	Label3
	Text	&Periodicals
periodicalsTextBox	Name	periodicalsTextBox
	Text	(blank)
Label4	Name	Label4
	Text	&Food
foodTextBox	Name	foodTextBox
	Text	(blank)
legendLabel	Name	legendLabel
	Text	Books: Blue, Periodicals: Yellow, Food: Red
	Visible	False
displayChartButton	Name	displayChartButton
	Text	&Display Chart
clearButton	Name	clearButton
	Text	&Clear
exitButton	Name	exitButton
	Text	E&xit

Plan the Event Procedures

Event Procedure	Actions—Pseudocode

displayChartButton_Click	If text fields are numeric
	    Create graphic objects
	    Find Total Sales
	    Calculate ratio of each department to total sales.
	    Draw portions of the pie for each department.

clearButton_Click	Set each text box and label to blanks. Set the focus in the first text box.
exitButton_Click	Exit the project.

Write the Project   Following the sketch in Figure 12.12, create the form. Figure 12.13 shows the completed form.

- Set the properties of each of the objects, as you have planned.

- Write the code. Working from the pseudocode, write each event procedure.

- When you complete the code, use a variety of test data to thoroughly test the project.

Figure 12.13

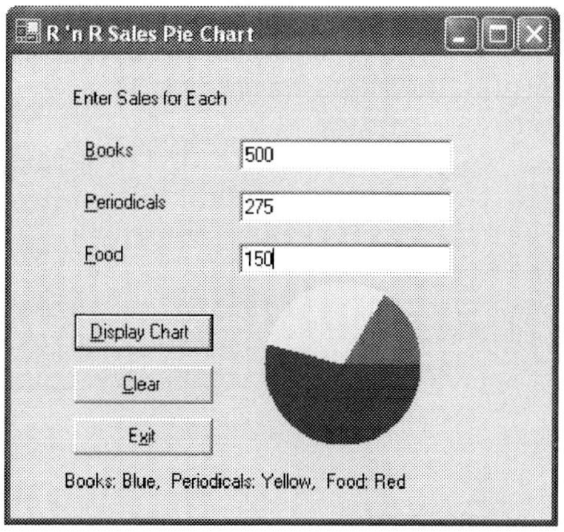

The form for the hands-on programming example.

Enter Sales for Each

Books   500

Periodicals 275

Food   150

Display Chart

Clear

Exit

Books: Blue, Periodicals: Yellow, Food: Red

R 'n R Sales Pie Chart

The Project Coding Solution

```
'Program:        Chapter 12 Pie chart
'Programmer:     Bradley/Millspaugh
'Date:           Jan 2004
'Description:    Draw a chart for relative sales amounts.
'Folder:         Ch12PieChart

Option Strict On

Public Class pieChartForm
    Inherits System.Windows.Forms.Form

    Private Sub displayChartButton_Click(ByVal sender As System.Object, _
      ByVal e As System.EventArgs) Handles displayChartButton.Click
        ' Display a pie chart showing relative sales by department.
        ' Need total sales amount.
        Dim totalSalesDecimal As Decimal
        Dim bookSalesDecimal As Decimal
        Dim periodicalSalesDecimal As Decimal
        Dim foodSalesDecimal As Decimal

        Try
            bookSalesDecimal = Decimal.Parse(booksTextBox.Text)
            Try
                periodicalSalesDecimal = Decimal.Parse(periodicalsTextBox.Text)
                Try
                    foodSalesDecimal = Decimal.Parse(foodTextBox.Text)
                    totalSalesDecimal = bookSalesDecimal + periodicalSalesDecimal + _
                      foodSalesDecimal

                    ' Create the pie chart.
                    Dim booksBrush As New SolidBrush(Color.Blue)
                    Dim periodicalsBrush As New SolidBrush(Color.Yellow)
                    Dim foodBrush As New SolidBrush(Color.Red)
                    ' Draw the chart.
                    ' Amounts are a portion of the total circle of 360 degrees.
                    ' The pie graphic includes a start angle and end angle.
                    If totalSalesDecimal <> 0 Then
                        legendLabel.Visible = True
```

```vbnet
                    ' Find the end of the book portion of 360 degrees.
                    Dim endBooksInteger As Integer = _
                      Convert.ToInt32(bookSalesDecimal / totalSalesDecimal * 360)
                    Me.CreateGraphics.FillPie(booksBrush, 160, 140, 100, 100, 0, _
                      endBooksInteger)
                    ' Find the end of the Periodicals portion.
                    Dim endPeriodicalsInteger As Integer = _
                      Convert.ToInt32(periodicalSalesDecimal / totalSalesDecimal * 360)
                    Me.CreateGraphics.FillPie(periodicalsBrush, 160, 140, 100, 100, _
                      endBooksInteger, endPeriodicalsInteger)
                    Dim endFoodInteger As Integer = _
                      Convert.ToInt32(foodSalesDecimal / totalSalesDecimal * 360)
                    Me.CreateGraphics.FillPie(foodBrush, 160, 140, 100, 100, _
                      endPeriodicalsInteger + endBooksInteger, endFoodInteger)
                End If

            Catch
                MessageBox.Show("Invalid Food Sales")
                foodTextBox.Focus()
            End Try
        Catch
            MessageBox.Show("Invalid Periodical Sales")
            periodicalsTextBox.Focus()
        End Try
    Catch
        MessageBox.Show("Invalid Book Sales")
        booksTextBox.Focus()
    End Try
End Sub

Private Sub exitButton_Click(ByVal sender As System.Object, _
  ByVal e As System.EventArgs) Handles exitButton.Click
    ' End the project.

    Me.Close()
End Sub

Private Sub clearButton_Click(ByVal sender As System.Object, _
  ByVal e As System.EventArgs) Handles clearButton.Click
    ' Clear the screen controls.
    Dim clearBrush As New SolidBrush(pieChartForm.DefaultBackColor)

    foodTextBox.Clear()
    periodicalsTextBox.Clear()
    With booksTextBox
        .Clear()
        .Focus()
    End With
    Me.CreateGraphics.FillEllipse(clearBrush, 160, 140, 100, 100)
    legendLabel.Visible = False
End Sub
End Class
```

Summary

1. A drawing surface is created with a Graphics object.
2. The graphics methods should appear in the form's Paint event procedure, so that the graphics are redrawn every time the form is repainted.
3. Pen objects are used for lines and the outline of shapes; brushes are used for filled shapes.
4. Measurements in drawings are in pixels.
5. The coordinate system begins with 0,0 at the upper-left corner of the container object.
6. You can declare a Point structure, a Size structure, or a Rectangle structure to use as arguments in the graphics methods.
7. You can generate random numbers using the Random class. Seed the random number generator when instantiating a variable of the class; use the Next method to generate a series of numbers.
8. An animated .gif file can be displayed in a PictureBox control to display animation on a Windows Form or in an Image control on a Web Form.
9. Animation effects can be created by using similar pictures and by controlling the location and visibility of controls.
10. Pictures can be loaded, moved, and resized at run time.
11. The Timer component can fire a Tick event that occurs at specified intervals, represented in milliseconds.
12. Scroll bar controls are available for both horizontal and vertical directions. Properties include Minimum, Maximum, SmallChange, LargeChange, and Value. Scroll and ValueChanged events are used to respond to the action.

Key Terms

Brush object *451*
DrawLine method *454*
DrawRectangle method *454*
FillEllipse method *454*
FromFile method *459*
graphics *450*
horizontal scroll bar *463*
Interval property *461*
LargeChange property *464*
Maximum property *464*
Minimum property *464*
Next method *456*
Pen object *451*

pixel *451*
Point structure *453*
Random class *456*
Rectangle structure *453*
Scroll event *465*
SetBounds method *461*
Size structure *453*
SmallChange property *464*
Tick event *461*
Timer component *461*
Value property *464*
ValueChanged event *465*
vertical scroll bar *463*

Review Questions

1. What is a pixel?
2. What class contains the graphics methods?
3. Describe two ways to add a Graphics object to a form.

4. Name three methods available for drawing graphics.
5. How is a pie-shaped wedge created?
6. Differentiate between using a Brush and a Pen object.
7. Which method loads a picture at run time?
8. How can you remove a picture at run time?
9. What steps are necessary to change an image that contains a turned-off light bulb to a turned-on light bulb?
10. What is the purpose of the Timer component?
11. Explain the purpose of these scroll bar properties: Minimum, Maximum, SmallChange, LargeChange, Value.

Programming Exercises

12.1 Create a project that contains two buttons labeled `Smile` and `Frown`. The `Smile` button will display a happy face; `Frown` will display a sad face. Use graphics methods to draw the two faces.

12.2 Use graphics methods to create the background of a form. Draw a picture of a house, including a front door, a window, and a chimney.

12.3 Use a PictureBox control with a .bmp file from Windows. Set the Size-Mode property to StretchImage. Use a scroll bar to change the size of the image.

12.4 Use graphics from any clip art collection to create a project that has a button for each month of the year. Have an appropriate image display in a PictureBox for each month.

12.5 Use the bicycle icon from Visual Basic and a Timer component to move the bicycle around the screen. Add a *Start* button and a *Stop* button. The *Stop* button will return the bicycle to its original position. (The bicycle icon is stored as *Graphics\Icons\Industry\Bicycle.ico* or in the Graphics folder on the text CD.)

12.6 Modify the snowman project (Chapter 12 Random Numbers) from the chapter by adding eyes, a mouth, and buttons.

12.7 Modify the chapter hands-on example to add two more categories: Drinks and Gifts. Allow the user to enter the additional values and make the pie chart reflect all five categories. Make sure to set the legend label at the bottom of the form to include the new categories.

Case Studies

VB Mail Order

Create a logo for VB Mail Order using graphics methods. Place the logo in the startup form for the project from Chapter 6. Add appropriate images and graphics to enhance each form. The graphics may come from .bmp files, .gif files, clip art, or your own creation from Paintbrush.

VB Auto Center

Have the startup screen initially fill with random dots in your choice of colors. Use graphics methods to draw an Auto Center advertisement that will appear on the screen. Have various appropriate images (icons) appear in different locations, remain momentarily, and then disappear.

Video Bonanza

Use the Timer component and the random number generator to create a promotional game for Video Bonanza customers. Create three image controls that will display an image selected from five possible choices. When the user clicks on the *Start* button, a randomly selected image will display in each of the image controls and continue to change for a few seconds (like a "slot machine") until the user presses the *Stop* button. If all three images are the same, the customer receives a free video rental.

Display a message that says "Congratulations" or "Better Luck Next Visit".

Very Very Boards

Modify your Very Very Boards project from Chapter 6 or 8 to add a moving graphic to the *About* form. Use the graphic *Skateboard.wmf* or other graphic of your choice. Include a Timer component to move the graphic across the form. When the graphic reaches the edge of the form, reset it so that the graphic appears at the opposite edge of the form and begins the trip again.

Note: For help in basing a new project on an existing project, see "Copy and Move a Windows Project" in Appendix C.

13

Additional Topics in Visual Basic

1. Validate user input in the Validating event and display messages using an ErrorProvider component.

2. Create a multiple document project with parent and child forms.

3. Arrange the child forms vertically, horizontally, or cascaded.

4. Store images in an image list.

5. Add toolbars and status bars to your forms.

6. Use calendar controls and date functions.

7. Create data reports using Crystal Reports.

This chapter introduces some topics that can make your programs a bit more professional. You can use an ErrorProvider component to display error messages to the user and perform field-level validation, rather than validate an entire form. You can improve the operation of multiple-form applications by using a multiple document interface (MDI), which allows you to set up parent and child forms. Most professional applications have toolbars and status bars, which you learn to create in this chapter.

Visual Studio .NET includes Crystal Reports, which provides an easy method to produce data reports directly from your applications.

Advanced Validation Techniques

You already know how to validate user input using Try/Catch, If statements, and message boxes. In addition to these techniques, you can use .NET Error-Provider components, which share some characteristics with the Web validation controls. Other useful techniques are to set the MaxLength and/or CharacterCasing properties of text boxes and to perform field-level validation using the Validating event of input controls.

The ErrorProvider Component

In Chapters 3 and 4 you learned to validate user input and display message boxes for invalid data. Now you will learn to display error messages directly on the form using an ErrorProvider component, rather than pop up messages in message boxes. Using an ErrorProvider component, you can make an error indication appear next to the field in error, in a manner similar to the validator controls in Web applications.

Although you can add multiple ErrorProvider components to a form, generally you use a single ErrorProvider for all controls on a form. Once you add the ErrorProvider into the component tray, you can validate a control. If the data value is invalid, the ErrorProvider component can display a blinking icon next to the field in error and display a message in a pop-up, similar to a ToolTip (Figure 13.1).

The logic of your program can be unchanged from a MessageBox solution. When you identify an error, you use the ErrorProvider.SetError method, which pops up the icon.

ErrorProvider.SetError Method—General Form

```
ErrorProviderObject.SetError(ControlName, MessageString)
```

ErrorProvider.SetError Method—Examples

```
ErrorProvider1.SetError(quantityTextBox, "Quantity must be numeric.")
ErrorProvider1.SetError(creditCardTextBox, "Required field.")
```

Figure 13.1

The ErrorProvider displays a blinking icon next to the field in error. When the user points to the icon, the error message appears in a pop-up.

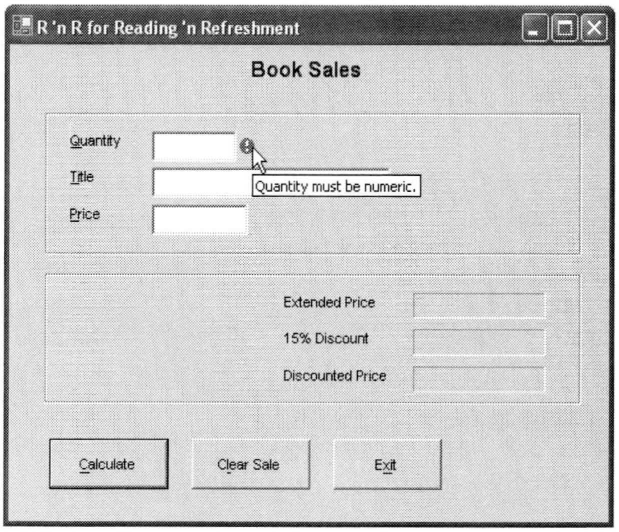

Figure 13.2

The calculation form from Chapter 3 with an ErrorProvider added.

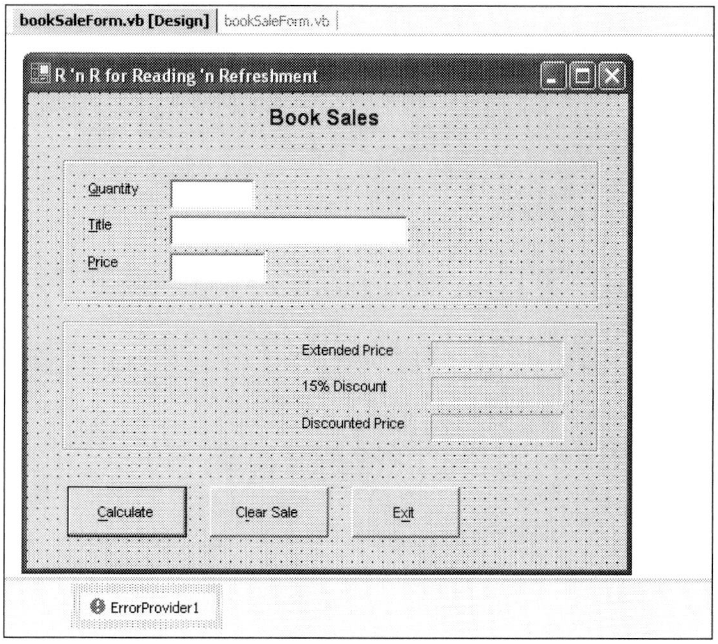

The following example is taken from Chapter 3. The message boxes have been removed and replaced with ErrorProvider icons and messages. Notice that all messages are cleared at the top of the calculateButton_Click procedure, so that no icons appear for fields that have passed validation. Figure 13.2 shows the form in design view.

```
Private Sub calculateButton_Click(ByVal sender As System.Object, _
  ByVal e As System.EventArgs) Handles calculateButton.Click
    ' Calculate the price and discount.
```

```
Dim quantityInteger As Integer
Dim priceDecimal, extendedPriceDecimal, discountDecimal, _
  discountedPriceDecimal As Decimal

' Clear any error messages.
ErrorProvider1.SetError(quantityTextBox, "")
ErrorProvider1.SetError(priceTextBox, "")

Try
    ' Convert quantity to numeric variables.
    quantityInteger = Integer.Parse(quantityTextBox.Text)
    Try
        ' Convert price if quantity was successful.
        priceDecimal = Decimal.Parse(priceTextBox.Text)

        ' Calculate values for sale.
        extendedPriceDecimal = quantityInteger * priceDecimal
        discountDecimal = extendedPriceDecimal * DISCOUNT_RATE_Decimal
        discountedPriceDecimal = extendedPriceDecimal - discountDecimal

        ' Format and display answers for the sale.
        extendedPriceLabel.Text = extendedPriceDecimal.ToString("C")
        discountLabel.Text = discountDecimal.ToString("N")
        discountedPriceLabel.Text = discountedPriceDecimal.ToString("C")

    Catch ex As Exception
        ' Handle a price exception.
        ErrorProvider1.SetError(priceTextBox, "Price must be numeric.")
        With priceTextBox
            .Focus()
            .SelectAll()
        End With
    End Try

Catch ex As Exception
    ' Handle a quantity exception.
    ErrorProvider1.SetError(quantityTextBox, "Quantity must be numeric.")
    With quantityTextBox
        .Focus()
        .SelectAll()
    End With
End Try
End Sub
```

The MaxLength and CharacterCasing Properties

You can use the **MaxLength** and **CharacterCasing properties** of text boxes to help the user enter correct input data. If you set the MaxLength property, the user is unable to enter more characters than the maximum. The user interface beeps and holds the insertion point in place to indicate the error to the user. The CharacterCasing property has possible values of Normal, Upper, or Lower, with a default of Normal. If you change the setting to Upper, for example, each character that the user types is automatically converted to uppercase, with no error message or warning. Figure 13.3 shows a State text box on a form. The user can enter only two characters, and any characters entered are converted to uppercase.

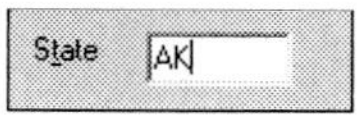

Figure 13.3

State [AK]

Note: Although the MaxLength property limits user input, the program can assign a longer value to the text box in code, if necessary.

Field-Level Validation

So far all of the validation you have coded is for the entire form, after the user clicks a button such as *OK, Calculate,* or *Save.* If the form has many input fields, the validation code can be quite long and complex. Also, the user can become confused or annoyed if multiple message boxes appear, one after another. You can take advantage of the Validating event, the CausesValidation property, and the ErrorProvider components to perform **field-level validation**, in which any error message appears as soon as the user attempts to leave a field with invalid data.

Using the Validating Event and CausesValidation Property

As the user enters data into input fields and tabs from one control to another, multiple events occur in the following order:

Enter
GotFocus
Leave
Validating
Validated
LostFocus

Although you could write event procedures for any or all of these events, the Validating event is the best location for validation code. The Validating event procedure's header includes a CancelEventArgs argument, which you can use to cancel the event and return the focus to the control that is being validated.

Each control on the form has a CausesValidation property that is set to True by default. When the user finishes an entry and presses Tab or clicks on another control, the Validating event occurs for the control just left. That is, the event occurs if the CausesValidation property of the *new* control is set to True. You can leave the CausesValidation property of most controls set to True, so that validation occurs. Set CausesValidation to False on a control such as Cancel or Exit to give the user a way to bypass the validation if he or she doesn't want to complete the transaction.

In the Validating event procedure you can perform any error checking and display a message for the user. If the data value does not pass the error checking, set the Cancel property for the *e* argument of the event procedure to True. This cancels the Validating event and returns the focus to the text box, making the text box "sticky." The user is not allowed to leave the control until the input passes validation.

```
Private Sub firstNameTextBox_Validating(ByVal sender As Object, _
  ByVal e As System.ComponentModel.CancelEventArgs) _
  Handles firstNameTextBox.Validating
    ' Validate for a required entry.

    ' Cancel any previous error.
    ErrorProvider1.SetError(firstNameTextBox, "")

    With firstNameTextBox
        ' Check for an empty string.
      If .Text = String.Empty Then
          ' Cancel the event.
          e.Cancel = True
          ErrorProvider1.SetError(firstNameTextBox, "Required Field.")
      End If
    End With
End Sub
```

One note of caution: If you use the validating event on the field that receives focus when the form is displayed, and the validation requires an entry, the user will be unable to close the form without filling in the text box. You can work around this problem by setting e.Cancel = False in the form's closing event procedure.

```
Private Sub validationForm_Closing(ByVal sender As Object, _
  ByVal e As System.ComponentModel.CancelEventArgs) _
  Handles MyBase.Closing
    ' Do not allow validation to cancel the form's closing.

    e.Cancel = False
End Sub
```

A Validation Example Program

The following program combines many of the techniques presented in this section. The form (Figure 13.4) has an ErrorProvider component and all controls

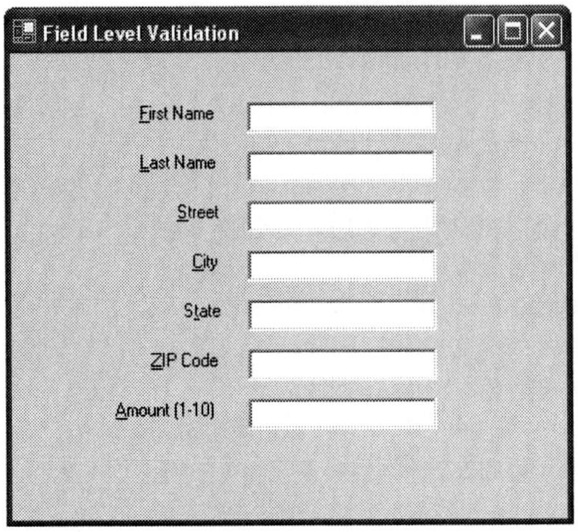

Figure 13.4

The Validation Example form, which provides field-level validation.

have their CausesValidation property set to True. The stateTextBox has its
MaxLength property set to 2 and its CharacterCasing property set to Upper. Although it seems out of place, the amountTextBox is included strictly to show an
example of numeric range validation.

```
'Program:          Ch 13 Validation
'Programmer:       Bradley/Millspaugh
'Date:             January 2004
'Description:      Demonstrate validation using the Validating event
'                  and an ErrorProvider component.
'Folder:           Ch13Validation

Public Class validationForm
    Inherits System.Windows.Forms.Form

    Private Sub firstNameTextBox_Validating(ByVal sender As Object, _
      ByVal e As System.ComponentModel.CancelEventArgs) _
      Handles firstNameTextBox.Validating
        ' Validate for a required entry.

        ' Cancel any previous error.
        ErrorProvider1.SetError(firstNameTextBox, "")

        With firstNameTextBox
            If .Text = String.Empty Then
                ' Cancel the event.
                e.Cancel = True
                ErrorProvider1.SetError(firstNameTextBox, "Required Field.")
            End If
        End With
    End Sub

    Private Sub lastNameTextBox_Validating(ByVal sender As Object, _
      ByVal e As System.ComponentModel.CancelEventArgs) _
      Handles lastNameTextBox.Validating
        ' Validate for a required entry.

        ' Cancel any previous error.
        ErrorProvider1.SetError(lastNameTextBox, "")

        With lastNameTextBox
            If .Text.Length = 0 Then
                ' Cancel the event.
                e.Cancel = True
                ErrorProvider1.SetError(lastNameTextBox, "Required Field.")
            End If
        End With
    End Sub

    Private Sub stateTextBox_Validating(ByVal sender As Object, _
      ByVal e As System.ComponentModel.CancelEventArgs) _
      Handles stateTextBox.Validating
        ' Make sure the state is two characters.
        ' The control's CharacterCasing property forces uppercase.
        ' The MaxLength property limits input to 2 characters.

        ' Cancel any previous error.
        ErrorProvider1.SetError(stateTextBox, "")
```

```
        With stateTextBox
            If .Text.Length <> 2 Then
                ' Cancel the event and select the text.
                e.Cancel = True
                .SelectAll()
                ErrorProvider1.SetError(stateTextBox, "Must be 2 characters.")
            End If
        End With
    End Sub

    Private Sub amountTextBox_Validating(ByVal sender As Object, _
      ByVal e As System.ComponentModel.CancelEventArgs) _
      Handles amountTextBox.Validating
        ' Validate a numeric amount for a range of values.
        Dim amountInteger

        ' Reset any previous error.
        ErrorProvider1.SetError(amountTextBox, "")

        With amountTextBox
            Try
                amountInteger = Integer.Parse(.Text)
                If amountInteger < 1 Or amountInteger > 10 Then
                    ' Cancel the event.
                    e.Cancel = True
                    .SelectAll()
                    ErrorProvider1.SetError(amountTextBox, _
                      "Amount must be between 1 and 10, inclusive.")
                End If
            Catch ex As Exception
                ' Cancel the event.
                e.Cancel = True
                .SelectAll()
                ErrorProvider1.SetError(amountTextBox, _
                  "Enter a numeric amount between 1 and 10, inclusive.")
            End Try
        End With
    End Sub

    Private Sub validationForm_Closing(ByVal sender As Object, _
      ByVal e As System.ComponentModel.CancelEventArgs) _
      Handles MyBase.Closing
        ' Do not allow validation to cancel the form's closing.

        e.Cancel = False
    End Sub
End Class
```

▶ Feedback 13.1

1. What is the purpose of the following code:

```
ErrorProvider1.SetError(quantityTextBox, "Quantity must be numeric.")
```

2. Name two properties of a TextBox control that help the user enter correct input data. Describe the function of each.
3. What is meant by field-level validation?

Multiple Document Interface

All of the projects so far have been **single document interface (SDI)**. Using SDI, each form in the project acts independently from the other forms. However, VB also allows you to create a **multiple document interface (MDI)**. For an example of MDI, consider an application such as Microsoft Word. Word has a **parent form** (the main window) and **child forms** (each document window). You can open multiple child windows, and you can maximize, minimize, restore, or close each child window, which always stays within the boundaries of the parent window. When you close the parent window, all child windows close automatically. Figure 13.5 shows an MDI parent window with two open child windows.

Figure 13.5

The main form is the parent and the smaller forms are the child forms in an MDI application.

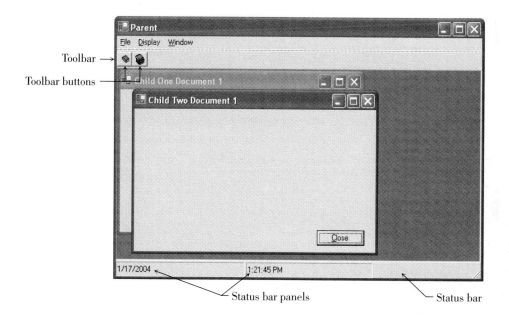

With MDI, a parent and child relationship exists between the main form and the child forms. One of the rules for MDI is that if a parent form closes, all of its children leave with it. Pretty good rule. Another rule is that children cannot wander out of the parent's area; the child form always appears inside the parent's area.

VB allows you to have forms that act independently from each other. You may have a parent form and several child forms *and* some forms that operate independently. For example, a splash form likely should remain SDI.

One feature of MDI is that you can have several documents open at the same time. The menu bar generally contains a *Window* menu that allows you to display a list of open windows and move from one active document to another.

Creating an MDI Project

You can make any form a parent. In fact, a form can be both a parent and a child form (just as a person can be both a parent and a child). To make a form into a parent, simply change its **IsMdiContainer property** to True in the Properties window of the designer. In a .NET project you can have multiple child forms and multiple parents.

Creating a child is almost as easy. Of course, your project must contain more than one form. You make a form into a child window in code at run time. Before displaying the child form from the parent, set the child's MdiParent property to the current (parent) form.

```
Private Sub displayChildOneMenuItem_Click(ByVal sender As System.Object, _
   ByVal e As System.EventArgs) Handles displayChildOneMenuItem.Click
   ' Display Child One form.

   Dim childOneForm As New childOneForm
   childOneForm.MdiParent = Me
   childOneForm.Show()
End Sub
```

Our example application allows the user to display multiple child windows. Therefore, the title bar of each child window should be unique. We can accomplish this by appending a number to the title bar before displaying the form. This is very much like Microsoft Word, with its Document1, Document2, and so forth.

```
' Module-level declarations.
Dim childOneCountInteger As Integer

Private Sub displayChildOneMenuItem_Click(ByVal sender As System.Object, _
   ByVal e As System.EventArgs) Handles displayChildOneMenuItem.Click
   ' Display Child One form.

   Dim childOneForm As New childOneForm
   childOneForm.MdiParent = Me
   childOneCountInteger += 1
   childOneForm.Text = "Child One Document " _
      & childOneCountInteger.ToString()
   childOneForm.Show()
End Sub
```

Adding a Window Menu

A parent form should have a *Window* menu (Figure 13.6). The *Window* menu lists the open child windows and allows the user to switch between windows and arrange multiple child windows. Take a look at the *Window* menu in an application such as Word or Excel. You will see a list of the open documents as well as options for arranging the windows.

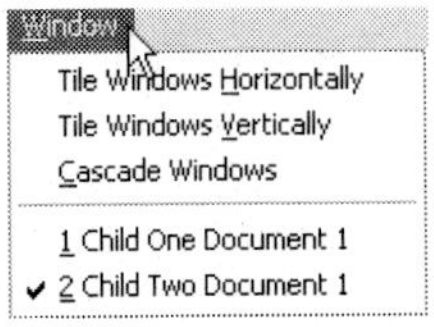

Figure 13.6

The Window menu in an MDI application lists the open child windows and allows the user to select the arrangement of the windows.

After you create a *Window* menu on your parent form, it's very easy to make it display the list of open child windows. Just set the menu's **MdiList property** to True for the windowMenu object. To actually arrange the windows requires a little code.

Layout Options

When several child windows are open, the windows may be arranged in several different layouts: tiled vertically, tiled horizontally, or cascaded. You set the type of layout with an argument of the **LayoutMdi method**.

```
Me.LayoutMdi(MdiLayout.TileHorizontal)
```

You can use one of the three constants: TileHorizontal, TileVertical, and Cascade.

```
Private Sub windowHorizontalMenuItem_Click(ByVal sender As System.Object, _
    ByVal e As System.EventArgs) Handles windowHorizontalMenuItem.Click
    ' Arrange the child forms horizontally.

    Me.LayoutMdi(MdiLayout.TileHorizontal)
End Sub

Private Sub windowVerticalMenuItem_Click(ByVal sender As System.Object, _
    ByVal e As System.EventArgs) Handles windowVerticalMenuItem.Click
    ' Arrange the child forms vertically.

    Me.LayoutMdi(MdiLayout.TileVertical)
End Sub

Private Sub windowCascadeMenuItem_Click(ByVal sender As System.Object, _
    ByVal e As System.EventArgs) Handles windowCascadeMenuItem.Click
    ' Cascade the child forms.

    Me.LayoutMdi(MdiLayout.Cascade)
End Sub
```

Toolbars and Status Bars

You can enhance the usability of your programs by adding features such as a toolbar and/or status bar. You probably find that you use the toolbars in applications as an easy shortcut for menu items. Status bars normally appear at the bottom of the screen to display information for the user.

To create a toolbar, you need a **toolbar control** and an **image list component**, which holds the graphics that appear on the toolbar buttons.

Image Lists

When you need several images to display in an application, you can store them in an image list component. Then you can assign the individual images to other controls, as needed. The toolbar control requires that its images be stored in an image list.

You add an image list to a form in the same way as any other component. Simply drag the ImageList component (Figure 13.7) from the toolbox and a new object appears in the component tray.

Figure 13.7

The ImageList component in the toolbox.

ImageList

After adding the image list to the form, you add images to the component's Images collection. In the Properties window, locate the Images property and click the Builder (ellipses) button to open the Image Collection Editor (Figure 13.8). Click on the *Add* button in the left pane to add images to the collection. An index is automatically assigned to each image in the collection. You use the index of each image to assign the pictures to the toolbar buttons, but you will be able to see a preview of each image.

Image index ⟶

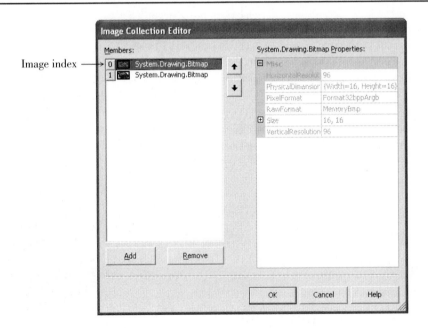

Toolbars

You use the ToolBar tool (Figure 13.9) in the toolbox to create a Toolbar object for your project. The new toolbar does not yet contain any buttons. You add the buttons using the Buttons collection in the Properties window. Refer to Figure 13.5 to see a toolbar.

Figure 13.9

The ToolBar control in the toolbox.

ToolBar

Setting Up the Buttons

Before you add buttons to the new toolbar, assign your image list component to the ImageList property of the toolbar. Then simply click on the Builder (ellipses) button for the Buttons collection to open the ToolBarButton Collection Editor (Figure 13.10). Click the *Add* button, which adds a new button to the collection. Then you set the properties for the new button in the right pane of the window. When you drop down the list for the ImageIndex property, the index and images from the image list appear (Figure 13.11).

*Add buttons to the new toolbar by clicking the **Add** button in the left pane of the ToolBarButton Collection Editor.*

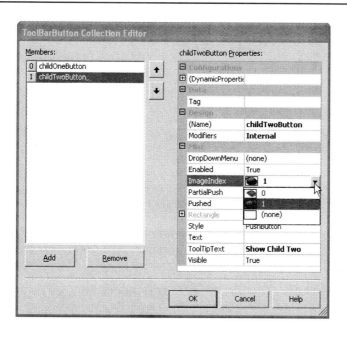

Set the properties of each toolbar button in the right pane of the ToolBarButton Collection Editor. Drop down the list for the ImageIndex property to view the images and select the correct index.

A big improvement in VB .NET over previous versions is that you can add images to the image list after you attach the image list to the toolbar.

Coding for the Toolbar

The toolbar has a single ButtonClick event that occurs when the user clicks on any of the buttons. You can use the event arguments to determine which button was clicked. For example, assuming that the toolbar is named ToolBar1, you can find the index of the selected button with this code:

```
ToolBar1.Buttons.IndexOf(e.Button)
```

You can use the index of the selected button in a `Select Case` statement to send the user to the appropriate menu procedure.

```
Private Sub parentToolbar_ButtonClick(ByVal sender As System.Object, _
  ByVal e As System.Windows.Forms.ToolBarButtonClickEventArgs) _
  Handles parentToolbar.ButtonClick
  ' Execute appropriate procedure for button clicked.

  Select Case parentToolbar.Buttons.IndexOf(e.Button)
    Case 0
        displayChildOneMenuItem_Click(sender, e)
    Case 1
        displayChildTwoMenuItem_Click(sender, e)
  End Select
End Sub
```

Status Bars

A **status bar** is usually located at the bottom of a form (refer to Figure 13.5). A status bar displays information such as date, time, status of the Caps Lock or Num Lock key, or error or informational messages. If you want a status bar on your form, you need to take two steps: add a **StatusBar control** (Figure 13.12) to your form and add **StatusBarPanel objects** to the status bar.

After adding a status bar to your form, you need to set a few properties. By default, the **ShowPanels property** is set to False; change this to True. The status bar can display either the Text property of the status bar or the Text properties of the panels, but not both.

You add panels to the status bar by selecting the Panels collection. Click the *Add* button in the StatusBarPanel Collection Editor, add a panel, and set its properties in the right pane of the window (Figure 13.13). You may find that you need to adjust the panel width to display the information completely.

Note: You can use a status bar with or without panels. If you don't use panels, you set the status bar's Text property to a single value.

> **✓ TIP**
>
> Set the ToolTipText property of each toolbar button to aid the user, in case the meaning of each graphic is not perfectly clear. ∎

Figure 13.12

The StatusBar control in the toolbox.

Figure 13.13

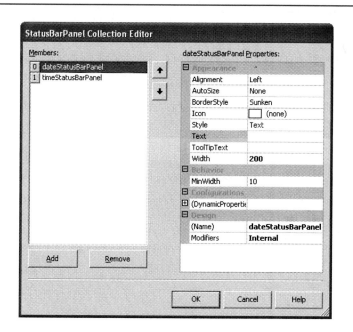

Assigning Values to Panels

You assign values to the Text property of panels at run time:

```
dateStatusBarPanel.Text = Now.ToShortDateString()
timeStatusBarPanel.Text = Now.ToLongTimeString()
informationStatusBarPanel.Text = "It's very late."
```

Displaying the Date and Time

You use the properties and methods of the **DateTime structure** to retrieve and format the current date and time. The **Now property** holds the system date and time in a numeric format that can be used for calculations. You can format the date and/or time for display using one of the following methods: `ToShortDateString`, `ToLongDateString`, `ToShortTimeString`, or `ToLongTimeString`. The actual display format of each method depends on the local system settings.

You can set the display value of status bar panels in any procedure; however, the display does not update automatically. Generally, you will set initial values in the Form_Load event procedure and use a Timer component to update the time.

```
Private Sub clockTimer_Tick(ByVal sender As System.Object, _
  ByVal e As System.EventArgs) Handles clockTimer.Tick
    ' Update the date and time on the status bar.
    ' Interval = 1000 milliseconds (one second).

    dateStatusBarPanel.Text = Now.ToShortDateString()
    timeStatusBarPanel.Text = Now.ToLongTimeString()
End Sub
```

```
Private Sub parentForm_Load(ByVal sender As Object, _
  ByVal e As System.EventArgs) Handles MyBase.Load
  ' Display the date and time in the status bar.

    dateStatusBarPanel.Text = Now.ToShortDateString()
    timeStatusBarPanel.Text = Now.ToLongTimeString()
End Sub
```

Don't forget to set the Enabled and Interval properties of your timer.

Feedback 13.2

1. Write the statements to display aboutForm as a child form.
2. Assume that you have a toolbar called ToolBar1 that has buttons for *Exit* and *About* with indexes of 0 and 1. Write the code to execute the correct procedure when the user clicks one of the buttons. Make up your own procedure names.
3. What steps are necessary to display the current time in a status bar panel called currentTimeStatusBarPanel?

Some Helpful Date Controls

There are many other controls in the toolbox. You may want to experiment with some of them to see how they work. This section demonstrates two more controls: the DateTimePicker and MonthCalendar controls.

The DateTimePicker and the MonthCalendar controls (Figure 13.14) provide the ability to display calendars on your form. One advantage of the Date-TimePicker is that it takes less screen space; it displays only the day and date unless the user drops down the calendar. You can use either control to allow the user to select a date, display the current date, or set a date in code and display the calendar with that date showing.

Figure 13.14

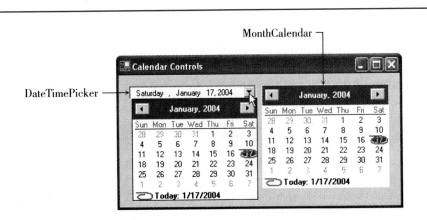

The calendar controls: The DateTimePicker drops down a calendar when selected and shows the current day and date when not dropped down; the MonthCalendar control displays the calendar.

The DateTimePicker control contains a Value property for the date. When the control initially displays, the Value is set to the current date. You can let the user select a date and then use the Value property or you can assign a Date value to the property.

The following example allows the user to enter a birthdate in a text box. It converts the text box entry in a `Try/Catch`, in order to trap for illegal date formats.

```
birthdateDateTimePicker.Value = Convert.ToDateTime(birthdateTextBox.Text)
```

This example program demonstrates the use of the calendar, date functions, and some interesting features of Visual Basic. Figure 13.15 shows the form for the project.

Figure 13.15

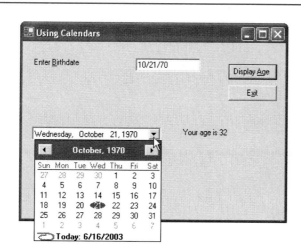

The birthday form with the calendar for the DateTimePicker dropped down.

```
'Program          Chapter 13 Calendar control
'Programmer:      Bradley/Millspaugh
'Date:            January 2004
'Description:     Enters and tests a date, displays a calendar, and uses
'                 Date functions.
'Folder:          Ch13Calendar

Option Strict On

Public Class calendarForm
    Inherits System.Windows.Forms.Form

    Private Sub displayButton_Click(ByVal sender As System.Object, _
      ByVal e As System.EventArgs) Handles displayButton.Click
        ' If the date is valid, set the calendar and display.

        Try
            With birthdateDateTimePicker
                .Value = Convert.ToDateTime(birthdateTextBox.Text)
                .Visible = True
            End With
        Catch err As Exception
            MessageBox.Show("Invalid Date")
            birthdateTextBox.Focus()
        End Try
    End Sub
```

```
Private Sub birthdateDateTimePicker_ValueChanged(ByVal sender As System.Object, _
    ByVal e As System.EventArgs) Handles birthdateDateTimePicker.ValueChanged
    ' Calculate the age when the calendar value changes.
    Dim yearsInteger As Integer

    With birthdateDateTimePicker.Value
        ' If birthday already passed this year.
        If .DayOfYear <= Now.DayOfYear Then
            yearsInteger = Now.Year - .Year
        Else
            ' Birthday yet to come this year.
            yearsInteger = Now.Year - .Year - 1
        End If
    End With

    With ageLabel
        .Text = "Your age is " & yearsInteger.ToString()
        .Visible = True
    End With
End Sub

Private Sub exitButton_Click(ByVal sender As System.Object, _
    ByVal e As System.EventArgs) Handles exitButton.Click
    ' Terminate the project.

    Me.Close()
End Sub
End Class
```

Notice the statements in the ValueChanged event procedure for the DatePicker. You can use all of the properties of the system time on the Value property of the control.

```
yearsInteger = Now.Year - birthdateDateTimePicker.Value.Year
```

You can see all of the methods and properties using Visual Studio's IntelliSense feature.

► ### Feedback 13.3

1. Write the code to assign the date from appointmentDateTimePicker to the variable appointmentDateTime.
2. Use the IntelliSense feature or Help to list five properties of the Value property for a DateTimePicker control.
3. Which of the five properties listed in question 2 are also available for the Now property?

Crystal Reports

One of the powerful features of Visual Basic is the report designer by Crystal Decisions called **Crystal Reports**. The Crystal Report Gallery contains "experts" to guide you in creating standard reports, forms, and even mailing labels, or you can use an existing report or generate a new one. Using Crystal Reports you can publish reports on Windows Forms or on Web Forms.

Note: The Standard Edition of Visual Basic .NET does not include Crystal Reports. If you are using the Standard Edition, you won't be able to complete the exercise in this section.

It takes two steps to create and display a report:

1. Add a Report Designer and design the report template. The template includes the settings for connection to the database and the layout of the report.
2. Add a **CrystalReportViewer control** to a form and connect it to the report template.

Once you have added the report to a project and run the project, you can view the report and send the report to the printer, if you wish.

Adding a Report Designer

You add a new Report Designer to a project by selecting *Add New Item* from the *Project* menu and choosing the *Crystal Report* icon. Give the report a name before pressing the Enter key (Figure 13.16).

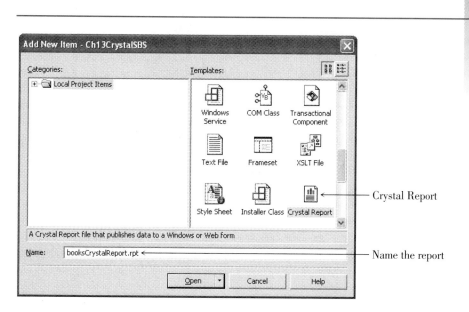

Figure 13.16

Add a new Crystal Report item and give it a name on the Add New Item *dialog box.*

Next you are given a choice of the type of report to create (Figure 13.17). You can choose *Using the Report Expert* to open a wizard that steps you through the report creation process. Or you can choose *As a Blank Report* to create your own report from scratch. The third choice, *From an Existing Report,* allows you to create a modification of a report you have already created. The example in this chapter uses the wizard.

Creating a Report—Step by Step

The following tutorial walks you through the steps for creating a Crystal Report for R 'n R. Figure 13.18 shows the completed report. *Note that the Standard*

Edition of Visual Basic .NET does not include Crystal Reports. You cannot complete this exercise if you are using the Standard Edition.

Create the Project

STEP 1: Create a new Windows Application project called "Ch13CrystalSBS".

STEP 2: Change the form's Text property to "R 'n R Book Report".

STEP 3: Change the form's Name property to reportForm, display the project properties, and set the project's startup object to the new form name.

STEP 4: Using Windows Explorer or My Computer, copy RnrBooks.mdb into your Ch13CrystalSBS folder. (You can find RnrBooks.mdb on the text CD.) Make sure that the file is not ReadOnly.

F i g u r e   1 3 . 1 7

Select the type of new report for the Crystal Reports Designer.

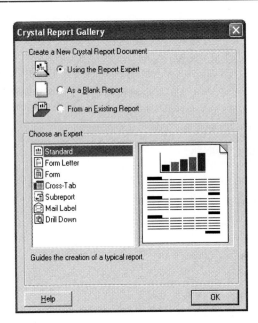

F i g u r e   1 3 . 1 8

The completed report from the step-by-step example.

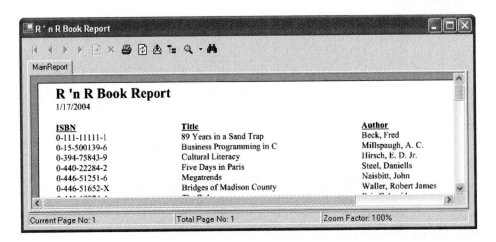

Design the Report

STEP 1: Select *Add New Item* from the *Project* menu and click on the *Crystal Report* icon.

STEP 2: Type the name "booksCrystalReport" and press Enter (refer to Figure 13.16). The Registration Wizard may appear; click *Register Later*.

STEP 3: Make sure the option for *Using the Report Expert* and the *Standard* report type are selected (refer to Figure 13.17). Click *OK*.

STEP 4: On the first screen of the Standard Report Expert (the wizard), click on the plus sign to expand the node for Database Files (Figure 13.19). An *Open* dialog box appears; browse to find RnrBooks.mdb in your project folder, select the filename, and click *Open*.

   The names of the tables in the database should appear.

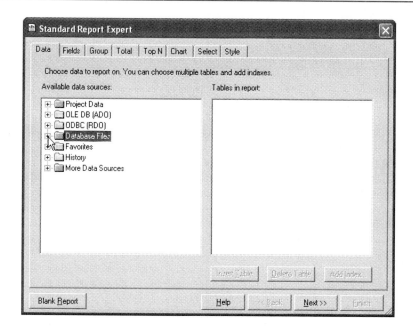

Figure 13.19

The first screen of the Standard Report Expert wizard. Expand the node for Database Files to connect to your database file.

STEP 5: Select the Books table and click *Insert Table* (or double-click the Books table). The table name will appear in the right pane (Figure 13.20).

   You can click through every tabbed page of the wizard, or use the tabs to go directly to the pages that you want to use.

STEP 6: Click *Next*, which takes you to the *Fields* page of the wizard.

   On this screen you select the fields that you want to include on the report. Select the field names from the list on the left and add them to the list on the right. You can either click the field name and click *Add* or double-click the field name.

STEP 7: Add ISBN, Title, and Author to the *Fields to Display* list (Figure 13.21).

STEP 8: Click on the *Style* tab at the top of the wizard. (If you want to view the other tabs, you can click *Next* through each page. For this report, you only need the *Style* tab.)

STEP 9: For *Title*, type "R 'n R Book Report". Click on each of the entries in the *Style* box to see the possibilities. Then click on *Standard* and click

Click on a field in the *Available Fields* list and select *Browse Data* to see the actual data in the table. ■

Figure 13.20

Select the Books table and add it to the right pane.

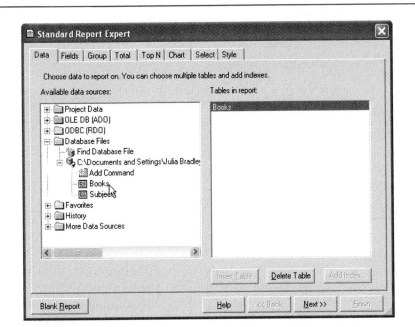

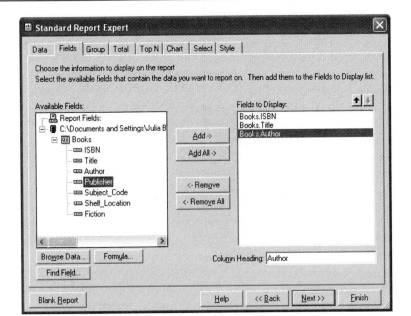

Finish. The report designer appears with the entries that you selected (Figure 13.22).

At this point, the report template is complete. However, you can make lots of adjustments and changes to the content and format. The various parts of the report layout screen are covered later in "The Report Designer" section (page 498).

Figure 13.22

The Crystal Reports report designer with the layout created by the wizard.

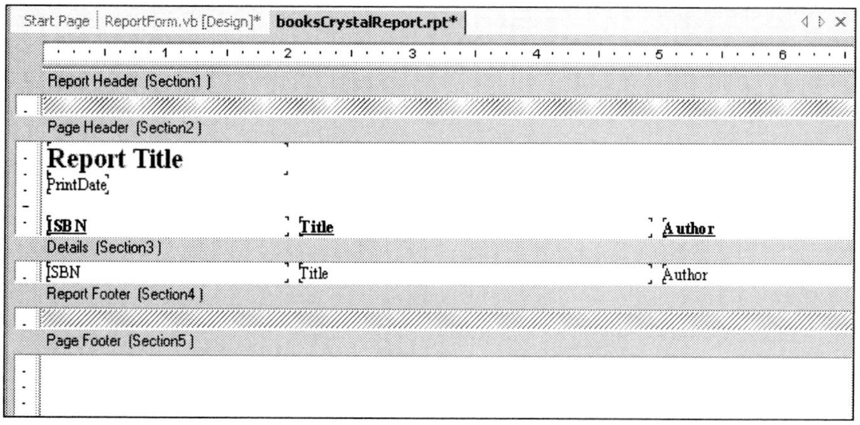

Start Page | ReportForm.vb [Design]* | **booksCrystalReport.rpt*** | ◁ ▷ ✕

Report Header (Section1)

Page Header (Section2)

Report Title
PrintDate

ISBN   Title   Author
Details (Section3)
ISBN   Title   Author
Report Footer (Section4)

Page Footer (Section5)

Display the Report

STEP 1: Return to the Form Designer window.
STEP 2: Drag a CrystalReportsViewer control to the form. (It's the last tool in the list if you have not sorted the toolbox in alphabetic order.)
STEP 3: Increase the size of the form and of the viewer.
STEP 4: Set the ReportSource property to booksCrystalReport.rpt by using the *Browse* option and finding the file in the Ch13CrystalSBS folder.
STEP 5: Change the DisplayGroupTree property to False.
     Figure 13.23 shows the form at this point.
STEP 6: Set the Anchor property of the control to anchor to all four edges (top, bottom, left, and right). This will make the control resize if you resize the form.

Figure 13.23

The form with the Crystal Reports viewer control. Expand the form and the control to allow space for the report to display.

Run the Project

STEP 1: Run the project. The report should appear with the data you selected.

Take note of the spacing and formatting, to see if there is anything you'd like to change. You'll have a chance to make adjustments in a minute. Also, try resizing and/or maximizing the form.

STEP 2: Close the form to return to design mode. You can make any desired adjustments to the report layout or to the form. See the section "Modifying Report Design" (on the next page) for some help.

The Report Designer

When the Crystal Reports Report Designer displays, you have many options. You can see two new toolbars, a separate section in the toolbox, and a **Field Explorer** window (Figure 13.24), which appears as a separate tab in the Toolbox window (Figure 13.25). You can use the Field Explorer to add new fields to your report. Use the items in the toolbox to add elements such as lines, boxes, or additional text that is not bound to a data field, such as explanations or additional title lines.

The report template contains several bands for information. Refer to Figure 13.22.

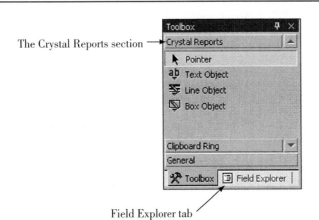

The Crystal Reports section

Field Explorer tab

Figure 13.24

The toolbox section for Crystal Reports.

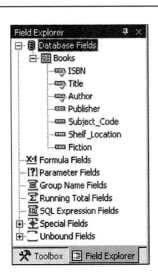

Figure 13.25

The Crystal Reports Field Explorer.

- The Report Header appears one time at the beginning of the report. You can place any item in this section that you want to appear on only the first page of a multipage report.

- The Page Header appears at the top of each page. Generally the Page Header section holds the report title and column headings.

- The Details section holds the data for the body of the report. Here you place the fields that you want to appear on each line of the report. Generally, these are the data from each record.

- The Report Footer appears once at the end of the report.

- The Page Footer appears at the bottom of each page.

Modifying Report Design

You can move, resize, and reformat the fields in the designer. Click on any field and resize it using the sizing handles, or drag the control to move it. To reformat a field, right-click and select *Format* from the shortcut menu.

If you want to recall the Report Expert (the wizard) or change the style of the report, right-click on the report design. On the context menu, select *Report* (Figure 13.26). From the pop-up menu, you can choose *Report Expert* to open the wizard or *Style Expert* to select a new report style.

F i g u r e   1 3 . 2 6

Make changes to the report design by selecting **Report Expert** *from the context menu. Or select* **Style Expert** *to choose a new report style.*

Do you want to change the page margins? If so, right-click on the designer and select *Designer* and *Page Setup* (Figure 13.27).

Adding a Report to a Web Form

You can display reports from Web Forms, but there are a few differences from Windows Forms. Just as with all controls, you use a different CrystalReportsViewer control on your Web Form. You will find the correct control in the Web Forms section of the toolbox. The Web version of the report viewer does not have a printer option; you can only display the report on the screen.

You must set the viewer's ReportSource property in code, rather than the Properties window. Add this code to the Web Form's Page_Load event procedure, substituting the path and report designer name for the actual name on your system.

Figure 13.27

```
Private Sub Page_Load(ByVal sender As System.Object, _
   ByVal e As System.EventArgs) Handles MyBase.Load
   ' Initialize the page.

   CrystalReportViewer1.ReportSource = _
     "C:\inetpub\wwwroot\CrystalReports\CrystalReport1.rpt"
End Sub
```

Moving a Crystal Reports Project

When you move a project that has a Crystal Report, you must make two changes:

1. Change the data source for the report template. In the Field Explorer, right-click on the *Database Fields* icon and choose *Set Location* from the context menu. In the *Set Location* dialog box, you can browse to find the current location of the database file.
2. Change the ReportSource property of the CrystalReportViewer control on the form. You can browse to locate the project's current folder.

Summary

1. An ErrorProvider component can provide an icon and pop-up error message next to the field that does not pass validation. Specify the text box and the message in the ErrorProvider.SetError method.
2. A text box MaxLength property limits the number of characters the user is allowed to enter into the control.
3. The CharacterCasing property of a text box can automatically convert user input to uppercase or lowercase.
4. You can validate individual fields in the Validating event procedure for the controls. The Validating event occurs when the user attempts to move the focus to another control that has its CausesValidation property set to True.
5. A multiple document interface (MDI) contains parent and child forms. Closing the parent also closes all child forms. The child forms stay within the bounds of the parent form.

6. To create an MDI parent form, set a form's IsMdiContainer property to True. To create a child form, set the form's MdiParent property to the parent form in code.

7. MDI applications generally have a *Window* menu, which displays a list of open child windows and provides choices for arranging the child windows.

8. An image list component contains a collection of the images for other controls, such as the buttons on a toolbar.

9. To create a toolbar, add the control, attach the image list, and add buttons to the Buttons collection. Set each button to one of the images in the image list.

10. A toolbar provides shortcuts to menu options. A `Select Case` statement can be used in the toolbar's ButtonClick event procedure to determine which button was clicked and take appropriate action.

11. A status bar contains information for the user along the bottom of a form. After adding a status bar to a project, add panels to its Panels collection.

12. The date can be assigned to the Text property of a panel during the Form_Load event procedure, but the time display requires an update routine using a Timer component.

13. The DateTimePicker and MonthCalendar controls have accurate calendars for displaying and inputting dates.

14. Crystal Reports make it easy to generate reports for database applications.

15. The Crystal Report Designer is used to create a report template.

16. The CrystalReportViewer control is placed on a form to display the data.

Key Terms

CharacterCasing property *478*
child form *483*
Crystal Reports *492*
CrystalReportViewer control *493*
DateTime structure *489*
Field Explorer *498*
field-level validation *479*
image list component *485*
IsMdiContainer property *484*
LayoutMdi method *485*
MaxLength property *478*
MdiList property *485*

multiple document interface
  (MDI) *483*
Now property *489*
parent form *483*
ShowPanels property *488*
single document interface
  (SDI) *483*
status bar *488*
StatusBar control *488*
StatusBarPanel object *488*
toolbar control *485*

Review Questions

1. Explain how to use an ErrorProvider component to validate the value in a text box.

2. What properties of a text box determine how many characters a user can enter and the case (upper or lower) of the input?

3. What is meant by *MDI*?

4. What are the advantages of having parent and child forms?

5. What are the layouts available for arranging child windows?

6. How can a child form be created? A parent form?

7. What steps are necessary to create a toolbar and have its buttons execute menu procedures?
8. What must be done to create a status bar? To display a panel with the current time? To keep the time display current?
9. Describe two controls that you can use for displaying dates on a form.
10. Describe the steps necessary to add a database report to a form.

Programming Exercises

13.1 Convert any of your earlier programs that use message boxes for error messages to use an ErrorProvider component. Remove all message boxes from the program and display meaningful messages in the pop-up Error-Text.

13.2 Write an MDI project that is a simple text editor. Allow the user to open multiple documents, each in a separate child form. For the text editor, use one big TextBox control with its Multiline property set to True or a Rich-TextBox control. Set the control's Anchor property to all four edges so the control fills its form.

   Each form should have its own Load File and Save File functions. Use the FileStreams that you learned about in Chapter 11.

13.3 Add a toolbar to a previous project to provide shortcuts to the menu items.

13.4 Add a toolbar to the calendar program from this chapter.

13.5 Add a report to your database project from Chapter 10. You can add a form to display the report.

Answers to Feedback Questions

▶ Feedback 1.1

These exercises are designed to become familiar with the Help system. There are no "correct" answers.

▶ Feedback 2.1

Property	Setting
Name	iconPictureBox
BorderStyle	Fixed3D
SizeMode	StretchImage
Visible	True

▶ Feedback 2.2

1. ```
   companyTextBox.Text = ""
   companyTextBox.Focus()
   ```
2. ```
   customerLabel.Text = ""
   orderTextBox.Focus()
   ```
3. (a) Places a check in the check box.
   (b) Radio button is deselected.
   (c) Makes the picture invisible.
   (d) Makes the label appear sunken.
   (e) Assigns the text value in cityTextBox.Text to the text value of cityLabel.Text.

▶ Feedback 3.1

1. Does not specify a data type.
2. Identifiers cannot contain special characters, such as "#".
3. An identifier cannot contain blank spaces.
4. Periods are used to separate items such as Object.Property.
5. Identifiers cannot contain embedded special characters such as "$".
6. *Sub* is a reserved word.
7. The name is valid; however, it does not indicate anything about what the variable is used for.
8. *Text* is a property name and therefore it is a reserved word.
9. The name is valid; however, the data type should be specified.
10. Valid.

11. Valid.
12. Valid.

▶ Feedback 3.2

Note: Answers may vary; make sure that the data type is included in each name.

1. (a) hoursDecimal
   (b) employeeNameString
   (c) departmentNumberString
2. (a) quantityInteger
   (b) descriptionString
   (c) partNumberString
   (d) costDecimal
   (e) sellingPriceDecimal

▶ Feedback 3.3

Note: Answers may vary; make sure the data type is included in each name.

1. `Private totalPayrollDecimal As Decimal`
   Declared at the module level.
2. `Const SALES_TAX_Decimal As Decimal = .08D`
   Declared at the module level.
3. `Dim participantCountInteger As Integer`
   Declared at the module level.

▶ Feedback 3.4

1. 18
2. 1
3. 6
4. 5
5. 22
6. 2048
7. 22
8. 38

▶ Feedback 3.5

1. (a) `countInteger = countInteger + 5`
   (b) `countInteger += 5`
2. (a) `balanceDecimal = balanceDecimal – withdrawalDecimal`
   (b) `balanceDecimal –= withdrawalDecimal`

3. (a) `priceDecimal = priceDecimal * countInteger`
   (b) `priceDecimal *= countInteger`

Feedback 3.6

1. `averagePayLabel.Text = averagePayDecimal.ToString("C")`
   $123.46
2. `quantityLabel.Text = quantityInteger.ToString()`
   176123
3. `totalLabel.Text = totalCollectedDecimal.ToString("N")`

Feedback 4.1

1. True
2. True
3. True
4. False
5. False
6. True
7. True
8. False
9. True
10. True

Feedback 4.2

1. frogsRadioButton will be checked.
   toadsRadioButton will be unchecked.
2. "It's the toads and the polliwogs"
3. "It's true"
4.
```
If Convert.ToInteger(orangesTextBox.Text) _
  > Convert.ToInteger(applesTextBox.Text) Then
    mostLabel.Text = "Oranges"
Else
    mostLabel.Text = "Apples"
End If
```
5.
```
If balanceDecimal > 0 Then
    fundsCheckBox.Checked = True
    balanceDecimal = 0
    countInteger += 1
Else
    fundsCheckBox.Checked = False
End If
```

▶ Feedback 4.3

Convert the following If statements to Select Case statements.

1.
```
Select Case tempInteger
    Case Is > 80
        commentLabel.Text = "Hot"
    Case Is > 32
        commentLabel.Text = "Moderate"
    Case Else
        commentLabel.Text = "Freezing"
End Select
```
2.
```
Select Case countInteger
    Case 0
        MessageBox.Show("No items entered.")
    Case 1 To 10
        MessageBox.Show("1 - 10 items entered.")
    Case 11 To 20
        MessageBox.Show("11 - 20 items entered.")
    Case Else
        MessageBox.Show("More than 20 items were entered.")
End Select
```

▶ Feedback 5.1

1. Function procedure; a value will be returned.
2.
```
Private Function Average(valueOneInteger As Integer,
    valueTwoInteger As Integer, _
    valueThreeInteger As Integer) As Integer
```
3.
```
Return (valueOneInteger + valueTwoInteger + _
    valueThreeInteger) / 3
```
4. The answer appears on a Return statement or is assigned to the field with the same name as the function.

▶ Feedback 6.1

1. An object is an instance of a class. A class defines an item type (like the cookie cutter defines the shape), whereas the object is an actual instance of the class (as the cookie made from the cookie cutter).
2. aProduct is an object, an instance of the Product class.
3. The numeric value of quantityTextBox is assigned to the Quantity property of aProduct.
4.
```
Private lastNameString As String
Private firstNameString As String
Private studentIDString As String
Private gpaDecimal As Decimal
```
These statements will appear at the module level.

```
5.  Property LastName() As String
        Get
            LastName = lastNameString
        End Get
        Set(ByVal Value As String)
            lastNameString = Value
        End Set
    End Property
6.  ReadOnly Property GPA() As Decimal
        Get
            GPA = gpaDecimal
        End Get
    End Property
```

▶ Feedback 7.1

1. Alphabetizes the items in a list box or combo box.
2. Stores the index number of the currently selected (highlighted) item; has a value of −1 if nothing is selected.
3. Is a collection that holds the objects, usually text, of all list elements in a list box or combo box.
4. Determines whether or not a list box will also have a text box for user input. It also determines whether or not the list will drop down.
5. Stores the number of elements in a list box or combo box.
6. Adds an element to a list at run time.
7. Adds an element to a list and inserts the element in the chosen position (index).
8. Clears all elements from a list box or combo box.
9. Removes an element from the list by referring to its index.
10. Removes an element from a list by looking for a given string.

▶ Feedback 7.2

```
itemFoundBoolean = False ' Set the initial value of the found switch to False.
itemIndexInteger = 0 ' Initialize the counter for the item index.
' Loop through the items until the requested item is found _
    or the end of the list is reached.
Do Until itemFoundBoolean Or itemIndexInteger = itemsListBox.Items.Count
    ' Check if the text box entry matches the item in the list.
    If newItemTextBox.Text = itemsListBox.Items(itemIndexInteger).ToString() Then
        itemFoundBoolean = True ' Set the found switch to True.
    End If
    itemIndexInteger += 1 ' Increment the counter for the item index.
Loop
```

➤ Feedback 7.3

1. (a) There should not be a comma after the test value.
   (b) The `Next` statement must contain the same variable that follows the `For` statement, indexInteger in this case.
   (c) The item following the word `For` must be a variable and the same variable must be used on the `Next` statement. 4 is not a proper variable name and `For` is a reserved word.
   (d) Valid.
   (e) Valid.
   (f) This loop will never be executed; needs to have a negative `Step` argument.
2. (a) Will be executed 3 times; countInteger will have an ending value of 4.
   (b) Will be executed 4 times; have an ending value of 14 in countInteger.
   (c) Will be executed 10 times; countInteger will have an ending value of 0.
   (d) Will be executed 7 times; counterDecimal will have an ending value of 6.5.
   (e) Will never be executed because the starting value is already greater than the test value; countInteger will have an ending value of 5.

➤ Feedback 7.4

1. A component used to set up output for the printer. Add the component to the form's component tray at design time. Begin the printing process by executing the `Print` method of the component; the component's PrintPage event occurs.
2. Starts the printing process. Belongs in the Click event procedure for the *Print* button.
3. The PrintPage event is a callback that occurs once for each page to print. The PrintPage event procedure contains all the logic for printing the page.
4. Sends a line of text to the graphics object. The `DrawString` method is used in the PrintPage event procedure.
5. An argument passed to the PrintPage event procedure. Holds items of information such as the page margins.
6. MarginBounds.Left is one of the properties of the PrintPageEventArgs argument passed to the PrintPage event procedure. The property holds the left margin and can be used to set the X coordinate to the left margin.
7. A component that allows the user to view the document in *Print Preview*. The component is added to the component tray at design time. In the event procedure where the user selects *Print Preview*, the print document is assigned to this component.

➤ Feedback 8.1

1. Valid.
2. Valid.

3. Valid.
4. Invalid, beyond the range of the array.
5. Valid.
6. Invalid; negative number.
7. Gives a decimal number but Visual Basic will round the fraction and use that integer.
8. Valid.

➤ Feedback 8.2

1.
```
Structure Student
    Dim lastNameString As String
    Dim firstNameString As String
    Dim studentNumberString As String
    Dim unitsCompletedDecimal As Decimal
    Dim gpaDecimal As Decimal
End Structure
```
2.
```
Dim infoStudent(99) As Student
```
3.
```
Structure Project
    Dim projectNameString As String
    Dim formNameString As String
    Dim folderNameString As String
End Structure
```
4.
```
Dim myProject As Project
```
5.
```
Dim ourProjects(99) As Project
```

➤ Feedback 8.3

1.
```
Dim temperatureDecimal(2, 4) As Decimal
```
2.
```
For columnInteger = 0 To 4
    temperatureDecimal(0, columnInteger) = 0
Next columnInteger
```
3.
```
For columnInteger = 0 To 4
    temperatureDecimal(1, columnInteger) = 75
Next columnInteger
```
4.
```
For columnInteger = 0 To 4
    temperatureDecimal(2, columnInteger) = temperatureDecimal(0, columnInteger) _
        + temperatureDecimal(1, columnInteger)
Next columnInteger
```
5.
```
For rowIndexInteger = 0 To 2
    For columnIndexInteger = 0 To 4
        e.Graphics.DrawString(temperatureDecimal _
            (rowIndexInteger, columnIndexInteger).ToString(), printFont, Brushes.Black, _
            printXSingle, printYSingle)
        printXSingle += 200
Next columnIndexInteger
```

```
   ' Begin a new line.
   printXSingle = e.MarginBounds.Left
   printYSingle += lineHeightSingle
Next rowIndexInteger
```

Feedback 9.1

1. Right-click on the control and choose *Run As Server Control*.
2. So that the control will respond to events and can execute an event procedure when clicked.
3. .aspx; Holds the information about the user interface.
   .aspx.vb; Holds the code that runs behind the .aspx file.
4. Right-click on the form and select *View in Browser*.

Feedback 9.2

1. Grid Layout allows you to determine the exact placement of controls. Flow Layout places each control immediately following the insertion point.
2. (a) Press the Enter key until the insertion point is at the bottom of the form.
   (b) Add a table to the form and place the button in a cell at the bottom of the table.
3. An HTML table works on the client side only; the data must be added at design time. A Web Table can be changed dynamically at run time.
4. Store images in the project folder or a graphics folder.

Feedback 9.3

Attach a RequiredFieldValidator control, so that the field cannot be left blank. Attach a CompareValidator to make sure that the entry can be converted to numeric. Attach a RangeValidator to check if the input falls within the specified range by setting the MinimumValue = 0 and the MaximumValue = 1000.

Feedback 9.4

The Page_Load event occurs and the page is redisplayed for every round-trip to the server. If you have initialization code in the Page_Load event procedure, you don't want to perform the initialization each time the procedure executes.

Feedback 9.5

1. The NavigateURL property.
2. Add a HyperLink control to both pages. Set the NavigateURL of each to point to the other page.

Feedback 10.1

1. The *file* is the database.
   The *table* contains the *rows* and *columns,* which hold the information about your friends.
   Each *row/record* contains information about an individual friend.
   A *column* or *field* contains an element of data, such as the name or phone number.
   The *key field* is the field used to organize the file; it contains a unique value that identifies a particular record, for example, the telephone number field.
2. XML is stored as text, which can pass through Internet firewalls and can be edited using any text editor.

Feedback 10.2

The connection object creates a link between the data source and the program. The data adapter passes information back and forth between the data source and the dataset. The dataset holds a copy of the data retrieved from the data source and is used in your program to access the data, either field by field (for labels and text boxes) or by connecting it to a grid.

Feedback 10.3

1. Set the DataSource to the DataSet and the DisplayMember to the field that you want to display in the list.
2. Set the DataBindings.Text property to the field in the table from which you want to display information.
3. To sort the list, modify the SQL SELECT statement used by the data adapter.

Feedback 11.1

1.
```
Dim inventoryStreamWriter _
    As New StreamWriter("Inventory.txt")
```
2. `inventoryStreamWriter.WriteLine(descriptionTextBox.Text)`
3. The declaration for the StreamReader object needs to be in a `Try/Catch` block in case the file does not exist. The declaration for the StreamWriter

object does not need to be in a `Try`/`Catch` block because, in this case, the
program is generating a file, not trying to locate one.

4.
```
If inventoryStreamReader.Peek <> -1 Then
    descriptionLabel.Text = inventoryStreamReader.ReadLine()
    productNumberLabel.Text = inventoryStreamReader.ReadLine()
End If
```

▶ Feedback 11.2

1.
```
Text Files (*.txt)|*.txt)
```
2.
```
OpenDialog1.InitialDirectory = Application.StartupPath
```
3.
```
If Not phoneStreamWriter Is Nothing Then
    phoneStreamWriter.Close()
End If
```

▶ Feedback 11.3

1.
```
countInteger = namesListBox.Items.Count - 1
For indexInteger = 0 To countInteger
    namesStreamWriter.WriteLine(namesListBox.Items(indexInteger))
Next indexInteger
```
2. The above code should be placed in a Save procedure, which should be
called from the form's Closing event procedure.
3.
```
Try
    Dim namesStreamReader As New StreamReader("Names.txt")
    Do Until namesStreamReader.Peek = -1
        namesListBox.Items.Add(namesStreamReader.ReadLine())
    Loop
    namesStreamReader.Close()
Catch
```

▶ Feedback 12.1

1.
```
Dim gr As Graphics = e.Graphics
Dim greenPen As New Pen(Color.Green)
Dim xInteger As Integer
Dim yInteger As Integer
yInteger = Convert.ToInteger(Me.Height)
xInteger = Convert.ToInteger(Me.Width / 2)
gr.DrawLine(greenPen, xInteger, 0, xInteger, yInteger)
```
2.
```
gr.DrawEllipse(greenPen, xInteger, yInteger, 100F, 100F)
gr.DrawEllipse(bluePen, xInteger + 25, yInteger + 25, 50F, 50F)
```

3.
```
Dim firstPoint As New Point(20, 20)
Dim secondPoint As New Point(100, 100)
Dim thirdPoint As New Point(200, 50)
gr.DrawLine(greenPen, firstPoint, secondPoint)
gr.DrawLine(greenPen, secondPoint, thirdPoint)
gr.DrawLine(greenPen, thirdPoint, firstPoint)
```

▶ Feedback 12.2

1.
```
Static xInteger As Integer = commandButton.Left − 10
Static yInteger As Integer = commandButton.Top
Static widthInteger As Integer = commandButton.Width
Static heightInteger As Integer = commandButton.Height
commandButton.SetBounds(xInteger, yInteger, widthInteger, heightInteger)
```
or
```
With commandButton
    .SetBounds(.Left − 10, .Top, .Width, .Height)
End With
```
2. A little less than half a second.
3. The Tick event fires each time the specified interval has elapsed.

▶ Feedback 13.1

1. When the code is place inside a `Catch` block, it will place an icon next to the quantityTextBox control when the user inputs invalid data. The message appears as a ToolTip when the user places the pointer over the icon.
2. The MaxLength and CharacterCasing properties.
   - MaxLength: Sets a maximum number of characters that may be entered into a text box. A beep occurs if the user attempts to exceed the maximum.
   - CharacterCasing: Automatically converts data entry to uppercase, lowercase, or normal
3. With field-level validation the user is notified of an error as the focus leaves a field, rather than wait until a button's Click event occurs.

▶ Feedback 13.2

1.
```
Dim aboutMyForm As New aboutForm()
aboutMyForm.MdiParent = Me
aboutMyForm.Show()
```

2.
```
Select Case ToolBar1.Buttons.IndexOf(e.Button)
    Case 0
            CloseMe()   ' Make up your own procedure names.
    Case 1
            ShowAboutForm()
End Select
```
3. In the Form_Load event procedure:

```
currentTimeStatusBarPanel.Text = Now.ToLongTimeString()
```

Add a timer component; set the Interval property and include this statement in the timer's Tick event procedure:

```
currentTimeStatusBarPanel.Text = Now.ToLongTimeString()
```

► Feedback 13.3

1. `appointmentDateTime = appointmentDateTimePicker.Value`
2. Hour; Millisecond; Minute; Second; Month; Day; Year; Now
3. All of the above properties are available for the Now property.

B

Methods and Functions for Working with Dates, Financial Calculations, Mathematics, and String Operations

Visual Basic and the .NET Framework include many functions and methods that you can use in your projects. This appendix introduces some functions and methods for handling dates, for performing financial calculations and mathematical operations, for converting between data types, and for performing string operations.

Working with Dates

Chapter 13 has a section introducing dates and the Calendar control. You can use the date functions and the methods of the DateTime structure to retrieve the system date, break down a date into component parts, test whether the contents of a field are compatible with the Date data type, and convert other data types to a Date.

The DateTime Structure

When you declare a variable of Date data type in VB, the .NET Common Language Runtime uses the DateTime structure, which has an extensive list of properties and methods. You can use the shared members of the DateTime structure (identified by a yellow *S* in the MSDN Help lists) without declaring an instance of Date or DateTime. For example, to use the Now property:

```
todayDateTime = Now
```

Following is a partial list of some useful properties and methods of the DateTime structure.

Property or Method	Purpose
Add	Add the specified number to an instance of a date/time. Variations include `AddDays`, `AddHours`, `AddMilliseconds`, `AddMinutes`, `AddMonths`, `AddSeconds`, `AddTicks`, `AddYears`.
Date	Date component.
Day	Integer day of month; 1–31
DayOfWeek	Integer day; Enum expression for each day in the form of DayOfWeek.Sunday.
DayOfYear	Integer day; 1–366
Hour	Integer hour; 0–23
Minute	Integer minutes; 0–59
Second	Integer seconds; 0–59
Month	Integer month; 1 = January.
Now	Retrieve system date and time.

(continued)

Property or Method	Purpose
`Subtract`	Finds the difference between date/time values; returns a TimeSpan object.
Today	Retrieve system date.
Year	Year component.
`ToLongDateString`	Date formatted as long date. (U.S. default: Wednesday, May 05, 2004)
`ToLongTimeString`	Date formatted as long time. (U.S. default: 12:00:00 AM)
`ToShortDateString`	Date formatted as short date. (U.S. default: 5/5/2004)
`ToShortTimeString`	Date formatted as short time. (U.S. default: 12:00 AM)

Retrieving the System Date and Time

You can retrieve the system date and time from your computer's clock using the Now property or the Today property. Now retrieves both the date and time; Today retrieves only the date.

Examples

```
Dim dateAndTimeDate As Date
dateAndTimeDate = Now

Dim todayDate As Date
todayDate = Today
```

To display the values formatted:

```
dateAndTimeLabel.Text = dateAndTimeDate.ToLongDateString()
dateLabel.Text = todayDate.ToShortDateString()
todayLabel.Text = Today.ToShortDateString()
```

In addition to the date formatting methods, you also can format dates and times with the `ToString` method by using an appropriate format specifier. The table below lists some of the format specifiers. See "Date and Time Format

Format Specifier	Description	Example for U.S. Default Setting
d	Short date pattern	5/5/2004
D	Long date pattern	Monday, May 5, 2004
t	Short time pattern	12:00 AM
T	Long time pattern	12:00:00 AM
f	Full date/time (short)	Monday, May 05, 2004 12:00 AM
F	Full date/time (long)	Monday, May 05, 2004 12:00:00 AM

Strings" in MSDN for a complete list. The actual format depends on the local format for the system.

Examples of formatting using `ToString`:

```
dateAndTimeLabel.Text = dateAndTimeDate.ToString("D")
todayLabel.Text = Today.ToString("d")
```

User-Defined Date Formatting

VB .NET provides format characters that you can use to create custom formatting for dates. Note that the format characters are case sensitive.

Character	Purpose
/	Separator; the actual character to print is determined by the date separator specified for your locale.
d	Day; displays without a leading zero.
dd	Day; displays with a leading zero.
ddd	Day; uses a three letter abbreviation for the day, such as Mon.
dddd	Day; spelled out, such as Monday.
M	Month; displays without a leading zero.
MM	Month; displays with a leading zero.
MMM	Month; uses a three letter abbreviation for the month, such as Jan.
MMMM	Month; spelled out, such as January.
Y	Year; displays as two characters without a leading zero.
YY	Year; displays as two characters with a leading zero.
YYY or YYYY	Year; displays as four characters.

Examples using January 1, 2005

Format	Result
M/d/yy	1/1/05
MM/dd/yy	01/01/05
MMMM d, yyyy	January 1, 2005

Date Variables

The Date data type may hold values of many forms that represent a date. Examples could be May 24, 2004 or 5/24/04 or 5-24-2004. When you assign a literal value to a Date variable, enclose it in # signs:

```
Dim aDate As Date
aDate = #5/24/2004#
```

Converting Values to a Date Format

If you want to store values in a Date data type, you need to convert the value to a Date type. The `Date.Parse` method and the `Convert.ToDateTime` method convert a value to Date type, but throw an exception if unable to create a valid date from the argument. Use a `Try/Catch` block to make sure you have a valid date value and catch the exception.

```
Try
    aDate = Date.Parse(dateTextBox.Text)
Catch
    MessageBox.Show("Invalid date.")
End Try
```

Finding the Difference between Dates

You can use the `Subtract` method to find the difference between two Date objects. The result is in the format of days, hours, minutes, and seconds. Perhaps you only want the number of days between two dates. The .NET Framework includes the TimeSpan class that stores the time differences with the properties that you need.

```
Dim enteredDate As Date

enteredDate = Date.Parse(dateTextBox.Text)
Dim daysTimeSpan As TimeSpan = enteredDate.Substract(Today)
dateDifferenceLabel.Text = daysTimeSpan.Days.ToString()
```

The user enters a date into a text box. That date object uses its `Subtract` method to compare to today's date.

A similar `Add` method allows you to set a date at a specified time in the future.

```
Dim nextWeekDate As Date

' Add methods require Double arguments.
nextWeekDate = Today.AddDays(7D)
nextWeekLabel.Text = "Next week is: " & nextWeekDate.ToString("D")
```

Checking for the Day of the Week

Sometimes a program may need to check for the day of the week. Maybe you have a set day for a meeting or perhaps the rates differ on weekends compared to weekdays.

```
If enteredDate.DayOfWeek = DayOfWeek.Saturday Or _
   enteredDate.DayOfWeek = DayOfWeek.Sunday Then
      weekendCheckBox.Checked = True
Else
      weekendCheckBox.Checked = False
End If
```

Financial Functions

Visual Basic provides functions for many types of financial and accounting calculations, such as payment amount, depreciation, future value, and present value. When you use these functions, you eliminate the need to know and code the actual formulas yourself. Each financial function returns a value that you can assign to a variable or to a property of a control. The functions belong to the Financial module of the VisualBasic namespace.

Category	Purpose	Function
Depreciation	Double-declining balance.	DDB
	Straight line.	SLN
	Sum-of-the-years' digits.	SYD
Payments	Payment.	Pmt
	Interest payment.	IPmt
	Principal payment.	PPmt
Return	Internal rate of return.	IRR
	Rate of return when payments and receipts are at different rates.	MIRR
Rate	Interest rate.	Rate
Future value	Future value of an annuity.	FV
Present value	Present value.	PV
	Present value when values are not constant.	NPV
Number of periods	Number of periods for an annuity (number of payments).	NPer

You must supply each function with the necessary arguments. You specify the name of the function, followed by parentheses that enclose the arguments.

IntelliSense helps you type the arguments of functions. When you type the parentheses, the arguments appear in order. The one to be entered next is in bold. The order of the arguments is important because the function uses the values in the formula based on their position in the argument list. For example, the following Pmt function has three arguments: the interest rate, the number of periods, and the amount of the loan. If you supply the values in a different order, the Pmt function will calculate with the wrong numbers.

The Pmt Function

You can use the `Pmt` function to find the amount of each payment on a loan if the interest rate, the number of periods, and the amount borrowed are known.

The Pmt Function—General Form

```
Pmt(InterestRatePerPeriod, NumberOfPeriods, AmountOfLoan)
```

The interest rate must be specified as Double and adjusted to the interest rate per period. For example, if the loan is made with an annual rate of 12 percent and monthly payments, the interest rate must be converted to the monthly rate of 1 percent. Convert the annual rate to the monthly rate by dividing by the number of months in a year (AnnualPercentageRate / 12).

The number of periods for the loan is the total number of payments. If you want to know the monthly payment for a five-year loan, you must convert the number of years to the number of months. Multiply the number of years by 12 months per year (NumberOfYears * 12).

The `Pmt` function requires Double arguments and returns a Double value.

The Pmt Function—Example

```
Try
    monthlyRateDouble = Double.Parse(rateTextBox.Text) / 12
    monthsDouble = Double.Parse(yearsTextBox.Text) * 12
    amountDouble = Double.Parse(amountTextBox.Text)
    monthlyPaymentDouble = –Pmt(monthlyRateDouble, monthsDouble, amountDouble)
    monthlyPaymentLabel.Text = monthlyPaymentDouble.ToString()
Catch
    MessageBox.Show("Invalid data.")
End Try
```

Notice in the example that the fields used in the payment function are from text boxes that the user can enter, and the answer is displayed formatted in a label.

Also notice the minus sign when using the `Pmt` function. When an amount is borrowed or payments made, that is considered a negative amount. You need the minus sign to reverse the sign and make a positive answer.

The Rate Function

You can use the `Rate` function to determine the interest rate per period when the number of periods, the payment per period, and the original amount of the loan are known.

The Rate Function—General Form

```
Rate(NumberOfPeriods, PaymentPerPeriod, LoanAmount)
```

The `Rate` function requires Double arguments and returns a Double value.

The Rate Function—Example

```
Try
    monthsDouble = Double.Parse(yearsTextBox.Text) * 12
    paymentDouble = Double.Parse(paymentTextBox.Text)
    amountDouble = Double.Parse(loanAmountTextBox.Text)
    periodicRateDouble = Rate(monthsDouble, -paymentDouble, amountDouble)
    annualRateDouble = periodicRateDouble * 12
    yearlyRateLabel.Text = annualRateDouble.ToString("P")
Catch
    MessageBox.Show("Invalid data.")
End Try
```

Notice that the `Rate` function, like the `Pmt` function, needs a minus sign for the payment amount to produce a positive result.

Functions to Calculate Depreciation

If you need to calculate the depreciation of an asset in a business, Visual Basic provides three functions: the double-declining-balance method (DDB), the straight-line method, and the sum-of-the-years' digits method.

The DDB function calculates the depreciation for a specific period within the life of the asset, using the double-declining-balance method formula. Once again, you do not need to know the formula but only in what order to enter the arguments. Incidentally, the salvage value is the value of the item when it is worn out.

The DDB (Double-Declining Balance) Function—General Form

```
DDB(OriginalCost, SalvageValue, LifeOfTheAsset, Period)
```

The `DDB` function returns a Double value and requires Double arguments.

The DDB Function—Example

```
costDouble = Double.Parse(costTextBox.Text)
salvageDouble = Double.Parse(salvageTextBox.Text)
yearsDouble = Double.Parse(yearsTextBox.Text)
periodDouble = Double.Parse(periodTextBox.Text)
depreciationLabel.Text = DDB(costDouble, salvageDouble, yearsDouble, _
    periodDouble).ToString("C")
```

The other financial functions work in a similar manner. You can use Help to find the argument list, an explanation, and an example.

Mathematical Functions

In Visual Studio .NET, the mathematical functions are included as methods in the System.Math class. To use the methods, you must either import System.Math or refer to each method with the Math namespace.

For example, to use the `Abs` (absolute value) method, you can use either of these techniques:

```
answerDouble = Math.Abs(argumentDouble)
```

or

```
Imports System.Math              ' At the top of the file.
answerDouble = Abs(argumentDouble)   ' In a procedure.
```

A few functions are not methods of the Math class, but are Visual Basic functions. These functions, such as `Fix` and `Int`, cannot specify the Math namespace.

A good way to see the list of math functions is to type "Math" in the Editor; IntelliSense will pop up with the complete list. The following table presents a partial list of the Math methods.

Method	Returns	Argument Data Type	Return Data Type
`Abs(x)`	The absolute value of x. $\|x\| = x$ if $x \geq 0$ $\|x\| = -x$ if $x \leq 0$	Overloaded: All numeric types allowed.	Return matches argument type.
`Atan(x)`	The angle in radians whose tangent is x.	Double	Double
`Cos(x)`	The cosine of x where x is in radians.	Double	Double
`Exp(x)`	The value of e raised to the power of x.	Double	Double
`Log(x)`	The natural logarithm of x, where $x \geq 0$.	Double	Double
`Max(x1, x2)`	The larger of the two arguments.	Overloaded: All types allowed. Both arguments must be the same type.	Return matches argument type.
`Min(x1, x2)`	The smaller of the two arguments.	Overloaded: All types allowed. Both arguments must be the same type.	Return matches argument type.
`Pow(x1, x2)`	The value of $x1$ raised to the power of $x2$.	Double	Double
`Round(x)` `Round(x, DecimalPlaces)`	The rounded value of x, rounded to the specified number of decimal positions. *Note:* 0.5 rounds to the nearest even number.	Overloaded: Double or Decimal; Integer DecimalPlaces	Return matches argument type.
`Sign(x)`	The sign of x. -1 if $x < 0$ 0 if $x = 0$ 1 if $x > 0$	Overloaded: All numeric types allowed	Return matches argument type.
`Sin(x)`	The sine of x where x is in radians.	Double	Double
`Sqrt(x)`	The square root of x where x must be ≥ 0.	Double	Double
`Tan(x)`	The tangent of x where x is in radians.	Double	Double

Here are some useful VB mathematical functions:

Function	Returns	Argument Data Type	Return Data Type
`Fix(x)`	The integer portion of *x* (truncated).	Any numeric expression.	Integer
`Int(x)`	The largest integer ≤ *x*.	Any numeric expression.	Integer
`Rnd()`	A random number in the range 0–1 (exclusive).		Single

Working with Strings

Visual Basic provides many methods for working with text strings. Although several of the methods are covered in this text, many more are available.

Strings in Visual Studio are **immutable**, which means that once a string is created, it cannot be changed. Although many programs in this text seem to modify a string, actually a new string is created and the old string is discarded.

For string handling, you can use any of the many methods of the String class. You also can use the StringBuilder class, which is more efficient if you are building or extensively modifying strings, since the string *can* be changed in memory. In other words, a StringBuilder is *mutable* (changeable) and a String is *immutable*.

Following is a partial list of the properties and methods in the String class. For shared methods, you don't need to specify a String instance; for nonshared methods, you must attach the method to the String instance. Examples of shared methods and nonshared methods follow:

Shared Method

```
If Compare(aString, bString) > 0 Then
    ' . . .
```

Nonshared Method

```
If myString.EndsWith("ed") Then
    ' . . .
```

Method	Returns

`Compare(aString, bString)` (Shared)	Integer:
	  Negative if *aString* < *bString*
	  Zero if *aString* = *bString*
	  Positive if *aString* > *bString*

Method	Returns

Compare(*aString, bString, ignoreCaseBoolean*)
(Shared)
	Case insensitive if ignoreCaseBoolean is True.
	Integer:
	    Negative if *aString < bString*
	    Zero if *aString = bString*
	    Positive if *aString > bString*

Compare(*aString, startAString, bString, startBString, lengthInteger*)
(Shared)
	Compare substrings; start position indicates beginning character to compare for a length of lengthInteger.
	Integer:
	    Negative if *aString < bString*
	    Zero if *aString = bString*
	    Positive if *aString > bString*

Compare(*aString, startAString, bString, startBString, lengthInteger, ignoreCaseBoolean*)
(Shared)
	Case insensitive if ignoreCaseBoolean is True.
	Compare substrings; start position indicates beginning character to compare for a length of lengthInteger.
	Integer:
	    Negative if *aString < bString*
	    Zero if *aString = bString*
	    Positive if *aString > bString*

EndsWith(*anyString*)	Boolean. True if the String instance ends with anyString. Case sensitive.
Equals(*anyString*)	Boolean. True if the String instance has the same value as anyString. Case sensitive.

IndexOf(*anyString*)	Integer. Index position in String instance that anyString is found.
	    Positive: String found at this position.
	    Negative: String not found.

IndexOf(*anyString, startPositionInteger*)	Integer. Index position in String instance that anyString is found, starting at startPositionInteger.
	    Positive: String found at this position.
	    Negative: String not found.

IndexOf(*anyString, startPositionInteger, numberCharactersInteger*)	Integer. Index position in String instance that anyString is found, starting at startPositionInteger, for a length of numberCharactersInteger.
	    Positive: String found at this position.
	    Negative: String not found.

Insert(*startIndexInteger, anyString*)	New string with anyString inserted in the String instance, beginning at startIndexInteger.
LastIndexOf(*anyString*)	Integer. Index position of anyString within String instance, searching from the right end.
LastIndexOf(*anyString, startPositionInteger*)	Integer. Index position of anyString within String instance, searching leftward, beginning at startPositionInteger.
LastIndexOf(*aString, startPositionInteger, numberCharactersInteger*)	Integer. Index position of anyString within String instance, searching leftward, beginning at startPositionInteger, for a length of numberCharactersInteger.
PadLeft(*totalLengthInteger*)	New String with String instance right justified; padded on left with spaces for a total length of totalLengthInteger.

Method	Returns
PadLeft(*totalLengthInteger*, *padCharacter*)	New String with String instance right justified; padded on left with the specified character for a total length of totalLengthInteger.
PadRight(*totalLengthInteger*)	New String with String instance left justified; padded on right with spaces for a total length of totalLengthInteger.
PadRight(*totalLengthInteger*, *padCharacter*)	New String with String instance left justified; padded on right with the specified character for a total length of totalLengthInteger.
Remove(*startPositionInteger*, *numberCharactersInteger*)	New String with characters removed from String instance, beginning with startPositionInteger for a length of numberCharactersInteger.
Replace(*oldValueString*, *newValueString*)	New String with all occurrences of the old value replaced by the new value.
StartsWith(*anyString*)	Boolean. True if the String instance starts with anyString. Case sensitive.
Substring(*startPositionInteger*)	New String that is a substring of String instance; beginning at startPositionInteger, including all characters to the right.
Substring(*startPositionInteger*, *numberCharactersInteger*)	New String; a substring of String instance, beginning at startPositionInteger for the specified length.
anyString.ToLower()	New String; the String instance converted to lowercase.
anyString.ToUpper()	New String; the String instance converted to uppercase.
anyString.Trim()	New String; the String instance with all white-space characters removed from the left and right ends.
anyString.TrimEnd()	New String; the String instance with all white-space characters removed from the right end.
anyString.TrimStart()	New String; the String instance with all white-space characters removed from the left end.

Methods for Conversion between Data Types

Each of the following methods converts an expression to the named data type.

Function	Return Type
Convert.ToBoolean(*Expression*)	Boolean
Convert.ToDateTime(*Expression*)	Date
Convert.ToDecimal(*Expression*)	Decimal
Convert.ToDouble(*Expression*)	Double

Function	Return Type
Convert.ToInt16(*Expression*)	Short
Convert.ToInt32(*Expression*)	Integer
Convert.ToInt64(*Expression*)	Long
Convert.ToSingle(*Expression*)	Single
Convert.ToString(*Expression*)	String
Convert.ToUInt16(*Expression*)	Unsigned Short
Convert.ToUInt32(*Expression*)	Unsigned Integer
Convert.ToUInt64(*Expression*)	Unsigned Long

You also can use functions from the VisualBasic namespace for conversion. Note that the Convert methods shown above are used in all .NET languages; the following functions are for Visual Basic only.

Function	Return Type
CBool(*Expression*)	Boolean
CDate(*Expression*)	Date
CDbl(*Expression*)	Double
CDec(*Expression*)	Decimal
CInt(*Expression*)	Integer
CLng(*Expression*)	Long
CObj(*Expression*)	Object
CShort(*Expression*)	Short
CSng(*Expression*) .	Single
CStr(*Expression*)	String
CType(*Expression*, *New Type*)	Specified Type

Functions for Checking Validity

The Visual Basic namespace also contains functions that you can use to check for validity or type. These functions were used extensively in earlier versions of VB, but the preferred technique is to use the methods in the .NET Framework.

Function	Returns
IsNumeric(*Expression*)	Boolean: True if the expression evaluates as a valid numeric value.
IsDate(*Expression*)	Boolean: True if the expression evaluates as a valid date value.
IsNothing(*ObjectExpression*)	Boolean: True if the object expression currently does not have an instance assigned to it.

Functions for Formatting Output

In Chapter 3 you learned to format data using specifier codes with the ToString method. Visual Basic also has some formatting functions that are included in the VisualBasic namespace. Using the ToString method, rather than the Visual Basic functions, is the preferred technique for compatibility among .NET languages.

Function	Effect
FormatCurrency(*ExpressionToFormat* [, *NumberOfDecimalPositions* [, *LeadingDigit* [, *UseParenthesesForNegative* [, *GroupingForDigits*]]]])	Format currency for output.
FormatDateTime(*ExpressionToFormat* [, *NamedFormat*])	Format dates and time for output.
FormatNumber(*ExpressionToFormat* [, *NumberOfDecimalPositions* [, *LeadingDigit* *UseParenthesesForNegative* [, [, *GroupingForDigits*]]]])	Format numbers with decimals, rounding as needed.
FormatPercent(*ExpressionToFormat* [, *NumberOfDecimalPositions* [, *LeadingDigit* [, *UseParenthesesForNegative* [, *GroupingForDigits*]]]])	Format percents for output.

C

Tips and Shortcuts for Mastering the Environment

Set Up the Screen for Your Convenience

As you work in the Visual Studio integrated development environment (IDE), you will find many ways to save time. Here are some tips and shortcuts that you can use to become more proficient in using the IDE to design, code, and run your projects.

Close or Hide Extra Windows

Arrange your screen for best advantage. While you are entering and editing code in the Editor window, you don't need the toolbox, the Solution Explorer window, the Properties window, or any other extra windows. You can hide or close the extra windows and quickly and easily redisplay each window when you need it.

Hiding and Displaying Windows

You can use AutoHide on each of the windows in the IDE. Each window except the Document window in the center of the screen has a pushpin icon that you can use to AutoHide the window or "tack" it into place.

You can AutoHide each window separately, or select *Window / Auto Hide All*. In this screen, all extra windows are hidden.

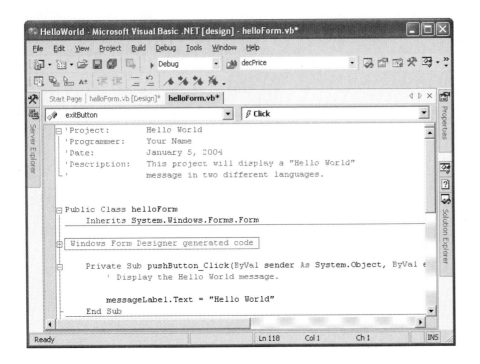

Point to the icon for one of the hidden windows to display it. In the next example, notice the mouse pointer on the *Solution Explorer* icon, which opens the Solution Explorer window temporarily. When you move the mouse pointer out of the window, it hides again.

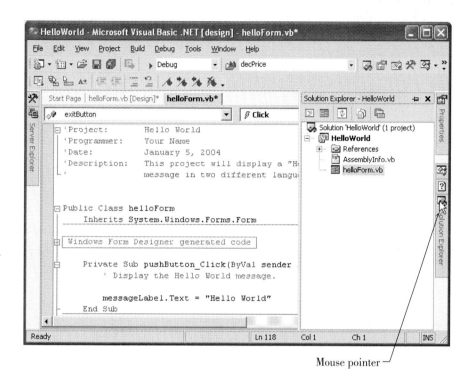

Mouse pointer

To undo the AutoHide feature, display a window and click its pushpin icon.

Closing Windows

You can close any window by clicking its Close button. You also can close any extra tabs in the Document window; each document has its own Close button.

Displaying Windows

You can quickly and easily open each window when you need it. Each window is listed on the *View* menu, or use the buttons on the Standard toolbar.

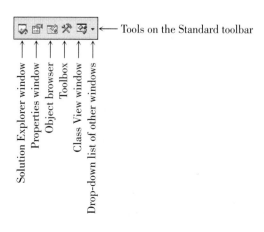

← Tools on the Standard toolbar

Solution Explorer window
Properties window
Object browser
Toolbox
Class View window
Drop-down list of other windows

Display Windows Using Keyboard Shortcuts

Solution Explorer window	Ctrl + Alt + L
Properties window	F4
Toolbox	Ctrl + Alt + X

Switch between Documents

When you have several tabs open in the Document window, you can switch by clicking on their tabs or use keyboard shortcuts.

Editor window for form's code	F7
Form Designer	Shift + F7
Cycle through open document tabs	Ctrl + Tab *or* Ctrl + F6
Navigate backward (to previous Help page)	Backspace key *or* Alt + Left arrow
Navigate forward (after navigating backward)	Alt + Right arrow

Use the Full Screen

When you are designing a form or editing code, you can work in full-screen mode. This gives you maximum screen space by getting rid of all extra windows. Unfortunately, it also hides all toolbars (the Edit toolbar can be a great timesaver while editing code). Select *View / Full Screen* to display in full-screen mode. A small *Full Screen* button appears, which you can use to switch back to regular display. You also can press Shift + Alt + Enter or select *View / Full Screen* a second time to toggle back. If you want to display the Edit toolbar while in full-screen mode, select *View / Toolbars / Text Editor*.

Modify the Screen Layout

For most operations, the Visual Studio tabbed Document window layout works very well and is an improvement over the older VB 6 environment. However, if you prefer, you can switch to MDI (multiple document interface), which is similar to the style used in VB 6. Set this option in the *Tools / Options / Environment / General / Settings*.

Each of the windows in the IDE is considered either a Tool window or a Document window. The Document windows generally display in the center of the screen with tabs. The rest of the windows—Solution Explorer, Properties window, Task List, Output, Server Explorer, and so forth—are Tool windows and share many characteristics. You can float each of the windows, tab-dock them in groups, and move and resize individual windows or groups of windows. For example, you can point to a window's title bar and drag it on top of another window to tab-dock them together. Drag on a tab to separate a window from its tabbed group. The following floating window has the Properties window, toolbox, Solution Explorer, Class View, Server Explorer, Help Index, and Help Contents all docked together. The window also was resized to make the tabs more readable.

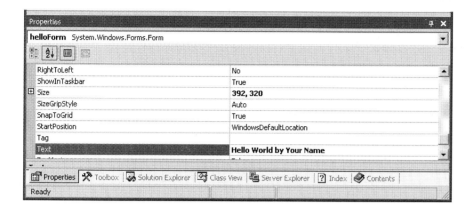

This combined window is *not* a recommended layout. It is intended only to show the possibilities. You may want to experiment with moving and resizing windows for your own convenience. You also can float a window, which makes it appear on top of the other windows, or dock the window along the top, bottom, left, or right. Experiment!

If you want to return to the default layout, choose *Tools / Options / Environment / General / Reset Window Layout*.

Split the Screen Vertically

You can view the Editor window and the form design at the same time. With at least two tabs open, select *Window / View Vertical Tab Group*. You may want to close the extra window to allow more room for the two large windows.

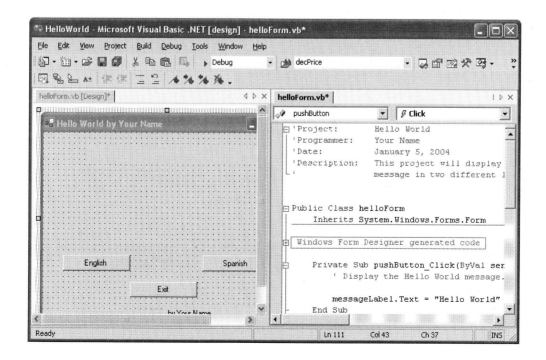

Set Options for Your Work

You can change many options in the VS IDE. Choose *Tools / Options* to display the *Options* dialog box. You may want to click on each of the categories to see the options that you can select.

    Note: If you are working in a shared lab, check with the instructor or lab technician before changing options.

Environment

General:	If it isn't already set, you may want to set the *At startup* option to *Show Start Page.*
Dynamic Help:	Set categories and topic types to limit the help available. See the next section, "Turn Off Dynamic Help."
Projects and Solutions:	Set the default folder for your projects. It's best to leave the *Build* and *Run* options to automatically save changes, but you may prefer to have a prompt or save them yourself.

Text Editor

You can set options for all languages or for Basic, which is Visual Basic. The following presumes that you first select Basic.

General:	Make sure that *Auto list members* is selected and *Hide advanced members* is deselected. You may want to turn on *Word wrap,* so that long lines wrap to the next line instead of extending beyond the right edge of the screen.
Tabs:	Choose *Smart* indenting; *Tab size* and *Indent size* should both be set to 4.
VB Specific:	All five options should be selected.

Windows Forms Designer

Grid Settings:	Notice that you can change the spacing of the grid dots, turn the grid on or off, and set the snap-to-grid option.

Turn Off Dynamic Help

Dynamic Help can be very useful; it displays a series of links that relate to the current operation. However, unless you have a very fast computer with lots of memory, the option can slow the IDE response time considerably. Try creating a project with Dynamic Help turned on and then again with it turned off to see which way works best for you.

    Turn off Dynamic Help by closing its window; display it again by selecting *Help / Dynamic Help.* You also can adjust the number and types of links displayed in *Tools / Options / Environment / Dynamic Help.*

Use Shortcuts in the Form Designer

You can save time while creating the user interface in the Form Designer by using shortcuts.

Create Multiple Controls of the Same Type

When you want to create several controls of the same class, you must select the toolbox tool each time you draw a new control. That is, unless you use this method: When you select the toolbox tool for the first control, hold down the Ctrl key as you click. After you create the first new control, the tool stays selected so that you can create as many more controls of that class as you wish.

When you are finished, click on the Pointer to deselect the tool, or click on another toolbox tool.

Use the Layout Toolbar

The Layout toolbar is great for working with multiple controls. You must have more than one control selected to enable many of the buttons. The same options are available from the *Format* menu.

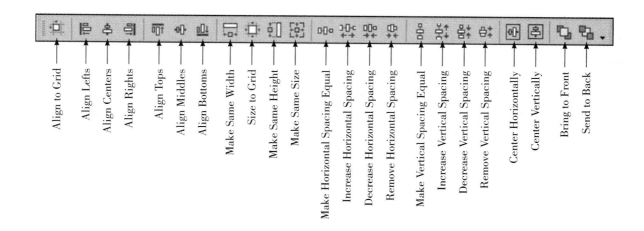

Nudge Controls into Place

Sometimes it is difficult to place controls exactly where you want them. Of course, you can use the alignment options of the *Format* menu or the Layout toolbar. You also can nudge controls in any direction by holding down the Ctrl key and pressing one of the arrow keys. Nudging moves a control one pixel in the direction you specify. For example, Ctrl + right arrow moves a selected control one pixel to the right.

Copy Controls Quickly

When you need to create several controls of the same type, you can save time by creating one control, setting any properties that you want for all controls (such as the font or text alignment), and making copies. Although you can use copy-and-paste, there is a quicker way: Hold down the Ctrl key and drag the control, which makes a copy that you can drop in the location that you choose.

Use Shortcuts in the Editor

Several features of the Editor can save you time while editing code. These are summarized in the following sections.

Use the Text Editor Toolbar

By default the Text Editor toolbar displays when the Editor window is open.

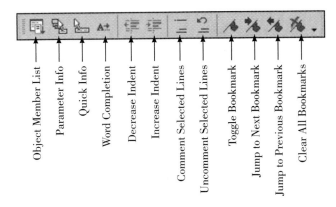

You can save yourself considerable time and trouble if you become familiar with and use some of these shortcuts.

- *Comment Selected Lines:* Use this command when you want to convert some code to comments, especially while you are testing and debugging projects. You can remove some lines from execution, to test the effect, without actually removing them. Select the lines and click the *Comment Selected Lines* button; each line will have an apostrophe appended at the left end.

- *Uncomment Selected Lines:* This command undoes the *Comment Selected Lines* command. Select some comment lines and click the button; the apostrophes at the beginning of the lines are deleted.

- *Increase Indent* and *Decrease Indent:* You can use these buttons to indent or outdent single lines or blocks of code. The buttons work the same as the Tab and Shift + Tab keys.

- *Toggle Bookmark:* This button sets and unsets individual bookmarks. Bookmarks are useful when you are jumping around in the Editor window. Set a bookmark on any line by clicking in the line and clicking the *Toggle Bookmark* button; you will see a mark in the gray margin area to the left of the marked line. You may want to set bookmarks in several procedures where you are editing and testing code.

- *Jump to Next Bookmark* and *Jump to Previous Bookmark:* Use these buttons to quickly jump to the next or previous bookmark in the code.

- *Clear All Bookmarks:* You can clear individual bookmarks with the *Toggle Bookmark* button or clear all bookmarks using this button.

- *Object Member List, Parameter Info,* and *Quick Info:* Generally, these Intelli-Sense options are turned on and the information pops up automatically. You might prefer to keep these options turned off (*Tools / Options / Text Editor / All Languages*) and click the buttons when you actually want the lists to appear.

- *Word Completion:* This is an especially useful one! Try clicking the *Word Completion* button as you are typing the name of an object or a variable. If you have typed enough for the Editor to identify the word, it will automatically fill in the rest when you press Enter or another character such as a space bar or equal sign. Or better yet, use one of the keyboard shortcuts: Ctrl + Spacebar or Alt + right arrow.

Use Keyboard Shortcuts When Editing Code

While you are editing code, save yourself time by using keyboard shortcuts.

Task	Shortcut
Delete the current line (insertion point anywhere in the line).	Ctrl + L
Delete from the insertion point left to the beginning of the word.	Ctrl + Backspace
Delete from the insertion point right to the end of the word.	Ctrl + Delete
Complete the word.	Ctrl + Spacebar *or* Alt + right arrow
Jump to a procedure (insertion point on procedure name). Use this shortcut while working on the sub procedures and functions that you write. For example, when writing a call to a function, you might want to check the coding in the function. Point to the procedure name in the *Call* and press F12. If you want to return to the original position, set a bookmark before the jump.	F12
Jump to the top of the current code file.	Ctrl + Home
Jump to the bottom of the current file.	Ctrl + End
Indent a block of code.	Select the lines and use the Tab key or the *Increase Indent* toolbar button.
Outdent (decrease indent) a block of code.	Select the lines and use the Shift + Tab keys or the *Decrease Indent* toolbar button.
View the form's Designer window.	Shift + F7
Return to the Editor window.	F7

You will find that most of the editing and selecting keyboard shortcuts for Microsoft Word also work in the Editor window.

Split the Editor Window

You can view more than one section of code at a time by splitting the Editor window. Point to the Split bar at the top of the vertical scroll bar and drag the bar down to the desired location. To remove the split, you can either drag the split bar back to the top or double-click the split bar.

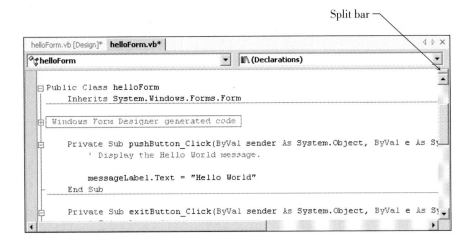

Split bar

Use Drag-and-Drop Editing

You can use drag-and-drop to move or copy text to another location in the Editor window or to another project. To move code, select the text, point to the selection, and drag it to a new location. You can copy text (rather than move it) by holding down the Ctrl key as you drag.

Drag Commonly Used Code to the Toolbox

When you have some lines of code that you use frequently, you can select the text and drag it to the toolbox. Then when you need to insert the code, drag it from the toolbox to the Editor window. The text appears in the toolbox when the Editor window is open, but not when a form is in design mode.

Caution: This shortcut should not be used on shared computers in a classroom or lab, as the text remains in the toolbox. Use it only on your own computer. You can delete previously stored text from the toolbox by right-clicking and selecting *Delete* from the context menu.

Use the Task List

The Task List displays error messages after your program is compiled. This makes sense—your tasks are to fix each of the errors. You also can add items to the Task List as a reminder to yourself, so that you don't forget to do something. A very easy way to add items to the Task List is to write a comment in your code with the *TODO* keyword.

```
'TODO Come back here and write this code.
'TODO Check on this.
```

You also can add tasks to the Task List by clicking at the top of the list; this creates a new line where you can enter text. If the Task List is filtered, as shown in its title bar, select *View / Show Tasks* and choose *All*.

Use the Task List to quickly jump to a line in code by double-clicking on a message in the list.

Use the Class View Window

The Class View window shows your project in a hierarchical tree view. You can view the classes, objects, event procedures, general procedures, and variables in your projects. You can view the declaration of the various symbols and jump directly to locations in your code.

Each type of object displays with a different symbol. In addition, the symbols may display signal icons that indicate the object's accessibility, such as Public, Private, Protected, or Friend.

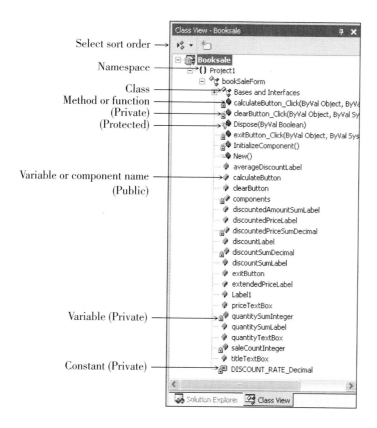

You can jump to the definition of any symbol in the Editor window. This is especially helpful for jumping to procedures in a large project. Point to the name of an event procedure, such as calculateButton_Click; then double-click, or right-click and select *Go To Definition* from the shortcut menu. If you choose to go to a definition that is in your code, the Editor window opens (if necessary), and the insertion point appears on the selected line. If you choose to go to a definition that is in another class, the Object Browser opens with that symbol selected.

Use the Object Browser

The Visual Studio Object Browser can be a valuable source of information. You can use the Object Browser to examine namespaces, objects, properties, methods, events, and constants for your project and for all .NET Framework namespaces. Use the *Find Symbol* button to look up any symbol that you want to examine.

The Object Browser and the Class View window use the same symbols and signal icons.

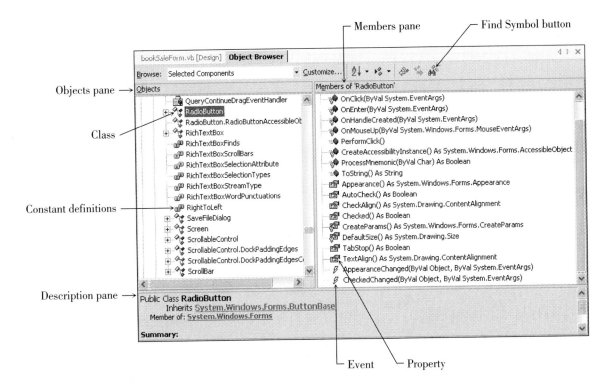

Use Context-Sensitive Help

The quickest way to get Help is to use context-sensitive Help. Click on a control or a line of code and press F1; Help displays the closest matching item it can locate. You also can get help on the IDE elements: Click in any area of the IDE and press Shift + F1; the Help explanation will be about using the current window or IDE element, rather than about the objects and language.

Copy and Move Projects

In a programming class, you often must move projects from one computer to another and must base one project on another one. To create a new project based on a previous one, you should copy the project folder. Then you can move it as necessary.

Windows projects that do not connect to a database file are very easy to copy and move. The problems occur for Web projects and database projects.

Copy and Move a Windows Project

You can copy an entire Windows project folder from one location to another using Windows Explorer or My Computer. Make sure that the project is not open in Visual Studio and copy the entire folder.

To base one project on a previous project, take the following steps:

- Make sure the project is not open.

- Copy the folder to a new location using Windows Explorer or My Computer.

- Rename the new folder for the new project name, still using Windows Explorer or My Computer.

- Open the new project (the copy) in the Visual Studio IDE.

- In the IDE's Solution Explorer, rename the solution and the project. The best way to do this is to right-click on the name and choose the *Rename* command from the shortcut menu.

- Rename the forms, if desired. If you rename the startup form, you must open the *Project Properties* dialog box and set the Startup Object.

Warning: Do not try to copy a project that is open using the *Save As* command, attempting to place a copy in a new location. The original solution and project files are modified, and you won't be able to open the original project.

Copy and Move a Web Project

If you plan to copy and/or move a Web project, make sure to explicitly save the solution file in the same folder as the project. By default, VB creates two folders for your Web projects: one in Inetpub\wwwroot and one in your default location for project files. If you save the solution file in the same folder as the rest of the project (in Inetpub\wwwroot), then you can delete or ignore the second project folder.

You can make a copy of a Web project by copying the entire folder using Windows Explorer or My Computer. To make a project in a copied or moved project run in IIS, see "Moving a Project" in Chapter 9 (page 369).

If you change the name or path of a Web project, you must manually change the solution file. With the project closed, open the solution file (.sln extension) in a text editor such as Notepad. Locate the line with the full path (*http://localhost/...*), change the folder name to the new name, and save the file. After you create the virtual folder (see page 369), you can open the solution, set the startup page, and run the project.

What if you didn't save the solution file in the project's folder? If you don't have a .sln file, open and edit the vbproj.webinfo file in the project's folder. You will find the complete path for the folder, which you can modify to the new folder name. Then create the virtual directory (see page 369) and open the project file (vbproj).

Copy and Move a Database Project

The problem with moving a database project is that the Connection object is tied to a physical file that includes the file's path. There are several ways that you can make the project portable, however. These instructions are for Access files (.mdb extension).

When you know that a project must be portable, store the database file in the project's bin folder. Then you need to set the Connection object's ConnectionString property. You can change the property in the Properties window or in code in the Form_Load event procedure, just before filling the dataset. Notice that the Data Source does not include a path, so the program will look in the folder from which the application is running (ProjectName\bin).

```
Private Sub booksForm_Load(ByVal sender As System.Object, _
    ByVal e As System.EventArgs) Handles MyBase.Load
        ' Fill the dataset.

        ' Statement added to make the project portable.
        RnRConnection.ConnectionString = _
        "Provider=Microsoft.Jet.OLEDB.4.0;Data Source=RnrBooks.mdb"

        booksDataAdapter.Fill(BooksDataset1)
End Sub
```

By changing the ConnectionString property in code, you can leave the connection information in the designer alone. However, if you need to modify the connection or dataset definition on the destination computer, you will have to change the ConnectionString of the Connection object. Here is the easiest way to do so:

- In the Properties window for the Connection object, click on the value for ConnectionString; a drop-down arrow will appear.

- Drop down the list and choose the connection for the desired database. If no connection exists, choose the *New Connection* option and set up the connection.

Once you reset the ConnectionString for the Connection object, the data adapters and datasets should work without any modification.

D

.NET Security

As a programmer, you must be aware of many aspects of security. You must not allow any unauthorized access to programs or data. But you must be able to access all needed resources while you are developing applications. For both sides of the security issue, you need a basic understanding of security topics.

The .NET Framework includes many features for implementing security. And as time passes and hackers and virus writers discover ways to circumvent the security, Microsoft is forced to tighten security. Because of this fact, you may sometimes find that programs or procedures that worked previously no longer work after you apply updates to Windows, which include updates to the .NET Framework and CLR.

For programmers security means information assurance. The .NET Framework provides many object-oriented features to assist in the process. The topic of security can fill multiple books and courses; this appendix is intended as an overview for introductory programmers.

Authentication Authorization

The two topics of authentication and authorization are frequently lumped together because they are so closely related. **Authentication** determines who the user is and **authorization** decides if the user has the proper authority to access information.

Authentication is based on credentials. When you are working with a Windows application, you only need to be concerned with Windows authentication. However, if your application is Web Forms–based (ASP.NET), authentication might be IIS Authentication or Forms-based (not recommended; it is an HTML request for credentials), or it might use Microsoft Passport, which is a centralized profile service for member sites. It is also possible to create a custom authentication method or use none at all. The settings in the Web.config file determine the method of authentication.

The following excerpt from the Web.config file describes each of the authentication methods:

```
<!-- AUTHENTICATION
    This section sets the authentication policies of the application. Possible modes are
    "Windows", "Forms", "Passport" and "None"

    "None" No authentication is performed.
    "Windows" IIS performs authentication (Basic, Digest, or Integrated Windows)
    according to its settings for the application. Anonymous access must be disabled
    in IIS.
    "Forms" You provide a custom form (Web page) for users to enter their credentials,
    and then you authenticate them in your application. A user credential token is stored
    in a cookie.
    "Passport" Authentication is performed via a centralized authentication service
    provided by Microsoft that offers a single logon and core profile services for
    member sites.
-->
<authentication mode = "Windows"/>
```

For no authentication, you can change the following line in the Web.config file to:

```
<authentication mode = "None"/>
```

IIS Authentication

Chapter 10 introduces database access from a Web page. A Web Form runs on IIS (Internet Information Server). When IIS is installed, the Setup creates a user account for anonymous access. The username is IUSR_*computername*. For example, if the machine is called SteveL, the username is IUSR_SteveL. This same anonymous-logon user is then used for all IIS services installed on the computer. The password for the account is randomly generated. The following dialog can be displayed by going to the *Control Panel / Administrative Services / Computer Management* and then expanding the *Local Users and Groups*.

The *Authentication Methods* dialog is accessed through IIS. From a project's *Properties* dialog, select the *Directory Security* tab and then click on the *Edit* button under *Anonymous access and authentication control*.

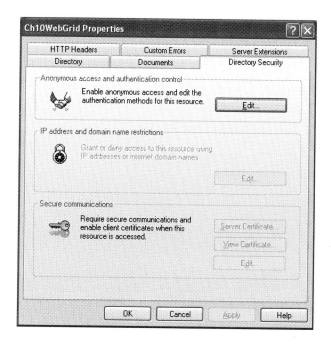

Anonymous access uses the anonymous user account. In the example programs, we have been removing the check mark for anonymous access and allowing Windows to perform the authentication.

Another authentication method is Basic authentication. This requires a Windows username and password. As you can see in the *Authentication Methods* dialog, this technique sends the password in clear text.

The Digest authentication, available on Windows domain servers, encrypts the password before it is sent across a network.

The final check box is the *Integrated Windows authentication*, which requires users to run Internet Explorer 3.1 or later.

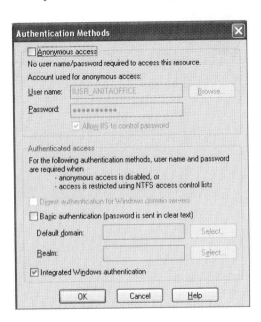

For more information, see Microsoft Knowledge Base article #142868: `http://support.microsoft.com/default.aspx?scid=kb;[LN];142868`.

If you are working with a SQL Server database or MSDE, you should refer to Knowledge Base article #247931: `http://support.microsoft.com/default.aspx?scid=kb;[LN];247931`.

Authorization and Impersonation

After the user is authenticated, another step checks for authorization. If ASP.NET does not use impersonation, the ASP.NET user that is created when the Framework is installed runs without any privileges. If impersonation is turned on, ASP.NET takes on the identity from IIS. If anonymous access is turned off, ASP.NET takes on the credentials of the authenticated user; otherwise it impersonates the account that IIS uses.

This is where the following code applies.

```
<identity impersonate = "true"/>
```

For a specific user you can use

```
<identity impersonate = "true" name = "Domain/username" password = "password"/>
```

The default authorization in the Web.config file has commented fields to specify users and roles.

```
<!-- AUTHORIZATION
    This section sets the authorization policies of the application. You can allow or
    deny access to application resources by user or role. Wildcards: "*" means everyone,
    "?" means anonymous (unauthenticated) users.
-->
<authorization>
    <allow users="*" /> <!-- Allow all users -->

        <!- <allow  users="[comma separated list of users]"
              roles="[comma separated list of roles]"/>
          <deny  users="[comma separated list of users]"
              roles="[comma separated list of roles]"/>
    -->
</authorization>
```

Writing Secure Code

Programmers need to be aware of how hackers are able to gain access to a database or a network through code. Two primary areas of importance are string injections and error messages that may give away important information about a data source.

SQL Injection

Proper validation of the code is extremely important. A system vulnerability occurs when code is "injected" into a string. A text box or a combo box control allows the user to type in information. It is the responsibility of the programmer to make sure that the code typed does not contain any scripting code or disruptive characters. When a program is working with a database, there must be no way for the user to inject code into that database.

It is wise to validate the keystrokes to be sure that the input text contains only valid characters.

Error Messages

Another technique that hackers use to find information about a database is to input wrong data hoping that the error message will give significant information. The default error messages indicate the name of the field containing an error. Plan your error messages so that you don't allow someone to determine valid field names or values.

Code Access Security

Basically, code access security determines what code is allowed to do on a computer; specifically, what resources such as hardware or files the code can access.

The settings of the computer ultimately determine if the code can execute or if a resource can be used by the code.

Code access security is based on several Permission classes. The Permission classes are organized into three types: code access, identity, and role-based. Examples of the code access type include the PrintingPermission class and the RegistryPermission class; the SiteIdentityPermission and the URLIdentityPermission class fall into the identity permission type. The PrincipalPermission class is the role-based type for user credentials.

If your program has an OpenFileDialog component, it may be necessary to request permission to access the files from a given system. The following code would appear at the top of the file.

```
Imports System.Security.Permissions
<Assembly: FileDialogPermissionAttribute(SecurityAction.RequestMinimum, Unrestricted: =
True)>
```

TroubleShooting

If you receive an error trying to access a database in a Web application, you must set the program up for Windows authentication and impersonation. The error message is `The Microsoft Jet database engine cannot open the file 'C:\Inetpub\wwwroot\`*filename*`\bin\`*databasename*`.mdb'. It is already opened exclusively by another user, or you need permission to view its data.`

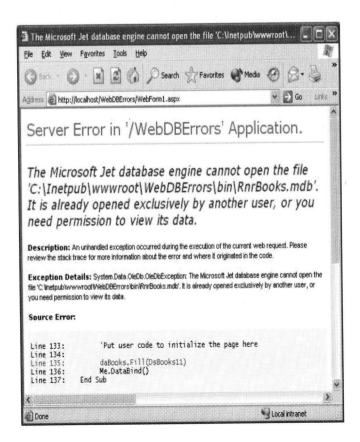

1. In the Web.config file, add a line following the Windows authentication line instructing the program to use impersonation.

    After the line `<authentication mode="Windows" />`, type:

```
<identity impersonate = "true"/>
```

2. Disable Anonymous Access. Run *inetmgr*, expand to the default Web site, and locate your program. From the *Properties* dialog, select the *Directory Security* tab, click on the *Edit* button, and deselect the *Anonymous access* check box.

Unspecified Error

When an Unspecified Error occurs on the `Fill` method of your data adapter, check to make sure that the *Anonymous access* box has been deselected in IIS.

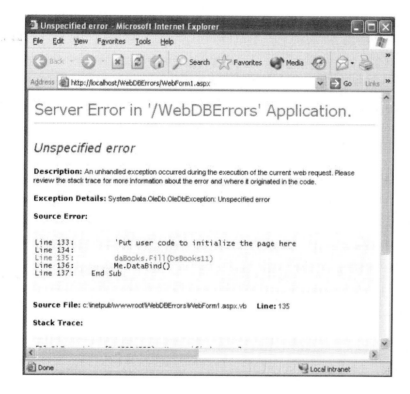

Glossary

A

abstract class   A class that cannot be instantiated but instead is used for inheritance.

abstract method   An empty method declared with the *MustOverride* keyword; must be overridden in the derived class.

AcceptButton property   Form property that sets the default button, which is activated with the Enter key.

access key   Underlined character that allows the user to select using the keyboard rather than the mouse; also called a *hot key*.

accessor method   The `Get` and `Set` methods written to allow external objects to access the private properties of a class.

ANSI code   A coding method used to represent characters on a microcomputer (American National Standards Institute).

Application.StartupPath   The folder from which the application begins execution. In a VB program running from the VS IDE, the project's bin folder.

argument   The expression to operate upon in a function or method. A value being passed to or from a procedure.

array   A series of variables; each individual element can be referenced by its index position. Also called a *list*.

assignment operator   An equal sign (=); assigns a value to the variable or property named on the left side of the sign.

assignment statement   Assigns a value to a variable or property using an assignment operator.

authentication   The policies used to determine who the user is; may be Windows-based, forms-based, Passport-based, or none (no authentication performed).

authorization   Determination of the rights allowed for a particular user. For ASP.NET applications, can allow access from any user by turning on impersonation.

Autos window   Window that opens in IDE during execution; automatically displays all variables and control contents that are referenced in the current statement and three statements on either side of the current one.

B

base class   Class that is inherited from; also called a *superclass* or *parent class*.

Binary formatter   Object serialization format that stores the data in binary form.

block-level variable   A variable declared inside a block of code; only accessible within that block.

BorderStyle property   Property of a control that allows the control to appear flat or three-dimensional.

break time   Temporary break in execution of a program; used for debugging.

breakpoint   Indicated point in project code where execution should break; used for debugging.

browser   An application used to render and display HTML code; used to display Web pages; in VB used to execute Web Forms.

Brush object   Graphical object for drawing filled shapes.

Button   Control used to activate a procedure.

ByRef   Declares that an argument passed to a procedure should be passed as the address of the data so that both calling and called procedures have access to the same memory location.

ByVal   Declares that an argument passed to a procedure should be passed as a copy of the data. The calling and called procedures do not have access to each other's variables.

C

Call (procedure call)   Execute a procedure.

callback   An object notifies the program that it needs to do something or that a situation exists that the program needs to handle. The object notifies the program of the situation by firing an event.

camel casing   The naming convention that specifies mixed-case names; the first character must be lowercase and the first character of each word within the name must be uppercase; the rest of the characters must be lowercase.

CancelButton property   Form property that sets the cancel button, which is activated with the Esc key.

Case structure   Selection structure; can be used in place of an *If* statement.

casting   Converting from one data type to another.

CharacterCasing property   Property of text boxes that specifies whether input should be left as entered or converted to uppercase or lowercase.

check box   A control used to indicate a value that may be True or False. In any group of check boxes, any number may be selected.

Checked property   Determines if a check box is checked or not.

child class   A class inherited from another class, called the *parent*. Also called a *derived class* or *subclass*.

child form   A child form belongs to a parent form, is displayed inside the parent, and closes when the parent does. See *multiple document interface (MDI)*.

class   A prototype or blueprint for an object; includes specifications for the properties and methods.

class module   A file that contains code for a class; has no visual component.

clean compile   Code compiles to Common Language Runtime without errors.

Close method   Closes forms or files; releases resources used by the object.

Closing event   Occurs before a form unloads. A good location to place the code to prompt the users if they wish to save any changes.

code   Programming statements in the Basic language.

collection   A series of objects or an object that can contain a series of objects; has properties and methods.

color constant   Values assigned in the Color class. Examples: Color.Red and Color.Blue.

column   A vertical section of a grid control.

ComboBox control   A control that is a combination of a list box and a text box.

common dialog   A set of Windows dialog boxes available to Visual Basic programmers for Open, Save, Fonts, Print, and Color.

complex binding   Connects multiple fields in a dataset to a control, such as a grid.

component tray   Area across the lower edge of a Form Designer window; used to store components that are not visible on the form.

compound condition   Multiple conditions combined with the use of the logical operators *And* or *Or*.

concatenation   Joining string (text) fields. The ampersand (&) is used to concatenate text.

condition   An expression that will evaluate True or False. May be a comparison of two values (variables, properties, constants) using relational operators.

connection   Object that establishes a link to a data source.

constant   A value that cannot change during program execution.

constructor   A procedure that runs automatically when an object is instantiated from that class. In VB, a constructor is coded with Sub New.

context menu   A pop-up menu, sometimes referred to as a *shortcut menu* or a *right-mouse menu*.

context-sensitive Help   Use of the F1 function key to directly access the Help topic related to the code or object containing the cursor.

control   An object used on a graphical interface such as a radio button, text box, button, or label.

Criteria   Conditions for selection.

Crystal Reports   A robust report generator for database files.

CrystalReportViewer control   Provides application the ability to display reports generated through Crystal Reports.

CType function   Converts from one object type to another; used with a shared event procedure to access the sender object.

D

data adapter   An object that handles retrieving and updating of the data in a dataset.

data binding   Connecting a control or property to one or more data elements.

data file   A file used to store small amounts of information such as the contents of a list box.

data type   Specifies the type of data a variable or constant can hold, such as Integer, Decimal, or String.

dataset   A temporary set of data stored in the memory of the computer.

DateTime structure   Used to retrieve and format the current date and time.

Debug.WriteLine method   Statement to write a line in the Debug window; used to write a message for debugging.

debugging   Finding and eliminating computer program errors.

declaration   Statements to establish a project's variables and constants, give them names, and specify the type of data they will hold.

Declaration section   Code outside of a procedure, used to declare module-level variables.

derived class   A subclass inherited from a base class.

deserialization   Reads an object that has been serialized or saved to a file. Recreates the saved object.

design time   The status of the Visual Studio environment while a project is being developed, as opposed to run time or break time.

destructor   A method that is called as an object goes out of scope.

DialogResult object   Used to determine which button the user clicked on a message box.

direct reference   Accessing an element of an array by a subscript when the value of the subscript is known.

disabled   Enabled property set to False; user can see the control but cannot access it.

Do and Loop statements   Statements to indicate the beginning and ending of a loop. A condition can appear on the Do or on the Loop.

Document window   IDE window that displays the Form Designer, the Code Editor, the Object Browser, and the pages of Help that you request.

DrawLine method   Method of the Graphics object.

DrawRectangle method   Method of the Graphics object; used to draw squares and rectangles.

DrawString method   Method of the Graphics object; sends a line of text to the graphics page.

drop-down combo box   A combo box control with a down-pointing arrow that allows the user to drop down the list. Allows efficient use of space on a form.

drop-down list   A list box with a down-pointing arrow that allows the user to drop down the list. Allows efficient use of space on a form.

E

element   Single item within a table, array, list, or grid.

empty string   A string containing no characters; also called a *null string* or *zero-length string*.

Enabled property   Determines if the control is available to the user.

encapsulation   OOP feature that specifies that all methods and properties of a class be coded within the class. The class can hide or expose the methods and properties, as needed.

End If   Terminates a block `If` statement.

Enterprise Architect Edition   The version of Visual Studio with the most features.

Enterprise Developer Edition   A version of Visual Studio more robust than the Professional Edition but with fewer features than the Enterprise Architect Edition.

event   An action that may be caused by the user, such as a click, drag, key press, or scroll. Events also can be triggered by an internal action, such as repainting the form or validating user input.

event procedure   A procedure written to execute when an event occurs.

exception   An error that occurs at run time.

explicit conversion   Writing the code to convert from one data type to another; as opposed to implicit conversion.

F

field   A group of related characters used to represent one characteristic or attribute of an entity in a data file or database.

Field Explorer   Window for adding fields to a Crystal Report layout.

field-level validation   Checking the validity of input data in each control as entered, rather than waiting until the user clicks a button.

file   A collection of related records.

FileStream   Class used for object serialization; used to transfer a series of characters to or from a file.

Fill method   Retrieves the data and creates the DataSet; based on the SQL SELECT statement in the data adapter's SelectCommand property.

FillEllipse method   Method of the graphics object; used to draw circles and ovals.

flow layout   Design for Web Forms; each element follows the previous one, similar to a word-processing document.

focus   The currently selected control on the user interface. For controls such as buttons, the focus appears as a light dotted line. For text boxes, the insertion point (also called the *cursor*) appears inside the box.

Focus method   Sets the focus to a control.

For and Next statements   A loop structure; usually used when the number of iterations is known.

For/Next loop   A loop structure; usually used when the number of iterations is known.

ForeColor property   Property that determines the color of the text.

form   An object that acts as a container for the controls in a graphical interface.

Form Designer   The IDE window for creating the user interface.

format   A specification for the way information will be displayed, including dollar signs, percent signs, and number of decimal positions.

format specifiers   Codes used as arguments for the `ToString` method; used to make the output easier to read. Can specify dollar signs, commas, decimal positions, percents, and date formats.

FromFile method   Retrieves an image from a file.

function   Performs an action and returns a value.

function procedure   A procedure that returns a value.

G

garbage collection   Automatic deletion of objects from memory after they are out of scope.

general procedure   A procedure not attached to an event; may be a sub procedure or a function procedure.

global   Variable that may be used in all procedures of a project.

graphical user interface (GUI)   Program application containing icons, buttons, and menu bars.

graphics   Lines, shapes, and images. An image file assigned to a PictureBox control; methods of the Graphics class, such as `DrawString`, `DrawLine`, and `DrawEllipse`.

grid layout   Default layout for Web Forms; controls may be placed anywhere on the form; location specified with X and Y coordinates.

group box   A control used as a container for other controls, such as a group of radio buttons.

H

handle   A small square on a selected control at design time; used to resize a control. Also called a *resizing handle*.

Help   The collection of reference pages about programming in VB and using the Visual Studio IDE.

horizontal scrollbar   A Windows control that provides a scroll bar that appears horizontally on the form.

I

IDE   See *integrated development environment, Visual Studio development environment*.

identifier   A name for a variable, procedure, and named constant; supplied by the programmer.

If ... Then ... Else   Statement block for testing a condition and taking alternate actions based on the outcome of the test.

image list component   Contains a collection of images to use for other controls, such as a toolbar.

Image property   A graphic file with an extension of .bmp, .gif, .jpg, .png, .ico, .emf, or .wmf.

immutable   The inability of a string to be modified once it is created. A new string must be created for any modifications.

implicit conversion   A conversion from one data type to another that occurs automatically or by default according to specified rules.

increment operator   Shortcut operator for increasing the value of a variable by 1 (+=).

index   Position within a list or array.

inheritance   Ability to create a new class based on an existing class.

instance   An object created from a class.

instance property   See *instance variable*.

instance variable   Each object created from the class has a separate occurrence of the variable.

instantiate Create an object using the New keyword.

integrated development environment (IDE) Tool for writing projects and solutions, includes an editor, tools, debugger, and other features for faster development.

Interval property Determines the amount of time until a Timer component fires a Tick event; measured in milliseconds.

intranet Network within a company.

intrinsic constant Constants supplied with a language or application such as Color.Blue.

IsMdiContainer property Used to create a parent form for MDI.

Items property Collection of elements for a list box or combo box control.

Items.Add method Adds elements to the Items collection of a list box.

Items.Clear method Clears all elements from a list box.

Items.Count property Property that holds the number of elements in a list box.

Items.Insert method Inserts an element in a list for a list box.

Items.Remove method Removes the currently selected item from a list.

Items.RemoveAt method Removes the specified item from a list.

iteration A single pass through the statements in a loop.

K

key field The field (or fields) on which a data file is organized; used to search for a record.

L

Label A control that displays text; cannot be altered by the user.

LargeChange property A property of a scroll bar that determines how far to scroll for a click in the gray area of the scroll bar.

late binding Program elements cannot be determined at compile time, but must be determined at run time. Should be avoided, if possible, for performance reasons.

LayoutMdi method Arranges MDI child windows vertically, horizontally, or cascaded.

lifetime The period of time that a variable exists.

line-continuation character A space and underscore; used in program code to indicate that a Basic statement continues on the next line.

ListBox control A control that holds a list of values; the user cannot add new values at run time.

local The scope of a variable or constant that limits its visibility to the current procedure.

Locals window Window that opens in IDE during execution; displays all objects and variables that are within scope at break time.

logic error An error in a project that does not halt execution but causes erroneous results in the output.

logical operator The operators And, Or, and Not; used to construct compound conditions and to reverse the truth of a condition.

loop A control structure that provides for the repetition of statements.

loop index A counter variable used in a For/Next loop.

M

Maximum property Scrollbar property for highest possible value.

MaxLength property Property of text boxes that limits the number of characters the user can enter as input.

MdiList property Determines whether the menu will display a list of open MDI child windows; used on the *Window* menu.

menu A list of choices; the available commands displayed in a menu bar.

Menu Designer Feature of the development environment for creating menus; accessed by adding a Main Menu component to the component tray.

MessageBox A dialog box that displays a message to the user.

method Predefined actions (procedures) provided with objects.

Minimum property Scrollbar property for lowest possible value.

modal A dialog box that requires a user response before continuing program execution.

modeless A dialog box that does not require a user response before continuing program execution.

module level A variable that can be used in any procedure within the current file.

multiple document interface (MDI) Multiple-form project that has parent and child forms.

multitier application A program designed in components or services, where each segment performs part of the necessary actions. Each of the functions of a multitier application can be coded in a separate component and the components may be stored and run on different machines.

MustInherit Modifier on a class definition. The class cannot be instantiated, but instead must be used for inheritance.

MustOverride Modifier on a procedure definition; requires that the procedure be overridden in an inherited class.

N

Name property The property of an object that is used to reference the object in code.

named constant Constant created and named by the developer.

namespace Used to organize a group of classes in the language library; the hierarchy used to locate the class. No two classes may have the same name within a namespace.

namespace-level variable A variable that can be used in any procedure within the current namespace, which is generally the current project.

nested If An If statement completely contained within another If statement.

Nested Try/Catch block A Try/Catch block completely contained within another Try/Catch block.

New keyword Used to instantiate an object; creates an object and assigns memory for property values.

NewLine   The Visual Studio constant `ControlChars.NewLine` used to determine line endings.

Next method   Returns the next in a series of random numbers for an object of the Random class.

Nothing   An object variable that does not have an instance of an object assigned. Formerly used to destroy an object.

Now property   Current date and time from the DateTime structure.

O

object   An occurrence of a class type that has properties and methods; a specific instance of a control type, form, or other class.

object-oriented programming (OOP) An approach to programming that uses classes to define the properties and methods for objects. Classes may inherit from other classes.

OpenFileDialog   Common dialog component used to display the Windows *Open File* dialog box; allows the user to view files and select the file to open.

Option Explicit   Setting this option On forces variables and objects to be declared before they can be used.

Option Strict   Setting this option On enforces strong data typing.

order of precedence   Hierarchy of mathematical operations; the order in which operations are performed.

overloading   Allows a method to act differently for different arguments. Multiple procedures in the same class with the same name but with different argument lists.

overriding   A method in a derived (inherited) class with the same name and argument list as a method in the parent (base) class. The method in the derived class overrides (supersedes) the one in the parent class for objects of the derived class.

P

PageLayout property   A setting for a Web page that determines the method of laying out the page. May be set to FlowLayout or GridLayout.

parameterized constructor   A constructor (`Sub New`) that contains an argument list; as opposed to an empty constructor.

parameterized query   Allows a value for a query to be supplied at run time.

parent class   The base class for inheritance, also called a *superclass*.

parent form   MDI container for child forms.

pascal casing   The naming convention that specifies mixed-case names; the first character must be uppercase and the first character of each word within the name must be uppercase; the rest of the characters must be lowercase.

Peek method   Used to look ahead to determine if records remain in a file stream.

Pen object   Graphical object for drawing lines and shapes.

PictureBox control   A control used to display an image.

pixel   Picture element; a single dot on the screen; a unit of measurement for displaying graphics.

Point structure   Holds X and Y coordinates as a single unit.

polymorphism   OOP feature allowing methods to take different actions depending on the situation. Methods may have the same name but different argument lists. Also refers to the naming convention of naming methods with similar actions the same in each class.

postback   A round-trip to the server.

posttest   A loop that has its test condition after the body of the loop; the statements within the loop will always be executed at least once; also called an *exit test*.

pretest   A loop that has its test condition at the top; the statements inside the loop may never be executed; also called an *entry test*.

Print method   A method of the PrintDocument class to begin executing code for printing.

print preview   View the printer's output on the screen and then choose to print or cancel.

PrintDocument component   Contains methods and events to set up output for the printer.

PrintPage event procedure   Contains the logic for printing.

PrintPreviewDialog component Used to allow print previews for an application.

private   Variable or procedure declared with the `Private` keyword; available only inside the current class.

procedure   A unit of code; may be a sub procedure, function procedure, or property procedure.

Professional Edition   A version of Visual Basic that includes fewer features than the Enterprise editions. The trial edition included with this text is based on the Professional Edition.

project file   A text file that contains information about the current project. Displays in the Solution Explorer and can be viewed and edited in a text editor.

Properties window   A window in the IDE used to set values for properties at design time.

property   Characteristic or attribute of an object; control properties may be set at design time or run time depending on the specific property.

property procedure   Procedure written with `Set` and `Get` keywords to pass values to and from private variables in a class.

Protected   Access modifier for a variable or procedure; behaves as private but allows inheritance.

pseudocode   Planning tool for code using an English expression or comment that describes the action.

R

radio button   A control used to indicate a value that may be True or False (selected or not selected). In any group of radio buttons, only one button may be selected.

Random class   Used to create Random numbers.

ReadLine method   Reads one record from a file; reads to the end of the line.

ReadOnly   A property that can be retrieved but not set by external classes; indicates that only a `Get` method exists for the property.

record   A group of related fields; relates to data files and database tables.

Rectangle structure   Defines a rectangular region, specified by its upper-left corner and its size.

relational operator   Used to compare two fields for greater than >, less than <, or equal to =.

remark   A Basic statement used for documentation; not interpreted by the compiler; also called a *comment*.

return value   Value returned from a function.

reusability   Code modules that can be used in multiple projects.

row   A horizontal section of a grid control.

run time   During the time a project is executing.

run-time error   An error that occurs as a program executes; causes execution to break.

S

scope   The extent of visibility of a variable or constant. The scope may be namespace, module level, local, or block.

Scroll event   Scrollbar event that occurs as the user moves the scroll box.

Select Case   Selection structure; can be used in place of an `If` statement.

SelectedIndex property   Index of the item currently selected in a list box or combo box.

separator bar   A horizontal line used to separate groups of menu commands.

serialization   A series of bits used to save the state of an object's properties so that the object can be recreated at a later time.

SetBounds method   Sets the location of a control; used to move a control.

Shared property   A property that can be used by all objects of the class; generally used for totals and counts. Only one copy exists for all objects of the class.

shared variable   One variable that can be used by all objects of the class; generally used for totals and counts.

short circuit   Skipping the evaluation of parts of a compound condition that are not required to determine the result.

shortcut menu   The menu that pops up when the right mouse button is clicked. Also called a *pop-up menu*, *context menu*, or *right-mouse menu*.

Show method   Displays a form or message box.

ShowDialog method   Displays a common dialog box.

ShowPanels property   Determines whether the panels in a status bar display or not.

signature   The argument list of a method or procedure.

simple binding   Connecting a single data field to a single control, such as a label or text box.

simple combo box   Fixed-size combo box.

simple list box   Fixed-size list box.

single document interface (SDI)   Forms act independently in a multiple-form project.

Size structure   A size specified by width and height; measured in pixels.

SizeMode property   Allows the size of an image in a picture box to resize to fit the control.

SmallChange property   Scrollbar property for amount of movement by a click on an arrow.

SOAP formatter   Format for storing objects following the standards for simple object access protocol (SOAP).

solution   A Visual Basic application; can consist of one or more projects.

Solution Explorer window   An IDE window that holds the filenames for the files included in your project and a list of the classes it references.

solution file   A text file that holds information about the solution and the projects it contains.

Sorted property   Property of a list box and combo box that specifies that the list items should be sorted.

Standard Edition   A version of Visual Basic with fewer features than the Professional and Enterprise versions; the version provided by Microsoft for inclusion with this text.

StartPosition property   Determines the screen location of the first form in a project when execution begins.

stateless   Does not store any information about its contents from one invocation to the next.

static local variable   A local variable with a lifetime that matches the module. The variable retains its value as long as the form is loaded.

status bar   An area along the lower edge of a window used to display information for the user.

StatusBar control   A control to create a status bar at the bottom of a form.

StatusBarPanel object   Individual item on a StatusBar control.

Step Into   Debugging command; executes each statement, including those in called procedures.

Step Out   Debugging command; continues rapid execution until the called procedure completes, and then returns to break mode at the statement following the `Call`.

Step Over   Debugging command; executes each statement in the main procedure but does not show statements in called procedures.

stream   An object used to transfer a series of bytes from one location to another.

StreamReader   Object used to input small amounts of information stored in a disk file.

StreamWriter   Object used to write small amounts of information to disk.

StretchImage   Setting for the value of the SizeMode property of a PictureBox control.

string literal   A constant enclosed in quotation marks.

strongly typed   A feature of VB that requires the programmer to always be aware of the data type. If you assign data to a wider type, VB can implicitly (automatically) convert for you; if you are assigning data to a narrower type, where precision or accuracy might be lost, VB will generate a compiler error.

structure   A grouping that combines multiple fields of related data.

style   Formatting for a Web Form.

Style Builder   An IDE feature for adding styles to HTML pages.

sub procedure   A procedure that performs actions but does not return a value.

subclass   A derived class; also called a *child class.*

submenu   A menu within a menu.

subscript   The position of an element within an array; also called an *index.*

subscripted variable   An element of an array.

superclass   A base class for inheritance, also called a *parent class.*

syntax error   An error caused by failure to follow the syntax rules of the language; often caused by typographical errors. The Editor informs you of syntax errors.

System.IO namespace   Holds the stream objects for persistence and serialization.

T

TabIndex property   Determines the order the focus moves as the Tab key is pressed.

table   A two-dimensional array.

table lookup   Logic to find an element within an array.

TabStop property   Determines if a control can receive focus.

text box   A control for data entry; its value can be entered and changed by the user.

Text property   The value that displays on a control such as the words in a text box or label.

TextAlign property   Used to change the alignment of text within the control.

Tick event   One firing of a timer component; each time the interval passes, another Tick event occurs.

Timer component   Fires Tick events at a specified time interval.

ToLower method   Converts text to lowercase letters.

toolbar   The bar beneath the menu bar that holds buttons; used as shortcuts for menu commands.

toolbar control   Displays buttons for shortcuts to menu items.

toolbox   A window that holds icons for tools; used to create controls and components on a form.

ToolTip   Small label that pops up when the mouse pointer pauses over a toolbar button or control.

ToolTip component   Placed on a form to allow the individual controls to display ToolTips. A ToolTip property is added to each control.

ToolTip on ToolTip1 property   The new property added to each control when a ToolTip component is added to the form.

ToUpper method   Converts text to all uppercase.

Try/Catch block   Traps user errors or program errors.

U

user interface   The display and commands seen by a user; how the user interacts with an application. In Windows, the graphical display of an application that contains controls and menus.

V

validation   Checking to verify that appropriate values have been entered.

validator controls   Controls that can automatically validate input data; used on Web Forms.

Value keyword   Incoming value for a Set clause in a property procedure.

Value property   Holds the current setting of a scroll bar control.

ValueChanged event   Event that occurs when a scroll bar control is scrolled.

variable   Memory location that holds data that can be changed during project execution.

vertical scrollbar   A Windows control that provides a scroll bar that appears vertically on the form.

Visible property   Determines if a control can be seen or not.

visual inheritance   Inheritance of the visual elements of a form.

Visual Studio environment   The development environment including tools for designing the interface, editing program code, and running and debugging applications; also called the *IDE.*

W

Web Form   Form in Visual Studio for creating pages that display in a browser.

Web page   A static page consisting of HTML elements; displayed in a browser application.

With and End With statements   A block of code that refers to the same object. The object name appears in the With statement; all subsequent statements until the End With relate to that object.

Write method   Writes one record to a stream object; does not include a carriage return.

WriteLine method   Writes one record to a stream object; includes a carriage return character at the end.

X

XML   Extensible Markup Language. A format for data; popular for data storage and transfer on the Internet.

Index